THEORY AND PRACTICE
OF GROUP COUNSELING

SIXTH EDITION

THEORY AND PRACTICE OF GROUP COUNSELING

Gerald Corey

California State University, Fullerton
Diplomate in Counseling Psychology,
American Board of Professional Psychology

THOMSON

™

BROOKS/COLE

Australia • Canada • Mexico • Singapore • Spain • United Kingdom • United States

THOMSON

BROOKS/COLE

Executive Editor: *Lisa Gebo*
Sponsoring Editor: *Julie Martinez*
Marketing Manager: *Caroline Concilla*
Marketing Assistant: *Mary Ho*
Assistant Editor: *Shelley Gesicki*
Editorial Assistant: *Amy Lam*
Technology Project Manager: *Barry Connolly*
Project Manager, Editorial Production:
Kim Svetich-Will
Permissions Editor: *Sue Ewing*

Production Service: *The Cooper Company*
Copy Editor: *Kay Mikel*
Interior Design: *Roy R. Neuhaus*
Cover Design: *Lisa Berman*
Cover Photo: *David Wasserman*
Print/Media Buyer: *Kristine Walker*
Compositor: *UG / GGS Information Services, Inc.*
Printing and Binding: *QuebecorWorld-Taunton*

For more information about our products, contact us at:
Thomson Learning Academic Resource Center
1-800-423-0563

For permission to use material from this text, contact us by:
Phone: 1-800-730-2214
Fax: 1-800-730-2215
Web: http://www.thomsonrights.com

Library of Congress Control Number:
2002113769

Student Edition with InfoTrac College
Edition: ISBN 0-534-59697-5

Instructor's Edition: ISBN 0-534-59699-1

Brooks/Cole–Thomson Learning
10 Davis Drive
Belmont, CA 94002

Asia
Thomson Learning
5 Shentonway 01-01
UIC Building
Singapore 068808

Australia/New Zealand
Thomson Learning
102 Dodds Street
Southbank, Victoria 3006
Australia

Canada
Nelson
1120 Birchmount Road
Toronto, Ontario M1K 5G4
Canada

Europe/Middle East/Africa
Thomson Learning
Holborn House
50/51 Bedford Row
London, WC1R 4LR
United Kingdom

Latin America
Thomson Learning
Seneca, 53
Colonia Polanco
11560 Mexico D.F.
Mexico

Spain/Portugal
Paraninfo
Calle Magallanes, 25
28015 Madrid
Spain

To my mother, Josephine Corey

> *You taught me how to work hard and be happy*
> *You led by example for 94 years*
> *Your presence enriched my life and those who knew you*
> *The power of your life continues to influence me*
> *Your spirit will always be a part of mine*

About the Author

Gerald Corey is Professor Emeritus of Human Services at California State University at Fullerton. He received his doctorate in counseling from the University of Southern California. He is a Diplomate in Counseling Psychology, American Board of Professional Psychology; a licensed psychologist; a National Certified Counselor; a Fellow of the American Psychological Association (Counseling Psychology); and a Fellow of the Association for Specialists in Group Work.

Jerry received the Outstanding Professor of the Year Award from California State University at Fullerton in 1991. He teaches both undergraduate and graduate courses in group counseling, as well as courses in experiential groups, the theory and practice of counseling, and professional ethics. He is the author or co-author of 15 textbooks in counseling currently in print, along with numerous journal articles. His book, *Theory and Practice of Counseling and Psychotherapy*, has been translated into Arabic, Indonesian, Portuguese, and Chinese. *Theory and Practice of Group Counseling* has been translated into Chinese and Spanish.

Along with his wife, Marianne Schneider Corey, Jerry often presents workshops in group counseling. In the past 25 years the Coreys have conducted group counseling training workshops for mental health professionals at many universities in the United States as well as in Mexico, China, Germany, Belgium, Scotland, Canada, and Ireland. In his leisure time, Jerry likes to travel, hike and bicycle in the mountains, and drive his 1931 Model A Ford.

Recent publications by Jerry Corey, all with Brooks/Cole–Wadsworth Publishing Company, include:

- *Theory and Practice of Group Counseling*, Sixth Edition, (and *Manual*) (2004)
- *Group Techniques*, Third Edition (2004, with Marianne Schneider Corey, Patrick Callanan, and J. Michael Russell)
- *Clinical Supervision in the Helping Professions: A Practical Guide* (2003, with Robert Haynes and Patrice Moulton).

- *Issues and Ethics in the Helping Professions*, Sixth Edition (2003, with Marianne Schneider Corey and Patrick Callanan)
- *Becoming a Helper*, Fourth Edition (2003, with Marianne Schneider Corey)
- *Groups: Process and Practice*, Sixth Edition (2002, with Marianne Schneider Corey)
- *I Never Knew I Had a Choice*, Seventh Edition (2002, with Marianne Schneider Corey)
- *Theory and Practice of Counseling and Psychotherapy*, Sixth Edition (and *Manual*) (2001)
- *Case Approach to Counseling and Psychotherapy*, Fifth Edition (2001)
- *The Art of Integrative Counseling* (2001)

Jerry is co-author, with his daughters Cindy Corey and Heidi Jo Corey, of an orientation-to-college book entitled *Living and Learning* (1997), published by Wadsworth. He is also co-author (with Barbara Herlihy) of *Boundary Issues in Counseling: Multiple Roles and Responsibilities* (1997) and *ACA Ethical Standards Casebook*, Fifth Edition (1996), both published by the American Counseling Association.

He has also made three videos on various aspects of counseling practice: (1) *Student Video and Workbook for the Art of Integrative Counseling* (2001, with Robert Haynes); (2) *The Evolution of a Group: Student Video and Workbook* (2000, with Marianne Schneider Corey and Robert Haynes); and (3) *Ethics in Action*: CD-ROM (2003, with Marianne Schneider Corey and Robert Haynes). All of these student videos and workbooks are available through Brooks/Cole–Thomson Learning.

Contents

10 The Person-Centered Approach to Groups   268

11 Gestalt Therapy in Groups   299

12 Transactional Analysis   335

13 The Behavioral Approach to Groups   359

14 Rational Emotive Behavior Therapy in Groups   395

15 Reality Therapy in Groups   421

PART INTEGRATION AND APPLICATION   449

16 Comparisons, Contrasts, and Integration 451

17 The Evolution of a Group: An Integrative Perspective 473

Name Index 501

Subject Index 505

Preface

Group counseling is an increasingly popular form of therapeutic intervention in a variety of settings. Although many textbooks deal with groups, very few of them present an overview of various theoretical models and describe how these models apply to group counseling. This book outlines the basic elements of group process, deals with ethical and professional issues special to group work, and presents an overview of the key concepts and techniques of ten approaches to group counseling. The book also attempts an integration of these approaches and encourages students to develop a framework that leads to their own synthesis.

Theory and Practice of Group Counseling is written in a clear and simple style, so that you will have no difficulty understanding the theoretical concepts and their relationship to group practice. Of course, many of you may have taken a course in counseling theories before your group counseling course, and that background will certainly be useful in understanding and applying the material in this book.

This updated sixth edition emphasizes the practical applications of the theoretical models to group work. The central purpose is to help you to develop your own synthesis of various aspects of these approaches. This book also has two detailed chapters on the stages of a group's development, providing a guide for leaders in the practice of counseling.

Part One (Chapters 1 through 5) treats the basic elements of group process and practice that you'll need to know regardless of the types of groups you may lead or the theoretical orientation you may hold. Chapter 1 presents an overview of the various types of groups and discusses some general principles that can be applied in working with the reality of cultural diversity in groups. Chapter 2 deals with basic concerns of group leadership, such as the personal characteristics of effective leaders, the problems they face, the different styles of leadership, the range of specific skills required for effective leading, and the components of an effective multicultural group counselor. Chapter 3 addresses important ethical issues that you will inevitably encounter as you lead groups. The emphasis is on the rights of group members and the responsibilities of group leaders. The ASGW's "Best Practice Guidelines" are presented in the Student Manual that accompanies this book. In Chapters 4 and 5 you are introduced to the major developmental tasks confronting a group as it goes through its various stages from formation to termination, including evaluation and follow-up. The central characteristics of the stages that make up the life history of a group are examined, with special attention paid to the major functions of the group leader at each stage. These chapters also focus on the functions of the members of a group and the possible problems that are associated with each stage in the group's evolution. The references and suggested readings for Part One have been updated.

Part Two (Chapters 6 through 15) examines ten theoretical approaches to group counseling. Most of the revisions for this edition are found in Part Two, in which about 14% of the material is new. These chapters are designed to provide you with a good overview of a variety of theoretical models underlying group counseling, so that you can see the connection between theory and practice. Each of these theoretical orientations has something valid to offer you as a future group leader. In this sixth edition some of the chapters have been significantly rewritten to reflect recent trends, whereas other chapters have undergone only minor revisions. The following chapters dealing with theory and practice of group work have been extensively revised: psychodrama, person-centered therapy, Adlerian, existential therapy, reality therapy, and behavior therapy. These revisions were based on the recommendations of expert reviewers, who provided suggestions for updating the discussions of the various theories with regard to current trends, new studies, and recent developments in the practice of the approach. Each of the theory chapters has been revised to reflect contemporary practice and to include the latest references for each theory. New to this edition is a section dealing with some of the concepts and techniques that have particular relevance and applicability to group work in the schools with children and adolescents.

To provide a framework that will help you integrate the theoretical models, these 10 chapters have a common structure. Each chapter begins by describing the key concepts of the theory and their implications for group practice. This is followed by a discussion of the role and functions of the group leader according to the particular theory and, when applicable, the stages of development of that particular group process. Next are discussions of how each theory is applied to group practice; the major techniques employed under each theory; concepts and techniques that have applicability to group work in the school; and how the approach can be applied with diverse client populations. Illustrative examples make the use of these techniques more concrete. Each chapter contains my evaluation of the approach under discussion—an evaluation based on what I consider to be its major strengths and limitations.

The necessity for flexibility and a willingness to adapt techniques to fit the client's cultural background is emphasized in each chapter. You are given recommendations regarding where to look for further training in each of the theoretical approaches. Updated annotated lists of reading suggestions and extensive references at the end of these chapters are offered to stimulate you to expand on the material and broaden your learning through further reading.

Part Three (Chapters 16 and 17) focuses on the practical application of the theories and principles covered in Parts One and Two, making these applications more vivid and concrete. Chapter 16 is designed to help you pull together the various methods and approaches, realizing commonalities and differences among them. The chapter concludes with a description of an "integrative eclectic model of group counseling," which combines concepts and techniques from all the approaches that have been examined and which should help students attempt their own personal integration. The model I present integrates "thinking," "feeling," and "doing" perspectives, with varying emphases at each stage of a group's development. My purpose is to show which aspects of each theory I draw on at the various stages of the group, as well as to offer a basis for blending what may look like diverse approaches to the practice of group work. I strive to give you some guidance in thinking about ways to develop your own synthesis of the various group approaches. Chapter 17 follows a group in action and applies an integrative perspective, demonstrating how my co-leader (Marianne Schneider Corey) and I draw from various approaches as we work with a group. This final chapter consists of our version of an integrative approach in working with certain typical themes that might emerge in a group, emphasizing the theoretical and therapeutic rationale behind our interventions with specific members. This is a case of the unfolding of a group in action, an actual three-day residential group co-led by Marianne and Jerry Corey.

Chapter 17 is based on the two-hour student video, *Evolution of a Group*. Central themes for each of the stages of a group are addressed in this chapter and demonstrated in the video. These illustrative samples of group work are intended to make the theoretical perspectives come alive, to provide some flavor of the differences and similarities among the approaches, and to show some ways of drawing on the diverse approaches in working with material that emerges from a group. The video also emphasizes the application of techniques in working with the material that unfolds in the here-and-now context of the group. The video depicts central features that illustrate the development of the group process and how co-leaders facilitate a process as the group moves through the various stages: initial, transition, working, and ending. Chapters 4 and 5 deal with the early and later stages of group respectively, and the video is structured around these stages of development.

For the purpose of getting a general overview of basic issues and of comparisons among the 10 theories, I recommend that you read Part Three (Chapters 16 and 17) early in the course (after reading Chapters 1 through 5) to get a general overview of the approaches. Of course, these two chapters will be most important as tools for integrating and synthesizing concepts after you have studied the contemporary approaches in Part Two.

This book is for graduate or undergraduate students in any field involving human services. It is especially suitable for students enrolled in any of the courses under the general designation of "Theory and Practice of Group Counseling." The book is also for practitioners who are involved in group work or for students and trainees who are interested in leading various types of groups. Those who may find this book useful are psychiatric nurses, ministers, social workers, psychologists, marriage and family therapists, rehabilitation counselors, community agency counselors, school counselors, licensed professional counselors, and mental health professionals who lead groups as a part of their work.

A sixth edition of the *Student Manual for Theory and Practice of Group Counseling* is available to help you gain maximum benefit from this book and actually experience group process and techniques. The manual includes questions for reflection and discussion, suggested activities for the whole class and for small groups, ideas for supervised training groups, summary charts, self-inventories, study guides, comprehension checks and quizzes, self-tests, group techniques, examples of cases with open-ended alternatives for group counseling practice, and a glossary of key terms. An ideal learning package is *Theory and Practice of Group Counseling; Student Manual for Theory and Practice of Group Counseling; Evolution of a Group* (student video and workbook); and *Group Techniques* (3rd ed., 2004).

An *Instructor's Resource Manual* is also available; it has been revised to reflect the changes in both the textbook and the student manual.

Acknowledgments

Many of the revisions that have become a part of this textbook since its original edition in 1981 have come about in the context of discussions with students, colleagues, and professors who use the book. Those students and professionals whom I teach continue to teach me in return, and most of my ideas are stimulated by interactions with them. The supportive challenge of my friends and colleagues (with whom I offer classes and workshops and with whom I co-lead groups) continues to keep my learning fresh and provides me with encouragement to keep practicing, teaching, and writing. These friends and colleagues are Patrick Callanan, Cindy Corey, Marianne Schneider Corey, Lynn Henning, Mary Moline, J. Michael Russell, and Veronika Tracy-Smith. I especially want to recognize the influence on my life and my books of my wife and colleague, Marianne Schneider Corey, with whom I regularly work professionally. Her critique and feedback have been especially valuable in preparing these revisions, and many of the ideas in the book are the product of our many hours of discussions about group work.

The comments of those who provided reviews either before or after the manuscript was revised have been most helpful in shaping up the final product. Those who reviewed the entire manuscript of the sixth edition and offered useful feedback are: Maureen Callahan, Long Island University, C.W. Post Campus; David Demetral, California State University, Sacramento; Judy DeTrude, Sam Houston State University, Dana Edwards, Georgia State University; Darcy Haag Granello, Ohio State University; Pam Remer, University of Kentucky; Wayne Rickard, Western Kentucky University, Owensboro; Marty Sapp, University of Wisconsin, Milwaukee; Muriel Stockburger, Eastern Kentucky University; and Allen Weber, St. Bonaventure University. I thank Paul Pedersen of the University of Hawaii, who reviewed all the sections on multicultural group counseling. I very much appreciate the numerous ideas regarding applications of group work with school-age students provided by

Wallace Kahn of West Chester University and his students including: Sabrina Blando, Jennifer Borzillo, Tia Crozier, Edward Cultrona, Mega Dawes, Kristen Donahue, Jennifer Goodballet, Kara Heilman, Kate Lawhorne, Carolyn Myers, Nicole Pappas, Lisa Ruggiano, and Nicole Small.

I value the detailed commentaries I received from single-chapter reviewers. Many people contributed by sharing their expertise in certain areas. I thank the following for their assistance in updating the various theory chapters:

Chapters 1 to 5: Jamie Bludworth, doctoral student, Arizona State University

Chapter 6: William Blau, Copper Mountain College, Joshua Tree, California

Chapter 7: James Bitter, East Tennessee State University; William G. Nicoll, Florida Atlantic University

Chapter 8: Adam Blatner, Private Practice, Sun City/Georgetown, Texas; and Zerka T. Moreno, of Zerka T. Moreno Workshops, Beacon, New York

Chapter 9: William Gould, University of Dubuque; and J. Michael Russell, California State University, Fullerton

Chapter 10: David J. Cain, Director of the Counseling Center at United States International University, San Diego; and Jo Cohen Hamilton, Kutztown University

Chapter 11: Gary Yontef, Private Practice, Gestalt Therapy Institute of the Pacific, Los Angeles; and Jon Frew, Private Practice, Vancouver, Washington

Chapter 12: Tim Schnabel, A Growing Place of Atlanta

Chapter 13: David C. Guevremont, Woonsocket Education Department; and Michael D. Spiegler, Providence College

Chapter 14: Albert Ellis, President of the Albert Ellis Institute in New York

Chapter 15: Robert E. Wubbolding, Center for Reality Therapy, Cincinnati, Ohio

Chapter 17: This case example is based on an actual group that is the subject of a video, *Evolution of a Group*. Let me recognize the courage of the participants in this group for being themselves in the video and providing a real example of the unfolding of a group through all its stages. These individuals reviewed the chapter and gave suggestions that have been incorporated: Jacqueline, SusAnne, Jyl, James, Andrew, Darren, Casey, and Jackie.

This book is the result of a team effort, which includes the combined talents of several people at Brooks/Cole–Thomson Learning. I appreciate the opportunity to work with a dedicated and talented group of professionals in the publishing business. They include Julie Martinez, counseling editor; Shelley Gesicki, assistant editor; Caroline Concilla, marketing manager; and Kim Svetich-Will, project manager. I also thank Cecile Joyner and Benjamin Kolstad of The Cooper Company, who coordinated the production of this book, and Kay Mikel, the manuscript editor of this edition, whose exceptional editorial talents continue to keep this book reader-friendly. I also appreciate the careful work that Mimi Lawson did in preparing the index. Their efforts and dedication certainly contribute to the quality of this edition. With the professional assistance of these people, the ongoing task of revising this book continues to be a source of more joy than pain.

Gerald Corey

PART 1

BASIC ELEMENTS OF GROUP PROCESS: AN OVERVIEW

1

Introduction to Group Work

Today, more than ever, mental health practitioners are being challenged to develop new strategies for both preventing and treating psychological problems. Although there is still a place in a community agency for individual counseling, limiting the delivery of services to this model is no longer practical. Group counseling offers real promise in meeting today's challenges. Group counseling enables practitioners to work with more clients—a decided advantage in these tight financial times—in addition, the group process also has unique learning advantages. Group counseling may well be the treatment of choice for many populations. If group work is to be effective, however, practitioners need a theoretical grounding and will have to find ways to use these theories creatively in practice.

The Increasing Use of Groups

In conducting workshops around the United States and Europe, my colleagues and I are finding a surge of interest in group work. Professional counselors are creating an increasing variety of groups to fit the special needs of a diverse clientele. In fact, the types of groups that can be designed are limited only by one's imagination. This expanded interest underscores the need for broad education and training in both the theory and the practice of group counseling. This book attempts to provide you with a fundamental base of knowledge applicable to the many kinds of groups you will be leading.

Groups can be used for therapeutic or educational purposes or for a combination of the two. Some groups deal primarily with helping people make fundamental changes in their ways of thinking, feeling, and behaving. Other groups, those with an educational focus, teach members specific coping skills. This chapter provides a brief overview of various types of groups and the differences among them.

In the human services field, you will be expected to be prepared to use group approaches with a variety of clients for a variety of purposes. In a psychiatric hospital, for example, you may be asked to design and lead groups for patients with various problems, for those who are about to leave the hospital and reenter the community, or for patients' families. Insight groups, remotivation groups, assertion training groups, bereavement groups, and recreational/vocational therapy groups are commonly found in these hospitals.

If you work in a community mental health center, a college counseling center, or a day-treatment clinic, you will be expected to provide therapeutic services in a wide range of group settings. Your client population will most likely be diverse with respect to age, problems, socioeconomic status, level of education, race or ethnicity, sexual orientation, and cultural background. Community agencies are making increased use of groups, and it is not uncommon to find groups for women, consciousness raising groups for men, groups for children of alcoholics, support groups, parent education groups, groups for cancer patients, eating disorders groups, crisis intervention groups, groups for senior citizens, HIV/AIDS support groups, and groups aimed at reducing substance abuse. Your theoretical approach may be based primarily on a single system, such as reality therapy, or on one of the many forms of behavior therapy done in a group setting. Increasingly, however, practitioners are becoming more eclectic as they draw techniques from various approaches. You may find this flexibility useful as well.

Special groups in schools are designed to deal with students' educational, vocational, personal, or social problems. If you work in a school, you may be asked to form a career exploration group, a self-esteem group, a group for children of divorce, a group for acting-out children, a group aimed at teaching interpersonal skills, or a personal growth group. Elementary school counselors are now leading therapeutic groups as well as educational groups. On the high school level, groups are aimed at helping students who are in drug rehabilitation, who have been victims of crime, or who are going through a crisis.

In sum, a group approach can help people meet almost any need. One of the main reasons for this popularity is that the group approach is frequently more effective than the individual approach. This effectiveness stems from the fact that group members can practice new skills both within the group and in their everyday interactions outside of it. Moreover, members of the group benefit from the feedback and insights of other group members as well as those of the practitioner. Groups also offer many opportunities for modeling. Members learn how to cope with their problems by observing others with similar concerns. There are practical reasons for the popularity of groups, too, such as lower costs and a broader distribution of the available counselors and therapists.

Even practitioners with advanced degrees in one or another of the helping professions often have very little exposure to the theory and techniques of group work. Many of these professionals find themselves thrust into the role of group leader without adequate preparation and training. It is not surprising that some of them become anxious and don't know where to begin. Although this book is not intended to be an exclusive means of preparing competent group leaders, it is aimed at providing some preparation for coping with the demands of group leadership.

Overview of the Counseling Group

Group counseling has preventive as well as remedial aims. Generally, the counseling group has a specific focus, which may be educational, vocational, social, or personal. The group involves an interpersonal process that stresses conscious thoughts, feelings, and behavior. Counseling groups are often problem oriented, with their content and aim determined largely by the members. These group members don't require extensive personality reconstruction, and their concerns generally relate to the developmental tasks of the life span. Group counseling tends to be growth oriented in that the emphasis is on discovering internal resources of strength. The participants may be facing situational crises and temporary conflicts, or they may be trying to change self-defeating behaviors. The group provides the empathy and support necessary to create the atmosphere of trust that leads to sharing and exploring these concerns. Group members are assisted in developing their existing skills in dealing with interpersonal problems so that they will be better able to handle future problems of a similar nature.

The group counselor uses verbal and nonverbal techniques as well as structured exercises. Common techniques include reflection (mirroring the verbal and nonverbal messages of a group member), clarification (helping members understand more clearly what they are saying or feeling), role playing, and interpretation (connecting present behaviors with past decisions). Other common techniques used in group counseling are described in more detail in Chapter 2. Basically, the role of the group counselor is to facilitate interaction among the members, help them learn from one another, assist them in establishing personal goals, and encourage them to translate their insights into concrete plans that involve taking action outside of the group. Counselors perform this role largely by teaching members to focus on the here-and-now and to identify the concerns they wish to explore in the group.

Goals

Ideally, members decide for themselves the specific goals of the group experience. Here are some general goals often shared by members of counseling groups:

- To learn to trust oneself and others
- To increase awareness and self-knowledge; to develop a sense of one's unique identity
- To recognize the commonality of members' needs and problems and to develop a sense of universality
- To increase self-acceptance, self-confidence, self-respect, and to achieve a new view of oneself and others
- To develop concern and compassion for others
- To find alternative ways of dealing with normal developmental issues and of resolving certain conflicts

- To increase self-direction, interdependence, and responsibility toward one-self and others
- To become aware of one's choices and to make choices wisely
- To make specific plans for changing certain behaviors and to commit oneself to follow through with these plans
- To learn more effective social skills
- To become more sensitive to the needs and feelings of others
- To learn how to challenge others with care, concern, honesty, and directness
- To clarify one's values and decide whether and how to modify them

Advantages

Group counseling has a number of advantages as a vehicle for helping people make changes in their attitudes, beliefs about themselves and others, feelings, and behaviors. One advantage is that participants can explore their styles of relating with others and learn more effective social skills. Another is that members can discuss their perceptions of one another and receive valuable feedback on how they are being perceived in the group.

In many ways the counseling group provides a re-creation of the participants' everyday world, especially if the membership is diverse with respect to age, interests, background, socioeconomic status, and type of problem. As a microcosm of society, the group provides a sample of reality—members' struggles and conflicts in the group are similar to those they experience outside of it—and the diversity that characterizes most groups also results in unusually rich feedback for the participants, who can see themselves through the eyes of a wide range of people.

The group offers understanding and support, which foster the members' willingness to explore problems they have brought with them to the group. The participants achieve a sense of belonging, and through the cohesion that develops they learn ways of being intimate, of caring, and of challenging. In this supportive atmosphere, members can experiment with alternative behaviors. As they practice these behaviors in the group, they receive encouragement as well as suggestions on how to apply what they are learning in the outside world.

Ultimately, it is up to the members themselves to decide what changes they want to make. They can compare the perceptions they have of themselves with the perceptions others have of them and then decide what to do with this information. In essence, group members get a clearer glimpse of the kind of person they would like to become, and they come to understand what is preventing them from becoming that person.

Value for Specific Populations

Group counseling can be designed to meet the needs of specific populations such as children, adolescents, college students, or the elderly. Examples of these counseling groups are described in *Groups: Process and Practice* (M. Corey & Corey, 2002), which offers suggestions on how to set up these groups and techniques to use for dealing with the unique problems of each of them. Following is a brief discussion of the value of counseling groups for several specific populations.

Counseling Groups for Children   Counseling groups for children can serve preventive or remedial purposes. In schools, group counseling is often suggested for children who display behaviors or attributes such as excessive fighting, inability to get along with peers, violent outbursts, chronic tiredness, lack of supervision at home, or neglected appearance. Small groups can provide children with the opportunity to express their feelings about these and related problems. Identifying children who are developing serious emotional and behavioral problems is extremely important. If these children can receive psychological assistance at an early age, they stand a better chance of coping effectively with the developmental tasks they must face later in life.

Counseling Groups for Adolescents   The adolescent years can be extremely lonely ones, and it is not unusual for an adolescent to feel that no one is there to help. Adolescence is also a time when key decisions are made that can affect the course of one's life.

Group counseling is especially suited for adolescents because it gives them a place to express conflicting feelings, to explore self-doubts, and to come to the realization that they share these concerns with their peers. A group allows adolescents to openly question their values and to modify those that need to be changed. In the group, adolescents learn to communicate with their peers, they benefit from the modeling provided by the leader, and they can safely experiment with reality and test their limits. Another unique value of group counseling for adolescents is that it offers a chance for them to be instrumental in one another's growth. Because of the opportunities for interaction available in the group situation, the participants can express their concerns and be heard, and they can help one another on the road toward self-understanding and self-acceptance.

Counseling Groups for College Students   Counseling groups are a valuable vehicle for meeting the developmental needs of the many students who feel that their college or university is preoccupied with their intellectual development to the exclusion of their emotional and social growth. During the years I spent working in the counseling centers at two universities, I became aware of the need for groups on campus. Today, many college counseling centers offer groups designed for relatively healthy students who are experiencing developmental crises. The main purpose of these groups is to provide participants with an opportunity for growth and a situation in which they can deal with career decisions, interpersonal relationships, identity problems, educational plans, feelings of isolation on an impersonal campus, and other concerns related to becoming an autonomous person.

Many university and college counseling centers now offer a wide range of structured groups to meet the diverse needs of students, a few of which are assertion groups, consciousness raising groups for women and men, groups for ethnic minorities, groups for the physically challenged, stress reduction groups, groups for middle-aged returning students considering career and lifestyle changes, and test anxiety reduction groups.

Counseling Groups for the Elderly   Counseling groups can be valuable for the elderly in many of the same ways they are of value to adolescents. As people grow older, they often experience isolation. Like adolescents, the elderly often feel unproductive, unneeded, and unwanted. Seeing no hope of meaning—let alone excitement—in their future, many resign themselves to a useless life. Many older people accept myths about aging, which then become self-fulfilling prophecies. An example is the misconception that older people cannot change or that once they retire they will be doomed to depression. Counseling groups can do a lot to help older people challenge these myths and deal with the developmental tasks that they, like any other age group, must face in such a way that they can retain their integrity and self-respect. The group situation can assist people in breaking out of their isolation and offer the elderly the encouragement necessary to find meaning in their lives so that they can live fully and not merely exist.

Other Types of Groups

Although the focus of this book is on counseling groups, the practice of group work has broadened to encompass psychotherapy groups, psychoeducation groups, and task groups as well as counseling groups. Many of these groups share some of the procedures, techniques, and processes of counseling groups. They differ, however, with respect to specific aims, the role of the leader, the kind of people in the group, and the emphasis given to issues such as prevention, remediation, treatment, and development. Let's take a brief look at how psychotherapy groups, psychoeducation (structured) groups, task groups, and self-help groups differ from counseling groups.

Group Psychotherapy

A major difference between group *therapy* and group *counseling* lies in their goals. Whereas counseling groups focus on growth, development, enhancement, prevention, self-awareness, and releasing blocks to growth, therapy groups typically focus on remediation, treatment, and personality reconstruction. Group psychotherapy is a process of reeducation that includes both conscious and unconscious awareness and both the present and the past. Some therapy groups are primarily designed to correct emotional and behavioral disorders that impede one's functioning or to remediate in-depth psychological problems. The goal may be either a minor or a major transformation of personality structure, depending on the theoretical orientation of the group therapist. Because of this goal, therapy groups tend to be more long-term than

other kinds of groups. The people who make up the g.
from severe emotional problems, deep neurotic conflicts
and some may exhibit socially deviant behavior. Many of t
in need of remedial treatment rather than developmental an

Group therapists are typically clinical or counseling
censed mental health counselors, and clinical social workers.
range of verbal modalities (which group counselors also use),
ploy techniques to induce regression to earlier experiences, to ta   us
dynamics, and to help members reexperience traumatic situat   so that
catharsis can occur. As these experiences are relived in the group, members become aware of and gain insight into past decisions that interfere with current
functioning. The group therapist assists members in developing a corrective
emotional experience and in making new decisions about the world, others,
and themselves. Working through unfinished business from the past that has
roots in the unconscious is a primary characteristic of group therapy. This
focus on past material, unconscious dynamics, personality reconstruction, and
development of new patterns of behavior based on insight also accounts for
the longer duration of group therapy.

Psychoeducation Groups

Psychoeducation groups, or groups structured by some central theme, seem to
be gaining in popularity. When my colleagues and I conduct group process
workshops, the practitioners we meet are often very creative in designing
short-term groups that deal with a specific theme or a particular population.
These group workers perceive needs in the community and address these
needs by creating groups. Such groups serve a number of purposes: imparting
information, sharing common experiences, teaching people how to solve problems, offering support, and helping people learn how to create their own support systems outside of the group setting. These groups can be thought of as
educational and therapeutic groups in that they are structured along the lines
of certain content themes aimed at imparting information and that they also
have a self-development component.

It is clear that psychoeducation groups—as opposed to counseling groups
or ongoing personal growth groups—are finding a place in many settings.
They appear to be increasingly used in community agencies and in schools.
Many college and university counseling centers offer a variety of special
groups for particular populations in addition to their unstructured personal
growth groups and counseling groups. For example, consider the group counseling programs available for students at Colorado State University. There are
both therapy groups for adult children of alcoholics and also education and
support groups for these clients. This counseling center also offers an anxiety
management group, an eating disorders group, a family issues group, a group
for students of nontraditional age, a relationship concerns group, a self-esteem
group, a group for adult female survivors of childhood sexual abuse, and a
personal identity group for women.

Psychoeducation groups are structured in such a way as to help people develop specific skills, understand certain themes, or go through difficult life transitions. Although the topics obviously vary according to the interests of the group leader and the clientele, such groups have a common denominator of providing members with increased awareness of some life problem and tools to better cope with it. The goal is to prevent an array of educational and psychological disturbances. Typically, the sessions are two hours each week, and the groups tend to be relatively short term. They may last only 4 or 5 weeks, or up to a maximum of one semester, about 16 weeks.

Members may be asked to complete a questionnaire at the beginning of the group that pertains to how well they are coping with the particular area of concern. Structured exercises and homework assignments are typically introduced as ways of teaching new skills to group members. Another questionnaire is often used at the final session to assess members' progress. A contract is frequently drawn up as a way of helping members pinpoint specific goals that will guide their participation in the group and stimulate them to practice new skills outside of the group.

Many psychoeducation groups are based on a learning theory model and use behavioral procedures. Chapter 13 provides detailed descriptions of such groups, including social skills training and assertiveness training groups, stress management groups, cognitive therapy groups, and multimodal therapy groups.

Psychoeducation groups for women have become increasingly popular. The formats vary from support to general therapy groups. The themes emphasize self-esteem and relationship issues in general and may highlight specific concerns such as sexual abuse or eating disorders (McManus, Redford, & Hughes, 1997). Juntunen, Cohen, and Wolszon (1997) describe one psychoeducation group for women that focuses on anger. The group meets for eight sessions and is structured around themes such as identifying anger, learning to express anger without blame, clarifying values and rights, learning how to deal with barriers to change, and negotiating relationships.

Another psychoeducation group for women is aimed primarily at helping women connect to themselves and to others (McManus, Redford, & Hughes, 1997). It is also based on feminist principles. During the six sessions, nine dimensions are explored:

- Understanding the impact of gender role socialization
- Identifying personal strengths, limitations, and resources
- Learning to develop empathy for oneself
- Learning to care for self
- Accepting and trusting feelings
- Learning to be assertive
- Examining the healthy aspects of relationships
- Learning empowerment to change relationships
- Affirming the importance of relationships in one's life

This kind of group offers women a chance to learn about themselves and ways of relating to others in a safe and supportive environment. Through the group experience, women have the opportunity to create a balance between being autonomous and being connected to others.

Psychoeducation groups are well suited to all age populations. Here are a few examples of such groups for various developmental levels; they are described in detail in *Groups: Process and Practice* (M. Corey & Corey, 2002):

- An elementary school group for children of divorce
- A high school group for children of alcoholics
- A group for unwed teenage fathers
- An HIV/AIDS support group
- A men's group in a community agency
- A relational women's support group
- A domestic violence group
- A women's support group for survivors of incest
- An elderly bereavement group

All of these groups are psychoeducational in that they contain certain content themes to provide structure for the sessions, they encourage sharing and feedback among the members, they are designed to increase self-awareness, and they are aimed at facilitating change in the members' daily lives. These groups can be designed for just about every client group and can be tailored to the specific needs of the individuals represented.

Task Facilitation Groups

Task facilitation groups are designed to assist task forces, committees, planning groups, community organizations, discussion groups, study circles, learning groups, and other similar groups to correct or develop their functioning. The focus is on the application of principles and processes of group dynamics that may improve practice and foster accomplishment of identified work goals. Increasingly, human services workers are being asked to help improve program planning and evaluation within organizations. Whether task groups are created for organizational purposes or to meet certain needs of clients, the tasks of these groups center around decision making and problem solving (Conyne, Wilson, & Ward, 1997).

Professionals who work in the community are often called on to apply their group work expertise to meet the needs of the community. Task groups have many uses in community intervention. Many of the problems people face are the result of being disenfranchised as individuals or as members of the community. The challenge of professionals engaged in community work is to assist individuals and the community in acquiring access to valued resources in moving toward a greater degree of enfranchisement. Group workers need to understand how sociopolitical influences impinge on the experiences of racial and ethnic minority groups. For example, immigration issues, racism, stereotyping, poverty, and powerlessness can all severely damage individuals (Arredondo et al., 1996).

Working with the community usually means working with a specific group or in a situation in which competing or collaborating groups are dealing with an issue or set of issues in a community. Most of the work in community change will be done in a small group context, and skills in organizing task groups are essential (M. Corey & Corey, 2003).

Self-Help Groups

The last 25 years have seen a burgeoning of self-help groups, which enable people with a common problem or life predicament to create a support system that protects them from psychological stress and gives them the incentive to begin changing their lives. These groups serve a critical need for certain populations, which is not met by professional mental health workers. The members share their experiences, provide one another with emotional and social support, learn from one another, offer suggestions for new members, and provide some direction for people who do not see any hope for their future.

Self-help groups and therapy groups have some common denominators. Both are based on the assumption that people suffer from unexpressed feelings and thoughts, and they encourage members to express their emotions. Both types of groups encourage support, stress the value of affiliation, and aim for behavioral change.

Despite these commonalities between self-help and therapy groups, some critical differences remain (Riordan & Beggs, 1987, 1988). Self-help groups have as their central issue a single topic such as addiction, cancer, or obesity, and such groups emphasize support and inspiration. Therapy groups have more global goals such as improving general mental health, increasing self-understanding, or enhancing one's interpersonal functioning.

A further difference between the two types of groups involves the kind of leadership employed. Self-help groups are generally led by individuals who are struggling with the same issues as the members of the group. In most self-help groups the leadership emerges rather than being designated.

With counseling groups and therapy groups, as we have seen, a basic assumption is that the group represents a social microcosm. These groups attempt to reflect in some ways all of the dimensions of the members' real social environment. The therapeutic factor that accounts for change in the participants is the group process, which provides a living example of the interpersonal conflicts members confront in their daily lives.

In contrast, self-help groups are not a social microcosm. The interactions of members within the group are not viewed as the primary catalyst for change. Instead, attention is placed on providing an accepting and supportive climate in the group itself. The group becomes a means of helping people modify their beliefs, attitudes, and feelings about themselves. Self-help groups stress a common identity based on a common life situation to a far greater extent than do most other groups.

People seem to have an increasing interest in banding together to find ways of helping themselves. Although professionally led counseling and therapy groups serve a vital role, perhaps it is a healthy sign that people are seeking other avenues for the help they need. Many self-help groups serve a unique function that cannot always be met in professionally led counseling or therapy groups. The challenge is to train future professionals in how best to collaborate with self-help groups. Clearly, both self-help groups and therapy groups have a distinct contribution to make in our society.

Brief Group Work

Although, strictly speaking, brief groups are not a type of group, many of the groups already described are characterized by a time-limited format. In the era of managed care, brief interventions and short-term groups have become a necessity. Economic pressures and a shortage of resources have resulted in major changes in the way mental health services are delivered, and these pressures are reshaping group therapy practices (MacKenzie, 1994). Managed care also has influenced the trend toward developing all forms of briefer treatment, including group treatment. A variety of approaches to brief group treatment have been developed, and there is evidence that these treatments are both effective and economical (Rosenberg & Wright, 1997).

In their review of research on brief, time-limited *outpatient* group therapy, Rosenberg and Zimet (1995) found clear evidence for the effectiveness of time-limited group therapy. Their review also showed that behavioral and cognitive behavioral approaches were particularly well suited to brief group therapy. In addition, they found that, if modifications were made, long-term psychodynamic approaches could be as useful. Klein, Brabender, and Fallon (1994) report positive results with short-term *inpatient* therapy groups with a variety of client populations and a broad range of problems. Brief interventions and time limitations are especially relevant for a variety of counseling groups, structured groups, psychoeducational groups, and self-help groups. The realistic time constraints in most settings demand that practitioners employ briefer approaches with demonstrated effectiveness.

Rosenberg and Wright (1997) maintain that it is clear that brief group therapy is well suited to the needs of both clients and managed care. Brief group therapy and managed care both require the group therapist to set clear and realistic treatment goals with the members, to establish a clear focus within the group structure, to maintain an active therapist role, and to work within a limited time frame. Rosenberg and Wright conclude: "In an era of increasingly limited resources, brief group treatment remains underutilized despite clear evidence of its efficacy and efficiency. There is little doubt that group psychotherapy can make important contributions to the provision of mental health services within managed care settings" (p. 116).

Group Counseling in a Multicultural Context

In a pluralistic society, the reality of cultural diversity is recognized, respected, and encouraged. Within groups, the worldviews of both the group leader and the members also vary, and this is a natural place to acknowledge and promote pluralism. Multicultural group work involves strategies that cultivate understanding and appreciation of diversity in such areas as culture, ethnicity, race, gender, class, religion, and sexual orientation. We each have a unique multicultural identity, but as members of a group we share a common goal—the success of the group. To that end, we want to learn more about ourselves as individuals and as members of diverse cultural groups.

DeLucia-Waack (1996) states that the multicultural context of group work requires attention to two tasks: (a) the application and modification of theories and techniques of group work to different cultures in ways that are congruent with cultural beliefs and behaviors, and (b) the development of the theory and practice of group work that makes full use of the diversity among members as a way to facilitate change and growth. Multiculturalism is inherent in all group work, and our uniqueness as individuals is a key factor in how groups operate.

In addition to understanding the range of clients' cultural similarities and differences, group counselors must be willing and able to challenge the culturally encapsulated view of a group's structure, goals, techniques, and practices. A fundamental step for group counselors is reexamining the underlying culturally learned assumptions of all the major theories in light of their appropriateness in a multicultural context. This multicultural perspective does not seek to compete with these major theories or to displace them. Rather, adopting a culture-centered perspective will strengthen the value of major theories and increase their practical relevance to multicultural groups in our pluralistic society (Paul Pedersen, pers. comm., June 5, 2002).

In their discussion of *multicultural intentionality* in group counseling, Ivey, Pedersen, and Ivey (2001) state that it is no longer adequate to mainly look to internal dynamics within the individual as a source of problems. Instead, it is essential that we examine ourselves as contextual/cultural beings. We must expand our awareness of issues pertaining to gender, sexual orientation, degree of physical and emotional ability, spirituality, and socioeconomic status. It is not necessary to discard traditional theories and techniques of counseling, but we must conceptualize them in ways that recognize the environmental influences on individual distress.

Multicultural counseling and psychotherapy challenge the notion that personal problems are exclusively within the person. Going beyond this stance of "blaming the victim," the multicultural approach emphasizes the social and cultural context of human behavior and deals with the self-in-relation. It is essential that group workers recognize that many problems reside outside the person—prejudice and discrimination, for example—and not within the person. If workers hope to make culturally effective interventions, they need to assume nontraditional roles that may include advocate, change agent, consultant, adviser, and facilitator of indigenous support or healing systems (Atkinson, Thompson, & Grant, 1993).

It is likely that culturally skilled group counselors will need to revise their theories and techniques if they hope to better serve individuals from diverse cultural backgrounds. Part Two addresses some of the major strengths and limitations of 10 major theories from a multicultural perspective. The general principles of effective multicultural group counseling discussed here provide some background for understanding that more detailed discussion later in the book.

Multiculturalism: Some Definitions and Implications

In multicultural counseling, two or more people with different ways of perceiving their social environment attempt to work together in a helping relationship (Pedersen, 2000). The term *multicultural* refers to the complexity of culture as it pertains to delivery of services. Other terms that are used in discussing group practice in a multicultural context include race, ethnicity, minority, and culture. Pedersen defines these terms as follows:

Race pertains to presumed genetic, biological, and physical characteristics shared within a group. Although the scientific basis of racial categories has been discredited, the political reality of race continues to be an important factor in everyday life.

Ethnicity involves a shared sociocultural heritage of religion, history, or common ancestry. Ethnic groups are defined by their shared history.

Culture, broadly defined, includes ethnographic (ethnicity, nationality), demographic (age, gender, residence), status (educational, socioeconomic), and affiliation (formal and informal) variables.

Minority refers to the differential and unequal treatment of an oppressed group due to discrimination by the dominant and more powerful majority. This term is used less often today as the stigma of powerlessness has become attached to it, which impedes efforts toward empowerment for group members.

Multicultural counseling focuses on understanding not only racial and ethnic minority groups (African Americans, Asian Americans, Latinos, Native Americans, and white ethnics) but also women, gay men and lesbians, people with physical disabilities, elderly people, and a variety of special needs populations.

According to Pedersen (1991, 1997), the multicultural perspective seeks to provide a conceptual framework that both recognizes the complex diversity of a pluralistic society and suggests bridges of shared concern that link all people, regardless of their differences. This enables group counselors to look both at the unique dimensions of a person and at how this person shares themes with those who are different. Such a perspective respects the needs and strengths of diverse client populations, and it recognizes the experiences of these clients. Mere knowledge of certain cultural groups is not enough; it is important to understand the variability within groups. Each individual must be seen in the context of his or her cultural identities, the degree to which he or she has become acculturated, and the level of multicultural self-awareness.

Pedersen (1997, 2000) emphasizes the importance of understanding both group and individual differences in making accurate interpretations of behavior.

Whether practitioners pay attention to cultural variables or ignore them, culture will continue to influence both group members' and group leaders' behavior, and the group process as well. Group counselors who ignore culture will provide less effective services. If group counselors hope to successfully lead multicultural groups, it is essential that they possess an awareness of their own cultural heritage and have a level of ethnic self-knowledge (DeLucia-Waack, 1996).

Three Perspectives on Multiculturalism

We have discussed one perspective on multiculturalism in the preceding section; that is, acknowledging a broader definition of culture that includes ethnographic, demographic, status, and affiliation variables. Two other perspectives are equally important for understanding and working with the diverse worldviews of client populations.

The universal perspective is grounded on the premise that basic human dimensions are universally important across cultural categories (Fukuyama, 1990). The emphasis is on the ways people of different cultural groups, whether broadly or narrowly defined, are similar rather than different. The universal approach to multicultural counseling explores the commonalities of the experiences of people and proposes transcultural models for training effective multicultural counselors. Fukuyama proposes a training program that involves these competencies:

- Understanding the concept of culture as a whole and how it affects the individual, society, and the helping process
- Defining culture broadly to encompass gender, sexual orientation, age, ethnicity, and race
- Providing information on all forms of oppression, including racism, sexism, and homophobia
- Exploring the importance of gender roles
- Facilitating the individual's identity development as a member of a culture
- Facilitating an understanding of one's own worldview and how it relates to family and one's cultural background
- Encouraging loyalty and pride in one's own culture and family ties

According to Fukuyama, overemphasizing the differences that separate one cultural group from another may promote stereotyping. She contends that her students have been able to adapt universal concepts covered in a multicultural counseling course and apply these notions to a variety of counseling situations.

In contrast, the focused perspective is grounded on the premise that basic human dimensions unique to each cultural group are more important (Locke, 1990). The emphasis is on the ways people from different cultural groups, whether broadly or narrowly defined, are different rather than similar. In Locke's challenge of the broad, universal approach, he asserts that counselors must gain cultural expertise about specific groups that they are likely to en-counter in their practice. This narrow approach rests on three key elements:

- A willingness by counselors to examine their racial beliefs and attitudes as they relate to specific culturally different individuals or groups
- A willingness to discuss specific racially relevant issues at an institutional level
- A willingness to view clients both as individuals and as members of a group

Locke contends that this perspective is requisite for an adequate philosophy of multicultural counseling.

The Need for a Multicultural Emphasis in Group Work

The changing demographics of North America make it imperative that coun-selors assume a proactive stance on cultural diversity. According to Comas-Diaz (1992), these demographic changes will alter the sociological, political, and economic realities of people of color. Diversity will become the blueprint of North American society. This reality will lead to flexibility and increased choices in psychotherapeutic practice.

It is not possible to apply the assumptions that suit a monocultural society to a multicultural society. Our perceptions of the world are learned within the context of a culture, and people from different cultural backgrounds perceive the world differently. Regardless of your ethnic, cultural, and racial back-ground, if you hope to build bridges of understanding between yourself and group members who are different from you, it is essential that you guard against stereotyped generalizations about social and cultural groups. Counsel-ing requires an accurate and profound understanding of the world of each client (Pedersen, 1991), and group counseling expands that from one individ-ual to many. DeLucia-Waack (1996) identifies three goals that all multicultural groups have in common:

- Helping members conceptualize problems within a personal and cultural framework so that an action plan reflects the individual's worldview
- Encouraging members to explore their behaviors to determine if such be-haviors are helping them in their relationships
- Assisting members in understanding new behaviors and beliefs within a cultural context

Johnson, Torres, Coleman, and Smith (1995) write about issues that group counselors are likely to encounter as they attempt to facilitate culturally di-verse counseling groups. They point out that group members typically bring with them their values, beliefs, and prejudices, which quickly become evident in a group situation. For Johnson and her colleagues, one goal of multicultural group counseling is to provide new levels of communication among members. This can be instrumental in assisting members in challenging their stereotypes by providing accurate information about individuals. Another goal of a di-verse group is to promote understanding, acceptance, and trust among mem-bers of various cultural groups.

The Challenges and Rewards of a Multicultural Perspective

The literature dealing with multicultural counseling indicates that ethnic and minority clients underuse mental health and social services (Atkinson, Morten, & Sue, 1998; Chu & Sue, 1984; Ho, 1984; Lee, Juan, & Hom, 1984; Leong, 1992; Mokuau, 1985, 1987; Pedersen, 2000; D. W. Sue, 1992; D. W. Sue & Sue, 2003). There are a number of reasons for this failure to make full and appropriate use of existing counseling services. One explanation involves the failure of mental health providers to assess, monitor, and address cultural issues. At times, counselors may be insensitive to cultural realities. In addition, clients' cultural values may inhibit the utilization of services. In some cultures, informal helping processes are used more than professional resources. Some clients hold values that call for them to work out their problems by themselves, and doing so indicates greater maturity than seeking help from others (Ho, 1984). Other explanations for the underuse of services include a lack of knowledge of available services, language difficulties, stigma and shame, geographic or community inaccessibility, and conflicts between a client's value system and the values underlying contemporary Western therapeutic approaches (Mokuau, 1985). Because this pattern of underutilization will not be changed in the short term, it is important to explore the nature and effectiveness of helping mechanisms preferred by various cultural groups in North America.

Practitioners writing about multicultural counseling often assert that many counseling approaches fail to meet the complex needs of various ethnic and minority clients because of stereotyped narrow perceptions of those needs. Asian Americans, African Americans, Latinos, Native Americans, and members of other minority groups (such as gay and lesbian clients) leave counseling significantly earlier than do Euro-American clients. This tendency is often attributed to cultural barriers such as language difficulties, class-bound values, and culture-bound values that hinder the formation of an effective counseling relationship (Atkinson et al., 1998; Ivey, 1995; Merta, 1995; Mokuau, 1987; Pedersen, 2000; Sue, Ivey, & Pedersen, 1996; D. W. Sue & Sue, 2003).

If you expect to have diversity within your groups, which is the case in most work settings, it will be important to accept the challenge of modifying your strategies to meet the unique needs of these populations. It is the responsibility of counselors to know their clients' cultural values before delivering mental health services. For example, an Afrocentric approach to group counseling involves understanding the worldview, set of social standards, and ethical values that reflect African values. Understanding the values associated with the spiritual and communal nature of African American people is basic to effective group work not only with African Americans but with many different cultural groups (Pack-Brown, Whittington-Clark, & Parker, 1998). Group leaders need to have a sociocultural framework from which to consider diverse values, interaction styles, and cultural expectations of a wide range of client populations. Effective multicultural practice in group work with diverse populations requires both knowledge and skills.

Although it is unrealistic to expect that you will have an in-depth knowledge of all cultural backgrounds, it is feasible for you to have a comprehensive grasp of general principles for working successfully amid cultural diversity. While upholding a belief in your own values, you must avoid assuming a stance of superiority that leads you to impose your values unthinkingly on others. Indeed, some clinicians use differences in values as justification for excluding a range of clients from their practice. If you are able to appreciate cultural differences and do not associate them with superiority or inferiority, however, diversity can expand your group members' perceptions of problems, increase your psychological resourcefulness, and result in a sense of community.

Pedersen (2000) asserts that adopting a multicultural perspective enables one to think about diversity without polarizing issues into "right" or "wrong." When two people's arguments are based on culturally different assumptions, they can disagree without one being right and the other being wrong. Depending on the cultural perspective from which a problem is considered, there may be several appropriate solutions. Culture is complicated, not simple; it is dynamic, not static. Nevertheless, the tapestry of culture that is woven into the fabric of all helping relationships need not be viewed as a barrier through which you must break. As Pedersen says, multiculturalism can make your job as a helper easier and more fun; it can also improve the quality of your life if you adopt a perspective that cultural differences are positive attributes that add richness to relationships. DeLucia-Waack (1996) suggests that addressing diversity issues within a group enhances the effectiveness of the process and outcomes of that group.

Transcending Cultural Encapsulation

Cultural encapsulation, or provincialism, can afflict both group members and the group leader. As group counselors, we have to confront our own distortions as well as those of the members. Culture-specific knowledge about a client's background should not lead counselors to stereotype him or her. Culturally competent group leaders recognize both differences among groups and differences within groups. It is essential that you do not get into the trap of perceiving individuals as simply belonging to a group. Indeed, the differences between individuals within a group are often greater than the differences among the various groups (Pedersen, 2000). Not all Native Americans have the same experiences, nor do all African Americans, Asians, women, elderly people, or people with disabilities. It is important to explore individual differences among members of the same cultural group and not to make general assumptions based on an individual's group. Counselors need to be prepared to deal with the complex differences among individuals from every cultural group. Effective group work from a multicultural perspective involves challenging stereotypes about an individual within a given group and modifying them to fit reality.

Practitioners may encounter resistance from some people of color because they are using traditional white, middle-class values to interpret these clients' experiences. Such culturally encapsulated practitioners are not able to view the world through the eyes of all of their clients. Wrenn (1985) defines the "culturally encapsulated counselor" as one who has substituted stereotypes for the real world, who disregards cultural variations among clients, and who dogmatizes technique-oriented definitions of counseling and therapy. Such individuals, who operate within a monocultural framework, maintain a cocoon by evading reality and depend entirely on their own internalized value assumptions about what is good for society and the individual. These encapsulated people tend to be trapped in one way of thinking, believing their way is the universal way. They cling to an inflexible structure that resists adaptation to alternative ways of thinking.

Western models need to be adapted to serve the members of certain ethnic groups, especially those clients who live by a different value system. Many clients from non-Western cultures, members of ethnic minorities, and women from nearly all cultural groups tend to value interdependence more than independence, social consciousness more than individual freedom, and the welfare of the group more than their own welfare. Western psychological thought emphasizes self-sufficiency, independence from family, and self-growth. However, many Asian Americans emphasize the collective good and make plans with the family in mind (Chu & Sue, 1984; Leong, 1992). In Asian cultures, moreover, family roles tend to be highly structured, and "filial piety" exerts a powerful influence; that is, obligations to parents are respected throughout one's life, especially among the male children. The roles of family members are highly interdependent, and family structure is arranged so that conflicts are minimized while harmony is maximized. Traditional Asian values emphasize reserve and formality in most social situations, restraint and inhibition of intense feelings, obedience to authority, and high academic and occupational achievement. The family structure is traditionally patriarchal in that communication and authority flow vertically from top to bottom. The inculcation of guilt and shame are the main techniques used to control the behavior of individuals within a family (D. Sue & Sue, 1993).

These traditional values are shared by other cultural groups. For instance, Latinos emphasize *familismo*, which stresses interdependence over independence, affiliation over confrontation, and cooperation over competition. Parents are afforded a great deal of respect, and this respect governs all interpersonal relationships. The role of fate is often a pervasive force governing behavior. Latinos typically place a high value on spiritual matters and religion (Comas-Diaz, 1990).

It is important to keep in mind that these are general cultural traits and that individuals within a culture may exhibit variability from these norms. The central point, however, is that if the group experience is largely the product of values that are alien to certain group members, it is easy to see that such members will not embrace the group. Group counselors who practice exclusively with a Western perspective are likely to meet with a considerable amount of resistance from clients with a non-Western worldview. Culturally sensitive group practice can occur only when leaders are willing to reveal the underlying values of the group process and determine whether these values are congruent with the cultural values of the members. Group members can also be encouraged to express their values and needs. The major challenge for group leaders is to determine what techniques are culturally appropriate for which individuals.

In writing about a multicultural perspective of group work, Merta (1995) indicates that the values of some cultural populations are congruent with group work, yet some populations have values that do not fit a group structure. Group counselors who have training in multicultural awareness and who know how to recruit, screen, select, and prepare group members consider cultural diversity as a basic component of an effective group.

General Guidelines for Serving Multicultural Populations

Racial and ethnic minority clients may display behavior that group leaders interpret as resistance. It is important to make a distinction between uncooperative behavior as a manifestation of resistance and as a hesitation to participate fully in the group process. Often, these clients are not so much resistant as they are reluctant or, in some cases, simply politely respectful. Such clients are not helped to participate more actively by leaders or other members who demonstrate little understanding or appreciation of these clients' underlying cultural values. For example, silence in a group should not always be interpreted as a refusal to participate. In traditional Asian cultures, silence is a customary sign of respect for elders and authority figures; talking too much or interrupting others is considered impolite (Chen & Han, 2001). Quiet clients may think that being silent is better than talking excessively or than verbalizing without careful thought. Their quietness could reflect their fear of being perceived as seeking attention. They may be waiting to be called on by the group leader, whom they view with respect. Some clients may be hesitant to talk about members of their family. This hesitation should not necessarily be interpreted as a stubborn refusal to be open and transparent. Instead, such clients may be influenced by taboos against openly discussing family matters.

Preparing Clients for a Group Experience

Multicultural group counseling demands adequate preparation by members. Screening and selecting members and orienting them to group procedures are especially critical in working with clients from certain cultural groups. In working with Asian members, Chen and Han (2001) state that the importance of screening cannot be overemphasized. This preparation is so critical because many of the behaviors expected in a group may be foreign to what people do in their everyday lives. For example, some cultures (such as Latino and Asian) value indirect communication; however, group members are told to be direct as they speak to one another. In daily life, people are often encouraged to mask their real feelings so that they will not offend others. In some cultures, individuals are not encouraged to express their feelings openly, to talk about their personal problems with people whom they do not know well, or to tell others what they think about them.

Many group members, regardless of their cultural background, may be hesitant in revealing personal matters for fear of being judged and of being rejected. This fear is generally much stronger in Asians than in other ethnic groups due to their reluctance to reveal personal matters in public. They often view expressing strong emotions as a sign of immaturity (Chen & Han, 2001). Yet in a group situation members are expected to abide by norms of openness, honesty, and directness, and they are expected to make themselves emotionally vulnerable. Depending on one's cultural background, some group norms may be very demanding and may go against the grain of a member's personal and cultural value system.

It is important for group leaders to help members clearly identify why they are in a group. Clients need to identify what they want to get for themselves from this process. Group leaders can help by focusing them on where they are now and where they want to go. It is important that members fully realize that group counseling involves change. They should be made aware of the possible consequences of change, not only for themselves but also for others in their lives. Some clients may be shunned by family members if they become too outspoken or move toward individualism.

During the pregroup screening and orientation process, it is a good practice for leaders to inform members about basic values that are implicit in the group process. For example, some groups operate on these value assumptions:

- Taking risks is essential for growth and change
- Self-determination is preferable to living by the standards of others
- Expressing emotions is healthier than repressing them
- Being open and expressing vulnerability can lead to intimacy
- Self-disclosure is a key to building solid relationships
- Striving for independence and interdependence is a primary goal
- Directness in communicating what you want and need from others is valued
- Trust in a group is attained by investing oneself personally in the group

Some of these values may conflict with the values of individual members. Certainly, ethical practice implies that members become aware of these values and what will be expected of them. It is useful to explore potential value conflicts during early group sessions. Ethical group leaders spend time in the initial sessions clarifying their cultural assumptions and the clients' cultural values and beliefs. Furthermore, leaders need to establish goals and processes that match the cultural values of the members of the group.

Adequate preparation of members is one of the best ways to increase the chances of a successful group experience for all clients. The preparation can include a discussion of members' values and how the group can help them achieve their personal goals. It is essential for clients with diverse cultural backgrounds that the goals and the purposes of the group be appropriate for their cultural context. This is why a discussion of the aims of a group and the importance of members' establishing their own goals is most important. At times, the goals may be consistent with the clients' cultural values, but the process or methods used to attain these goals can be antagonistic to these values.

Self-Disclosure and Confrontation in Multicultural Groups

Pushing for early disclosure of highly personal material or expecting members to be completely open can entrench resistance in certain clients. Some individuals from a variety of cultural backgrounds may take longer to develop trust and to participate in the disclosure that is based on this trust. Group leaders who understand the worldview of their clients are better able to be patient in helping these clients begin to speak. If such clients feel that they are respected, there is a greater chance that they will begin to challenge their hesitation.

Part of the group process is confrontation. Confrontation is therapeutic when it invites clients to more deeply explore a particular issue in their lives and when it is appropriate and well timed. However, confrontation that is harsh, attacking, hostile, and uncaring does not have a beneficial impact. Even therapeutic confrontation may not always be appropriate for clients from certain cultures, especially if it is done too soon. In fact, confronting client resistance too quickly and too directly is often counterproductive. For example, Asian cultures place a high value on authority, and Asian clients may not be willing to confront the group leader, whom they view as an authority figure (DeLucia-Waack, 1996). Asian clients may perceive the directness associated with confrontation as a personal attack; they often view confrontation as a negative behavior and avoid it at all costs (Chen & Han, 2001; Ho, 1984; Leong, 1992). Individuals from many cultures may associate confrontation with a significant sense of shame, making it difficult for them to return to the group setting. If such individuals feel insulted, the chances are that they will also feel rejected or angry, and such feelings may deter them from becoming involved in a group. For such clients, confrontation may be a factor in premature termination from the group.

Some Points to Remember

Reflecting on these guidelines may increase your effectiveness in serving diverse client populations:

- Learn more about how your own cultural background influences your thinking and behaving. Become familiar with some of the ways that you may be culturally encapsulated. What specific steps can you take to broaden your base of understanding both of your own culture and of other cultures?
- Identify your basic assumptions—especially as they apply to diversity in culture, ethnicity, race, gender, class, religion, and sexual orientation—and think about how your assumptions are likely to affect your practice as a group counselor.
- Attempt to move beyond a perspective of looking within the individual for the sources of his or her problems. Instead, strive to adopt a self-in-relation

perspective. Take into account the environmental and systemic factors that often contribute to an individual's struggles.

- Respect individual differences and recognize that diversity enhances a group.
- Learn to pay attention to the common ground that exists among people of diverse backgrounds. What are some of the ways that we all share universal concerns?
- Realize that it is not necessary to learn everything about the cultural background of your clients before you begin working with them. Allow them to teach you how you can best serve them.
- Spend time preparing clients for a successful group experience, especially if some of their values may differ from some of the values that form the foundation of a group. Teach clients how to adapt their group experience to meet the challenges they face in their everyday lives.
- Recognize the importance of being flexible in applying the methods you use with clients. Don't be wedded to a specific technique if it is not appropriate for a given group member.
- Remember that practicing from a multicultural perspective can make your job easier and can be rewarding for both you and your clients.

As you study the 10 theories explored in Part Two of this book, give careful consideration to the underlying value issues that are likely to have a clear impact on your practice. It is apparent that the direct application of many contemporary models of therapy is inappropriate for some clients. However, certain concepts and techniques drawn from the various therapeutic schools do have cultural relevance. As a group practitioner, you will use a range of concepts and techniques. It is important to develop selection criteria that will enable you to systematically integrate those tools that best meet the needs of diverse client populations. Assess the particular attributes that your clients bring to you and tailor the interventions that you make in a group to those attributes. In working with diverse populations, you will be challenged to develop a wide variety of strategies, which you can learn from the 10 theoretical approaches presented in Part Two.

At this point, I suggest that you take time to read the two chapters in Part Three. Chapter 16 deals with comparisons, contrasts, and integration of the various theoretical models of group counseling. Many students have said they found it helpful to read the illustration of the evolution of a group (Chapter 17) at various points during the course because it provides a framework for applying the different perspectives to an actual group.

CHAPTER 2

Group Leadership

This chapter focuses on the influence of the group leader—as a person and as a professional—on the group process. After discussing the personal characteristics of effective leaders, I analyze the skills and techniques that are necessary for successful leadership and the specific functions and roles of group leaders. This chapter will give you enough information about these crucial topics to allow you to benefit fully from the discussion in the next three chapters, which deal with the ethics of group practice and the stages in a group's development. The topics covered here also represent an important prelude to the theory chapters in Part Two.

The Group Leader as a Person

Group counseling techniques cannot be divorced from the leader's personal characteristics and behaviors. Thus, I don't agree with those who attribute the success or failure of a group mainly to the characteristics of the participants or to the specific techniques being used to get the group moving. These are no doubt important variables, but by themselves they do not determine the outcome of a group.

Group leaders can acquire extensive theoretical and practical knowledge of group dynamics and be skilled in diagnostic and technical procedures yet be ineffective in stimulating growth and change in the members of their groups. Leaders bring to every group their personal qualities, values, and life experiences. To promote growth in the members' lives, leaders need to live growth-oriented lives themselves. To foster honest self-investigation in others, group leaders need to have the courage to engage in self-appraisal. If they hope to inspire others to break away from deadening ways of being, leaders need to be willing to seek new experiences themselves. In short, the most effective group direction is found in the kind of life the group members see the leader demonstrating and not in the words they hear the leader saying.

I am not implying that group leaders must be self-actualized beings who have successfully worked through all of their problems. The issue is not whether leaders have personal problems but whether they are willing to make serious attempts to live the way they encourage members to live. More important than being a finished product is the willingness to continually look at oneself to see whether one's life reflects life-giving values. The key to success as a group leader is the commitment to the never-ending struggle to become more effective as a human being.

Personality and Character

Some personal characteristics are vitally related to effective group leadership; their presence or absence can facilitate or inhibit the group process. As you read about these characteristics, evaluate your own strengths and areas for improvement.

Presence Being emotionally present means being moved by the joy and pain that others experience. If leaders recognize and give expression to their own emotions, they can become more emotionally involved with others. The ability of leaders to draw on these experiences makes it easier for them to empathize with and be compassionate toward group members. Presence also has to do with "being there" for the members, which involves genuine caring and a willingness to enter their psychological world. Being present means that leaders are not fragmented when they come to a group session, that they are not preoccupied with other matters, and that they are open to their reactions in the group.

Personal Power Personal power involves self-confidence and an awareness of one's influence on others. If group leaders do not feel a sense of power in their own lives (or if they do not feel in control of their destiny), it is difficult for them to facilitate members' movement toward empowerment. In short, it is not possible to give to others what you do not possess. It should be stressed that power does not mean domination and exploitation of others. These are abuses of power. Truly powerful leaders use the effect they have on group participants to encourage members to get in contact with their own unused power, not to foster their dependency. Group leaders promote a sense of empowerment by encouraging group members to become *client colleagues*. If members risk change, the bulk of the credit belongs to them.

Courage Effective group leaders are aware that they need to exhibit courage in their interactions with group members and that they cannot hide behind their special role as counselors. They show courage by taking risks in the group and admitting mistakes, by being occasionally vulnerable, by confronting others and revealing their own reactions to those they confront, by acting on intuitions and beliefs, by discussing with the group their thoughts and feelings about the group process, and by being willing to share their power with group members. They can model important lessons to members by taking a stance toward life and acting in spite of the fact that they are imperfect. When members push themselves to leave familiar and secure patterns, they often report being anxious and scared. Group leaders can demonstrate, through their own behavior, their willingness to move ahead in spite of being uncertain about the terrain and somewhat fearful.

Willingness to Confront Oneself   One of the leader's central tasks is to promote self-investigation in clients. Since group counselors cannot expect participants to do something that they themselves are not prepared to do, they must show that they are willing to question themselves.

Self-awareness entails the willingness to confront oneself. This essential characteristic of effective leadership includes awareness not only of one's needs and motivations but also of personal conflicts and problems, of defenses and weak spots, of areas of unfinished business, and of the potential influence of all of these on the group process. Leaders who are self-aware are able to work therapeutically with the transferences that emerge within the group setting, both toward themselves and toward other members. Furthermore, they are aware of their own vulnerabilities, especially their potential countertransference. Leaders take responsibility for their own reactions, and they do not use the group as a place to seek their own therapy.

Sincerity and Authenticity   One of the leader's most important qualities is a sincere interest in the well-being and growth of others. Because sincerity involves being direct, it can also involve telling members what may be difficult for them to hear. For a group leader, caring means challenging the members to look at parts of their lives that they are denying and discouraging any form of dishonest behavior in the group. Giving members feedback that is honest and helpful also requires sincerity, in the sense that the client's best interest is paramount.

Authenticity is a close cousin to sincerity. Authentic group leaders do not live by pretenses and do not hide behind masks, defenses, sterile roles, or facades. Authenticity entails the willingness to appropriately disclose oneself and share feelings and reactions to what is going on in the group. But, as we will examine in more detail, authenticity does not imply indiscriminately "letting it all hang out." It is surely possible to be authentic without sharing every fleeting thought, perception, fantasy, and reaction. For instance, even though a leader might initially be sexually attracted to a member, it would not be wise to disclose this reality at the initial session. Such "holding back" does not imply inauthenticity.

Sense of Identity   If group leaders are to help others discover who they are, leaders need to have a clear sense of their own identity. This means knowing what you value and living by internally derived standards, not by what others expect. It means being aware of your own strengths, limitations, needs, fears, motivations, and goals. It means knowing what you are capable of becoming, what you want from life, and how you are going to get what you want. A vital component of this identity is awareness of one's cultural heritage and ethnic self-knowledge.

Belief in the Group Process and Enthusiasm   The leader's deep belief in the value of the group process is essential to the success of the group. Why should members believe the group experience will be of value to them if the leader is without enthusiasm for it? Too often practitioners lead groups in an agency simply because they are expected to without being convinced that group interventions make a difference.

The enthusiasm group leaders bring to their groups can have an infectious quality. If leaders radiate life, the chances are slim that they will be consistently leading "stale groups." Leaders need to show that they enjoy their work and like being with their groups. A leader's lack of enthusiasm is generally reflected in members' lack of excitement about coming to group sessions and in their resistance to doing significant work.

Inventiveness and Creativity   Leaders should avoid getting trapped in ritualized techniques and programmed presentations that are void of life. It may not be easy to approach each group with new ideas. Inventive and creative leaders are open to new experiences and to lifestyles and values that differ from their own. One of the main advantages of group work is that it offers so many avenues for being inventive.

A Concluding Comment

As you review the characteristics of effective group leaders, do not burden yourself with thinking that you have to possess all of these qualities to the utmost. Consider such qualities on a continuum. For instance, it is not a matter that either you have traits such as courage, self-awareness, and a clear sense of identity or you don't. Instead, as your self-awareness increases, it will be easier for you to facilitate members' self-exploration. The challenge is for you to take an honest look at your personal qualities and make an assessment of your ability as a person to inspire others. Your own commitment to living up to your potential is a key tool. The best way to lead others is to demonstrate what you believe in through your own life. Experiencing your own therapy (either individually or in groups) is one way to remain open to looking at the direction of your life. It is certainly not a matter of being the perfectly integrated group leader who has "arrived." Once you have arrived, after all, there is no place to go!

The personal dimensions described in the preceding pages are essential, but they are not sufficient for successful leadership. Specialized knowledge and skills, as identified by the Association for Specialists in Group Work (ASGW) in "Professional Standards for the Training of Group Workers" (ASGW, 2000) and described in Chapter 3, are central to effective group leadership. Later in this chapter we will examine these leadership skills in greater detail.

Special Problems and Issues for Beginning Group Leaders

Through my work in training and supervising group leaders and providing in-service workshops, I have come across a number of issues with special relevance for beginning leaders. These issues must be faced by all group leaders, regardless of their experience, but they are especially significant for those who are relatively inexperienced.

You may wonder whether you have what it takes to be an effective leader. My advice is to be patient with yourself and not to demand that you immediately become the "perfect group leader." Most practitioners I know (including myself) struggled over their competence when they began leading groups and still have difficult times. Such self-doubts are less of a problem if you are willing to continue to seek training and to work under supervision.

Initial Anxiety

Before you lead your first group, you will no doubt be anxious about getting the group started and about keeping it moving. In other words, you will probably be asking yourself questions like these with a certain degree of trepidation:

- What do the participants really expect of me?
- Will I be able to get the group started? How?
- Will I run out of things to say or do before the end of the session?
- What if members of my group find out that I really don't know what I'm doing?
- Should I take an active role, or should I wait for the group to start on its own?
- Should I have an agenda, or should I let the group members decide what they want to talk about?
- Do I possess the cultural competence to lead this group?
- What techniques shall I use during the early stages of the group?
- What if nobody wants to participate? And what if too many people want to participate? How will I be able to take care of those who want to get involved?
- Will the group members want to come back?

It is essential for group counselors to identify and examine their internal dialogue. Even the most effective group leaders may find themselves slipping into distorted ways of thinking and engaging in negative thinking. Corey, Ellis, and Cooker (1998) contend that it is not easy to erase self-defeating thought patterns. However, it is possible to question the assumptions we make and the conclusions we form. By being willing to continue challenging the grounds for our beliefs, it is certainly possible to avoid being controlled by negative internal dialogue.

In supervising and training beginning leaders, I encourage them to recognize that these doubts and concerns are perfectly normal. Moderate anxiety is beneficial because it can lead to honest self-appraisal. Anxiety can be counterproductive, however, if it begins to feed on itself and is allowed to freeze one into inactivity. Therefore, I encourage beginning leaders to voice their questions and concerns and to explore them in the course of the training sessions. Their very willingness to do this can allay some unnecessary anxiety, for the trainees discover that their peers share their concerns. Students frequently say that their peers appear to be so much more knowledgeable, skilled, talented, and self-confident than they themselves are. When they hear their peers express anxieties and feelings of inadequacy, these students realize that those who appear to be extremely self-confident are also struggling with self-doubts. The interchanges that occur when trainees are willing to openly discuss their anxieties offer invaluable opportunities for personal and professional growth. Exploring these feelings with peers and a supervisor can help the beginning leader distinguish between realistic and unrealistic anxiety and thus defuse unwarranted and counterproductive anxiety.

Self-Disclosure

Regardless of their years of experience, many group leaders struggle with the problem of self-disclosure. For beginning leaders, the issue is of even greater concern. Although *what* to reveal and *when* are factors in determining the appropriateness of self-disclosure, the issue centers on *how much* to reveal. It is not uncommon to err on either extreme, disclosing too little or disclosing too much.

Too Little Self-Disclosure   If you try very hard to maintain stereotyped role expectations and keep yourself mysterious by hiding behind your professional facade, you can lose your personal identity in the group and allow very little of yourself to be known. The reasons for functioning in a role (rather than as a person who has certain functions to perform) are many. One may be the fear of appearing unprofessional or of losing the respect of the members. Another may be the need to keep a distance or to maintain a "doctor/patient" relationship.

In addition to being unwilling to share your personal life, you may also be hesitant to disclose how you feel in the group or how you feel toward certain members. As a way of avoiding sharing your own reactions to what is occurring within the group, you might limit your interventions to detached observations. Such "professional" aloofness may be expressed by making interpretations and suggestions, asking questions rather than making personal statements, acting as a mere coordinator, providing one structured exercise after another to keep the group moving, and clarifying issues.

In my opinion, the most productive form of sharing is disclosure that is related to what is going on in the group. For instance, if you have a persistent feeling that most members are not very motivated and are not investing themselves in the session, you are likely to feel burdened by the constant need to keep the meetings alive all by yourself, with little or no support from the participants. Disclosing how you are affected by this lack of motivation is generally very useful and appropriate.

Too Much Self-Disclosure   At the other end of the continuum are the problems associated with excessive self-disclosure. Most beginning group leaders (and many experienced ones) have a strong need to be approved of and accepted by group members. It is easy to make the mistake of "paying membership dues" by sharing intimate details to prove that you are just as human as the members. There is a fine line between appropriate and inappropriate self-disclosure. It is a mistake to assume that "the more disclosure, the better." Considering the reasons for your disclosures, the readiness of the members, the impact your sharing of intimate details is likely to have on them, and the degree to which your disclosures are relevant to the here-and-now process of the group should go hand-in-hand with self-disclosure.

You may be tempted to submit to group pressure to share more of yourself. Members often say to leaders: "We don't know much about you. Why don't you say more about yourself? For example, tell us about your hang-ups. We talked about ourselves, and now we'd like to see you come down to our level and open up too!" The members can exert more subtle, but no less strong, pressures for you to "become a member" of the group you are leading. In an attempt to avoid getting lost in a professionally aloof role, you may try too hard to be perceived as a friend and a fellow group member. If you decide to share personal concerns, it should be for the benefit of your clients. The place to explore these concerns (and thus serve your own needs) is in a group in which you are a participant yourself. Group leading is demanding work, and you can make this work even more difficult by confusing your role and functions with those of the participants.

Appropriate and Facilitative Self-Disclosure   Facilitative and appropriate self-disclosure is an essential aspect of the art of group leading. It is not necessary to disclose details of your past or of your personal life to make yourself known as a person or to empathize with the participants. A few words can convey a great deal, and nonverbal messages—a touch, a look, a gesture—can express feelings of identification and understanding. Appropriate disclosure does not take the focus away from the client and is never a contrived technique to get group members to open up. Your sensitivity to how people respond can teach you a lot about the timeliness and value of your disclosures. Timeliness is a truly critical factor, for what might be inappropriate to disclose during the early stages of a group could be very useful at a later stage.

Yalom (1983, 1995) stresses that a leader's self-disclosure must be instrumental in helping the members attain their goals. He calls for selective disclosure that provides members with acceptance, support, and encouragement. For Yalom, group leaders who disclose here-and-now reactions rather than detailed personal events from their past facilitate the movement of the group.

The Challenges of Dealing with a System

Most groups that you lead will be under the auspices of some type of institution—a school system, a community mental health organization, a state mental hospital, a clinic, or a local or state rehabilitation agency. When conducting groups in an institutional setting, one quickly discovers that mastering group leadership theory and practice doesn't guarantee successful groups. Being able to deal effectively with institutional demands and policies may at times be as important as being professionally competent.

A common problem among those who regularly do group work in an institutional setting is the constant struggle to retain dignity and integrity in a system where the administrators are primarily concerned with custodial care or with putting out "crisis fires" and are relatively indifferent to the pursuit of genuine group therapy or counseling. Another common problem besetting counselors in an institution relates to demands that they function as leaders of groups that they are unequipped or ill-equipped to handle. This problem is intensified by the fact that few institutions provide the training needed for the type of group leadership they demand and burden their counselors with such a workload that they don't have time for continuing education during their regular working hours. Thus, many institutional counselors are forced to take courses or attend workshops on their own time and at their own expense.

The point is that these problems exist and that it is up to you to deal with them and to work within the system while, at the same time, maintaining your professional standards and integrity. Ultimately, the responsibility for conducting successful groups is yours. Beware of blaming external factors for failures in your group counseling programs.

I'm not implying that these complaints don't reflect real obstacles. I know from personal experience how taxing and draining any battle with a bureaucracy can be. There are times when the hassle of merely trying to get a group started in some institutions may overwhelm us to the point of questioning whether the effort is worth it. My point is that whatever the external obstacles, it is our responsibility to face them and not allow them to render us powerless.

Professional impotency of any kind is a condition that feeds on itself. When counselors abdicate their own power, they assume the role of victims, or they develop the cynical attitude that all their proposals and efforts are doomed—that nothing they do matters or makes any difference. So, by way of summary and restatement, when we surrender our power by placing all the responsibility for the failure of our programs outside of ourselves, we are in jeopardy of having our work devitalize us when it should be having the opposite effect.

Group Leadership Skills

It is a mistake to assume that anyone with certain personal qualities and a desire to help will be an effective group leader. Successful leadership requires specific group leadership skills and the appropriate performance of certain functions. Like most skills, leadership skills need to be learned and practiced. Think about your own skill level as you read about these essential leadership skills for group counselors.

Active Listening   Active listening involves paying total attention to the speaker and being sensitive to what is being communicated at both the verbal and nonverbal levels. Your ability to hear what is being communicated improves as your expertise improves. Many leaders make the mistake of focusing too intently on the content and, in doing so, don't pay enough attention to the way in which group members express themselves. Being a skilled group leader entails picking up the rich cues provided by members through their style of speech, body posture, gestures, voice quality, and mannerisms. (Active listening will be dealt with in greater detail in Chapter 10; attending and listening are key concepts of the person-centered approach to group work.)

Restating   In a sense, restating (or paraphrasing) is an extension of listening. It means recasting what someone said into different words so that the meaning is clearer to both the speaker and the group. Effective restating zeroes in on the core of a person's message, brings into sharper focus the meaning of what was said, and eliminates ambiguity. By capturing the essence of a member's message and reflecting it back, the leader helps the person continue the self-exploration process on a deeper level.

Restating is not an easy skill to master. Some group leaders, for example, confine themselves to simply repeating what was said, adding little new meaning and not really clarifying the message. Others overuse the technique, with the result of sounding mechanical and repetitive. The value of accurate and concise restating is twofold: it tells the participants that they are being understood, and it helps them see more clearly the issues they are struggling with and their own feelings and thoughts about these issues.

Clarifying   Clarifying, too, is an extension of active listening. It involves responding to confusing and unclear aspects of a message by focusing on underlying issues and helping the person sort out conflicting feelings. Members often say that they have ambivalent feelings or are feeling many things at once; clarification can help sort out these feelings so that members can focus more sharply on what are actually experiencing. The same procedure applies to thinking. In clarifying, the group leader stays within the individual's frame of reference but, at the same time, helps the client put things into perspective; this, in turn, may lead to a slightly deeper level of self-exploration on the part of the client.

Summarizing   The skill of pulling together the important elements of a group interaction or part of a session is known as summarizing. This ability is particularly useful when making a transition from one topic to another. Rather than merely proceeding from issue to issue, identifying common elements can increase learning and maintain continuity.

Summarizing is especially needed at the end of a session. It is a mistake for a group leader to end a session abruptly, with little attempt to pull the session together. One of the leader's functions is to help members reflect on and make sense of what has occurred in their group. Summarizing encourages participants to think about what they have learned and experienced in a session and about ways of applying it to their everyday lives. At the end of the session, group leaders may offer their own brief summary or ask each member in turn to summarize what has taken place, what the highlights of the session were, and how they responded to the interaction.

Questioning   Questioning is probably the technique that novice group leaders tend to overuse most. Bombarding members with question after question does not lead to productive outcomes and may even have a negative impact on the group interaction. There are several problems with the ineffective use of questioning. Members feel violated, as if they had been subjected to the "third degree." The questioner probes for personal information while remaining safe and anonymous behind the interrogation. Also, a low-level questioning style on the leader's part provides a poor model for the members, who soon begin to imitate the leader's ineffective questioning style when they deal with one another.

Not all questioning is inappropriate, but closed questions—those that require a mere "yes" or "no" response—are generally fruitless. And so are "why" questions, because they usually lead to intellectual ruminating. Instead, use open-ended questions that elicit alternatives and new areas of self-investigation. These questions can be of real value. For example, "What are you experiencing right now?" "What is happening with your body at this moment?" and "How are you dealing with your fear in this group?" are questions that can help participants become more focused and feel their emotions more deeply. It is important that leaders ask questions that explore issues in greater depth. (The topic of questioning will be dealt with in greater detail in Chapter 15 as a special procedure used in reality therapy.)

Interpreting   The leader interprets when he or she offers possible explanations for a participant's thoughts, feelings, or behavior. By offering tentative hypotheses concerning certain patterns of behavior, interpreting helps the individual see new perspectives and alternatives. Interpreting requires a great deal of skill. Interpreting too soon, presenting an interpretation in a dogmatic way, or encouraging the members to become dependent on the leader to provide meanings and answers are common mistakes. Timing is especially important. Interpretations not only have to be made at a time when the person is likely to be willing to consider them but also need to be expressed in a tentative way that gives the person a chance to assess their validity. Although an interpretation may be technically correct, it may be rejected if the leader is not sensitive to the client's willingness or unwillingness to accept it. (I will return to the topic of interpreting in Chapters 6, 7, and 11.)

Confronting   Confrontation can be a powerful way of challenging members to take an honest look at themselves. However, if it is handled poorly, it also has the potential of being detrimental both to the person being confronted and to the group process. Many beginning leaders shy away from confrontation because they fear its possible repercussions: blocking the group interaction, hurting someone, or becoming the target of retaliation. The problem with confrontation is that it can easily be seen as an uncaring attack. That is why skilled group counselors confront only when they care about the person, and they do so in a way that gives the person ample opportunity to consider what is being said. Skillful confrontation specifies the behavior or the discrepancies between verbal and nonverbal messages that are being challenged so that no labeling can possibly occur. (Confrontation will be discussed in more detail in Chapters 11, 14, and 15.)

Reflecting Feelings Reflecting feelings is the skill of responding to the essence of what a person has communicated. The purpose is to let members know that they are being heard and understood. Although reflection entails mirroring certain feelings that the person has expressed, it is not merely a bouncing-back process. Reflection is dependent on attention, interest, understanding, and respect for the person. When reflection is done well, it fosters further contact and involvement; feeling understood and achieving a clearer grasp of one's feelings are very reinforcing and stimulate the person to seek greater self-awareness.

Supporting Supporting means providing group members with encouragement and reinforcement, especially when they are disclosing personal information, when they are exploring painful feelings, and when they are taking risks. A leader can provide support by being fully present at the appropriate time. This full presence requires a combination of skills: listening actively to what is being said, being psychologically present with the client, and responding in a way that encourages the client to continue working and to move forward.

The essence of this skill is in knowing when it will be facilitative and when it will be counterproductive. Some group leaders make the mistake of being overly supportive, of supporting without challenging, or of supporting too soon. If leaders limit themselves to a style that is almost exclusively supportive, they deprive the members of potentially valuable challenges. Leaders who offer support too quickly when someone is exploring painful material tend to defuse the intensity of the experience and pull group members away from their feelings. (I will return to this topic in Chapter 10.)

Empathizing The core of the skill of empathy lies in the leader's ability to sensitively grasp the subjective world of the participant and yet retain his or her own separateness. To empathize effectively, a leader needs to care for and respect the group members. A background that includes a wide range of experiences can help the leader identify with others. (Empathy, too, is discussed in more detail in Chapter 10.)

Facilitating Facilitating is aimed at enhancing the group experience and enabling the members to reach their goals. Facilitation skills involve opening up clear and direct communication among the participants and helping them assume increasing responsibility for the direction of the group. Facilitating is a vital tool in the person-centered approach, and it will be explored in more depth in Chapter 10. Here are some specific ways group leaders can facilitate the group process:

- Focus on resistances within the group and help members realize when they are holding back and why.
- Encourage members to express their feelings and expectations openly.
- Teach members to focus on themselves and their feelings.
- Teach members to talk directly and plainly to one another.
- Work to create a climate of safety that will encourage members to take risks.
- Provide support for members as they try new behaviors.
- Foster a member-to-member rather than a member-to-leader interaction style.
- Encourage open expression of conflict.
- Assist members in overcoming barriers to direct communication.
- Help members integrate what they are learning in the group and find ways to apply it to their everyday lives.
- Help members achieve closure by taking care of any unfinished business in the group.

Initiating Good initiating skills on the leader's part keep the group from floundering without direction. These skills include using catalysts to get members to focus on meaningful work, knowing how to employ various techniques that promote deeper self-exploration, and providing links among the various themes being explored in the group. Whereas appropriate leader direction can give the group a focus and keep it moving, too much direction can lead to passivity on the part of members.

Setting Goals Productive goal setting is at the core of group counseling. Note that group leaders do not set goals for members; they help group members select and clarify their own specific goals. Although goal setting is especially important during the initial stages of a group, throughout the group's life leaders need to encourage participants to take another look at their goals, to modify them if necessary, and to determine how effectively they are accomplishing them. Leaders who don't develop the intervention skills of challenging members to formulate concrete goals often find that their groups are characterized by aimless and unproductive sessions. (This topic is dealt with in more detail in Chapters 13 and 15.)

Evaluating Evaluating is an ongoing process that continues for the duration of a group. After each session, the leader should assess what is happening in the group as a whole and within individual members. Leaders must also teach participants how to evaluate themselves and how to appraise the movement and direction of their group. For example, if at the end of a session most participants agree that the session was superficial, they can be challenged to find the reasons for the unsatisfactory outcome and to decide what they are willing to do to change the situation. (This topic is also explored in more depth in Chapters 13 and 15.)

Giving Feedback   A skilled group leader gives specific and honest feedback based on his or her observation of and reaction to the members' behaviors and encourages the members to give feedback to one another. One of the great advantages of groups is that participants can tell each other their reactions to what they observe. The purpose of feedback is to provide a realistic assessment of how a person appears to others. The skill involved in productive feedback relates to the ability to present the feedback so that it is acceptable and worthy of serious consideration. Feedback that is specific and descriptive rather than global and judgmental is the most helpful.

Suggesting   Suggestion is a form of intervention designed to help participants develop an alternative course of thinking or action. It can take many forms, a few of which are giving information and advice, giving "homework assignments," asking members to think of experiments they might try inside and outside of the group, and encouraging members to look at a situation from a different perspective. Giving information and providing appropriate suggestions for alternative plans of action can hasten the progress members make in a group. Suggestions need not always come from the leader; members can make suggestions for others to consider.

The overuse of persuasion, suggestions, and advice entails some dangers. One is that members can be led to believe that simple and neat solutions exist for complex problems. Another is that members may remain dependent on other people to suggest what they should do in the face of future problems instead of growing toward autonomy. There is a fine line between suggesting and prescribing, and the skill consists in using suggestions to enhance an individual's movement toward independence.

Protecting   Without assuming a parental attitude toward the group, leaders need to be able to safeguard members from unnecessary psychological or physical risks associated with being in a group. Although the very fact of participating in a group does entail certain risks, leaders can step in when they sense that psychological harm may result from a series of group interactions. For example, intervention is called for when a member is being treated unfairly or when an avalanche of feelings from the group is directed toward one person.

Disclosing Oneself   When leaders reveal personal information, they usually have an impact on the group. The skill consists of knowing what, when, how, and how much to reveal. If the leader shares appropriately, the effects on the group are likely to be positive. If the leader shares too much too soon, the effects are likely to be adverse because the members may not be able yet to handle such openness comfortably. The most productive disclosure is related to what is taking place within the group. The skill involved in appropriate self-disclosure lies in the ability to present the information in such a way that the members are encouraged to share more of themselves.

Modeling   Group members learn by observing the leader's behavior. If leaders value honesty, respect, openness, risk taking, and assertiveness, they can foster these qualities in the members by demonstrating them in the group. From a leader who shows respect by really listening and empathizing, members learn a direct and powerful lesson in how respect is shown behaviorally. In short, one of the best ways to teach more effective skills of interpersonal relating is by direct example. (Modeling is discussed more fully in Chapter 13.)

Linking   One way of promoting interaction among the members is to look for themes that emerge in a group and then to connect the work that members do to these themes. Group leaders with an interactional bias—that is, those who develop the norm of member-to-member rather than leader-to-member communication—rely a great deal on linking. They encourage members to address others in the group directly rather than looking at the leader and talking about others who are present. Members often have shared concerns, and through effective linking they can be helped to work through their problems by talking to others with similar concerns. By being alert for common concerns, the leader can promote interaction and increase the level of group cohesion. Through linking several members together, the leader is also teaching members how to take responsibility for involving themselves in the work of others. When members learn how to bring themselves into group interactions, they become more independent of the leader and are also likely to feel a greater sense of belongingness by being connected to others.

Blocking   Sometimes a leader must intervene to stop counterproductive behaviors within the group. Blocking is a skill that requires sensitivity, directness, and the ability to stop the activity without attacking the person. The focus should be on the specific behavior and not on the person as a whole, and labeling should be avoided. For example, if a member is invading another member's privacy by asking probing and highly personal questions, the leader will point to this behavior as being unhelpful, without referring to the person as a "peeping tom" or an "interrogator." When members judge or criticize others, pressure others to take a specific course of action or to express feelings in a group, or habitually ask questions of others, the group leader may need to block this behavior. Other behaviors that group leaders need to watch for and block when necessary include making excuses to justify failure to make changes, breaking confidences, invading a member's privacy, perpetually giving advice, storytelling, gossiping, offering support inappropriately, and making inaccurate or inappropriate interpretations. Whatever the behavior, blocking must be carried out gently and sensitively.

Terminating   Group leaders need to learn when and how to terminate their work with individuals as well as groups. The skills required in closing a group session or ending a group successfully include providing members with suggestions for applying what they've learned in the group to their daily lives, preparing the participants to deal with the problems they may encounter outside of the group, providing for some type of evaluation and follow-up, suggesting sources of further help, and being available for individual consultation should the need arise.

Don't Overwhelm Yourself!

It is not unusual for beginning group counselors to feel somewhat overwhelmed when they consider all these skills. If you, too, feel overwhelmed and discouraged, think about what it was like when you were learning to drive a car. If you had tried to think of all the rules simultaneously, you would have become frustrated and incapable of responding appropriately. The same applies to developing specific leadership skills. By systematically learning certain principles and practicing certain skills, you can expect to gradually refine your leadership style and gain the confidence you need to use these skills effectively. Participating in a group as a member is one way of developing these skills, for you can learn a lot by observing experienced people. Of course, you also need to practice these skills by leading groups under supervision. Feedback from group members, your co-leader, and your supervisor is essential to the refinement of your leadership skills. Seeing yourself in action on videotape can be a powerful source of feedback that will help you identify the specific areas you most need to strengthen.

Like all skills, group leadership skills exist in degrees, not on an all-or-nothing basis. They may be developed only minimally, or they may be highly refined and used appropriately. But through training and supervised experience, these skills can continually be improved. The *Student Manual for Theory and Practice of Group Counseling* (Corey, 2004) has a checklist and self-evaluation of the 22 skills discussed here. This inventory is useful for rating yourself on the leadership skills and can be used in rating your co-leader. Of course, your co-leader can rate you on each of the skills too. This instrument can provide topics for you and your co-leader to discuss in your meetings.

Table 2-1 presents an overview of the group leadership skills discussed in the preceding pages.

Table 2-1 ■ Overview of Group Leadership Skills

Skill	Description	Aims and Desired Outcomes
Active listening	Attending to verbal and non-verbal aspects of communication without judging or evaluating.	To encourage trust and client self-disclosure and exploration.
Restating	Paraphrasing what a participant has said, to clarify its meaning.	To determine if the leader has understood correctly the client's statement; to provide support and clarification.
Clarifying	Grasping the essence of a message at both the feeling and the thinking levels; simplifying client statements by focusing on the core of the message.	To help clients sort out conflicting and confused feelings and thoughts; to arrive at a meaningful understanding of what is being communicated.
Summarizing	Pulling together the important elements of an interaction or session.	To avoid fragmentation and give direction to a session; to provide for continuity and meaning.
Questioning	Asking open-ended questions that lead to self-exploration of the "what" and "how" of behavior.	To elicit further discussion; to get information; to stimulate thinking; to increase clarity and focus; to provide for further self-exploration.
Interpreting	Offering possible explanations for certain thoughts, feelings, and behaviors.	To encourage deeper self-exploration; to promote full use of potentials; to bring about awareness of self-contradictions.
Confronting	Challenging members to look at discrepancies between their words and actions or their bodily and verbal messages; pointing to conflicting information or messages.	To encourage honest self-investigation; to promote full use of potentials; to bring about awareness of self-contradictions.
Reflecting feelings	Communicating understanding of the content of feelings.	To let members know that they are being heard and understood beyond the level of words.
Supporting	Providing encouragement and reinforcement.	To create an atmosphere that encourages members to continue desired behaviors; to provide help when clients are facing difficult struggles; to create trust.
Empathizing	Identifying with clients by assuming their frames of reference.	To foster trust in the therapeutic relationship; to communicate understanding; to encourage deeper levels of self-exploration.
Facilitating	Opening up clear and direct communication within the group; helping members assume increasing responsibility for the group's direction.	To promote effective communication among members; to help members reach their own goals in the group.

Table 2-1 ■ **Overview of Group Leadership Skills** (continued)

Skill	Description	Aims and Desired Outcomes
Initiating	Promoting participation and introducing new directions in the group.	To prevent needless group floundering to increase the pace of the group process.
Setting goals	Planning specific goals for the group process and helping participants define concrete and meaningful goals.	To give direction to the group's activities; to help members select and clarify their goals.
Evaluating	Appraising the ongoing group process and the individual and group dynamics.	To promote better self-awareness and understanding of group movement and direction.
Giving feedback	Expression of concrete and honest reactions based on observation of members' behaviors.	To offer an external view of how the person appears to others; to increase the client's self-awareness.
Suggesting	Offering advice and information, direction, and ideas for new behavior.	To help members develop alternative courses of thinking and action.
Protecting	Safeguarding members from unnecessary psychological risks in the group.	To warn members of possible risks in group participation; to reduce these risks.
Disclosing oneself	Revealing one's reactions to here-and-now events in the group.	To facilitate deeper levels of group interaction; to create trust; to model ways of revealing oneself to others.
Modeling	Demonstrating desired behavior through actions.	To provide examples of desirable behavior; to inspire members to fully develop their potential.
Linking	Connecting the work that members do to common themes in the group.	To promote member-to-member interactions; to encourage the development of cohesion.
Blocking	Intervening to stop counter-productive group behavior.	To protect members; to enhance the flow of group process.
Terminating	Preparing the group to close a session or end its existence.	To help members assimilate, integrate, and apply in-group learning to everyday life.

Note: The format of this chart is based on Edwin J. Nolan's article "Leadership Interventions for Promoting Personal Mastery," *Journal for Specialists in Group Work*, 1978, 3(3), 132–138.

Becoming a Diversity-Competent Group Counselor

Special knowledge and skills are required for dealing with culturally diverse groups. If you are open to the values inherent in a diversity perspective, you will find ways to avoid getting trapped in provincialism, and you will be able to challenge the degree to which you may be culturally encapsulated (Wrenn,

1985). Take an inventory of your current level of awareness, knowledge, and skills that have a bearing on your ability to function effectively in multicultural situations, by reflecting on these questions:

- Are you aware of how your own culture influences the way you think, feel, and act?
- What could you do to broaden your understanding of both your own culture and other cultures?
- Are you able to identify your basic assumptions, especially as they apply to diversity in culture, ethnicity, race, gender, class, religion, and sexual orientation?
- How are your assumptions likely to affect the manner in which you function as a group counselor?
- Can you be flexible in applying the techniques you use in your groups, depending on the specific makeup of the membership?
- How prepared are you to understand and work with individuals from different cultural backgrounds in a group?
- Is your academic program preparing you to work with diverse client populations in different kinds of groups?
- What life experiences have you had that will help you to understand and make contact with group members who have a different worldview from yours?
- Can you identify any areas of cultural bias that could inhibit your ability to work effectively with people who are different from you? If so, what steps might you take to challenge your biases?

Becoming a diversity-competent group counselor demands self-awareness and an open stance on the part of the practitioner. You must be willing to modify strategies to fit the needs and situations of the individuals within the group. It is clear that no one "right" technique can be utilized with all clients, irrespective of their cultural background. It is important to realize that it takes time, study, and experience to become an effective multicultural group counselor. Multicultural competence cannot be reduced simply to cultural awareness and sensitivity, to a body of knowledge, or to a specific set of skills. Multicultural expertise requires that counselors have sufficient breadth and depth in all three of these areas (Leong & Kim, 1991).

D. W. Sue, Arredondo, and McDavis (1992), and more recently Arredondo and her colleagues (1996), have developed a conceptual framework for multicultural counseling competencies in three areas: (1) awareness of beliefs and attitudes, (2) knowledge, and (3) skills. What follows is a modified and brief version of the multicultural competencies identified by D. W. Sue and Sue (2003), Sue and his colleagues (1992, 1998), Arredondo and her colleagues (1996), and the ASGW's (1999) "Principles for Diversity Competent Group Workers."

Beliefs and Attitudes   Diversity-competent group leaders recognize and understand their own values, biases, ethnocentric attitudes, and assumptions about human behavior. They do not allow their personal values or problems to interfere with their work with clients who are culturally different from them. They are aware of their negative and positive emotional reactions toward other racial and ethnic groups that may prove detrimental to establishing collaborative relationships within the group. They seek to understand the world from the vantage point of their clients. Rather than maintaining that their cultural heritage is superior, they are able to accept and value cultural diversity. They welcome diverse value orientations and diverse assumptions about human behavior, and thus, they have a basis for sharing the worldview of their clients as opposed to being culturally encapsulated. They respect clients' religious and spiritual beliefs and values and are comfortable with differences between themselves and others in gender, race, ethnicity, culture, sexual orientation, different abilities, age, and beliefs. They value bilingualism and do not view another language as an impediment to counseling.

Effective multicultural group workers monitor their functioning through consultation, supervision, and continuing education. They realize that group counseling may not be appropriate for all clients or for all problems. If necessary, they are willing to refer a client if it becomes evident that group counseling is not an appropriate form of treatment for the client or if, for example, a more homogeneous support group seems warranted.

Knowledge   Diversity-competent group practitioners possess certain knowledge. They know specifically about their own racial and cultural heritage and how it affects them personally and professionally. Because they understand the dynamics of oppression, racism, discrimination, and stereotyping, they are aware of the institutional barriers that prevent minorities from accessing the mental health services available in their community. They acknowledge their own racist attitudes, beliefs, and feelings. They do not impose their values and expectations on their clients from differing cultural backgrounds, and they avoid stereotyping clients. They strive to understand the worldview of their clients. They possess knowledge about the historical background, traditions, and values of the groups with whom they are working. They have knowledge of minority family structures, hierarchies, values, and beliefs. They are knowledgeable about communication style differences and how their style may clash with or foster the group process. Because they understand the basic values underlying the therapeutic group process, they know how these values may differ from the cultural and family values of various minority groups. Furthermore, these practitioners are knowledgeable about community characteristics and resources. They know how to help clients make use of indigenous support systems. In areas where they are lacking in knowledge, they seek resources to assist them. The greater their depth and breadth of knowledge of culturally diverse groups, the more likely they are to be effective group workers.

Skills and Intervention Strategies   Effective group counselors have acquired certain skills in working with culturally diverse populations. Multicultural counseling is enhanced when practitioners use methods and strategies and define goals that are consistent with the life experiences and cultural values of their clients. Such practitioners modify and adapt their interventions in a group to accommodate cultural differences. They are able to exercise institutional intervention skills on behalf of their clients. They become actively involved with minority individuals outside of the group setting (community events, celebrations, and neighborhood groups) as this is called for and to the extent possible. They are not limited to one approach in helping and recognize that helping strategies may be culture bound. They do not force their clients to fit within one counseling approach. They are able to send and receive both verbal and nonverbal messages accurately and appropriately. They are willing to seek out educational, consultative, and training experiences to enhance their ability to work with culturally diverse clients. They consult regularly with other professionals regarding issues of culture to determine whether or where referral may be necessary. Diversity-competent group counselors take responsibility in educating the members of their groups about the way the group process works, including matters such as goals, expectations, legal rights, and alternative resources for continued growth.

Recognize Your Limitations   As a diversity-competent group leader, you can acquire general knowledge and skills that will enable you to function effectively with diverse group members. However, it is not realistic to expect that you will know everything about the cultural background of all of these members. You do yourself an injustice if you overwhelm yourself with all that you do not know or if you feel guilty over your limitations or parochial views. You will not become more effective by expecting that you must be completely knowledgeable about the cultural backgrounds of all the members of your groups, by thinking that you should have a complete repertoire of skills, or by demanding perfection as a multicultural group worker. Instead, recognize and appreciate your efforts toward becoming a more effective person and professional. The first step is to become more comfortable in accepting diversity as a positive value and in taking actions to increase your ability to work with a range of clients. In developing models for counseling culturally diverse clients, Vontress (1996) emphasizes that we need to recognize simultaneously the commonalities and the differences of human beings. He writes, "Cross-cultural counseling, in short, does not intend to teach specific interventions for each culture, but to infuse the counselor with a cultural sensitivity and tolerant philosophical outlook that will befit all cultures" (p. 164).

Ivey, Pedersen, and Ivey (2001) write about the notion of multicultural intentionality, or the ability to work effectively with many types of individuals with diverse cultural backgrounds. To the key components of awareness, knowledge, and skills, they add the characteristics of humility, confidence, and recovery skills as critical to becoming a diversity-competent group counselor. These attributes mean that group counselors do not have to possess all the answers, that they can learn from their mistakes, and that they can develop confidence in their ability to become flexible with challenging situations. The ability to recover from mistakes gracefully is more important than not making any mistakes.

Remember, there is much to be said for letting group members teach you and other group members about relevant aspects of their culture. It is a good practice to ask members to provide you and the others in the group with the information they will need to effectively interact with them. It is helpful to assess a client's degree of acculturation and identity development. This is especially true for individuals who have the experience of living in several cultures. Although they often have allegiance to their own home culture, they may also find certain characteristics of their new culture attractive and experience conflicts in integrating the two cultures. These core struggles can be productively explored in a group context if you and the other members respect this cultural conflict.

If you truly respect the members in your group, you will patiently attempt to enter their world as much as possible. It is not necessary that you have the same experiences as your clients, but it is important that you attempt to be open to a similar set of feelings and struggles. If this respect exists, all of the members benefit from cultural diversity within a group.

As you study the contemporary theories and apply them to group counseling, strive to think about the cultural implications of the techniques that grow out of them. Consider which techniques may be more appropriate with specific client populations and in specific contexts. Even more important, think about ways to adapt the techniques you will be learning to a group member's cultural background. Perhaps most important of all, consider how you might acquire the personal characteristics required to become a diversity-competent group counselor.

If your groups are composed of individuals from a variety of ethnic and cultural backgrounds that differ from your own, you can benefit from reading articles that address diversity perspectives. I recommend the following sources for educating yourself about issues of multicultural competence: Atkinson, Morten, and Sue (1998); Pedersen (1997, 2000); D. W. Sue and D. Sue (2003); Sue, Ivey, and Pedersen (1996); and D. W. Sue and his colleagues (1998).

In the *Student Manual for Theory and Practice of Group Counseling* (Corey, 2004), you will find a checklist for becoming a diversity-competent group counselor. Use this checklist to assess your current level of skill development in the multicultural competencies. Chapter 2 of the Student Manual also contains the full text of the ASGW's (1999) "Principles for Diversity Competent Group Workers." Take time to think about these principles and how they might apply to your group work.

Special Skills for Opening and Closing Group Sessions

If you open a group session effectively, it will set the tone for the rest of the session. In training and supervising group leaders, I have found that many leaders lack the skills necessary to open and close a group session effectively. For example, some simply select one member and focus on that person while the rest of the group sits passively waiting. Because of the leader's anxiety to "get things going," any member who raises a question is likely to receive attention without any attempt to involve the other participants in the interaction. When a group session begins poorly, it may be difficult to accomplish any sustained work during the rest of the meeting.

The way each session is closed is as important as the way it is initiated. I have observed group leaders who simply allow the time to elapse and then abruptly announce, "Our time is up; we'll see you all next week." Because of the leader's failure to summarize and offer some evaluation of the session, much of the potential value of the meeting is lost. Effectively opening and closing each session ensures continuity from meeting to meeting. Continuity makes it more likely that participants will think about what occurred in the group when they are outside of it, and they will be more likely to try to apply what they have learned to their everyday lives. Together with encouragement and direction from the leader, it also facilitates the members' task of assessing their own level of participation at each session.

Procedures for Opening a Group Session

With groups that meet on a weekly or regular basis, group leaders have a variety of options for opening the session.

1. Participants can be asked to briefly state what they want to get from the session. I prefer a quick "go-around" in which each group member identifies issues or concerns that could be explored during the session. Before focusing on one person, give all members a chance to at least say what they want to bring up during the meeting. In this way a loose agenda can be developed, and if a number of people are concerned with similar issues, the agenda will allow the repeated involvement of several members.

2. Give members a chance to express any thoughts they may have had about the previous session or to bring up for consideration any unresolved issues from an earlier meeting. Unresolved issues among members themselves or between members and the leader can make progressing with the current agenda most difficult. The hidden agenda will interfere with productive work until it has surfaced and been dealt with effectively.

3. Participants can be asked to report on the progress or difficulties they experienced during the week. Ideally, they have been experimenting with other ways of behaving outside of the group, they are getting involved in carrying out "homework assignments," and they are working on concrete plans that are action-oriented. Even if not all of these desirable activities have taken place, time can be profitably used at the beginning of a session to share successes or to bring up specific problems.

4. The group leader may want to make some observations about the previous meeting or relate some thoughts that have occurred to him or her since the group last met.

5. In an open group (one where membership changes somewhat from week to week), it is a good idea to encourage those members who have been part of the group for a while to share with newcomers what the group has

meant to them. Those who are just joining the group can say something about what they hope to get from the experience and perhaps share any of their anxieties pertaining to coming to the group.

One way to open a group session is through the use of a structured exercise as a way to assist members in identifying what concerns they want to explore. Depending on how, when, and why they are used, structured exercises can enhance interaction and provide a focus for work, or they can promote member dependence on the leader for continuing to provide direction. In their eagerness to get a group moving and keep it moving, some leaders try one exercise after another in a hit-or-miss fashion. Exercises that relate to the overall plan of the group and are appropriately applied in a timely manner can be useful tools for promoting change. However, lacking proper application, they can be counterproductive to the group process and to an individual's growth.

Structured exercises can be very useful during the initial and the final stages of a group or as a way to open a meeting. At the beginning of a group, I use certain exercises designed to assist members in clarifying their personal goals, in dealing with their expectations and fears, and in building trust. These exercises may consist of asking members to work in pairs or in small groups on some selected topic—for example, what they hope to get from a group session.

Procedures for Closing a Group Session

Before closing a session, allow time for integrating what has occurred, for reflecting on what has been experienced, for talking about what the participants may do between now and the next session, and for other summarizing. The leader may also find it useful to check with the group around the midpoint of the session and say something like this: "I'm aware that we still have an hour left before we close today. So I want to check with you to see if there are any matters you want to bring up before we close"; or this: "I'd like each of you to give me an idea of how you feel about this session. So far, have you gotten what you wanted from it?" Although these assessments in the middle of a session don't have to be made routinely, doing so from time to time can encourage members to evaluate their progress. If they are not satisfied with either their own participation or what is going on in the session, there is still time to change the course of the group before it ends.

Generally, members do not automatically evaluate the degree of their investment in the group or the extent of the gains they have made. The leader can do a great deal to guide participants into reflecting on the time limitations of their group and on whether they are satisfied with their participation. Members also need guidance in appraising how fully their goals are being achieved and how effectively the group is operating. If this periodic appraisal is done well, members have a chance to formulate plans for changes in the group's direction before it is too late. Consequently, it is less likely they will leave the group feeling that they didn't get what they had hoped for when they joined.

In sum, the leader's closing skills bring unity to the group experience and consolidate the learning that has occurred during a session. Here are some steps group leaders can take toward the end of each weekly session to help members evaluate their participation and bridge the gap between the group and their daily existence.

1. Group leaders should strive to close the session without closing the issues raised during the session. It may not be therapeutic to wrap up an issue or solve a problem too quickly. Many leaders make the mistake of forcing resolution of problems prematurely. Being task-oriented, they feel uncomfortable about allowing members the time they need to explore and struggle with personal problems. In such instances, the leader's intervention has the effect of resolving quite superficially what may be complex matters that need to be fully explored. It is good for people to leave a session with unanswered questions. They will be motivated to think more about their concerns and to come up with some tentative solutions on their own. Leaders need to learn the delicate balance between bringing temporary closure to an issue at the end of a session and closing the issue completely.

2. Summarizing can be effective at the end of each session. It is helpful to ask members to summarize both the group process and their own progress toward their goals. Comments can be made about common themes and issues that have emerged. The group leader can add summary comments, especially as they pertain to group process, but it is even better to teach members how to integrate what they have learned for themselves.

3. Participants can be asked to tell the group how they perceived the session, to offer comments and feedback to other members, and to make a statement about their level of investment in the session. By doing this regularly, members share in the responsibility of deciding what they will do to change the group's direction if they are not satisfied with it. For example, if participants report week after week that they are bored, they can be asked what they are willing to do to relieve their boredom.

4. It is helpful to focus on positive feedback too. Individuals who get involved should be recognized and supported for their efforts by both the leader and other participants.

5. Members can report on their homework assignments, in which they tried to put into practice some of their new insights, and they can make plans for applying what they have learned to problem situations outside the group.

6. Participants can be asked whether there are any topics or problems they would like to put on the agenda for the next session. Besides linking sessions, this procedure prompts participants to think about ways of exploring these concerns in the next meeting—that is, to work between sessions.

7. Group leaders may want to express their own reactions to the session and make some observations. These reactions and comments about the direction of the group can be very useful in stimulating thought and action on the part of the members.

8. In a group with changing membership, it is good to remind members a week before that certain members will be leaving the group. Those who are terminating need to talk about what they have gotten from the group and

what it is like for them to be leaving. Other members will most likely want to give feedback to the terminating member.

In summary, the leader interventions I have described illustrate that careful attention to opening and closing group sessions facilitates learning. It has the effect of challenging members to recognize their role in determining the outcomes of the group.

Co-Leading Groups

There are pluses for both you and your group if you are able to arrange to have a co-leader. Leading a group can be a lonely experience at times, and the value of meeting with a co-leader for planning and processing should not be underestimated. The co-leadership style has many advantages and a few disadvantages. Here are some of the advantages:

- Group members can benefit from the life experience and insights of two therapists; the leaders may have different perspectives on any given situation. Co-leaders with different theoretical orientations can work well together by keeping each other balanced.
- Two leaders can complement each other; a group can benefit from the combined strengths of the co-leading team.
- If one of the leaders is female and the other is male, they can re-create some of the original dynamics involved in the members' relationships with their parents; the opportunities for role playing are various.
- Co-leaders can serve as models for the participants with respect to how they relate to each other and to the group.
- The co-leaders can provide each other with valuable feedback; they can discuss what happened in the session and how to improve their skills. This discussion is especially important if one of the co-leaders needs some assistance in understanding countertransference.
- Each leader can grow from observing, working with, and learning from the other.
- Co-leaders provide more opportunities to facilitate linking among the work of members. While one leader is working with a particular member, the other leader can scan the group to get a sense of how other members are involved.
- If one of the co-leaders needs to be absent, the group can continue.
- The participants have the opportunity of getting feedback from two leaders instead of one; occasional differing reaction may inject vitality into the group and offer opportunities for reflection and further discussion.

Most of the disadvantages of the co-leading model arise when the two leaders fail to create and maintain an effective working relationship. A central factor in determining the quality of this relationship is *respect*. The two leaders are likely to have their differences in leadership style, and they may not always agree or share the same perceptions or interpretations. But if there is mutual respect, they will be open and direct with each other, trust each other, work cooperatively instead of competitively, and be secure enough not to need to "prove" themselves. If this trust is lacking, the members are bound to sense the absence of harmony, and the group will be negatively affected.

The choice of a co-leader, therefore, is an important one. A power struggle between incompatible co-leaders can have the effect of dividing the group. If the co-leaders do not work as a harmonious team, the group may follow their example and become fragmented. If the co-leaders evidence even subtle ongoing friction, they are providing a poor model of interpersonal relating. This friction can lead to unexpressed hostility among the members, which interferes with effective group work. If there are conflicts between leaders, it might be helpful to explore them openly in the group session, but ideally the two leaders will have talked about any emerging differences between them in their private meetings.

Although co-leaders do not necessarily have to work from the same theoretical approach, there are bound to be problems if they have vastly different perceptions about what the purpose of a group is or about their own role and function. For example, consider the situation in which one leader is intent on intervening with a great deal of advice aimed at providing answers for every problem a member raises, whereas the other leader is not interested in quick problem solving but, rather, encourages the members to struggle and to find their own direction. It is likely that they will be working at cross purposes and that their clients will get different messages about the purpose of the group.

It is important that co-leaders get together regularly to discuss any matters that may affect their work—for example, how they feel about working together, how they see their group, and how they can enhance each other's contribution. Ideally, co-leaders will spend time together before and after each session so they can plan for the upcoming session, share their perceptions, and address any difficulties that arise between them. Chapters 4 and 5 highlight some specific issues co-leaders might talk about in their meetings at each of the various stages of a group.

I prefer the co-leadership model both for leading groups and for training and supervising leaders. Co-leading offers a certain safety, especially when practitioners are leading a group for the first time. It is typical for beginning group leaders to experience self-doubt and anxiety. Facing a group for the first time with a co-leader whom you trust and respect can make what might seem like an anxiety-provoking task a delightful learning experience.

Developing Your Group Leadership Style

There are as many styles of group counseling as there are leaders, and even leaders who subscribe to a primary therapeutic model, such as behavior therapy or transactional analysis, show considerable variation in the way they lead groups. As a group leader, you bring your background of experiences and your personality, value systems, biases, and unique talents and skills to the group you lead. You also bring to it your theoretical preferences.

One determinant of your leadership style is whether you lead short-term or long-term groups. As you will see in Chapter 6, psychoanalytic groups tend to be long term, with the major aim of bringing about change in character structure. However, such a broad goal is not possible in short-term groups. As a group leader, your role in short-term groups is quite different from the leadership role in long-term therapy groups.

Most likely you will be expected to set up and conduct a variety of short-term groups, which means you will need to be active, directive, conscious of time limitations, and concerned with assisting members in identifying specific problem areas dealing with their current life situation. Brief groups require a more structured style so that members can attain specific goals. For example, you will be more concerned with present issues than with exploring the members' past. In conducting short-term groups the leader must pay particular attention to pregroup screening and preparation of potential members prior to the group; maintain a focus on a particular set of themes during the sessions; strive to develop group cohesion quickly; remind members of the time limits on the group's duration; and do follow-up work once the group ends. Leaders are more active in brief group work than in long-term groups, both in setting up the group and in conducting group sessions, because of the necessity of attending to the foregoing tasks within a relatively short time duration (Rosenberg & Wright, 1997).

Regardless of whether you work mostly with short- or long-term groups, what is most important is that you know yourself and develop a style that fits your personality. My goal is to help you develop a leadership style that is your own and that expresses your uniqueness as a person. If you attempt to copy someone else's style, you can lose much of your potential effectiveness as a group leader. Surely you will be influenced by supervisors, co-leaders, and the leaders of groups and workshops you attend as a participant. But it is one thing to be influenced by others—most leaders borrow from many resources in developing their style of group leadership—and another to deny your own uniqueness by copying others' therapeutic styles, which may work well for them but may not be suited to you.

The theoretical stance that you are challenged to develop must be closely related to your values, beliefs, and personal characteristics. You may advocate an approach that emphasizes thinking, one that stresses experiencing and expressing feelings, or one that focuses on action-oriented methods. Or your approach may integrate the thinking, feeling, and acting dimensions. Regardless of the approach you favor, your theoretical preferences will no doubt influence your style, especially with regard to the aspects of the group interaction on which you choose to focus.

One way to build a foundation for a personal leadership style is to know the diverse range of theories of group counseling and their implications for styles of leading. Leading a group without an explicit theoretical rationale is somewhat like flying a plane without a map and instruments. Some students think of a theoretical model as a rigid structure that prescribes step by step what to do in specific situations. That's not my understanding of theory. I see theory as a set of general guidelines that you can use in your practice. A theory is a map that provides direction and guidance in examining your basic assumptions about human beings, in determining your goals for the group, in clarifying your role and functions as a leader, in explaining the group interactions, and in evaluating the outcomes of the group.

Developing a theoretical stance involves more than merely accepting the tenets of any one theory. It is an ongoing process in which group leaders keep questioning the "what," "how," and "why" of their practice. I encourage my students to take a critical look at the key concepts of the various theories and also to consider the theorists behind them, because a theory is generally a personal expression of the person who developed it. I further encourage them not to uncritically follow any theory in totality. It is important to remain open and to seriously consider the unique contributions as well as the limitations of different approaches. If someone swallows a theory whole, the theory never gets properly digested and integrated. When practitioners settle on one theory and don't recognize its limitations, they are likely to misuse it and to assume that it is an axiom and a set of proven facts rather than a tool for inquiry. If your theoretical perspective causes you to ignore all others, you may force your clients to fit its confines instead of using it to understand them.

Many group workers align their practice with one particular theoretical orientation on the grounds that their theory of choice provides a good explanation of human behavior and provides them with a unified and consistent basis for intervening in their groups. I have no quarrel with practitioners who have carefully evaluated a theory and identify with a particular orientation. However, some adopt a theory without knowing why they prefer the approach, and in doing so they often maintain a closed stance to incorporating alternative perspectives. In adopting a closed stance, one can become a "true believer," and the problem with true believers is that they limit their vision by screening out anything that doesn't fit their preconceived structures. Also, since they assume that their approach contains the whole truth, they are likely to try to impose it on others and to expect the same complete acceptance from them.

I also warn my students of the danger of discarding a theory in its entirety because of their objections to some aspects of it. For example, some students initially see little practical relevance in the psychoanalytic approach. They object to the lengthy period of time required by analysis, consider the analysis of unconscious material as being beyond their scope of competence, and typically don't appreciate the anonymous role of the therapist. I encourage these students to examine the model to see what concepts they can incorporate.

As you study the 10 theoretical models of group counseling presented in Part Two, the commonalities and differences among these models and the ways in which the various perspectives can shape your style as a group leader will become clear. As you study each theory, reflect on the applications for developing short-term groups. Given the managed care emphasis on being both efficient and effective, today's group leaders need to learn as much as possible about short-term groups. Among all of the theories described, the psychoanalytic approach is most geared to long-term therapy groups, yet even here short-term psychodynamic groups have begun to be developed. All of the other theoretical approaches covered in Part Two lend themselves well to brief interventions and to time-limited groups. The cognitive behavioral group approaches also provide leaders with a variety of techniques that are well suited to short-term groups.

Encouraging Practitioner Research

As a group practitioner, you will be expected to demonstrate the efficacy of your interventions. Familiarity with research in the group work field is becoming an essential part of practice in the era of managed care. You will likely be expected to gather evaluation data that will support the value of group services. Research can help you come to a better understanding of the specific factors that contribute to successful outcomes of groups. Applied research can help you refine your interventions and identify factors that interfere with group effectiveness. Many schools and agencies are requiring some form of evaluation of the effectiveness of a group. As a practitioner, it is also essential that what you do in your groups is informed by research on the process and outcomes of groups. Part of your development as a group practitioner involves thinking of ways to make evaluation research a basic part of your group practice.

Many group workers are not willing to devote time to devising evaluative instruments as part of their clinical practice. Certainly, combining research and practice is challenging. Because of the demands of each role, it is difficult to be both a group practitioner and a researcher. Although some group practitioners express interest in research, they rarely engage in group research, citing restrictions such as lack of time and funds, not having expertise in research methods, and working in settings that do not support research (Riva & Smith, 1997). Yalom (1995) admits that few group practitioners will ever have the time, funding, and institutional backing to engage in large-scale research, yet he contends that "many can engage in intensive single-patient or single-group research, and all clinicians must evaluate published clinical research" (p. 529).

In their article on perspectives on research in group work, Bednar and colleagues (1987) commented on overcoming obstacles to the future development of research. These authors mention a number of common conceptual, methodological, and attitudinal impediments. They conclude that reducing these obstacles will require a commitment by researchers and other professionals:

- To improve conceptualizations of variables studied in relation to groups
- To use research designs and methods that can assess the subtle nature of interactions among the leader and members
- To improve reporting of the characteristics of treatment and control groups that are studied
- To focus on the applications of research findings

These results can only be achieved through meaningful collaboration between researchers and group practitioners. Even if practitioners do not have the time or the expertise required to conduct research themselves, it is possible for them to work with researchers so that they can integrate research findings in their group practice. Collaboration between practitioners and researchers can benefit both parties as well as the field of group work (Kalodner & Riva, 1997).

The Current Status of Group Work Research

Both consumers and funding agencies are increasingly demanding that practitioners demonstrate the value of their therapeutic strategies. Based on empirical investigations of more than four decades of group work, Dies (1992) finds that there is relatively little difference in outcome between individual and group treatments. With the pressures to justify the expense of psychotherapy, Dies suggests that clinicians are likely to face increased challenges to explain why the treatment of choice for most clients is not group therapy. In writing of the future of group therapy, Dies states that research on group interventions is expected to reflect growing efforts to link group process and outcome, provide a more congenial collaboration between practitioners and researchers, and offer a more sophisticated blending of research designs to study group process and outcomes.

Although research on group counseling has improved over the past two decades, many research studies of group work suffer from serious methodological problems. Future group research needs to inform practice, and, at the same time, research needs to be guided by the expertise of those who conduct groups (Riva & Kalodner, 1997).

Over the past 15 years, the focus of group studies has shifted from an emphasis on process research to an examination of outcome studies. There are many unanswered questions related to group process variables, such as matching certain individuals to specific groups, member selection and group composition, style of group leadership, and interventions at various stages of a group (Riva & Smith, 1997). During the 1990s, research focused on very specific applications of types of group interventions with specific client populations, with much less effort aimed at understanding group dynamics. Research continues on a wide range of problem areas, a few of which include group treatment of depression, eating disorders, obesity, panic and phobia, dissociative disorders, behavioral change programs, couples therapy, parent training, older adults, support groups for specific disabilities, and bereavement groups for people of different ages (Horne & Rosenthal, 1997; White & Freeman, 2000).

A survey of more than 45 years of research provides an abundance of evidence that group approaches are associated with clients' improvement in a variety of settings and situations (Bednar & Kaul, 1994). But the general consensus among experts is that the current knowledge of the effects of specific group treatments is modest at best. Researchers know little about how group processes mediate change in participants, how members influence group processes, and what dimensions of psychological functioning are most amenable to change in small groups. Quite simply, although researchers know that group treatments can be effective, they don't know much about why this is so.

In their description of the history of research on group work, Horne and Rosenthal (1997) indicate that we have learned much about the complex nature of group work. They state that the efficacy of group treatment appears to have less to do with a specific theoretical orientation than with finding an optimum combination of pregroup training, client characteristics, therapeutic factors, group structure, and stages of group development.

The Challenge of Combining Research and Practice

Make systematic observation and assessment basic parts of your practice of group work. Instead of thinking exclusively in terms of rigorous empirical research, practitioners can begin to consider alternatives to traditional scientific methods. One such alternative is evaluative research, which is aimed at gathering and assessing data that can be of value in making decisions about programs and in improving the quality of professional services (Dies, 1983a). In group work, pure research should not be seen as the only type of inquiry that has value. Practitioners and researchers can choose to do good field research instead (Morran & Stockton, 1985).

Yalom (1995) claims that group trainees need to know more than how to implement techniques in a group—they also need to know how to learn. Faculty should teach and model a basic research orientation characterized by an open, self-critical inquiring attitude toward clinical and research evidence. He writes that students need to critically evaluate their own work and maintain sufficient flexibility to be responsive to their own observations.

According to Yalom, a research orientation enables group therapists, throughout their career, to remain flexible and responsive to new evidence. Practitioners who lack a research orientation will have no basis to critically evaluate new developments in the field of group work. Without a consistent framework to evaluate evidence of the efficacy of innovations in the field, practitioners run the risk of being unreasonably unreceptive to new approaches. Or, in contrast, they uncritically embrace one fad after another.

In learning how to become a group practitioner, it is necessary to progress from a beginner to a skilled clinician in stages. Likewise, a developmental approach can be useful for teaching students about group research. Rex Stockton advocates an apprenticeship model. Students improve their clinical skills through practice, consultation, supervision, and discussion with mentors and peers. Likewise, they can learn about group research techniques through the same kind of exposure, practice, consultation, and collaboration with those who are doing research (Stockton & Toth, 1997).

As a group practitioner, whether or not you actually conduct research with your groups is less important than your willingness to keep yourself informed about the practical applications of research on group work. At the very least, you need to be up to date with the research implications for practice. One way to do this is to read professional journal articles that deal with research in the field of group work. For example, the *Journal for Specialists in Groups Work*, published four times a year, contains a variety of excellent articles of interest to group practitioners and researchers.

CHAPTER 3

Ethical and Professional Issues in Group Practice

Those who seek to be professional group leaders must be willing to examine both their ethical standards and their level of competence. The ethical issues treated in this chapter include the rights of group members, including informed consent and confidentiality; the psychological risks of groups; personal relationships with clients; socializing among members; the impact of the group leader's values; working sensitively and ethically with diverse clients; and the uses and misuses of group techniques. In my opinion, a central ethical issue in group work pertains to the group leader's competence. Thus, I give special attention to ways of determining competence, professional training standards, and adjuncts to academic preparation of group counselors. Also highlighted are ethical issues involved in training group workers. The final section outlines issues of legal liability and malpractice.

As a responsible group practitioner, you are challenged to clarify your thinking about the ethical and professional issues discussed in this chapter. Although you are obligated to be familiar with, and bound by, the ethics codes of your professional organization, many of these codes offer only general guidelines. Thus, you need to learn how to make ethical decisions in practical situations. The ethics codes will give you a general framework from which to operate, but you must apply these principles to concrete cases. The Association for Specialists in Group Work (ASGW, 1998) "Best Practice Guidelines" is reproduced in the Student Manual that accompanies this textbook. You may want to refer to these guidelines often, especially as you study Chapters 1 through 5.

The Rights of Group Participants

My experience has taught me that those who enter groups are frequently unaware both of their basic rights as participants and of their responsibilities. It is your function as a group leader to help prospective members learn what their rights are. This section offers a detailed list of group participants' rights.

A Basic Right: Informed Consent

If basic information about the group is discussed at the initial session, the participants are likely to be far more cooperative and active. A leader who does this as a matter of policy demonstrates honesty and respect for the members and fosters the trust necessary if group members are to be open and active. Such a leader has obtained the *informed consent* of the participants. Members have a right to receive basic information *before* joining a group, and they have a right to expect certain other information *during* the course of the group.

Pregroup Disclosures   Here is a list of what group participants have a right to expect before they make the decision to join a group:

- A clear statement regarding the purpose of the group
- A description of the group format, procedures, and ground rules
- An initial interview to determine whether this particular group with this particular leader is at this time appropriate to their needs
- An opportunity to seek information about the group, to pose questions, and to explore concerns
- A discussion of ways the group process may or may not be congruent with the cultural beliefs and values of group members
- A statement describing the education, training, and qualifications of the group leader
- Information concerning fees and expenses including fees for a follow-up session; also, information about length of group, frequency and duration of meetings, group goals, and techniques being employed
- Information about the psychological risks involved in group participation
- Knowledge of the circumstances in which confidentiality must be broken because of legal, ethical, or professional reasons
- Clarification of what services can and cannot be provided within the group
- Help from the group leader in developing personal goals
- A clear understanding of the division of responsibility between leader and participants
- A discussion of the rights and responsibilities of group members

Clients' Rights During the Group   Here is a list of what members have a right to expect during the course of the group:

- Guidance concerning what is expected of them
- Notice of any research involving the group and of any audio- or videotaping of group sessions
- The right to stop any recording if it restricts member participation
- Assistance from the group leader in translating group learning into action in everyday life
- Opportunities to discuss what one has learned in the group and to bring some closure to the group experience so participants are not left with unnecessary unfinished business

- A consultation with the group leader should a crisis arise as a direct result of participation in the group, or a referral to other sources of help if further help is not available from the group leader
- The exercise of reasonable safeguards on the leader's part to minimize the potential risks of the group; respect for member privacy with regard to what the person will reveal as well as to the degree of disclosure
- Observance of confidentiality on the part of the leader and other group members
- Freedom from having values imposed by the leader or other members
- The right to be treated as an individual and accorded dignity and respect

The leader should stress that participation in groups carries certain responsibilities as well as rights. These responsibilities include attending regularly, being prompt, taking risks, being willing to talk about oneself, giving others feedback, maintaining confidentiality, and asking for what one needs. Some of these group norms may pose problems for certain members because of their cultural background. It is essential that the expectations for group members be clear from the outset and that members be in agreement with such expectations. Of course, part of the group process involves the participation of members in developing norms that will influence their behavior in a group situation.

Issues in Involuntary Groups

When participation is mandatory, informed consent is particularly important. Much effort needs to be directed toward fully informing involuntary members of the nature and goals of the group, the procedures to be used, their rights and responsibilities, the limits of confidentiality, and what effect their level of participation in the group will have on critical decisions about them outside of the group. When groups are involuntary, every attempt should be made to enlist the cooperation of the members and encourage them to continue attending voluntarily. One way of doing this is to spend some time with involuntary clients helping them reframe the notion "I have to come to this group." They do have some choice whether they will attend group or deal with the consequences of not being in the group. If "involuntary" members choose not to participate in the group, they will need to be prepared to deal with consequences such as being expelled from school, doing jail time, or being in juvenile detention.

Another alternative would be for the group leader to accept involuntary group members only for an initial limited period. There is something to be said for giving reluctant members a chance to see for themselves what a group is about and then eventually (say, after three sessions) letting them decide whether they will return. Group leaders can inform members that it is their choice of how they will use the time in the group. The members can be encouraged to explore their fears and reluctance to fully participate in the group, as well as the consequences of not participating in the group. Ethical practice would seem to require that group leaders fully explore these issues with clients who are sent to them.

The Freedom to Leave a Group

Leaders should be clear about their policies pertaining to attendance, commitment to remaining in a group for a predetermined number of sessions, and leaving a particular session if they do not like what is going on in the group. If members simply drop out of the group, it makes it extremely difficult to develop a working level of trust or to establish group cohesion. The topic of leaving the group should be discussed during the initial session, and the leader's attitudes and policies need to be clear from the outset.

In my view, group members have a responsibility to the leaders and other members to explain why they want to leave. There are a number of reasons for such a policy. For one thing, it can be deleterious to members to leave without having been able to discuss what they considered threatening or negative in the experience. If they simply leave when they become uncomfortable, they are likely to be left with unfinished business, and so are the remaining members. A member's dropping out can surely damage the cohesion and trust in a group, for the remaining members may think that they in some way "caused" the departure. It is a good practice to tell members that if they are even thinking of withdrawing they should bring the matter up for exploration in a session. It is critical that members be encouraged to discuss their departure, at least with the group leader.

If a group is counterproductive for an individual, that person has a right to leave the group. Ideally, both the group leader and the members will work cooperatively to determine the degree to which a group experience is productive or counterproductive. My position is that if, at a mutually agreed-upon time, members still choose not to participate in a group, then they should be allowed to drop out without being subjected to pressure by the leader and other members to remain.

Freedom from Coercion and Undue Pressure

Members can reasonably expect to be respected by the group and not to be subjected to coercion and undue group pressure. However, some degree of group pressure is inevitable, and it is even therapeutic in many instances. People in a group are confronted with some of their self-defeating beliefs and behaviors and are challenged to admit what they are doing and determine whether they want to remain the way they are. Further, there is pressure in sessions to speak up, to make personal disclosures, to take certain risks, to share one's reactions to the here-and-now events within the group, and to be honest with the group. It is essential for group leaders to differentiate between destructive pressure and therapeutic pressure. People may need a certain degree of pressure to challenge them to take the risks involved in becoming fully invested in the group.

It is well to keep in mind that the purpose of a group is to help participants find their own answers, not to pressure them into doing what the group thinks is the appropriate course. Members can easily be subjected to needless anxiety if they are badgered to behave in a certain way. Members may also be pressured to take part in communication exercises or nonverbal exercises designed to promote interaction. It is essential that leaders be sensitive to the values of members who decline to participate in certain group exercises. Leaders must make it genuinely acceptable for members to abstain by mentioning this option periodically whenever it is appropriate. It is a good practice for group leaders to teach members how to resist undue group pressure and how to decline gracefully from participating in activities if they so choose.

The Right to Confidentiality

Confidentiality is a central ethical issue in group counseling, and it is an essential condition for effective group work. As a leader, you are required to keep the confidences of group members, but you have the added responsibility of impressing on the members the necessity of maintaining the confidential nature of whatever is revealed in the group. This matter bears reinforcement along the way, from the initial screening interview to the final group session. If the rationale for confidentiality is clearly presented to each individual during the preliminary interview and again to the group as a whole at the initial session, there is less chance that members will treat this matter lightly. Confidentiality is often on the minds of people when they join a group, so it is timely to fully explore this issue.

A good practice is to remind participants from time to time of the danger of inadvertently revealing confidences. My experience continues to teach me that members rarely gossip maliciously about others in their group. However, people do tend to talk more than they should outside the group and can unwittingly offer information about fellow members that should not be revealed. If the maintenance of confidentiality seems to be a matter of concern, the subject should be discussed fully in a group session.

In groups in institutions, agencies, and schools, where members know and have frequent contact with one another outside of the group, confidentiality becomes especially important and is more difficult to maintain. Clearly, there is no way to ensure that group members will respect the confidences of others. As a group leader, however, you can discuss the matter, express your feelings about the importance of maintaining confidentiality, have members sign contracts agreeing to it, and even impose some form of sanction on those who break it. Realize that your own modeling and the importance that you place on maintaining confidentiality will be crucial in setting norms for members to follow. If the members sense that you take confidentiality seriously, there is a greater likelihood that they also will be concerned about the matter. Ultimately, it is up to the members to respect the need for confidentiality and to maintain it. The American Counseling Association's *Code of Ethics and Standards of Practice* (ACA, 1995) makes this statement concerning confidentiality in groups:

> In group work, counselors clearly define confidentiality and the parameters for the specific group being entered, explain its importance, and discuss the difficulties

related to confidentiality involved in group work. The fact that confidentiality cannot be guaranteed is clearly communicated to group members. (B.2.a.)

Members have the right to know of any tape recordings or videotapes that might be made of group sessions, and the purpose for which they will be used. Written permission should be secured before recording any session. If the tapes will be used for research purposes or will be critiqued by a supervisor or other students in a group supervision session, the members have the right to deny permission.

Exceptions to Confidentiality   Other aspects of confidentiality that group leaders should address from the outset of a group are the limits of confidentiality. For instance, leaders can explain to members when they are legally required to break confidentiality. Leaders can add that they can assure confidentiality on their own part but not on the part of other members. It is important to encourage members to bring up matters pertaining to confidentiality whenever they are concerned about them. The ACA's *Code of Ethics* (1995) identifies exceptions to confidentiality that members should understand:

> The general requirement that counselors keep information confidential does not apply when disclosure is required to prevent clear and imminent danger to the client or others or when legal requirements demand that confidential information be revealed. Counselors consult with other professionals when in doubt as to the validity of an exception. (B.1.c.)

It is a good policy for group workers to give a written statement to each member setting forth the limitations of confidentiality and spelling out specific situations that would demand the breaching of confidences. It seems that such straightforwardness with members from the outset does a great deal to create trust, for at least members know where they stand.

Of course, it is imperative that those who lead groups become familiar with the state laws that have an impact on their practice. Group leaders do well to let members know that legal privilege does not apply to group treatment, unless provided by state statute (ASGW, 1998). Counselors are legally required to report clients' threats to harm themselves or others. This requirement also covers cases of child abuse or neglect, incest, or child molestation. Taking an extreme case, if one of your group members convincingly threatens to seriously injure another person, you may have to consult your supervisor or other colleagues, warn the intended victim, and even notify the appropriate authorities. The threat need not involve others; clients may exhibit bizarre behavior that requires you to take steps to have them temporarily hospitalized, such as having "visions" or "hearing voices" telling them to maim themselves.

If you lead a group at a correctional institution or a psychiatric hospital, you may be required to act as more than a counselor; for instance, you may have to record in a member's file certain behaviors that he or she exhibits in the group. At the same time, your responsibility to your clients requires you to inform them that you are recording and passing on certain information. Generally speaking, you will find that you have a better chance of gaining the cooperation of group members if you are candid about a situation rather than hiding your disclosures and thereby putting yourself in the position of violating their confidences.

Confidentiality with Minors   In a group for children in a school setting, care needs to be exerted to ensure that what goes on within the group is not a subject for discussion in class or on the playground. If children begin to talk about other members outside of the group, this will certainly block progress and damage the cohesion of the group. As is the case for adults and adolescents, children require the safety of knowing they will be treated respectfully. Group leaders must also be careful in how they talk about the children to teachers and administrators. Those who do groups with children need to be clear about what will be kept confidential and what may need to be shared with school personnel.

Do parents have a right to information that is disclosed by their children in a group? The answer to that question depends on whether you are looking at it from a legal, ethical, or professional viewpoint. It is a good practice to require written permission from parents before allowing a minor to enter a group. It is useful to have this permission include a brief statement concerning the purpose of the group, along with comments regarding the importance of confidentiality as a prerequisite to accomplishing such purposes and your intention not to violate any confidences. Clearly, it may be useful to give the parents information about their child, but this can be done without violating confidences. One useful practice to protect the privacy of what goes on in the group is to provide feedback to parents in a session with the child and one or both parents. In this way the child will have less cause to doubt the group leader's integrity in keeping his or her disclosures private.

Group leaders have a responsibility in groups that involve children and adolescents to take measures to increase the chances that confidentiality will be kept. It is important to work cooperatively with parents and guardians as well as to enlist the trust of the young people. It is also useful to teach minors, in terms that they are capable of understanding, about the nature, purposes, and limitations of confidentiality. In summary, group leaders would do well to continue to remind members to bring up their concerns about confidentiality for discussion whenever the issue is on their minds.

The Issue of Psychological Risks in Groups

Groups can act as powerful catalysts for personal change, and they can also pose definite risks for group members. The nature of these risks—which include life changes that cause disruption, hostile and destructive confrontations, scapegoating, and harmful socializing among members—and what the leader can do about them are the subject of this section. It is unrealistic to expect that a group will not involve risk, for all meaningful learning in life involves taking risks. However, it is the ethical responsibility of the group leader to ensure that prospective group members are aware of the potential risks and to take every precaution against them.

The ACA *Code of Ethics* (1995) specifies: "In a group setting, counselors take reasonable precautions to protect clients from physical or psychological trauma" (A.9.b.). This includes discussing the impact of potential life changes and helping group members explore their readiness to deal with such changes. A minimal expectation is that group leaders discuss with members the advantages and disadvantages of a given group, that they prepare the members to deal with any problems that might grow out of the group experience, and that they be alert to the fears and reservations that members might have.

It is also incumbent on group leaders to have a broad and deep understanding of the forces that operate in groups and how to mobilize those forces for ethical ends. Unless leaders exert caution, members not only may miss the benefits of a group but also could be harmed by it psychologically. Ways of reducing these risks include knowing members' limits, respecting their requests, developing an invitational style as opposed to a pushy or dictatorial style, avoiding abrasive confrontations, describing behavior rather than making judgments, and presenting hunches in a tentative way rather than forcing interpretations on members.

Here are a few of the problems group leaders can warn members about and work toward minimizing:

1. Members should be made aware of the possibility that participating in a group (or any other therapeutic endeavor) may disrupt their lives. As members become increasingly self-aware, they may make changes in their lives that, although constructive in the long run, can create turmoil along the way. For example, changes that a woman makes as a result of what she gains in a group may evoke resistance, even hostility, in her husband, with a resulting strain on their marriage. Furthermore, the rest of her family may not appreciate her changes and may prefer the person she was before getting involved in counseling.

2. Occasionally an individual member may be singled out as the scapegoat of the group. Other group members may "gang up" on this person, blaming him or her for problems of the group. Clearly, the group leader must take firm steps to deal with such occurrences.

3. Confrontation, a valuable and powerful tool in any group, can be misused, especially when it is employed to destructively attack another. Intrusive interventions, overly confrontive leader tactics, and pushing members beyond their limits often produce negative outcomes. Here, again, leaders (and members as well) must be on guard against behavior that can pose a serious psychological risk for group participants. To lessen the risks of nonconstructive confrontation, leaders can model the type of confrontation that focuses on specific behaviors and can avoid making judgments about members. They can teach members how to talk about themselves and the reactions they are having to a certain behavior pattern of a given member.

One way to minimize psychological risks in groups is to use a contract in which the leader specifies his or her responsibilities and the members specify their commitment by stating what they are willing to explore and do in the group. Such a contract reduces the chances that members will be exploited or will leave the group feeling that they have had a negative experience.

Another safeguard against unnecessary risk is the ability of leaders to recognize the boundaries of their competence and to restrict themselves to working only with those groups for which their training and experience have properly prepared them. Ultimately, it is the group leader who is responsible for minimizing the inevitable psychological risks associated with group activity. To best assume this responsibility, the leader will undergo the supervised practice and course work that is described later in this chapter.

The Ethics of Group Leaders' Actions

Being a group practitioner demands sensitivity to the needs of the members of your group and to the impact your values and techniques can have on them. It also demands an awareness of community standards of practice, the policies of the agency where you work, and the state laws that govern group counseling. In the mental health professions in general, there is a trend toward accountability and responsible practice. Graduate programs in counseling and social work are increasingly requiring course work in ethics and the law. In part, these trends may have something to do with the increased vulnerability of mental health practitioners to malpractice suits.

Almost all of the professional organizations have gone on record as affirming that their members should be aware of prevailing community standards and of the impact that conformity to or deviation from these standards will have on their practice. These organizations state explicitly that professionals will avoid exploitation of the therapeutic relationship, will not damage the trust that is necessary for a relationship to be therapeutic, and will avoid dual relationships if they would interfere with the primary therapeutic aims. Typically, the ethics codes caution against attempting to blend social or personal relationships with professional ones and stress the importance of maintaining appropriate boundaries.

Personal Relationships Between Leaders and Members

What criteria can a group counselor use to determine whether personal and social relationships with group members are appropriate? A key factor is whether such a social relationship is interfering with the therapeutic relationship. The ACA (1995) *Code of Ethics* states the issue this way:

> Counselors are aware of their influential positions with respect to clients, and they avoid exploiting the trust and dependency of clients. Counselors make every effort to avoid dual relationships with clients that could impair professional judgment or increase the risk of harm to clients. When dual relationships cannot be avoided, counselors take appropriate professional precautions such as informed consent, consultation, supervision, and documentation to ensure that judgment is not impaired and no exploitation occurs. (A.6.a.)

Another principle of the general concept of avoiding exploitation cautions counselors about misusing their role and power to meet their personal needs at the expense of clients. The core issue in this guideline deals with using power appropriately. When group leaders meet their personal needs for power and prestige at the expense of what is best for the members, they commit an ethical violation. The role of leaders is to help members meet their goals, not to become friends with their clients. Of course, leaders who develop sexual relationships with current group members are acting unethically.

Socializing Among Group Members

A related issue is whether socializing among group members hinders or facilitates the group process. This concern can become an ethical issue if members are forming cliques and gossiping about others in the group or if they are banding together and talking about matters that are best explored in the group sessions. If hidden agendas develop through various splinter groups within the group, it is likely that the progress of the group will come to an abrupt halt. Unless the hidden agenda is brought to the surface and dealt with, it seems very likely that many members will not be able to use the group therapeutically or meet their personal goals.

Yalom (1995) writes that a therapy group teaches people how to form intimate relationships but does not provide these relationships. He also points out that members meeting outside of the group have a responsibility to bring information about their meeting into the group. Any type of out-of-group socialization that interferes with the functioning of the group is counterproductive and should be discouraged. This is especially true in those situations in which participants discuss issues relevant to the group but avoid bringing up the same issues in the group itself.

In some cases, out-of-group contact and socialization can be beneficial. From the perspective of feminist group therapy, out-of-group socialization is not viewed as harmful. This is especially true if members are selected carefully and are able to manage out-of-group contact so that it works to their own best interests and to the good of the group as a whole. During out-of-group contact, members often have the opportunity to relate to others in a genuine and safe manner. If members recognize the pitfalls of socializing outside of group, and if they are willing to bring to the group whatever they discuss in these out-of-group encounters, they are well on the road to learning how to safely and productively manage such extra-group socialization.

One of the best ways for the group leader to prevent inappropriate and counterproductive socialization among group members is to bring this issue up for discussion. It is especially timely to explore the negative impact of forming cliques when the group seems to be stuck and is getting nowhere or when it appears that members are not talking about their reactions to one another. The members can be taught that what they do not say in the group itself might very well prevent their group from attaining any level of cohesion.

The Impact of the Leader's Values on the Group

In all controversial issues related to the group process, the leader's values play a central role. Your awareness of how your values influence your leadership style is in itself a central ethical issue. You may be under the impression that the ideal behavior is to be neutral and to keep your values separate from your leadership function. My position is that it is neither possible nor desirable for you to be scrupulously neutral with respect to values in the therapeutic relationship. Although it is not your proper function to persuade clients to accept a certain value system, it is appropriate that you be clear about your own values and that you express them openly when it is relevant to the work of the group.

In my view, the crux of the ethical concern in this area involves leaders who use their group to advance their personal agenda, or to meet their own needs at the expense of the members. Group counseling is not a forum in which leaders impose their worldview on the members; it is a way to assist members in exploring their own cultural values and beliefs. The ACA's (1995) standard here is that "counselors are aware of their own values, attitudes, beliefs, and behaviors and how these apply in a diverse society, and avoid imposing their values on clients" (A.5.b.). Value-laden issues are often brought to a group—religion, spirituality, abortion, divorce, and family struggles, to name just a few. The purpose of the group is to help members clarify their beliefs and examine options that are most congruent with their own value system.

There is a real difference between *imposing* and *exposing* one's values. As a group leader, when you impose your values, you are showing disrespect for the members' integrity. Expecting members to adopt your value system gives them the message that they are incapable of discovering a meaningful set of values and acting on them by themselves. When you expose your values, in contrast, members are free to test their own thinking against the background of your beliefs, but they can still make their own choices without being burdened with guilt that they are not meeting your expectations.

You need to be clear about your own values and remain objective when working with values that are different from your own. Doing this may necessitate that you seek supervision, especially if you become aware of a value conflict that interferes with your ability to respect a particular value of a member. It is critical that group counselors increase their awareness of how their personal reactions to members may inhibit the group process. They must monitor their countertransference and recognize the danger of stereotyping individuals on the basis of race, ethnicity, gender, age, or sexual orientation.

Members are best served if they learn to evaluate their own behavior to determine how it is working for them. If they come to the realization that what they are doing is not serving them well, it is appropriate for you to challenge them to develop alternative ways of behaving that will enable them to reach their goals. A group is an ideal place for members to assess the degree to which their behavior is consistent with their own values. They can get feedback from others, yet it will be their responsibility to make their own decisions.

Ethical Issues in Multicultural Group Counseling

The values leaders bring to the group process must consciously acknowledge the reality of human diversity in our society. If leaders ignore some basic differences in people, they can hardly be doing what is in the best interests of these clients. The ASGW (1998) "Best Practice Guidelines" offers this guidance on recognizing the role of diversity in the practice of group work:

> Group workers practice with broad sensitivity to client differences including but not limited to ethnic, gender, religious, sexual, psychological maturity, economic class, family history, physical characteristics or limitations, and geographic location. Group workers continuously seek information regarding the cultural issues of the diverse population with whom they are working both by interaction with participants and from using outside resources. (B.8.)

The ASGW (1999) "Principles for Diversity Competent Group Workers" reinforces this requirement of self-awareness:

> Diversity-competent group workers demonstrate increased awareness of how their own race, ethnicity, culture, gender, SES, sexual orientation, abilities, and religion and spiritual beliefs are impacted by their own experiences and histories, which in turn influence group process and dynamics. (I.A.3.)

The APA's Office of Ethnic Minority Affairs has developed a useful set of guidelines that focus on the ethical implications of working with culturally diverse clients. These guidelines are not specifically designed for group counselors, but they can be adapted for the group process.

- Group leaders should acquire the knowledge and skills they need to effectively work with the diverse range of members in their groups. If they do not have this essential background, they should seek consultation, supervision, and further education and training.
- Group leaders are aware of how their own cultural background, attitudes, values, beliefs, and biases influence their work, and they make efforts to correct any prejudices they may have.
- Group leaders acknowledge that ethnicity and culture influence behavior.
- Group leaders respect the roles of family and community hierarchies within a client's culture.
- Group leaders respect members' religious and spiritual beliefs and values.
- Group leaders consider the impact of adverse social, environmental, and political factors in assessing problems and designing interventions.
- Group leaders make efforts to eliminate biases, prejudices, and discriminatory practices. In their practice, they develop sensitivity to issues of oppression, sexism, and racism.

I agree with Pate and Bondi (1992) who maintain that religious beliefs and values are part of the cultural background of clients and should be considered vital components of counselor training programs. I also support their stand that counseling students need to be taught the importance of religious and spiritual beliefs in the lives of many of their clients. It is essential that group counselors also understand their own spiritual beliefs and values.

Being sensitive to how cultural and spiritual values influence their own thinking and behavior will help group leaders work ethically and effectively with members who are culturally different from themselves. Furthermore, ethical practice demands that group counselors possess the self-awareness, knowledge, and skills that are basic components of multiculturally competent practitioners. (See Chapter 2 for more discussion on this.)

Uses and Misuses of Group Techniques

In leading groups, it is essential that you have a clear rationale for each technique you use. This is an area in which theory is a useful guide for practice. As you will see, the 10 theories at the core of this book give rise to many therapeutic strategies and techniques. Such techniques are a means to increase awareness, to accomplish change, or to promote exploration and interaction. They can certainly be used ethically and therapeutically, yet they can also be misused.

Some of the ways in which leaders can practice unprofessionally are using techniques with which they are unfamiliar, using techniques in a mechanical way, using techniques to serve their own hidden agendas or to enhance their power, or using specific techniques to pressure members. Many techniques that are used in a group do facilitate an intense expression of emotion. For example, guided fantasies into times of loneliness as a child can lead to deep psychological experiences. If leaders use such techniques, they must be ready to deal with any emotional release.

Leaders should avoid pushing members to "get into their emotions." Some group leaders measure the efficacy of their group by the level of catharsis, and members can be exploited by a leader who has a need to see them experience intense emotions. This expression of emotion can sometimes be more important in meeting the leader's needs than in meeting the needs of the member.

Techniques have a better chance of being used appropriately when there is a rationale underlying their use. Techniques are aimed at fostering the client's self-exploration and self-understanding. At their best, they are invented in each unique client situation, and they are a collaborative effort between the leader and members. Techniques assist the group member in experimenting with some form of new behavior. It is critical that techniques be introduced in a timely and sensitive manner, with respect for the client, and that they be abandoned if they are not working.

In working with culturally diverse client populations, leaders may need to modify some of their interventions to suit the client's cultural and ethnic background. For example, if a client has been taught not to express his feelings in public, it may be inappropriate to quickly introduce techniques aimed at bringing out his feelings. It would be useful first to find out if this member is interested in exploring what he has learned from his culture about expressing his feelings. In another situation, perhaps a woman has been socialized to obey her parents without question. It could be inappropriate to introduce a role-playing technique that would have her confronting her parents directly. Leaders can respect the cultural values of members and at the same time encourage them to think about how these values and their upbringing have a continuing effect on their behavior. In some cases members will decide to modify certain behaviors because the personal price of retaining a value is too high. In other cases they will decide that they are not interested in changing certain cultural values or behaviors. The techniques used by leaders can help such members examine the pros and cons of making these changes. For a more detailed discussion of ethical considerations in using group techniques, see G. Corey, Corey, Callanan, and Russell (2004).

Group Leader Competence

Determining One's Own Level of Competence

How can leaders determine whether they have the competence to use a certain technique? Although some leaders who have received training in the use of a technique may hesitate to use it (out of fear of making a mistake), other overly confident leaders without training may not have any reservations about trying out new methods. It is a good policy for leaders to have a clear theoretical and therapeutic rationale for any technique they use. Further, it is useful if leaders have experienced these techniques as members of a group. The issue of whether one is competent to lead a specific group or type of group is an ongoing question that faces all professional group leaders. You will need to remain open to struggling with questions such as these:

- Am I qualified through education and training to lead this specific group?
- What criteria can I use to determine my degree of competence?
- How can I recognize the boundaries of my competence?
- If I am not as competent as I'd like to be as a group worker, what specifically can I do?
- How can I continue to upgrade my leadership knowledge and skills?
- What techniques can I effectively employ?
- With what kinds of clients do I work best?
- With whom do I work least well, and why?
- When and how should I refer clients?
- When do I need to consult with other professionals?

There are no simple answers to these questions. Different groups require different leader qualities. For example, you may be fully competent to lead a group of relatively well-adjusted adults or of adults in crisis situations yet not be competent to lead a group of seriously disturbed people. You may be well trained for, and work well with, adolescent groups, yet you may not have the skills or training to do group work with younger children. You may be successful leading groups dealing with substance abuse yet find yourself ill-prepared to work successfully with family groups. In short, you need specific training and supervised experience for each type of group you intend to lead.

Degrees and credentials may be necessary but are not sufficient in themselves; all they indicate is a certain background of content and experience, which usually means that you have completed a minimum number of years of training and experience. The breadth and quality of training and experience indicated by credentials varies greatly.

Most practitioners have had their formal training in one of the branches of the mental health field, which includes counseling psychology, clinical psychology, community counseling, educational psychology, marriage and family counseling, nursing, pastoral psychology, rehabilitation counseling, mental health counseling, clinical social work, and psychiatry. Generally, however, those who seek to become group practitioners find that formal education, even at the master's or doctoral level, does not give them the practical grounding they require to effectively lead groups. Thus, practitioners often find it necessary to take a variety of specialized group therapy training workshops.

Professional competence is not arrived at once and for all, but is an ongoing developmental process for the duration of your career. The "Best Practice Guidelines" (ASGW, 1998), which are reproduced in the Student Manual, provide some general suggestions for enhancing your level of competence as a group worker:

- Remain current and increase your knowledge and skill competencies through activities such as continuing education, consultation, supervision, and participation in personal and professional development activities.
- Be open to getting professional assistance for your own personal problems or conflicts that may impair your professional judgment or ability to facilitate a group.
- Utilize consultation and supervision to ensure effective practice when you are working with a group for which you need to acquire more knowledge and skill competencies.

Part of being a competent group counselor involves being able to explain to group members the theory behind your practice, telling members in clear language the goals of the group and how you conceptualize the group process, and relating what you do in a group to this model. As you acquire competence, you will be able to continually refine your techniques in light of your model. Competent group counselors possess the knowledge and skills that are described in the following section.

Professional Training Standards for Group Counselors

Effective group leadership programs are not developed by legislative mandates and professional codes alone. For proficient leaders to emerge, a training program must make group work a priority. Unfortunately, in most master's programs in counseling generally, only one group course is required, and it is typical for this single course to cover both the didactic and experiential aspects of group process. This course often deals both with theories of group counseling and with group process, and as well, it provides students with opportunities to experience a group as a member. It is a major undertaking to train group counselors adequately in a single course!

The expanded ASGW (2000) "Professional Standards for the Training of Group Workers"* specifies two levels of competencies and related training. First is a set of *core knowledge* and *skill competencies* that provides the foundation on which *specialized* training is built. At a minimum, one group course should be included in a training program, and it should be structured to help students acquire the basic knowledge and skills needed to facilitate a group.

Areas of knowledge that are considered basic include identifying one's strengths and weaknesses and one's values, being able to describe the characteristics associated with the typical stages in a group's development, being able to describe the facilitative and debilitative roles and behaviors of group members, knowing the therapeutic factors of a group, understanding the importance of group and member evaluation, and being aware of the ethical issues special to group work.

Skill competencies that group leaders should have include being able to open and close group sessions, modeling appropriate behavior for group members, engaging in appropriate self-disclosure in the group, giving and receiving feedback, helping members attribute meaning to their experience in the group, helping them integrate and apply their learning, and demonstrating the ability to apply ethical standards in group practice.

The ASGW (2000) training standards state that these group work skills are best mastered through supervised practice, which should include observation and participation in a group experience. Although there is a minimum of 10 hours of supervised practice, 20 hours is recommended as part of the core training. Furthermore, these training standards require that all counselor trainees complete core training in group work during their entry-level education. This group work core includes both basic knowledge and the foundational skills needed to facilitate a group in a competent way (Conyne, 1996; Conyne & Wilson, 1998; Conyne, Wilson, & Ward, 1997).

Once counselor trainees have mastered the core knowledge and skill domains, they have the platform to develop a group work specialization in one or more of four areas: (1) task and work groups, (2) psychoeducational groups, (3) group counseling, and (4) group psychotherapy. The standards outline specific knowledge and skill competencies for these specialties and also specify the recommended number of hours of supervised training for each.

---

*These group skills are adapted from the ASGW's (2000) revised and expanded "Professional Standards for the Training of Group Workers," which was adopted January 22, 2000, and is reproduced by permission of the Association for Specialists in Group Work, a division of the American Counseling Association, 5999 Stevenson Avenue, Alexandria, VA 22304.

A *task/work group* features the application of group dynamics principles and processes such as collaborative group problem solving, team building, and program development consultation. The training for this kind of group involves course work in the broad area of organizational development and management. Specialist training requires a minimum of 30 hours of supervised experience in leading or co-leading a task facilitation group.

A *psychoeducational group* features the presentation and discussion of factual information and skill building through the use of planned skill-building exercises. Specialist training for this kind of group involves course work in the broad area of community psychology, health promotion, marketing, consultation, and curriculum design. These specialists should have content knowledge in the topic areas in which they intend to work (such as substance abuse prevention, stress management, parent effectiveness training, AIDS). This specialty requires an additional 30 hours of supervised experience in leading or co-leading a guidance group in field practice.

Group counseling focuses on interpersonal communication and interactive feedback and support methods within a here-and-now time frame. The specialist training for this type of group should ideally include as much course work in group counseling as possible, with at least one course beyond the generalist level. Group counselors should have knowledge in the broad areas of human development, problem identification, and treatment of normal personal and interpersonal problems of living. For this specialization there is a minimum of 45 hours of supervised experience in leading or co-leading a counseling group.

Group psychotherapy features exploration of the antecedents to current behavior, using interpersonal and intrapersonal assessment, diagnosis, and interpretation to connect historical material to the present. Specialist training for psychotherapy groups consists of courses in the area of abnormal psychology, psychopathology, and diagnostic assessment to ensure capabilities in working with more disturbed populations. For this specialization there is a minimum of 45 hours of supervised experience in working with therapy groups.

The current trend in training group workers focuses on learning group process by becoming involved in supervised experiences. Certainly, the mere completion of one graduate course in group theory and practice does not equip one to lead groups. Both direct participation in planned and supervised small groups and clinical experience in leading various groups under careful supervision are needed to provide leaders with the skills to meet the challenges of group work.

Three Adjuncts to the Training of Group Counselors

If you expect to lead groups, you will want to be prepared for this work, both personally and academically. If your program has not provided this preparation, it will be necessary for you to seek in-service workshops in group processes. It is not likely that you will learn how to lead groups merely through reading about them and listening to lectures.

I recommend at least three experiences as adjuncts to a training program for students learning about group work: (1) participation in personal therapy, (2) participation in group counseling or a personal growth group, and (3) participation in a training and supervision group. Following is a discussion of these three adjuncts to the professional preparation of group counselors.

Personal Psychotherapy for Group Leaders   I agree with Yalom's (1995) recommendation that extensive self-exploration is necessary if trainees are to perceive countertransference feelings, recognize blind spots and biases, and use their personal attributes effectively in groups. Although videotapes, work with a co-leader, and supervision all are excellent sources of feedback, Yalom maintains that some type of personal therapy is usually necessary for fuller understanding and correction. Group leaders should demonstrate the courage and willingness to do for themselves what they expect members in their groups to do—expand their awareness of self and the effect of that self on others.

Increasing self-awareness is a major reason to seek out personal counseling. In leading a group, you will encounter many instances of transferences, both among members and toward you. Transference refers to the unconscious process whereby clients project onto their therapist past feelings or attitudes that they had toward significant people in their lives. Of course, group leaders can easily become entangled in their own feelings of countertransference, unconscious emotional responses to group members. Leaders also have unresolved personal problems, which they can project onto the members of their group. Through personal counseling, trainees can work through some of their unfinished business that could easily interfere with their effective functioning as a group leader.

Self-Exploration Groups for Group Leaders   Being a member of a variety of groups can prove to be an indispensable part of training for group leaders. By experiencing their own resistances, fears, and uncomfortable moments in a group, by being confronted, and by struggling with their problems in a group context, practitioners can experience what is needed to build a trusting and cohesive group.

In addition to helping interns resolve personal conflicts and increase self-understanding, a personal growth group can be a powerful teaching tool. One of the best ways to learn how to assist group members in their struggles is to participate yourself as a member of a group.

Yalom (1995) strongly recommends a group experience for trainees. Some of the benefits that he suggests are experiencing the power of a group, learning what self-disclosure is about, coming to appreciate the difficulties involved in self-sharing, learning on an emotional level what one knows intellectually, and becoming aware of one's dependency on the leader's power and knowledge. Yalom cites surveys indicating that 60 to 70% of group therapy training programs offer some type of personal group experience.

In their preliminary naturalistic inquiry of the significance of the group experience for students in counseling programs, Kline, Falbaum, Pope, Hargraves, and Hundley (1997) found two main outcomes. First, students who had a group experience generally had positive reactions to it, even though the group involved an uncomfortable level of anxiety. Student reactions consistently indicated that they valued the opportunity to challenge their interpersonal fears and that they were satisfied with the gains they made from taking risks. Furthermore, the conflicts among members and the authority conflicts common to unstructured groups were viewed as a positive learning experience by most participants.

Unstructured self-exploration groups that emphasize feedback and interpersonal learning appear to be an invaluable component in counselor training. Such group experiences often lead to increased personal awareness and result in insights into counseling issues that are basic to counseling practice and interpersonal relationships. However, further qualitative research is needed to confirm the observations and encouragement in the literature on the value of interpersonal groups as a part of counselor training programs (Kline et al., 1997).

Participation in Experiential Training Workshops   I have found training workshops most useful in helping group counselors develop the skills necessary for effective intervention. The trainees can also learn a great deal about their response to criticism, their competitiveness, their need for approval, their concerns over being competent, and their power struggles. In working with both university students learning about group approaches and with professionals who want to upgrade their group skills, I have found an intensive weekend workshop effective. In these workshops the participants all have ample opportunity to lead their small group for a designated period. After a segment in which a participant leads the group, my colleagues and I intervene, giving feedback and promoting discussion by the entire group. By the end of the weekend each participant has led the group at least twice (for an hour each time) under direct supervision.

Ethical Issues in Training Group Counselors

Training programs differ on whether participating in a group is optional or required. Requiring participation in a therapeutic group as part of a training program can present some practical and ethical problems of its own. A controversial ethical issue in the preparation of group workers involves combining experiential and didactic training methods.

I consider an experiential component to be essential when teaching group counseling courses. Admittedly, there are inherent problems in teaching students how groups function by involving them on an experiential level. Such an arrangement entails their willingness to engage in self-disclosure, to become active participants in an interpersonal laboratory, and to engage themselves on an emotional level as well as a cognitive one. Time and again, however, my colleagues and I hear both students and professionals who participate in our group training workshops comment on the value of supervised experience in which they have both leadership and membership roles. Through this format, group process concepts come alive. Trainees experience firsthand what it takes to create trust and what resistance feels like. They often say that they have gained a new appreciation for the resistance of their clients.

In talking with many other counselor educators throughout the country who teach group courses, I find that it is common practice to combine the experiential and didactic domains. Sometimes students co-lead a small group with a peer and are supervised by the instructor. Of course, this arrangement is not without problems, especially if the instructor also functions in the roles of facilitator and supervisor. Students may fear that their grade will be influenced by their participation (or lack of it) in the experiential part of the class.

In grading and evaluating students in group courses, the professionalism of the instructor is crucial. Ethical practice requires instructors to spell out their grading criteria clearly. The criteria may include the results of written reports, oral presentations, essay tests, and objective examinations. Most group counselor educators agree that students' performance in the experiential group should not be graded, but they can be expected to attend regularly and to participate. Clear guidelines need to be established so that students know what their rights and responsibilities are at the beginning of the group course.

In a national survey of the training of group counselors, Merta, Wolfgang, and McNeil (1993) found that a large majority of counselor educators continue to use the experiential group in preparing group counselors although there was significant diversity in the way they employed various training models. In group classes that are taught both experientially and didactically, the first half of the class meeting often deals with counseling theories and group process issues. The content of the discussions may be very similar to the material in this textbook. During the second half of the class meeting, many instructors conduct a group in which the students have an opportunity to be members. Sometimes students co-lead a small group with a peer and are supervised by the instructor or an advanced graduate student.

The experiential group aspect of a group course might well focus on here-and-now interactions. Even if members choose not to bring up highly personal matters, dealing with their reactions to other people in the group provides plenty to talk about. If they learn to deal with one another in the group setting, they are making great strides in learning how to facilitate a group. Sklare, Thomas, Williams, and Powers (1996) describe a "here-and-now" model of a group course that is led by the instructor, outlining a specific format to maximize students' experiential participation and at the same time safeguard their rights to privacy and informed consent. In situations where the instructor is also a group leader, they emphasize that it is essential to balance evaluative and therapeutic skills for the benefit of students. Instructors need to be aware of the position of their students and exercise caution in using power appropriately. This model provides a structure that optimally combines didactic, experiential, and supervisory experiences.

Anderson and Price (2001) conducted a survey of students in master's degree courses in group counseling to assess their attitudes toward the use of an experiential group activity as a component of training, as well as the level of instructor involvement in these experiential groups. Approximately 41% of [studen]ts in this survey indicated that their instructor did not lead their ex-[ ]group and did not observe the group but did receive feedback about [ ]'s process or members' participation; 33% indicated that their in-[ ]id not lead their experiential group but did observe the group at [ ] indicated that the instructor did not lead, observe, or receive feed-[ ]t their group; and 3% indicated that their instructor led the experien-[ ]. Based on the students' responses to the survey items, it is apparent [m]ajority of the students (93%) believe experiential groups are neces-[th]eir development as group workers. Most of the students (92%) indi-cated that they benefited from their involvement in the experiential group, even though they felt anxiety and discomfort at times. Anderson and Price maintain that there is research support for the value of experiential groups and that these groups are an effective and necessary part of the training of group counselors. They also suggest that programs need to have safeguards in place, including informed consent, pregroup preparation, and training in appropri-ate self-disclosure (Forester-Miller & Duncan, 1990; Merta et al., 1993; Pierce & Baldwin, 1990).

The challenge of educators is to provide the best training available. For more detailed discussions of various perspectives on multiple relationship controversies in the preparation of group counselors, see Herlihy and Corey (1997) and the journal articles cited in this section. These resources will help you formulate your own position and guidelines on these topics.

Liability and Malpractice

Although the topics of professional liability and malpractice are not strictly a part of ethical practice, these are legal dimensions with implications for group practitioners. Group leaders are expected to practice within the code of ethics of their particular profession and also to abide by legal standards. Practitioners are subject to civil penalties if they fail to do right or if they actively do wrong to another. If group members can prove that personal injury or psychological harm was caused by a leader's failure to render proper service, either through negligence or ignorance, the leader is open to a malpractice suit. Negligence consists of departing from the standard and commonly accepted practices of others in the profession. Practitioners who are involved in a malpractice ac-tion may need to justify the techniques they use. If their therapeutic interven-tions are consistent with those of other members of their profession in their community, they are on much firmer ground than if they employ uncommon techniques.

Group leaders need to keep up to date with the laws of their state as they affect their professional practice. Those leaders who work with groups of chil-dren and adolescents, especially, must know the law as it pertains to matters of confidentiality, parental consent, the right to treatment or to refuse treatment, informed consent, and other legal rights of clients. Such awareness not only protects the group members but also protects group leaders from malpractice suits arising from negligence or ignorance.

The best way to protect yourself from getting involved in a malpractice suit is to take preventive measures, which means not practicing outside the boundaries of your competence. Following the spirit of the ethics codes of your professional organization is also important. The key to avoiding a malpractice suit is maintaining reasonable, ordinary, and prudent practices. Here are some prudent guidelines for professional standards of practice:

- Give the potential members of your groups enough information to make informed choices about group participation. Do not mystify the group process.
- Develop written informed consent procedures at the outset of a group. Using contracts, signed by both members and the leader, is an example of such a procedure.
- Become aware of local and state laws that limit your practice, as well as the policies of the agency for which you work. Inform members about these policies and about legal limitations (such as exemptions to confidentiality, mandatory reporting, and the like).
- Emphasize the importance of maintaining confidentiality before the group begins and at various times during the life of a group.
- Restrict your practice to client populations for which you are prepared by virtue of your education, training, and experience.
- Have a standard of care that can be applied to your services, and communicate this standard to the members of your groups.
- Be alert for symptoms of psychological debilitation in group members, which may indicate that their participation should be discontinued. Be able to put such clients in contact with appropriate referral resources.
- Do not promise the members of your group anything that you cannot deliver. Help them realize that their degree of effort and commitment will be key factors in determining the outcomes of the group experience.
- In working with minors, secure the written permission of their parents, even if this is not required by state law.
- Keep lines of communication open with your members.
- Always consult with colleagues or supervisors whenever there is an ethical or legal concern. Document the nature of these consultations.
- Keep adequate clinical notes.
- Make it a practice to assess the general progress of a group, and teach members how to evaluate their progress toward their personal goals.
- Learn how to assess and intervene in cases in which clients pose a threat to themselves or others.
- Be willing to devote the time it takes to adequately screen, select, and prepare the members of your group.
- Provide an atmosphere of respect for diversity within the group.
- Incorporate ethical standards in your practice of group work.
- Avoid blending professional relationships with social ones.

- Avoid engaging in sexual relationships with either current or former group members.
- Remain alert to ways in which your personal reactions might inhibit the group process, and monitor your countertransference. Avoid using the group as a place where you work through your personal problems.
- Strive to develop procedures to evaluate the effectiveness of your groups.
- Continue to read the research and use group interventions and techniques that are supported by the research, as well as community practice.
- Have a theoretical orientation that serves as a guide to your practice. Be able to describe the purpose of the techniques you use in your groups.

As you read about the stages of group development in Chapters 4 and 5, reflect on the issues raised in this chapter as they apply to the tasks and challenges you will face as a group leader during various group phases. Realize that there are few simple answers to the ethical aspects of group work. Learn how to think through the ethical considerations that you will face as a group practitioner. Being willing to raise questions and think about an ethical course to follow is the beginning of becoming an ethical group counselor. The *Student Manual for Theory and Practice of Group Counseling* (6th Edition) contains a number of resources that will help you develop your awareness of ethical group practice. I urge you to consult these resources frequently as you begin to formulate your own ideas about ethical practice in group work.

CHAPTER 4

Early Stages in the Development of a Group

This chapter and the next one are meant to be a road map of the stages through which a group progresses. This map is based on my own experience, as well as on the experience and writings of others, and describes the essential issues that characterize the development of a group.

The stages described in this chapter don't correspond to discrete and neatly separated phases in the life of a real group. There is considerable overlap between the stages, and groups don't conform precisely to some preordained time sequence that theoretically separates one phase from the next. Also, the content of the group process varies from group to group, and different aspects of the process may be stressed depending on the theoretical orientation of the leader, the purpose of the group, and the population that makes up the group. In spite of these differences, however, there does seem to be a general pattern to the evolution of a group.

A clear grasp of the stages of group development, including an awareness of the factors that facilitate group process and of those that interfere with it, will maximize your ability to help the members of your groups reach their goals. By learning about the problems and potential crises of each stage, you learn when and how to intervene. As you gain a picture of the systematic evolution of groups, you become aware of the developmental tasks that must be successfully met if a group is to move forward, and you can predict problems and intervene therapeutically. Finally, knowledge of the developmental sequence of groups will give you the perspective you need to lead group members in constructive directions by reducing unnecessary confusion and anxiety.

This chapter begins with an examination of the leader's concerns in forming a group: getting prepared, announcing the group, screening and selecting the members, and preparing them for a successful experience. Stage 1 of a group, under my six-stage breakdown, is the *formation stage* of the group. Stage 2, the *orientation phase*, is a time of exploration during the initial sessions. Stage 3, the *transition stage*, is characterized by dealing with conflict, defensiveness, and resistance.

Chapter 5 continues with Stage 4, the *working stage*. This stage is marked by action—dealing with significant personal issues and translating insight into action both in the group and outside of it. In Stage 5, the *consolidation stage*, the focus is on applying what has been learned in the group and putting it to use in everyday life. I conclude with an examination of postgroup concerns in Stage 6, which includes *evaluation* and *follow-up* issues. The description of these stages is based largely on my observations of the way in which groups typically evolve.

Stage 1: Pregroup Issues—Formation of the Group

If you want a group to be successful, you need to devote considerable time to planning. In my view planning should begin with drafting a written proposal containing the basic purposes of the group, the population to be served, a clear rationale for the group—namely, the need for and justification of that particular group—ways to announce the group and recruit members, the screening and selection process for members, the size and duration of the group, the frequency and time of meetings, the group structure and format, the methods of preparing members, whether the group will be open or closed, whether membership will be voluntary or involuntary, and the follow-up and evaluation procedures.

It cannot be overstressed that leader preparation at this formative phase is crucial to the outcome of a group. Thus, it is time well spent to think about what kind of group you want and to get yourself psychologically ready. If your expectations are unclear, and if the purposes and structure of the group are vague, the members will surely engage in unnecessary floundering.

Announcing a Group and Recruiting Members

How a group is announced influences the way it will be received by potential members and the kind of people who will be attracted to it. It is imperative that you say enough to give prospective members a clear idea about the group's rationale and goals.

Although printed announcements have their value if they can reach the population they are intended for, they also have limitations. Regardless of how specific you are in these announcements, people—at least some of them—are likely to misunderstand them. Because of this risk, I am in favor of making direct contact with the population that is most likely to benefit from the group. For example, if you are planning a group at a school, make personal visits to several classes to introduce yourself and to tell the students about the group. You could also distribute a brief application form to anyone who wanted to find out more about the group.

Screening and Selecting Group Members

The ACA's (1995) ethical standard pertaining to screening group members reads as follows:

> Counselors screen prospective group counseling/therapy participants. To the extent possible, counselors select members whose needs and goals are compatible

with goals of the group, who will not impede the group process, and whose well-being will not be jeopardized by the group experience. (A.9.a.)

As you screen and select group members, ask yourself these questions: How can I decide who is most likely to benefit from the group I plan to create? Who is likely to be disturbed by group participation or become a negative influence for the other members?

The setting in which leaders work may make it difficult to screen members individually, but there are alternative ways of accomplishing this. For example, leaders can ask prospective members to complete a written questionnaire and then arrange group interviews with them. If these methods of screening are not realistic, the initial group meeting can be used as an information and screening session. In agency settings, clients are often court-ordered to a group, which makes screening impractical. However, even in these instances, the group leader can still attempt to meet with each client for a pregroup interview rather than a formal screening session.

Once potential members have been recruited, the leader must determine who (if anyone) should be excluded. Careful screening will lessen the psychological risks of inappropriate participation in a group. During the screening session, the leader can spend some time exploring with potential members any fears or concerns they have about participating in a group.

The leader can help them make an assessment of their readiness for a group and discuss the potential life changes that might come about. Members can benefit from knowing that there is a price for remaining the way they are as well as for making substantive changes. If they go into a group unaware of the potential impact of their personal changes on others in their lives, their motivation for continuing is likely to decrease if they encounter problems with their family.

Screening should be a two-way process, and potential members should have an opportunity at the private screening interview to ask questions to determine whether the group is right for them. Group leaders should encourage prospective members to be involved in the decision concerning the appropriateness of their participation in the group.

Of course, there is always the possibility that the leader may have real reservations about including some people who are quite determined to join the group. I find that it is at times difficult to determine which candidates will benefit from a group. During the private interview, people can be vague about what they hope to get from the group. They may be frightened, tense, and defensive, and they may approach the personal interview as they would a job interview, especially if they are anxious about being admitted to the group. The basic question for the selection of group members is, "Will the group be productive or counterproductive for this individual?"

Some people can quite literally drain the energy of the group so that little is left for productive work. Also, the presence of certain people can make group cohesion difficult to attain. This is especially true of individuals who have a need to monopolize and dominate, of hostile or aggressive clients with a need to act out, and of people who are extremely self-centered and who seek a group as an audience.

Others who should generally be excluded from most groups are people who are in a state of extreme crisis, who are suicidal, who have sociopathic personalities, who are highly suspicious, or who are lacking in ego strength and are prone to fragmented and bizarre behavior. It is difficult to say categorically that a certain kind of person should be excluded from all groups, but the type of group should determine who is accepted. Thus, an alcoholic might be excluded from a personal growth group but be an appropriate candidate for a homogeneous group of individuals who suffer from addiction problems, be it addiction to alcohol, to other drugs, or to food.

The screening session is an opportunity for the leader to evaluate candidates and to determine what they want from the group experience. It is also a chance for prospective members to get to know the leader and to develop a feeling of confidence. The manner in which this initial interview is conducted has a lot to do with establishing the trust level of the group. During this interview, I stress the two-way exchange, hoping that members will feel free to ask questions that will help them determine whether they want to join this group at this particular time. Here are some questions I consider in screening: Does this person appear to want to do what is necessary to be a productive group member? Has the decision to join the group been made by the person? Will a prospective member be able to attend to the group tasks? Does the candidate have clear goals and an understanding of how a group might help him or her attain them? Is the individual open and willing to share something personal? How is a prospective member likely to fit with other members so that work can proceed?

The selection of members to ensure optimum group balance often seems an impossible task. Yalom (1995) proposes that cohesiveness be the main criterion in the selection of participants. Thus, the most important thing is to choose people who are likely to be compatible, even though the group may be a heterogeneous one.

In the context of group psychotherapy, Yalom (1995) argues that unless careful selection criteria are employed clients may end up discouraged and not helped. He maintains that it is easier to identify those who should be excluded from a therapy group than it is to identify those who should be included. Citing clinical studies, he lists the following as poor candidates for a heterogeneous, outpatient, intensive-therapy group: brain-damaged people, paranoid clients, hypochondriacs, those who are addicted to drugs or alcohol, acutely psychotic individuals, and sociopathic personalities. In terms of criteria for inclusion, Yalom contends that the client's level of motivation to work is the most important variable. From his perspective, groups are useful for people who have interpersonal problems such as loneliness, an inability to make or maintain intimate contacts, feelings of being unlovable, fears of being assertive, and dependency. Clients who lack meaning in life, who suffer from diffuse anxiety, who are searching for an identity, who fear success, and who are compulsive workers might also profit from a group experience.

Whether a client is to be included or excluded has much to do with the purposes of the group. You have a responsibility to make a determination as to whether or not a prospective member is suitable for a given group, which is for the protection of both the prospective member and the group itself. At times, you may have to inform prospective members that a particular group could be more harmful than helpful to them. If you decide that certain members are not appropriate for your group, provide these individuals with the reasons for your decision and make appropriate referrals.

Practical Concerns in the Formation of a Group

Open Versus Closed Groups   As a result of managed care, many groups tend to be short term, solution-oriented, and characterized by changing membership. Whether the group will be open or closed may in part be determined by the population and the setting. But the issue needs to be discussed and decided before the group meets, or at the initial session. There are some distinct advantages to both kinds of groups. In the closed group, no new members are added for the predetermined duration of its life. This practice offers a stability of membership that makes continuity possible and fosters cohesion. If too many members drop out of a closed group, however, the group process is drastically affected.

In an open group, new members replace those who are leaving, and this can provide for new stimulation. A disadvantage of the open group is that new members may have a difficult time becoming part of the group because they are not aware of what has been discussed before they joined. Another disadvantage is that changing group membership can have adverse effects on the cohesion of the group. Therefore, if the flow of the group is to be maintained, the leader needs to devote time and attention to preparing new members and helping them become integrated.

Voluntary Versus Involuntary Membership   Should groups be composed only of members who are there by their own choice, or can groups function even when they include involuntary members? Obviously, there are a number of advantages to working with a group of clients who are willing to invest themselves in the group process. Yalom (1995) maintains that to benefit from the group experience a person must be highly motivated. Attending a group because one has been "sent" there by someone greatly curtails the chances for success. Yalom believes that people with a deeply entrenched unwillingness to enter a group should not be accepted. However, he thinks that many of the negative attitudes that involuntary candidates have about groups can be changed by adequately preparing members for a group.

I have found that many involuntary members learn that a group counseling experience can help them make some of the changes they want to achieve. In many agencies and institutions, practitioners are expected to lead groups with an involuntary clientele. It is important for these counselors to learn how to work within such a structure rather than hold to the position that they can be effective only with a voluntary population. By presenting the group experience in a favorable light, the leader can help involuntary members see the potential benefits of the experience and the chance of productive work taking place will be increased. The key to successful participation lies in thorough member orientation and preparation and in the leader's belief that the group process has something to offer to these prospective members.

Homogeneous Versus Heterogeneous Groups   Group leaders need to decide the basis for the homogeneity of their groups. By homogeneous I mean composed of people who, for example, are similar in ages, such as a group for children, for adolescents, or for the elderly. Other homogeneous groups are those based on a common interest or problem. Short-term groups usually are characterized by homogeneous membership. The unitary focus in a homogeneous group tends to foster group cohesion, and common problem areas of group members promote sharing experiences and learning from one another.

At times, a group composed of homogeneous members may be more functional than one composed of people from different populations. Consider, for example, a group for young African Americans. Vontress (1995) recommends that such a group be segregated by gender because African American males are generally unable to engage in frank and open discussion in the presence of female peers. He contends that a group could be a useful intervention in helping these young men talk about how they are affected by racism and also show them how to succeed despite it.

Although homogeneous membership can be more appropriate for certain target populations with definite needs or with short-term groups, heterogeneous membership has some definite advantages for many personal growth groups, whether short or long term. A heterogeneous group represents a microcosm of the social structure that exists in the everyday world and offers participants the opportunity to experiment with new behaviors, develop social skills, and get feedback from many diverse sources. If a simulation of everyday life is desired, it is well to have a range of ages, races, cultural and ethnic backgrounds, and a variety of concerns.

Meeting Place   Another pregroup concern is the setting. Privacy, a certain degree of attractiveness, and a place that allows for face-to-face interaction are crucial. A poor setting can set a negative tone that will adversely affect the cohesion of the group, so every effort should be made to secure a meeting place that will facilitate in-depth work.

Group Size   The desirable size for a group depends on factors such as the age of the clients, the type of group, the experience of the group counselors, and the type of problems explored. Another element to be taken into consideration is whether the group has one leader or more. For ongoing groups with adults, about eight members with one leader seems to be a good size. Groups with children may be as small as three or four. In general, the group should have enough people to afford ample interaction so that it doesn't drag and yet be small enough to give everyone a chance to participate frequently without, however, losing the sense of "group."

Frequency and Length of Meetings   How often should groups meet and for how long? These issues, too, depend on the type of group and, to some extent, on the experience of the leader. Once a week is a typical format for most counseling groups. With children and adolescents, it is usually better to meet more frequently for shorter sessions. For adults who are functioning relatively well, a two-hour group each week is long enough to allow for some intensive work. Outpatient groups often meet for a 90-minute session, whereas inpatient groups may have shorter sessions. Groups do not necessarily have to meet weekly, even though this is typical. One pattern is to meet a group weekly for six weeks, then every other week for two weeks, and then once a month for several months. This pattern may be particularly useful for group members working on specific forms of behavioral change (such as weight control, assertion training, stress management). At this time no systematic research data are available to answer the question of what length of session and frequency of meetings are most desirable for what type of clients using what type of group approach (Klein, Brabender, & Fallon, 1994).

Short-Term Versus Long-Term Groups   It is wise to set a termination date at the outset of a closed group so members have a clear idea of their commitment. The duration varies from group to group, depending on the type of group, the population, and the requirements of the agency. Many community agencies have policies that limit groups to a relatively short duration. For brief group therapy, length of treatment is a defining characteristic. Time-limited groups have a specific focus, and interventions have the aim of being as efficient as possible. The length of treatment in short-term groups might well vary from several weeks to 15 weeks, with the number of sessions generally around 20 (Rosenberg & Wright, 1997).

Some closed groups have long-term goals that require long-term commitments of members. This is particularly true of psychodynamic groups that aim for character restructuring. In private practice, groups can be either short or long term. Some of these groups last for 12 to 20 weeks, some for 30 to 50 weeks, and some for over a year. Many college and high school groups typically run for the length of a semester (about 15 weeks). The group should be long enough to allow for cohesion and productive work yet not so long that it seems to drag on interminably.

The Uses of a Pregroup Meeting or the Initial Session

After the group membership has been established, the next question is: What is the group leader's responsibility in preparing members to get the maximum benefit from their group experience? My bias is that systematic preparation is essential and that it begins at the private screening interview and continues during the first few sessions. Preparation consists essentially of exploring with members their expectations, fears, goals, and misconceptions; the basics of group process; the psychological risks associated with group membership and ways of minimizing them; the values and limitations of groups; guidelines for getting the most from the group experience; and the necessity of confidentiality. This preparation can be done through a preliminary meeting of all those who will be joining a group.

In addition to the private interview with each person before the group is formed, I use the initial session as a group screening device. The initial session is a good place to talk about the purposes of the group, to let members know how they will be using group time, to explore many of the possible issues that might be considered in the group, to discuss the ground rules and policies, and to begin the getting-acquainted process. Because I prefer to have people decide early if they are ready for a group and willing to become active members, I encourage participants to consider the first session as an opportunity to help them make such a decision.

Structuring the group, including the specification of norms and procedures, should be accomplished early in the group's history. Although structuring begins at the private intake session, it will be necessary to continue this process the first time the group actually meets. In fact, structuring is an ongoing process, one that will be a vital part of the early phases of your group. Some group members expect a low degree of structure, and others prefer a group that is highly structured with clearly defined tasks.

Preparation is particularly important for ethnic and minority clients. Many group members hold values and expectations that make it difficult for them to participate fully in a group experience. For example, the free participation and exchange of views in therapy groups appear to be in conflict with Asian values of humility and modesty. Furthermore, many Asians do not share Western values of independence, individualism, directness of communication, expressiveness of feelings, and assertiveness (Lee et al., 1984; Leong, 1992). Asian clients may feel threatened in a group experience, especially if they are expected to make deeply personal disclosures too quickly. Therefore, adequate preparation will be essential for Asian American clients who have had no prior therapeutic experience in a group setting. Careful preparation will reduce the dropout rate of these clients and will help them maximize their gains (Ho, 1984). For individuals of other ethnic groups, preparation is no less important. It is essential that members know the purpose of the group as well as how the group experience can be of personal value to them. Group workers need to be aware that reluctance or resistance may be more the result of cultural background than of an uncooperative attitude.

Pack-Brown and her colleagues (1998) suggest that African American women benefit more from a group counseling experience when they are properly prepared. These authors list some of the following reasons for group preparation: reducing anxiety, assisting members in understanding the group process, clarifying expectations, demystifying the therapeutic process, enhancing group effectiveness, and reducing fear by providing information about the group. In their *Images of Me* groups with African American women, Pack-Brown and her colleagues find that pregroup preparation serves a number of functions including building rapport, which is a first step toward establishing therapeutic alliances; assessing members' ability to communicate with others; and clarifying therapeutic goals and pinpointing a specific agenda for achieving these goals.

Bowman and DeLucia (1993) maintain that there is increasing support for preparation methods that reduce clients' initial anxiety, clarify their expectations, and educate them about the group process. Their study found that preparation can have a positive impact on clients' beliefs, attitudes, and expectations about therapy. They also conclude that it can help members acquire skills that contribute to a successful group experience. Finally, preparation can give beginning group leaders a greater understanding of the group process and increase their confidence in their leadership role. Adequate preparation is particularly important in short-term groups; a good preparation process will sharply reduce dropout rates in these groups (Budman, Simeone, Reilly, & Demby, 1994).

Another advocate of systematic preparation for group members is Yalom (1995). His preparation includes explaining his theory of group work, exploring misconceptions and expectations, predicting early problems and stumbling blocks, discussing how the participants can best help themselves, talking about trust and self-disclosure, and exploring the risks associated with experimenting with new behavior. Yalom also discusses matters such as the goals of group therapy, confidentiality, and extra-group socialization.

Although I believe strongly in the value of systematic and complete preparation of group members, I also do see the danger of overpreparation. For example, I typically ask members to talk early in the group about any fears or reservations they might have. I also explore a few common risks of participating in a group. In this particular area, however, if the leader becomes too specific, some members may end up developing concerns or even fears that they never had before and that may become self-fulfilling prophecies. In addition, too much structure imposed by the leader can stifle any initiative on the part of the members. The risks inherent in overpreparation should be balanced against those that accompany insufficient preparation. Excessive floundering and useless conflict during the group's later stages are often the result of a failure to acquire basic skills and a lack of understanding of the group process.

Guidelines for Orientation and Preparation of Members

I begin my preparation program at the time of screening each potential member, and I devote most of the first group meeting (what I call the pregroup meeting) to orientation about group process. This orientation continues during the initial phase of the group. Group process issues emerge naturally while the group is taking shape, and these concerns are dealt with as they arise.

I start by discussing with the participants the importance of their own preparation for group work. I stress that what they get from their group will depend largely on their level of investment. During the pregroup meeting and continuing into the initial group sessions, I view my role as helping members examine and decide on their level of commitment. We focus on what they want to get from participating in a group, and I assist them in defining clear, specific, and meaningful personal goals. After they have decided on some personal goals that will guide their work in the group, they are asked to refine these goals by developing a contract. (For details on ways to help members define personal goals and formulate contracts, see the discussions of transactional analysis, behavioral group therapy, rational emotive behavior therapy, and reality therapy in Chapters 12 through 15.)

At the pregroup meeting I ask members to talk about their expectations, their reasons for being in the group, their fears about participating, and their hopes. I also provide them with some pointers on what they can do to maximize the benefit of the group in enabling them to make the changes they desire in their lives. I talk with them about appropriate self-disclosure. They hear that it is their decision to select the life issues they want to explore in the group. They are also told that it is critical that they be willing to share persistent reactions they are having to here-and-now group interactions. My purpose is to teach them that the group will function only if they are willing to express what they are thinking and feeling about being in the group. In fact, their reactions provide the direction in which we typically proceed during the first few sessions. I also encourage them to bring up any questions or concerns they have about group process.

I ask the members to give some thought before they come to each session about personal issues they are willing to bring up for exploration. Although they may have a specific agenda when they come to a group meeting, I also encourage them to remain flexible by being willing to work on other issues that may emerge spontaneously as others are interacting in the group. Because I continue to find that reading, reflecting, and writing do help members focus on themes for themselves, I attempt to get them to read selected books.

Group members are typically asked to keep a journal and to spontaneously write about the range of reactions they have while they are in the group as well as reactions to what they experience between the sessions. They are encouraged to bring into the group the gist of what they have been writing in their journals. In this way they are taught about the value of continuing work that was begun during a session. Group members uniformly comment about the value of the writing they do throughout the life of a group. Their journaling not only keeps them focused on their issues but also provides them with a basis for identifying ways that they have changed. Journal entries also provide a mechanism for self-assessment of their involvement in the group.

Riordan and White (1996) explain the value of journals as a therapeutic adjunct in groups. They indicate that during the beginning stage of a group, it is common for members to exhibit some reluctance in sharing feelings about themselves and others. Leaders can encourage members to write about their observations and reactions. Eventually members may be able to bring these issues and feelings out in the group. In their experience in using journals, Riordan and White find that the vast majority of group members report favorable reactions to the practice. Journals often help members sift through their thoughts and feelings, which they can then express in the group as they develop a greater degree of safety.

Members hear over and over about the importance of using the group to practice new behaviors. I continually remind them that the group is not an end in itself but only a means to help them acquire new ways of thinking, feeling, and behaving. Thus, they are continually invited to try out new styles of behavior during the sessions to see if they might want to make certain changes. I suggest that members write in their journals about their reactions to behavior they have experimented with during the group sessions and also about new behaviors they have implemented in everyday life.

Chapter 1 of the Student Manual that accompanies this book contains a set of suggestions entitled "Ways of Getting the Most from Your Group Experience." These guidelines serve as one method of teaching members how to become active participants.

Summary of Pregroup Issues

Member Functions and Possible Problems   Before joining a group, individuals need to have the knowledge necessary for making an informed decision concerning their participation. Members should be active in the process of deciding if a group is right for them. Here are some issues that pertain to the role of members at this stage:

- Members should have adequate knowledge about the nature of the group and understand the impact the group may have on them.
- Members need to determine if a particular group is appropriate for them at this time.
- Members can profit by preparing themselves for the upcoming group by thinking about what they want from the experience and identifying personal themes that will guide their work in a group.

Problems can arise if members are coerced into a group, do not have adequate information about the nature of the group, or are passive and give no thought to what they want or expect from the group.

Leader Functions   These are the main tasks of group leaders during the formation of a group:

- Identify general goals and specific purposes of the group.
- Develop a clearly written proposal for the formation of a group.
- Announce the group in a way that provides adequate information to prospective participants.
- Conduct pregroup interviews for screening and orientation purposes.
- Make decisions concerning the selection of members.
- Organize the practical details necessary to launch a successful group.
- Get parental permission (if appropriate).

- Prepare psychologically for leadership tasks and meet with co-leader (if appropriate).
- Arrange for a preliminary group session for the purposes of getting acquainted, presenting ground rules, and preparing members for a successful group experience.
- Make provisions for informed consent and exploring with participants the potential risks involved in a group experience.

Final Comments   Many groups that get stuck at an early developmental stage do so because the foundations were poorly laid at the outset. What is labeled "resistance" on the part of group members is often the result of the leader's failure to give members adequate orientation. The nature and scope of pregroup preparation are determined largely by the type of group, yet common elements can be addressed in most groups, such as member and leader expectations, basic procedures of the group, misconceptions about groups, and the advantages and limitations of group participation. This preparation can begin at the individual screening and can be continued during the initial session. Although building pregroup preparation into the design of a group takes considerable effort, the time involved pays dividends as the group evolves. Many potential barriers to a group's progress can be avoided by careful planning and preparation.

Stage 2: Initial Stage—Orientation and Exploration

Characteristics of the Initial Stage

The initial stage of a group is a time of orientation and exploration: determining the structure of the group, getting acquainted, and exploring the members' expectations. During this phase, members learn how the group functions, define their own goals, clarify their expectations, and look for their place in the group. At the initial sessions members tend to keep a "public image"; that is, they present the dimensions of themselves they consider socially acceptable. This phase is generally characterized by a certain degree of anxiety and insecurity about the structure of the group. Members are tentative because they are discovering and testing limits and are wondering whether they will be accepted.

Typically, members bring to the group certain expectations, concerns, and anxieties, and it is vital that they be allowed to express them openly. At this time the leader needs to clear up any misconceptions and, if necessary, demystify groups.

Primary Tasks of the Initial Stage: Inclusion and Identity

Finding an identity in the group and determining the degree to which one will become an active group member are the major tasks of the initial stage. Members often ask themselves these questions at the initial sessions:

- Will I be in or out of this group?
- How much do I want to reveal of myself?

- How much do I want to risk?
- How safe is it to take risks?
- Can I really trust these people?
- Do I fit and belong in here?
- Whom am I drawn to, and whom do I feel distant from?
- Will I be accepted or rejected?
- Can I be myself and, at the same time, be a part of the group?

The Foundation of the Group: Trust

Establishing trust is vital to the continued development of the group. Without trust, group interaction will be superficial, little self-exploration will take place, constructive challenging of one another will not occur, and the group will operate under the handicap of hidden feelings.

It is a mistake to assume that people will "naturally" trust one another as soon as they enter a group—and why should they trust without question? How do they know that the group will offer a more accepting and safer climate than society at large? My view is that people make a decision whether to trust a group. Such a decision depends in part on the leader's ability to demonstrate that the group is a safe place where members can reveal themselves. Also, by encouraging members to talk about any factors that inhibit their trust, the leader supports the therapeutic atmosphere necessary for openness and risk taking on the part of the members.

Ways of Establishing Trust   The manner in which leaders introduce themselves can have a profound effect on the group's atmosphere. Is the leader enthusiastic, personable, psychologically present, and open? To what degree does the leader trust him- or herself? To what degree does the leader show trust and faith in the group? I have often heard members comment that it felt good to be trusted by their leaders.

The leader's success in establishing a basic sense of trust and security depends in large part on how well he or she has prepared for the group. Careful selection of members and efforts to make sure that the group is appropriate for them are very important, and so is the way in which the leader presents the ground rules of the group. Leaders who show that they are interested in the welfare of individual members and of the group as a whole engender trust. Talking about matters such as the rights of participants, the necessity of confidentiality, the diversity that exists within the group, and the need for respecting others demonstrates that the leader has a serious attitude toward the group. If the leader cares, chances are that the members will also care enough to invest themselves in the group to make it successful.

Trust building is not the exclusive province of group leaders, however. True, leaders can engender trust by their attitudes and actions, but the level of trust also depends in large part on the members—individually and collectively. Members usually bring to the group some fears as well as their hopes. Participants will trust the group more if they are encouraged to expose their fears, because talking about them is likely to reveal that their fears are shared by others. If one member, for example, is concerned about not being able to express herself effectively, and someone else expresses the same concern, almost invariably a bond is established between the two.

Silences and awkwardness are characteristically part of the beginning session. The more unstructured the group, the greater the anxiety and ambiguity about how one is to behave in a group. The members are floundering somewhat as they seek to discover how to participate. More often than not, in these initial sessions, the issues raised tend to be safe ones, and there is some talking about other people and there-and-then material. This is one way that members go about testing the waters. It is as though they are saying, "I'll show a part of myself—not a deep and sensitive one—and I'll see how others treat me." As the sessions progress, members generally find it easier to raise issues and participate in the discussion.

Ways of Maintaining Trust   Another characteristic of this initial phase is the tendency for some participants to jump in and try to give helpful advice as problems are brought up. It is the leader's task to make sure that these "problem-solving interventions" do not become a pattern; they may cause enough irritation in other members to precipitate a confrontation with those who are quick to offer remedies for everyone's troubles.

The group's atmosphere of trust is also affected by the negative feelings members often experience at the initial stage toward certain other members or toward the leader and over the fact that the group is not proceeding the way they would like to see it proceed. This is an important turning point in a group, and trust can be lost or enhanced depending on the manner in which negative feelings are dealt with. If conflict is brought out into the open and negative feelings are listened to nondefensively, there's a good chance that the situation producing these feelings can be changed. Members need to know that it is acceptable to have and express a range of feelings. Only then can the group move ahead to a deeper level of work.

As members reveal more of themselves to one another, the group becomes cohesive; in turn, this emerging cohesion strengthens the trust that exists in the group and creates the right atmosphere for members to try new ways of behaving in the group. When the members trust one another, they also trust the feedback they receive, which they can use as they try to carry these newly acquired behaviors into their daily lives.

Role of the Group Leader at the Initial Stage

Modeling   When you lead a group, you set the tone and shape the norms as a model-setting participant as well as a technical expert (Yalom, 1995). It is important to state your own expectations for the group openly during the first session and to model interpersonal honesty and spontaneity. You need to be aware of your own behavior and of the impact you have on the group and to practice the skills that create a therapeutic milieu. To be effective as a leader, you must be psychologically present in the group and be genuine. How can you expect the participants to get involved and believe in the potential of your group if you don't believe in what you are doing or if you are apathetic?

With regard to empathy—both cognitive and affective—you can create a therapeutic situation by being able to see and understand the world from the internal vantage point of the members. Another key characteristic is your sensitivity in attending and responding not only to what is said but also to the subtle messages conveyed beyond words. This applies to individual members as well as to the group as a whole. Finally, the people who make up your group need to sense that you have respect and positive regard for them.

All of these comments acquire special meaning if you keep in mind that at the initial stage the participants depend very much on you. They turn to you for direction and structure and often focus so much on you that they neglect their own resources. This situation, which exists in most groups, requires that you be constantly aware of your own need to be seen as an authority figure and to keep tight control on the group. If you are not aware of these needs in yourself, you may keep the members of your group from becoming autonomous.

Helping Identify Goals   Another of your main tasks as a group leader is to help the participants get involved. You can do a lot to motivate, inspire, and challenge people to want to get the most from their group. At this stage you do it mostly by helping them identify, clarify, and develop meaningful goals. There are general group goals, which vary from group to group because they depend on the purpose of the group, and there are group process goals, which apply to most groups. Some examples of process goals are staying in the here-and-now, making oneself known to others, challenging oneself and others, taking risks, giving and receiving feedback, listening to others, responding to others honestly and concretely, dealing with conflict, dealing with feelings that arise in the group, deciding what to work on, acting on new insights, and applying new behavior in and out of the group.

In addition to establishing these group process goals, you need to help members establish their own goals. Typically, people in the early stages of a group have vague ideas about what they want from a group experience. These vague ideas need to be translated into specific concrete goals with regard to the desired changes and to the efforts the person is actually willing to make to bring about these changes. It is during the initial phase that this process needs to take place if the members are to derive the maximum benefit from the group.

One of the leader's basic tasks, and a most challenging one, is to bring hidden agendas out into the open. For example, some members may have hidden goals that are at cross-purposes with group goals. They may have an inordinate need to be the center of attention, or they may sabotage intimacy in a group because of their discomfort with getting close to others. A leader's function is to do what is needed to make these hidden agendas explicit. If such personal goals remain hidden, they are bound to undermine the effectiveness of the group.

The Division of Responsibility   A basic issue that group leaders must consider is responsibility for the direction and outcome of the group. Is a nonproductive group the result of the leader's lack of skill, or does the responsibility rest with the group members?

One way of conceptualizing the issue of leader responsibility is to think of it in terms of a continuum. At one end is the leader who assumes a great share of the responsibility for the direction and outcomes of the group. Such leaders tend to have the outlook that unless they are highly directive the group will flounder. They see their role as that of the expert, and they actively intervene to keep the group moving in ways that they deem productive. A disadvantage of this extreme form of responsible leadership is that it robs the members of the responsibility that is rightfully theirs. If members are perceived by the leader as not having the capacity to take care of themselves, they soon begin to live up to this expectation by being irresponsible, at least in the group.

At the other end of the responsibility continuum is the leader who proclaims: "I am responsible for me, and you are responsible for you. If you want to leave this group with anything of value, it is strictly up to you. I can't do anything for you—make you feel something or take away any of your defenses—unless you allow me to."

Ideally, as a leader you will discover a balance, accepting a rightful share of the responsibility but not usurping the members' responsibility. This issue is central because a leader's approach to other issues (such as structuring and self-disclosure) hinges on his or her approach to the responsibility issue. Consider your own personality in the determining how much responsibility to assume and what, specifically, this responsibility will include.

Structuring   Like responsibility, structuring exists on a continuum. The leader's theoretical orientation, the type of group, and the membership population are some factors that determine the amount and type of structuring employed. Providing therapeutic structuring is particularly important during the initial stage when members are typically confused about what behavior is expected in the group and are therefore anxious. Structure can be either useful or inhibiting in a group's development. Too little structure results in members' becoming unduly anxious, which inhibits their spontaneity. Too much structuring and direction can foster dependent attitudes and behavior. The members may wait for the leader to "make something happen" instead of taking responsibility for finding their own direction.

In my own groups, the type of structure provided in the initial stage is aimed at assisting members to identify and express their fears, expectations, and personal goals. For example, members participate in dyads, go-arounds, and structured questions as ways of making it easier for them to talk to one another about their life issues. After talking to several people on a one-to-one basis, they feel more comfortable talking openly to the entire group. From the outset I try to help them become aware of what they are thinking and feeling in the here-and-now and encourage them to express their reactions. My interventions are aimed at promoting a high degree of interaction within the group, as opposed to creating the norm of having a few individuals do prolonged work while other members merely observe. This type of structuring is designed to let members assume increased responsibility for getting the most out of the group. As they learn basic norms, they tend to take the initiative rather than waiting for my direction.

What does research teach us about the value of providing structure during the initial stages of a group? Yalom (1995) cites a body of evidence indicating that ambiguity with respect to the goals and procedures of the group and to the behavior expected of members increases members' anxiety, frustration, and disengagement. Yalom found that both too much and too little leader activity or leader management were detrimental to the members' growth as well as to the autonomy of the group. Too much leader direction tends to limit the growth of members, and too little results in aimless groups. Yalom sees the basic task of the group leader as providing enough structure to give a general direction to the members while avoiding the pitfall of fostering dependency on the leader. His message to leaders is to structure the group in a way that promotes each member's autonomous functioning. Instead of inviting or calling on members to speak, for example, leaders can show them how to bring themselves into the interactions without being called on.

Research has shown the value of an initial structure that builds supportive group norms and highlights positive interactions among members. The leader must carefully monitor and assess this therapeutic structure throughout the life of a group rather than waiting to evaluate it during the final stage. Structuring that offers a coherent framework for understanding the experiences of individuals and the group process will be of the most value. When therapeutic goals are clear, when appropriate member behaviors are identified, and when the therapeutic process is structured to provide a framework for change, members tend to engage in therapeutic work more quickly (Dies, 1983b). Leader direction during the early phases of a group tends to foster cohesion and the willingness of members to take risks by making themselves known to others and by giving others feedback (Stockton & Morran, 1982).

Another leader task during the early stage of a group involves being aware of the nature of members' concerns about self-disclosure. Leaders can intervene by helping members identify and process their concerns early in the life of a group. Robison, Stockton, and Morran (1990) cite research indicating that early structure imposed by the leader tends to increase the frequency of therapeutically meaningful self-disclosure, feedback, and confrontation. It appears that this structuring can also reduce negative attitudes about self-disclosure.

In summary, although many variables are related to creating norms and trust during the early phase of development, the optimum balance between too much and too little leader direction is one of the most important. The art is to provide structuring that is not so tight that it robs group members of the responsibility of finding their own structure. Involving group members in a continual process of evaluating their own progress and that of the group as a whole is one effective way of checking for the appropriate degree of structure.

Members need to be taught specific skills of monitoring group process if they are to assume this responsibility.

Summary of the Initial Stage

Stage Characteristics   The early phase of a group is a time for orientation and determining the structure of the group. These are some of the distinguishing events of this stage:

- Participants test the atmosphere and get acquainted.
- Members learn what is expected, how the group functions, and how to participate in a group.
- Members display socially acceptable behavior; risk taking is relatively low and exploration is tentative.
- Group cohesion and trust are gradually established if members are willing to express what they are thinking and feeling.
- Members are concerned with whether they are included or excluded, and they are beginning to define their place in the group.
- A central issue is trust versus mistrust.
- There are periods of silence and awkwardness; members may look for direction and wonder what the group is about.
- Members are deciding whom they can trust, how much they will disclose, how safe the group is, whom they like and dislike, and how much to get involved.
- Members are learning the basic attitudes of respect, empathy, acceptance, caring, and responding—all attitudes that facilitate trust building.

Member Functions and Possible Problems   Early in the course of the group, these specific member roles and tasks are critical to shaping the group:

- Taking active steps to create a trusting climate
- Learning to express one's feelings and thoughts, especially as they pertain to interactions in the group
- Being willing to express fears, hopes, concerns, reservations, and expectations concerning the group
- Being willing to make oneself known to others in the group
- Being involved in the creation of group norms
- Establishing personal and specific goals that will govern group participation
- Learning the basics of group process, especially how to be involved in group interactions

   Some of the problems that can arise are these:

- Members may wait passively for "something to happen."
- Members may keep to themselves feelings of distrust or fears pertaining to the group and thus entrench their own resistance.
- Members may keep themselves vague and unknown, making meaningful interaction difficult.

- Members may slip into a problem-solving and advice-giving stance with other members.

■ **Leader Functions**   The major tasks of group leaders during the orientation and exploration phase of a group are these:

- Teaching participants some general guidelines and ways to participate actively that will increase their chances of having a productive group
- Developing ground rules and setting norms
- Teaching the basics of group process
- Assisting members in expressing their fears and expectations and working toward the development of trust
- Modeling the facilitative dimensions of therapeutic behavior
- Being open with members and being psychologically present for them
- Clarifying the division of responsibility
- Helping members establish concrete personal goals
- Dealing openly with members' concerns and questions
- Providing a degree of structuring that will neither increase member dependence nor promote excessive floundering
- Assisting members to share what they are thinking and feeling about what is occurring within the here-and-now group context
- Teaching members basic interpersonal skills such as active listening and responding
- Assessing the needs of the group and facilitating in such a way that these needs are met

Exercises and activities designed to develop leadership skills for each of the stages of a group are included in the Student Manual accompanying this book.

Stage 3: Transition Stage—Dealing with Resistance

Before a group can begin doing a deeper level of work, it typically goes through a somewhat challenging transition phase. During this stage, members deal with their anxiety, defensiveness, conflict, and ambivalence about participating in the group. The leader helps the members learn how to begin working on the concerns that brought them to the group.

Characteristics of the Transition Stage

■ **Anxiety**   The transition stage is generally characterized by increased anxiety and defensiveness. These feelings normally give way to genuine openness and trust in the stages that follow. Participants may articulate their anxieties in the form of statements or questions such as these, directed to themselves or to the group:

- I wonder whether these people really understand me and whether they care.
- I don't know how much I have in common with folks in here. I'm not sure they will understand me.

- What good will it do to open myself up in here? Even if it works, what will it be like when I attempt to do the same outside of this group?
- What if I lose control? What if I cry?
- I see myself standing before a door but unwilling to open it for fear of what I'll find behind it. I'm afraid to open the door into myself, because once I open it a crack I'm not sure I'll be able to shut it again.
- How close can I get to others in here? How much can I trust these people with my inner feelings?

Anxiety grows out of the fear of letting others see oneself on a level beyond the public image. Anxiety also results from the fear of being judged and misunderstood, from the need for more structure, and from a lack of clarity about goals, norms, and expected behavior in the group situation. As the participants come to trust more fully the other members and the leader, they become increasingly able to share of themselves, and this openness lessens their anxiety about letting others see them as they are.

Conflict and Struggle for Control   Many writers point out the central role that conflict plays during the transition stage of a group. Yalom (1995) sees this stage as characterized by negative comments and criticism. People may be quite judgmental of others and yet unwilling to open up to the perceptions that others have of them. In Yalom's eyes, the transition stage is a time of struggling for power—among the members and with the leader—and establishing a social pecking order: "The struggle for control is part of the infrastructure of every group. It is always present, sometimes quiescent, sometimes smoldering, sometimes in full conflagration" (p. 298).

Before conflict can be dealt with and constructively worked through, it must be recognized. Too often both the members and the leader want to bypass conflict out of the mistaken assumption that it is something to be feared and avoided at all costs. If conflict exists and is ignored in a group, what originally produced the conflict festers and destroys the chance for genuine contact. When conflict is recognized and dealt with in such a way that those who are involved can retain integrity, the foundations of trust between the parties are established. Recognizing that conflict is often inevitable and that it can strengthen trust is likely to reduce the probability that members and the leader will try to dodge the conflicts that are a natural part of a group's development.

Ignoring conflicts and negative reactions requires energy, and that energy can be better employed to develop an honest style of facing and working through inevitable conflicts. As a group evolves, members continue to discover whether the group is a safe place to disagree, to have and express the full range of feelings, and to experience interpersonal conflict. They are testing the degree to which they can be accepted when they are not living up to social expectations. The way conflict is recognized, accepted, and worked with has critical effects on the progress of the group. If it is poorly handled, the group may retreat and never reach a productive stage of development. If it is dealt with openly and with concern, the members discover that their relationships are strong enough to withstand an honest level of challenge.

Certain group behaviors tend to elicit negative reactions that reflect conflict:

- Remaining aloof and hiding behind the stance of observer
- Talking too much and actively interfering with the group process through questioning, giving abundant advice, or in other ways distracting people from their work
- Dominating the group, using sarcasm, belittling the efforts that are being made, and demanding attention

Intermember conflict is often the result of transference. Members may have intense reactions to one another; through exploring these reactions to specific individuals in a group, they can discover some important connections to the ways in which they transfer feelings from significant people in their lives to others. Here are some statements that can represent transference reactions:

- You seem so self-righteous. Every time you begin to talk, I want to leave the room.
- You bother me because you look like a well-functioning computer. I don't sense any feeling from you.
- Your attempts to take care of everyone in here really bother me. You rarely ask anything for yourself, but you're always ready to offer something.

Challenging the Group Leader   Conflicts also often involve the group leader. You may be challenged on professional as well as personal grounds. You may be criticized for being "too standoffish" and not revealing enough of yourself, or you may be criticized for being "one of the group" and revealing too much of your private life. Here are some of the comments you may hear from your group members:

- You're judgmental, cold, and stern.
- No matter what I do, I have the feeling that it'll never be enough to please you. You expect too much from us.
- You really don't care about us personally. I sense that you're just doing a job and that we don't count.
- You don't give us enough freedom. You control everything.
- You push people too much. I feel you aren't willing to accept a "no."

It is helpful to distinguish between a challenge and an attack. An attack can take the form of "dumping" or "hit-and-run" behavior. Members who attack group leaders with "This is how you are" statements don't give leaders much chance to respond. The leader has already been judged, categorized, and dismissed. It is quite another matter to openly confront a leader with how the members perceive and experience that person. A member leaves room for dialogue when she says: "I'm aware that I'm not opening up in here. One reason is that if I do I feel that you'll push me beyond where I want to go." This member openly states her fears but leaves enough room for the leader to respond and to explore the issue further. This is a challenge, not an attack.

Challenging the leader is often a participant's first significant step toward autonomy. Most members experience the struggle of dependence versus independence. If members are to become free of their dependency on the leader that is characteristic of the initial group stage, the leader must deal directly with these revealing challenges to his or her authority. It is well for leaders to be aware that some members, because of their cultural values and socialization, will be very hesitant to challenge a leader. In these cases, it is not generally facilitative for leaders to expect or to push members to express everything they are feeling.

The way in which you accept and deal with challenges to you personally and to your leadership style greatly determines your effectiveness in leading the group into more advanced levels of development. If you can learn to appreciate the opportunities that challenges from group members offer, you have a better chance of dealing with these challenges directly and honestly. You are also in a better position to share how you are affected by the confrontation, to ask members to check out their assumptions, and to tell them how you see yourself in regard to their criticism. By keeping the lines of communication open, and by consistently trying to avoid slipping into a "leader role" that entails diluting the challenge as a means of self-defense, you are modeling appropriate ways of dealing with personal challenges.

Resistance   Resistance is behavior that keeps members from exploring personal issues or painful feelings in depth. It is an inevitable phenomenon in groups, and unless it is recognized and explored, it can seriously interfere with the group process. An integral part of one's typical defensive approach to life, resistance must be recognized as a protective force that reduces anxiety. For group leaders not to respect members' resistances is akin to not respecting the members themselves. An effective way of dealing with resistances is to treat them as an inevitable aspect of the group process; that is, the leader acknowledges that resistance is a member's natural response to getting personally involved in a risk-taking course. An open atmosphere that encourages people to acknowledge and work through whatever hesitations and anxieties they may be experiencing is essential. The participants must be willing to recognize their resistance and to talk about what might be keeping them from full participation.

Before proceeding with this discussion, two points need to be made. One is that the members' unwillingness to cooperate is not always a form of resistance in the proper sense of the term. There are times when member "resistance" is the result of factors such as an unqualified leader, conflict between co-leaders, a dogmatic or authoritarian leadership style, a leader's failure to prepare the participants for the group experience, or a lack of trust engendered by the leader. In other words, group members may be unwilling to share their feelings because they don't trust the group leader or because the group is simply not a safe place in which to open up. It is imperative that those who lead groups look honestly at the sources of resistance, keeping in mind that not all resistance stems from the members' lack of willingness to face unconscious and threatening sides of themselves.

The second point is a warning against the danger of categorizing people and reducing them to labels such as "the monopolist," "the intellectualizer," "the dependent one," or "the quiet seducer." Although it is understandable that prospective leaders will be interested in learning how to handle "problem members" and the disruption of the group that they can cause, the emphasis should be on *actual behaviors* rather than on labels. Regardless of the type of behavior a member exhibits as a characteristic style, he or she is more than that particular behavior. If you see and treat a person just as a "monopolizer" or an "advice giver" or a "help-rejecting complainer," you contribute to cementing that particular behavior instead of helping the person work on the problems behind the behavior.

For example, if Maria is treated as a "monopolizer" and is not encouraged to explore the impact she has on the group, she will continue to see herself as others see her and respond to her. You can help Maria, as well as the entire group, by investigating the reasons for her need to keep the spotlight on herself and the effects of her behavior on the group. People need to become aware of the defenses that may prevent them from getting involved in the group and of the effects of these defenses on the other members. However, they should be confronted with care and in such a way that they are *challenged* to recognize their defensive behaviors and invited to go beyond them.

Another limitation of identifying "problem members" rather than problem behaviors is that most of those who participate in groups exhibit, at one time or another, some form of resistance. Occasional advice giving, questioning, or intellectualizing is not in itself a problem behavior. As a matter of fact, the group leader needs to be aware of the danger of letting participants become overly self-conscious of how they behave in the group. If clients become too concerned about being identified as "problem group members," they will not be able to behave spontaneously and openly.

Difficult Group Member, or Difficult Group Leader?

Many students in group counseling classes want to talk about the "difficult" members in the groups they are leading. At times certain members may display problematic behaviors such as monopolizing the group's time, story-telling, asking many questions, making interpretations for others, being overly intellectual and detached, being overly silent, or giving advice or reassurance when it is not appropriate. Such behavior often gets in the way of those members who want to work on their concerns.

Members become problematic at times because of problematic behaviors on the part of group leaders. Even in effective groups, certain members may manifest problematic behaviors that are a source of difficulty to themselves, other members, and the leader. Learning how to deal therapeutically with resistance and the many forms it takes is a central challenge for group leaders. When beginning counselors encounter members who are highly resistant, they often take the matter personally. They seem to view themselves as not being competent enough to cope with certain problematic members. If they were able to "break through" the layers of defenses of some of these difficult members, they believe, they would then feel competent.

In working with behaviors of members that are problematic, leaders would do well to reflect on ways their attitudes and interventions can either decrease or escalate difficult behavior patterns. Some common denominators characterize appropriate group leader interventions when dealing with difficult behaviors of group members. Below are some guidelines for effectively dealing with members who sometimes can be challenging.

- Express annoyance and anger at a member without denigrating the character of the person.
- Avoid responding to a sarcastic remark with sarcasm.
- Educate the member about how the group works to demystify the process.
- Encourage a member to explore his or her fears or any form of resistance rather than ignore them.
- Avoid labeling and judging any member and instead describe the behavior of the member.
- State observations and hunches in a tentative way rather than being dogmatic.
- Demonstrate sensitivity to a member's culture and avoid stereotyping the individual.
- Let members who are difficult know how they are affecting you in a non-blaming way.
- Avoid using the role and power of the leader to intimidate members.
- Monitor your own countertransference reactions.
- Challenge members in a caring and respectful way to do things that may be painful and difficult.
- Confront in a caring manner.
- Avoid retreating when conflict arises.
- Provide a balance between support and challenge.
- Refrain from taking member reactions in an overly personal way.
- Facilitate a more focused exploration of a problem rather than give simple solutions.
- Meet the member's needs, not your own.
- Invite group members to state how they are personally affected by problematic behaviors of other members but block judgments, evaluations, and criticisms.

When working with a group member who exhibits difficult behaviors, put these behavioral patterns into the context of the meaning and purpose of this behavior for the individual. People in a group are likely doing the best they know how, even if they become aware that what they are doing is not working well for them. It is always useful to remind ourselves that the very reason people seek a group is to assist them in finding more effective ways of expressing themselves and dealing with others.

Dealing with Your Own Reactions to Member Resistance

Look at how you are being personally affected by the wide variety of problem behaviors you encounter, and avoid categorizing people as "problem types." The fact is that many of us would display a variety of avoidance strategies if we were in a group. As old patterns are challenged and as we experience the anxiety that accompanies personal change, we are likely to be very creative in devising a pattern of resistive strategies. Remember, resistance does make sense and emerges from members for a purpose.

When group members exhibit what you consider to be problematic behavior, examine your own desire to respond with strong feelings. You may feel threatened by those members who dominate and attempt to control the group; you may be angered by members who display resistive behavior; you may blame certain clients or the group as a whole for the slow pace or lack of productivity of the group; and you may take any signs of resistance personally. If you ignore your own reactions, you are in essence leaving yourself out of the interactions that occur in the group. Your own responses—be they feelings, thoughts, or observations—are often the most powerful resource at your disposal in effectively handling resistant behaviors.

One rationale for group leaders to experience their own group therapy is that this kind of self-exploration increases the chances that they will gain awareness of their own blind spots and potential vulnerabilities. Frequently, those members whom we perceive as being "difficult" and who affect us the most are those who remind us of aspects of ourselves.

In dealing with countertransference, supervision is most helpful. As a trainee, you have the opportunity to explore with your supervisor and fellow group leaders your feelings of attraction or dislike toward certain members and to learn a lot about yourself in the process. If you are leading a group alone and no longer have supervision, it is important that you be willing to consult with a qualified professional to work through unresolved problems that may lie behind your feelings of countertransference. One of the advantages of working with a co-leader is that your partner can offer valuable feedback from an objective point of view and thus help you see things that may be blocked from your awareness. Handling countertransference is discussed further in Chapter 6.

Summary of the Transition Stage

Stage Characteristics   The transitional phase of a group's development is marked by feelings of anxiety and defenses in the form of various resistances. At this time members experience a variety of feelings and may once again question their involvement with the group process:

- Wondering what they will think of themselves if they increase their self-awareness, and wondering about others' acceptance or rejection of them
- Testing the leader and other members to determine how safe the environment is
- Experiencing some struggle for control and power and some conflict with other members or the leader
- Learning how to work through conflict and confrontation
- Feeling reluctant to get fully involved in working on their personal concerns because they are not sure others in the group will care about them

- Observing the leader to determine if he or she is trustworthy and learning from this person how to resolve conflict
- Learning how to express themselves so that others will listen to them

Member Functions and Possible Problems   A central role of members at this time is to recognize and deal with the many forms of resistance. These tasks include the following:

- Recognizing and expressing the range of feelings and thoughts
- Respecting one's own struggles, yet continuing to explore them in group
- Moving from dependence to independence
- Taking increased responsibility for what they are doing in the group
- Learning how to confront others in a constructive manner
- Being willing to face and deal with reactions toward what is occurring in the group
- Being willing to work through conflicts, rather than avoiding them

Some problems can arise with members at this time:

- Members can be categorized as a "problem type," or they can limit themselves with a self-imposed label.
- Members may refuse to express persistent negative reactions, thus contributing to the climate of distrust.
- If confrontations are poorly handled, members may retreat into defensive postures and issues will remain hidden.
- Members may identify a scapegoat to project their own feelings on.
- Members may collude by forming subgroups and cliques, expressing negative reactions outside of the group but remaining silent in the group.

Leader Functions   Perhaps the central challenge that leaders face during the transition phase is the need to intervene in the group in a sensitive manner and at the right time. The basic task is to provide both the encouragement and the challenge necessary for the members to face and resolve the conflicts that exist within the group and their own resistances and defenses against anxiety. As I indicated earlier, the genuine cohesion that allows for productive exploration and interaction to develop demands that this difficult phase of defensiveness and conflict be experienced and dealt with successfully.

Here are some of the major tasks you need to perform during this critical period in a group's development:

- Teach group members the importance of recognizing and expressing their anxieties, reluctances, and here-and-now reactions to what is happening in the sessions.
- Help participants recognize the ways in which they react defensively and create a climate in which they can deal with their resistances openly.
- Teach the members the value of recognizing and dealing openly with conflicts that occur in the group.

- Point out behavior that is a manifestation of the struggle for control, and teach members how to accept their share of responsibility for the direction of the group.
- Assist the group members in dealing with any matters that will influence their ability to become both independent and interdependent.
- Encourage members to keep in mind what they want from the group and to ask for it.
- Provide a model for the members by dealing directly and honestly with any challenges to you as a person or as a professional.
- Continue to monitor your own reactions to members who display problematic behavior. Explore your potential countertransference through supervision or personal therapy.

Leaders need to be especially active during the first and second stages of a group. During the transition stage, active intervention and structuring are important because generally the participants have not yet learned to work effectively on their own. If a conflict arises, for example, some members may attempt to move on to more pleasant topics or in some other way ignore the conflict. Group leaders need to teach members the value of expressing their feelings, thoughts, and reactions.

Destructive confrontations, with an attacking quality, can lead to entrenchment of resistance and breed hostility and mistrust. But confrontation is appropriate even during the early stages of a group if it is done with sensitivity and respect. In fact, trust is often facilitated by caring confrontations on the leader's part. To avoid challenging a group in its early phases is to treat the members as though they were fragile. How leaders deal with conflict, resistance, anxiety, and defensiveness does much to set the tone of the group. In my view, members have a tendency to follow the leader's manner of confronting.

Concluding Comments

This chapter has addressed various issues of group membership and group process that are central to your effectiveness as a group leader. I have focused on key concerns as the group is being formed, at its initial phase, and at the transitional period in a group's history. I have emphasized the central characteristics of the group at each phase, the member functions and possible problems, group process concepts, and the leader's key tasks. Your approach to leadership functions and skills hinges on your understanding of the roles that members play at the various stages in the group. Only if you are clear in your own mind about the various aspects of productive and unproductive member behaviors can you help group participants acquire the skills necessary for a successful group experience and correct behaviors that hinder self-exploration and involvement in the group. The next chapter continues this account of the unfolding of a group.

CHAPTER 5

Later Stages in the Development of a Group

Continuing the discussion of the evolutionary process of a group in action, this chapter focuses on the working stage, the final stage, and the postgroup issues of evaluation and follow-up. We will look at the major characteristics of the group at each phase, the member functions and possible problems that are likely to occur, and the group leader's key functions.

Stage 4: Working Stage—Cohesion and Productivity

The line between expressing conflicts and resistance, so characteristic of the transition stage, and working them through to move the group into a more advanced stage of development is thin indeed. There are no arbitrary dividing lines between the phases of a group. In actual practice there is considerable overlapping of stages, and this is especially true of movement from the transition stage to the working stage.

The working stage is characterized by a more in-depth exploration of significant problems and by effective action to bring about the desired behavioral changes. This stage is characterized by the commitment of members to explore significant problems they bring to the sessions and by their attention to the dynamics within the group. At this time in a group's evolution, I find that my degree of structuring and intervention is lower than during the initial and transition stages. By now the participants have learned how to involve themselves in group interactions in more spontaneous ways.

To be sure, work and learning do occur during the initial and transition stages. However, a higher degree of cohesion, a clearer notion of what members want from their group, and a more intensive level of interaction among the members is characteristic of the working stage. This is the time when participants need to realize that they are responsible for their lives. Thus, they must be encouraged to decide what issues to explore in the group and to learn how to become an integral part of the group and yet retain their individuality. Group members must filter the feedback they receive and decide what they will do about it. Consequently, it is very important at this stage that neither the group leader nor other members attempt to decide on a course of action or make prescriptions for another member.

Development of Group Cohesion

Nature of Group Cohesion   Group cohesion involves a sense of belonging, inclusion, and solidarity. Cohesiveness is the result of all the forces acting on the members that make them want to remain in the group. It refers to the condition of members experiencing caring and comfort in the group, a sense that they belong, a sense of being valued, and the feeling of being accepted and supported in the group (Yalom, 1995).

Although cohesion may begin to develop in the early stages of a group, at the working stage it becomes a key element of the group process. If trust has been established, and if conflict and negative feelings have been expressed and worked through, the group becomes a cohesive unit. Groups do not have to experience conflict before they become cohesive. But if conflict is present in the group and is smoothed over or somehow ignored, it will get in the way of building cohesion. If the group has successfully navigated a testing period, members will conclude, "If it's OK to express negative reactions and conflict, then maybe it's OK to get close." Cohesion is not fixed, however; it fluctuates throughout the life of the group depending on the interactions of group members.

When cohesion occurs, people open up on a deeper level and are willing to reveal painful experiences and take other risks. Often, the route to this increased level of interaction within the group is due to a willingness of members to stay in the here-and-now, especially their willingness to express persistent reactions they are having to one another. The honest sharing of deeply significant personal experiences and struggles binds the group together, because the process of sharing allows members to identify with others by seeing themselves in others. Cohesion provides the group with the impetus to move forward and is a prerequisite for the group's success. Without a sense of "groupness," the group remains fragmented, members become frozen behind their defenses, and their work is of necessity superficial. Groups do not become cohesive automatically. Cohesion is the result of a commitment by the participants and the leader to take the steps that lead to a group-as-a-whole feeling.

Although group cohesion is not in itself a sufficient condition for effective group work, in a sense all the characteristics of a well-functioning group are contingent on it. Cohesiveness is necessary for other group therapeutic factors to operate (Yalom, 1995). Cohesion fosters action-oriented behaviors such as immediacy, mutuality, confrontation, risk taking, and translation of insight into action. Also, without group cohesion the participants don't feel secure enough to maintain a high level of self-disclosure.

Yalom (1995) maintains that cohesion is a strong determinant of a positive group outcome. If members experience little sense of belonging or attraction to the group, there is little likelihood that they will benefit, and they may well experience negative outcomes. According to Yalom, groups with a here-and-now focus are almost invariably vital and cohesive. In contrast, groups in which members merely talk about issues with a "there-and-then" focus rarely develop much cohesiveness.

Cohesion as a Unifying Force   Although cohesiveness is necessary for effective group work, it can potentially hinder the group's development. When cohesiveness is not accompanied by a challenge to move forward by both the members and the leader, the group can reach a plateau. Group members may settle for feeling secure and comfortable rather than being open to taking risks necessary for growth.

In many of the adult groups that I lead, common human themes arise that most of the members can relate to personally, regardless of their age, sociocultural background, or occupation. Whereas members are likely to be aware in the earlier stages of the group of the differences that separate them, it is quite common as the group reaches a level of cohesion for members to comment on how alike they are in the feelings that connect them. These commonalties can be expressed in a variety of ways:

- I'm not alone in my pain and with my problems.
- I'm more lovable than I thought I was.
- I used to think I was too old to change and that I'd just have to settle for what I have in life. Now I see that what I feel is no different from what the younger people in here feel.
- I'm hopeful about my future, even though I know I have a long way to go and that the road will be rough.
- There are a lot of people in here I feel close to, and I see that we earned this closeness by letting others know who we are.
- I learned that the loneliness I felt was shared by most of the people in this group.

As a group becomes cohesive, it is not uncommon for a woman in her early twenties to discover that she is very much like a man in his late fifties. Both of them may still be searching for parental approval, and they may both be learning how futile it is to look outside of themselves for confirmation of their worth. A man learns that his struggles with masculinity are not too different from a woman's struggles with her femininity. A woman learns that she is not alone when she discovers that she feels resentment over the many demands her family makes on her. An older man sees in a younger male member "his son" and allows himself to feel tenderness and compassion that he did not let himself experience earlier.

Other common themes evolving in this stage lead to an increase of cohesion: remembering painful experiences of childhood and adolescence, becoming aware of the need for and fear of love, becoming able to express feelings that have been repressed, discovering that our worst enemy often lives within ourselves, struggling to find a meaning in life, recognizing commonalties that link us together as humans, coming to an increased appreciation of our differences and the ways we are unique, feeling guilt over what we have done or failed to do, longing for meaningful connections with significant people, and beginning a process of finding our identity. The leader can foster the development of cohesion by pointing out the common themes that link members of the group.

Characteristics of an Effective Working Group

Stage 4 is characterized by productiveness that builds on the effective work done in the initial and transition stages. Now that members have truly become a group and have developed relationship skills that allow them a greater degree of autonomy, they are less dependent on the leader. Mutuality and self-exploration increase, and the group is focused on producing lasting results. Although the specific characteristics of a cohesive and productive group vary somewhat with the type of group, here are some general trends that identify a group in its working stage:

- There is a here-and-now focus. People have learned to talk directly about what they are feeling and doing in the group sessions, and they are generally willing to have meaningful interactions. They are talking to one another, not about one another. They focus more on what is going on in the group than on stories about people outside of the group. When outside issues are brought up, they are often related to what is going on within the group.

- Members more readily identify their goals and concerns, and they have learned to take responsibility for them. They are less confused about what the group and the leader expect of them.

- Members are willing to work and practice outside the group to achieve behavioral changes. They are carrying out "homework assignments," and they bring into the sessions any difficulties they have had in practicing new ways of thinking, feeling, and behaving. They are willing to try to integrate thoughts, emotions, and behaviors in their everyday situations. They are better able to catch themselves when they are thinking and acting in old patterns.

- Most of the members feel included in the group. Those who are not active know that they are welcome to participate, and their lack of participation does not discourage others from doing meaningful work. A few members may be on the periphery and may feel distant from those members who are doing intensive work. Members who are having a difficult time feeling a sense of connection or belonging will hopefully bring this problem up in the sessions.

- The group has almost become an orchestra in that individuals listen to one another and do productive work together. Although the participants may still look to the leader for direction, as musicians look to the conductor for cues, they also tend to initiate a direction in which they want to move.

- Members continually assess their level of satisfaction with the group, and they take active steps to change matters if they see that the sessions need changing. In a productive group, members realize that they have a part in the outcome. If they are not getting what they want, they generally say so.

Therapeutic Factors of a Group

The following brief overview provides a summary of the specific factors that ensure that a group will move beyond the security of cohesiveness into productive work. The major aspects of the working stage are addressed in detail.

Trust and Acceptance   Group members at the working stage trust one another and the leader, or at least they openly express any lack of trust. Trust is manifested in the participants' attitude of acceptance and in their willingness to take risks by sharing meaningful here-and-now reactions. Feeling that they are accepted, the members recognize that in the group they can be who they are without risking rejection. They dare to assert themselves, for example, because they know that they don't have to please everybody. At the working stage trust is generally high because members have been willing to deal with any barriers to its establishment and maintenance. As is the case with other interpersonal relations, however, trust is not a static entity. Even during the advanced stages of a group, trust may ebb and flow, and there is an ongoing challenge for members to talk about how safe they feel in their group.

Empathy and Caring   Empathy involves a deep capacity to recall, relive, and tap one's feelings through the intense experiences of others. By understanding the feelings of others—such as the need for love and acceptance, hurt about past experiences, loneliness, joy, and enthusiasm—members come to see themselves more clearly. Empathy means caring, and caring is expressed in a group by genuine and active involvement with the other members. It is also expressed by compassion, support, tenderness, and even confrontation. As people open themselves to others by showing their pain, struggles, joy, excitement, and fears, they make it possible for others to care for them, and even to love them. It is empathy that bridges the gap between peoples of different ethnic and cultural groups and allows them to share in universal human themes. Although clients' specific life circumstances may differ depending on their cultural background, groups allow a diverse range of people to come to realize what they have in common.

Intimacy   Genuine intimacy develops in a group after people have revealed enough of themselves for others to identify with them. I have found that intimacy increases as people work through their struggles together. Members see that, regardless of their differences, they all share certain needs, wants, anxieties, and problems. When members learn that others have similar problems, they no longer feel isolated; identification with others eventually brings about closeness, which enables the members to help one another work through fears related to intimacy. The group setting provides an ideal arena for members to discover their fears of intimacy and their resistances to getting close to others. The ultimate goal is to understand how one has avoided intimacy outside of the group and how one can accept intimacy in life without fear.

During the working phase, members ideally not only recognize their resistances to interpersonal intimacy but also demonstrate a willingness to work through the fears associated with getting close to others. If they do get close, members may fear that they will not be able to control their impulses; if they care, they may suffer abandonment again; if they allow intimacy, they will merge with others and lose a sense of their own identity; and if they experience intimacy, they are opening themselves up to being emotionally wounded in various ways by others.

A productive group offers many opportunities for members to face and challenge these fears. They are able to use the here-and-now group experience as a way of working through past hurts and early decisions that block intimacy. Old and unfinished issues are relived in the group context, and new decisions are made possible. Members are able to see connections between ways in which they are avoiding interpersonal intimacy both in the group and with significant others. Ormont (1988) describes what occurs within a group as the members develop mature forms of intimacy: members make emotional space for one another; talk is simple and direct; there are no hidden agendas in the group; members are openly taking risks with one another; powerful feelings are present; members regard one another with a freshness that they have not shown before; and they are able to live in the moment, for the lingering remnants of their past hurts have been worked through successfully.

Bemak and Epp (1996) have written about the healing power of love in a group and contend that love has traditionally been ignored by group counselors. Bemak and Epp believe "love is a powerful therapeutic tool that can aid in the transition of group clients from a pattern of failed or unhealthy love relationships to a greater understanding of love's reality" (p. 125). The authentic experience of empathy, acceptance, caring, and intimacy that develop within a group certainly can be a manifestation of love in the best sense. The intimacy and love that develop among members is often the outcome of the commitment of members to let themselves be known in significant ways, which makes it possible to genuinely love others. Group counselors have the significant role of harnessing the healing power of love and assisting members in appreciating the dynamics of love in the group situation.

Hope   If change is to occur, members must believe that change is possible, that they need not remain trapped in their past, and that they can take active steps to make their lives richer. Hope is therapeutic in itself, for it gives members the confidence to commit themselves to the demanding work that a group requires and motivates them to explore alternatives. Hope is characteristic of effective group leaders and underlies their beliefs about their clients, themselves, and the basic purposes to be achieved through group counseling (Couch & Childers, 1987).

As Yalom (1995) has indicated, instilling and maintaining hope are crucial in group therapy so that members will remain in the group and other therapeutic factors can take effect. He cites research demonstrating that clients' high expectations that therapy will help them are significantly correlated with positive outcomes. Research also substantiates that the therapist's belief in the group process is critical to motivating clients.

A number of leadership strategies for fostering hope have been proposed (Couch & Childers, 1987). Some of these are using the pregroup interview as an opportunity to instill hope in members by creating positive (but realistic) expectations, acknowledging and validating concerns common to many of the participants, calling attention to improvements that members make, encouraging any signs of subtle and positive movement, letting members acknowledge one another's progress, and helping members assume responsibility for their own progress.

Freedom to Experiment   Experimentation with different modes of behavior is a significant aspect of the working stage. The group is a safe place in which to try out novel behavior. After such experiments members can decide what behaviors they want to change. In everyday transactions people often behave in rigid and unimaginative ways, for they don't dare deviate from familiar and predictable patterns. With group support, participants can practice more functional ways of being. Role playing is often an effective way to practice new skills in interpersonal situations; then these skills can be applied to out-of-group situations. This topic is explored more fully in the discussions of psychodrama (Chapter 8) and Gestalt groups (Chapter 11).

Catharsis   The expression of pent-up feelings can be therapeutic because it releases energy that has been tied up in withholding certain threatening feelings. This emotional release, which often occurs in an explosive way, leaves the person feeling freer. Also, keeping a lid on anger, pain, frustration, hatred, and fear means preventing spontaneous feelings such as joy, affection, delight, and enthusiasm from emerging. This emotional release plays an important part in many kinds of groups, but both group leaders and members sometimes make the mistake of concluding that mere catharsis implies "real work." Some disappointed members who do not have emotional releases are convinced that they are not really getting involved. They may be convinced that they are not getting as much from the group as those who have had more catharses than they have. Although it is often healing, catharsis by itself is limited in producing long-lasting changes.

Yalom (1995) notes that catharsis is an interpersonal process. People do not get enduring benefits from ventilating feelings in an empty closet. It is a mistaken assumption that a strong emotional experience is in itself a sufficient force to lead to change. Although catharsis is related to a positive outcome and is often necessary for change, Yalom stresses that it is certainly not enough to produce change by itself. He puts the impact of catharsis into perspective: "The open expression of affect is without question vital to the group therapeutic process; in its absence a group would degenerate into a sterile academic exercise. Yet it is only a part of the process and must be complemented by other factors" (p. 81).

My experience has taught me that catharsis may be a vital part of a person's work in a group, especially if the client has a reservoir of unrecognized and unexpressed feelings. I have also learned that it is a mistake to assume that no real work occurs without a strong ventilation of feelings; many people appear to benefit in the absence of catharsis. After catharsis has occurred, it is extremely important to work through the feelings that emerged, to gain some understanding of the meaning of the experience, and to make new decisions based on such understanding. The topic of catharsis is explored in greater detail in Chapters 8 and 11.

Cognitive Restructuring   A central part of the work done in a group consists of challenging and exploring beliefs about situations. Understanding the meaning of intense emotional experiences is essential to further self-exploration. This cognitive component includes explaining, clarifying, interpreting, providing the cognitive framework needed for change, formulating ideas, and making new decisions. Groups offer members many opportunities to evaluate their thinking and to adopt constructive beliefs in place of self-limiting ones. This process of cognitive restructuring forms a central role in several therapeutic approaches, including Adlerian groups (Chapter 7), transactional analysis (Chapter 12), cognitive behavioral groups (Chapter 13), and rational emotive behavior therapy (Chapter 14).

Commitment to Change   For change to occur, a person must believe that change is possible, but hoping for change is not enough. Constructive change requires a firm resolve to actually do whatever is necessary in order to change. This means deciding what to change as well as how to change it. Participants need to formulate a plan of action, commit themselves to it, and use the tools offered by the group process to explore ways of carrying it out. The support offered by the group is invaluable in encouraging the members to stick with their commitments even when they experience temporary setbacks. An inherent advantage of groups is that members can use one another to help themselves maintain their commitments. They can agree to call another member when they encounter difficulties in carrying out their plans, or they can call when they have made a successful breakthrough. A "buddy system" can be instrumental in teaching members how to ask for help and how to give this help to others. The topic of commitment in group counseling is examined in more detail in the discussion of reality therapy (Chapter 15).

Self-Disclosure   Disclosure is not an end in itself; it is the means by which open communication can occur within a group. If disclosure is limited to safe topics or if it is equated with exposing secrets, the group cannot move beyond a superficial level. As Chen and Han (2001) note, if cultural conflicts have not been sensitively acknowledged during the initial and transition stage, an Asian member may have difficulty during the working stage in engaging in a deeper level of self-disclosure. There are many barriers within us that keep us from self-disclosure—for example, fear of the intimacy that accompanies self-revelation, avoidance of responsibility and change, feelings of guilt and shame, fear of rejection, and cultural taboos. The willingness to overcome these barriers and make oneself known to others is a basic requirement at every stage of a group.

During the working stage, most members have developed enough trust to risk disclosing threatening material.

Self-disclosure is the principal vehicle of group interaction, and it is critical that group participants have a clear understanding of what self-disclosure is— and what it is not. One level of self-disclosure involves sharing one's persistent reactions to what is happening in the group. Another level entails revealing current struggles, unresolved personal issues, goals and aspirations, joys and hurts, and strengths and weaknesses. If people are unwilling to share of themselves, they make it very hard for others to care for them. In the process of talking about concerns that occurred outside of the group or in the past, it is important for members to relate these issues to the here-and-now. By focusing on the here-and-now, participants make direct contact with one another and generally express quite accurately what they are experiencing in the present. The interactions become increasingly honest and spontaneous as members become more willing to risk revealing their reactions to one another.

Self-disclosure does not mean revealing one's innermost secrets and digging into one's past. Nor does it mean "letting everything hang out" or expressing every fleeting reaction to others. Self-disclosure should not be confused with telling stories about oneself or with letting group pressure dictate the limits of one's privacy. At times, in striving to be "open and honest" or in perceiving pressure from others in the group, some members say more than is necessary for others to understand them. They disclose so much that nothing remains private, and as a result they may feel deprived of their dignity.

Self-disclosure is highly valued in most of the traditional counseling approaches covered in this book, but keep in mind the fact that self-disclosure is foreign to the values of some cultural groups. This premium that is placed on self-disclosure by most therapeutic approaches is often in conflict with the values of some European ethnic groups that stress that problems should be kept "in the family." Generally, group members may be slow to self-disclose until they are fairly certain that it is safe to do so, which usually involves some testing of the leader.

Unless clients challenge the obstacles to disclosure, their participation in a group will be very limited. As a group leader, you can recognize that individuals from some ethnic and cultural backgrounds will have difficulties in readily sharing their feelings and reactions, let alone revealing their deeper struggles. You can help such clients by demonstrating respect for their cultural values and at the same time encouraging them to express what they want from you and from the group. With your support and the understanding of other members, they are in a position to clarify their values pertaining to self-disclosure and can decide the degree to which they are willing to make themselves known to others. A good starting point is for them to talk about their difficulty in revealing themselves in a group setting. The topic of self-disclosure is addressed more fully in later chapters as it applies to existential groups (Chapter 9) and person-centered groups (Chapter 10).

Confrontation   Like self-disclosure, confrontation is a basic ingredient of the working stage; if it is absent, stagnation results. Constructive confrontation is an invitation to examine discrepancies between what one says and what one does, to become aware of unused potential, and to carry insights into action. When confrontation takes place in the supportive environment of a group, it can be a true act of caring.

In a successful group, confrontation occurs in such a way that the confronters share their reactions to the person being confronted rather than their judgments of the person. Avoid using a negative style of confrontation—that is, confrontation done in a hostile, indirect, or attacking way—because it may leave people feeling judged and rejected. Done with care and sensitivity, confrontation by others ultimately helps members develop the capacity for the self-confrontation necessary to work through the problems they need to resolve.

Confrontation is an issue that group members, as well as group leaders, frequently misunderstand; it is often feared, misused, and seen as a negative act to be avoided at all costs. In my opinion, although support and empathy are certainly essential to group process, they can become counterproductive if carried to excess. A group can cease to be effective if its members have colluded to interact only on a supportive level and agreed to focus almost exclusively on strengths and positive feedback. Unwillingness to challenge the others to take a deeper look at themselves results in overly polite and supportive exchanges that bear little resemblance to everyday interactions and that provide no incentive to extend oneself.

Group leaders can productively devote time to helping the participants clear up their misconceptions regarding confrontation and learn what to confront and how to confront in a constructive way. One of the most powerful ways of teaching constructive and caring confrontation is for leaders to model this behavior in their interactions in the group. By being direct, honest, sensitive, respectful, and timely in their confrontations, leaders provide the members with valuable opportunities to learn these skills through observing the leader's behavior.

I typically emphasize the following points about effective confrontation:

- Remember that confrontation must be based on respect for others and that it is aimed at challenging others to look at unrecognized and unexplored aspects of themselves.
- Use confrontation only if you want to get closer to a client and only if you are willing to stay with the person after the confrontation.
- Learn to discriminate between what may be a judgmental attack and a caring challenge. For example, instead of saying, "All you do is take from the group; you never give anything of yourself," you may say, "I miss hearing from you. I'm wondering whether you'd like to be saying more. Are you aware of anything that's preventing you from expressing your feelings and thoughts?"
- When you confront a person, address his or her specific behaviors that affect others in the group and explain exactly what the effect is.
- Take responsibility for your behaviors instead of blaming others for how you respond. Instead of saying, "You're boring," say, "I have a hard time staying with you when you speak, and I find that I'm getting impatient."

In sum, confrontation should be done so as to preserve the dignity of the one being confronted, without prejudice to the client, and with the purpose of helping the person identify and see the consequences of his or her behavior. Effective positive confrontation should open up the channels of communication, not close them.

Benefiting from Feedback   Although I treat the topics of self-disclosure, confrontation, and feedback separately for the purpose of discussion, these therapeutic factors have some degree of overlap in actual practice. Most feedback entails self-disclosure, and sometimes feedback can be confrontational. Take, for example, the group member who says this to another member: "I was very affected by the way you role-played talking to your father. It reminded me of my own father and the way I struggle with getting close to him." This is an example of both giving feedback and self-disclosing. Now consider the group member who says this: "When you talked about your father, your fists were clenched, yet you were smiling. I don't know which to believe—your fists or your smile." This type of feedback illustrates a confrontation, as well as some degree of self-disclosure. The person giving feedback disclosed some here-and-now reactions to another member.

The exchange of feedback among group members is widely considered to be a key element in promoting interpersonal learning (Morran, Stockton, & Bond, 1991). One study found that incorporating structured feedback exercises into a group contributed to the attainment of members' goals (Rohde & Stockton, 1992). For members to benefit from feedback, they need to be willing to listen to a range of reactions that others have to their behavior. It is important that there be a balance between "positive" feedback and corrective feedback (sometimes referred to as "negative" feedback). If members give one another their reactions and perceptions honestly and with care, all participants are able to hear what impact they have had on others and can decide what, if anything, they want to change. Such feedback is one of the most important ways in which learning takes place in a group. It can be of great help to the person who is exploring a problem, attempting to resolve a difficult situation, or trying different ways of behaving. Here are some points that can help members learn how to give and receive feedback:

• Global feedback is of little value. Reactions to specific behavior in the group, in contrast, provide clients with an immediate, independent assessment that they can compare with their own view.

• Concise feedback given in a clear and straightforward manner is more helpful than qualified statements and interpretive or mixed feedback (Stockton & Morran, 1980).

• Positive feedback is almost invariably rated as more desirable, more acceptable, more influential, and more conducive to change than corrective feedback. Such feedback focuses on the person's strengths as well as behaviors that might be a source of difficulty (Dies, 1983b; Morran, Robison, & Stockton, 1985; Morran & Stockton, 1980; Morran, Stockton, & Harris, 1991).

• Difficult feedback must be timed well and given in a nonjudgmental way, otherwise the person receiving it is likely to become defensive and reject it.

• Corrective feedback seems to be more credible and helpful when it is focused on observable behaviors and when it comes at a later phase of the group; it is also more likely to be accepted when it has been preceded by positive feedback (Morran, Stockton, & Harris, 1991; Stockton & Morran, 1981).

• Group members are often more reluctant to deliver corrective feedback than positive feedback. This reluctance is due partly to fears of rejection by other members and partly to fears of causing harm to the feedback recipient (Morran, Stockton, & Bond, 1991). Thus, it can be helpful for members to explore their fears about giving and receiving feedback. Members need to be taught the value of giving a range of feedback, as well as ways to deliver their reactions.

• Negative feedback is easier to take if the speaker says how he or she has been affected by the other member's behavior. This practice lessens the chances that members will be judged, for those who give feedback are focusing on themselves at the same time that they are talking to others about their behavior.

• Feedback with a quality of immediacy—that is, feedback given as a here-and-now reaction—is especially valuable and is far better than "stored up" reactions.

• Leader feedback is generally of higher quality than member feedback, but it is not more readily accepted (Morran, Robison, & Stockton, 1985).

• Feedback is best directed toward a behavior the receiver can do something about or has control over.

• Feedback should not be imposed on others. There are times when members are not able to hear feedback because of emotional vulnerability, and this should be respected.

Members sometimes make a global declaration such as "I'd like feedback!" If such clients have said very little, it is difficult to give them many reactions. Members need to learn how to ask for specific feedback and how to receive it. There is value in listening nondefensively to feedback, in really hearing what others want to say to us, and then in considering what we are willing to do with this information. As the group progresses to a working stage, members are typically more willing to freely give one another their reactions.

Commentary   As my colleagues and I have written elsewhere (Corey, Corey, Callanan, & Russell, 2004), not all groups reach the working stage described here. This does not necessarily mean that the leader is ineffective. Changing membership in a group can block its progress. Some populations simply may not be ready for the level of intensity that is often part of a working phase.

If the tasks of the initial and transition stages were never mastered, it can be expected that the group will get stuck. For instance, some groups don't get beyond the hidden agendas and unspoken conflicts that were typical of earlier sessions. Or the members may simply not be willing to give much of themselves beyond safe and superficial encounters. They may have made a decision to stop at a safe level characterized by mutual support rather than also challenging one another to move into unknown territory. Early interchanges between members and the leader or among members may have been abrasive, creating a climate of hesitancy and an unwillingness to trust others. The group may be oriented toward solving problems or patching up differences. This orientation can discourage self-exploration, for as soon as a member raises a problem, other members may rush in with advice on how to remedy the situation. For these reasons and others, some groups never progress beyond the initial stage or the transition stage.

When a group does get to the working stage, it doesn't necessarily progress as tidily as this characterization may suggest. Earlier themes of trust, unconstructive conflict, and the reluctance to participate surface time and again in a group's history. Trust is not a matter that is dealt with once and for all during the early stages of development. As the group faces new challenges, deeper levels of trust have to be earned. Also, considerable conflict may be resolved during the initial stage or transition stage, but new conflicts emerge in the advanced phases and must be faced and worked through. As is true with any intimate relationship, the relationships in the group are not static. Utopia is never reached, and the smooth waters may well turn into stormy seas for a time.

Summary of the Working Stage

Stage Characteristics   When a group reaches the working stage, it has these central characteristics:

- The level of trust and cohesion is high.
- Communication within the group is open and involves an accurate expression of what is being experienced.
- Members interact with one another freely and directly.
- There is a willingness to risk threatening material and to make oneself known to others.
- Conflict among members is recognized and dealt with directly and effectively.
- Confrontation occurs in a way in which those doing the challenging avoid labeling others in judgmental ways.
- Participants feel supported in their attempts to change and are willing to risk new behavior.
- Members feel hopeful that they can change if they are willing to take action; they do not feel helpless.

Member Functions and Possible Problems   The working stage is characterized by the exploration of personally meaningful material. To reach this stage, members must fulfill these tasks and roles:

- Bring into group sessions issues they are willing to discuss.
- Give others feedback and be open to receiving it.

- Share how they are affected by others' presence and work in the group.
- Practice new skills and behaviors in daily life and bring the results to the sessions.
- Continually assess their satisfaction with the group and actively take steps to change their level of involvement in the sessions if necessary.

Some problems may arise at this time:

- Members may gain insights in the sessions but not see the necessity of action outside of the group to bring about change.
- Members may withdraw because of anxiety over others' intensity.

Leader Functions   The central leadership functions at this stage are these:

- Provide systematic reinforcement of desired group behaviors that foster cohesion and productive work.
- Look for common themes among members' work that provide for some universality.
- Continue to model appropriate behavior, especially caring confrontation, and disclose ongoing reactions and perceptions.
- Interpret the meaning of behavior patterns at appropriate times so that members will be able to reach a deeper level of self-exploration and consider alternative behaviors.
- Be aware of the therapeutic factors that operate to produce change and intervene in such a way as to help members make desired changes in thoughts, feelings, and actions.

Stage 5: Final Stage—Consolidation and Termination

One of the group leadership skills that is especially important as a group evolves and is moving toward a final stage is the capacity to assist members in transferring what they have learned in the group to their outside environments. During each stage of the group, participants are applying lessons learned in the sessions to their daily lives. The consolidation of this learning takes on special meaning as a group moves toward termination; this is a time for summarizing, pulling together loose ends, and integrating and interpreting the group experience.

I see the initial and final stages as the most decisive times in the group's life history. If the initial phase is effective, the participants get to know one another and establish their own identities in the group. An atmosphere of trust develops, and the groundwork is laid for later intensive work. Throughout the life of a group, the members are engaging in the cognitive work necessary to make decisions regarding what they are learning about themselves and others. As a group evolves into its final stage, cognitive work takes on particular importance. To maximize the impact of the group experience, participants need to conceptualize what members learned, how they learned it, and what they will do about applying their insights to situations once the group ends. If the final phase is handled poorly by the group leader, the chances that the members will be able to use what they have learned are greatly reduced. Worse yet, members can be left with unresolved issues and without any direction for how to bring these issues to closure.

It is essential that termination issues be brought up early in the course of a group's history. In every beginning the end is always a reality, and members need periodic reminders that their group will eventually end. As a group leader, unless you recognize your own feelings about termination and are able to deal with them constructively, you are in no position to help members deal with separation issues. It may be that you find endings difficult, for a variety of reasons, which will likely mean that you'll want to ignore feelings of sadness as a group comes to an end.

Avoiding acknowledging a group's completion may reflect an unconscious desire on the part of the leader or members not to deal with the role that endings play in their lives. I have found that many people have had negative experiences with endings in their personal relationships. Frequently, people leave us with the assurance they will keep in contact, yet many of them fade away in spite of our efforts to keep in touch. Some of us have friends and relatives who have ended a relationship with anger, leaving us with unfinished business. In our everyday lives, we often lack the modeling for dealing effectively with termination, which is the reason that doing so becomes especially important in group counseling. When termination is not dealt with, the group misses an opportunity to explore an area about which many members have profound feelings. Even more important, much of what clients take away from a group is likely to be lost and forgotten if they do not make a sustained effort to review and think through the specifics of work they have done. Dealing with termination is essential for all types of groups, whatever their duration.

There is a danger that as group members become aware that the end of the group is nearing they will isolate themselves so that they do not have to deal with the anxiety that accompanies separation. Work generally tapers off, and new issues are rarely raised. If members are allowed to distance themselves too much, they will fail to examine the possible effects of their group experience on their out-of-group behavior. Thus, it is crucial that you help the participants put into meaningful perspective what has occurred in the group.

Effective Ways of Terminating a Group

This section deals with ways of terminating the group experience by exploring questions such as these: How can members best complete any unfinished business? How can members be taught, as they leave the group, to carry what they have learned with them and to use it to deal more effectively with the demands of their daily existence? What are the relevant issues and activities in the closing phases of a group? Because of space limitations, most of my discussion focuses on the termination of a *closed group*, that is, a group that consists of the same members throughout its life and whose termination date has been decided in advance.

■ **Dealing with Feelings**   During the final stages of the group, it is a good practice for the leader to remind members that there are only a few sessions remaining. This allows members to prepare themselves for termination and to achieve successful closure of the group experience. Members need help in facing the reality that their group will soon end. Feelings about separation, which often take the form of avoidance or denial, need to be fully explored. It is the leader's job to facilitate an open discussion of the feelings of loss and sadness that accompany the eventual termination of an intense and highly meaningful experience. The members can be helped to face separation by the leader's disclosure of his or her own feelings about terminating the group.

During the initial phase, members are often asked to express their fears of *entering* fully into the group. Now, members should be encouraged to share their fears or concerns about *leaving* the group and having to face day-to-day realities without the group's support. It is not uncommon for members to say that they have developed genuine bonds of intimacy and have found a trusting and safe place where they can be themselves without fear of rejection. They may dread the prospect of being deprived of this intimacy and support. Also common are concerns of not being able to be so trusting and open with people outside the group. One of your leadership tasks is to remind the participants that if their group is special—close, caring, and supportive—it is because the members made the choice and the commitment to work together. Therefore, they can make similar choices and commitments, and be equally successful, in their relationships outside the group. This "boost of confidence" is not intended to deny the sense of loss and the sadness that may accompany the ending of a group. On the contrary, mourning the separation can be an enriching experience if the members of the group are encouraged to fully express their feelings of loss and anxiety.

■ **Examining the Effects of the Group on Oneself**   Toward the end of the group it is useful to give all members an opportunity to put into words what they have learned from the entire group experience and how they intend to apply their increased self-understanding. I routinely discuss the various ways in which participants can go further with what they have learned in the group. This is a time for making specific plans for ways members can continue to build on what they learned in their group. To be fruitful, this discussion must be concrete and specific. Statements such as "This group has been great. I really grew a lot, and I learned a lot about people as well as myself" are so general that the person who made the comments will soon forget what specifically was meaningful about the group experience. When someone makes this kind of sweeping statement, you can help the person express his or her thoughts and feelings more concretely by asking these questions: "How has the group been good for you? In what sense have you grown a lot? What do you mean by 'great'? What are some of the things you actually learned about others and yourself?" Emphasizing the importance of being specific, helping members to conceptualize, and encouraging the open expression of feelings about endings and the meaning of the group can increase the chances that members will retain and use what they have learned. If members have kept up their writing about their group experience in their journal, they often have an excellent basis for assessing the impact of the group as a factor in bringing about significant change. During the final stage, I suggest that members of my groups write about most of the topics that are addressed in this section.

Giving and Receiving Feedback   Giving and receiving feedback are crucial during the final phase. Although members of an effective group have been sharing their perceptions and feelings at each session, the opportunity to give and receive summary feedback has a value of its own. To help participants take advantage of this opportunity, during one of the last few sessions I generally ask members to give a brief summary of how they have perceived themselves in the group, what conflicts have become clearer, what the turning points were, what they expect to do with what they have learned, and what the group has meant to them. Then the others in the group say how they have perceived and felt about that person. I have found that concise and concrete feedback that also relates to the hopes and fears that the person has expressed is most valuable. Vague comments such as "I think you're a neat person" are of little long-term value. It is useful to ask members to write down specific feedback in their journals. If they do not record some of the things that people say to them, they tend to forget quickly. If they make a record, months later they can look at what others told them to determine if they are progressing toward their goals.

Completing Unfinished Business   Time should be allotted for working through any unfinished business relating to transactions between members or to the group process and goals, yet addressing unfinished business should not be done at the very last session. Even if some issues cannot be resolved, members should be encouraged to talk about them. For example, a member who has been silent throughout most of the group may say that she never felt safe enough to talk about her real concerns. Although it may be too late to work through this issue to everyone's satisfaction, it is still important to look at this statement rather than completely ignoring it.

Summary of the Final Stage

Stage Characteristics   During the final phase of a group, the following characteristics are typically evident:

- There may be some sadness and anxiety over the reality of separation.
- Members are likely to pull back and participate in less intense ways in anticipation of the ending of the group.
- Members are deciding what courses of action they are likely to take.
- Members may express their hopes and concerns for one another and tell one another how they were experienced.
- There may be talk about follow-up meetings or some plan for accountability so that members will be encouraged to carry out their plans for change.

Member Functions and Possible Problems   The major task facing members during the final stage of a group is consolidating their learning and transferring what they have learned to their outside environment. Of course, they have probably been doing this to some extent between sessions if the group has been meeting on a weekly basis. This is the time for members to review the process and outcomes of the entire group and put into some cognitive framework the meaning of the group experience. After their group has ended, the members' main functions are to continue applying what they have learned to an action program in their daily lives and to attend a follow-up group session (if appropriate). Here are some of the tasks for members at this time:

- Deal with their feelings and thoughts about separation and termination.
- Complete any unfinished business, either issues they have brought into the group or issues that pertain to people in the group.
- Make decisions and plans concerning ways they can generalize what they have learned to everyday situations.
- Identify ways of reinforcing themselves so that they will continue to grow.
- Explore ways of constructively meeting any setbacks after termination of a group.
- Evaluate the impact of the group experience.

    Some problems can occur at this time:

- Members may avoid reviewing their experience and fail to put it into some cognitive framework, thus limiting the generalization of their learning.
- Due to separation anxiety, members may distance themselves.
- Members may consider the group an end in itself and not use it as a way of continuing to grow.

Leader Functions   The group leader's central tasks in the consolidation phase are to provide a structure that enables participants to clarify the meaning of their experiences in the group and to assist members in generalizing their learning from the group to everyday situations. The leader should focus on these tasks:

- Reinforce changes members have made and ensure that members have information about resources to enable them to make further changes.
- Assist members in determining how they will apply specific skills in a variety of situations in daily life, including helping them to develop specific contracts aimed at change.
- Assist participants to develop a conceptual framework that will help them understand, integrate, consolidate, and remember what they have learned in the group.

Stage 6: Postgroup Issues—Evaluation and Follow-Up

Just as the formation of a group and the leader's preparatory activities greatly affect the group's progress through its various stages, the work of the leader once the group has come to an end is also highly important. The last session of the group is not a signal that the leader's job is finished, for there are important considerations after termination. Two issues are dynamically related to the successful completion of a group's development: evaluation and follow-up.

What is the group leader's responsibility in evaluating the outcomes of a group? How can the leader help members evaluate the effectiveness of their group experience? What kind of follow-up should be provided after the termination of a group? What are the ethical considerations in evaluating a group and arranging for follow-up procedures?

Part of effective practice entails developing strategies to ensure continuing assessment and designing follow-up procedures for a group. Here are the ASGW's (1998) "Best Practice Guidelines" of procedures to keep in mind when conducting evaluation and follow-up of groups:

- Group Workers process the workings of the group with themselves, group members, supervisors or other colleagues, as appropriate. This may include assessing progress on group and member goals, leader behaviors and techniques, group dynamics and interventions, as well as developing understanding and acceptance of meaning. Processing may occur both within sessions and before and after each session, at time of termination, and later follow-up, as appropriate. (C.1.)
- Group Workers attend to opportunities to synthesize theory and practice and to incorporate learning outcomes into ongoing groups. Group Workers attend to session dynamics of members and their interactions and also attend to the relationship between session dynamics and leader values, cognition and affect. (C.2.)
- Group Workers evaluate process and outcomes. Results are used for ongoing program planning, improvement and revisions of current group and/or to contribute to professional research literature. Group Workers follow all applicable policies and standards in using group material for research and reports. (C.3.a.)
- Group Workers conduct follow-up contact with group members, as appropriate, to assess outcomes or when requested by a group member(s). (C.3.b.)

Evaluating the Process and Outcomes of a Group

Evaluation is a basic aspect of any group experience, and it can benefit both members and the leader. Ethical practice requires a realistic assessment of the learning that has occurred. Evaluation is not a procedure to use only at the termination of a group. It should be an ongoing process throughout the life of a group—or at least at important turning points in the group—that tracks the progress of individual members and the group as a whole. Fuhriman and Burlingame (1998) identify both methods and measures of evaluating group process and outcomes. The chapters in this edited volume deal with conceptual and methodological foundations of group counseling and offer useful evaluation methods for group counseling and for psychotherapy groups. Another resource for a review and analysis of process and outcome measures of group work is DeLucia-Waack (1997).

In many agencies, group counselors are required to use objective measures as a means of demonstrating the effectiveness of a group. Standardized instruments can assess individual changes in attitudes and values. Some type of rating scale can also be devised to give the leader a good sense of how each member experienced and evaluated the group. Such practical evaluation instruments can help members make a personal assessment of the group and can also help the leader know what interventions were more, or less, helpful. A willingness to build evaluation into the structure of the group is bound to result in improving the design of future groups.

Writing done by members about the group experience is a very useful basis for subjectively evaluating the meaning of a group experience. Generally, I ask people before they enter a group to put down in writing what their concerns are and what they expect from the group. I strongly encourage members to keep an ongoing journal of their experiences in the group and in their everyday lives between sessions. This writing process helps participants focus on relevant trends and on the key things they are discovering about themselves and others through group interaction. Journal writing gives participants a chance to recall significant occurrences in the group and helps them identify what specifically they liked most and least about the group. The writing process is a useful tool for self-evaluation and is in itself therapeutic. As Riordan and White (1996) have pointed out, the journals kept by members not only act as a therapeutic tool that often makes the group experience a richer one but provide leaders with valuable feedback about the group. This is a useful source of evaluation of the group process from the members' perspective. Of course, any feedback the leader can offer members in their journals can help them consolidate significant learnings.

Finally, I often ask members to fill out a brief questionnaire when we come together for the postgroup meeting. The members evaluate the techniques used, the group leader, the impact of the group on them, and the degree to which they think they have changed because of their participation in the group. These questions are designed to get information on key matters:

- Did the group have any negative effects on you?
- How has the group influenced you in relation to others?
- Have your changes been lasting so far?

The questionnaire is a good way to get members focused before the exchange of reactions that occurs in the follow-up session. It also provides useful data for evaluating the group. If the group was co-led, it is important that the co-leaders make time to meet to discuss what they can learn from the members' evaluations and to make revisions and plans for future groups.

The Follow-Up Group Session

It is wise at the final session of a group to decide on a time for a follow-up session to discuss the group experience and put it in perspective. This session is valuable not only because it offers the group leader an opportunity to assess the outcomes of the group but also because it gives members the chance to gain a more realistic picture of the impact the group has had on them and their peers.

At the follow-up session members can discuss the efforts they have made since termination of the group to implement their learnings in the real world. They can report on the difficulties they have encountered, share the joys and successes they have experienced in life, and recall some of the things that occurred in the group. A follow-up session also provides people with the opportunity to express and work through any afterthoughts or feelings connected with the group experience. At this time the mutual giving of feedback and support is extremely valuable. It is also a good time to assist members in locating specific referral resources for further growth once the group ends. All members can be encouraged to find some avenues of continued support and challenge so that the ending of the group can mark the beginning of a search for self-understanding.

The element of accountability that a follow-up session encourages maximizes the chances of long-lasting benefits from the group experience. Many people have reported that simply knowing that they would be coming together as a group one, two, or three months after the group's termination and that they would be giving a self-report provided the stimulus they needed to stick with their commitments. Finally, the follow-up session offers leaders another opportunity to remind participants that they are responsible for what they become and that if they hope to change their situation they must take active steps to do so.

Individual Follow-Up Sessions

Besides the group follow-up, I endorse the idea of leaders' arranging for a one-to-one follow-up session with each member, if it is practical. If you administered any pretests to assess beliefs, values, attitudes, and levels of personal adjustment before the group sessions began, it is a good idea to administer some of these same instruments during one of the final sessions for comparison purposes. When you meet with members on an individual basis at the follow-up session to review how well they have accomplished their personal goals, these assessment devices can be of value in discussing specific changes in attitudes and behaviors.

These individual interviews after the termination of a group, which may last only 20 minutes, help the leader determine the degree to which members have accomplished their goals. Members may reveal reactions in the individual session that they would not share with the entire group. Also, this one-to-one contact tells the participants that the leader is concerned and does care. The individual interview provides an ideal opportunity to discuss referral sources and the possible need for further professional involvement—matters that are probably best handled individually.

Although it is ideal to conduct individual follow-up sessions, I realize that this may not be practical in some settings. In a community mental health clinic, for example, it might be difficult to arrange for this kind of follow-up. One option is a telephone call.

Concluding Comments

I have mentioned more than once that the stages in the life of a group do not generally flow neatly and predictably in the order described in the last two chapters. In actuality there is considerable overlap between stages, and once a group moves to an advanced stage of development there may be temporary regressions to earlier developmental stages.

However, knowledge of the major tasks that commonly confront participants and leader during the different stages of the group's evolution allows you to intervene at the right time and with a clear purpose. Having a clear grasp of typical stages of group development gives you a conceptual map from which to operate. Knowledge of the group's critical turning points enables you to assist the members in mobilizing their resources to successfully meet the demands facing them as their group progresses. Knowledge of the typical pattern of groups gives you an overall perspective that enables you to determine which interventions might be more useful at a particular time. Also, this perspective allows you to predict and prepare for certain crises in the life of the group and to manage them more effectively.

Chapter 17 describes a real group as it progresses from the initial through the final stages of development. I highly recommend that you read Chapter 17 now, prior to delving into the survey of theories contained in Part Two. Rereading Chapter 17 after you have completed Part Two will then provide a good way for you to pull all the theories together.

References and Suggested Readings for Part One

American Counseling Association. (1995). *Code of ethics and standards of practice*. Alexandria, VA: Author.

Anderson, R. D., & Price, G. E. (2001). Experiential groups in counselor education: Student attitudes and instructor participation. *Counselor Education and Supervision, 41*(2), 111–119.

Arredondo, P., Toporek, R., Brown, S., Jones, J., Locke, D., Sanchez, J., & Stadler, H. (1996). Operationalization of multicultural counseling competencies. *Journal of Multicultural Counseling and Development, 24*(1), 42–78.

Association for Specialists in Group Work. (1998). Best practice guidelines. *The Group Worker, 28*(3),1–5. [Special insert]

Association for Specialists in Group Work. (1999). Principles for diversity competent group workers. *The Group Worker, 28*(3), 1–6. [Special insert]

Association for Specialists in Group Work. (2000). Professional standards for the training of group workers. *The Group Worker, 28*(3), 1–10. [Special insert]

Atkinson, D. R., Morten, G., & Sue, D. W. (1998). *Counseling American minorities: A cross-cultural perspective* (5th ed.). Boston, MA: McGraw-Hill.

Atkinson, D. R., Thompson, E. E., & Grant, S. K. (1993). A three-dimensional model for counseling racial/ethnic minorities. *The Counseling Psychologist, 21*(2), 257–277.

Bednar, R. L., Corey, G., Evans, N. J., Gazda, G. M., Pistole, M. C., Stockton, R., & Robison, F. F. (1987). Overcoming obstacles to the future development of research on group work. *Journal for Specialists in Group Work, 12*(3), 98–111.

Bednar, R. L., & Kaul, T. J. (1994). Experiential group research: Can the cannon fire? In A. E. Bergin & S. L. Garfield (Eds.), *Handbook of psychotherapy and behavior change* (pp. 631–663). New York: Wiley.

Bemak, F., & Epp, L. R. (1996). The 12th curative factor: Love as an agent of healing in group psychotherapy. *Journal for Specialists in Group Work, 21*(2), 118–127.

Borkman, T. J. (1991). Introduction to the special issue. *American Journal of Community Psychology, 19*(5), 643–650.

Bowman, V. E., & DeLucia, J. L. (1993). Preparation for group therapy: The effects of preparer and modality on group process and individual functioning. *Journal for Specialists in Group Work, 18*(2), 67–79.

Brabender, V. (2002). *Introduction to group therapy*. New York: Wiley.

Budman, S. H., Simeone, P. G., Reilly, R., & Demby, A. (1994). Progress in short-term and time-limited group psychotherapy: Evidence and implications. In A. Fuhriman & G. Burlingame (Eds.), *Handbook of group psychotherapy: An empirical and clinical synthesis* (pp. 319–339). New York: Wiley.

Chen, M., & Han, Y. S. (2001). Cross-cultural group counseling with Asians: A stage-specific interactive approach. *Journal for Specialists in Group Work, 26*(2), 111–128.

Chu, J., & Sue, S. (1984). Asian/Pacific-Americans and group practice. In L. E. Davis (Ed.), *Ethnicity in social group work practice* (pp. 23–35). New York: Haworth Press.

Comas-Diaz, L. (1990). Hispanic/Latino communities: Psychological implications. *Journal of Training and Practice in Professional Psychology, 4*(1), 14–35.

Comas-Diaz, L. (1992). The future of psychotherapy with ethnic minorities. *Psychotherapy, 29*(1), 88–94.

Conyne, R. K. (1996). The Association for Specialists in Group Work Training Standards: Some considerations and suggestions for training. *Journal for Specialists in Group Work, 21*(3), 155–162.

Conyne, R. K. (1999). *Failures in group work: How we can learn from our mistakes.* Thousand Oaks, CA: Sage.

Conyne, R. K., & Wilson, F. R. (1998). Toward a standards-based classification of group work offerings. *Journal for Specialists in Group Work, 23*(2), 117–184.

Conyne, R. K., Wilson, F. R., & Ward, D. E. (1997). *Comprehensive group work: What it means and how to teach it.* Alexandria, VA: American Counseling Association.

Corey, G. (2004). *Student manual for theory and practice of group counseling* (6th ed.). Pacific Grove, CA: Brooks/Cole.

Corey, G., & Corey, M. (2002). *I never knew I had a choice* (7th ed.). Pacific Grove, CA: Brooks/Cole.

Corey, G., Corey, M., & Callanan, P. (2003). *Issues and ethics in the helping professions* (6th ed.). Pacific Grove, CA: Brooks/Cole.

Corey, G., Corey, M., Callanan, P., & Russell, J. M. (2004). *Group techniques* (3rd ed.). Pacific Grove, CA: Brooks/Cole.

Corey, G., Corey, M., & Haynes, R. (2000). *Student video and workbook for the evolution of a group.* Pacific Grove, CA: Brooks/Cole.

Corey, G., Corey, M., & Haynes, R. (2003). *Ethics in action* (CD-ROM). Pacific Grove, CA: Brooks/Cole.

Corey, G., Ellis, A., & Cooker, P. (1998). Challenging the internal dialogue of group counselors. *Journal of the Mississippi Counseling Association, 6*(1), 36–44.

Corey, M., & Corey, G. (1986). Experiential/didactic training and supervision workshop for group leaders. *Journal of Counseling and Human Service Professions, 1*(1), 18–26.

Corey, M., & Corey, G. (1993). Difficult group members—difficult group leaders. *New York State Journal for Counseling and Development, 8*(2), 9–24.

Corey, M., & Corey, G. (2002). *Groups: Process and practice* (6th ed.). Pacific Grove, CA: Brooks/Cole.

Corey, M., & Corey, G. (2003). *Becoming a helper* (4th ed.). Pacific Grove, CA: Brooks/Cole.

Couch, R. D., & Childers, J. H. (1987). Leadership strategies for instilling and maintaining hope in group counseling. *Journal for Specialists in Group Work, 12*(4), 138–143.

DeLucia-Waack, J. L. (1996). Multiculturalism is inherent in all group work. *Journal for Specialists in Group Work, 21*(4), 218–223.

DeLucia-Waack, J. L. (1997). Measuring the effectiveness of group work: A review and analysis of process and outcome measures. *Journal for Specialists in Group Work, 22*(4), 277–293.

Dies, R. R. (1983a). Bridging the gap between research and practice in group psychotherapy. In R. R. Dies & K. R. MacKenzie (Eds.), *Advances in group psychotherapy: Integrating research and practice* (pp. 1–16). New York: International Universities Press.

Dies, R. R. (1983b). Clinical implications of research on leadership in short-term group psychotherapy. In R. R. Dies & K. R. MacKenzie (Eds.), *Advances in group psychotherapy: Integrating research and practice* (pp. 27–78). New York: International Universities Press.

Dies, R. R. (1992). The future of group therapy. *Psychotherapy, 29*(1), 58–64.

Donigian, J., & Hulse-Killacky, D. (1999). *Critical incidents in group therapy* (2nd ed.). Pacific Grove, CA: Brooks/Cole.

Earley, J. (2000). *Interactive group therapy: Integrating interpersonal, action-oriented, and psychodynamic approaches.* Philadelphia, PA: Brunner/Mazel (Taylor & Francis Group).

Forester-Miller, H., & Duncan, J. A. (1990). The ethics of dual relationships in the training of group counselors. *Journal for Specialists in Group Work, 15*(2), 88–93.

Fuhriman, A., & Burlingame, G. (Eds.) (1998). *Handbook of group psychotherapy: An empirical and clinical synthesis.* New York: Wiley.

Fukuyama, M. A. (1990). Taking a universal approach to multicultural counseling. *Counselor Education and Supervision, 30*(1), 6–17.

Gazda, G. M., Ginter, E. J., & Horne, A. M. (2001). *Group counseling and group psychotherapy: Theory and application.* Boston: Allyn & Bacon.

Gladding, S. (2003). *Group work: A counseling specialty* (4th ed.). Upper Saddle River, NJ: Prentic-Hall.

Herlihy, B., & Corey, G. (1996). *ACA ethical standards casebook* (5th ed.). Alexandria, VA: American Counseling Association.

Herlihy, B., & Corey, G. (1997). *Boundary issues in counseling: Multiple roles and relationships.* Alexandria, VA: American Counseling Association.

Ho, M. K. (1984). Social group work with Asian/Pacific-Americans. In L. E. Davis (Ed.), *Ethnicity in social group work practice* (pp. 49–61). New York: Haworth Press.

Horne, A. M., & Rosenthal, R. (1997). Research in group work: How did we get where we are? *Journal for Specialists in Group Work, 22*(4), 228–240.

Ivey, A. E. (1995). Psychotherapy as liberation: Toward specific skills and strategies in multicultural counseling and therapy. In J. G. Ponterotto, J. M. Casas, L. A. Suzuki, & C. M. Alexander (Eds.), *Handbook of multicultural counseling* (pp. 53–72). Newbury Park, CA: Sage.

Ivey, A. E., Pedersen, P. B., & Ivey, M. B. (2001). *Intentional group counseling: A microskills approach.* Pacific Grove, CA: Brooks/Cole.

Jacobs, E., Masson, R. L., & Harvill, R. L. (2002). *Group counseling: Strategies and skills* (4th ed.). Pacific Grove, CA: Brooks/Cole.

Juntunen, C. L., Cohen, B. B., & Wolszon, L. R. (1997). Women and anger: A structured group. *Journal for Specialists in Group Work, 22*(2), 97–110.

Kalodner, C. R., & Riva, M. T. (1997). Group research: Encouraging a collaboration between practitioners and researchers—A conclusion. *Journal for Specialists in Group Work, 22*(4), 297.

Katz, A. H. (1981). Self-help and mutual aid: An emerging social movement? *American Review of Sociology, 7,* 129–155.

Klein, R., Brabender, V., & Fallon, A. (1994). Inpatient group therapy. In A. Fuhriman & G. Burlingame (Eds.), *Handbook of group psychotherapy: An empirical and clinical synthesis* (pp. 370–415). New York: Wiley.

Kline, W. B., Falbaum, D. F., Pope, V. T., Hargraves, G. A., & Hundley, S. F. (1997). The significance of the group experience for students in counselor education: A preliminary naturalistic inquiry. *Journal for Specialists in Group Work, 22*(3), 157–166.

Kottler, J. A. (2001). *Learning group leadership: An experiential approach.* Boston: Allyn & Bacon.

LaFountain, R. M., & Garner, N. E. (1996). Solution-focused counseling groups: The results are in. *Journal for Specialists in Group Work, 21*(2), 128–143.

Lee, P. C., Juan, G., & Hom, A. B. (1984). Group work practice with Asian clients: A sociocultural approach. In L. E. Davis (Ed.), *Ethnicity in social group work practice* (pp. 37–47). New York: Haworth Press.

Leong, F. T. L. (1992). Guidelines for minimizing premature termination among Asian American clients in group counseling. *Journal for Specialists in Group Work, 17*(4), 218–228.

Leong, F. T. L., & Kim, H. H. W. (1991). Going beyond cultural sensitivity on the road to multiculturalism: Using the intercultural sensitizer as a counselor training tool. *Journal of Counseling and Development, 70,* 112–118.

Locke, D. C. (1990). A not so provincial view of multicultural counseling. *Counselor Education and Supervision, 30*(1), 18–25.

MacKenzie, K. R. (1994). Where is here and when is now? The adaptational challenge of mental health reform for group psychotherapy. *International Journal of Group Psychotherapy, 44,* 407–428.

McManus, P. W., Redford, J. L., & Hughes, R. B. (1997). Connecting to self and others: A structured group for women. *Journal for Specialists in Group Work, 22*(1), 22–30.

Meissen, G. J., Mason, W. C., & Gleason, D. F. (1991). Understanding the attitudes and intentions of future professionals toward self-help. *American Journal of Community Psychology, 19*(5), 699–714.

Merta, R. J. (1995). Group work: Multicultural perspectives. In J. G. Ponterotto, J. M. Casas, L. A. Suzuki, & C. M. Alexander (Eds.), *Handbook of multicultural counseling* (pp. 567–585). Newbury Park, CA: Sage.

Merta, R. J., Johnson, P., & McNeil, K. (1995). Updated research on group work: Educators, course work, theory, and teaching methods. *Journal for Specialists in Group Work, 20*(3), 132–142.

Merta, R. J., & Sisson, J. A. (1991). The experiential group: An ethical and professional dilemma. *Journal for Specialists in Group Work, 16*(4), 236–245.

Merta, R. J., Wolfgang, L., & McNeil, K. (1993). Five models for using the experiential group in the preparation of group counselors. *Journal for Specialists in Group Work, 18*(4), 200–207.

Mokuau, N. (1985). Counseling Pacific Islander-Americans. In P. Pedersen (Ed.), *Handbook of cross-cultural counseling and therapy* (pp. 147–155). Westport, CT: Greenwood Press.

Mokuau, N. (1987). Social workers' perceptions of counseling effectiveness for Asian American clients. *Journal of the National Association of Social Workers, 32*(4), 331–335.

Morran, D. K., Robison, F. F., & Stockton, R. (1985). Feedback exchange in counseling groups: An analysis of message content and receiver acceptance as a function of leader versus member delivery, session, and valence. *Journal of Counseling Psychology, 32,* 57–67.

Morran, D. K., & Stockton, R. (1980). Effect of self-concept on group member reception of positive and negative feedback. *Journal of Counseling Psychology, 27,* 260–267.

Morran, D. K., & Stockton, R. (1985). Perspectives on group research programs. *Journal of Specialists for Group Work, 10*(4), 186–191.

Morran, D. K., Stockton, R., & Bond, L. (1991). Delivery of positive and corrective feedback in counseling groups. *Journal of Counseling Psychology, 38*(4), 410–414.

Morran, D. K., Stockton, R., & Harris, M. (1991). Analysis of group leader and member feedback messages. *Journal of Group Psychotherapy, Psychodrama, and Sociometry, 43,* 126–135.

Nolan, E. (1978). Leadership interventions for promoting personal mastery. *Journal for Specialists in Group Work, 3*(3), 132–138.

Ormont, L. R. (1988). The leader's role in resolving resistances to intimacy in the group setting. *International Journal of Group Psychotherapy, 38*(1), 29–46.

Pack-Brown, S. P., Whittington-Clark, L. E., & Parker, W. M. (1998). *Images of me: A guide to group work with African-American women.* Boston: Allyn & Bacon.

Pate, R. H., & Bondi, A. M. (1992). Religious beliefs and practice: An integral aspect of multicultural awareness. *Counselor Education and Supervision, 32*(2), 108–115.

Pedersen, P. (1991). Multiculturalism as a generic approach to counseling. *Journal of Counseling and Development, 70*(1), 6–12.

Pedersen, P. (1997). Culture-centered counseling interventions: Striving for accuracy. Thousand Oaks, CA: Sage.

Pedersen, P. (2000). *A handbook for developing multicultural awareness* (3rd ed.). Alexandria, VA: American Counseling Association.

Pierce, K. A., & Baldwin, C. (1990). Participation versus privacy in the training of group counselors. *The Journal for Specialists in Group Work, 18*, 200–207.

Remley, T. (1992). A model for teaching a graduate course in group counseling. *Together: Association for Specialists in Group Work Newsletter, 20*(2), 10–11.

Riordan, R. J., & Beggs, M. S. (1987). Counselors and self-help groups. *Journal of Counseling and Development, 65*(8), 427–429.

Riordan, R. J., & Beggs, M. S. (1988). Some critical differences between self-help and therapy groups. *Journal for Specialists in Group Work, 3*(1), 24–29.

Riordan, R. J., & White J. (1996). Logs as therapeutic adjuncts in group. *Journal for Specialists in Group Work, 21*(2), 94–100.

Riva, M. T., & Kalodner, C. R. (1997). Group research: Encouraging a collaboration between practitioners and researchers. *Journal for Specialists in Group Work, 22*(4), 226–227.

Riva, M. T., & Smith, R. D. (1997). Looking into the future of group research: Where do we go from here? *Journal for Specialists in Group Work, 22*(4), 266–276.

Robison, F. F., Stockton, R., & Morran, D. K. (1990). Anticipated consequences of self-disclosure during early therapeutic group development. *Journal of Group Psychotherapy, Psychodrama, and Sociometry, 43*(1), 3–18.

Rohde, R., & Stockton, R. (1992). The effect of structured feedback on goal attainment, attraction to the group, and satisfaction with the group in small group counseling. *Journal of Group Psychotherapy, Psychodrama, and Sociometry, 44*(4), 172–180.

Rosenberg, S., & Wright, P. (1997). Brief group psychotherapy and managed mental health care. In R. M. Alperin & D. G. Phillips (Eds.), *The impact of managed care on the practice of psychotherapy: Innovation, implementation, and controversy* (pp. 105–119). New York: Brunner/Mazel.

Rosenberg, S., & Zimet, C. (1995). Brief group treatment and managed mental health care. *International Journal of Group Psychotherapy, 45*, 367–379.

Schubert, M. A., & Borkman, T. J. (1991). An organizational typology for self-help groups. *American Journal of Community Psychology, 19*(5), 769–787.

Shapiro, J. L., Peltz, L. S., & Bernadett-Shapiro, S. (1998). *Brief group treatment: Practical training for therapists and counselors.* Pacific Grove, CA: Brooks/Cole.

Sklare, G., Thomas, D. V., Williams, E. C., & Powers, K. A. (1996). Ethics and an experiential "here and now" group: A blend that works. *Journal for Specialists in Group Work, 21*(4), 263–273.

Stockton, R., & Morran, D. K. (1980). The use of verbal feedback in counseling groups: Toward an effective system. *Journal for Specialists in Group Work, 5*, 10–14.

Stockton, R., & Morran, D. K. (1981). Feedback exchange in personal growth groups: Receiver acceptance as a function of valence, session, and order of delivery. *Journal of Counseling Psychology, 28*, 490–497.

Stockton, R., & Morran, D. K. (1982). Review and perspective of critical dimensions in therapeutic small group research. In G. M. Gazda (Ed.), *Basic approaches to group psychotherapy and group counseling* (3rd ed., pp. 37–85). Springfield, IL: Charles C Thomas.

Stockton, R., & Toth, P. L. (1997). Applying a general research training model to group work. *Journal for Specialists in Group Work, 22*(4), 241–252.

Sue, D., & Sue, D. W. (1993). Ethnic identity: Cultural factors in the psychological development of Asians in America. In D. R. Atkinson, G. Morten, & D. W. Sue (Eds.), *Counseling American minorities: A cross-cultural perspective* (pp. 199–210). Madison, WI: Brown & Benchmark.

Sue, D. W. (1992). The challenge of multiculturalism: The road less traveled. *American Counselor, 1*(1), 6–14.

Sue, D. W. & colleagues. (1998). *Multicultural counseling competencies: Individual and organizational development.* Thousand Oaks, CA: Sage.

Sue, D. W., Arredondo, P., & McDavis, R. J. (1992). Multicultural counseling competencies and standards: A call to the profession. *Journal of Counseling and Development, 70*(4), 477–486.

Sue, D. W., Ivey, A. E., & Pedersen, P. (1996). *A theory of multicultural counseling and therapy.* Pacific Grove, CA: Brooks/Cole.

Sue, D. W., & Sue, D. (2003). *Counseling the culturally diverse: Theory and practice* (4th ed.). New York: Wiley.

Toseland, R. W., & Rivas, R. F. (2001). *An introduction to group work practice* (4th ed.). Boston: Allyn & Bacon.

Vontress, C. E. (1995). The breakdown of authority: Implications for counseling young African American males. In J. G. Ponterotto, J. M. Casas, L. A. Suzuki, & C. M. Alexander (Eds.), *Handbook of multicultural counseling* (pp. 457–473). Newbury Park, CA: Sage.

Vontress, C. E. (1996). A personal retrospective on cross-cultural counseling. *Journal of Multicultural Counseling and Development, 24*(3), 156–166.

White, J. R., & Freeman, A. (Eds.) (2000). *Cognitive-behavioral group therapy for specific problems and populations.* Washington, DC: American Psychological Association.

Wrenn, C. G. (1985). Afterward: The culturally encapsulated counselor revisited. In P. Pedersen (Ed.), *Handbook of cross-cultural counseling and therapy* (pp. 323–329). Westport, CT: Greenwood Press.

Yalom, I. D. (1983). *Inpatient group psychotherapy.* New York: Basic Books.

Yalom, I. D. (1995). *The theory and practice of group psychotherapy* (4th ed.). New York: Basic Books.

PART II

THEORETICAL APPROACHES TO GROUP COUNSELING

CHAPTER 6

The Psychoanalytic Approach to Groups

Introduction

Psychoanalytic theory has influenced most of the other models of group work presented in this textbook. Some of these other approaches are extensions of the analytic model, some are modifications of analytic concepts and procedures, and some have emerged as a reaction against psychoanalysis. It is fair to say that most theories of group counseling have borrowed concepts and techniques from psychoanalysis. As a group counselor, you may have neither the training nor the motivation to conduct analytic groups. However, even if you may not use psychoanalytic *techniques*, the basic psychoanalytic *concepts* can become an integral part of your own theoretical approach.

This chapter includes an overview of the psychoanalytic and psychosocial perspectives, a brief introduction to contemporary trends in psychoanalytic thinking, and the stages of development in an individual's life. Sigmund Freud made significant contributions to our understanding of the individual's *psychosexual development* during early childhood. However, he wrote little about the *psychosocial* influences on human development beyond childhood. Therefore, I have given special emphasis to Erik Erikson's (1963, 1982) psychosocial perspective, which provides a comprehensive framework for understanding the individual's basic concerns at each stage of life from infancy through old age. Erikson can be considered a psychoanalyst as well as an ego psychologist; he built on Freudian concepts by continuing the story of human development where Freud left off.

The person credited with first applying psychoanalytic principles and techniques to groups is Alexander Wolf, a psychiatrist and psychoanalyst. He began working with groups in 1938 because he did not want to turn away patients who needed but could not afford intensive individual therapy. His experiences increased his interest in this approach, and he made it his primary mode of therapy.

Goal of the Analytic Group

The goal of the analytic process is restructuring the client's character and personality system. This goal is achieved by making unconscious conflicts conscious and examining them. Specifically, psychoanalytic groups reenact the family of origin in a symbolic way via the group so that the historical past of each group member is repeated in the group's presence. Wolf (1963, 1975) developed group applications of basic psychoanalytic techniques such as working with transference, free association, dreams, and the historical determinants of present behavior. He stresses the re-creation of the original family, which allows members to work through their unresolved problems in the group. Their reactions to fellow members and to the leader are assumed to reveal symbolic clues to the dynamics of their relationships with significant figures from their family of origin. Although these reactions are taken from the here-and-now, there is a constant focus on tracing them back to the early history of the members (Tuttman, 1986). Wolf's approach is aimed at a controlled and systematic regression of the personality in the service of strengthening the ego.

Mullan and Rosenbaum (1978) speak of the process of re-creating one's family as the *regressive-reconstructive* approach to psychoanalytic group therapy. This term refers to a regression into each member's past to achieve the therapeutic goal of personality reconstruction, which is characterized by social awareness and the ability to be creatively involved in life. The group in many respects duplicates the original family. The group leader applies understanding to the family-like connections that arise among the members and between the members and the therapist. The leader imposes a minimum of structure, and the group, like a family, is heterogeneous. Members reexperience conflicts that originated in the family context.

Key Concepts

Influence of the Past

Psychoanalytic work focuses on the influence of the past on current personality functioning. Experiences during the first six years of life are seen as the roots of one's conflicts in the present. When I consider typical problems that bring many clients to therapy groups, the following come to mind: inability to freely give and accept love; difficulty in recognizing and dealing with feelings such as anger, resentment, rage, hatred, and aggression; inability to direct one's own life and resolve dependence/independence conflicts; difficulty in separating from one's parents and becoming a unique person; need for and fear of intimacy; difficulty in accepting one's own sexual identity; and guilt over sexual feelings. According to the psychoanalytic view, these problems of adult living have their origin in early development. Early learning is not irreversible, but to change its effects one must become aware of how certain early experiences have contributed to one's present personality structure.

Although practitioners with a psychoanalytic orientation focus on the historical antecedents of current behavior, it is a mistake to assume that they dwell on the past to the exclusion of present concerns. A common misconception about psychoanalytic work is that it resembles an archaeologist digging up relics from the past. Modern analytically oriented practitioners are interested in their clients' past, but they intertwine that understanding with the present (DeAngelis, 1996). As Locke (1961) points out, psychoanalytic group work consists of "weaving back and forth between past and present, between present and past. . . . It is essential that the therapist move back and forth in time, trying always to recapture the past or to see the repetition in the present and to become aware of the early traumatic event which made for the neurotic pattern of the individual today" (pp. 30–31). Kernberg (1997) indicates that there is an increasing interest in contemporary psychoanalytic therapy to focus on the unconscious meanings in the here-and-now before attempting to reconstruct the past.

It is essential that participants understand and use historical data in their group work, but they also need to be aware of the pitfalls of getting lost in their past by recounting endless and irrelevant details of their early experiences. In the view of Wolf and Kutash (1986), the recital of yesterday's events can be uselessly time consuming and can inhibit progress. They see this use of history as essentially a form of resistance, and they suggest that talking about events in one's childhood is not as useful as dealing with the past in relation to here-and-now interactions within the group.

The Unconscious

The concept of the unconscious is one of Freud's most significant contributions and is the key to understanding his view of behavior and the problems of personality. The unconscious consists of those thoughts, feelings, motives, impulses, and events that are kept out of awareness of the conscious ego. Freud believed that most of human behavior is motivated by forces outside conscious experience. What we do in everyday life is frequently determined by these unconscious motives and needs. Painful experiences during early childhood and the feelings associated with them are buried in the unconscious. These early traumas are such that conscious awareness would cause intolerable anxiety to the child. The child's repression of them does not automatically lift with time, and the client reacts to threats to the repression as if the anxiety associated with the early events would still be intolerable if these were recalled. Thus, the "shadow of the past" haunts the present. But the trauma was intolerable only to the child; with an adult perspective on the world, the client can handle the memory with relative ease. The therapist helps make the unconscious conscious, and the client realizes that the anxiety is not intolerable. The client is thus helped to be free of the tyranny of past repressions.

Unconscious experiences have a powerful impact on our daily functioning. Indeed, Freud's theory holds that most of our "choices" are not freely made; rather, they are determined by forces within us of which we are unaware. Thus, we select mates to meet certain needs that may never have been satisfied; we select a job because of some unconscious motive; and we continually experience personal and interpersonal conflicts whose roots lie in unfinished experiences that are outside the realm of our awareness.

According to psychoanalytic theory, consciousness is only a small part of the human experience. Like the greater part of the iceberg that lies below the surface of the water, the larger part of human experience exists below the surface of awareness. The aim of psychoanalysis is to make the unconscious material conscious, for it is only when we become conscious of the motivations underlying our behavior that we can choose and become autonomous. The unconscious can be made more accessible to awareness by working with dreams, by using free-association methods, by learning about transference, by understanding the meaning of resistances, and by employing the process of interpretation. Analytic therapists move back and forth between reality and fantasy, the conscious and the unconscious, the rational and the nonlogical, and thought and feeling.

The concept of the unconscious has deep significance for analytic group therapy. In the psychoanalytic view, a group that ignores the role of the unconscious and focuses exclusively on conscious here-and-now interactions among participants is an encounter group more than a therapy group. Although it is true that exhaustive work with the unconscious determinants of behavior and personality reconstruction is beyond the scope of group counseling as it is generally practiced, group counselors should have an understanding of how unconscious processes operate. This understanding provides counselors with a conceptual framework that helps them make sense of group interactions, even if the unconscious is not directly dealt with by the members.

Anxiety

To appreciate the psychoanalytic model, one must understand the dynamics of anxiety. Anxiety is a feeling of dread and impending doom that results from repressed feelings, memories, desires, and experiences bubbling to the surface of awareness. It is triggered by something in the environment or within the individual. Anxiety stems from the threat of unconscious material breaking through the wall of repression. We experience anxiety when we sense that we are dealing with feelings that threaten to get out of our control. Anxiety is often "free-floating"; that is, it is vague and general, not yet having crystallized into specific form. The next section deals with the function of ego-defense mechanisms, which are an integral part of the individual's attempt to cope with anxiety.

Ego-Defense Mechanisms

The ego-defense mechanisms were first formulated by psychoanalytic theory as a way of explaining behavior. These defense mechanisms protect the ego from threatening thoughts and feelings. Conceptually, the ego is that part of the personality that performs various conscious functions, including keeping in contact with reality. When there is a threat to the ego, anxiety is experienced. Although we may be interested in the growth that comes from facing reality directly, we attempt to protect ourselves from experiencing anxiety. The ego defenses enable us to soften the blows that come with emotional wounding, and they are one way of maintaining a sense of personal adequacy. Although the ego defenses do involve self-deception and distortion of reality, they are not considered essentially pathological. It is only to the degree that they impair a person's ability to deal effectively with the tasks of life that their use becomes problematic. Even though these mechanisms are learned and become a habitual mode of defense against anxiety, they typically operate outside one's consciousness.

In a group situation there are many opportunities to observe a variety of defensive behaviors. In many cases the defenses that we used in childhood when we were threatened continue into adulthood and are activated when we feel threatened in the group. A main therapeutic value of a group is that, through feedback from the leader and the other members, clients can become increasingly aware of their defensive styles of interaction. With awareness, members are eventually able to choose direct forms of dealing with anxiety-producing situations as they emerge in a group.

Several common ego defenses are typically manifested in the pattern of interactions in the therapeutic group:

- *Repression* involves excluding from consciousness threatening or painful thoughts and desires. By pushing distressing thoughts or feelings into the unconscious, people manage the anxiety that grows out of situations involving guilt and conflict. If adults were physically or emotionally abused in childhood, they might well have blocked out the pain and anxiety associated with these traumatic events by pushing the memories into the unconscious. For example, adults may have no recollection of the details of incestuous events that occurred in early childhood. However, as other members experience a catharsis and work through the pain associated with recalled incest, a member who has repressed an incestuous experience may be emotionally triggered, and unconscious material may surface to awareness.

- *Denial* plays a defensive role similar to that of repression, yet it generally operates at the preconscious or conscious level. In denial there is an effort to suppress unpleasant reality. It consists of coping with anxiety by "closing our eyes" to the existence of anxiety-producing reality. In a therapy group members sometimes refuse to accept that they have any problems. They may attempt to deceive both themselves and others by saying that they have "worked on" certain problems and that they therefore no longer have any concerns to deal with in the group.

- *Regression* involves returning to a less mature developmental level. In the face of severe stress or crisis, we sometimes revert to old patterns that worked for us earlier. For instance, a man in a therapy group may retreat to childlike behaviors and become extremely frightened and dependent as he faces a crisis precipitated by his wife's decision to leave him.

- *Projection* involves attributing our own unacceptable thoughts, feelings, behaviors, and motives to others. In a group setting, members may be very able to see the faults of others. They may also attribute to other members certain feelings and motives that would lead them to feel guilty if they owned these feelings and motives themselves. Of course, groups offer many opportunities to view projection in action. Members who have difficulty accepting their aggressive or sexual feelings may see other group members as hostile or seductive. Group leaders should be aware, however, that members who do make inappropriate hostile or seductive comments often defend themselves by labeling as "projection" any negative feedback they receive in the group.

• *Displacement* entails a redirection of some emotion (such as anger) from a real source to a substitute person or object. Group members who are frustrated are likely to feel angry. If the leader confronts members for pouting or employing some other attention-seeking behaviors, for example, they may lash out in a hostile way toward some member who is relatively nonthreatening. Although their anger may be a result of a group leader's confrontation, they pick a safer target on whom to vent their hostility.

• *Reaction formation* involves behaving in a manner that is opposite to one's real feelings. It serves as a defense against anxiety that would result from accepting feelings that one is striving to disown. This defense is exhibited in a group by the woman who is "sugary sweet" yet really harbors many hostile feelings that she dares not express. It is also displayed by the man who tries to convince himself and others in his group that he does not care if others reject him, either in this group or at home (yet who underneath very much wants the acceptance of others). These behaviors cover up one's real feelings, for dealing with hostility or rejection would be painful. In these cases there is an exaggeration of being sweet or of being emotionally indifferent to rejection. The excessive quality of these behaviors is what makes them recognizable as a form of defense.

• *Rationalization* is a defense mechanism whereby we try to justify our behavior by imputing logical and admirable motives to it. Some people manufacture "good" reasons to explain away a bruised ego. This defense involves an attempt to minimize the severity of disappointment over losses or failures. In groups there are many opportunities to observe this behavioral pattern in action. Members may devote a great deal of energy to focusing on "others out there" as the source of their problems.

Everyone uses ego-defense mechanisms, and they have some adaptive value; nevertheless, their overuse can become problematic. It is true that self-deception can soften harsh reality, but the fact is that reality does not change through the process of distorting those aspects of it that produce anxiety. In the long run, when these defensive strategies do not work, the result is even greater anxiety. The group situation is ideal for enabling individuals to learn to recognize the indirect methods that they resort to when they feel emotionally threatened. To avoid judging such behavior, it is possible to work with members in therapeutic ways so that they can increase their tolerance for coping with anxiety and can learn direct ways of dealing with difficult interpersonal situations.

Resistance

In psychoanalytic therapy, resistance is defined as the individual's reluctance to bring into conscious awareness threatening unconscious material that has been previously repressed or denied. It can also be viewed as anything that prevents members from dealing with unconscious material and thus keeps the group from making progress. Resistance is the unconscious attempt to defend the self against the high degree of anxiety that the client fears would result if the material in the unconscious were uncovered. As Locke (1961) puts it, group members need to protect themselves against the "flooding of the conscious by the forbidden feeling, fantasy, or memory" (p. 72). Resistance is the "fight to maintain the defense"; thus, it is "the defense of the defense."

One method of therapeutically dealing with resistance is through free association, an uncensored and uninhibited flow of ideas produced by the client that offers clues about the person's unconscious conflicts. According to Wolf (1983) and Wolf and Schwartz (1962), resistances emerge with clarity as members continue to free-associate with one another and as old feelings recur in the present. When these defenses surface, they are observed, analyzed, and interpreted. Support offered by the group helps the person break through his or her defenses. Durkin (1964) stresses that resistance is a basic part of the analytic group, and she warns group leaders not to be surprised by or impatient with it. She also warns leaders not to view resistance, which is a natural phenomenon of all groups, as a sign of their own ineptness.

There are many kinds of resistances, some relating to apprehension about joining a group, some to participation in the group process, and some to the desire to leave the group (Locke, 1961). One common resistance stems from the belief that one cannot benefit from the group situation because help cannot come from people who are themselves in trouble. Wolf (1963) lists other sources of resistance in group members: fear that one's privacy will be invaded; need to "own" the therapist exclusively; fear of "meeting" again one's original family in the group—namely, recognizing one's parents or siblings in some of the participants—and having to deal with the anxiety produced by these encounters; unconscious fear of giving up neurotic trends; and anxiety about the freedom that a group offers, including the freedom to discuss anxiety.

Wolf also explores other forms of resistance that surface during the advanced stages of group analysis. Members may "go blank" when they are asked to free-associate about other group members, or they may escape personal exploration by simply watching others and refusing to participate. Some members hide behind the analysis of other members, and some engage in lengthy recitations of their life histories, thus avoiding the challenge of facing the present. Additional manifestations of resistance include these behaviors:

- Typically arriving late or not showing up at all
- Maintaining an attitude of complacency or indifference
- Hiding behind a wall of silence or talking incessantly
- Intellectualizing
- Exhibiting an exaggerated need to help others in the group
- Showing distrust
- Behaving uncooperatively
- Inappropriate or impulsive behavior, including comments or gestures offensive to any group members
- Using the group for mere socializing

These are by no means the only manifestations of resistive behavior; what they all have in common is the fear of recognizing and dealing with that part of oneself that is locked in the unconscious.

How do group analysts deal with resistance? Durkin (1964) maintains that to penetrate and work through resistances the therapist needs to enlist the co-operation of members. Therefore, he or she must start with the client's immediate problems as they are manifested through resistive behaviors. Durkin stresses the importance of dealing with disappointments and resentments; otherwise, members will become increasingly angry, less desirous of opening up, and more resistant. Thus, resistances are not just something to be overcome. Because they are valuable indications of the client's defenses against anxiety, they should be acknowledged and worked through by therapist and client together, with the clear understanding that they are both working toward the same ends. Generally, it is best to call attention to those manifestations of resistance that are most readily observable and to work with these behaviors first. In doing so, leaders should take care not to label or censure group members; unacceptable criticism will only increase resistive behaviors. It can also be useful to bring other group members into the analysis of individual member's resistances.

Transference

Transference is a basic concept of the psychoanalytic approach. It refers to the client's unconscious shifting to the therapist (or to other group members) of feelings, attitudes, and fantasies (both positive and negative) that stem from reactions to significant persons from the client's past. The key issue of transference is the distortion imposed on the therapeutic relationship by prior relationships, usually childhood ones. Analytic technique is designed to foster the client's transference. But the therapeutic setting, unlike the original situation, does not punish the person for experiencing or expressing these feelings. If a client perceives the therapist as a stern and rejecting father, he or she does not receive from the therapist the expected negative responses. Instead, the therapist accepts the client's feelings and helps the client understand them.

By reliving their past through the transference process, clients gain insight into the ways in which the past is obstructing present functioning. Insight is achieved by working through unresolved conflicts that keep the person fixated and that make full emotional growth impossible. Basically, the negative effects of painful early experiences are counteracted by working through similar conflicts in the therapeutic setting.

Transference also manifests itself in groups through the member's attempts to win the approval of the leader, and these attempts can be explored to find out whether they reflect the client's need for universal approval and how such a need governs the person's life. Remember that groups can provide a dynamic understanding of how people function in out-of-group situations.

Group therapy also offers the possibility of multiple transferences. In individual therapy, the client's projections are directed toward the therapist alone;

in group therapy, they are also directed toward other members. The group constellation provides rich possibilities for reenacting past unfinished events, especially when other members stimulate such intense feelings in an individual that he or she "sees" in them some significant figure such as a father, mother, sibling, spouse, ex-lover, or boss.

The element of rivalry that often exists in a group can also be valuable therapeutic material to explore. Group participants tend to compete for the attention of the leader—a situation reminiscent of earlier times when they had to vie for their parents' attention with their brothers and sisters. Thus, sibling rivalry can be explored in group as a way of gaining increased awareness of how the participants dealt with competition as children and how their past success or lack of it affects their present interactions with others.

The opportunity that psychoanalytic groups offer for multiple transferences is stressed by several authors. The group is a conducive milieu in which to relive significant past events because "the group of today becomes the family of yesterday" says Locke (1961, p. 102). Wolf (1963) and Wolf and Schwartz (1962) observe that group members serve as transference figures for other members and that the main work of the analytic group consists of identifying, analyzing, and resolving these projections onto family surrogates in the group. The leader has the task of helping members discover the degree to which they respond to others in the group as if they were their parents or siblings. By interpreting and working through their transferences, participants become increasingly aware of their fixations and deprivations and of the ways in which past events interfere with their ability to appraise and deal with reality.

Countertransference

From time to time the therapist's own feelings become entangled in the therapeutic relationship, obstructing or even destroying objectivity. According to psychoanalytic theory, countertransference consists of a therapist's unconscious emotional responses to a client, resulting in a distorted perception of the client's behavior. Wolf (1983) makes it clear that no analytic leader is totally free of involvement in transference or countertransference. Kutash and Wolf (1983) describe countertransference as the leader's "unconscious, involuntary, inappropriate, and temporarily gratifying response to the patient's transference demands" (p. 135). Vontress (1996) gives an example of countertransference involving minority counselors who expect their minority clients to feel the same way that they do about racial situations in society. It would not be therapeutic for the counselor to consciously or unconsciously judge the client by this expectation because each individual has learned to cope with his or her minority status differently.

To the degree that countertransference is present, group therapists react to members as if they were significant figures of their own original family. Group leaders need to be alert to signs of unresolved conflicts within themselves that could interfere with the effective functioning of a group and create a situation in which members are used to satisfy their own unfulfilled needs. If, for example, group leaders have an extreme need to be respected, valued, and confirmed, they can become overdependent on the members' approval and reinforcement. The result is that much of what they do is designed to please the group members and ensure their continued support. It is important to differentiate between appropriate emotional reactions and countertransference. Following are some manifestations of countertransference:

- Seeing oneself in certain clients and overidentifying with them to the point of becoming less able to work effectively with them
- Projecting onto clients some traits that one despises in oneself and regarding such clients as not amenable to treatment or impossible to work with
- Engaging in seductive behavior and taking advantage of the leader's role to win the special affection of certain group members

Group therapists' unresolved conflicts and repressed needs can seriously interfere with the group process and can lead them to abuse their position of leadership. The difficulty in recognizing one's own countertransference and the necessity that such reactions be acknowledged and therapeutically dealt with provide a rationale for group leaders to experience their own therapy. The analytic approach requires that therapists undergo psychoanalysis or analytic psychotherapy to become conscious of their own dynamics and of the ways in which these dynamics can obstruct therapeutic tasks.

Brabender (1987) states that countertransference can be an avenue for understanding the dynamics of a group, but she reminds us that group therapists are not immune to feelings of hate, envy, guilt, admiration, and love. Her position is that "the full experience and tolerance of all of these therapist feelings within the inpatient group enables group members to realize the richness of their humanity in relation to one another" (p. 566). It is essential that the therapist's feelings be conscious and self-acknowledged. Bemak and Epp (2001) identify five typical countertransference patterns that a group counselor may experience: (1) becoming emotionally withdrawn and remaining unavailable to the group; (2) passivity; (3) being overly controlling; (4) regressing to maladaptive behaviors based on one's own unresolved personal issues; and (5) being paternalistic and adopting a role as a rescuer. Brabender (1987) maintains that understanding and exploring a group therapist's countertransference is more important than his or her theoretical orientation. The resolution of countertransference is an essential skill that requires systematic reflection and exploration: "The group counselor's countertransference has the potential to be utilized as a powerful therapeutic force for the group and its leader, given good supervision and training" (Bemak & Epp, 2001, p. 310).

Based on their review of the literature on countertransference in group work and their experience in training group counselors, Bemak and Epp identify some important aspects of this issue for both groups and students:

- Countertransference is a phenomenon that group counselors commonly experience.
- Relatively little emphasis is given to learning about countertransference in graduate-level training and supervision of group counselors.

- Given the number of clients in a group, there is an increased opportunity and likelihood that group leaders will encounter countertransference.
- If group leaders are unaware of their unresolved personal issues and their emotional responses, it will be difficult for them to effectively facilitate a group.
- Understanding one's own countertransference leads to enhanced effectiveness in facilitating groups and adds to the potential richness of the group experience.
- Countertransference is often associated with a range of emotionally charged responses such as withdrawal, anger, love, hate, annoyance, powerlessness, avoidance, collusion, overidentification, control, and sadness.
- It is essential that graduate programs create a context that facilitates a critical self-analysis of countertransference by students.

Analysis of countertransference can be considered as a form of self-therapy that is essential for the personal and professional development of group counselors.

Role and Functions of the Group Leader

Leadership styles vary among psychoanalytically oriented group therapists, ranging from leaders characterized by objectivity, warm detachment, and relative anonymity to those who favor a role that is likely to result in a collaborative relationship with group members. If they remain more anonymous, some psychoanalytically oriented leaders believe members will project onto them more of their own images of what they expect leaders to be, images that are seen as expressions of the members' unconscious needs. Although such analysis of transference is still viewed as a hallmark of psychodynamic therapy, the model of the impersonal therapist is far from ideal and today "represents a serious and frequently noxious miscarriage of the therapeutic role" in the minds of many practitioners (Strupp, 1992, p. 23). Indeed, one of the most significant developments of psychoanalytically oriented therapy is the growing recognition of the central importance of the therapeutic relationship. In contrast to the classical model of the impersonal and detached analyst, the contemporary formulation places emphasis on the therapeutic alliance, a working relationship whereby the therapist "communicates commitment, caring, interest, respect, and human concern for the patient" (p. 23).

According to Strupp, the redefinition of the therapeutic climate in more personal terms does not prevent the emergence of transference. He maintains that transference and countertransference still remain the cornerstones of psychodynamic therapy. A central task of the leader is to work out and work through these transference reactions, toward the leader as well as other members, as they are manifested in the group. Exploring transference reactions should be done with care so as not to create resistance within the client. On this point Kernberg (1997) issues a warning: "Transference is to be handled like radioactive material, very responsibly, and with an awareness of how easily it can be misused" (p. 22).

As group interaction increases, the leader pursues participants' unconscious motivations and investigates the historical roots of these motivations through analysis and interpretation. In addition, the group leader also performs these functions:

- Gives support when support is therapeutic and the group is not providing it
- Helps members face and deal with resistances within themselves and in the group as a whole
- Attracts members' attention to the subtle aspects of behavior and, through questions, helps them explore themselves in greater depth

These additional functions and tasks of the leader are identified by Wolf (1963) and Wolf and Schwartz (1962):

- Makes efforts to acknowledge errors and is secure enough to transfer some leadership functions to the group
- Welcomes manifestations of transference in the group as opportunities for fruitful work
- Guides members toward full awareness and social integration
- Sees the group as a potentially powerful catalytic agent
- Employs the skills necessary to resolve intragroup conflict
- Sets the tone of emotional freedom by being open about one's own feelings
- Watches for destructive alliances within the group
- Notices if any group member is becoming an isolate or is otherwise being harmed rather than helped by the group

To carry out these many functions effectively, group leaders have the paramount obligation of understanding their own dynamics and countertransference throughout the therapeutic process. To do so, they may need consultation and occasional supervision. Their own personal therapy can be most valuable in helping them recognize signs of countertransference and ways in which their own needs and motivations influence their group work.

Application: Therapeutic Techniques and Procedures

The Therapeutic Process

The therapeutic process focuses on re-creating, analyzing, discussing, and interpreting past experiences and on working through defenses and resistances that operate at the unconscious level. (*Working through* is a psychoanalytic concept that refers to repetition of interpretations and overcoming of resistance, thus allowing the client to resolve dysfunctional patterns that originated in childhood and to make choices based on new insights.) Insight and intellectual understanding are important, but the feelings and memories associated with self-understanding are crucial. Because clients need to relive and reconstruct their past and work through repressed conflicts to understand how the unconscious affects them in the present, psychoanalytic group therapy is usually a long-term and intensive process.

Modern analytic practitioners are leaving behind the "detached-observer" model of classical psychoanalysis for a more intersubjective style called *relational analysis* (DeAngelis, 1996). All analytically oriented therapists consider the process of analyzing and interpreting transference feelings as the core of the therapeutic process, because it is aimed at achieving insight and personality change.

A group format that uses psychoanalytic concepts and techniques has some specific advantages over individual analysis:

- Members are able to establish relationships similar to those that existed in their own families; this time, however, the relationships occur in a group setting that is safe and conducive to favorable outcomes.
- Group participants have many opportunities to experience transference feelings toward other members and the leader; they can work through these feelings to increase their self-understanding.
- Participants can gain more dramatic insight into how their defenses and resistances work.
- Dependency on the authority of the therapist is not as great as in individual therapy because group members also get feedback from other members.
- From observing the work of others in a group, members learn that it is acceptable to have and to express intense feelings that they may have kept out of awareness.
- Members have many opportunities to learn about themselves and others, in fact and in fantasy, through interactions with peers as well as with the leader. The material for analysis is available not only in terms of historical recollection but also on the basis of interaction with fellow members.
- The group setting encourages members to examine their ego defenses. Resistance melts away in the atmosphere of mutual revelation and exploration in a group to a greater extent than is typically true of one-to-one therapy.
- Analysis in groups therapeutically works with a member's idealistic expectation of having an exclusive relationship with the therapist. The experience of supporting others and the discovery of universal struggles encourage a fuller range of responses than does individual therapy.
- Analytic group therapy provides a context for addressing contemporary social issues, including class, race, and cultural differences.

Exploring Anxiety in the Group Situation

How the group leader recognizes and deals with anxiety, both within the individual and within the group as a whole, is a key technique in the psychoanalytic group. Mullan and Rosenbaum (1978) view anxiety as a necessary part of regressive-reconstructive group therapy. Therapeutic regression involves re-experiencing primitive patterns associated with earlier developmental stages and is a necessary element of the analytic group process. In a sense, the members must take one step backward to advance therapeutically. This regression involves some dissolving of the members' ego defenses, which also results in an increase in their experience of anxiety. Thus, anxiety is not something to overcome; it is essential to recognize, understand, and explore the function that the defenses against it serve. Anxiety is a necessary by-product of taking risks in the group, a process that eventually leads to constructive changes.

Free Association

The basic tool for uncovering repressed or unconscious material is free association—communicating whatever comes to mind regardless of how painful, illogical, or irrelevant it may seem. Group members are expected to report feelings immediately, without trying to exercise censorship, and the group discussion is left open to whatever the participants may bring up rather than revolving around an established theme. Foulkes (1965) refers to this process as "free-floating discussion" or "free group association."

One adaptation of free association to groups is the "go-around technique," which uses free association to stimulate member interaction (Wolf, 1963). After a good rapport has developed in the conducive atmosphere fostered by sharing dreams and fantasies, members are encouraged to free-associate about each person in the group. Each participant goes around to each of the other members and says the first thing that comes to mind about that person. According to Wolf, the go-around method makes all the members adjunct therapists; that is, instead of remaining passive recipients of the leader's insights, the participants actively contribute to the interpretation of key meanings. Wolf (1963) contends that if group members say whatever comes into their heads about another "they will intuitively penetrate a resistive facade and identify underlying attitudes" (p. 289). As a result, the participants reveal inner feelings, become less guarded, and often develop the ability to see underlying psychic conflicts. Also, all group members have an opportunity to know how the other participants view them.

Wolf and Kutash (1986) suggest that it is useful when a client reports a dream to ask other members to free-associate with it. In this way they are being active and do not feel excluded as they listen to the details of another member's dream. The group can explore not only the dreamer's but also the other members' associations.

In summary, free association encourages members to become more spontaneous and to uncover unconscious processes, which leads to the discovery of keener insights into their psychodynamics. This procedure also promotes unity and active participation in the group process.

Interpretation

Interpretation is a therapeutic technique used in the analysis of free associations, dreams, resistances, and transference feelings. In making interpretations, the group therapist points out and explains the underlying meaning of behavior. Interpretations are designed to accelerate the therapeutic process of uncovering unconscious material. The assumption is that well-timed and accurate interpretations can be used by the client to integrate new data that will lead to new insights. Interpretation requires considerable skill. If therapists force their interpretations on clients in a dogmatic fashion, clients are likely to close off and become increasingly defensive. If clients are presented with an accurate interpretation at an inappropriate time, they may fight the therapeutic process and resist other interventions.

Scheidlinger (1987) maintains that an interpretation is simply a hypothesis and that, no matter how elegantly conceived, it is still subject to confirmation or refutation. When group members reject a therapist's interpretation, he suggests that it may mean the interpretation is inaccurate, not that members are being resistant. He writes that the correct timing of an interpretation in group therapy involves both a given member's readiness to understand and accept it and also the readiness of other group members. He adds that premature interpretations are likely to promote undue anxiety and lead to considerable resistance. The way interpretations are phrased and their manner of presentation, according to Scheidlinger, will certainly affect the degree to which they are considered by members. He formulates his interpretations in the form of questions, a practice that conveys the notion that they are merely hypotheses.

Interpretations presented as hypotheses and not as facts are more likely to be considered by clients. For example, Sam keeps making inappropriate interventions when other members express intense feelings and thus causes the others to lose contact with their feelings. The leader finally intervenes and says: "Sam, you seem to want to reassure Julie by trying to convince her that everything will work out for her. I have a hunch that you become uncomfortable when you see a person in pain; so you rush in, trying to take that person's pain away. Could it be that you're trying to avoid painful experiences yourself?" This comment alerts Sam to a possible reason for his behavior in the group. If he thinks about the leader's interpretation, he may discover other meanings of which he is not now conscious. Whether he will respond nondefensively has a lot to do with the manner in which the interpretation is made. In this case, the leader's tentative approach doesn't pose a threat and doesn't push Sam into accepting something that he may not be ready to accept.

In making interpretations, a few other general rules are useful:

- Interpretation should deal with material that is close to the client's awareness. In other words, the therapist needs to interpret material that clients have not yet seen for themselves but that they are ready and able to incorporate.
- Interpretation should begin from the surface and go as deep as the client can emotionally tolerate.
- It is best to point out a form of defense or resistance before interpreting the feeling or conflict that lies underneath it.

Some therapists direct interpretation to the group as a whole as well as to individual participants. For example, group members may be operating under the unspoken agreement that they will be polite and supportive and that they will not challenge one another. By observing the group process and sharing these observations with the group, the therapist can be instrumental in helping the members see their hidden motives and reach a deeper level of interaction. Here, too, *how* the leader presents the observations is crucial.

One of the advantages of the psychoanalytic method in groups is that members are encouraged to share their insights about other participants. This process can be very supportive and can accelerate progress. Even though the members do not systematically make interpretations, leaving that function to the therapist, they can have a deep effect on other members by being direct, unrehearsed, and confrontive. As members become more familiar with one another, they become increasingly able to recognize defensive strategies and offer perceptive observations. Fellow members' reactions may elicit more consideration and thought than those coming from an expert, but they may also be resisted with more tenacity. Some group therapists are concerned that a member may make inappropriate comments—that is, insights that the person in question is not ready to handle. This concern is somewhat lessened by what typically happens when someone is presented with an insight that is timed poorly or inaccurately: generally the person rejects the insight or in some way discounts it on the ground that it comes from a peer rather than from an expert.

Dream Analysis

Freud saw dreams as "the royal road to the unconscious." Dreams express unconscious needs, conflicts, wishes, fears, and repressed experiences. When a dream is shared in a group and worked through, the participant gains new insight into the motivations and unresolved problems behind it. Some motivations are so unacceptable to the person that they can be expressed only in disguised or symbolic form. Thus, an advantage of working with dreams in a group is that it enables members to deal in a concrete way with feelings and motivations that they otherwise could not face. After exploring the various facets and possible meanings of a dream in a supportive group, members may be more willing to accept themselves and explore other unresolved problems that elicit feelings of guilt and shame.

It should be noted that dreams have both a *manifest* (or conscious) content and a *latent* (or hidden) content. The manifest content is the dream as it appears to the dreamer; the latent content consists of the disguised, unconscious motives that represent the hidden meaning of the dream. A psychoanalytic group works at both levels. Because dreams are viewed as the key that unlocks what is buried in the unconscious, the goal is to search for the latent beneath the manifest and to gradually uncover repressed conflicts.

In the first session, group members are told that sharing their dreams, fantasies, and free associations is essential to the analysis and understanding of the dynamics behind confused thinking, feeling, and behaving. Even though therapists may have a great deal of insight into clients' dreams, they generally give little analysis during the early stages of a group. Instead, the members are encouraged to offer their own analyses (Mullan & Rosenbaum, 1978). Kolb

(1983) takes the position that dreams can be viewed from both an intrapersonal and an interpersonal perspective. She contends that the dream experience itself, often without interpretation, taps unconscious mental activity in a manner unequaled by most other clinical experiences.

According to Wolf (1963), the interpretation of dreams is an essential aspect of the analytic process and should continue throughout the various stages of a group. It is an essential technique because the unconscious material that dreams reveal has a liberating effect on the participants. Members are encouraged to interpret and to free-associate with one another's dreams to reach the deepest levels of interaction. Wolf reports that the entire group becomes "engrossed in dream analysis with its attendant associations, catharsis, sense of liberation and mutuality, all of which contribute toward the group unity which is so important in the first stages of treatment" (p. 287). He stresses the importance of a nonjudgmental attitude on the part of the leader toward the emerging unconscious material. The leader's tolerant approach encourages a similar attitude in the members, and the group may soon become a compassionate and supportive family.

Besides their value for unblocking unconscious material from the client's past, dreams also contain a wealth of meaningful material concerning what is going on in the group. Members' dreams often reveal their reactions to the therapist and to other group members (Locke, 1961). The dreamer reports the dream and tells the group what meanings and associations it has for him or her. Then the group as a whole responds; other group members give their reactions to the dream and suggest cross-associations. The result is stimulation within the group.

Exploring dreams in a group has another valuable aspect. As members analyze the dreams of others and offer their own associations, they also project significant dimensions of themselves. In other words, the group members are both interpreting and projecting, a process that often leads to extremely valuable insights. Wishes, fears, and attitudes are revealed as members associate with one another's dreams. One person's dream becomes the dream of the whole group, a process that is the "true essence of dream work in group psychoanalysis" (Locke, 1961, p. 133).

Insight and Working Through

Insight means awareness of the causes of one's present difficulties. In the psychoanalytic model, insight is also an awareness, intellectual as well as emotional, of the relationship between past experiences and present problems. As clients develop keener insight, they become increasingly able to recognize the many ways in which these core conflicts are manifested, both in the group and in their daily lives. New connections are formed, and dominant themes begin to emerge. For example, if in the course of group work some members discover that they need to please everyone at all costs, they come to see the effects of their need for approval on their lives.

But the analytic process doesn't stop at the insight level; working through core problems and conflicts is an essential aspect of analytically oriented group and individual therapy. Thus, if group members hope to change some aspect of their personality, they must work through resistances and old patterns—typically a long and difficult process. Working through is one of the most complex aspects of analysis, and it requires deep commitment. The working-through process involves reexperiencing the unfinished business in the context of transference (multiple transference, in group analysis).

Working through represents the final phase of the analytic group and results in increased consciousness and integration of the self. According to Wolf and Schwartz (1962), after discovering the dynamics of an individual's problems and symptoms, the leader carefully maps a course of action to deal with them. These authors maintain that participants make progress and change as a result of a cooperative effort between the group leader and the client within the context of a thoughtful and flexible treatment plan.

Early conflicts are rarely completely worked through. Most individuals will have to deal again with these deeply rooted issues from time to time. Thus, it is a mistake to think of working through as a technique that frees the individual from any vestige of old patterns.

Developmental Stages and Their Implications for Group Work

This section describes a developmental model that has significant implications for group work. The model is based on Erikson's eight stages of human development and on the Freudian stages of psychosexual development. Such a combination provides group leaders with the conceptual framework required for understanding trends in development, major developmental tasks at each stage of life, critical needs and their satisfaction or frustration, potentials for choice at each stage of life, critical turning points or crises, and the origins of faulty personality development that can lead to later personality conflicts.

Erikson (1963, 1982) built on and extended Freud's ideas by stressing the psychosocial aspects of development. Although he was intellectually indebted to Freud, he did not accept all of Freud's views. Erikson's theory of development holds that psychosexual and psychosocial growth occur together and that at each stage of life we face the task of establishing an equilibrium between ourselves and our social world. Psychosocial theory stresses the integration of the biological, psychological, and social aspects of development. Erikson describes development in terms of the entire life span, which he divides into eight stages, each of which is characterized by a specific crisis to be resolved. According to Erikson, each crisis represents a *turning point* in life. At these turning points, we either achieve successful resolution of our conflicts and move forward or fail to resolve the conflicts and regress. To a large extent, our lives are the result of the choices we make at each stage.

This conceptual framework is useful for all group leaders, regardless of their theoretical orientation. Irrespective of the model underlying one's group practice, the following questions need to be raised as group work proceeds:

- What are some of the themes that give continuity to a person's life?
- What are the client's ongoing concerns and unresolved conflicts?
- What is the relationship between this individual's current problems and significant events in earlier years?
- What influential factors have shaped the person's character?
- What were the major turning points and crises in the client's life?
- What choices did the individual make at these critical periods, and how did he or she deal with these various crises?
- In what direction does the person seem to be moving now?

Stage 1: Infancy—Trust Versus Mistrust (Birth to 12 Months)

Freud labeled the first year of life the *oral stage*; sucking the mother's breast satisfies the infant's need for food and pleasure. According to the psychoanalytic view, the events of this period are extremely important for later development. Infants who don't get enough love and food may later develop greediness and acquisitiveness as material things become substitutes for what they really wanted and didn't get. Later personality problems that stem from the oral stage include a mistrustful view of the world, a tendency to reject love, a fear of loving and trusting, and an inability to establish intimate relationships.

According to Erikson (1963), an infant's basic task is to develop a sense of trust in self, others, and the world. Infants need to count on others and to feel wanted and secure. If, however, parents are not responsive to infants' needs, they develop an attitude of mistrust toward the world, especially toward interpersonal relationships.

Implications for Group Work The connection between these ideas and the practice of group psychotherapy seems quite clear. A common theme explored in groups is the feeling of being unloved and uncared for and the concomitant acute need for someone who will deeply care and love. Time after time, group members recall early feelings of abandonment, fear, and rejection, and many of them have become fixated on the goal of finding a symbolic "parent" who will accept them. Thus, much of their energy is directed to seeking approval and acceptance. The problem is compounded by the fact that, being unable to trust themselves and others, they are afraid of loving and of forming close relationships.

Group leaders can assist these clients to express the pain they feel and to work through some of the barriers that are preventing them from trusting others and fully accepting themselves. Erikson (1968) observes that these clients tend to express their basic mistrust by withdrawing into themselves every time they are at odds with themselves, others, or the world. It should be noted that each stage builds on the psychological outcomes of the previous stage(s).

In this regard, establishing a sense of basic trust is a foundation for later personality development.

Problems associated with each of these developmental stages may become manifest in an analytic group in which the family of origin is recapitulated. Some regression to behaviors associated with earlier developmental stages is common in this type of group. For example, in this first stage members may project hostile feelings onto the leader or other members. These individuals may feel justified in harboring unrealistic fears and may not have enough trust to check such projections for accuracy. It is essential that leaders do what is necessary to establish a group atmosphere that allows members to feel safe so they can explore possible projections. If a member does not develop this trust, he or she could easily become isolated in the group.

Analytic group therapists use their knowledge of developmental stages to understand patterns in which the members may be "stuck." The group leader's comments, questions, and interpretations can then be framed to help the participants resolve fixations and crises linked to specific developmental stages.

Stage 2: Early Childhood—Autonomy Versus Shame and Doubt (12 Months to 3 Years)

Freud called the next two years of life the *anal stage*. The main tasks that children must master during this stage include learning independence, accepting personal power, and learning how to express negative feelings such as jealousy, rage, aggression, and destructiveness. It is at this stage that children begin their journey toward autonomy. They play an increasingly active role in taking care of their own needs and begin to communicate what they want from others. This is also the time when they continually encounter parental demands: they are restricted from fully exploring their environment, and toilet training is being imposed on them. The Freudian view is that parental feelings and attitudes during this stage have significant consequences for later personality development.

From Erikson's viewpoint the years between age 1 and 3 are a time for developing a sense of *autonomy*. Children who don't master the task of gaining some measure of self-control and the ability to cope with the world develop a sense of *shame* and *doubt* about themselves and their adequacy. At this age children need to explore the world, to experiment and test their limits, and to be allowed to learn from their mistakes. If parents do too much for their children and try to keep them dependent, they are likely to inhibit the children's autonomy and hamper their capacity to deal with the world successfully.

Implications for Group Work   By understanding the dynamics of this stage of life, the group leader can gain access to a wealth of useful material. Many of those who seek help in a group have not learned to accept their anger and hatred toward those they love. They need to get in touch with the disowned parts of themselves that are at the bottom of these conflicting feelings. To do this, they may need to relive and reexperience situations in their distant past in which they began to repress intense feelings. In the safe environment of the group, they can gradually learn ways of expressing their locked-up feelings, and they can work through the guilt associated with some of these emotions. Groups offer many opportunities for catharsis (expressing pent-up feelings) and for relearning.

Stage 3: The Preschool Age—Initiative Versus Guilt (3 to 6 Years)

In Freud's *phallic stage* sexual activity becomes more intense. The focus of attention is on the genitals, and sexual identity takes form. Preschool children become curious about their bodies. They explore them and experience pleasure from genital stimulation. And they show increased interest in the differences between the sexes and ask questions about reproduction. The way in which parents respond, verbally and nonverbally, to their children's emerging sexuality and sexual interest is crucial in influencing the kinds of attitudes, sexual and otherwise, their children develop.

According to the Freudian view, the basic conflict of the phallic stage centers on the unconscious incestuous desires that children develop for the parent of the opposite sex. These feelings are highly threatening, so they are repressed; yet they remain as powerful determinants of later personality development. Along with the wish to possess the parent of the opposite sex comes the unconscious wish to displace the parent of the same sex, a wish epitomized by the slaying of the father in the Oedipus myth.

Erikson, in contrast, emphasizes that the basic task of the preschool years is to establish a sense of *competence* and *initiative*. This is the time for becoming psychologically ready to pursue activities of one's own choosing. If children are allowed the freedom to select meaningful activities, they tend to develop a positive outlook characterized by the ability to initiate and follow through. But if they are not allowed to make at least some of their own decisions or if their choices are ridiculed, they are likely to develop a sense of guilt over taking initiative. Typically, they will refrain from taking an active stance and will increasingly let others make decisions for them.

Implications for Group Work   In most therapy and counseling groups, participants struggle with issues related to sex-role identity. Many individuals have incorporated stereotypical notions of what it means to be a woman or a man, and they have consequently repressed many of their feelings that don't fit these stereotypes. A group can be the place where individuals challenge such restricting views and become more whole.

Because concerns about sexual feelings, attitudes, values, and behavior are often kept private, people feel very much alone with their sexual concerns. Groups offer the chance to express these concerns openly, to correct faulty learning, to work through repressed feelings and events, and to begin to formulate a different view of oneself as a female or male sexual being. Perhaps the most important function of a group is that it gives clients permission to have feelings and to talk honestly about them.

Stage 4: The School Age—Industry Versus Inferiority (6 to 12 Years)

Freudians call middle childhood the *latency stage*. After the torrent of sexual impulses of the preceding years, this period is relatively quiescent. There is a decline in sexual interests, which are replaced by interests in school, playmates, sports, and a whole range of new activities. Around age 6, children begin to reach out for new relationships.

Erikson stresses the active, rather than the latent, aspect of this stage and the unique psychosocial tasks that must be met at this time if healthy development is to take place. Children need to expand their understanding of the physical and social worlds and continue to develop appropriate sex-role identities. They must also form personal values, engage in social tasks, learn to accept people who are different from them, and acquire the basic skills needed for schooling. According to Erikson, the central task of middle childhood is the achievement of a sense of *industry*, and the failure to do so results in a sense of *inadequacy* and *inferiority*. Industry refers to setting and achieving goals that are personally meaningful. If children fail at this task, they are unlikely to feel adequate as adults, and the subsequent developmental stages will be negatively influenced.

Implications for Group Work   Some problems originating at this stage that group leaders may expect to encounter include a negative self-concept, feelings of inadequacy relating to learning, feelings of inferiority in establishing social relationships, conflicts about values, a confused sex-role identity, unwillingness to face new challenges, dependency, and lack of initiative.

To see how the leader's knowledge of the problems and promises of this period of life can help the therapeutic process, let's look at a participant who suffers from feelings of inferiority. Rachel fears failure so much that she shies away from college because she is convinced she could never make it. In a group, she can be helped to see possible connections between her feelings of inadequacy and some events that occurred when she was in elementary school. Perhaps she had a series of negative learning experiences, such as being told, openly or not, by her teachers that she was stupid and couldn't learn. Before Rachel can overcome her feelings that she cannot meet the demands of college, she may have to go back to the traumatic events of her childhood, relive them, and express the pain she felt then. Through the support of the group she can experience many of these buried feelings and begin to put the events of her past in a different perspective. Eventually, she may also come to realize that she doesn't have to wreck her academic career now because of something that happened in grade school.

Rachel could be harmed more than helped by a group experience. She could very well fear that she will also fail as a member. She might set herself up for failure and also bias others to view her as a failure and as a "group reject." If the other members eventually come to share her negative feelings about her involvement in the group, this vicious circle may be difficult to break and skillful intervention by the leader may be required. It is crucial that members learn to recognize patterns that originated during childhood because those patterns will inevitably unfold in a group.

Stage 5: Adolescence—Identity Versus Identity Confusion (12 to 18 Years)

Adolescence is a stage of transition between childhood and adulthood. It is a time for continually testing limits, rejecting ties of dependency, and establishing a new identity. It is most of all a time of conflict, especially between the desire to break away from parental control and the fear of making independent decisions and living with the consequences. Adolescence is marked by a resurgence of Oedipal feelings.

In Freudian theory the final psychosexual stage of development, the *genital stage*, is the longest and extends far beyond adolescence; it begins at the time of puberty and lasts until senility sets in, at which time the individual tends to regress to earlier stages. Erikson picked up where Freud left off and devoted a great deal of attention to the later stages, especially adolescence. He saw the crisis that characterizes adolescence—the identity crisis—as the most important of life.

What does Erikson mean by *identity crisis*? He means that most conflicts of the adolescent years are related to the development of a personal identity. Adolescents struggle to define who they are, where they are going, and how they will get there. Because all kinds of changes—physical as well as social—are taking place and because society applies diverse pressures, many adolescents have difficulty finding a stable identity. They experience pressure from school, from their parents, from their peer group, from members of the other sex, and from society at large, and these demands are often conflicting. In the midst of this turmoil, the adolescent has the task of ultimately deciding where he or she stands in the face of these varying expectations. If the adolescent fails, *identity confusion* results, and the person will lack purpose and direction in later years.

Implications for Group Work In many groups a good deal of time is devoted to the exploration and resolution of the dependence/independence conflicts that are so prevalent in adolescence. A central struggle involves the process of separation and individuation.

At times one or several members may manifest a rebellious attitude toward the leader. Although challenging the leader often signals a move toward independence, attacking a leader may well be a symptom of rebellion against parents or any other authority. There could be an attempt to psychologically slay the therapist, which is an example of a recapitulation of adolescent themes within the group context. It is essential that leaders be aware of their own dynamics, especially when they are confronted by members. Leaders will be less likely to react defensively if they understand the transference nature of this behavior.

The unresolved problems of adolescence are manifest in many of the problems that adults bring to a group. In many of the groups I have led, one of the most persistent themes is the search for identity: "Who am I? How did I get this way? What do I really stand for? Where am I going, and how will I get there? If I get there, what will it ultimately mean?" Until adults recognize this unfinished issue from their earlier years, they cannot effectively meet the challenges presented by other stages of life.

Stage 6: Young Adulthood—Intimacy Versus Isolation (18 to 35 Years)

In Erikson's view we enter adulthood after we have mastered the conflicts of adolescence and established a firm personal identity. During the sixth stage, young adulthood, our sense of identity is tested again by the challenge of *intimacy* versus *isolation*.

An essential characteristic of the psychologically mature person is the ability to form intimate relationships. To achieve true intimacy with others, we need to have confidence in our own identity. Intimacy involves commitment and the ability to share and to give from our own centeredness; the failure to achieve intimacy leads to alienation and isolation. Young adulthood is also a time for focusing on one's interests, for becoming established in an occupation, and for carving out a satisfying lifestyle. It is a time for dreams and life plans but also a time for productivity.

Implications for Group Work   In many adult groups considerable time is devoted to exploring the members' priorities. Participants struggle with concerns of interpersonal intimacy, talk about their unfulfilled dreams, question the meaningfulness of their work, wonder about the future, and reevaluate the patterns of their lives to determine what changes they need to make. Perhaps the greatest value of a group for people engaged in these struggles is the opportunity to take another look at their dreams and life plans and determine the degree to which their lives reflect these aspirations. If the gap is great, the participants are encouraged to find ways of changing the situation.

Typically, young adults bring to a group the problems related to living with another person and establishing a family. The central struggle of this period is the intimacy crisis, a conflict between the need to maintain a sense of one's own separateness and the need to establish close relationships. The successful resolution of the intimacy crisis involves achieving a balance between taking care of oneself and actively caring for others. Those who fail to strike this balance either focus exclusively on the needs of others, thus neglecting their own needs, or are so self-centered that they have little room for concern about others. Of course, the quality of the young adult's ability to form interpersonal relationships is greatly influenced by what took place during early development.

How members deal with intimacy within the group reveals patterns they learned about getting close or keeping distant during their young adulthood. For many people in groups, forming close bonds with others is extremely difficult. This pattern of being uncomfortable and frightened of both receiving and giving love and compassion is bound to unfold in the group sessions. The group is an ideal place for members who are struggling with intimacy issues to recognize and confront their fears. If members are not aware of their tendencies to keep themselves distant from others, they could easily try to mold the therapy group into their family-of-origin group, which had injunctions against intimacy.

Stage 7: Middle Age—Generativity Versus Stagnation (35 to 60 Years)

The seventh stage is characterized by a need to go beyond ourselves and our immediate family and to be actively involved with helping and guiding the next generation. The mature years can be one of the most productive periods of our lives, but they can also entail the painful experience of facing the discrepancy between what we set out to accomplish in young adulthood and what we have actually accomplished.

Erikson sees the stimulus for continued growth during this stage in the conflict between *generativity* and *stagnation*. Generativity is a broad concept that is manifested in the ability to love well, work well, and play well. If people fail to achieve a sense of personal competence, they begin to stagnate and to die psychologically. When we reach middle age, we become more sharply aware of the inevitability of our own eventual death. This awareness of mortality is one of the central features of the midlife crisis and colors our evaluations of what we are doing with our lives.

Implications for Group Work   The changes that occur during this life stage and the crises and conflicts that accompany them represent valuable opportunities for group work. Participants are often challenged to make new assessments, adjustments, and choices to open up new possibilities and reach new levels of meaning. Knowledge of adult development allows the group leader to watch for the hopelessness that some people experience during middle age and to help them go beyond the destructive view that "that's all there is to life." It takes caring and skilled leadership to inspire people to look for new meanings and to "invent themselves" in novel ways.

Stage 8: Later Life—Integrity Versus Despair (above 60 Years)

The eighth, and last, stage of life confronts the individual with crucial developmental tasks, such as adjusting to the death of a spouse or friends, maintaining outside interests, adjusting to retirement, and accepting losses in physical and sensory capacities. But the central task of the final stage is reviewing the past and drawing conclusions.

According to Erikson, the successful resolution of the core crisis of this stage—the conflict between *integrity* and *despair*—depends on how the person looks back on the past. Ego integrity is achieved by those who feel few regrets. They see themselves as having lived productive and worthwhile lives, and they feel that they have coped with their failures as well as their successes. They are not obsessed with what might have been and are able to derive satisfaction from what has been. They see death as a part of the life process and can still find meaning and satisfaction in the time left. Failure to achieve ego integrity often leads to feelings of despair, hopelessness, guilt, resentment, and self-rejection.

Implications for Group Work   The salient issues of this stage of life have implications not only for group leaders working with older adults but also for those who work with young or middle-aged adults. Often these younger people express the fear of getting older. As they begin to see the years slip by, they feel the increasing pressure of making something of their lives. Some worry about being alone when they are old, and some are afraid of financial or physical dependency on others. Group leaders can help these people realize that perhaps the only way to deal constructively with these fears is to prepare now for a satisfying life as they grow old. Asking the question "What would you like to be able to say about your life when you reach old age?" is a good way to start. What the members say in answer to this question (to themselves and in the group) can dictate the decisions they need to make now and the specific steps they must take to achieve a sense of integrity at a later age.

Contemporary Trends in Psychoanalytic Group Theory

Psychoanalytic theory, rather than being closed or static, is continually evolving. Freud's ideas were based on an id psychology, characterized by conflicts over the gratification of basic needs. Later, writers in the social-psychological school moved away from Freud's orthodox position and contributed to the growth and expansion of the psychoanalytic movement by incorporating the cultural and social influences on personality. Then, ego psychology, with its stress on psychosocial development throughout the life span, was developed by Erikson, among others. Anna Freud, with her identification of defense mechanisms, is a central figure in ego psychology although she is not particularly associated with the life-span interests of Erikson.

According to DeAngelis (1996), psychoanalysis has evolved to the point where it can creatively meet modern challenges while still retaining its original focus on depth and the inner life. Psychoanalytic approaches are being applied to both family systems therapy and group therapy. DeAngelis informs us that some contemporary psychoanalysts with an object relations orientation are stressing the relational more than the insight aspects of therapy. Neil Altman (cited in DeAngelis, 1996) has been adapting psychoanalytic theory to low-income urban populations, applying psychoanalytic concepts to issues of class, race, and gender.

Strupp (1992) writes that the notion of unconscious conflict is still fundamental to psychodynamic thought. However, more attention is now being given to internal structures of personality that are significantly influenced by experiences with significant figures during one's infancy and early childhood. Strupp notes that the Oedipus complex is no longer considered a universal phenomenon. Instead, there is an increased focus on disturbances and arrests in infancy and early childhood that stem from deficiencies in the mother/child relationship.

Object Relations Theory

The evolution of psychoanalytic theory and practice did not cease with the development of the psychosocial perspective. A new trend in psychoanalytic thinking characterized the 1970s and the 1980s. These newer approaches are often classified as *self psychology, object relations theory*, or *relational psychoanalysis*. There is no single, generally accepted school or theory of object relations, and theories of object relations continue to evolve. Many theorists have contributed ideas to an evolving body of concepts that deal with object relationships (St. Clair, 2000).

Object relations are interpersonal relationships as they are represented intrapsychically. The term *object* was used by Freud to refer to that which satisfies a need, or to the significant person or thing that is the object or target of one's feelings or drives. It is used interchangeably with the term *other* to refer to an important person to whom the child and, later, the adult becomes attached. At birth, the infant has no sense of separateness; self and other are fused. The process of separation/individuation begins when the infant perceives that pleasure and discomfort are related to objects external to the self. The infant at this stage will typically make an attachment to the mother's breast before any recognition of her as a whole person.

Mahler (1968) believes the individual begins in a state of psychological fusion with the mother and progresses gradually to separation. The unfinished crises and residues of the earlier state of fusion, as well as the process of individuating, have a profound influence on later relationships. Object relations of later life build on the child's search for a reconnection with the mother (St. Clair, 2000). Virtually all psychoanalytic thinkers believe there is continuity in the development of self/other relations from their infantile origins to mature involvement with other persons. Thus, object relations are interpersonal relationships that shape the individual's current interactions with people (St. Clair, 2000).

The contemporary theoretical trends in psychoanalytic thinking center on predictable developmental sequences in which the early experiences of the self shift in relation to an expanding awareness of others. Once self/other patterns are established, it is assumed, they influence later interpersonal relationships. This influence occurs through a process of searching for a type of experience that comes closest to the patterning established by the early experiences. These newer theories provide insight into how an individual's inner world can cause difficulties in living in the actual world of people and relationships (St. Clair, 2000).

Psychological development can be thought of as the evolution of the way in which individuals differentiate themselves from others. In group work, participants can experience how they are bringing very early patterns into their present interactions. For example, a group member who appears closely involved with others at one meeting may seem distant and removed at the next, leaving everyone wondering what happened to the level of work that seemed to have been achieved. This pattern might repeat what Mahler (1968) calls the "ambitendency" of an infant who goes back and forth between wanting to be held by its mother and wanting to be left free to roam and explore.

Dealing with Borderline and Narcissistic Personalities

Perhaps the most significant developments of recent psychoanalytic theory involve borderline and narcissistic personality disorders. The essential features of the borderline personality are an unstable view of one's self and instability in relating to others. With *borderline* individuals, relationships are dominated by the need to defend against the fear of abandonment or depression. The essential features of the *narcissistic* personality disorder are a pervasive pattern of grandiosity, hypersensitivity to the evaluations of others, and a lack of empathy. Every relationship with a narcissistic individual requires adulation and perfect responsiveness from the partner (Masterson, 1997). Both of these personality patterns begin by early adulthood. Among the most significant theorists in this area are Kernberg (1975, 1976) and Kohut (1971, 1977, 1984). Kohut maintains that people are their healthiest and best when they can feel both independence and attachment, taking joy in themselves and also being able to idealize others.

Object relations theory sheds new light on the understanding of personality disorders. According to St. Clair (2000), borderline and narcissistic disorders seem to result from traumas and developmental disturbances during separation/individuation. However, the full manifestations of the personality and behavioral symptoms tend to develop in adolescence or early adulthood. Narcissistic and borderline symptoms, such as omnipotence, splitting (a defensive process of keeping incompatible feelings separate), and grandiosity, are behavioral manifestations of developmental tasks that were disturbed or not completed earlier.

Borderline Personality A borderline personality disorder is characterized by bouts of irritability, self-destructive acts, impulsive anger, and extreme mood shifts. People with borderline dynamics typically experience extended periods of disillusionment punctuated by occasions of euphoria. Interpersonal relations are often intense and unstable, with marked changes of attitude over time. There is frequently impulsive and unpredictable behavior that can cause physical harm. A marked identity disturbance is generally manifested by uncertainty about life issues pertaining to self-image, sexual orientation, career choice, and long-term goals. Kernberg (1975) describes the syndrome as including a lack of clear identity, a lack of deep understanding of other people, poor impulse control, and the inability to tolerate anxiety. In recent years a great deal more clarity about individuals with borderline dynamics has emerged, especially due to the work of Kernberg and other theorists. They may be more disorganized than neurotics but more integrated than psychotics. People who manifest borderline dynamics have not fully achieved separation/individuation and tend to have a chaotic, primitive personality structure.

William Blau (personal communication, March 6, 2001) points out that the diagnosis of a borderline personality is being applied rather broadly in clinical settings. Although such a diagnosis originally referred to individuals occupying a border area between neurosis and psychosis, the current DSM IV diagnostic criteria are broad enough to include many people who have fully intact reality testing but serious problems in the classic Freudian areas of love and work. Blau believes these clients are amenable to treatment, although their difficulties may be more difficult to resolve than simple neuroses because they are embedded in relatively permanent personality patterns. He also prefers to refer to borderline "dynamics" rather than borderline "personalities."

Implications for Group Work   Some psychologists are seeking to dispel the notion that borderline personality disorder is largely intractable (Sleek, 1997). Jeffrey Magnavita (cited in Sleek, 1997) uses a short-term psychodynamic approach with personality disorders. However, it should be noted that some analysts believe borderline personality disorders cannot be treated in brief therapy. For example, Bertram Karon (cited in Sleek, 1997) questions the effectiveness of short-term interventions with people with borderline disorders and also sees dangers in arbitrarily limiting the length of treatment as a cost-cutting measure.

According to Yalom (1995), the core problem of borderline individuals lies in the area of intimacy, and a group setting offers the therapeutic factors of cohesiveness and reality testing. He contends that if these individuals can accept feedback and observations provided by other members, and if their behavior is not highly disruptive, the group can offer them supportive refuge from daily stresses. Although individuals with borderline dynamics may express primitive, chaotic needs and fears, they are continually confronted with reality through the group process, which helps keep these feelings somewhat under control. If the group begins to ignore borderline members, they will assume deviant roles and act out in the group, and therapy fails.

Borderline clients may be treated with a group format developed by Linehan (1993b), which is based on her dialectical behavior therapy (DBT). DBT includes some psychodynamic concepts in a cognitive behavioral framework. DBT skills training groups should be used with borderline clients in conjunction with individual psychotherapy. DBT groups validate the client's behavior "as it is in the moment," confront resistance, and emphasize "the therapeutic relationship as essential to treatment" while teaching clients skills necessary to change (Linehan, 1993b, pp. 5–6).

Narcissistic Personality   Children who lack the opportunity either to differentiate or to idealize others while also taking pride in themselves may later suffer from narcissistic personality disorders. This syndrome is characterized by an exaggerated sense of self-importance and an exploitive attitude toward others, which serves the function of masking a frail self-concept. Such individuals tend to display exhibitionistic behavior. They seek attention and admiration from others, and they tend toward extreme self-absorption. Narcissism may also present itself as very low self-esteem and an overreadiness to idealize others (see Gabbard, 2000).

Kernberg (1975) characterizes people with narcissistic dynamics as focusing on themselves in their interactions with others, having a great need to be admired, possessing shallow affect, and being exploitive and at times establishing parasitic relationships with others. He writes that individuals who are narcissistically oriented have a shallow emotional life, enjoy little other than tributes received from others, and tend to depreciate those from whom they expect few narcissistic pleasures.

There is also a growing trend to see narcissism as a striking lack of self-esteem. Kohut (1971) characterizes narcissistically oriented people as being highly threatened in maintaining their self-esteem and as having feelings of emptiness and deadness. These individuals are typically searching for someone who will serve as an object to feed the famished self. Kohut uses the term *selfobject* to refer to a person who is used to foster the narcissist's self-esteem and sense of well-being. These clients look for people whom they can admire for their power because they see themselves as worthwhile only if they are associated with such selfobjects. Yet their inner void cannot be filled, so their search for confirmation by others is never-ending. These people attempt to merge with powerful or beautiful selfobjects. Because of their impoverished sense of self and their unclear boundaries between self and others, they have difficulty differentiating between their own thoughts and feelings and those of the selfobject.

Implications for Group Work   Yalom (1995) discusses the problems that arise when individuals with narcissistic dynamics enter group therapy. They typically have difficulty sharing group time, understanding and empathizing with others, and forming relationships with other members. These clients have a constant need for center stage. They often assess a group's usefulness to them in terms of how much time is devoted to them and how much attention they receive from the therapist. They are likely to be bored and impatient while other members are working, and they also tend to divert the discussion back to themselves. These individuals have unrealistic expectations of the other members. They feel that they are special and deserve the group's attention, yet they are not willing to give attention to others. According to Yalom, a major task of the therapist is to manage such highly vulnerable members in the group. The leader must focus on the nature of the current forces, both conscious and unconscious, that are influencing the way members who display narcissistic traits relate to others in the group.

In his book, *Interactive Group Therapy*, Jay Earley (2000) has an informative discussion about the challenges of dealing with members who exhibit borderline and narcissistic tendencies. One of the main problems for group leaders is the potential countertransference reactions that are stirred up in them. The intense anger and splitting defenses that people with borderline disorders often display can result in a leader becoming intimidated by the client's anger or by becoming angry in return. The grandiosity, self-centeredness, and demeaning comments of a narcissistic member can also elicit intense feelings of anger in both the leader and the members. Earley states that although group therapists can develop countertransference reactions in response to any group member, borderline and narcissistic members tend to provoke more intense reactions. This makes it particularly important for group leaders to become aware of their reactions toward certain members, to avoid acting on their feelings as much as possible, and to seek supervision when needed.

The spirit of psychoanalysis requires taking the time to form a deep relationship with a minimum agenda in a carefully structured frame. Some of the most powerful tools for understanding borderline and narcissistic personality organization have emerged within this tradition. This way of working draws from the developmental models of Mahler and the competing visions of transference and countertransference put forward by Kernberg and Kohut.

Future of Psychoanalytically Oriented Therapy

Forecasting the future of psychodynamic therapy, Strupp (1992) contends that the various modifications of psychoanalysis "have infused psychodynamic psychotherapy with renewed vitality and vigor" (p. 25). He suggests that this approach will undergo further revisions and that it will maintain its prominence in individual, group, marital, and family therapy. Although contemporary psychodynamic forms diverge considerably in many respects from the original Freudian emphasis on drives, the basic concepts of unconscious motivation, influence of early development, transference, countertransference, and resistance are still central. Further, Strupp notes a decline in practices based on the classical analytic model, due to reasons such as time commitment, expense, limited applications to diverse client populations, and questionable benefits. He acknowledges that the realities stemming from managed care will place increasing emphasis on short-term treatments for specific disorders, limited goals, and containment of costs. Some of the current trends and directions in psychodynamic theory and practice that Strupp identifies are these:

• The emphasis on treatment has shifted from the "classical" interest in curing neurotic disorders to the problems of dealing therapeutically with chronic personality disorders, borderline conditions, and narcissistic personality disorders.

✓ • There is increased attention on establishing a good therapeutic alliance early in the course of psychodynamic therapy. A collaborative relationship is now viewed as a key factor related to a positive therapeutic outcome.

• There is a renewed interest in development of briefer forms of psychodynamic therapy, largely due to societal pressures for accountability and cost-effectiveness. The indications are that time-limited therapy will receive increasing attention in the future.

• Psychodynamic group therapy is becoming more popular and it is receiving widespread acceptance. This approach provides clients with opportunities to learn how they function in groups and it offers a unique perspective on understanding problems.

In keeping with this context of future developments of psychoanalytic practice, Messer and Warren (2001) describe brief psychodynamic therapy (BPT). This adaptation applies the principles of psychoanalytic theory and therapy to treating selective disorders within a preestablished time limit of generally 10 to 25 sessions. BPT makes use of key psychoanalytic concepts such as the enduring impact of psychosexual, psychosocial, and object relational stages of development; the existence of unconscious processes; and reenactment of the client's past emotional issues in relationship to the therapist. Most forms of this brief approach call upon the therapist to assume an active role in quickly formulating a therapeutic focus that goes beneath the surface of presenting problems and symptoms and treats underlying issues. Some possible goals of this approach might include conflict resolution, greater access to feelings, increasing choice possibilities, improving interpersonal relationships, and symptom remission. The goals, therapeutic focus, and active role of the therapist have implications for both individual and group therapy. Although BPT is not suitable for all clients, it does fit a variety of clients' needs. This briefer treatment approach has become increasingly important in the climate of cost containment for health care. BPT "has an important role in sustaining the values of psychoanalytic treatment, which is to understand and treat people's problems in the context of their current situation and earlier life experience" (p. 83).

Applying the Psychoanalytic Approach to Group Work in the Schools

The analytic model provides a conceptual framework for understanding a child's or an adolescent's current problems. Although the use of psychoanalytic techniques is beyond the scope of group counseling in the school setting, group counselors can draw upon certain psychoanalytic concepts that have been elaborated in this chapter. Exploring the historical context of an elementary or high school student's problems is clearly beyond the scope and limitations of school groups. However, understanding how past events may continue to have a present influence on the problems can reframe the counselor's approach. A group leader can be aware of factors such as resistance, transference, anxiety, and the functioning of the ego-defense mechanisms. This awareness will add some depth to the interventions the counselor makes, even though he or she does not encourage or allow excursions into past trauma or unconscious conflicts. Understanding these psychoanalytic concepts affords counselors a way to develop empathy and to work compassionately with here-and-now problems of children and adolescents.

The developmental stages and the implications that flow from a life-span perspective were addressed in considerable detail earlier in this chapter. This developmental perspective is useful for group counselors working in schools. Group work with children is enhanced by the counselor's understanding of the developmental needs and tasks related to themes of industry versus inferiority. Adolescent groups function better if the counselor understands core struggles around identity versus identity confusion. Groups can be structured to assist the members in learning age-appropriate skills to enhance daily living. The development of the ego functions can be facilitated by conceptualizing and structuring a remedial counseling group as a supportive surrogate family.

Applying the Psychoanalytic Approach with Multicultural Populations

When considering whether a given theory is appropriate for working with diverse client populations in a group setting, one key criterion is the consistency between the concepts and techniques of a theory with the cultural values of the group members. Consider how well the underlying assumptions and key concepts mesh with the cultural values of diverse client groups. Although the basic concepts of psychoanalytic theory can be applied to understanding people from diverse cultures, the analytic therapist must also consider those instances when specific psychotherapeutic techniques may not fit with a client's cultural background.

Many cultural groups place a high priority on family history. A review of a client's past and of how this past is having an important bearing on current functioning may be appropriate as a conceptual framework. Working in symbolic ways can also be powerful, especially with clients who are reluctant to talk about their personal problems. For example, there is value in using pictures of the family at different periods of the client's childhood. The leader might say: "Select a picture that has particular meaning for you. Tell me what you remember during these times. As you look at the picture, what thoughts and feelings come to you?" Once group members begin talking to one another about their memories based on these pictures, they are likely to be more open in dealing with emotional material.

As we have seen, group therapists need to be aware of the ways in which the interpretations they make are influenced by their cultural background and their theoretical assumptions. Although practitioners can still conceptualize the struggles of their clients from an analytic perspective, it is critical that they adopt a stance of flexibility. Group counselors need to exercise vigilance lest they misuse their power by turning the group into a forum for pushing clients to adjust by conforming to the dominant cultural values at the expense of losing their own worldviews and cultural identities. Group practitioners also need to be aware of their own potential sources of bias. The concept of countertransference can be expanded to include unacknowledged bias and prejudices that may be conveyed unintentionally through the techniques used by a group therapist.

Although some are critical of the limited scope of psychoanalytic practice with diverse client populations, others seek a broader range of clients, from gay men and lesbians to people of color to the seriously mentally ill. Psychoanalysis is now also being applied to short-term therapy and community psychology (DeAngelis, 1996).

Evaluation of the Psychoanalytic Approach to Groups

Contributions and Strengths of the Approach

There is much in the psychoanalytic approach that I consider of great value. The analytic model provides a conceptual framework for understanding an individual's history, and in this regard group practitioners can learn to *think* psychoanalytically even if they do not *practice* psychoanalytically. Although some psychoanalytic techniques may have limited utility for the group counselor, many analytic concepts help explain the dynamics operating both in individuals and in the group as a whole.

It is important to consider the past to fully understand present behavior. Many of the conflicts brought to a group are rooted in early childhood experiences. Although I am not advocating a preoccupation with the past—digging it up and then dwelling on it—ignoring the influence of the past can lead to superficial group work. Understanding this influence gives people more control over their present behavior.

Students sometimes think of Freudian theory as antiquated and without scientific support. However, the scientific status of Freud's basic discoveries continues to improve in the 21st century. An issue of *Science News* cites research that describes "an everyday form of induced forgetting that may provide scientific footing for Freudian repression" (Bower, 2001, p. 164). Similarly, an article in *Discover* on the nature of dreams reports that "new brain research suggests that the often-derided Sigmund Freud may have been right after all—those crazy nighttime scenes are an open door to your unconscious mind" (Sapolsky, 2001, p. 37). As you have seen in this chapter, the concepts of both repression and dreams have implications for the psychoanalytic approach to groups.

A psychoanalytic concept I find of particular importance is resistance. Even when members are in a group by their own choice, I observe resistances, especially during the early development of the group. These resistances are manifestations of various fears; unless they are dealt with, they are not going to go away. In fact, I typically ask members to share with the group the ways in which they expect their own resistance to interfere with their group work. Even though resistance is typically unconscious, group members will often be surprisingly revealing. Some members seem to know quite well that they may sabotage their best efforts and resist change by intellectualizing, by being overly nurturing or overly critical with fellow members, or by convincing themselves that their problems are not as pressing as others in the group. If members can recognize their avoidant behaviors when they occur, they have a chance to change them. Some of the more subtle forms of defense may become evident over time, such as displacing feelings and projecting.

The psychoanalytic concepts of anxiety and the ego-defense mechanisms that emerge as a way to cope with this anxiety are most useful for group practitioners. Although in some groups the leader may not interpret and work through these defensive structures, it is essential to learn to respect defenses and to recognize how they develop and how they manifest themselves in group interactions. Dealing with the defenses against anxiety provides a useful framework for intense group work. Members have the opportunity to challenge some of their defensive strategies, and in the process of learning how to communicate in nondefensive ways they can also learn new ways of responding.

Transference and countertransference have significant implications for group work. Although not all feelings between members and the leader are the result of these processes, a leader must be able to understand their value and role. I find the analytic concept of projection quite useful in exploring certain feelings within the group. Projections onto the leader and onto other members are valuable clues to unresolved conflicts within the person that can be fruitfully worked through in the group.

The group can also be used to re-create early life situations that are continuing to have an impact on the client. In most groups individuals elicit feelings of attraction, anger, competition, avoidance, aggression, and so forth. These feelings may be similar to those that members experienced toward significant people in the past. Thus, members will most likely find symbolic mothers, fathers, siblings, and lovers in their group. These transferences within the group and the intense feelings that often characterize them are fruitful avenues to explore.

Modifications of Classical Analytic Practice

An approach that integrates Freud's psychosexual stages of development with Erikson's psychosocial stages is, in my view, most useful for understanding key themes in the development of personality. I do not think that working solely on an insight level will result in changes; it is essential to explore sociocultural factors as they pertain to the struggles of individuals at the various phases of their development. Unless group practitioners have a good grasp of the major tasks and crises of each stage, they have little basis for determining whether developmental patterns are normal or abnormal. Also, a synthesis of

Freud's and Erikson's theories offers a general framework for recognizing conflicts that participants often explore in groups.

The newer developments—object relations theories, self psychology, and relational psychoanalysis—offer valuable conceptions for group therapists. There have been a number of breakthroughs in working with borderline and narcissistic dynamics in group therapy, and the group offers some unique advantages over the one-to-one relationship in working with borderline personalities.

Many practitioners who were trained in classical psychoanalysis have modified analytic concepts and techniques to fit group situations. I have encountered a number of therapists who think in psychoanalytic terms but draw on other therapeutic models. They work with analytic concepts such as the unconscious, defenses, resistances, transference, and the significance of the past, but they also borrow techniques from other approaches. Some analytic therapists demonstrate an openness toward integrating various methods. For example, Marmor (1997), a psychoanalyst, states: "I try to avoid putting every patient on a Procrustean bed of a singular therapeutic method but rather adapt my approach to the patient's own unique needs" (p. 32).

Limitations of the Approach

From a feminist perspective, there are distinct limitations to a number of Freudian concepts, especially the notion of the Oedipus and Electra complexes and the assumptions about the inferiority of women. In her review of feminist counseling and therapy, Enns (1993) notes that the object relations approach has been criticized for its emphasis on the role of the mother/child relationship as a determinant of later interpersonal functioning. This approach gives great responsibility to mothers for deficiencies and distortions in development, whereas fathers are conspicuously absent from the hypothesis. Enns writes that some feminist therapists have addressed the limitations of psychoanalysis by incorporating family systems work within their psychoanalytic model.

In addition to the criticisms of psychoanalysis from feminist writers, the approach has been accused of failing to adequately address the social, cultural, and political factors that result in an individual's problems. There are likely to be some difficulties in applying a psychoanalytic approach with low-income clients. This is especially true when working within the framework of long-term, in-depth analysis, which may be in direct conflict with some clients' social framework and interpersonal and environmental perspective.

Psychoanalytic therapy is less concerned with short-term problem solving than it is with long-term personality reconstruction. Poor people generally do not have the time, resources, or inclination to begin and maintain the extended and expensive journey of psychoanalytic self-exploration. Instead, they are likely to be motivated more by the need to have psychological security and provide for their family. If they seek professional help, they are generally concerned with dealing with a crisis situation and with finding answers, or at least some direction, in addressing survival needs pertaining to housing, employment, and child care.

A major limitation of psychodynamic group therapy is the relatively long time span required to accomplish analytic goals. Indeed, Alperin (1997) raises the question "Is psychoanalytically oriented psychotherapy compatible with managed care?" (p. 185). He persuasively argues that managed care violates many of the basic premises upon which psychoanalytic therapy rests. For example, analytic therapists who offer services under managed care cannot provide their clients with privacy and confidentiality, and the requirements and justifications for treatment of managed care plans negatively affect the therapeutic relationship and are injurious to the client. Psychodynamic therapy focuses on the resolution of conflicts within the underlying character structure, and its basic principles are both different from and incompatible with the philosophy of managed care. Alperin goes so far as to state that, because of the power and control big businesses now have over health practices, psychodynamic therapy may be in danger of extinction.

In his critique of long-term psychodynamic therapy, Strupp (1992) acknowledges that this approach will clearly remain a luxury for most people in our society. Recognizing that most practitioners have been influenced by an eclectic spirit, he predicts this outlook for psychodynamic practice: "This [new] movement reflects a decisive departure from orthodoxy, together with much greater openness by most therapists to adapt to changing circumstances and to tailor techniques to the changing needs of patients as well as to the demands of our multifaceted society" (p. 25).

Psychoanalysts are attempting to creatively meet modern challenges without losing their original focus on depth and inner life (DeAngelis, 1996). Many psychoanalytically oriented group therapists support the move to the use of briefer therapy, especially when this is indicated by the client's needs rather than arbitrarily set by third-party payers. However, analytically oriented therapists tend to be skeptical of "quick fix" techniques and simplistic solutions to complex psychodynamic problems. Hence, it is understandable that many psychoanalytically oriented group therapists resist pressures to limit their work to short-term, managed care therapy. In their view the economic pressures promote superficial therapy, the benefit of which is only illusory.

Where to Go from Here

If you would like to learn more about psychoanalytic groups, you would do well to join the American Group Psychotherapy Association (AGPA). Membership includes a subscription to an excellent journal, the *International Journal of Group Psychotherapy*, which is published four times a year. The journal contains a variety of articles dealing with both the theory and practice of group therapy, and many of the articles relate to psychoanalytic groups. Each year in February the AGPA sponsors a five-day annual meeting that features a variety of institutes, seminars, open sessions, and workshops. Although psychodynamic groups are featured, other group orientations are offered as well. Many of these full-day and half-day workshops are directed toward issues of interest to psychodynamic practitioners. The AGPA does have a student-member category. For further information about journal subscriptions and membership requirements contact:

American Group Psychotherapy Association, Inc.
25 East 21st Street, 6th Floor
New York, NY 10010
TELEPHONE: (212) 477-2677 or Toll Free: (877) 668-2472
FAX: (212) 979-6627
E-MAIL: info@agpa.org
WEB SITE: www.agpa.org

Recommended Supplementary Readings

Object Relations and Self Psychology: An Introduction (St. Clair, 2000) provides an overview and critical assessment of two streams of psychoanalytic theory and practice: object relations theory and self psychology. The book looks at how different theorists vary from one another and how they depart from the classical Freudian model. This is a good place to start if you want an update on the contemporary trends in psychoanalysis.

Psychoanalytic Theory: An Introduction (Elliott, 1994) provides thorough coverage of the psychoanalytic implications for "postmodern" theories, systems approaches, and feminist thought.

Techniques of Brief Psychotherapy (Flegenheimer, 1982) is useful in describing the processes of client selection, therapist training, and modifications of techniques used in brief psychoanalytic therapy.

The Psychoanalytic Conspiracy (Langs, 1982) describes the search for truth in analytic therapy. Criticism of other schools is somewhat extreme in its severity, but the book provides a useful admonition to counselors to be self-aware.

References and Suggested Readings*

*Alperin, R. M. (1997). Is psychoanalytically oriented psychotherapy compatible with managed care? In R. M. Alperin & D. G. Phillips (Eds.), *The impact of managed care on the practice of psychotherapy: Innovation, implementation, and controversy* (pp. 185–198). New York: Brunner/Mazel.

*American Psychiatric Association. (2000). *Diagnostic and statistical manual of mental disorders text revision*, (4th ed.). (DSM-IV-TR). Washington, DC: Author.

Bemak, F., & Epp, L. (2001) Countertransference in the development of graduate student group counselors: Recommendations for training. *Journal for Specialists in Group Work, 26*(4), 305–318.

Bower, B. (2001). Repression tries for experimental comeback. *Science News, 159*(11), 164.

---

*Books and articles marked with an asterisk are suggested for further study.

Brabender, V. M. (1987). Vicissitudes of countertransference in inpatient group psychotherapy. *International Journal of Group Psychotherapy, 37*(4), 549–567.

Brand, J. (1995). Does contemporary cognitive psychology favor or oppose psychoanalytic theory? *American Psychologist, 50*(9), 799–800.

*DeAngelis, T. (1996). Psychoanalysis adapts to the 1990s. *APA Monitor, 27*(9), 1, 43.

Durkin, H. (1964). *The group in depth.* New York: International Universities Press.

*Earley, J. (2000). *Interactive group therapy: Integrating interpersonal, action-oriented, and psychodynamic approaches.* Philadelphia, PA: Brunner/Mazel (Taylor & Francis Group).

*Elliott, A. (1994). *Psychoanalytic theory: An introduction.* Cambridge: Blackwell.

Enns, C. Z. (1993). Twenty years of feminist counseling and therapy: From naming biases to implementing multifaceted practice. *The Counseling Psychologist, 21*(1), 3–87.

*Epstein, S. (1994). Integration of the cognitive and the psychodynamic unconscious. *American Psychologist, 49,* 709–724.

Erikson, E. H. (1963). *Childhood and society* (2nd ed.). New York: Norton.

Erikson, E. H. (1968). *Identity: Youth and crisis.* New York: Norton.

Erikson, E. H. (1982). *The life cycle completed.* New York: Norton.

*Flegenheimer, W. V. (1982). *Techniques of brief psychotherapy.* New York: Aronson.

Foulkes, S. H. (1965). *Therapeutic group analysis.* New York: International Universities Press.

Freud, S. (1955). *The interpretation of dreams.* New York: Basic Books.

Gabbard, G. O. (2000). *Psychodynamic psychiatry in clinical practice* (3rd ed.). Washington, DC: American Psychiatric Press.

*Horgan, J. (1996). Why Freud isn't dead. *Scientific American, 275*(6), 106–111.

Kernberg, O. F. (1975). *Borderline conditions and pathological narcissism.* New York: Aronson.

Kernberg, O. F. (1976). *Object-relations theory and clinical psychoanalysis.* New York: Aronson.

*Kernberg, O. F. (1997). Convergences and divergences in contemporary psychoanalytic technique and psychoanalytic psychotherapy. In J. K. Zeig (Ed.), *The evolution of psychotherapy: The third conference* (pp. 3–22). New York: Brunner/Mazel.

Kohut, H. (1971). *The analysis of the self.* New York: International Universities Press.

Kohut, H. (1977). *The restoration of the self.* New York: International Universities Press.

Kohut, H. (1984). *How does psychoanalysis cure?* Chicago: University of Chicago Press.

Kolb, G. E. (1983). The dream in psychoanalytic group therapy. *International Journal of Group Psychotherapy, 33*(1), 41–52.

Kutash, I. L., & Wolf, A. (1983). Recent advances in psychoanalysis in groups. In H. I. Kaplan & B. J. Sadock (Eds.), *Comprehensive group psychotherapy* (2nd ed.). Baltimore: Williams & Wilkins.

*Langs, R. (1982). *The psychotherapeutic conspiracy.* New York: Aronson.

Linehan, M. M. (1993a). *Cognitive-behavioral treatment of borderline personality disorder.* New York: Guilford.

Linehan, M. M. (1993b). *Skills training manual for treating borderline personality disorder.* New York: Guilford.

Locke, N. (1961). *Group psychoanalysis: Theory and technique.* New York: New York University Press.

Mahler, M. S. (1968). *On human symbiosis and the vicissitudes of individuation.* New York: International Universities Press.

*Marmor, J. (1997). The evolution of an analytic psychotherapist: A sixty-year search for conceptual clarity in the tower of Babel. In J. K. Zeig (Ed.), *The evolution of psychotherapy: The third conference* (pp. 23–36). New York: Brunner/Mazel.

*Masterson, J. F. (1997). The disorders of the self and intimacy: A developmental self and object relations approach. In J. K. Zeig (Ed.), *The evolution of psychotherapy: The third conference* (pp. 37–52). New York: Brunner/Mazel.

*Messer, S. B., & Warren, C. S. (2001). Brief psychodynamic therapy. In R. J. Corsini (Ed.), *Handbook of innovative therapies* (2nd ed., pp. 67–85). New York: Wiley.

*Mullan, H., & Rosenbaum, M. (1978). *Group psychotherapy: Theory and practice* (2nd ed.). New York: Free Press.

St. Clair, M. (2000). *Object relations and self psychology: An introduction* (3rd ed.). Pacific Grove, CA: Brooks/Cole.

Salter, A. (1961). *Conditioned reflex therapy*. New York: Capricorn Books. (original work published 1949)

Sapolsky, R. (2001). Wild dreams. *Discover, 22*(4), 36–43.

Scheidlinger, S. (1987). On interpretation in group psychotherapy: The need for refinement. *International Journal of Group Psychotherapy, 37*(3), 339–352.

Sleek, S. (1997). Treating people who live on the borderline. *APA Monitor, 28*(7), 20–21.

Strupp, H. H. (1992). The future of psychodynamic psychotherapy. *Psychotherapy, 29*(1), 21–27.

Tuttman, S. (1986). Theoretical and technical elements which characterize the American approaches to psychoanalytic group psychotherapy. *International Journal of Group Psychotherapy, 36*(4), 499–515.

*Vontress, C. E. (1996). A personal retrospective on cross-cultural counseling. *Journal of Multicultural Counseling and Development, 24*(3), 156–166.

Wolf, A. (1963). The psychoanalysis of groups. In M. Rosenbaum & M. Berger (Eds.), *Group psychotherapy and group function*. New York: Basic Books.

Wolf, A. (1975). Psychoanalysis in groups. In G. M. Gazda (Ed.), *Basic approaches to group psychotherapy and group counseling* (2nd ed.). Springfield, IL: Charles C Thomas.

Wolf, A. (1983). Psychoanalysis in groups. In H. I. Kaplan & B. J. Sadock (Eds.), *Comprehensive group psychotherapy* (2nd ed.). Baltimore: Williams & Wilkins.

Wolf, A., & Kutash, I. L. (1986). Psychoanalysis in groups. In I. L. Kutash & A. Wolf (Eds.), *Psychotherapist's casebook* (pp. 332–352). San Francisco: Jossey-Bass.

Wolf, A., & Schwartz, E. K. (1962). Psychoanalysis in groups. New York: Grune & Stratton.

Yalom, I. D. (1995). *The theory and practice of group psychotherapy* (4th ed.). New York: Basic Books.

CHAPTER 7

Adlerian Group Counseling

Introduction

While Freud was developing his system of psychoanalysis, a number of other psychiatrists also interested in the psychodynamic approach were independently studying the human personality.* One of these was Alfred Adler. Freud and Adler attempted to collaborate, but Freud's basic concepts of sexuality and biological determinism were unacceptable to Adler. Freud believed sexual repression caused neurotic disorders. Adler (1996a, 1996b), in contrast, contended that neurosis was the result of a person's retreat from the required tasks in life with the symptoms serving an ego-protective or safeguarding function to protect the individual from perceived failure in a life task. Adler focused on the struggle of individuals to become all that they might be. This psychology of growth was quite different from Freud's psychology of the abnormal personality, and after about nine years of loose association the two parted company, with Freud taking the position that Adler had deserted him.

Another major difference between Freud and Adler involves the populations with whom they worked. Freud focused on the individual psychodynamics of a neurotic population, and Freudian psychoanalysis was largely confined to more affluent clients. By contrast, Adler was a politically and socially oriented psychiatrist who showed great concern for the common person; part of his mission was to bring psychological understanding to the general population and to translate psychological concepts into practical methods for helping a varied population meet the challenges of life.

Alfred Adler made significant contributions to contemporary therapeutic practice. Adler believed in the social nature of human beings, and he was interested in working with clients in a group context. He established more than 30 child guidance clinics in which he pioneered live demonstrations by interviewing children, adults, teachers, and parents in front of community groups. He was the first psychiatrist to use group methods in a systematic way in child guidance centers in the 1920s in Vienna.

---

*I appreciate James Bitter's collaboration with me on this chapter over the various revisions of this textbook.

To fully appreciate the development of the practice of Adlerian psychology, one must recognize the contributions of Rudolf Dreikurs, who was largely responsible for transplanting Adler's ideas to the United States. It was Dreikurs who developed and refined Adler's concepts into a clear-cut, teachable system with practical applications for family life, education, preventive mental health, and, especially, group psychotherapy (Terner & Pew, 1978). Dreikurs (1960) was likely to have been the first to use group psychotherapy in private practice. He did a great deal to translate Adlerian principles into the practice of group psychotherapy (see Dreikurs, 1960, 1967, 1997). Dreikurs was a key figure in developing the Adlerian family education centers in the United States. Work with children and their parents in a group setting paved the way for Dreikurs's pioneering group psychotherapy.

Adlerian interventions have been widely applied to diverse client populations of all ages in many different settings. Adlerian group therapy is an integration of key concepts of Adlerian psychology with socially constructed, systemic, and brief approaches based on the holistic model developed by Dreikurs (Sonstegard, Bitter, Pelonis-Peneros, & Nicoll, 2001).

Key Concepts

Overview of the Adlerian View of the Person

Adler's system emphasizes the social determinants of behavior rather than its biological aspects; its goal directedness rather than its origins in the past; and its purposeful, rather than its unconscious nature. This "socioteleological" approach implies that people are primarily motivated by social forces and are striving to achieve certain goals. Adler's view is that we create for ourselves an idiosyncratic view of self, life, and others from which we then create goals, both short- and long-term, that motivate our behavior and influence our development. It is especially our long-term goals that guide our movement toward an envisioned completion and sometimes even toward perfection. The search for significance is related to our basic feelings of inferiority with regard to others, which motivates us to strive toward ever-greater mastery, superiority, power, and, ultimately, perfection. Inferiority feelings can thus be the wellspring of creativity; perfection, though never reached, is the ultimate goal of life. Since most of us do not reach completion or perfection, our goals are always fictions—pictures of personal fulfillment that we adopt "as if" they were true. Adler's socioteleological approach provides an ideal foundation for group work (Sonstegard, 1998b).

Adler's system stresses self-determination and consciousness—rather than the unconscious posited by Freud—as the center of personality. We are not the victims of fate but creative, active, choice-making and meaning-making beings whose every action has purpose and is directed toward some goal. Movement toward goals and our anticipation of the future are far more important than what has happened to us in the past. Behavior can be understood only if one takes a holistic approach and looks at all actions from the perspective of the individual's chosen style of life. Each of us has a unique lifestyle, or personality, which starts to develop in early childhood to compensate for and overcome some perceived inferiority. Our lifestyle orders our experiences of life and guides interactions with others. It consists of our views about ourselves, others, and the world, and the distinctive behaviors we use to pursue our goals.

Because of its stress on responsibility, on the striving for superiority, and on the search for value and meaning in life, Adler's approach is basically a growth model. The striving for superiority is best conceived of as "moving from a perceived minus to a perceived plus" (Ansbacher & Ansbacher, 1956). Adlerians reject the idea that some individuals are psychologically "sick" and in need of a "cure." Instead, Adlerians view their work as primarily an educational process—helping people learn better ways to meet the challenges of life tasks, providing direction, helping people change their mistaken notions, and offering encouragement to those who are discouraged.

Holism

The Adlerian approach, also known as *Individual Psychology*, is based on a holistic view of the person. (The word *individual* does not imply a focus on the individual client as opposed to people in groups.) Individuals are always more than the sum of their parts. Thoughts, feelings, beliefs, behavioral patterns, traits and characteristics, convictions, attitudes, and fundamental selves are all expressions of the uniqueness of the person. Adler stressed understanding the whole person—not just parts but an indivisible whole.

One implication of this holistic view is that the client is seen as an integral part of a social system. There is more focus on interpersonal factors than on intrapersonal ones. The therapist is oriented toward understanding the client's social situation and the attitudes he or she has about it. Viewing people in relationship to social systems is basic to group and family therapy.

Adler's theory is, in essence, a field theory of personality focusing on how the individual attempts to find his or her place within the social environment. Adler saw behavior as inherently social and therefore all behavior is understandable only with reference to its function within the social context in which this behavior occurs. To understand an individual, one must learn how the person operates within this social context. Group counseling is a natural setting for addressing relationships, for it is in a group that members can experiment with interactions that result in transforming the mistaken goals and notions they are pursuing (Sonstegard & Bitter, 2001).

Teleology

According to Adler, all forms of life are characterized by a trend toward growth and expansion. He rejected Freud's causal determinism in favor of teleological explanations: humans live by goals and purposes, they are moved by anticipation of the future, and they create meaning. Adler's basic assumption was that we create meaning for our lives and based on this "private logic" we develop goals, both immediate and long-term, which motivate both behavior and development. Long-term goals especially guide our movement toward an envisioned completion or self-actualization. Very early in life we begin to envision what we might be like if we were complete, whole, and in some cases, perfect. Since we rarely reach self-actualization or perfection, the goals are always fictions—pictures of personal fulfillment that we adopt and then function "as if" they were true and that one day we will reach these goals (Sonstegard & Bitter, 2001). The group setting provides an ideal place for members to identify and explore their core beliefs and the goals toward which they are striving.

Individual Psychology contends that we can be understood best by looking at where we are going and what we are striving to accomplish. Thus, in contrast to the Freudian psychoanalytic emphasis on the past, Adlerians are more interested in the future. The three aspects of time are dynamically interrelated: our behavioral decisions are based on the conclusions we have made from what we have experienced in the past, which we use to then provide a framework for understanding our present situation, and for choosing, albeit unconsciously, the goals toward which we move. In short, Adlerians look for a continuity or pattern in a client's life, but always with the emphasis on the goal-directed nature of all behavior.

Phenomenology

Adler was perhaps the first major theorist to stress a phenomenological orientation toward therapy. His psychological approach pays attention to the subjective fashion through which people perceive their world. This personal perspective includes the individual's views, beliefs, perceptions, and conclusions. From the Adlerian perspective, objective reality is less important than how we interpret reality and the meanings we attach to what we experience. Humans are creative beings who decide on their actions based on their subjective perceptions.

As you will see in later chapters, many contemporary theories have incorporated this notion of the client's subjective perception of reality, or personal worldview, as a basic factor explaining behavior. Some of the other group approaches that have a phenomenological perspective are psychodrama, existential therapy, person-centered therapy, Gestalt therapy, the cognitive therapies, reality therapy, and narrative therapy.

Creativity and Choice

From the Adlerian perspective, humans are not defined solely by heredity and environment; rather, these are the foundations, or building blocks, of life. The socioteleological approach is grounded on the notion that humans are self-determining beings. We have the capacity to influence and create events. We express ourselves in diverse ways that are consistent with our past experiences, present attitudes, and anticipations about the future (Sonstegard, 1998b). Adler believed that what we are born with is not as crucial as the use we make of our natural endowment. Adlerians do recognize, however, that biological and environmental conditions limit our capacity to choose and to create. Although they reject the deterministic stance of Freud, they do not go to the other extreme by maintaining that individuals can become whatever they want to be. This approach is based on the premise that within a framework of limitations a wide range of choices is open to us.

From the Adlerian viewpoint, healthy people strive toward perfection or completion, but they are not perfectionistic. They attempt to become masters of their fate. Adlerians base their practice on the assumption that people are creative, active, and self-determining. They have little sympathy with perspectives that cast a client in the role of a passive victim. As an illustration of the implications of this view, consider Dreikurs's typical remark to a man who complained about his wife's behavior and who tried to play a helpless role. Dreikurs (1967) confronted him with the question "And what did you do?" He developed a style of challenging clients to become aware of the ways in which they were active participants in situations they perceived as problematic. In other words, he explored with them how they were part of a circular pattern of causality and thus capable of breaking that pattern. His therapy was aimed at showing clients that, although they could not directly change the behavior of others, they did have the power to change their own reactions and attitudes toward others.

Social Interest and Community Feeling

Social interest and community feeling, derived from the German word *Gemeinschaftsgefühl*, is a fundamental and distinctive notion in Individual Psychology (Eckstein & Baruth, 1996). This concept embodies the feeling of being connected to all of humanity—past, present, and future—and to being involved in making the world a better place. The term *social interest* refers to an action line of one's community feeling. Social interest is the individual's positive attitude toward other people in the world. Adlerians believe this connecting, community feeling is innate and that, when developed, it expresses an active, social interest (Sonstegard, 1998b). As an antidote to social isolation and self-absorption, social interest leads to courage, optimism, and a true sense of belongingness. Adler equates social interest with a sense of identification and empathy with others.

Individual Psychology rests on a central belief that our happiness and success are largely related to social connectedness. As social beings, we have a need to be of use to others and to establish meaningful relationships in a community. Because we are embedded in a society, we cannot be understood in isolation from that social context. We are primarily motivated by a desire to belong. Only within the group can we actualize our potentialities.

Adler (1964) notes that we have strong needs to feel united with others and that only when we do so can we act with courage in facing and dealing with life's problems. He contends that we must successfully master at least three universal life tasks. All people need to address these life tasks, regardless of age, gender, time in history, culture, or nationality. These tasks are building friendships (social task), establishing intimacy (love/marriage task), and contributing to society (occupational task). These life tasks are so fundamental to human living that dysfunction in any one of them is often an indicator of psychological disorders (American Psychiatric Association, 2000). Each of these areas can be fruitfully discussed in a group. Most members have core beliefs surrounding key life tasks such as work, love, self-acceptance, and friendship. These beliefs can be critically examined within the group, and it is possible to eliminate faulty beliefs and replace them with more constructive or useful beliefs.

Dreikurs and Mosak (1966, 1967) discuss two additional life tasks: the self task (getting along with ourselves) and the spiritual task. Adler (1964) maintains that the degree to which we successfully share with others and are concerned with the welfare of others is an index of our overall personality adjustment and level of maturity. In other words, social interest is the measure of mental health, insofar as it is reflected in our capacity to give and receive and in our willingness to cooperate for the common benefit of all (Sherman & Dinkmeyer, 1987).

These key concepts of community feeling and social interest have significant implications for group counseling; the general goals of the group are to increase self-esteem and to develop social interest. The group focuses on discovering the members' mistaken assumptions that are keeping them from feeling adequate and from being oriented toward and engaged with others. This concept is applied to group counseling by structuring the group so that members can meet some of their needs for affiliation with others.

Self-centeredness and the alienation it produces are the opposite of social interest and are seen as a major problem in contemporary society. It is hoped that one of the outcomes of a group experience will be that members grow to accept themselves and others, even though all of us are imperfect. For this reason, most Adlerians reject the idea of prescreening in groups. They believe the process tends to destroy heterogeneity and works against accepting different levels of imperfection common in the larger society. Sonstegard and Bitter (1998a, 2001) assert that, generally, prescreening excludes the very people who could most use a group experience—those who are self-absorbed, noncommunicative, disruptive, and isolated. Such people may best find solutions to their problems in a group setting. Adlerians contend that refusing to give an individual the opportunity to participate in a group experience is antidemocratic. Adlerians believe groups ought to welcome all who want to join and not exclude the people who need it most (Bitter, 1996; Sonstegard, 1998b).

Inferiority/Superiority

From our earliest years, we recognize that we are helpless or less capable than we need to be, which is characterized by feelings of inferiority or of being less than we should be. This inferiority is not a negative force. On the contrary, our basic inferiority is the springboard for our attempts to master our environment. To compensate for feelings of inferiority, we strive for a better position in life. In Adler's words, we *strive for superiority*, or to move from a felt minus position in life to a perceived plus position. It is through this striving that we find ways to control the forces in our lives rather than being controlled by them.

Inferiority feelings, therefore, can be the wellspring of creativity; and life goals of perfection, though never reached, can draw us forward into new possibilities for which our past has not otherwise prepared us. Since inferiority feelings and striving for success are two sides of the same coin, both are grist for the mill in group work. Rather than attempting to make members feel better quickly, it is useful to explore the basis of feelings of inferiority. It is also useful for members to explore their own current strategies for managing their personal feelings of insignificance and inferiority. Members are encouraged to talk about any inferiority feelings and feelings of significance they may be experiencing within the group context itself. This can lead to very productive work with early recollections where members have made assumptions about their personal worth based all too often on remembered failure experiences. The group experience provides members with an opportunity to see these experiences in a new light and to put a new ending to a painful story.

Role of the Family

Adlerians place great emphasis on family processes, which play a significant role in the development of the personality during childhood. The climate of relationships among family members is known as the *family atmosphere*. The *family constellation* is the social configuration of the family group, the system of relationships in which self-awareness develops. This system includes and is maintained by the individual, the parents and siblings, and any others living in the household (Powers & Griffith, 1987).

Children incorporate many of the personal characteristics of their parents, and they learn a great deal about life by observing and interacting with their parents (Christensen, 1993; Sherman & Dinkmeyer, 1987). Dreikurs (1967) takes the position, however, that sibling relationships are more influential in personality development than relationships between children and parents. In addition, the meaning that people give to their own position in the family constellation and the positions of their siblings is more important than the actual chronological ages of the siblings. The personality characteristics of each person in the family, the emotional bonds between family members, the size of the family, and the sex of the siblings are all factors in the family constellation. The child's position and role in the family influence later personality development (Powers & Griffith, 1987).

Powers and Griffith believe young family members rehearse a way of relating to others that will become a vital part of their style of life. They add that the family is not an encapsulated system apart from the community. Once material is gathered about the client's family constellation, a summary is developed so that interpretations can be made. The summary contains the client's strengths and weaknesses, and it is used in helping clients gain a fuller understanding of the current influence of their family on them. It is also important to take into account the ethnic, religious, social, and economic milieu reported by the client. These factors serve as the material for one's self-perception and one's view of the world, but they are not causal factors.

Style of Life

Our basic concept of self in relation to the world—our personal orientation toward social living—is expressed in a discernible pattern that characterizes our existence. Bitter (1995) says that this pattern is called the *lifestyle*, or the "story of our life." He contends that the purpose of counseling is to help enlarge the client's story by making it fuller and richer. As already mentioned, the style of life is drawn first from one's family constellation and family atmosphere. The formative experiences within the family, particularly among siblings, contribute to establishing guidelines for understanding life that eventually make up the style of life (Sherman & Dinkmeyer, 1987). No two persons develop exactly the same style of life. In striving for the goal of success, some people develop their intellect, others develop their physical being, and so on.

In striving for goals that are meaningful to us, we develop this unique approach to life (Ansbacher, 1974). Basic convictions and assumptions underlie the lifestyle pattern and form the *private logic* on which we operate. This concept helps explain how all our behavior fits together so that there is some consistency to our actions. Everything we do is related to our fictional goal of perfection. Adlerians refer to this process as *fictional finalism*, which is the imagined central goal that gives direction to behavior and unity to the personality. It is an image of what people would be like if they were perfect and perfectly secure. Adlerian group counselors work with both the patterns for living and the logic supporting it as a way to facilitate a more socially useful life (Sonstegard, 1998b).

Although our style of life is created primarily during the first six years of life, other events that occur later can have a profound effect on our development. It is not childhood experiences in themselves that count but our *interpretation* of these events, which may lead us to develop a faulty style of life based on mistaken notions in our private logic. Although we are not determined by our past, we are significantly influenced by our perceptions and interpretations of past events. Once we become aware of the patterns and continuity of our lives, especially of certain mistaken, self-defeating or self-limiting notions that we have developed, then we are in a position to modify those faulty assumptions and make basic changes. We can reframe childhood experiences and *consciously* create a new style of life.

Behavioral Disorders

Adler sees emotional and behavioral disorders as "failures in life." Psychological and behavioral disorders can be considered erroneous ways of living, or mistaken assumptions. They can include a faulty lifestyle, a mistaken goal of success, or an underdeveloped social interest. Since Adlerians maintain that clients do not suffer from a disease but from discouragement and a failure to solve the problems and tasks set by life, therapy is based on an educational model, not a medical model (Adler, 1996a, 1996b). Applied to group counseling, this emphasis means that much of what goes on in a group is a process of encouraging clients and teaching ways to move toward personal growth and connectedness with others as equals.

Role and Functions of the Group Leader

Adlerian group leaders promote an egalitarian, person-to-person relationship, which is basic to the Adlerian approach to groups. The Adlerian facilitator has feelings and opinions and is free to express them (Mosak, 2000). Group leaders serve as models for the members, who often learn more from what leaders do in the group than from what they say.

A number of specific personal attributes are essential for group counselors and are prerequisites for effectively fulfilling their role and function in a group (Sonstegard, 1998b). Some of these characteristics include presence, self-confidence, demonstrating the courage to be imperfect, willingness to take risks, acceptance, caring, willingness to model, collaborative spirit, sense of humor, listening for purposes and motives, and belief in the usefulness of the group process. For optimum results, counselors need to have a clear sense of their own identity, beliefs, and feelings. They must also be aware of the basic conditions essential for the growth of the group members.

Adlerian group counselors have the role of tending to the group process. They do this by leading each group session *as if* it were the last. Group leaders have the task of creating a structure that promotes involvement and interaction. Adlerian leaders tend to be quite active, especially during the initial group session. They provide structure for the sessions by assisting members to define personal goals, they conduct psychological assessments of individuals in the group, they offer interpretations, and they guide group assessment (Sonstegard & Bitter, 2001).

Sonstegard (1998b) identifies four key tasks that Adlerian group counselors perform in building a community sense within the group: (1) establish and maintain a group relationship; (2) examine the patterns and purposes of group members' actions and behaviors; (3) disclose to individuals the goals pursued and the private logic that supports these goals; and (4) implement a reeducation experience that tends to increase members' community feeling and social interest. These tasks are the goals of Adlerian group counseling, and they correspond to the stages in the development of a group, which are described next.

Stages of the Adlerian Group

Like the psychoanalytic approach to groups, Adlerian group counseling involves the investigation and interpretation of one's early life. As the following discussion indicates, however, there are some fundamental differences between

Adlerians and Freudians. Sonstegard and Bitter (1998b, 2001) outline the four stages of group counseling, which correspond to the four goals of counseling listed previously and which overlap to some extent:

Stage 1: establishing and maintaining cohesive relationships with members
Stage 2: initiating a psychological investigation emphasizing the motivation in understanding the individual (assessment)
Stage 3: communicating to the individual an understanding of self (insight)
Stage 4: seeing new alternatives and making new cognitive and behavioral choices (reorientation)

Let's examine each of these stages in more detail.

Stage 1: Establishing and Maintaining Cohesive Relationships with Members

In the initial stage the emphasis is on establishing a good therapeutic relationship based on cooperation and mutual respect. By focusing on the relationship from the first session, counselors are laying a foundation for cohesiveness and connection (Sonstegard et al., 2001). Group participants are encouraged to be active in the process, for they are responsible for their own participation in the group. It is not always easy to create an active atmosphere. Even those clients most eager to make progress may be unwilling to do the work required for effective group participation and may be determined to prove that they are helpless (Dreikurs, 1969). Dreikurs sees the group as conducive to a good client/counselor relationship. In the group situation there is ample opportunity to work on trust issues and to strengthen the relationship between member and leader. Also, by witnessing positive changes in peers, participants can see how well the group works.

The Adlerian therapeutic relationship is one between equals. A democratic atmosphere prevails, and the effective group counseling relationship is based on mutual respect. This does not mean that members do anything they please, however, for firmness in a spirit of kindness is necessary in all group counseling. Nor does social equality mean that everyone in the group is the same. What democracy and social equality imply is mutual respect and involvement.

Winning the client's cooperation is essential for effective group counseling. The process of creating a therapeutic relationship supports the development of common tasks to which the group counselor needs to win the cooperation of the members. Group process facilitates a sense of cooperation and collaboration (Sonstegard, 1998b; Sonstegard & Bitter, 2001). Both the leader and the members work together toward mutually agreed-upon goals. Adlerians believe that counseling, individual or group, progresses only when the therapeutic process focuses on what participants see as personally significant and on areas that they want to explore and change.

Stage 2: Analysis and Assessment
(Exploring the Individual's Dynamics)

The aim of the second stage is twofold: understanding one's lifestyle and seeing how it is affecting one's current functioning in all the tasks of life (Mosak, 2000). The leader may begin by exploring how the participants are functioning at work and in social situations and how they feel about themselves and their gender-role identities.

According to Dreikurs (1969), the individual's goals and current lifestyle become much more obvious in interactions with others in the group. Also, clients may respond differently when confronted by fellow participants than when confronted by the counselor alone. Adlerian group counselors use any number of assessment techniques. Process assessment techniques include examining such areas as the members' family constellation, birth order, relationship difficulties, early recollections, dreams, and artwork, all of which produce clues to each person's goals, purposes, and lifestyle. Each of these approaches to psychological investigation can reveal a group member's interpretations of self, life, and the world as well as any mistaken notions that may be connected to these interpretations (Sonstegard, 1998b). Analysis and assessment rely heavily on exploration of the client's family constellation, which includes evaluating the conditions that prevailed in the family when the person was a young child in the process of forming lifestyle convictions and basic assumptions.

Another assessment procedure is asking clients to report their *early recollections* along with the feelings and thoughts that accompanied these childhood incidents. Early memories cast light on the "story of my life," for they are more like metaphors for our current views on life rather than what actually happened long ago. From a series of early memories, it is possible to get a clear sense of our mistaken notions, guiding goals in life, present attitudes, social interests, and possible future behavior. Exploring early recollections involves discovering how mistaken notions based on faulty goals and values fly in the face of social interest and create problems in people's lives.

Adlerian counselors collect early recollections by asking group members to think back to when they were much younger, before the age of 8, and to tell the group about some specific event they recall happening at one time: "One time, I _____."

Early recollections provide an understanding of how we view and feel about ourselves, how we see the world, what our life goals are, what motivates us, what we believe in, and what we value. Early recollections represent a significant contribution for group counselors who use a variety of techniques. They are easy to obtain, and because of their projective nature, they offer practitioners a wealth of information that can be used in both the assessment and intervention phases of group counseling.

The lifestyle investigation, which includes exploration of one's family background and life story, reveals a pattern of *basic mistakes*. Mosak (2000) writes that the lifestyle can be conceived of as a personal mythology; people behave as if the myths were true, because, for them, they are true. Mosak lists five basic mistakes: (1) overgeneralizations, (2) false or impossible goals of "security," (3) misperceptions of life and its demands, (4) minimization or denial of one's basic worth, and (5) faulty values.

Dreikurs maintains that it is essential to obtain a thorough social history of the client to understand his or her lifestyle and to provide a foundation for treatment. This social history is made up of both objective and subjective dimensions. The subjective interview precedes the objective interview and involves carefully listening to the client's story. The counselor attends to the client's presentation, lets questions follow from the client's answers, and helps the client develop a complete picture of who he or she is (Dreikurs, 1997; Carr & Bitter, 1997).

An integral aspect of the subjective interview is the use of "The Question." A question Dreikurs typically asked was, "How would life be different if illness and/or symptom(s) were not present?" Other ways of posing the question are "What would change in your life if you could have a pill that would make you completely well?" "What would be different in your life if you felt completely free of your complaint?" The client's answer is crucial to the assessment process; it is used as a basis to determine whether an illness is due to organic or psychological factors. The answer clearly indicates the purpose and the direction of the symptoms. If nothing would change, this indicates a greater chance that organic causes are operating in the client's illness (Dreikurs, 1997). However, if a group member were to say, "I would be doing better in school or have more friends if it were not for my anxiety," Dreikurs believed the client's anxiety was serving a functional purpose of justifying lack of success or lack of friends (Sonstegard et al., 2001).

During the assessment stage, the group counselor's main task is to integrate and summarize data from the lifestyle investigation and to interpret how the mistaken notions and personal mythology are influencing the client. This is done in a clear and concise way so that clients can recognize their own dynamics and pinpoint their assets. The analysis of the lifestyle is an ongoing process and helps client and counselor develop a plan for counseling.

Stage 3: Awareness and Insight

Whereas the classical analytic position is that personality cannot change unless there is insight, the Adlerian view is that insight is a special form of awareness that facilitates a meaningful understanding within the counseling relationship and acts as a foundation for change. It is a means to an end, however, not an end in itself. People can make abrupt and significant changes without much insight. Mosak (2000) defines insight as "understanding translated into constructive action" (p. 76). He contends that the Freudian notion that insight must precede behavioral change frequently results in extended treatment and encourages clients to postpone taking action to change. Mere intellectual insight can lead to the endless "Yes, but" game of "I know I should stop, but _____." Adlerians believe change begins with present-centered awareness, a recognition that one has options or choices in regard to both perception and behavior, yet this awareness is not in and of itself enough to bring about significant change.

According to Sonstegard (1998b), groups are more effective than individual counseling in helping people gain awareness and redirect their mistaken goals and mistaken notions. The interaction within a group provides an ideal setting for learning about oneself. In groups, awareness is heightened by the feedback and support of other members. The reactions of members may carry more weight than what the group leader says. Group members accept feedback from each other because they feel that a certain equality exists among them. Furthermore, the sense of social connectedness that develops in groups enables members to see parts of themselves in others.

In a group context the awareness and insight stage is concerned with helping participants understand why they are functioning as they are. Members learn about themselves by exploring their own goals, personal mythology, private logic, mistaken goals, and lifestyle. The group facilitates the process of gaining insight because, as members experience resistance in themselves, they can also observe resistance in other members. There is enough similarity in basic mistaken attitudes and faulty motivations among all participants to allow the members to observe themselves in others and to help one another.

Interpretation is a technique that facilitates the process of gaining insight into one's lifestyle. Interpretation deals with members' underlying motives for behaving the way they do in the here-and-now. Interpretations are never forced on the client; they are presented tentatively in the form of hypotheses: "Could it be that _____?" "I have a hunch that I'd like to share with you." "It seems to me that _____." "Perhaps _____." "I get the impression that _____."

Interpretations are open-ended sharings that can be explored in group sessions. Interpretations are achieved collaboratively within groups with group members offering hunches about possible meanings. The group is invited to investigate meaning in each other's lives as a foundation for achieving desired changes (Sonstegard et al., 2001). Sonstegard (1998b) states that the beauty of offering interpretations in this collaborative manner is that group members are free to consider what they hear without feeling that an expert has handed down a final dogma. If the interpretation fits, members tend to respond with statements that give a new understanding. If it does not fit, the group often looks for a more accurate interpretation. The ultimate goal of this process is that participants will come to a deeper psychological understanding of themselves. The aim is for members to acquire deeper awareness of their own role in creating a problem, the ways in which they are maintaining the problem, and what they can do to improve the situation.

Stage 4: Reorientation

The end product of the group process is reorientation and reeducation. The reorientation stage consists of both the group leaders and the members working together to challenge erroneous beliefs about self, life, and others. The emphasis is on considering alternative beliefs, behaviors, and attitudes.

There is a change in members' attitudes toward their current life situation and the problems they need to solve. This reorientation is an educational experience. Adlerian groups are characterized by an attempt to reorient faulty living patterns and teach a better understanding of the principles that result in cooperative interaction (Sonstegard, 1998b). Members are helped to redirect their mistaken goals and mistaken notions. One of the aims is teaching participants how to become more effective in dealing with the tasks of life. Another aim is challenging and encouraging clients to take risks and make changes.

During the reorientation phase, members are encouraged to take action based on what they have learned in the group. The group becomes an agent in bringing about change because of the improved interpersonal relationships among members. The group process allows members to see themselves as others do and to recognize faulty self-concepts or mistaken goals that they are pursuing. Change is facilitated by the emergence of hope. Members accept that there are options, that others have shown they can be different, and that life can work out well. This sense of faith and hope contradicts the negative social influences members are imbued with in daily life (Sonstegard, 1998b).

Encouragement refers to the "building of courage," and it is derived from strengths. Encouragement is a process that expresses respect, trust, and belief in oneself and others. It communicates a deep sense of caring for others, whereas discouragement leads to diminished self-esteem and alienation from others (Eckstein, 1995). Encouragement is a basic aspect of all stages but is essential during reorientation. If encouragement is absent, the counseling efforts will not take root. Through encouragement, group participants begin to experience their own inner resources and the power to choose for themselves and direct their own lives. Peer encouragement often plays the most significant role in this reorientation and reeducation. The greatest encouragement comes from feeling that the members have found a place in the group. Members are encouraged when they realize they are accepted through their differences as well as the common ground they share (Sonstegard & Bitter, 2001). According to Sonstegard, Bitter, Pelonis-Peneros, and Nicoll (2001), groups have the potential for providing the necessary ingredients of encouragement. They state: "Encouragement flows from the faith members come to have in each other, from the hope that comes from group support, and from a communication of caring that often comes from both group members and the therapist" (p. 23).

Reorientation is the action stage of a group, during which new decisions are made and goals are modified. To challenge self-limiting assumptions, members are encouraged to act _as if_ they were the persons they want to be. They are asked to "catch themselves" in the process of repeating old patterns that have led to ineffective or self-defeating behavior. If clients hope to change, they need to set tasks for themselves and do something specific about their problems. Commitment is needed to translate new insights into concrete action.

Application: Therapeutic Techniques and Procedures

Rationale for a Group Approach

Adler and his co-workers used a group approach in their child guidance centers in Vienna as early as 1921. Adler appears to have been the first psychiatrist to use group methods in a systematic way. As noted earlier, Dreikurs extended and popularized Adler's work, especially with regard to group applications, and used group psychotherapy in his private practice for more than 40 years.

A rationale for group counseling is based on the premise that the problems of individuals are mainly of a social nature. Based on this assumption, group work takes on special significance from both diagnostic and treatment perspectives. The group provides the social context in which members can develop a sense of belonging and a sense of community. Group participants come to see that many of their problems are interpersonal in nature, that their behavior has social meaning, and that their goals can best be understood in the framework of social purposes. Sonstegard (1998a) writes that in the action and interaction within a group the participants express their goals, their sense of belonging, their intentions, and their social connectedness. Inferiority feelings can be challenged and counteracted effectively in groups, and the mistaken concepts and values at the root of social and emotional problems can be deeply influenced by the group because it is a value-forming agent.

Applications to Brief Group Therapy

Adlerian group counseling lends itself to brief interventions and to short-term formats. From the beginning, both Adler and Dreikurs developed and used group methods as a way to reach a greater number of people in a shorter period of time. To this day, Adlerian group counseling can be considered a brief approach to treatment (Sonstegard et al., 2001). Bitter and Nicoll (2000) identify five characteristics that form the basis for an integrative framework in brief therapy: time limitation, focus, counselor directiveness, symptoms as solutions, and the assignment of behavioral tasks. One advantage of the time limitation concept is that it conveys to clients the expectation that change will occur in a short period of time. Specifying the number of sessions can motivate both client and therapist to stay focused on desired outcomes and to work as efficiently as possible. Bitter and Nicoll claim that practitioners of Adlerian brief therapy strive to make a difference in the lives of their clients by staying focused on what is therapeutically possible in each engagement they have with their clients. Because there is no assurance that a future session will occur, brief therapists tend to ask themselves: "If I had only one session to be useful in this person's life, what would I want to accomplish" (p. 38).

What are the implications of these brief therapy concepts for the practice of group counseling? Adlerian group leaders recognize that many of the changes in the members take place between the group sessions. Thus, leaders create a structure that will help both them and the members stay focused on specific personal goals. Self-selected goals formulated once a group convenes become the focus of group work. Members can decide how they want to best use the time available to them, and they can formulate a set of understandings that will guide the group.

Sonstegard, Bitter, Pelonis-Peneros, and Nicoll (2001) have noted that many groups are time limited. These groups require at least a session or two for accomplishing the tasks of closure, completing unfinished business, suggesting referrals, and scheduling follow-up meetings. Bitter and Nicoll (2000) suggest that some time-limited groups consider meeting on a short-term basis at a later time (perhaps 6 months or a year after the initial sessions). This arrangement, which is structured with formal follow-up meetings, allows members to check in with one another, and the group may never officially terminate. This kind of group is an example of a form of brief, intermittent therapy.

Adlerians recognize that *focus*, combined with time limits and encouragement, helps group members gain hope that change is possible, and relatively soon (Bitter & Nicoll, 2000). Group leaders focus on empowerment, generating new behaviors from existing internal and external resources. They want group members to leave in better shape than when they came.

Applying the Adlerian Approach to Group Work in the Schools

Many Adlerian concepts, techniques, and procedures can be incorporated in groups for children in school settings where the entire history of the group may be limited to as few as six sessions. Because Adlerians focus on conscious aspects, on goals and motives, and deal with the present rather than exploring the past, short-term groups can be designed for a variety of populations in the schools.

Many Adlerian concepts and themes fit with counseling children and adolescents in various types of group counseling formats. One such example, an intervention based on the family constellation, is to invite children and adolescents to talk about their position in their family. Group members can be asked these questions: "How many children were in your family, and what was your birth order? Are you an only child? the first born? the last born? What do you remember about each of your siblings growing up? Which sibling did you feel the closest to? the most distant from? How do you think your relationship with your siblings has influenced your personality today?"

The concept of encouragement has relevance for group work with children and adolescents, for many of them feel a profound sense of discouragement. Without encouragement, group counseling will not make a difference (Sonstegard & Bitter, 1998b). The group process allows members to express the ways in which they experience their discouragement, and they also come to learn that they are not alone with their feelings. Groups using Adlerian basic concepts can be applied with at-risk high school students who are especially vulnerable to losing a sense of hope that life can be better. The four-stage model of Adlerian groups discussed earlier can be applied to adolescents who are lacking a sense of purpose. Through the reorientation process, at-risk adolescents are able to find a renewed sense of hope that they can change the direction of their lives. Bauer, Sapp, and Johnson's (2000) study provides quantitative and qualitative data that support the use of group counseling in a rural high school environment.

A concept that has great significance for group counseling in schools is social interest—which involves empathy, concern for others, cooperation, the ability to listen well, belonging, mutuality, and relatedness to others. Social interest is related to Goleman's (1995) notion of *emotional intelligence*, which pertains to the ability to control impulses, empathize with others, form responsible interpersonal relationships, and develop intimate relationships. Emotionally competent children and adolescents can be said to possess a high degree of social interest. Such people are able to express and control a range of emotions, they are accepting of the emotions of others, they strive for connections with others, and they have an interest in increasing both their self- and other-esteem (Hwang, 2000).

The focus of many counseling programs and self-improvement courses is the development of self-esteem. Children and adolescents also struggle with issues of feeling worthwhile, likable, and competent. Thompson and Rudolph (2000) state that for children to achieve a feeling of self-esteem they need to feel good about finding a place in life and about their progress in overcoming the unpleasant sense of inferiority typically associated with dependence and vulnerability, which often begins in early childhood. A well-adjusted child respects the rights of others, has tolerance for others, is cooperative and encouraging of others, has a positive self-concept and feelings of belonging, and identifies with socially acceptable goals. Sonstegard and Bitter (1998b) stress that the problems of most children stem from their interactions in groups and therefore these problems are best solved in groups. They explain how groups with children enhance social interest:

> Group counseling contributes to the dissolution of the social walls within which most children live. Over a period of time, group members develop a real interest in helping others in the group. We immediately know two things: (1) the group member offering help has already found a place in the group and may be on her or his way to finding a place in the larger world; (2) the help offered reflects an increase in social interest, not merely an attempt at self-elevation. (p. 264)

Hwang (2000) asserts that happiness entails possessing a healthy balance of both *self-esteem* and *other-esteem*. Rather than searching for ways to enhance self-esteem, Hwang makes a strong case for promoting personal and social responsibility. *Other-esteem* involves respect, acceptance, caring, valuing, and promoting others, without reservation. Hwang suggests that our challenge is to learn to see the world anew by reexamining our attitudes, values, and beliefs and developing a balance of caring for self and yet at the same time showing high esteem for others. Participating in a group can be instrumental in understanding others who may think, feel, and act differently from us. In a productive group, young people acquire increased self-esteem, but they also are able to enhance interest and esteem in others.

There is another use for groups in the schools. Children are often sent to a counseling group by a teacher because of misbehavior. Adlerians have an interesting perspective on the meaning of misbehavior. Children with a pattern of misbehavior are usually in pursuit of any of these mistaken goals: attention getting, power struggle, revenge, and inadequacy or withdrawal. Group counseling with children deals with these mistaken goals and with changes in the motivations that account for children's behavior. A group can provide a context for understanding the goal for which the child is striving, as well as the purpose underlying a "behavior problem," and can provide a basis for corrective action (Sonstegard & Bitter, 1998b; Thompson & Rudolph, 2000).

Applying the Adlerian Approach with Multicultural Populations

Adlerian theory is well suited to working with culturally diverse clients. Although the Adlerian approach is called Individual Psychology, the emphasis is on the person-in-the-environment, and culture can help define clients in a manner respectful of individual and cultural diversity (Carlson & Carlson, 2000). Adlerians' interest in helping others, in social interest, in pursuing meaning in life, in belonging, and in the collective spirit fits well with the group process. This approach respects the role of the family as influential in personality development and stresses social connectedness and establishing meaningful relationships in a community. Adlerian therapists tend to focus on cooperation and socially oriented values as opposed to competitive and individualistic values (Carlson & Carlson, 2000). The Native American, Latino, African American, and Asian American cultures likewise stress collectivism over the individual's welfare and emphasize the role of the family and the extended family. Many of the Adlerian key concepts have been applied to working with people from diverse cultures, for example, Latinos (Frevert & Miranda, 1998), Native Americans (Kawulich & Curlette, 1998), Vietnamese refugee women (Chung & Bemak, 1998), and Hindu women (Reddy & Hanna, 1998).

In Native American cultures spirituality is highly valued, and health and spirituality are generally viewed as inseparable (Kawulich & Curlette, 1998). A key component of group counseling with Native Americans is respect for the spiritual dimensions of their culture (Dufrene & Coleman, 1992). Adlerian psychology espouses a holistic view of the person that involves a unity of mind, body, and spirit—giving this approach some usefulness in working with Native Americans. However, Kawulich and Curlette (1998) state that the incidence of Native Americans seeking formal counseling is rare. They cite a number of reasons for the reluctance of Native Americans to seek counseling services. Seeking counseling from a Western-oriented program over a traditional healer is not considered the Indian way. Revealing one's highly personal thoughts and feelings is not easily done. It is not uncommon for Native Americans to be cautious in choosing those with whom they become open and trust. If they are referred to group counseling, they may be very reluctant to participate in the group discussions, or they may avoid sharing information that is likely to cast their family in a bad light. Likewise, Dufrene and Coleman (1992) indicate that there is general suspicion by Native Americans of non-Native populations, and group counseling may be seen as an intrusion. They also state that Native Americans tend not to disclose personal or family matters with outsiders. Although some of the philosophy of Individual Psychology may fit for working with Native Americans in groups, the group leader needs to assess the degree of congruence with the values of the Native American culture and the group.

Counseling Latinos from an Adlerian perspective has both strengths and limitations. The Adlerian emphasis on the family is congruent with the Latino cultural value given to family connections and social networks. Latinos derive most of their personal identity from their family and social networks (Frevert & Miranda, 1998). However, the Adlerian counselor who values equality and democracy may find many Latinos are not interested in equality in relationships, especially when it comes to parent–children relationships.

Adlerian concepts and methods lend themselves to the creation of a healing community, which is certainly a strength of the approach from a multicultural perspective. Kopp (1997) has written about creating a healing community through the application of Adlerian principles, methods, and skills. These Adlerian principles form the foundation for establishing a healing community:

- Democratic leadership does not imply anarchy, for order is essential. Decisions are made with the participation and input of all who are affected by these decisions.
- All individuals must be accorded equal worth. Attempts to achieve status, power, or superiority are never done by an individual at the expense of another person.
- Individuals have a basic need to contribute to the social good and to belong.
- Problem solving is based on mutual respect, which can be conveyed by an openness to diverse viewpoints, tolerance of differences, and listening to others. A climate of mutual respect and trust is essential for a healthy relationship and a healing community.

Kopp (1997) lists several methods that can be used in creating a healing community, all of which have implications for effective counseling groups:

- Replace interpersonal relationships based on an autocratic structure with relationships grounded on mutual respect among equals.
- Unify the group with a common purpose.
- Achieve unity of purpose through diversity of contribution.
- Employ action strategies that empower diverse groups and individuals.

Certain skills based on Adlerian psychology are necessary to implement these methods. A healing community is created by leaders who possess skills in winning cooperation, encouraging others, understanding group dynamics, conducting group discussions, conducting problem-solving discussions, being able to resolve conflicts, and establishing clear expectations and standards for evaluating progress. To be sure, these skills are essential for becoming an effective multicultural group counselor.

Although the Adlerian approach has some advantages in addressing diversity in a counseling group and in helping members apply what they learn in a group to create a therapeutic community where they live and work, there are also some potential limitations from a multicultural perspective. For example, applying the Adlerian concepts of belongingness and social interest to group counseling with Asian American clients may be difficult. Leong (1992) writes that in the collectivist orientation of many Asian Americans there is no clear distinction between individual and family problems. This could make disclosure about family dynamics in a group quite problematic. Many Asian Americans have been socialized to respect their family heritage, and some clients will be reluctant to reveal material that they believe brings dishonor to members of their family. Asian Americans are likely to be less verbally expressive in group situations, and they may be hesitant about admitting personal problems due to the shame it may cause. Leong points out that honor and the avoidance of losing face are important values for Asians. These factors need to be considered in an Adlerian group.

Leong (1992) also writes that in most Asian cultures interpersonal relationships tend to be hierarchical, with a strong respect for and loyalty to authority. Asian American group members will tend to view the group leader as the authority and expect him or her to have special expertise and power and to direct the group process. This is contrary to the Adlerian stress on the egalitarian, person-to-person spirit that reduces social distance and encourages self-disclosure. Adlerian group leaders may need to modify some techniques, especially the lifestyle assessment procedures, when working with Asian Americans.

Jim Bitter takes exception to the contention that the Adlerian approach may meet with resistance from people from Asian cultures who do not want to share personal matters about their families:

> This is only true if the therapist is insensitive and incompetent. Many Adlerians have worked very well in Japan, Hong Kong, and China, as well as with Asian Americans. We take into account cultural mandates, and we do our best to work compassionately with the people who put their lives in our trust. There are so many ways I can work with people and never ask them about family or even early recollections. (personal communication, January 25, 2002)

Carlson and Carlson (2000) note that a therapist's sensitivity and understanding of a client's culturally constructed beliefs about disclosing family matters are of paramount importance. If therapists are able to demonstrate an understanding of a client's cultural values, then this client is likely to show more openness to the assessment and treatment process. If therapists demonstrate sensitivity to and respect for the member's cultural values, then the chances are increased that the person will become more open to the assessment and exploration of his or her lifestyle.

In many respects Adlerian psychotherapy offers an ideal fit with Asian American clients. The Carlsons maintain that aspects of Adlerian psychotherapy that appear conducive to therapeutic work with Asian Americans are the emphasis on the client's social and cultural context, the value placed on collaborative goal setting, the importance given to the family environment, and the role of social interest in healthy functioning. Adlerian therapists encourage clients to define themselves within their social environments. Adlerians allow broad concepts of age, ethnicity, lifestyle, and gender differences to emerge in therapy. To their credit, Adlerians operate in flexible ways from a theory that can be tailored to work with individually and ethnically diverse clients. Employing this tailored approach, the therapeutic process is grounded within a client's culture and worldview. Instead of attempting to fit clients into preconceived models, they value fitting techniques to the particular needs of the individuals and families with whom they are working.

If the Adlerian approach is practiced appropriately and competently, it is difficult to find limitations from a multicultural perspective. The phenomenological nature of the Adlerian approach lends itself to understanding the worldview of clients, and Adlerians investigate culture in much the same way that they approach birth order and family atmosphere. Culture is a vantage point from which life is experienced and interpreted; it is also a background of values, history, convictions, beliefs, customs, and expectations that must be addressed by the individual. Adlerians do not decide for clients what they should change or what their goals should be; rather, they work cooperatively to enable clients to reach their self-defined goals.

Evaluation of the Adlerian Approach to Groups

Contributions and Strengths of the Approach

My group practice has been influenced by several Adlerian concepts, including emphasis on the social forces that motivate behavior and the search for mastery, superiority, and power. The patterns that people develop out of their relationships with their parents and siblings and the notion that we create a unique style of life as a response to our perceived inferiority are also intriguing to me.

The Adlerian approach deviates in many ways from the psychoanalytic model. Most Adlerians maintain that much of Adler's work was done independently of Freud. There are, however, some important commonalities between the two approaches, including a focus on critical periods of development, an interest in early recollections, and an emphasis on interpretation. The difference lies in Adler's social constructionist view of these areas as opposed to Freud's deterministic perspective.

A major Adlerian contribution to group counseling is the use of early recollections. Early memories cast light on the "story of my life," for they are consistent with our current view of life. From a series of early memories it is possible to get a clear sense of our mistaken notions, overriding goals in life, present attitudes, social interests, and possible future behavior (Eckstein, 1995).

One of the strengths of the Adlerian approach is its integrative nature. It is a holistic approach that encompasses the full spectrum of human experience, and practitioners have great freedom in working with clients in ways that are uniquely suited to their own therapeutic style. Adlerians use a wide variety of techniques, only a few of which are unique to Adlerian group counseling. An example of one such technique is the use of the family constellation as a means of learning the client's identity interpretations.

Even though all Adlerians accept the same theoretical concepts, they do not have a monolithic view of the therapeutic process. The methods of assessment and treatment differ substantially among practitioners who consider themselves to be Adlerians. Some Adlerian group practitioners are very directive, and others are not. Some are willing to disclose themselves, and others rarely make personal disclosures to clients. Adlerians who were trained by Adler tend to ask for one early recollection, whereas those who were trained by Dreikurs might routinely ask for as many as 6 to 12 recollections as part of the lifestyle interview. Adlerian group practitioners are not bound to follow a specific procedure, nor are they limited to using certain techniques. There can be almost as many methods as there are Adlerian therapists. The basic criterion is that therapeutic techniques fit the theory and the client. Thus, therapists are encouraged to grow both personally and professionally by being inventive.

Integration with Other Approaches

One of the strengths of the Adlerian approach is that its concepts have group applications in both clinical and educational settings (Sonstegard, 1998a; Sonstegard & Bitter, 1998b). As we have seen, its emphasis on social factors accounts for its success with individuals in groups, including parent education groups, teacher groups, and families—and also its widespread applicability to diverse client populations.

It is difficult to overestimate the contributions of Adler to contemporary therapeutic practice. Adler's influence has extended beyond group counseling into the community mental health movement, including the use of paraprofessionals. Abraham Maslow, Viktor Frankl, Rollo May, and Albert Ellis have all acknowledged their debt to Adler. Both Frankl and May see Adler as a forerunner of the existential movement because of his position that human beings are free to choose and are entirely responsible for what they make of themselves. This view also makes Adler a forerunner of the subjective, phenomenological approach to psychology, an approach that focuses on the internal determinants of behavior: values, beliefs, attitudes, goals, interests, personal meanings, perceptions of reality, and strivings toward self-actualization.

Furthermore, the Adlerian view is congruent with many other current psychological schools, such as Gestalt therapy, learning theory, transactional analysis, reality therapy, rational emotive behavior therapy, cognitive therapy, person-centered therapy, and logotherapy. All these approaches are based on a similar concept of the person as purposive and self-determining and as always striving for growth, value, and meaning in this world. In several important respects, Adler seems to have paved the way for the current developments in the cognitive behavior therapies. A basic premise in Adlerian practice is that if therapists can encourage clients to change their thinking, clients will then change their feelings and behavior. These connections to such a wide range of current theories and psychotherapies make the use of the Adlerian model ideal for integration purposes.

Limitations of the Approach

The Adlerian approach to group work shares some of the basic limitations of the psychoanalytic approach. Leaders of more structured groups may have difficulty incorporating some of the procedures geared toward understanding members' lifestyles and showing them how earlier experiences are influencing their current functioning. Members in structured or short-term groups may not be able to appreciate the value of exploring their childhood dynamics based on a comprehensive assessment.

Another basic limitation pertains to the practitioner. Unless group leaders are well trained, they can make significant mistakes, especially if they engage in interpreting members' dynamics. Leaders who have only a general understanding of Adlerian concepts could overstep the boundaries of their competence in attempting to teach members about the meaning of factors such as birth order and the family constellation. Using the procedures outlined in this chapter requires training.

Sperry (cited in Nystul, 1996) considers Adlerian psychology to be the most integrative and far ranging of any of the current or traditional models of human behavior, but he is concerned about the potential for stagnation of the theory. He asserts that there have been minor modifications in Adler's theory and techniques, yet he does not see much in the way of new developments in the last two decades. Unless the theory and methods are expanded, he believes the Adlerian approach will become a historical footnote. Similarly, in his keynote address at the International Congress for Individual Psychology, Nicoll (1996) cautioned that just as Adler stated that life is not a matter of being but of becoming, so too his theory must continuously be growing, developing, and becoming to face the new questions, issues, and knowledge in the field of counseling and psychology.

Where to Go from Here

If you find that your thinking is allied with the Adlerian approach, you might consider seeking training in Individual Psychology or becoming a member of the North American Society of Adlerian Psychology (NASAP). To obtain information on NASAP and a list of Adlerian organizations and institutes, contact:

North American Society of Adlerian Psychology (NASAP)
50 Northeast Drive

Hershey, PA 17033
TELEPHONE: (717) 579-8795
FAX: (717) 533-8616
E-MAIL: nasap@msn.com
WEB SITE: www.alfredadler.org

The society publishes a newsletter and a quarterly journal and maintains a list of institutes, training programs, and workshops in Adlerian psychology. The *Journal of Individual Psychology* presents current scholarly and professional research. Columns on counseling, education, and parent and family education are regular features. Information about subscriptions is available by contacting the society.

If you are interested in pursuing training, postgraduate study, continuing education, or a degree, contact NASAP for a list of Adlerian organizations and institutes. A few Adlerian training institutes are listed here:

Adler School of Professional Psychology
65 East Wacker Place, Suite 2100
Chicago, IL 60601-7298
TELEPHONE: (312) 201-5900
FAX: (312) 201-5917
E-MAIL: information@adler.edu
WEB SITE: www.adler.edu

Adlerian Training Institute
Dr. Bill Nicoll, Coordinator
P. O. Box 276358
Boca Raton, FL 33427-6358
TELEPHONE: (954) 757-2845

The Alfred Adler Institutes of San Francisco and Northwestern Washington
3320 Sussex Drive
Bellingham, WA 98226
TELEPHONE: (360) 935-1661
E-MAIL: HTStein@att.net
WEB SITE: http://ourworld.compuserv.com/homepages/hstein/

The Alfred Adler Institute of Quebec
4947 Grosvenor Avenue
Montreal, QC H3W 2M2
Canada
TELEPHONE: (514) 731-5675
FAX: (514) 731-9242
E-MAIL: aaiq@total.net
WEB SITE: www.total.net/~aaiq/index.html

The International Committee for Adlerian Summer Schools and Institutes (ICASSI)
Betty Haeussler
9212 Morley Road

Lanham, MD 20706
Telephone: (301) 577-8243
Fax: (301) 595-0669
E-mail: PeteHMSU64@aol.com

Recommended Supplementary Readings

Understanding Life-Style: The Psycho-Clarity Process (Powers & Griffith, 1987) is one of the best sources of information for doing a lifestyle analysis. This book comes alive with many good clinical examples. Separate chapters deal with interview techniques, lifestyle assessment, early recollections, the family constellation, and methods of summarizing and interpreting information.

The Theory and Practice of Life-Style Assessment (Eckstein & Baruth, 1996) is a useful workbook designed to introduce students to the lifestyle process. It contains an overview of Adlerian theory, guidelines to using a lifestyle assessment, and reorientation methods. The workbook contains a number of valuable inventories that can be used for personal growth and in therapeutic groups.

Superiority and Social Interest: A Collection of Later Writings (edited by H. Ansbacher & Ansbacher, 1979) contains various writings by Adler on topics such as his basic assumptions, his theory of the neuroses, case studies, and his views of religion and mental health. It also has a biographical essay on Adler and a chapter on the increasing recognition of his influence on current practice.

References and Suggested Readings[*]

Adler, A. (1964). *Social interest: A challenge to mankind.* New York: Capricorn.

Adler, A. (1996a). The structure of neurosis. *Individual Psychology, 52*(4), 318–333. (Original work published in 1935)

Adler, A. (1996b). What is neurosis? *Individual Psychology, 52*(4), 363–371.

American Psychiatric Association. (2000). *Diagnostic and statistical manual of mental disorders, text revision,* (4th ed.). (DSM-IV-TR). Washington, DC: Author.

Ansbacher, H. L. (1974). Goal-oriented Individual Psychology: Alfred Adler's theory. In A. Burton (Ed.), *Operational theories of personality* (pp. 99–142). New York: Brunner/Mazel.

Ansbacher, H. L., & Ansbacher, R. R. (Eds.). (1956). *The Individual Psychology of Alfred Adler.* New York: Basic Books.

*Ansbacher, H. L., & Ansbacher, R. R. (Eds.). (1979). *Superiority and social interest: A collection of later writings* (3rd rev. ed.). New York: Norton.

Bauer, S. R., Sapp, M., & Johnson, D. (2000). Group counseling strategies for rural at-risk high school students. *The High School Journal, 83*(2), 41–50.

Bitter, J. R. (1995, May 27). *The narrative study of lives: Lifestyle assessment as qualitative research.* Program presented at NASAP Annual Conference, Minneapolis, MN.

---

*Books and articles marked with an asterisk are suggested for further study.

*Bitter, J. R. (1996). An interview with Manford A. Sonstegard: A career in group counseling. *Journal for Specialists in Group Work, 21*(3), 194–213.

*Bitter, J. R., Christensen, O. C., Hawes, C., & Nicoll, W. G. (1998). Adlerian brief therapy with individuals, couples, and families. *Directions in Clinical and Counseling Psychology, 8*(8), 95–112.

*Bitter, J. R., & Nicoll, W. G. (2000). Adlerian brief therapy with individuals: Process and practice. *Journal of Individual Psychology, 56*(1), 31–44.

*Carlson, J. M., & Carlson, J. D. (2000). The application of Adlerian psychotherapy with Asian-American clients. *Journal of Individual Psychology, 56*(2), 214–225.

Carr, C. N., & Bitter, J. R. (1997). Dreikurs' holistic medicine: An introduction. *Individual Psychology: The Journal of Adlerian Theory, Research & Practice, 53*(2), 122–126.

Christensen, O. C. (Ed.). (1993). *Adlerian family counseling* (rev. ed.). Minneapolis, MN: Educational Media Corporation.

Chung, R. C-Y., & Bemak, F. (1998). Lifestyle of Vietnamese refugee women. *Journal of Individual Psychology, 54*(3), 373–384.

Corey, G. (1999). Adlerian contributions to the practice of group counseling: A personal perspective. *Journal of Individual Psychology, 55*(1), 4–14.

Dreikurs, R. (1960). *Group psychotherapy and group approaches: The collected papers of Rudolf Dreikurs*. Chicago: Alfred Adler Institute.

Dreikurs, R. (1967). *Psychodynamics, psychotherapy, and counseling: Collected papers*. Chicago: Alfred Adler Institute.

Dreikurs, R. (1969). Group psychotherapy from the point of view of Adlerian psychology. In H. M. Ruitenbeek (Ed.), *Group therapy today: Styles, methods, and techniques* (pp. 37–48). New York: Atherton.

*Dreikurs, R. (1997). Holistic medicine. *Individual Psychology, 53*(2), 127–205.

Dreikurs, R., & Mosak, H. H. (1966). The tasks of life: 1. Adler's three tasks. *The Individual Psychologist, 4*, 18–22.

Dreikurs, R., & Mosak, H. H. (1967). The tasks of life: 2. The fourth task. *The Individual Psychologist, 4*, 51–55.

Dufrene, P. M., & Coleman, V. D. (1992). Counseling Native Americans: Guidelines for group process. *Journal for Specialists in Group Work, 17*(4), 229–234.

*Eckstein, D. (1995). *The encouragement process in life-span development*. Dubuque, IA: Kendall/Hunt.

*Eckstein, D., & Baruth, L. (1996). *The theory and practice of life-style assessment*. Dubuque, IA: Kendall/Hunt.

Frevert, V. S., & Miranda, A. O. (1998). A conceptual formulation of the Latin culture and the treatment of Latinos from an Adlerian psychology perspective. *Journal of Individual Psychology, 54*(3), 291–309.

Goleman, D. (1995). *Emotional intelligence*. New York: Bantam.

Hwang, P. O. (2000). *Other esteem: Meaningful life in a multicultural society*. Philadelphia, PA: Accelerated Development (Taylor & Francis).

Kawulich, B. B., & Curlette, W. L. (1998). Life tasks and the Native American perspectives. *Journal of Individual Psychology, 54*(3), 359–367.

Kopp, R. R. (1997). Healing community: An Adlerian approach. *Individual Psychology: The Journal of Adlerian Theory, Research & Practice, 53*(1), 23–32.

Leong, F. T. L. (1992). Guidelines for minimizing premature termination among Asian American clients. *Journal for Specialists in Group Work, 17*(4), 218–228.

*Mosak, H. H. (2000). Adlerian psychotherapy. In R. J. Corsini & D. Wedding (Eds.), *Current psychotherapies* (6th ed., pp. 54–98). Itasca, IL: F. E. Peacock.

*Mosak, H. H., & Maniacci, M. P. (1998). *Tactics in counseling and psychotherapy.* Itasca, IL: F. E. Peacock.

*Mosak, H. H., & Maniacci, M. P. (1999). *A primer of Adlerian psychotherapy: The analytic-behavioral-cognitive psychology of Alfred Adler.* New York: Brunner/Mazel.

Nicoll, W. G. (1996). Keynote address at the International Congress of the International Association for Individual Psychology, August 1996, Cambridge, UK.

Nystul, M. S. (1996). An interview with Len Sperry. *Individual Psychology: The Journal of Adlerian Theory, Research & Practice, 52*(2), 200–207.

*Powers, R. L., & Griffith, J. (1987). *Understanding life-style: The psycho-clarity process.* Chicago: Americas Institute of Adlerian Studies.

Reddy, I., & Hanna, F. J. (1998). The lifestyle of the Hindu woman: Conceptualizing female clients of Indian origin. *Journal of Individual Psychology, 54*(3), 385–398.

Sherman, R., & Dinkmeyer, D. (1987). *Systems of family therapy: An Adlerian integration.* New York: Brunner/Mazel.

*Sonstegard, M. A. (1998a). A rationale for group counseling. *Journal of Individual Psychology, 54*(2), 164–175.

*Sonstegard, M. A. (1998b). The theory and practice of group counseling and group psychotherapy. *Journal of Individual Psychology, 54*(2), 217–250.

*Sonstegard, M. A., & Bitter, J. R. (1998a). Adlerian group counseling: Step by step. *Journal of Individual Psychology, 54*(2), 176–216.

*Sonstegard, M. A., & Bitter, J. R. (1998b). Counseling children in groups. *Journal of Individual Psychology, 54*(2), 251–267.

*Sonstegard, M. A., & Bitter, J. R. (2001). *Adlerian group therapy: Step-by-step.* Unpublished manuscript.

*Sonstegard, M. A., Bitter, J. R., Pelonis-Peneros, P. P., & Nicoll, W. G. (2001). Adlerian group psychotherapy: A brief therapy approach. *Directions in Clinical and Counseling Psychology, 11*(2), 11–12.

*Sweeney, T. J. (1998). *Adlerian counseling: A practitioner's approach* (4th ed.). Philadelphia: Accelerated Development (Taylor & Francis).

Terner, J., & Pew, W. L. (1978). *The courage to be imperfect: The life and work of Rudolf Dreikurs.* New York: Hawthorn Books.

Thompson, C. L., & Rudolph, L. B. (2000). *Counseling children* (5th ed.). Pacific Grove, CA: Brooks/Cole.

CHAPTER 8

Psychodrama

Introduction

Psychodrama is primarily a group therapy approach in which the client enacts past, present, or anticipated life situations and roles in an attempt to gain deeper understanding, achieve catharsis, and develop behavioral skills. This approach was created in the 1930s by J. L. Moreno (1889–1974) and later developed by his wife, Zerka Toeman Moreno, and by many other followers. Psychodrama weaves together imagination, intuitive impulse, physical action, and various dramatic devices to explore a wide range of psychological problems. It is the root of the more widely used approach known as role playing but has a depth to it that deserves more study and consideration.

The classical form of psychodrama is a complex group method. Blatner (2000) notes, however, that the various techniques and principles of psychodrama may have their greatest value as adjuncts to a wide range of therapies and educational approaches. Instead of viewing psychodrama as one "school of thought" among many, psychodrama should be recognized for offering tools to help people relate to one another more effectively. These tools can significantly enhance an integrative approach to therapy and can foster problem solving, communications, and self-awareness (Blatner, 2001). In this sense, "drama" doesn't refer to behaving in a histrionic fashion, nor to theatrics; rather, it pertains to reworking our lives as if they were dramatic situations and we were the playwrights.

Psychodrama had its origins in the Theater of Spontaneity, which Moreno started in Vienna in 1921. The troupe of actors directed by Moreno had no scripts; rather, they improvised scenes based on events drawn from the daily newspaper or topics suggested by the audience. People in the audience were invited to discuss their reactions to these scenes, and especially how they might have played one or another of the roles differently. Moreno found that both the actors and the audience members experienced a psychological release of pent-up feelings (catharsis) as a result. The Theater of Spontaneity led him to develop the group methods and specialized therapeutic techniques that he later incorporated into psychodrama. Moreno had a desire to see theater revitalized and applied as a real instrument for individual, group, and societal therapy.

Psychodrama allows group members to play various roles and to receive feedback about the impact of the way they behave. The techniques of psychodrama encourage people to express themselves more fully, explore both intrapsychic conflicts and interpersonal problems, get constructive feedback on how they come across to others, reduce feelings of isolation, and experiment with novel ways of approaching significant others in their lives. This approach certainly helps to enliven group interactions. Zerka Moreno (1983) writes that "psychodrama represents a major turning point away from the treatment of the individual in isolation and toward the treatment of the individual in groups, from treatment by verbal methods toward treatment by action methods" (p. 158). Rather than have individuals *talk about* their hopes, dreams, and struggles, Moreno asked people he worked with to *show* their feelings and situations in the unfolding group setting (Blatner & Blatner, 1997).

Key Concepts

Creativity

Moreno was unique in his belief that a major function of the therapeutic process is to promote the client's creativity in coping with life. Creativity often emerges best not from careful, reasoned planning but as surges of inspired action, and is often generated through active experimentation. Creativity is catalyzed by imagination, play, and improvisation (Blatner, 2001). Psychodrama aims at fostering creativity in the individual, the group, and ultimately in the culture as a whole. Moreno studied and was inspired by the work and lives of some of the great figures in history, including Socrates, Buddha, and Jesus. He was influenced by the themes of creativity and expressionism prevalent in the intellectual life of pre-World War I Vienna, which was one of the intellectual centers of Europe. Moreno thought people individually and collectively suffered from an overreliance on that which has already been created rather than being open to the challenge of creating anew. His view was that God was the source of creativity in every moment, operating through the creativity of every being. Psychodrama entails the idea that each person is responsible for becoming more creative and for promoting creativity in others (Blatner, 2000).

Spontaneity

Blatner (2000) considers Moreno's ideas about spontaneity to be among his most brilliant insights. People with problems require stimulation of their creativity, and the best way to achieve this is through a method that promotes spontaneity. Moreno made spontaneity his second most important concept, and it stands out because, in fact, so many of life's activities, and even some aspects of therapy, tend to inhibit spontaneity. Moreno sought to reverse this trend by creating contexts and activities that would maximize the courage to improvise.

From Moreno's perspective, spontaneity is an adequate response to a new situation or a novel response to an old situation. Spontaneity should not be thought of as impulsive behavior or as a license to act out; spontaneity involves reflection and gives people the ability to act according to the situations they face. Instead of encountering a new situation with anxiety, spontaneity fosters a sense of being capable of approaching a challenging situation (Moreno, Blomkvist, & Rutzel, 2000). Blatner (2000) believes that in spontaneity there are elements of courage, liveliness, engagement, openness, the willingness to take risks, and a stretching of the mind. "Spontaneity involves an inclination towards questioning, challenging, re-thinking, re-evaluating, taking a fresh look—it is a shift in attitude" (pp. 83–84).

One of Moreno's best insights is that creativity and spontaneity can be catalyzed through improvisational involvement. He observed that children, in contrast to adults, were relatively more able to enter into role-playing and fantasy situations and to express their feelings freely. As people grow older, they tend to become less and less spontaneous. To remedy this tendency, Moreno developed methods for training spontaneity aimed at freeing people from limiting "scripts" and rigid and stereotyped responses. He considered spontaneity training to be a prime way of enabling people to meet new situations from a fresh perspective.

It is important to create a climate that will facilitate the unfolding of spontaneity. People cannot effectively be pushed into "being spontaneous," and spontaneity does not imply impulsivity. Perhaps the most important way to facilitate spontaneity in group members is for the group leader to model spontaneous behavior. To be able to create a climate that fosters the development of spontaneity, group practitioners must be aware of their own feelings and draw upon them in intuitive ways.

Working in the Present Moment

Working in the present moment is a concept closely related to creativity and spontaneity. Pioneered by Moreno years before it became fashionable, action in the "here-and-now" is an important element of psychodrama. People subconsciously defensively distance themselves from their involvements in problems by thinking of them in the past. Psychodrama counters this tendency by encouraging participants to become involved in the immediacy of the issues and events. Thus, in psychodrama, clients enact conflicts "as if" they were occurring in the present moment rather than just narrating past events.

Psychodrama directors will often say to members, "Don't tell us, show us." Members may be asked: "Show us what happened when you were a young child and you found out your parents were divorcing" (Blatner, 2001). A basic tenet of psychodrama is that reliving and reexperiencing a scene from the past gives the participants both the opportunity to examine how that event affected them at the time it occurred and a chance to deal differently with the event *now*. By replaying a past event "as if" it were happening in the present, the individual is able to assign new meaning to it. Through this process, the client works through unfinished business and puts a new and different ending to that earlier situation.

Psychodrama can deal with a present conflict: "Show us the conflict you are now experiencing between staying in college versus quitting." And psychodrama can enable members to bring the future into the now: "Show us how you'd like to be able to talk with your partner one year from now." Thus, the past, present, and future are all significant tenses, yet the action is played out in the present moment. When members engage in *showing others* what they are thinking or feeling, they move toward concrete experiencing and cut through defenses. They also move away from abstract and impersonal discussions about a topic when they plunge into personal enactment of a concern.

Encounter

The underlying goals of immediacy and involvement were further supported when Moreno taught the principle of encounter, which he propounded long before the encounter group movement began in the 1960s. The *encounter* is that which occurs when individuals connect with one another in a meaningful way in an enactment. This encounter occurs in the context of the here-and-now, regardless of whether the enactment relates to a past event or to an anticipated future event. It involves a great degree of both directness of communication and self-disclosure. There is great power in encountering. Even when done only symbolically in the form of role playing, it is still more effective than merely reporting an incident.

In addition to directness of self-expression, Moreno also thought a true encounter involves opening the minds and hearts of both parties to the viewpoint of the other person through "role reversal." Encountering is at the very core of psychodrama, for through this process people not only meet but also understand one another on a deep and significant level. By their very nature, encounters entail an element of surprise; they are not rehearsed or forced. Containing dimensions of both transference and empathy, encounters go beyond these concepts to foster a sense of community in a group, which builds the trust that is necessary for productive work.

Tele

In the spirit of promoting an increased level of interpersonal freedom and spontaneity, Moreno pioneered the use of "sociometry," a method whereby people could be helped to more consciously recognize and choose their relationships. *Tele* is what is measured by sociometry, which includes the degrees of preference a member has toward others. The concept of *tele* (tay-lay) is derived from the Greek root for "action at a distance." It represents the basic tone associated with our interpersonal connections. J. L. Moreno (1964) defines tele as the two-way flow of feelings between people. He calls it a "feeling of individuals into one another, the cement which holds groups together" (p. xi). Tele is a therapeutic factor related to change. Healing of individuals occurs through a reciprocal empathic feeling. People naturally, or for not-so-obvious reasons, feel attracted to certain people and are repelled by others. When positive tele is reciprocated, it is sometimes called "rapport." When negative tele is reciprocated, it may be called "bad vibes." The level of positive tele in a group correlates with its cohesiveness.

Addressing the shifting tone of interest (attraction or repulsion) of the people in a group is essential to any understanding of the group's dynamics. Moreno believed the therapeutic relationship required development of positive tele. When tele is positive and reciprocal, the people involved tend to be more accurately empathic with each other. When tele is negative, misunderstandings multiply and are inclined to be compounded (Blatner, 2000). The dynamics go beyond mere projection or transference. This principle transcends the use of psychodramatic methods. Group therapists would benefit from knowing about these sociometric principles, utilizing them in helping group members become more sensitive to their own shifting currents of preference, and discussing these openly.

Surplus Reality

Psychotherapy is about helping people to become more conscious of their deeper attitudes and motives, and sometimes it helps to bring unspoken and unfulfilled fantasies into explicit awareness. Instead of just talking about what actually happened or what might in fact yet occur, it is often more important to help the client become clear about what was hoped for or feared, even if it is not realistic. Psychodrama includes the portrayal of such scenes, and Moreno gave the name "surplus reality" to these enactments that reflected the psychological world of the client apart from any concern for the limits of ordinary reality. Surplus reality is more than a clinical technique; it is a philosophical attitude toward life (Moreno, Blomkvist, & Rutzel, 2000).

These concrete expressions of the imagination enable psychotherapeutic exploration of dimensions of events that do not occur in actuality. Therapists often ask clients questions such as these: "What if you could have spoken up?" "What if she hadn't died?" "What if you could have a new mother or father?" In psychodrama, this "what if" perspective is made more explicit by being physically enacted in the present, going beyond the limits of being realistic to acknowledge the way emotions work in the realm of "what could have been *if only* _____." For example, a son can talk to a father who died before they had a chance to say goodbye to each other. A woman can encounter her wiser self from 20 years in the future. A man can go back and experience the perfect seventh birthday, to counter memories of what had been a humiliating or disappointing "actual" event. Using surplus reality, individuals can encounter lost others to talk out previously unexpressed emotions and ask and answer questions. Surplus reality can also be used to replay an unfortunate or even traumatic event so that the individual experiences a more empowered or satisfactory ending.

Moreno called psychodrama a "theater of truth" because the most poignant and central truths in the minds and hearts of people often go beyond ordinary reality and involve the extra dimension of what could have been or what might have happened if things were different. Helping clients to become conscious of their own repressed emotions and implicit beliefs and attitudes requires a context that evokes spontaneous responses and bypasses tendencies to defend oneself through verbal distancing, narration, describing circumstances, and explaining. All these are forgotten when the protagonist engages in a direct encounter with another.

Using surplus reality, clients are helped to discover viewpoints they had not otherwise entertained. From a different perspective, alternative basic assumptions can then be considered. Thus, psychodrama can offer a way for clients to express and reflect on their hopes, fears, expectations, unexpressed resentments, projections, internalizations, and judgmental attitudes. Clients are assisted in ventilating these feelings and are able to symbolically live through them. They are generally encouraged to maximize all expression, action, and verbal communication rather than to reduce it (Z. T. Moreno, 1965). The stage offers a way to symbolically live through so much that ordinarily remains suppressed in life, to maximize rather than dampen expression and action in the service of becoming more self-aware.

Catharsis and Insight

Although psychodrama has been considered a therapy that works because of the catharsis it engenders, this may be somewhat misleading. It isn't always necessary for therapists to press for catharsis itself. Indeed, in many enactments this may even be contraindicated. However, when an individual needs to rediscover repressed emotions, techniques that facilitate this reconnection of conscious and unconscious functions tend to evoke catharsis just as exercising tends to evoke sweat. Blatner (2000) points out that this emotional release occurs when the sense of self expands in any of four categories: abreaction, when one rediscovers one's previously disowned feelings; renewed hope, in discovering how those feelings can be integrated into one's life; relief that one's full being can be accepted and included in a group; and a deepened sense of significance as one finds meaning in life.

People tend to compartmentalize their emotions and attitudes, which is one of the main functions of most of the ego-defense mechanisms. When these complexes reconnect, emotions tend to be released—tears, laughter, anger, vulnerability, guilt, hope—and this is the catharsis that often accompanies the experiential aspect of therapy.

Catharsis is a natural part of the psychodramatic process, but it is not in itself a goal. Rather, it serves as an indicator of emotional expansion and integration. Blatner (2000) suggests that dramatic emotional releases should not become the exclusive focus of psychodrama, for subtle and gentle catharses can also result in healing: "Abreaction is not enough. People need to carry forward the healing into other levels" (p. 114). Simply rediscovering buried emotions will not bring about healing; these feelings must be worked with for integration to occur.

For those who have lost awareness of the roots of their feelings, emotional release may lead to insight, or to an increased awareness of a problem situation. Insight is the cognitive shift that connects awareness of various emotional experiences with some meaningful narrative or some growing understanding. Insight adds a degree of understanding to the catharsis. There are times in psychodrama when it is inappropriate to have protagonists verbalize their insight explicitly. The experience itself often provides sufficient "action insight." At other times, protagonists are helped to find the words that express their feelings through the use of various psychodramatic techniques and so achieve insight in this fashion. Or insight might occur following the enactment when others in the group are sharing with the protagonist their own feelings and reactions to what happened on the stage. Often the other players (auxiliaries) and audience members also experience varying degrees of insight regarding their own life situations.

Once people allow themselves the freedom to release intense emotions that have been controlling them and come to a cognitive and emotional (or experiential) understanding that they no longer have to continue living as they did before, they can begin the critical process of gaining control over inappropriate modes of either suppressing or expressing those feelings.

Reality Testing

The psychodramatic group offers an opportunity to find out how others feel and what the results of certain behaviors might be. The group is like a laboratory in that there is a protected context of "as if," which allows for unfinished business to be explored. This offers a relatively safe setting for trying out behaviors that are not generally socially accepted in "real life" situations.

For example, a young woman is in great emotional pain over what she sees as her father's indifference to her and the ways in which he has passed up opportunities to demonstrate whatever love he has for her. After concluding a psychodramatic enactment in which the young woman "tells" her father of her feelings of missing this love, she may still be angry with him and expect him to make the first move to change matters. During the discussion phase, the leader or the members can point out that she is making the assumption that he must be the person to initiate a closer relationship. In reality, the father may well be fearful of showing her affection and attention, thinking that she is not interested in such a relationship with him. The group can be instrumental in helping her see that she may have to make the first move if she wants to change her relationship with him. Then psychodrama can again be used as a reenactment for her to practice this new approach, which will facilitate translating insight into action. This enactment maximizes the process of interpersonal learning.

Role Theory

In the 1930s Moreno was one of the originators of social role theory—a way of thinking and talking about psychological phenomena that has many practical implications. Using psychodrama, we can examine the roles we play, renegotiate them, and choose different ways to play these roles. In psychodrama members are given the freedom to try out a diversity of roles, thereby getting a sharper focus on parts of themselves that they would like to present to others. Playing roles also enables participants to get in contact with parts of themselves that they were not aware of. They can challenge stereotyped ways of responding to people and break out of behaving within a rigid pattern, creating new dimensions of themselves.

Blatner (2000) writes that role theory suggests that we can become improvisational actors, creating our parts without scripts. We thus become not only actors but also playwrights. By thinking of our behavior patterns as roles in a drama, we are encouraged to bring a measure of reflection to the task, much as an actor stands back during rehearsal and considers how best to play the role assigned. We can go further and question which roles we want to take on or which roles are to be played out. More than merely performing social roles, we are able to actively modify certain roles. Indeed, we have the capacity to break out of roles when we discover that they no longer serve us.

Role playing, which is largely an extension of psychodrama, involves the sense of "playing with" the role, bringing a measure of creativity to it, refining it, and at times even redefining or radically renegotiating the role. Psychodrama is one way to help people become more conscious and creative in how they play the various roles in their lives.

Role and Functions of the Psychodrama Group Leader

The psychodrama director (or group leader) has a number of roles. According to J. L. Moreno (1964), the director has the role of producer, catalyst/facilitator, and observer/analyzer. Directors help in the selection of the protagonist and then decide which of the special psychodramatic techniques is best suited for the exploration of the person's problem. They organize the psychodrama, play a key role in warming up the group, and pay careful attention to what emerges in the drama. Directors function as catalysts and facilitators in that they assist the protagonist in developing a scene and facilitate the free expression of feelings. Only occasionally will they make therapeutic interpretations to help the protagonist gain a new understanding of a problem. Haskell (1975, pp. 161–164) describes these specific functions of psychodramatic directors:

- Plan the session.
- Provide an accepting and tolerant atmosphere.
- Warm up the group so that participants will be psychologically ready to identify their goals and explore personal issues.
- Provide support and direction for the protagonist.
- Suggest relationships that might be explored, scenes that might be enacted, and experiments that might be tried.
- Stop the action for clarification whenever necessary, and make sure roles are being properly enacted.

- Pay careful attention to the reactions of group members and, if it seems appropriate, try to bring other participants into the psychodrama.
- Protect the protagonist.
- Lead a group sharing after the action is over.
- Summarize the experience on the basis of the feedback obtained in the discussion and the enactments.

One crucial skill of the psychodramatist is learning how to work *with* any resistance or reluctance on the protagonist's part. When natural resistances are attacked by the therapist, participants are almost never facilitated into deeper expression and exploration of a conflict. If the leader does not respect the resistance of the members, they will not develop the trust in the leader and the group process necessary for facing their own fears. Blatner (1996) cites Moreno's advice on this issue: "We don't tear down the protagonist's walls; rather, we simply try some of the handles on the many doors, and see which one opens" (p. 78).

The Basic Components of Psychodrama

The psychodramatic method consists of the following components: a director (usually the main group therapist), a protagonist (the person who is presenting a problem to be explored), auxiliaries (who play roles of others in the enactment), and the audience (the others in the group, before whom the problem is actually explored), and the stage (usually a space in a room).

The Protagonist

The protagonist is the name of the role a person takes on when he or she becomes the focal actor in a psychodrama. Group members may interact for a while, and then, if an issue is raised with one of them so that person, the therapist, and the group agree that a psychodramatic exploration is warranted, the person for whom the issue is most relevant generally becomes the protagonist of the ensuing psychodrama. This role is assumed voluntarily, although it may be suggested by the therapist or the group. In general, it is important that members feel free to decline to be placed in the position of increased demand for disclosure.

The protagonist selects the event to be explored. He or she, in negotiation with the director, chooses a scene from the past, the future, or an alternative present, and that scene is played as if it is happening in the here-and-now. In the case of a past event, it is not necessary to remember exact words, but rather to portray the essential elements as experienced by the protagonist. The protagonist is the source of the imagery but requires the assistance of the director to explore a problem and to create a psychodrama. As soon as possible, the director encourages the protagonist to move spontaneously into action rather than merely talking about the event.

As the protagonist acts out a situation, it is important that he or she have the freedom to explore any aspect of the scene (and related relationships) that seems significant. Although the director may encourage the protagonist to reenact a situation or deal with an anticipated event, the protagonist decides whether he or she is willing to follow the director's suggestions. The protagonist's preferences, readiness for engaging in a given theme, and decisions should be given priority over the director's or group's desires. If this is done, there is a greater chance that the protagonist will feel supported in going as far as he or she chooses. It is essential to respect the protagonist's process and decisions. Directors function best when they accurately sense and work with the protagonist's flow. Also, the director may employ a particular technique, but protagonists always have the right to say that they don't want to move in that direction. Effective psychodrama never involves coercion; the auxiliaries and the director are there to serve the protagonist.

The Auxiliary Egos

Auxiliary egos (often simply called "auxiliary" or "supporting players") usually portray the roles of significant others in the life of the protagonist. These persons may be living or dead, real or imagined. Auxiliaries may also play the roles of inanimate objects, pets, or any emotionally charged object or being that is relevant to the protagonist's psychodrama.

Zerka Moreno (1987) notes four functions of the auxiliary: (1) to play out the perceptions held by the protagonist, at least in the beginning; (2) to investigate the interaction between the protagonist and their own roles; (3) to interpret this interaction and relationship; and (4) to act as therapeutic guides in helping the protagonist develop an improved relationship. Effective auxiliary egos can give a psychodrama greater power and intensity. A few ways in which they do this are by helping the protagonist warm up, by intensifying the action, and by encouraging the protagonist to become more deeply involved in the here-and-now of the drama.

The protagonist generally selects the group members who will serve as supporting players. These choices are made for both conscious and unconscious reasons. Some choices are made on the basis of characteristics of group members that are perceived as similar to those of the actual loved ones. When a choice is made on this basis, the interaction between the protagonist and auxiliary egos is likely to be more spontaneous, real, and effective. Directors may take exception to this rule if they want a group member to assume an auxiliary role with particular therapeutic potential.

Although the protagonist has ideas about a problem, both the protagonist and the director have the function of coaching auxiliaries in how to play their roles. This task sometimes entails giving an auxiliary some background on the person he or she is to play and a feeling for the style of that person. Protagonists may teach or coach an auxiliary on how best to portray the behavioral style of a significant other.

It is the director's responsibility to assess whether the auxiliary's role playing is working more for the protagonist's benefit or meeting the auxiliary's needs. In the latter case, the auxiliary may be redirected by the director. The director needs to be sure to discuss this development during the sharing phase of the group, because it usually has significant therapeutic implications for the auxiliary. It is important to remember that psychodrama is a *group process* and that auxiliary work has great therapeutic potential. Playing someone else's role often serves as a vehicle for getting in touch with parts of the self not uncovered while playing one's own role. At times, it is a good idea to permit auxiliaries some freedom of expression in their role portrayals. Often this introduces novel elements that are surprisingly evocative. In other situations, the director might want to help the auxiliary to restrain his or her performance so it fits the protagonist's perception. Zerka Moreno (1987) warns about possible dangers when the protagonist's psychodrama and the auxiliary's drama combine. She cautions both the auxiliary and the director to avoid doing their own psychodrama, thus taking the focus away from the protagonist's drama.

The Audience

Even group members who are not engaged in the action play a role. As members witness the self-disclosure of others, they function psychologically as a kind of externalized "mirror." This gives the protagonist the experience of knowing the others share in looking at the world from his or her point of view. The audience also functions in the ongoing improvisational process as the source of people who will volunteer or be chosen to enter the scene as auxiliaries, or as people who will share with the protagonist in an enactment on a future occasion.

Psychodrama benefits the whole group, not just the protagonist. Almost always some group members find a particularly moving resonance in the enactment, identifying with either the protagonist or one of the other roles. Usually, group members feel at least some empathy, and they can experience a release of their own feelings through their identification with others; they thus gain insight into some of their own interpersonal conflicts. These other group members—the audience—provide valuable support and feedback to the protagonist.

The Stage

The stage is the area where the enactment takes place. It represents an extension of the life space of the protagonist, and as such it should be large enough to allow for movement of the protagonist, the auxiliary egos, and the director. The stage is generally empty, but it is helpful to have available as props a few chairs, perhaps a table, a variety of pieces of colored fabrics for costuming and other uses, and other items. Props can be used to intensify the dramatic function. When a protagonist emerges from the group, he or she moves to this area to create the psychodrama. If a special psychodrama stage is not available, a section of the room can be designated. In that case, that area of the room can be preserved for "as if" action, and the group should not expect those involved in the action to also be reflective and interactive group members at the same time.

Stages of the Psychodrama Process

Psychodrama consists of the following three stages: (1) warm-up, (2) action, and (3) sharing and discussion. These stages are not absolute but are general intellectual constructs that help the practitioner to (1) build the spontaneity, (2) apply it, and (3) integrate the enactment with the group process.

The Warm-Up Stage

Warming up consists of the initial activities required for a gradual increase in involvement and spontaneity. It includes the director's warm-up, establishing trust and group cohesion, identifying a group theme, finding a protagonist, and moving the protagonist onto the stage (Blatner, 1996, 2001). It is essential that participants are helped to get ready for the methods used during the action phase. Such readiness involves being motivated enough to formulate one's goals and feeling secure enough to trust the others in the group. Physical techniques for warming up a group are commonly introduced and may include using music, dancing, and movement or other nonverbal exercises.

Early in a psychodrama certain group members may emerge who appear ready to benefit from an experiential exploration of a problem. It may be an individual's relationship to a personal situation outside of the group or some group members needing to clarify their own interactions within the group. In these instances, the flow of group process serves as a warm-up enactment. In settings in which a psychodrama is to be the primary mode for exploration, these warm-ups methods have been used:

- The director gives a brief talk about the nature and purpose of psychodrama, and participants are invited to ask questions.
- Each member is briefly interviewed by the director. A lead question may be, "Is there a present or past relationship that you'd like to understand better?" If each person in the group responds to this question, a basis for group cohesion is being established.
- Members can form several sets of dyads and spend a few minutes sharing a conflict that they are experiencing and that they'd like to explore in the session.
- The "go-around" technique can facilitate group interaction. Each member is asked to make some brief comments about what he or she is experiencing in the moment. Making the rounds can also focus members on personal work they would like to do during the session.
- In a long-term group with functional people, a nondirective warm-up is often used to get members ready for a session. Members may be asked to briefly state what they were aware of as they were coming to the session or to make any comments about their readiness to work.

Leveton (2001) states that the message of a successful warm-up to the members of the group is to actively participate and that all contributions will be rewarded. The warm-up is aimed at creating an atmosphere of spontaneity that eases resistive tendencies within members. Leveton describes a wide variety of both verbal and nonverbal warm-up techniques. There are scores of structured experiences that can work as warm-ups. In addition to structured techniques aimed at warming up a group for action, there are unstructured warm-ups, including the process by which a protagonist emerges from the spontaneous interaction at the beginning of a group session. It is critical that the leader pay close attention to verbal and nonverbal cues as the protagonist describes the issue to be explored. For example, a member (Umberto) may describe himself as reserved and distant from others. He may use some metaphoric or symbolic language that has rich implications. In talking about letting others get close to him, Umberto may allude to "shields" that he has carefully built to protect himself from the pain of rejection.

During the warm-up stage, members need to be reassured that the working environment is a safe one, that they are the ones to decide *what* they will reveal and *when* they will reveal it, and that they can stop whenever they want to. The techniques are less important than the spirit and purpose of the warm-up; anything that facilitates the cohesion of the group and establishes trust is a useful tool for the initial phase of a psychodrama.

According to Blatner (1996), the most important task during the warm-up period consists of creating an atmosphere that fosters spontaneity. In his view, these four conditions are necessary for spontaneous behavior to occur:

- A sense of trust and safety
- A receptivity to intuitions, images, and feeling
- An element of playfulness
- A willingness to take risks and engage in novel behavior

Blatner (1996) emphasizes the importance of the director's own warm-up as a key factor in creating a climate that encourages spontaneous behavior. It is during the warm-up period that directors are developing their own spontaneity. By communicating a sense of authenticity and warmth, they foster confidence and trust. Similarly, modeling risk taking, self-disclosure, humor, spontaneity, creativity, empathy, and the acceptability of expressing emotions and acting them out contributes to the group's cohesion. A theme may begin to emerge, and a protagonist may be selected and move onto the stage for action.

The Action Stage

The action stage includes the enactment and working through of a past or present situation or of an anticipated event. It is important to facilitate the process so that the protagonist can move into action as soon as possible. Because group members tend to slip into explaining and other verbal modes, it is important for the director to get the protagonist up and moving into action, setting the stage, bringing in the auxiliaries, and guiding the protagonist in establishing the scene in which some significant event took place. In doing this, the leader can draw on important cues that the protagonist gave in presenting his or her situation, including facial expressions, figures of speech, and body posture. The director helps the protagonist get a clear focus on a particular concern. Rather than having the protagonist give lengthy details and risk losing the energy of the psychodrama, the director can ask the protagonist questions such as these:

- With whom in your life are you having the most trouble at this time?
- What few words or phrases would best describe your father [mother]?
- What is the main message that you get from your mother [father]?
- When have you felt the most isolated or abandoned?
- What did you do when you felt rejected and unloved?
- How old are you feeling at this time?
- How do you wish your husband had been different with you?
- When do you feel most criticized by your wife?
- What are the things your husband tells you that upset you the most?
- What are a few lines you'd like to say to your son?
- What would you most like to hear from your daughter?

The point of these questions is to avoid lengthy commentaries on content and instead to focus the protagonist on the process of his or her struggle.

Once the protagonist has a clear sense of what he or she would like to explore, it is possible to create the scene and coach the auxiliary egos. After this focusing process, protagonists act out their problems and relationships on the stage. A single action phase may consist of one to several scenes. Scenes are constructed and enacted as they relate to the protagonist's issues. They may be interpersonal or intrapersonal in nature and usually progress from peripheral issues (presenting problems) to more central issues (the real or deeper problems). At the end of a scene the protagonist or the director may suggest that the protagonist assume a different role in the same scene to determine whether he or she can respond more effectively. Another suggestion is that the protagonist fantasize about the future by acting out how things might be a year afterward, thus sharing private thoughts with the audience. The duration of the action stage varies, depending on the director's evaluation of the protagonist's involvement and on the level of involvement of the group.

At times most of a session may be devoted to the group as a whole working through interpersonal issues among members. At other times a common theme such as loneliness, fear of intimacy, or feelings of rejection seems to touch everyone in the group. With skillful facilitation by the group leader, the work of many group members can be linked and a common theme can be pursued.

At the end of the action stage, it is important to help protagonists acquire a sense of closure for any work they have accomplished. One useful way to facilitate closure is to arrange for behavioral practice. This allows the protagonist to translate group learning to everyday life. The function of behavioral practice is to create a climate that allows for experimentation with a variety of new behaviors. Then the person can implement some of these new behaviors with significant others outside the group and cope with situations more effectively. To facilitate behavioral practice, the protagonist presents the situation as it was originally presented in the action stage. Various techniques, such as role reversal, future projection, mirroring, and feedback, are often used to help the protagonist get a clearer idea of the impact of his or her new behavior. (These techniques are described later in the chapter.)

The Sharing and Discussion Stage

The third stage of psychodrama involves sharing and discussion. After a scene is enacted, the psychodrama leader has the function of making sure that all the group members have an opportunity to participate in sharing how the enactment affected them personally. One reason for the sharing phase is that the protagonist has revealed a great deal from his or her life and now deserves to get something back from the group (Moreno, Blomkvist, & Rutzel, 2000). Sharing, which comes first, consists of nonjudgmental statements about oneself; a discussion of the group process follows. The participants are asked to share with the protagonist their observations of and reactions to the psychodrama in a constructive and supportive way, emphasizing what the enactment touched in their lives. Those who played roles in the enactment can also share their reactions to these roles. The audience's reactions can help the protagonist understand the impact he or she has on others.

Zerka Moreno (Moreno, Blomkvist, & Rutzel, 2000) believes that both members and leaders need to be taught to have an open heart, not just a head. Sharing is a deeply personal process, not a cognitive reflection, and Moreno has some excellent guidelines for making the sharing session a therapeutic experience:

- Group members should not offer advice or analysis to the protagonist but instead talk about themselves and how they were affected by the enactment.
- The protagonist has engaged in open sharing, and he or she deserves more than a cold analysis or critique.
- Sharing has healing effects. The disclosure of others' experiences gives people a sense that they are not alone and leads to bonding.
- Interpretation and evaluation come later, when the protagonist is not so vulnerable.

During the sharing phase of psychodrama, the director's function is to initiate and lead a discussion that includes as many participants as possible to maximize feedback. The director needs to watch for attempts by members to analyze the protagonist or confront the person harshly at a time when, having just finished revealing some intimate life experiences, he or she can be most vulnerable. It is important that protagonists be given an opportunity for some form of closure of their experience. If they have opened themselves up and expressed deep feelings, they need to be able to count on the support of the group to integrate through sharing and some exploration of the meaning of the experience. If no such opportunity is available, protagonists may leave the session feeling rejected and lost instead of feeling freer and more purposeful.

After an intense piece of work, the leader might ask the protagonist any one of these open-ended questions: "What are you experiencing now?" "What are you aware of right now?" "How was it for you to do and say what you just did?" If the protagonist is aware of what others are thinking or feeling, he or she can simply look at the eyes of each of the members in the room. Sometimes remaining silent and "taking in the energy of the group" is much more powerful than using too many words.

It is crucial that the sharing from the audience be personal and nonjudgmental. The director must reinforce the kind of sharing that entails self-disclosure, support, and emotional involvement on the part of the members. The sharing is best structured so that members discuss how they were affected by the session, and in this way their own involvement, transparency, and growth are fostered. As mentioned earlier, this is not a time for giving advice to the protagonist or, worse yet, attempting to "cure" the protagonist by providing insightful interpretations into his or her psychodynamics. If participants attempt to analyze or to provide solutions, the director needs to intervene, for example, by asking questions such as these:

- How has Enjolie's drama affected *you*?
- Who or what most touched you in what you just saw?
- What feelings were stirred up in you as you were participating in Enjolie's drama?
- What experiences in *your* life relate to Enjolie's situation?
- Are there any feelings you had toward Enjolie that you'd like to share with her?

During the sharing time, group cohesion is typically increased, for members are able to see commonalities. The participation in universal struggles is a way to bond members. Thus, after an effective sharing of experiences, protagonists are not left feeling as though they are alone in an unfriendly universe. They have a basis for feeling accepted, and the feedback from other members acts as a reinforcement for them to continue revealing personal concerns. Blatner (1996) writes that the sharing period gives all the members in a psychodrama group the chance to express their feelings: "The group members need this as much as the protagonist does. The catharsis in the drama may then spread, be reexperienced, and subside as the group realizes its common bond of human feelings" (p. 106).

Leveton (2001) stresses the importance of the director in helping the protagonist, auxiliaries, and other members find closure after a piece of work. Closure does not necessarily mean that a concern is resolved, but all who were involved in a psychodrama should have an opportunity to talk about how they were affected and what they learned. A key aspect of closure is the process of shedding the roles (debriefing) of protagonist and auxiliaries.

Closure depends on the client, the situation, and the group. The length of the session, the degree of cohesion, and the intensity of the work are other factors that determine what kind of closure is appropriate. If the group will not meet again, closure is essential; if the group meets on a regular basis, however, there might be times when the leader will defer closure to a later session. A period of discussion can be useful for "winding down" the emotional pitch to a more cognitive level and for helping the protagonist and the audience integrate key aspects of the session.

Although the emotional aspects of an enactment are of great therapeutic value, a degree of cognitive integration will maximize the value of the emotional components. Protagonists can be asked to express what they have learned from the particular enactment and the insights they have acquired. It is also a good practice to encourage protagonists to talk about the personal meaning of reliving a situation. They can be stimulated to think of a possible course of action that will permit them to cope with repressed feelings and of practical ways of dealing more effectively with similar problem situations in the future. Here are some of the tasks for closing a session that Blatner (1996) lists:

- Assist members in applying what they've learned in the group to daily living.
- Summarize some of the highlights of the session.
- Make plans for the next session or identify future themes.
- Provide additional support.
- Engage in some kind of closing ritual (if appropriate).
- Deal with feelings about separation.
- Address unfinished business or encourage members to briefly express unspoken reactions.

Several writers discuss the importance of dealing with unfinished business during the final stage of a psychodrama (Blatner, 1996; Goldman & Morrison 1984; Leveton, 2001; Z. T. Moreno, 1987). Before ending a session, the director may ask members to verbalize any unspoken feelings that have developed during the psychodrama. As mentioned earlier, it is not always necessary to work things out, but it is important that the existence of unfinished business be mentioned before the session closes. Some problems will probably be opened up and fruitfully explored, yet the protagonist may be far from having resolved the issue. After a successful sharing session, new work is likely to be shaping up as other members identify with what they just experienced. Of course, it is not wise to undertake further work in a given session if there is not ample time to address the issue adequately.

Members need to be warned of the danger of attempting premature and forced closure of an issue. It is essential that protagonists have ample opportunities to express their feelings, experience their conflicts, and explore the meaning of their emotional release. Clinicians, out of their own anxiety for wanting to see problems solved, sometimes suggest behavioral practice and an action plan before members have had a chance to ventilate and identify an area of personal concern. J. L. Moreno makes this important point: "Enactment comes first, retraining comes later. We must give the protagonist the satisfaction of act completion first, before considering retraining for behavioral changes" (as cited in Blatner, 1996, p. 100).

Leveton (2001) notes that some practitioners expect perfection. Unless everything is settled, these leaders feel that they have failed. To avoid such feelings, they may try to force closure in situations where participants are better off if they continue reflecting on what has occurred. One of the most challenging tasks for the director is learning to bring closure to a session without curtailing members' further self-exploration, which is necessary for an in-depth resolution of their problems.

Application: Therapeutic Techniques and Procedures

Psychodrama uses a number of specific techniques designed to intensify feelings, clarify confusions and implicit beliefs, increase insight and self-awareness, and practice new behaviors. These techniques should be used for specific purposes related to what the protagonist and other group members need to experience to optimize relearning. Drama itself is not the goal (J. L. Moreno, 1978).

Blatner (2001) points out that classical psychodrama is a powerful approach that requires specialized training on the director's part, adequate time for orientation and follow-up, a supportive group atmosphere, and members who are appropriate for these methods. For those who do not practice classical psychodrama, many psychodrama techniques can be part of a therapist's eclectic orientation to group work.

Directors have latitude to invent their own techniques or to modify standard psychodramatic ones. It is of the utmost importance that group leaders bring caution and commitment to the practice of their technical skills, and they need to know when and how to apply these methods. Effective psychodrama consists of far more than the mere use of certain techniques. Practitioners must learn to know, and work with, the members' psychological worlds in an educated, trained, sensitive, caring, and creative manner.

The techniques mentioned here are described in detail in the following sources: Blatner (1996, 1999), Blatner and Blatner (1997), Goldman and Morrison (1984), Leveton (2001), J. L. Moreno (1964), J. L. Moreno and Moreno (1958), Z. T. Moreno (1959, 1965, 1983, 1987), and Moreno, Blomkvist, and Rutzel (2000).

Some principles of psychodramatic techniques serve as useful guidelines for the practitioner (Blatner, 2000, pp. 227–228):

- Whenever possible, use physical action rather than talking about a situation.
- Promote authentic encounters as much as possible. Group members should speak directly to each other rather than explaining to the director.
- Look for ways to promote the active behavior of other members by getting them involved in an enactment as much as possible.
- Make abstract situations more concrete by working with specific scenes.
- Encourage participants to make affirmative statements about themselves by using sentences beginning with "I."
- Continue to encourage members to deal with situations in the past or future as if they were happening in the present moment.
- Recognize and tap the potential for redecisions, renegotiations, and corrective experiences in the present.

- Pay attention to the nonverbal aspects of communication.
- Work toward increasing levels of self-disclosure and honesty.
- When appropriate, weave in a degree of playfulness, humor, and spontaneity in a situation.
- Utilize symbols and metaphors, personifying them and making them more vivid.
- Include other artistic principles and vehicles, such as movement, staging, lighting, props, poetry, art, and music.
- Exaggerate or amplify behavior to explore a wider range of responses.
- Recognize and use the warming-up process as a prelude to facilitating creative and spontaneous behavior.
- Utilize the therapeutic factors of a group.
- Integrate psychodrama with other therapeutic approaches and the creative arts.

Self-Presentation

In the self-presentation technique, the protagonist gives a self-portrait to introduce the situation. Let us say that in the group Jack wants to explore his relationship with his daughter, Laura. The group is interested in this and wants to have it enacted. The director (group leader) has Jack stand up, come onto the stage area, and they begin to establish a scene in which Jack interacts with Laura. Someone from the group is picked to be the auxiliary playing the daughter. Jack states the problem as he sees it, and the director helps to translate the narrative into an action, so that "talking about" becomes "show us how you and your daughter interact."

Role Reversal

Role reversal is considered one of the most powerful tools of psychodrama. Role reversal means to look upon oneself through another individual's eyes. It allows expansion of the client's awareness and behavior. Through role reversal, people are able to get outside of their own frame of reference and enact a side of themselves they would rarely show to others (Moreno, Blomkvist, & Rutzel, 2000). In role reversal the protagonist takes on the part of another personality portrayed in his or her drama. Once an enactment is set up, the director may wish to have the protagonist use this technique (1) to better portray how he or she imagines or remembers the other personality and (2) to reach a fuller understanding of the viewpoint or situation of the other. Through reversing roles with a key person in his or her psychodrama, the protagonist is able to formulate significant emotional and cognitive insights into the situation of others. This technique builds empathy with others.

In setting a scene, the auxiliary ego chosen to play a particular part (mother, father, sibling, lover, close friend, teacher, or relative) does not know how to enact either the nonverbal or the verbal components of the assigned role. The protagonist is asked to reverse roles to demonstrate this. As the scene unfolds, if the auxiliary ego begins to take the role in a direction that does not apply to the protagonist, the director can again invite a role reversal so that the auxiliary can get back on track. The leader needs to intervene to reduce the chances that the auxiliary will contaminate the process with his or her own dynamics. The auxiliary is instructed to keep the drama true to the protagonist's perception of events.

The second and more important function of role reversal is to encourage protagonists to empathize with a significant person in their life. In assuming the role of that person in the psychodrama, they begin to develop a deeper appreciation for the person's world. This reversal allows them to experience the environment from a different perspective. Typically, the director suggests a role reversal when it appears that the protagonist would benefit by attempting to "walk in the shoes" of the person with whom he or she is experiencing conflict. The art of this technique lies in the director's ability to warm up the protagonist as if he or she were the other person (Blatner, 1995b).

Zerka Moreno (1983) makes the point that protagonists must act out the truth as they feel it and from their own subjective stance, regardless of how distorted their presentation may appear to the other members or the leader. For example, Jack presents his daughter, Laura. Preferably, he plays the role of Laura and demonstrates how she typically responds. As Jack "becomes" his daughter, another member can assume the role of Jack as father. By playing the role of Laura as he experiences her, Jack may begin to come to a clearer understanding of how she feels. To warm the protagonist up to this role shift, the director can interview Jack as he plays the role of his daughter. This technique also gives the director and the group a clearer picture of how Jack perceives his daughter and how he thinks she perceives him.

Zerka Moreno (1983) maintains that this technique encourages maximum expression in conflict situations. Protagonists' distortions of these relationships can be brought to the surface, explored, and corrected in action. First, clients must "own" their emotions through ventilation, or catharsis. Then, by reversing roles, protagonists can reintegrate, redigest, and grow beyond situations that are keeping them unfree. Role reversal allows members to fully express their perceptions of reality, to get feedback from others in the group about their subjective views, and to make modifications of their perceptions to the extent that they discover distortions. It can be used throughout the drama to correct or modify the principal auxiliary's role portrayal and to present additional information to the auxiliary.

Role reversal is a useful psychodramatic technique that has many applications outside of group work. For example, it can be applied to supervision and can enable trainees to get an experiential sense of what it is like to be one of their "difficult clients."

Double

The double involves an auxiliary playing a special role—that of the protagonist's "inner self." The double expresses the thoughts and feelings that might otherwise go unexpressed. Doubling performs the function of the "voice over" in cinema or television. The double stands to the side of the protagonist (so as to be able to see and mirror the protagonist's nonverbal communications and yet not intrude on the protagonist's perceptual field) and says the words that aren't being spoken. The director may introduce the techniques by saying: "This is your double. If she says what you're thinking, repeat it. If it's not what you're thinking, correct it." It is often wise to ask the protagonist if he or she wants a double. It is important that the protagonist accept the double. Then, as the encounter proceeds, the director might ask: "Is this double right for you? Is this what you are trying to express?" Doing this empowers the protagonist. Even if the protagonist wants someone to stand in as a double, it is important that the double not overwhelm or take over for the protagonist (Moreno, Blomkvist, & Rutzel, 2000).

As an auxiliary, the double assists with the specific job of finding a part of the protagonist that is below the surface. Doubling is not an avenue for the venting of the double's emotions, unless the emotional expression fits for the protagonist. The double needs to pay close attention to cues given by the protagonist. The double follows the lead of the protagonist rather than doing the leading (Leveton, 2001).

Doubling is aimed at expressing preconscious, not unconscious, material, facilitating the client's awareness of internal processes and often leading to an expression of unvoiced thoughts and feelings. The double also acts as a support of the protagonist and as a link between the director and the protagonist. Once an alliance is developed between the double and the protagonist, the director may coach the double to insert some mild provocations or confrontive statements as a way of facilitating expression of feeling and the clarification process. The double may serve an integrative function and also intensify the interaction between the protagonist and the auxiliary ego. It is useful for doubles to assume both the posture and the attitude of protagonists. However, these are merely tools that doubles use to help them fulfill their purpose. The purpose is to help protagonists increase their awareness of inner conflicts and repressed feelings and even express them.

The double attends to process events and the immediate moment and is available to the protagonist in role reversals and in other roles. In Jack's case, the double technique might be used if he felt stuck or felt overwhelmed by his daughter. The double would then help Jack stay in contact with and express his feelings. Effective doubling often results in the escalation of an interaction, and it is likely to provide the protagonist with the needed catalyst to say things that until now have remained unexpressed.

Multiple doubles may be used to represent and embody the various sides of the protagonist. They can represent the protagonist's different conflicting desires, assets, liabilities, or various roles he or she plays in life (Goldman & Morrison, 1984). With Jack, one double may represent the side of him that misses his daughter and wants to express love, and the other double can be the "cold father" who really wants to have nothing to do with her. The doubles may speak at the same time, or they may take turns. If the doubles are effective, the father's ambivalent feelings toward his daughter can be successfully portrayed on the stage, and Jack may come to see which side within him is stronger. Also, he may get a clearer picture of the feelings and attitudes he'd like to express to Laura.

A wide range of subtle variations is associated with the doubling technique, and it is one of the most powerful tools in psychodrama. Because of this, doubling must be used cautiously (Leveton, 2001).

Soliloquy

At times protagonists are asked to imagine themselves in a place alone where they can think out loud (soliloquize). The director may ask a protagonist to stop the action at some point, turn aside, and express her feelings at the moment. Or the director, on sensing ambivalence on the part of another protagonist, may stop the action and ask him to walk around the stage and say what he is thinking and feeling. Or the protagonist may be engaged in a solitary activity, such as walking home. As a variation, the protagonist may soliloquize by having an inner dialogue with a double as the two walk together.

Like the doubling technique, soliloquy facilitates an open expression of what the protagonist may be thinking and feeling but not verbally expressing. For example, Jack may be asked to verbalize his thoughts during the course of a role reversal. This soliloquy gives him the chance to get a sense of what he believes Laura is thinking and feeling but perhaps not expressing directly.

The Empty Chair

The empty chair technique was originated by Moreno and later refined by Fritz Perls, the founder of Gestalt therapy. The empty chair can be a useful technique when a psychodrama involves someone who is absent or who is dead. A group member, Adeline, can put her mother who suddenly died in the empty chair. Adeline can tell her mother what she meant to her and say many of the things that she did not get a chance to let her know before her death. During this time the director might sit or stand next to Adeline for support, or another member with a similar issue could be next to Adeline. A variation of this technique involves an extension of role reversal. Here Adeline is asked to sit in the empty chair, "become her mother," and speak to Adeline. This role reversal gives Adeline a chance to verbalize what she would like to have heard from her mother. In this way the empty chair technique can serve as a way to complete unfinished emotional work (Leveton, 2001).

Replay

One obvious technique, used widely in musical or dramatic rehearsals, is that of simply redoing an action—refining it, playing it with more expressiveness, or varying it in some other fashion. If you make a mistake, you might simply say, "That didn't work well enough. May I please do it over?" In psychodrama this approach may be used to accentuate the sense of awareness in an action, to intensify the sense of ownership and responsibility, or to broaden the protagonist's role repertoire. Replay is a fundamental technique that is modified and used in other approaches, especially in behavior therapy and Gestalt therapy.

Mirror Technique

To foster self-reflection, another member mirrors the protagonist's postures, gestures, and words as they appeared in the enactment. If Jack observes his own behavior as reflected by another person, he can see himself as others do. It is as if Jack had access to a live equivalent of videotape playback. This process may help Jack develop a more accurate and objective self-assessment.

The feedback for protagonists may help clarify any discrepancies between their self-perception and what they communicate of themselves to others (Goldman & Morrison, 1984). For example, if another member portrays Jack as demanding, critical, aloof, and cold, he is likely to wonder whether that's the way his daughter perceives him. This technique may be particularly useful if others in the group see Jack differently from the way he sees himself or if he has difficulty presenting himself verbally or in action. Blatner (2000) cautions that mirroring can be a powerful confrontation technique and must be used with discretion. It must be given in the spirit of concern and empathy rather than making the protagonist the object of ridicule.

Future Projection

The technique of future projection is designed to help group members express and clarify concerns they have about the future. In future projection, an anticipated event is brought into the present moment and acted out. These concerns may include wishes and hopes, dreaded fears of tomorrow, and goals that provide some direction to life. Members create a future time and place with selected people, bring this event into the present, and get a new perspective on a problem. Members may act out either a version of the way they hope a given situation will ideally unfold or their version of the most horrible outcome.

Zerka Moreno (1983) contends that the future has typically been a neglected dimension in therapeutic practice. When participants in psychodrama enact anticipated events as though they were taking place in the here-and-now, they achieve an increased awareness of their available options. Rehearsals for future encounters, coupled with constructive and specific feedback, can be of real value to those members who want to develop more effective ways of relating to significant people in their lives.

Once members clarify their hopes for a particular outcome, they are in a better position to take specific steps that will enable them to achieve the future they desire. To return to the case of Jack, he can be asked to carry on the kind of dialogue with his daughter that he would ideally like one year hence. He may even reverse roles, saying all those things that he hopes she will say to him. He can also project himself forward and tell her how he has acted differently toward her during the previous year. If he gets a clearer sense of the kind of relationship that he would like with her, and if he accepts his own responsibility for the quality of this relationship, he can begin to modify some of the ways in which he approaches his daughter.

The Magic Shop

The "magic shop" is occasionally used as a warm-up technique and may also be elaborated on throughout the action phase. The basic idea is that the protagonist must bargain with an auxiliary playing the "storekeeper," who has the power to grant his or her most pressing wish. This technique may be useful for protagonists who are unclear about what they value, who are confused about their goals, or who have difficulty assigning priorities to their values.

The magic shop is imagined and staged with various containers made up of personal qualities, which can be obtained like magic wishes, but only if there is an exchange for some other quality that the protagonist already possesses. Jack, for example, may want to exchange his competitive style for the ability to open up to his daughter in a loving way. This technique can help him assess his priorities and see what is keeping him from getting what he wants from his relationship with Laura. The magic shop is a powerful technique, but Leveton (2001) indicates that it is of limited use: it must be timed appropriately, and it cannot be repeated very often with the same group.

Role Training

As early as the mid-1930s Moreno developed a major technique of role training, which is now widely used in behavioral group therapy (behavioral rehearsal). Psychodramatic methods aren't used only to bring out emotions or even to foster insight. Sometimes they can be applied in the service of expanding or refining an individual's role repertoire. Role training allows a person to experiment with new behaviors in the safety of the group. Protagonists have many opportunities for replaying a scene until they discover a response that fits them personally. They are given support, reinforcement, and feedback on the effectiveness of their new behaviors. As a part of working through a problem, the director typically focuses on acquiring and rehearsing specific interpersonal skills, which are often learned through the modeling of other members.

Participants are likely to be coached and to receive role training in situations such as a job interview, with the aim of learning how to manage their anxiety. Not only can they come into contact with their feelings, but they can also gain insight into behaviors that are likely to impede an effective interview. They can get feedback on the way they present themselves in the interview, and they can practice various behavioral styles to prepare themselves psychologically for what they see as a stressful experience. Members work on developing and practicing concrete social skills that will help them deal effectively with a range of interpersonal situations. The techniques of behavioral rehearsal, coaching, modeling, and feedback, which are described in the behavioral approach to group counseling (Chapter 13), are all part of role training.

Applying Psychodrama to Group Work in the Schools

Psychodrama is insight oriented and is designed to bring into consciousness and expression the underlying attitudes, thoughts, and emotions of individuals (Blatner, 2001). This kind of work may be too intense for use with school-aged children, but role playing, which has been derived from psychodrama, can be very effective. Role playing is a solution-oriented approach that is well suited to group work with children and adolescents. Indeed, Blatner (1995a) views role playing as the prime vehicle for developing the kinds of psychosocial skills that are becoming recognized as essential for adapting to contemporary life. This method, which is widely used in education from preschool to professional graduate programs, offers an experiential mode that involves active integration of the imaginative and emotional dimensions of human experience (Blatner & Blatner, 1997).

Certain other psychodrama methods also can be useful with children and adolescents who are experiencing a conflict or a problem situation that can be enacted or dramatized in some form. Not only does the young person who is the focus of the action benefit, but other students in the group benefit as well. These action-oriented methods build group cohesion, offering opportunities for young people to become aware that their struggles are shared by others.

School groups are generally time-limited and structured around a topical theme, and many of the techniques described in this chapter can enliven the work of both children and adolescents. Dramatic role play of previous or anticipated situations can be *in vivo* or can utilize dolls, puppets, or masks with younger elementary school students. Just as cathartic release can occur as children reenact painful experiences, feelings of self-confidence and self-efficacy can emerge from successful rehearsals of future challenges.

Role reversal gives a young person a chance to understand the world of others by experiencing their situation through others' eyes. This method expands a member's vision and assists in the development of empathy. The future projection technique has many possibilities for children and adolescents, especially as a vehicle for clarifying their concerns about their future. In a group situation the members can create the kind of relationships that they would hope for with others, they can rehearse for future encounters, and they can get helpful feedback on how they are coming across to others. The magic shop technique can assist young people in identifying some of their core values and clarifying how their values are related to their behavior. Depending on what is going on within the group, other action-oriented techniques can tap the creativity, spontaneity, and imagination of the members. Of course, whatever methods group leaders draw from with this approach, it is essential that these methods be appropriate for the specific purpose of the group and for the school context. Leaders need to exert caution that they do not open up material that cannot adequately be dealt with within the limits imposed by the school setting or that exceeds their competence. The topic of training and supervision in psychodrama is addressed in detail later in this chapter.

Applying Psychodrama with Multicultural Populations

If practitioners take seriously the cautions that have been mentioned in this chapter, psychodrama can make unique contributions in helping ethnically and culturally diverse populations. The method is being used by thousands of professionals worldwide (Adam Blatner, personal communication, February 1, 2002). Rather than having a mother merely *talk about* her problems in relating to her children, for example, she can take on the roles of her children during therapeutic sessions.

For many people who have English as a second language, psychodrama has some interesting applications. My colleagues and I have often asked group members to speak to a significant other in their native language as they are engaged in a role-playing situation in a group session (Corey, Corey, Callanan, & Russell, 2004). When they do so, their emotions quickly come to the surface. I recall a German-born group member who was speaking in English to her "father" in a role-playing situation. She did this in a detached manner, and what she said had a rehearsed quality to it. We asked her to continue talking to her father, but to speak in German. She did so and was quickly overcome with emotion. It was difficult for her to keep up her defenses against experiencing her intense feelings when she used her native tongue. It was not important for the leaders or the other members to understand the exact words spoken. They could understand the underlying emotional message through the protagonist's nonverbal cues and tone of voice. After she finished her psychodrama, we asked her to put some English words to what she had been experiencing. She said that speaking in German had vividly brought back early images, which led to a powerful experience of reliving scenes from her childhood. This helped others who did not understand German to be more tuned into her work, and it also helped her put her emotional work into a cognitive perspective. (For a video on using role-play techniques in groups, including speaking to a parent in one's native language, see Corey, Corey, & Haynes, 2000.)

If group members are highly uncomfortable even talking about personal issues, let alone displaying their emotions in front of others, many psychodrama techniques are most likely not appropriate. However, some of these techniques can be adapted to a problem-solving approach that makes use of cognitive and behavioral principles. It is possible to combine both didactic and experiential methods in structured groups with multicultural populations. All psychodrama techniques do not have to be used to elicit emotions and to encourage members to express and explore their feelings. Role-playing techniques can be productively adapted to structured situations dealing with trying on a new set of specific behaviors.

For those members who have grave cultural injunctions against talking about their family in a group, role playing that involves "talking" to their mother or father will probably be met with reluctance. Before attempting such techniques, the leader should fully explore the clients' cultural values and any hesitation to participate in certain techniques. This demands a high level of training and skill on the leader's part. It is easy to see that an untrained and culturally unaware leader could be counterproductive.

Evaluation of Psychodrama

Contributions and Strengths of the Approach

The action-oriented methods that have been described in this chapter can be integrated into the framework of other group approaches. Increasing numbers of practitioners are creating their own synthesis of psychodramatic techniques within their theoretical orientation. I value psychodrama's active techniques and role playing mainly because these methods lead participants to the direct experience of real conflicts to a much greater degree than is the case when members *talk about* themselves in an objective and storytelling manner.

Psychodrama offers a lively approach to life's problems and provides members with alternative ways of coping with their concerns. People often do not see alternatives for dealing with the significant people in their lives. In psychodrama, group members can demonstrate other ways of responding and thus provide the person with different frames of reference. In a role-playing situation, for example, Noreen approaches her husband, Roger, with a litany of all his shortcomings: In talking about him she says that Roger is selfish, he doesn't care, and he doesn't show his feelings or truly share his life with her. Through some variation of role play, another member can demonstrate for Noreen a different way of relating to her husband that is not accusatory and that is less likely to cause him to become defensive and ignore her complaints.

Potential for Integration with Other Approaches

Learning about psychodrama is of value because of the many ways in which it can be integrated with other therapies that you will study in this book. Integrated into psychodynamic, humanistic, and cognitive behavioral approaches, psychodrama offers a more experiential process, adding imagery, action, and direct interpersonal encounter. In turn, psychodrama can utilize methods derived from the aforementioned approaches to ground participants in a meaningful process. For example, if a catharsis occurs, the protagonist and group members can work through it more completely.

As was discussed earlier, psychodrama frequently involves catharsis, yet this catharsis is not the goal of psychodrama. Instead, catharsis is a natural product of the process of integration or healing. Emotional ventilation does not in itself heal, but it does help clients become aware of feelings with which they had lost touch (Blatner, 2000). Although there is value in catharsis, my experience with groups has taught me time and again how essential it is to provide a context in which members can come to an understanding of how their bottled-up emotions have affected both themselves and their relationships. J. L. Moreno taught that every emotional catharsis should be followed by a catharsis of integration (Blatner, 2000).

Psychodrama can foster a healing catharsis when that is what is needed, and it can also be a useful force in integrating insights and developing and practicing more effective behaviors. From my perspective, deep personal changes will come about only if members are taught how to transfer what they have learned in their sessions to everyday situations, which is a vital part of psychodrama. It is also critical to teach members how to maintain these positive emotional and behavioral changes. This can be done by helping them plan ways of coping effectively when they meet with frustration in the world and when they regress by seeming to forget the lessons they have learned. An excellent time for this cognitive work and formulation of action plans is toward the end of the sharing session after the psychodrama has been brought to a close. One excellent way to help members achieve closure on some of their emotional issues is to have them begin to think about the meaning of heightened emotional states. They can be encouraged to formulate their own interpretations of their problem situations. Furthermore, they can reflect on how their beliefs and decisions may be contributing to some of the emotional turmoil they reexperienced in the psychodrama.

According to Blatner (1996), a major contribution of psychodrama is that it supports the growing trend toward technical eclecticism in psychotherapy. Although psychodrama can be usefully applied to various types of individual therapy, it is most powerful when used within the group context. Practitioners are challenged to draw on whatever tools will be useful in a given situation. Yet psychodrama is best viewed as an optional set of tools rather than a single approach for all group participants (Blatner, 1996).

In my view, from all the approaches discussed in this book, psychodrama is the most ideally suited for groups. In addition to group therapy, psychodrama can be adapted to individual, couple, and family therapy as well. Variations of psychodrama can work quite well in groups with people of all age groups. Psychodrama techniques can also be readily integrated with most of the other types of therapy covered in this book—Adlerian therapy, transactional analysis, behavior therapy, multimodal therapy, rational emotive behavior therapy, reality therapy, and Gestalt therapy, to mention a few. Psychodramatic methods can synergistically enhance techniques from those group approaches that stress a cognitive behavioral orientation. (See Blatner 1996, 2000, for a more detailed discussion of integrations with other therapies.) As you read about other group-therapeutic approaches, you will see how many of the basic concepts and techniques of psychodrama appear in what are sometimes referred to as "innovative therapies."

Keep in mind that the field of psychodrama is characterized by evolution. Psychodrama has continued to develop with significant refinements in theory and practice beyond the seminal work of J. L. Moreno. Zerka Moreno has made significant contribuztions to psychodramatic methodology, along with scores of other psychodramatists who have added their own significant innovations and applications (Blatner, 1996).

Limitations of the Approach

Blatner (1996) emphasizes that psychodrama is no panacea and that it must be used with good judgment and in a balance with other group therapy skills. Indeed, because enactment can evoke powerful emotions, therapists need to exercise humility in their commitment to continuing their professional education, in refining their own skills in the understanding and use of this most valuable method. Although spontaneity is one of the basic concepts of psychodrama, it can be misused. It is imperative that a group leader's spontaneity, inventiveness, and courage to try new techniques be tempered with a measure of caution, respect for the members, and concern for their welfare.

Practitioners who use psychodrama need to exercise caution in working with people who manifest acting-out behaviors and with seriously disturbed individuals. It is critical that leaders have the experience and knowledge to deal with underlying psychopathology. In addition, they must have considerable sensitivity so that they do not push disturbed clients past a point that is therapeutic. It is also important to use good judgment in structuring situations so that members are not likely to open up old wounds without getting some closure to their problems.

As with other approaches to psychotherapy, it is important that leaders using the powerful methods of psychodrama also become aware of how their own personal problems and unmet needs might interfere with their professional functioning. In this regard, countertransference issues must be worked through before leaders can hope to have a therapeutic impact on the group. For example, some group leaders may easily become impatient with what they perceive as the "slow progress" of clients. Out of their desire to see more immediate results, they may resort to a variety of manipulations designed to stir up emotions for the sake of drama. A continued commitment to the director's own personal development is essential. Becoming aware of countertransference is as relevant in psychodrama as it is in psychoanalysis (Blatner, 1996).

The underlying philosophy of psychodrama is based on many of the premises of person-centered therapy [see Chapter 10]. Although group counselors who employ psychodramatic methods assume an active and a directive role in facilitating a group, these methods will be most effective when the leader maintains the person-centered spirit (Blatner, 1996). Thus, group leaders who are authentic, who are successful in making good contact with members, who are able to be psychologically present, and who exhibit a high level of respect and positive regard for their clients are most effectively able to implement a range of psychodrama techniques. One of the best safeguards for using these techniques appropriately is for a leader's practice to be grounded on a person-centered philosophical foundation.

Training as a Safeguard

To minimize the limitations and potential problems that might be associated with psychodrama, ensure that those who practice psychodrama have the necessary training and supervision in this approach. Leveton (2001) warns about the irresponsible use of psychodramatic procedures. Skilled directors, she says, are willing to devote the time necessary to develop their skills, and they have undergone a training program under the supervision of an experienced clinician. According to Blatner (1995b), psychodrama works best in the hands of clinicians who are well grounded in professional judgment and open to applying an eclectic methodology in practice. It is important to remember that practitioners can use certain aspects of psychodrama without employing the full classical enactment for many populations.

According to Zerka Moreno (1987), the director's function is complicated and involves a combination of art and science. She contends that it takes approximately two years to train a director. The more fully the director lives, the better he or she will be able to fulfill the functions demanded in a psychodrama. Orchestrating the many variables in psychodrama is not simply a matter of learning a technique at a weekend workshop. Although some psychodramatic methods can be acquired at a beginning level of competence in this fashion, the skills of an effective psychodramatist require many hundreds of hours of supervision.

Psychodrama is a powerful method, and Blatner (1996) contends that it is essential that directors have theoretical, technical, and practical knowledge of psychodramatic techniques. To appreciate fully the potential values and risks inherent in these techniques, directors need to have participated in the process of experientially learning these techniques. The training required for full certification as a psychodramatist includes having at least a master's degree in the helping professions and more than 780 hours of didactic and experiential work with supervision. Certification involves an examination based on ethical issues, knowledge of theory and practice, and an observation of the candidate's skills in leading psychodrama (Blatner, 2001). Blatner (1996) summarizes his recommendations for training in this way:

> The student of psychodrama must balance several aspects of learning: (1) the knowledge that comes with reading and classroom work; (2) the understanding that comes with experiencing a variety of situations through the exercise of role reversal, as auxiliary, as protagonist, and simply in play; (3) the competence that comes with practice to the point of mastery; and (4) the wisdom that comes from integrating into the learning process one's own personal therapeutic journey, and with it the growing capacity to liberate and access one's higher self. (p. 175)

Students of psychodrama need to experience the process in all available roles: auxiliary ego, audience, director, and especially protagonist. By getting personally involved in the psychodrama process, trainees not only learn a great deal more about themselves but develop sensitivity toward the role of client. Inept leadership—manifested, for instance, in forcing people into situations with which they are not ready to deal—can have serious negative consequences for the participants. The sensitivity and expertise of the director are crucial if the experience is to be therapeutic.

Group practitioners who are interested in incorporating psychodrama into their style of leadership should realize that they do not have to be perfect in their first attempts to apply its methods. Some beginning group practitioners become overly intimidated when they think about the personal qualities, skills, and knowledge required to effectively carry out the role and functions of a psychodrama leader. With supervised practice, experience as a member of a psychodramatic group, and specialized training, group practitioners can acquire competence in this powerful approach.

If you are interested in learning more about the practical values and applications of psychodrama, you can make a good beginning by reading about the approach in journals and books. Also, consider seeking out advanced training and supervision and attending reputable workshops where you can experience psychodrama as a group member. Not only will you learn how this approach works in a group, but you will also be able to work on some personal concerns and find new ways of dealing with them.

Where to Go from Here

The American Society for Group Psychotherapy and Psychodrama (ASGPP) is geared to the needs of professionals who want to learn about the latest developments in the field. It is an interdisciplinary society with members from all of the helping professions. The goals of the organization are to establish standards for specialists in group therapy and psychodrama and to support the exploration of new areas of endeavors in research, practice, teaching, and training. The ASGPP holds national and regional conferences, provides a journal, the *International Journal of Action Methods*, and offers a number of membership benefits. For further information, contact them directly:

American Society for Group Psychotherapy and Psychodrama (ASGPP)
301 N. Harrison Street, Suite 508
Princeton, NJ 08540
TELEPHONE: (609) 452-1339
FAX: (609) 936-1659
E-MAIL: asgpp@asgpp.org
WEB SITE: www.asgpp.org

The American Board of Examiners in Psychodrama, Sociometry and Group Psychotherapy was formed to establish national professional standards in the fields of psychodrama, sociometry, and group psychotherapy, and to certify qualified professionals on the basis of these standards. Two levels of certification have been established by the board: Certified Practitioner (CP), and Trainer, Educator, and Practitioner (TEP). Applicants must be certified at the first level before becoming eligible for certification at the second. If you are interested in details about certification or if you want a geographic listing of approved trainers, educators, and practitioners in psychodrama, request a copy of the current *Directory of the American Board of Examiners in Psychodrama, Sociometry and Group Psychotherapy* from the board:

American Board of Examiners in Psychodrama,
Sociometry and Group Psychotherapy
P.O. Box 15572
Washington, DC 20003-0572
TELEPHONE: (202) 483-0514

Psychodrama is practiced by thousands of therapists worldwide, and a number of Web sites can help you locate training institutes, conferences, books, and other resources. In addition to the resources listed here, check the Web site of Dr. Adam Blatner (www.blatner.com/adam/) for references and papers on psychodrama.

Recommended Supplementary Readings

If you are seriously interested in psychodrama, I encourage you to read the works of J. L. Moreno and Zerka Moreno. Also, current and back issues of the *International Journal of Action Methods* contain important readings. This journal is published quarterly. Write to:

Heldref Publications
1319 Eighteenth Street, N.W.
Washington, DC 20036-1802

Psychodrama, Surplus Reality and the Art of Healing (Moreno, Blomkvist, & Rutzel, 2000) is a useful resource that will amplify some of the concepts and techniques of psychodrama such as role reversal, diagnosis in psychodrama, sharing in psychodrama, the technique of doubling, the protagonist, and group therapy and the individual.

Acting-In: Practical Applications of Psychodramatic Methods (Blatner, 1996) is an excellent introduction and a guide for practitioners interested in using psychodramatic techniques in a group setting. This brief book is written very clearly and deals with the basic elements of psychodrama—its methods, stages, principles, and applications—as well as some of its pitfalls. This has become one of the most widely used basic textbooks for this approach, and it has been updated with extensive references. If you have time to read only one source, this would be my recommendation.

Foundations of Psychodrama: History, Theory and Practice (Blatner, 2000) provides a comprehensive overview of psychodrama and gives readers an appreciation for the uniqueness of this therapeutic approach to group therapy. This most useful book deals with the history, theory, and practice of psychodrama.

The Art of Play: Helping Adults Reclaim Imagination and Spontaneity (Blatner & Blatner, 1997) demonstrates how imaginative role playing can be used by adults as recreation, as well as for educational and therapeutic purposes.

A Clinician's Guide to Psychodrama (Leveton, 2001) offers an excellent and eclectic view of psychodrama. The writing is clear, vivid, and interesting. A number of psychodramatic techniques are described and illustrated through case examples that attest to the author's skills and creativity in applying these techniques.

The Evolution of a Group: Student Video and Workbook (Corey, Corey, & Haynes, 2000) is a two-hour video depicting the stages of a group. The Coreys demonstrate an integrative approach to group work, drawing heavily on psychodramatic interventions and various role-playing techniques. The video with accompanying workbook (designed for student purchase as an interactive learning tool) illustrates ways of creating trust in a group through the use of experiential approaches.

References and Suggested Readings*

Blatner, A. (1995a). Drama in education as mental hygiene: A child psychiatrist's perspective. *Youth Theatre Journal, 9,* 92–96.

Blatner, A. (1995b). Psychodrama. In R. J. Corsini & D. Wedding (Eds.), *Current psychotherapies* (5th ed., pp. 399–408). Itasca, IL: F. E. Peacock.

*Blatner, A. (1996). *Acting-in: Practical applications of psychodramatic methods* (3rd ed.). New York: Springer.

*Blatner, A. (1999). Psychodramatic methods in psychotherapy. In D. J. Wiener (Ed.), *Beyond talk therapy: Using movement and expressive techniques in clinical practice* (pp. 125–143). Washington, DC: American Psychological Association.

*Blatner, A. (2000). *Foundations of psychodrama: History, theory, and practice* (4th ed.). New York: Springer.

*Blatner, A. (2001). Psychodrama. In R. J. Corsini (Ed.), *Handbook of innovative therapies* (2nd ed., pp. 535–545). New York: Wiley.

*Blatner, A., & Blatner, A. (1997). *The art of play: Helping adults reclaim imagination and spontaneity* (rev. ed.). New York: Brunner/Mazel.

*Corey, G., Corey, M., Callanan, P., & Russell, J. M. (2004). *Group techniques* (3rd ed.). Pacific Grove, CA: Brooks/Cole.

*Corey, G., Corey, M., & Haynes, R. (2000). *The evolution of a group: Student video and workbook.* Pacific Grove, CA: Brooks/Cole.

*Corsini, R. J. (Ed.). (2001). *Handbook of innovative therapy* (2nd ed.). New York: Wiley.

Goldman, E. E., & Morrison, D. S. (1984). *Psychodrama: Experience and process.* Dubuque, IA: Kendall/Hunt.

Haskell, M. R. (1975). *Socioanalysis: Self-direction via sociometry and psychodrama.* Long Beach, CA: Role Training Associates.

*Leveton, E. (2001). *A clinician's guide to psychodrama* (3rd ed.). New York: Springer.

Moreno, J. L. (1964). *Psychodrama: Vol. 1* (3rd ed.). Beacon, NY: Beacon House.

Moreno, J. L. (1978). *Who shall survive?* (3rd ed.). Beacon, NY: Beacon House.

Moreno, J. L., & Moreno, Z. T. (1958). *Psychodrama: Vol. 2.* Beacon, NY: Beacon House.

Moreno, J. L., & Moreno, Z. T. (1969). *Psychodrama: Vol. 3.* Beacon, NY: Beacon House.

*Moreno, Z. T. (1959). A survey of psychodramatic techniques. *Group Psychotherapy, 12,* 5–14.

*Books and articles marked with an asterisk are suggested for further study.

*Moreno, Z. T. (1965). Psychodramatic rules, techniques, and adjunctive methods. *Group Psychotherapy, 18,* 73–86.

Moreno, Z. T. (1983). Psychodrama. In H. I. Kaplan & B. J. Sadock (Eds.), *Comprehensive group psychotherapy* (2nd ed.). Baltimore: Williams & Wilkins.

Moreno, Z. T. (1987). Psychodrama, role theory, and the concept of the social atom. In J. K. Zeig (Ed.), *The evolution of psychotherapy* (pp. 341–366). New York: Brunner/Mazel.

*Moreno, Z. T., Blomkvist, L. D., & Rutzel, T. (2000). *Psychodrama, surplus reality and the art of healing.* Philadelphia: Routledge (Taylor & Francis).

*Yablonsky, L. (1992). *Psychodrama.* New York: Brunner/Mazel.

CHAPTER 9

The Existential Approach to Groups

Introduction

Existential therapy can best be considered as an approach, or philosophy, with which a therapist operates. It is not a separate school or a neatly defined, systematic model with specific therapeutic techniques. Rather, it is more appropriate to speak of *existential psychotherapies* (Walsh & McElwain, 2002). Universal human concerns and existential themes constitute the background of most groups. This chapter deals with the practical implications of existential themes that have relevance to a wide variety of groups.

Psychoanalysis views freedom as being restricted by unconscious forces, irrational drives, and past events. Behaviorists see freedom as being restricted by sociocultural conditioning. The existential approach rejects these deterministic views of human nature and emphasizes our freedom to choose what to make of our circumstances. It is a dynamic approach that focuses on four ultimate concerns that are rooted in human existence: death, freedom, existential isolation, and meaninglessness (Yalom, 1980). Existential therapy is grounded on the assumption that we are free and therefore responsible for our choices and actions. We need to be the pioneers of our lives and to find models that will give them meaning. A basic existential premise is that we are not the victims of circumstances because, to a large extent, we are what we choose to be. Thus, one of the goals of the therapeutic process is to challenge clients to discover alternatives and to choose among them. As van Deurzen-Smith (1997) has indicated, existential therapy is ultimately a process of exploring a client's values and beliefs that give meaning to living. The therapist's basic task is to encourage clients to consider what they are most serious about so they can pursue a direction in life. The existential approach assumes the individual's capacity to make well-informed choices about his or her life. Group leaders cannot assume that they alone know the purpose of the group; rather, it is up to each participant to create this purpose.

The Focus of Existential Psychotherapy

Existentialism is a branch of philosophical thought that began in Europe. Key existential writers, such as Martin Heidegger (1889–1976) and Jean-Paul Sartre (1905–1980), did not address themselves to psychotherapeutic concerns directly. The existential tradition emphasizes the limitations and tragic dimensions of human existence. It grew out of a desire to help people engage the dilemmas of contemporary life, such as isolation, alienation, and meaninglessness. The focus is on the individual's experience of being in the world alone and facing the anxiety of this isolation.

One of the key figures responsible for bringing existentialism from Europe and translating key concepts into psychotherapeutic practice is Rollo May. His writings have had a significant impact on existentially oriented practitioners. According to May, becoming a person is not an automatic process, yet people do have a desire to fulfill their potential. It takes courage to be, and our choices determine the kinds of people we become. There is a constant struggle within us. Although we want to grow toward maturity and independence, we realize that expansion is often a painful process. Hence, the struggle is between the security of dependence and the delights and pains of growth. Along with May, two other significant contemporary sources of existential therapy in the United States are James Bugental (1987) and Irvin Yalom (1980).

Existentialism focuses on understanding the person's subjective view of the world. As such, it is a phenomenological approach. Therapy is a journey taken by therapist and client into the world as perceived and experienced by the client. But this quest demands that the therapist also be in contact with his or her own phenomenological world. Bugental (1987) writes about life-changing psychotherapy, which is the effort to help clients examine how they have answered life's existential questions and challenge them to revise their answers and begin to live authentically.

This approach does not focus on merely applying problem-solving techniques to the complex task of authentic living. Existential counseling does not aim at curing people in the traditional medical sense. People are not viewed as being ill but as being sick of playing certain roles or being clumsy at living. What clients need is assistance in surveying the terrain so that they can decide which path to pursue. Clients are not changed by the therapist as much as they are helped in coming to terms with life in all its contradictions. Through the experience of existential therapy, clients get an enlarged vision of themselves as free to engage in action that aims at change, tempered by the wisdom to acknowledge that we are (as Heidegger puts it) "thrown" into a world we didn't create. Clients gradually learn how to accept life in all its complexities and paradoxes. This process involves learning to face the inevitable problems, difficulties, disappointments, and crises that are a part of living. Clients come to realize that they are not imprisoned by their responses but have the ability to achieve authentic freedom. They are better able to live with the givens and find the courage within themselves to deal with uncertainty. Therapy provides them with the opportunity to contemplate a life that is worthy of commitment (van Deurzen-Smith, 1988, 1990a).

The Purpose of an Existential Group

The existential group represents a microcosm of the world in which participants live and function. Its members meet for the purpose of discovering themselves as they are by sharing their existential concerns. An existential group can be described as people making a commitment to a lifelong journey of self-exploration with three goals: (1) enabling members to become truthful with themselves, (2) widening their perspectives on themselves and the world around them, and (3) clarifying what gives meaning to their present and future life (van Deurzen-Smith, 1990a). An open attitude toward life is essential, as is the willingness to explore unknown territory. Van Deurzen-Smith (1997) captures this idea well:

> Embarking on our existential journey requires us to be prepared to be touched and shaken by what we find on the way and to not be afraid to discover our own limitations and weaknesses, uncertainties and doubts. It is only with such an attitude of openness and wonder that we can encounter the impenetrable everyday mysteries, which take us beyond our own sorrows and which by confronting us with death, make us rediscover life. (p. 5)

The therapeutic process involves encouraging members to begin listening to themselves and paying attention to their subjective experience. A group can assist members in addressing their deepest human concerns. Attention is given to clients' immediate, ongoing experience with the aim of helping them develop greater presence in their quest for meaning and purpose (Sharp & Bugental, 2001). This phenomenological self-searching gives emphasis to what members discover within their own stream of awareness when this stream is not directed by the therapist. By openly sharing and exploring universal personal concerns, members develop a sense of mutuality. The close ties they feel with one another give them many opportunities to use the group culture differently from other aspects of their culture. The group becomes a place where people can be together in deeply meaningful ways.

Key Concepts

In this chapter we will examine some key concepts of the existential approach and their implications for group practice. These concepts are self-awareness, self-determination and responsibility, existential anxiety, death and nonbeing, the search for meaning, the search for authenticity, and aloneness/relatedness. These key existential concepts guide the practice of group work by providing a way to view and understand individuals in the group. Although existentially oriented group practitioners have the freedom to incorporate into their therapeutic style many techniques from other therapeutic orientations, these interventions are always secondary to the genuine relationship between the leader and members and among the members (Walsh & McElwain, 2002). In this spirit, rather than focusing on group techniques, I will stress understanding how these key concepts can be applied in a group.

Self-Awareness

The capacity for self-awareness separates us from other animals and enables us to make free choices. The greater our awareness, the greater our possibilities for freedom. We are all subject to the deterministic forces of sociocultural conditioning and to the limitations imposed by our genetic endowment, but we are still able to choose based on our awareness of these limiting factors. As May (1961) writes, "No matter how great the forces victimizing the human being, man has the capacity to know that he is being victimized and thus to influence in some way how he will relate to his fate" (pp. 41–42). Furthermore, because of our self-awareness, we come to recognize the responsibility associated with the freedom to choose and to act. Bugental (1997) sees the main task of existential therapy as being to increase both the range and the depth of the client's awareness: "Awareness of the main elements of one's self-and-world construct system is important to full living and potency in life" (p. 192).

Implications for Group Work   In group work, the basic existential goal of expanding self-awareness and thereby increasing the potential for choice is pursued by helping members discover their unique "being-in-the-world." By asking themselves key questions, participants seek to define themselves and become aware of the central dimensions of their existence: "To what degree am I aware of who I am and where I am going?" "How do I experience my world?" "What meanings do I attach to the events I experience?" "How can I increase my self-awareness?" "In what concrete ways does expanded consciousness increase my range of alternatives?" The challenge for members in a group is to become aware of their existence as fully as possible, which includes realizing their possibilities and learning to act on the basis of them. A central theme of the existential approach is taking existence seriously.

In the group situation participants have the opportunity to express their own unique feelings and their subjective views of the world. They are also explicitly confronted by others, and they learn to deal with the anxiety that arises from having to choose for themselves when they are stripped of the securities of their everyday roles. As we will see in detail later in the chapter, existentialists view anxiety in positive terms. Anxiety helps "individuate" us: Anxiety awakens us to the inauthenticity of merely being who others want us to be, and it reflects the understanding that we are unique.

I believe group leaders need to alert the members of their groups to the price they must pay for seeking greater self-awareness. As people become more aware, they find it increasingly difficult to "go back home again." If living in ignorance of the quality of one's existence can lead to staleness, it can also bring a certain degree of contentment or, at least, security. As we open doors that were previously closed, we can expect to encounter more struggles as well as the potential for enhancing the quality of our living. The experience can be exciting and joyful but also frightening and, at times, depressing. This is an issue that should be mentioned during the early phases of a group.

What are the options that a higher degree of self-awareness permits us to recognize? Here are some of them:

- We can choose to expand our awareness, or we can choose to limit our vision of ourselves.
- We can determine the direction of our own lives, or we can allow other people and environmental forces to determine it for us.
- We can use our potential for action, or we can choose not to act.
- We can choose to establish meaningful ties with others, or we can choose to isolate ourselves.
- We can search for our own uniqueness, or we can allow our identity to be lost in conformity.
- We can create and find meaning in our lives, or we can lead an empty and meaningless existence.
- We can engage in certain risks and experience the anxieties that accompany deciding for ourselves, or we can choose the security of dependence.
- We can make the most of the present by accepting the inevitability of our eventual death, or we can hide from this reality because of the anxiety it generates.

Example   Here is an example that illustrates how participants in a group can gradually achieve a higher level of awareness. This and other examples that illustrate key concepts in this chapter are drawn from my experience with groups I have led. To protect the identity of the clients, I have changed the names and the specific circumstances, and I have chosen examples that have a universal quality—that is, situations that occur frequently in a group.

When Crystal first entered the group, she could see no value in expressing intense emotions and insisted that she had to be rational no matter what. She tried very hard to keep her feelings harnessed at all times because she was afraid that she'd "go crazy" if she allowed herself to feel intensely. This need to tightly control her feelings manifested itself in several ways. For example, when other group members relived painful emotional events, Crystal panicked and tried to leave the room, and she often attempted to defuse the expression of intense emotions by others in the group. During one session, however, another person's work triggered some painful memories in Crystal that were associated with her childhood memories of her parents' divorce. Suddenly she became that frightened child again, pleading with her parents to stay together and letting herself "go emotionally out of control."

This unexpected experience made Crystal aware that she had been keeping a lid on her strong feelings and that her defenses against "hurting too much" had resulted in her difficulty in getting close to others, in expressing anger, and in manifesting the love she claimed she felt for her family now. She also learned that she wouldn't "go crazy" by permitting herself to experience the depth of her feelings. After that experience, Crystal chose to open herself to feelings and not to run out of the room when she was afraid she couldn't take the intense emotions of other members.

Self-Determination and Personal Responsibility

Another existential theme is that we are self-determining beings, free to choose among alternatives and therefore responsible for directing our lives and shaping our destinies. Although we are thrust into the world, the existentialist view is that how we live and what we become are the result of our own choices. As Sartre (1971) put it, our existence is a given, but we do not have, and cannot have, a fixed, settled "nature," or "essence." We are constantly faced with having to choose the kind of person we want to become, and as long as we live, we must continue to choose. Sartre remarks: "Man being condemned to be free carries the weight of the whole world on his shoulders; he is responsible for the world and for himself as a way of being" (p. 553). For Sartre, we are free in that we are nothing but what we do, and what we do is not the result of our past. However, we are much given to making excuses, thus acting in "bad faith."

Russell (1978) notes that in Sartre's view nothing in the world has a meaning independent of us, and we are responsible for the world as a significant place. Russell adds: "Each time we act we thereby choose and create ourselves as we want to be, and this is never finished—what we are is never settled—but is created in each of the deeds that constitute us" (p. 262). We are responsible for the consequences of our actions and any failure to act: "I author the meaningfulness of my world in giving significance to my situation. It is when I see myself as the author of my actions and (relatedly) of the significance I give my world that I get an enlarged sense of my responsibility for this" (p. 261).

Viktor Frankl, an existential psychiatrist, stresses the relationship between freedom and responsibility and insists that freedom can never be taken from us because we can at least choose our attitude toward any given set of circumstances. To support this statement, Frankl (1963) draws from his own experiences in a German concentration camp, where the prisoners were stripped of every semblance of outward freedom. He contends that even in a situation of such extreme powerlessness, people can ultimately be their own master because the attitude they assume toward their suffering is of their own choosing: "Life ultimately means taking responsibility to find the right answer to its problems and to fulfill the tasks which it constantly sets for each individual" (p. 122). Frankl believes human freedom is not freedom from conditions but the ability to take a stand in the face of conditions.

Frankl's brand of existential therapy, *logotherapy* (*logos* = meaning), teaches that meaning in life cannot be dictated but can only be discovered by searching in our own existential situation. Indeed, we have the will to meaning, and we have the freedom to find meaning in how we think and in what we do. Frankl believes the goal is not to attain peace of mind but to experience meaning in a healthy striving. This search for meaning, which is our central quest, enables us to make sense of our existence despite guilt, suffering, and the inevitability of death (Gould, 1993). We are also responsible for (but not to blame for) the symptoms that restrict our ability to live freely and fully. It is essential that we recognize and accept our part in creating the quality of our existence, for life does not simply happen to us. We are capable of actively influencing our thoughts, feelings, and actions. Until we accept our capacity for freedom, we will not change. If we wait around for others to change or for the environment to change, we may well increase our misery and hopelessness instead of taking action to make something happen differently.

Implications for Group Work   The members of an existential group are confronted over and over with the fact that they cannot escape from freedom and that they are responsible for their existence. Accepting this freedom and this responsibility generates anxiety, and so does the risk associated with making choices. Another goal of the existential group is to help participants face and deal with these anxieties. The main task for the group leader is to confront members with the reality of their freedom and of the ways in which they are restricting or denying it. Group participants sometimes present themselves as victims, talk about their feelings of helplessness and powerlessness, and place the blame for their miseries on others and on external circumstances. A good place for clients to start on the road to greater self-determination is to become aware of the roles they have been programmed to play. When people come to believe they can direct their own destinies, they ultimately assume control of their lives.

Lantz (1993) believes that some clients are so externally focused on the requirements of social living that they have limited awareness of their own feelings, goals, thoughts, responsibilities, fantasies, and expectations. He adds that these clients usually benefit from a treatment approach that introduces them to their own strengths and potentials. Because *group logotherapy* promotes internal reflection and develops internal self-awareness, Lantz recommends this approach "for emancipated adults who need to replace old interpersonal patterns that once were useful in the family of origin but now create difficulties for the client away from the original family" (p. 67). He also maintains that group logotherapy is often the treatment of choice for children, adolescents, and adults who are not living in a natural family group or who are living in a group that is unable to support their changes.

Yalom (1980) contends that the group provides the optimal conditions for therapeutic work on personal responsibility. If the group has a here-and-now focus, members can be encouraged to observe how they are creating a victim-like stance for themselves. In Yalom's view, members are responsible for the interpersonal position they assume in the group, which also gives a glimpse of how they behave in life situations. Members who describe themselves as being victimized by external conditions can be challenged. Through feedback, members learn to see themselves through others' eyes, and they learn the ways in which their behavior affects others. Further, they learn how the group situation represents situations in their everyday lives. Building on these discoveries, members can take responsibility for making changes. From Yalom's perspective, the existential group leader encourages the members to assume genuine responsibility for their functioning as a group.

It is important to recognize that the existential approach represents a way of thinking that influences group members. Over time, members are likely to acknowledge their own freedom and responsibility as they have significant moments of insight. However, it is a mistake to conduct the group with the superficial aim of changing the vocabulary of the members. A group leader who preaches the language of freedom and choice, who prematurely coaches members to merely talk about how they are "choosing" their existence, will only encourage people to go through the motions of accepting these ideas.

Example   Edward reluctantly joined one of my groups. I say "reluctantly" because he had serious misgivings about the value of participating in a group. At 62, Edward had settled into a dull, predictable, but comfortable and safe life as a successful business executive. When he joined, he presented himself with this statement: "I don't know if this group will do me any good or not. Frankly, I think that I'm too old to change and that what I have is the most I can hope to get from life. I believe that things will probably stay as they are." In spite of his own statement and in spite of the fact that his life was orderly and safe, he felt that he was "drying up" and that life had lost zest. He was ready for a change, even though he was not sure whether change was possible.

Through his involvement in the group, Edward began to realize that he did have options—many more than he had thought possible. All along, he had blamed his wife, his three sons, and his daughter for the fact that he couldn't change jobs and live the kind of life he wanted for himself. He was, of course, avoiding responsibility for his own problems by focusing on what his family expected, often without ever verifying whether they did expect what he thought they did.

The other members and I challenged Edward to begin thinking for himself about how he wanted his life to be different. I asked him these questions: "If you were to continue living for the rest of your life as you are now, with no basic changes, how would you feel about it?" "Assume that your family would be willing to make the changes in lifestyle that you want to make. How would your life be different a year from now? five years from now?" "What steps can you take today that will help you make some of the changes you want? What is preventing you from taking these steps?"

Another dimension of an existential approach consists of helping people face their own attitude and situation in life. For example, Edward might be encouraged to take note of the way in which he makes himself comfortable by choosing to settle for the same routines and pretending to himself that this is all there is to life, or at least all that he is capable of achieving for himself. Through the perspective of existentialist philosophy, Edward and I can work together to see how he avoids his freedom by defining himself in static terms (Russell, 1979). Van Deurzen-Smith (1990a) reminds us that we often pretend that life has determined our situation to the degree that we have no real choices left. Crises provide us with evidence to the contrary, however. The safety within a group allows members like Edward to explore the meaning of crisis as a place for rediscovering opportunities and challenges that have been forgotten. An existential group leader could help Edward face the actual process of decay that he is allowing to take place. Once he recognizes his ways of engaging in self-deception and sees that he is choosing to rest on his laurels, he can decide to take a different direction.

Existential Anxiety

Existential therapists view anxiety as providing potentially instructive signals that can assist individuals to live more authentically. Existential anxiety is the unavoidable product of being confronted with the "givens of existence": death, freedom, existential isolation, and meaninglessness (Yalom, 1980). From the existential viewpoint, anxiety is an experience of freedom and not just a symptom to be eliminated or "cured." Anxiety results from having to make choices without clear guidelines and without knowing what the outcome will be and from being aware that we are ultimately responsible for the consequences of our actions. In the words of the Danish philosopher Søren Kierkegaard (1813–1855), existential anxiety is "the dizziness of freedom." In the context of group, it is hoped that we will feel anxious! At some level we know that for new dimensions of ourselves to emerge old parts of ourselves must die. The knowledge that to grow we must exchange familiar and secure ways for new and unknown ones is in itself a source of anxiety.

From the perspective of van Deurzen-Smith (1988, 1990a, 1991), existential anxiety is basic to living with awareness and being fully alive. In fact, the courage to live fully entails accepting the reality of death and the anxiety associated with uncertainty. Although we may not welcome this anxiety, it is the price we must pay for becoming what we are capable of becoming. Some people dull their sensitivity as a way of avoiding the basic challenges of life, and others find different ways of disguising their anxiety. Yet underneath the surface of their coping styles, people experience anxiety as an ever-present threat. Paradoxically, it is equally a source of transformation.

Implications for Group Work   Bugental (1978) describes therapeutic work with existential anxiety as a stripping away of defenses, much like peeling an onion. At the core of therapy, clients eventually come to terms with the underlying conditions of being human. These sources of existential anxiety must be faced and worked through in therapy; they involve recognition of our separateness and our need to be with others, of our guilt over not living authentically, of the emptiness in the universe and lack of meaning, of the burden of responsibility associated with choosing for ourselves, and of our fear of death and nonbeing. As therapy progresses and the resistances are peeled away, clients often painfully recognize how much energy they have put into maintaining an idealized image of themselves that is impossible to achieve. They also see that they must let go of static images of themselves that lead to a restricted existence. As clients give up their phony roles, they are able to bring a renewed quality to their living. A death of their old self occurs, which allows room for some kind of breakthrough experience. Yet such a process is typically anxiety provoking, for clients are giving up rigid ways of being that are familiar.

In existential group therapy, members are assisted in coming to terms with the paradoxes of existence: that life can be undone by death, that success is precarious, that we are determined to be free, that we are responsible for a world we didn't choose, that we must make choices, and that these choices are decisive in the face of doubt and uncertainty. As members recognize the realities of their birth and death, their confrontation with pain and suffering, the need to struggle for survival, and their basic fallibility, anxiety surfaces. Thus, anxiety is an indicator of the level of awareness that group participants allow. Existential anxiety is exposed in a group, especially when members explore ways in which they have adjusted too comfortably to a status quo style of living designed to mask basic insecurity and anxiety. Van Deurzen-Smith (1991, 1997) maintains that a main aim of existential therapy is not to make life seem easier or safer but to encourage clients to be more receptive to recognizing and dealing with the sources of insecurity and anxiety. Facing existential anxiety involves viewing life as an adventure rather than hiding behind securities that seem to offer protection. As van Deurzen-Smith (1991) puts it: "We need to question and scrape away at the easy answers and expose ourselves to some of the anxiety that can bring us back to life in a real and deep way" (p. 46).

It is essential for the group leader to recognize existential anxiety and guide group members in finding ways of dealing with it constructively. Existential therapy does not aim at eliminating anxiety, for doing so would be to cut off a source of vitality. Leaders have the task of encouraging members to deal with their existential anxiety and to develop the courage to face life squarely (van Deurzen-Smith, 1988).

One of the leader's tasks is to encourage participants to accept anxiety as growth producing and to help them find the courage to face and to fully experience their anxieties. The next step is to encourage members to make a commitment to action. Through the support of the leader and of other participants in the group, the individual can be inspired to explore unknown paths and to investigate new dimensions of self. This search can lead to even greater anxiety, but if the person is in the process of growth, he or she knows that anxiety doesn't have to be devastating and that it is the price one must pay for breaking out of constricting modes of existence. Bugental (1997) views the chief function of the therapist as displaying to clients the ways in which they constrict their awareness and the cost of such constrictions.

Example For much of her life Ann had allowed others to make decisions for her. She had uncritically accepted her parents' religious values and had become dependent on her church to make decisions for her. At this time in her life, she was struggling with following the values she had grown up with. Through her work in a group, she came to see more and more clearly that if she wanted to grow she needed to take more responsibility for her choices. Thus, Ann decided to look within herself for strength and direction. It took Ann some time to begin to trust herself and even longer to let go of the need to rely on external authority for her answers and security. Although some of her values changed, she now has a sense of these values as being her own. Yet by making decisions for herself, she also experienced anxiety and self-doubt.

The task of existential therapy is to teach Ann how to understand her feelings of anxiety, which surface as she becomes aware that she is responsible for deciding who she will be. As Ann realizes she does not have to continue being her "old self," she begins to experience the uneasiness that accompanies not having a comfortable structure of how to behave.

Death and Nonbeing

The existentialist considers death as essential to the discovery of meaning and purpose in life. Life has meaning precisely because it must end and life is enhanced when we take seriously the reality of our mortality. The reality of our finiteness can stimulate us to look at our priorities and to ask what we value most. The present is precious because it is all we really have. It is our temporal nature that makes us feel the urgency to do something with our life, to make a choice between affirming life by trying to become the person we are capable of becoming or allowing life to slip by us and eventually realizing that we've never been truly alive. When we emotionally accept the reality of our eventual death, we realize more fully that our actions do count, that we do have choices concerning how we live our lives, and that we must accept the ultimate responsibility for how well we are living (Corey & Corey, 2002).

As the only creatures with a strong sense of the future, humans need to deal with the end of life, which Heidegger (1962) calls "cessation of possibility." Because many of us are afraid of facing the reality of our own death and the anxiety that goes with it, we might attempt to escape the awareness of this reality. But the price for trying to flee from the confrontation with nonbeing is awesome. In the words of May (1961): "The price for denying death is undefined anxiety, self-alienation. To completely understand himself, man must confront death, become aware of personal death" (p. 65). Frankl (1963) concurs and adds that it is not how long we live but how we live that determines the quality and meaningfulness of our life. Vontress (1996) suggests that counselors should address the implications of the fact that we are all mortal beings: "Counseling is a human encounter in which counselors accept their clients as fellow travelers, en route to the same destination, death" (p. 161). Vontress stresses that people all over the world are engaged in a lifelong quest to make sense out of life and of their significance in the world. Human mortality is a catalyst for giving meaning to life.

Existentialists view the acceptance of death as essential to discovering meaning and purpose in life. As humans, a key characteristic is our ability to grasp the concept of the future, and, thus, the inevitability of death. This awareness gives meaning to our existence, for it makes our every act and moment count.

Implications for Group Work   Awareness of death and the anxiety it generates has significant implications for the practice of group work. The concern with living life fully, rather than merely existing, is a recurrent theme in many groups. Generally I address this theme by encouraging group members to ask themselves honestly how they feel about the quality of their lives. Then I ask them to answer this same question as if they knew that they were about to die. How do the two answers differ? Have they made decisions that were not carried through? Have they ignored opportunities for change? By reflecting on their unfinished business, participants may come to realize that they are not living the kind of life they'd like to live, and they may be able to identify the reasons for this unsatisfactory existence. Sometimes dreams about one's dying may symbolize the coming to a close of one phase of life, of some interest, work, or relationship.

I find it valuable to expand the concept of physical death to other kinds of death. Even though we are physically alive, we may be dead or dying in important areas of life. Perhaps we are numb to our feelings or caught up in deadening roles. We may have lost our intellectual curiosity and wonderment about life. Perhaps our relationships with significant people are characterized by routine and devitalizing acts. What we do may have lost meaning. In fact, the end of the group is itself a sort of "death" that is often avoided. A group can be a good place to recognize the areas in which we have gone stale and to confront ourselves with what we are willing to do to change and flourish again.

The process of change always entails allowing parts of us to die to make room for new growth. And growth often demands that we be willing to let go of familiar ways of being. We may need to experience a period of mourning over our losses before we can move forward and establish new patterns. Groups offer a safe place to express this sadness, to explore the ambivalence that generally accompanies change, and to experiment with new ways of being.

Example   The stoics of ancient Greece proclaimed, "Contemplate death if you would learn how to live." Indeed, we can learn a great deal from those who have faced death or those with near-death experiences. People who are terminally ill have often said how they have a new appreciation of the gift of life and how a "death sentence" awakened them to living as fully as possible. Their confrontation with death results in their getting the most from a relatively brief period of time. The pressure of time forces them to choose how they will spend whatever time they have left. Kinnier, Tribbensee, Rose, and Vaughan (2001) conducted interviews with people who experienced life-threatening situations and found some common themes: advocating less materialism, more spirituality, and more caring for and serving others. Kinnier and his colleagues found that people who have faced death worry less about mundane issues and become more optimistic about the future of humankind.

This framework can be applied to group work, including those who are very young and those who have not experienced a life-threatening event. Members can be challenged to look at how they are living right now, and if they are not satisfied with the direction they are moving, they can make new choices. If they accept the reality that they have only a limited time to achieve their personal goals, they may discover a freshness in living.

Irvin Yalom (1980) found that cancer patients in group therapy had the capacity to view their crisis as an opportunity to bring about changes in how they were living. After discovering they had cancer, many of these individuals experienced the following inner changes that enabled them to find a powerful focus on life:

- A rearrangement of life's priorities; avoiding getting caught up in insignificant matters
- A sense of liberation; being able to choose the things they most wanted to do
- An increased sense of living in the present moment; living less for the future
- A vivid appreciation of the basic facts of life; noticing various aspects of nature
- A deeper communication with loved ones than before the crisis
- Fewer interpersonal fears, less concern over security, and more willingness to take risks (p. 35)

Group members do not have to wait until they are diagnosed with a terminal illness to begin living the way they would like. Members and leaders of a variety of groups can, however, learn a great deal from groups for cancer patients and others who are exploring end-of-life challenges.

The Search for Meaning

The struggle for a sense of significance and purpose in life is a distinctively human characteristic. We search for meaning and personal identity, and we raise existential questions: "Who am I? Where am I going and why? Why am I here? What gives my life purpose and meaning?" For the existentialists, life does not have positive meaning in itself; it is up to us to create meaning. Vontress (1996) believes that people all over the world try to understand life. We are engaged in an eternal quest to make sense out of our presence in the world. As we struggle in a world that often appears meaningless and even absurd, we challenge long-held values, discover new facets of ourselves, and try to reconcile conflicts and discrepancies. In so doing, we create meaning in our world.

Frankl (1963) has devoted his career to developing an existential approach to therapy that is grounded on the role of meaning in life. According to him, the central human concern is to discover meaning that will give one's life direction. On the basis of his clinical work and study, Frankl has concluded that a lack of meaning is the major source of existential stress and anxiety in modern times. He views existential neurosis as the experience of meaninglessness. Many people come to therapy because of an existential vacuum, a feeling of inner void that results from not fully addressing issues of meaning. Therefore, according to Frankl, therapy should help clients create meaning in their lives.

There are many ways of creating meaning—through work, through loving, through suffering, or through doing for others. According to Frankl, the therapist's function is not to tell clients what their particular meaning in life should be but to encourage clients to develop meaning for themselves. He believes that even suffering can be a source of growth and that if we have the courage to experience our suffering we can find meaning in it. Suffering can be turned into achievement by the stand we take in the face of it. By confronting pain, despair, and death, and by trying to understand their meaning for us, we turn the negative sides of life into triumph.

Implications for Group Work   It is common for groups to explore both the issue of creating meaning and the related question of challenging and perhaps discarding values that are no longer meaningful. Many participants are concerned that they will discard old values without finding new and more suitable ones to replace them. Some people live by a value system that they have never challenged, one that was handed down to them and merely incorporated. Others have lost their identity by conforming to social mores. This issue comes alive within the group, where there is considerable pressure to conform to the expectations of others.

One of the tasks of the therapeutic process is to confront clients with evidence of the fact that they are living by unexamined values that no longer contribute to a meaningful existence. We may not be responsible for having acquired values that don't help our quest for meaning, but we are certainly responsible for clinging to them and for failing to find new ones. Some useful questions that can be explored in a group setting are these:

- Do you like the direction of your life? If not, what are you doing about it?
- What are the aspects of your life that satisfy you most?
- What is preventing you from doing what you really want to do?

With the support of the group, participants can find the strength to create an internally derived value system that is consistent with their way of being. This process is likely to generate anxiety, at least for a time, and they will flounder in the absence of clear-cut values. The leader's job is to remind members that learning to develop the self-trust necessary to look within, discover one's own values, and live by them is a long and difficult process that requires determination and patience.

Example   Priscilla was reared with extremely conventional values, and she had never really examined them. She felt compelled to be a "proper lady" at all times, as if her parents were watching over her shoulder. Whenever Priscilla was doing something she thought her parents wouldn't approve of, she seemed to "hear mother and father speaking," telling her what she *should* do and what she *ought* to feel. In various group exercises, Priscilla "became" her parents and spoke for them by lecturing each of us about how we ought to change our ways.

At one point I urged her to act as if she had no choice but to remain forever the nice and proper lady her parents expected her to be and asked her to exaggerate this ladylike behavior in the group for several sessions. Afterward she reported that it "made her sick" to be so phony and so ready to conform. She decided she would change, no matter how difficult the task was going to be. Although Priscilla still respected some of the core values she had learned at home, she wanted the freedom to discard others without feeling guilty. Her work in the group and outside of it gave her new freedom to develop her own set of values—values that were meaningful to her and that freed her to live by her own expectations rather than by those of others.

The Search for Authenticity

The theologian Paul Tillich (1952) uses the phrase "the courage to be" to define a courage that can take all forms of "nonbeing" into itself because it is based on the ground of being. Such a grounding both centers our being and gives us the power to be self-transcending. It is a courage that "allows us to accept our acceptance."

Discovering, creating, and maintaining the core deep within our being is a difficult and never-ending struggle. Van Deurzen-Smith (1988) suggests that such authentic living is more of a process than a static end result. Living authentically entails engagement in doing what is worthwhile as we see it. Briefly put, it means that we are true to ourselves. This kind of living can provide a deep sense of inner peace, yet authenticity is no easy matter. It is only when we stop trying to be cured of the paradoxes of life, van Deurzen-Smith reminds us, that we can be truly alive.

When we lead an authentic existence, we are constantly becoming the person we are capable of becoming. Living authentically also entails knowing and accepting our limits. The "Serenity Prayer" offers a good example of this knowledge and acceptance: "God grant me the serenity to accept the things I cannot change, courage to change the things I can, and wisdom to know the difference."

A quote with a different twist that Frankl (1963) is fond of using is Goethe's admonition: "If we take man as he is, we make him worse; but if we take him as he should be, we help him become what he can be." Frankl sees it as the therapist's task to challenge clients to become their full and authentic selves by getting engaged in life and making commitments. His logotherapy, since it is concerned with people's spiritual dimensions and higher aspirations, provides inspiration to continually seek the meaning that is necessary to live authentically. The essence of defining oneself is captured in an adage I saw in a church in Hawaii: "Who you are is God's gift to you; what you make of yourself is your gift to God."

Those who typically ignore their inner promptings in a perennial quest for conformity lose themselves in the values and standards of others. One of the most common fears expressed by people in groups is that if they take an honest look at themselves they will discover they are just empty shells with no core and no substance. Therefore, they are afraid of shedding masks and pretenses because, once those are gone, nothing will be left.

A concept related to inauthenticity is guilt. Existential guilt grows out of a sense of incompleteness and the realization that we are viewing life through someone else's eyes. Ultimately, the loss of the sense of being becomes psychological sickness. To the extent that we allow others to design our lives, we experience a restricted existence.

■ **Implications for Group Work**   A group provides a powerful context in which to look at oneself, decide the degree to which one is a fully functioning person as opposed to reflecting what others expect, and consider what choices might be more authentically one's own. Members can openly share their fears related to living in unfulfilling ways and come to see how they have compromised their integrity. The group offers many opportunities for tackling life's challenges. Members can gradually discover ways in which they have lost their direction and can begin to be more true to themselves. They will learn that others cannot give them easy answers to the problems of living. Certainly, existential group leaders will not prescribe simple solutions, for they know that this is inconsistent with helping members live in authentic ways.

A major part of the group counseling experience involves members sorting out for themselves who they are and what identities they have assumed without conscious thought. When people live by outworn identities, their lives lose meaning. An existential group can be instrumental in assisting members to come to a full appreciation of themselves in relation to others. Through the group experience, members see that their identity is not cast in stone but that they can reshape the purpose of their life. Group leaders who themselves continue to reshape their personal meanings can be an encouragement to the members.

■ **Example**   Martha, who at 45 had devoted a major portion of her life to her family, is typical of many women who have been members of my groups and personal growth workshops. For most of her life, Martha had depended almost totally on her roles as wife, mother, and homemaker as sources of identity. As her daughters and sons entered high school and then college and finally left home, she asked herself more and more frequently: "Is there more to life than what I've done so far? Who am I besides all the roles I've responsibly filled? What do I want to do with the rest of my life?"

Martha returned to the university and obtained a degree in human services, a critical turning point in her life that opened many new doors for her. She engaged in a number of projects that enriched her life, including specialized work with the elderly. Through her program of studies, Martha joined several intensive personal growth workshops, which gave her the opportunity to pose and debate questions such as "Do I have the courage to find out if I can create a new identity for myself? Will I be able to withstand pressures from my family to remain the way they want me to be? Can I give to others and at the same time give to myself?" These questions indicated Martha's growing awareness that she needed to be a person in her own right and that she wanted to live an authentic existence. Martha's self-questioning also showed that she knew that making choices entails doubts and struggles that one must resolve for oneself.

Aloneness and Relatedness

Existentialists believe that ultimately we are alone—that only we can give a sense of meaning to our lives, decide how we will live, find our own answers, and decide whether we will be or not be. Because awareness of our ultimate aloneness can be frightening, some of us try to avoid it by throwing ourselves into casual relationships and frantic activities, trusting that they will numb our fear and anguish.

We also have the choice of experiencing our aloneness and trying to find a center of meaning and direction within ourselves. Only if we make this choice and succeed at establishing our own identity can we relate genuinely and meaningfully to others. We must stand alone before we can truly stand beside another.

There is a paradox in the proposition that we are existentially both alone and related. Yet it is this very paradox that describes the human condition. We are social beings, and we depend on interpersonal relationships for our human-ness. We have a desire for intimacy, a hope to be significant in another's world, and a desire to feel that another's presence is important in our world. But un-less we can find our own strength within ourselves, we cannot have nourishing relationships with others based on fulfillment rather than deprivation.

Implications for Group Work   In groups participants have the opportunity to relate to others in meaningful ways, to learn to be themselves in the com-pany of other people, and to find reward and nourishment in the relationships they establish. They also learn that it is not in others that they can find the an-swers to questions about significance and purpose in life. If their struggle for self-awareness is successful, they come to realize that no matter how valuable their relationships are they are ultimately on their own.

The relationships that participants establish within the group are valuable also because they teach people how to relate to others outside of the group. In a group, people recognize their own struggles in others, and this often results in a bond. Even though they may accept that ultimately they are existentially alone, they also come to realize that they are not alone in their struggles and that others, too, are courageously looking at themselves and trying to establish their own identities. In short, groups offer distinct possibilities for members to intimately relate to one another that individual therapy does not offer.

Example   The case of Zeke shows that a person can be with others and at the same time be very much alone. During a group session, Zeke said that he felt cut off from everyone in the group and described himself as a "spectator who seems out of place." I asked him if he would be willing to experiment with re-ally separating himself from the group and observing us from a distance. He agreed to leave the room, sit outside on the balcony, and observe what was going on through the window. I asked him to be aware of what he was think-ing and feeling as he sat out there observing. He was told to return to the group when he was ready to talk about what he had experienced sitting on the outside.

When he returned, Zeke said that for the first time he had realized how safe it was for him to keep himself in a spectator role and that he was ready to do something different. I asked him if he would go around to each person in the group and complete these two sentences: "One way I have kept you at a distance is by _____." and "One way I could be closer to you is by _____." After he had "made the rounds," Zeke described the circumstances in which he typically felt alone, even when surrounded by many people. He spoke of his desire to achieve intimacy and of his fears of approaching people. His work in the group had intensified his attempts to keep himself separate, which finally resulted in a desire to change.

Role and Functions of the Group Leader

In the existential view, therapy is a partnership and a shared venture between the therapist and the client. To develop this partnership, therapists focus on the human side of the person-to-person relationship. From the existential perspective, therapists must bring their own subjectivity into their work, and it is essential that they demonstrate presence if they are to develop an effective working relationship with members. High priority is given to the quality of the therapeutic relationship as a healing force, with an emphasis on I/Thou encounters and dialogue (Cain, 2002). A central role of existential leaders is to create a therapeutic alliance, for it is assumed that change comes from the relationship itself. (As you will see in Chapters 10 and 11, the relationship is also the core of the person-centered approach and of Gestalt therapy.)

Bugental (1997) writes about the therapeutic alliance: "The chief function of the psychotherapist is to display to the client the ways in which the client constricts her or his awareness (the resistances) and the costs of such constrictions" (p. 191). This climate for change will not come about if the leader maintains a strictly objective orientation, is psychologically absent from the group, and is merely a skilled but impersonal technician. Bugental (1987) puts this idea beautifully:

> The therapeutic alliance is the powerful joining of forces which energizes and supports the long, difficult, and frequently painful work of life-changing psychotherapy. The conception of the therapist here is not of a disinterested observer-technician but of a fully alive human companion for the client. In this regard my view is in marked contrast to the traditional notion of the therapist as a skilled but objective director of therapeutic processes. (p. 49)

Change is brought about not only by the relationship with the leader but also by relationships with other members. Thus, a primary role of the leader is to foster meaningful relationships among participants. This can be done by having members focus on key existential concerns and providing a climate in which these concerns can be fully explored. A therapeutic community is thus established based on the commonality of shared struggles. The members make a commitment to confront one another about their unused potentials and inauthentic behaviors and to support one another in the common endeavor to open the door to selfhood.

Existential group leaders assume a basic role of challenging the members of their groups to examine their lives. This involves encouraging members to assess ways their freedom may be restricted, reflect on how they might increase their choices, and assume responsibility for their choices. Cain (2002) writes: "Clients are challenged to wrestle with the basic question of how they are living, face the givens of their existence, confront the associated anxiety, and learn to live more fully, authentically, and responsibly" (p. 24).

Sharp and Bugental (2001) emphasize that the cornerstone of existential therapeutic work is the attention that is paid to *presence*. The therapist's job is to draw attention to what interferes with the client's presence and to invite him or her to recognize and deal with resistances to change. Bugental (1987) defines resistance as "the impulse to protect one's familiar identity and known world against perceived threat" (p. 175). Bugental views resistance as those ways in which clients avoid being subjectively present in the therapeutic work. A therapist's function often entails challenging clients to explore life-pattern resistance that leads to distress (Sharp & Bugental, 2001). A group can be instrumental in helping members see how some of the self-constricting patterns they are manifesting in the group are paralleled in their everyday life. By exploring their resistances, individuals may recognize, challenge, and modify their self-conception and their way of being in the world (Sharp & Bugental, 2001).

Application: Therapeutic Techniques and Procedures

Unlike many other group approaches, the existential model puts more emphasis on experiencing the client in the present moment than on using a particular set of techniques. May (1983) emphasizes that technique follows understanding. This means that the primary concern of the therapist is to be with the client and to understand his or her subjective world. Questions concerning therapeutic technique are subordinate to this quest for understanding. There are no "right" techniques in this approach; the task is accomplished through the therapeutic encounter and dialogue between client and therapist. Although existential group counselors are free to incorporate techniques from various approaches, they are not bound to use any particular technique.

The interventions existential group practitioners employ are based on philosophical views about the essential nature of human existence. Existential group therapists may incorporate a variety of techniques from various therapeutic schools. Vontress (1996) uses the phrase *Socratic dialogue* to describe his holistic intervention strategy, which addresses simultaneously the psychological, sociological, physical, and spiritual dimensions of human existence. Rejecting the term *eclectic*, Vontress will sometimes draw on phenomenological, cognitive, behavioral, and psychoanalytic insights during a single session with a client. Existential practitioners do not employ an array of unintegrated techniques. They have a set of assumptions and attitudes that guides their interventions in the groups they facilitate. The main guideline is that the existential therapist's practice is responsive to the uniqueness of each client (Walsh & McElwain, 2002).

Van Deurzen-Smith (1990a) points out that the existential approach is well known for placing primary emphasis on understanding the world of the client rather than on applying techniques in solving problems. She stresses the importance of therapists reaching sufficient depth and openness in their own lives to enable them to venture into their clients' subjective world without losing their own sense of identity. Van Deurzen-Smith (1997) reminds us that existential therapy is a collaborative adventure in which both client and therapist will be transformed if they allow themselves to be touched by life. She also emphasizes that "one of the fundamental characteristics of existential work is its openness to the individual creativity of the practitioner and the client" (p. 189). She encourages therapists to use interventions that reflect their own personality and style but to remain flexible in relation to what their clients need. Van Duerzen-Smith suggests several kinds of interventions, including the therapeutic use of silence, questions, and making interpretations:

• *Silence* is one of the most significant interventions a therapist can make. There needs to be a breathing space in between dialogue. Therapists have the task of listening with a receptive attitude so that clients can move forward in a way of their choosing.

• *Questions* have a place in therapy, yet they need to be based on what clients are saying rather than probing for more information. It is best for therapists to ask questions that are implied in the client's words and in the subtext of their messages.

• *Interpretations* are used in existential therapy as a way to make sense of the client's overall story by connecting individual statements and experiences to enhance meaning. Van Duerzen-Smith sums up the essence of this intervention thusly: "The duty of the existential therapist is to see to it that interpretations are made within the framework of meaning of the client, rather than within the framework of meaning of the therapist. The puzzle to be completed is the client's, not our own" (p. 229).

Group practitioners who work within an existential framework do use many of the techniques described in this book. Many of the procedures used by Adlerians and the techniques used by psychodramatists fit with an existential philosophy beautifully. Furthermore, it is possible to have an existential orientation that guides the interventions of a group leader and still rely heavily on techniques from transactional analysis, cognitive behavior therapy, and reality therapy. The techniques of these action-oriented therapeutic approaches can be grounded on existential concepts. However, existential group counselors never use techniques as the main menu. Instead, primary consideration is given to the nature of the relationships being formed in the group. When the deepest self of the group therapist meets the deepest part of the individual group members in the I/Thou encounter, the group process is at its best.

The leader sets the tone for the group not by introducing techniques and *doing something* but rather by *being* and *becoming* somebody. Mullan (1978, 1979) describes how challenges by the group leader foster personality changes in members (including changes in thinking, feeling, and behaving). The group sessions tend to shake up the conventional ways in which members view the world. When their status quo is jarred, members have a better chance of facing themselves and of changing.

Phases of an Existential Group

A therapeutic group is characterized by a creative, evolving process of discovery, which can be conceptualized in three general phases.

During the initial phase, group counselors assist the participants in identifying and clarifying their assumptions about the world. Group members are invited to define and question the ways in which they perceive and make sense of their existence. They examine their values, beliefs, and assumptions to determine their validity. For many group members this is a difficult task, because they may initially present their problems as resulting almost entirely from external causes. They may focus on what other people "make them feel" or on how others are largely responsible for their actions or inaction. The group leader teaches members how to reflect on their own existence and to examine their role in contributing to their problems in living.

During the middle phase of existential group counseling, the members are encouraged to more fully examine the source and authority of their present value system. This process of self-exploration typically leads to new insights and some restructuring of their values and attitudes. Group members get a better idea of what kind of life they consider worthy to live. They develop a clearer sense of their internal valuing process. Van Deurzen-Smith (1997) states that existential exploration addresses a spiritual dimension of finding meaning. The focus is on core life issues, and clients deal with moral issues of living.

The final phase focuses on helping members put what they are learning about themselves into action. The aim of a group experience is to empower the participants to implement their examined and internalized values in concrete ways. Through a therapeutic group experience, members are able to discover their strengths and put these capabilities to the service of living a meaningful existence.

Existential group counseling focuses on exploring options to help members create a meaningful life. For many of us, recognition of the ways in which we have kept ourselves in a victimlike stance marks the beginning of change. Through the group process, we begin to understand that we can choose to consciously become the authors of our lives.

Applying the Existential Approach to Group Work in the Schools

The existential approach has a great deal to offer when counseling adolescents in groups because they face so many existential challenges today. From elementary to high school level, violence is becoming more commonplace, and school counselors are called upon for crisis intervention and to devise programs to prevent violence. When tragedies do occur, these young people are certainly awakened to the reality of death. Such occurrences are a stark reminder that we do not know how much time we have on this earth and that we may not be able to accomplish our dreams. A crisis-oriented group gives students opportunities to verbally express their shock, grief, anger, and fear. During a period of crisis, existential themes involving death and nonbeing, life's meaning, and existential anxiety become very real. It is not necessary for those who conduct a school group to process feelings surrounding violence to come up with answers or to bring closure to such issues; rather, the leader can provide a valuable function by encouraging students to give full expression to their feelings and thoughts. Group members can acknowledge their common concerns and provide support in a time when it is sorely needed. Such a group can be a catalyst for young people to assess their lives and do what they can to make life-affirming choices. Groups can be a rich source of healing, for both young people in the group and the counselor who facilitates the open expression of reactions. Exploring the existential anxiety surrounding the unknown is a main task of a group with a crisis-oriented focus.

Existential concepts can be incorporated in groups with adolescents in other ways as well. One of my colleagues, Conrad, is a counselor at a middle school. He facilitates several different kinds of groups, including a bereavement group that he started in response to a number of students who had to cope with the death of a parent. Conrad finds that these junior high students are able to process a wide range of feelings and reactions associated with a significant loss, that they can be a genuine source of support for one another, and that they are able to begin healing from losses. As is the case for crisis-oriented groups, the members of Conrad's groups are challenged to reflect on their own mortality, to talk about their fears of death, and to explore what really counts in their lives. Conrad reports that his level of presence and compassion with the students is far more important than any techniques or exercises he might introduce.

Most key concepts of the existential approach have relevance for a wide variety of groups with both children and adolescents. Young people struggle with issues of freedom and responsibility, existential anxiety around the unpredictable nature of life, the reality of death, question the true purpose of their lives, and reflect on striving for authenticity. Even a psychoeducational group or a short-term school group can reach more depth if the group leader learns to listen for the existential underpinnings that form the concerns of the members. In addition to teaching coping skills or acquiring certain information, a group can be instrumental in beginning a reflection process that encourages young people to take seriously the existential challenges of their existence. In working with school-age students, the emphasis needs to be placed on personal responsibility and the choices they make. In talking about members' changes within the group, it is important to build an internal locus of control by processing the choices members make and the actions they take.

Applying the Existential Approach
with Multicultural Populations

According to van Deurzen-Smith (1990a), because the existential approach does not dictate a particular way of viewing or relating to reality, it is very suitable for working with multicultural groups. One quality of this approach is its flexibility in therapeutic style. Van Duerzen-Smith (1997) points out that existential therapists are willing to shift their stance when the situation requires it, especially in cross-cultural counseling situations. Existential therapists attempt to free themselves of their preconceptions and prejudices as much as possible. They respect the uniqueness of the particular situation of each client and do not impose their cultural values on the client. Van Duerzen-Smith (1997) writes: "Working within the relative values of a cross-cultural context is a challenge that can be met if we take a broadly philosophical stance, rather than buying into the ideology of our own culture or of our own particular system of psychotherapy" (p. 239).

Assuming an existential orientation does not mean that we have to preach to group members about the values of self-awareness, choice, and responsibility. The existential approach is particularly relevant for multicultural situations because it does not impose particular values and meanings; rather, it investigates the values and meanings of group members. Existential counselors respect the different elements that make up a client's philosophy of life. With this understanding of different worldviews, group practitioners are in a position to establish mutually agreed-upon goals with clients that will provide a direction for change.

Vontress (1996) points out that we are all multicultural in the sense that we are all products of many cultures. According to Vontress, existential counseling is especially useful in working with culturally different populations because of its focus on universality, the similarities we all share. He encourages counselors in training to focus on the universal commonalities of clients first and secondarily on areas of differences.

Those clients who are willing to participate in a group are frequently experiencing psychological pain. Faced with a crisis and feeling helpless, they often experience their lives as being out of their control. Some clients simply believe that they do not have a choice or that choice is mainly a middle-class notion. Even if they do have some freedom, societal factors (such as racism, discrimination, and lack of opportunity) may severely restrict their ability to choose for themselves. Existentially oriented group leaders would do well to take into account the sociocultural factors that restrict choices. Clients who come from the barrio or an inner-city environment, for example, may be motivated primarily by the need for safety and survival and may be seeking help in getting these basic needs met. Simply *telling* clients they have a choice in making their life better will not help, and it is likely to have a negative impact. Premature assurances that we are all free to give meaning to our lives will seem like insensitive clichés. It is real-life issues that provide grist for the mill for group work, assuming that the leader is willing to deal with them. Developing interventions that can help the client take action, even if it is only small steps toward change, can have a significant impact on a client's life in the long run (van Deurzen-Smith, 1997).

Pack-Brown, Whittington-Clark, and Parker (1998) maintain that existential approaches will resonate with many African American women, mainly because they encounter many difficult realities, suffering, and pain. Here are a few specific existential factors that often resonate with African American women:

- Life can be unfair and unjust.
- Ultimately there is no escape from pain and death.
- In spite of intimacy with others, one must still face life alone.
- The core challenge is to face and deal with basic issues of life and death.
- We must assume the ultimate responsibility for how we are living, regardless of the support and guidance we may get from others.

These authors state that the Afrocentric approach addresses the illumination and liberation of the spirit and focuses on the principles of harmony within the universe as a natural order of existence. In an individual's search for a meaningful existence, spiritual values should be viewed as a potential resource. Existential groups take up questions such as "Who am I?" and "What is the meaning of my life?" For many clients, spirituality can be a powerful force in fostering healing through an exploration of self by learning to accept oneself, forgiving others and oneself, admitting one's shortcomings, accepting personal responsibility, letting go of resentments, and dealing with guilt. Clearly, spirituality is an existential issue.

Evaluation of the Existential Approach to Groups

Contributions and Strengths of the Approach

I value many features of the existential approach and have incorporated them in my practice. I work on the basic assumption that people have the capacity to become increasingly self-aware and that expansion of awareness results in greater freedom to choose their own direction in life. I share the existentialists' view that we are not driven by instinctual forces, nor are we merely the products of conditioning. I base my group work on the assumption that people do not have to remain victims of their past or of the external world and that they have the power to decide for themselves and take action, at least to some extent. For me, this assumption has implications for conducting a wide range of groups for victims of rape, battering, crime, and various other forms of abuse. Although I agree that people can indeed be victims of forces outside of themselves, I also believe that existential therapy can help such individuals reclaim or acquire a sense of power so they will not remain victims. This approach is largely about empowerment of individuals.

I value the existential perspective because it has brought the person back into a central place and because it addresses itself to the basic question of what it means to be human. This approach humanizes psychotherapy and reduces the chances of its becoming a mechanical process in the hands of technicians. I especially value the emphasis on the therapist's being fully present in the therapeutic encounter. This full presence implies having access to one's own feelings and being able to express them appropriately and in a timely way. Bugental (1987) maintains that through the therapist's concern, sensitivity, and presence, clients are invited to disclose the core life issues they are struggling with. If therapists are not personally involved in their work, their clients will not be supported as they endure the painful and frightening self-confrontations that are necessary for major life changes to occur.

This approach encourages and challenges me as a group leader to bring my own experiences and my very humanness to my work. I cannot help clients face their existential concerns without doing the same in my own life. My willingness to remain open to my own struggles determines the degree to which I can be a significant and positive influence for others in a group.

An important contribution of the existential approach is the notion that techniques follow understanding. In my view, this basic concept lessens the danger of abusing techniques. Too often leaders use techniques merely to "get things going" in a group. When the emphasis is on understanding the world of the participant, the leader's first concern is with genuinely grasping the core struggles of others and then drawing on certain techniques to help participants explore these struggles more fully. Because existentially oriented group leaders can draw from the techniques of most of the other approaches discussed in this book, they can develop a highly flexible therapeutic style that is suitable for a variety of groups. Not only do I view the relationship-oriented and experiential approaches as being compatible with an existential orientation, but I also think cognitive behavioral therapies (Adlerian, TA, behavioral, and reality therapy) can be productively used along with an existential foundation.

Van Deurzen-Smith (1990a) identifies the clients and problems most suited to an existential approach as those who are interested in and committed to dealing with their problems about living. The approach has particular relevance for people who feel alienated from the current expectations of society or for those who are searching for meaning in their lives. It tends to work well with people who are at a crossroads, coping with the changes of personal circumstances such as bereavement or loss of employment. Van Deurzen-Smith believes existential therapy works better with individuals who are willing to challenge the status quo in the world. It can be useful for people who are on the edge of existence: those who are dying, those working through a developmental or situational crisis, or those who are starting a new phase of life.

One strength of the existential approach is its focus on spirituality. Some group members cannot be understood without appreciating the central role their religious or spiritual beliefs and practices exert in daily life. Universal concerns about freedom and responsibility, anxiety, guilt, meaning in life, and the relationship of death to finding purpose in life can all be explored in an existential group. Once members better understand these life issues, they may find resolution to some of their core struggles. Spiritual and religious values can be integrated with other therapeutic tools to enhance the process of a therapeutic group.

Bugental and Bracke (1992) write that the value and vitality of a psychotherapeutic approach depend on its ability to help clients deal with the sources of pain and dissatisfaction in their lives. They contend that the existential orientation is particularly suited to offering meaningful assistance to individuals who are experiencing a lack of a centered awareness of being. Cushman (1990) has written about the *empty self*—whose emptiness results from failing to listen to our internal voice or from not trusting our sense of direction. This emptiness is manifested in several ways: through depression, through the absence of a purpose for life, through a lack of clear priorities, through addiction to food or drugs, and through other means of striving to fill the void. Frankl (1963) refers to this condition of emptiness as an "existential vacuum." Many group members describe feeling as if there is a hole in their lives, and even though they attempt to fill this emptiness of self, they are not successful. Unless they confront their fears and the sources that are blocking their ability to live fully, they are likely to strive in vain to numb the pain created by this inner void. An existential group can be instrumental in encouraging members to face themselves courageously and deal with the inauthentic aspects of their lives.

There are some distinct advantages of existential group work over dyadic existential therapy. First, existential group counseling is comprehensive; it includes a consideration of the "worlds" in which people live. One of the most important of these worlds is the *Mitwelt*, the interpersonal environment in which we relate to others. From infancy to old age, we need others and develop a sense of empathy with others. We are fulfilled by fellowship with other people and are influenced by continued contact with others. People who learn to relate to others usually have little trouble relating to themselves. However, before people can relate meaningfully to others, they need to know and have a good relationship with themselves. The interpersonal perspective of the existential approach is well suited to this process of discovery (Vontress, 1996).

Existential groups can be either a long-term or a short-term venture. Exploring the deeper layers of human existence is an involved process, but the basic concepts of the existential approach can form the foundation of a short-term, structured group. The existential themes of death and mortality challenge members to examine what they are doing in their lives. Likewise, the reality of a time-limited group can be a catalyst for members to become actively and fully involved in each group session. Group members can be challenged to examine how they are relating to the here-and-now aspect of the group experience. They can be asked to evaluate the degree to which they are fully utilizing the resources within the group and the degree to which they are active in the group. A short-term group can actually help members keep their focus clearly in mind and can encourage them to make optimal use of the limited time they have to accomplish their personal goals.

Sharp and Bugental (2001) indicate that short-term groups require a clearly defined purpose and a limited goal. Thus, members would be asked to present their concerns in a succinct form, and a contract might be designed to work toward resolution of a particular concern. In using a briefer approach, members would still be taught the searching process of getting deeply centered to mobilize their concerns. Sharp and Bugental add that this short-term focus is often a compromise necessitated by managed care programs, which are characterized by cost containment, brevity, and quantifiable behavioral change. Most of the existential themes considered in this chapter would be viewed as being too abstract, complex, and amorphous to fit within a managed care context. In many instances, a short-term approach is not desirable for existential groups.

Limitations of the Approach

Many existentialist concepts are quite abstract and difficult to apply in practice. Existential theorists such as Kierkegaard, Heidegger, and Sartre were not writing for group counselors and therapists! Existentialism began as a formal philosophical movement, and although it eventually led to existential approaches within both psychology and psychiatry, its philosophical nature still dominates. Both beginning and advanced group practitioners who are not of a philosophical turn of mind tend to find many of the existential concepts lofty, abstract, and elusive. Even those group counselors who are sympathetic to the core ideas of this perspective sometimes struggle with knowing how to apply these concepts to the practice of group work. It is not so much a matter of applying existentialist philosophy as it is a matter of educating group leaders on the concrete and practical issues of life that are relevant to all human beings. To put it another way, as group members consolidate what they have learned from their efforts to be open with their struggles, they often find themselves saying the things these philosophers had also stated. They begin to talk about choices. In this sense, existential group work has little to do with existentialism and everything to do with life.

As van Deurzen-Smith (1990a) points out, some existential therapists tend to emphasize the cognitive aspects of a client's concerns, and some clients are attracted to the approach believing that they can avoid tapping their senses, feelings, and intuitions. She suggests that a good existential therapist would address all these different levels of human experience, believing that openness to exploring these aspects of being is a requisite for self-understanding.

Some other limitations of the existential approach have been identified by van Deurzen-Smith (1990a):

• It is not particularly relevant for people who are uninterested in examining their basic assumptions and who would rather not explore the foundation of their human existence.
• Those clients who want relief from specific symptoms or who are seeking problem-solving methods will generally not find much value in this orientation.

- The existential therapist functions in the role of a consultant who can provide clients with support in facing up to the truth of their lives. For those who are looking for a therapist who will direct them or who will function as a substitute parent, this approach will have little to offer.

An effective existential practitioner needs to have a great deal of maturity, life experience, and intensive supervision and training. It is easy to envision the dangers posed by therapists who have a shallow grasp of this approach and who deceive both themselves and their clients into thinking that they possess the requisite wisdom.

Where to Go from Here

The Society for Existential Analysis is a professional organization devoted to exploring issues pertaining to an existential/phenomenological approach to counseling and therapy. Membership is open to anyone interested in this approach and includes students, trainees, psychotherapists, philosophers, psychiatrists, counselors, and psychologists. Members receive a regular newsletter and an annual copy of the *Journal of the Society for Existential Analysis*. The society provides a list of existentially oriented psychotherapists for referral purposes. The School of Psychotherapy and Counselling at Regent's College in London offers an advanced diploma in existential psychotherapy as well as short courses in the field. For information on any of the above, contact:

Society for Existential Analysis
BM Existential
London
WCIN 3XX
England
E-MAIL: exist@cwcom.net
WEB SITE: www.existential.mcmail.com

Recommended Supplementary Readings

No books that I am aware of deal explicitly and exclusively with the application of the existential approach to group counseling. However, the books included here contain related material that you can use to apply this approach to your work with groups.

Existential Psychotherapy (Yalom, 1980) is a superb treatment of ultimate human concerns of death, freedom, isolation, and meaninglessness as these issues relate to therapy. This book has depth and clarity, and it is rich with clinical examples that illustrate existential themes. If you were to select just one book on existential therapy, this would be my recommendation.

Existential Counselling in Practice (van Deurzen-Smith, 1988) is highly recommended as a good overview of the basic assumptions, goals, and key concepts of the existential approach. The author puts into clear perspective topics such as anxiety, authentic living, clarifying one's worldview, determining values, discovering meaning, and coming to terms with life. This book provides a framework for practicing counseling from an existential perspective.

Everyday Mysteries: Existential Dimensions of Psychotherapy (van Deurzen-Smith, 1997) contains contributions of key existential psychotherapists. Topics such as therapeutic dialogue, the client/therapist relationship, the psychological and spiritual dimensions of therapy, and other aspects of existential worldviews are addressed.

The Art of the Psychotherapist (Bugental, 1987) is an outstanding book that bridges the art and science of psychotherapy, making places for both. The author is an insightful and sensitive clinician who writes about the psychotherapist's and the client's journey from an existential perspective.

I Never Knew I Had a Choice (Corey & Corey, 2002) is a self-help book written from an existential perspective. It contains many exercises and activities that leaders can use for their group work and that they can suggest as "homework assignments" between sessions. The topics covered include our struggle to achieve autonomy; the roles that work, love, sexuality, intimacy, and solitude play in our lives; the meaning of loneliness, death, and loss; and the ways in which we choose our values and philosophy of life.

References and Suggested Readings*

Bugental, J. F. T. (1978). *Psychotherapy and process: The fundamentals of an existential-humanistic approach*. Reading, MA: Addison-Wesley.

*Bugental, J. F. T. (1987). *The art of the psychotherapist*. New York: Norton.

*Bugental, J. F. T. (1997). There is a fundamental division in how psychotherapy is conceived. In J. K. Zeig (Ed.), *The evolution of psychotherapy: The third conference* (pp. 185–196). New York: Brunner/Mazel.

Bugental, J. F. T., & Bracke, P. E. (1992). The future of existential-humanistic psychotherapy. *Psychotherapy 29*(1), 28–33.

*Cain, D. J. (2002). Defining characteristics, history, and evolution of humanistic psychotherapies. In D. J. Cain, & J. Seeman, (Eds.), *Humanistic psychotherapies: Handbook of research and practice* (pp. 3–54). Washington, DC: American Psychological Association.

*Corey, G., & Corey, M. (2002). *I never knew I had a choice* (7th ed.). Pacific Grove, CA: Brooks/Cole.

Cushman, P. (1990). Why the self is empty: Toward a historically situated psychology. *American Psychologist, 45*(5), 599–611.

*Deurzen-Smith, E. van. (1988). *Existential counselling in practice*. London: Sage.

*Deurzen-Smith, E. van. (1990a). *Existential therapy*. London, England: Society for Existential Analysis Publications.

Deurzen-Smith, E. van. (1990b). What is existential analysis? *Journal of the Society for Existential Analysis, 1*, 6–14.

---

*Books and articles marked with an asterisk are suggested for further study.

Deurzen-Smith, E. van. (1991). Ontological insecurity revisited. *Journal of the Society for Existential Analysis, 2*, 38–48.

*Deurzen-Smith, E. van. (1995). *Existential therapy*. London: Society for Existential Analysis.

*Deurzen-Smith, E. van. (1997). *Everyday mysteries: Existential dimensions of psychotherapy*. London: Routledge.

*Frankl, V. (1963). *Man's search for meaning*. New York: Washington Square Press.

*Gould, W. B. (1993). *Viktor E. Frankl: Life with meaning*. Pacific Grove, CA: Brooks/Cole.

Heidegger, M. (1962). *Being and time* (John Macquarrie & Edward Robinson, Trans.). New York: Harper & Row.

*Kinnier, R. T., Tribbensee, N. E., Rose, C. A., & Vaughan, S. M. (2001). In the final analysis: More wisdom from people who have faced death. *Journal of Counseling and Development, 79*(2), 171–177.

Lantz, J. (1993). Treatment modalities in logotherapy. *International Forum for Logotherapy, 16*(2), 65–73.

*May, R. (1953). *Man's search for himself*. New York: Norton.

May, R. (Ed.). (1961). *Existential psychology*. New York: Random House.

May, R. (1983). *The discovery of being: Writings in existential psychology*. New York: Norton.

*May, R., & Yalom, I. (2000). Existential psychotherapy. In R. Corsini & D. Wedding (Eds.), *Current psychotherapies* (6th ed., pp. 273–302). Itasca, IL: F. E. Peacock.

Mullan, H. (1978). Existential group psychotherapy. In H. Mullan & M. Rosenbaum (Eds.), *Group psychotherapy: Theory and practice* (2nd ed.). New York: Free Press.

Mullan, H. (1979). An existential group psychotherapy. *International Journal of Group Psychotherapy, 29*(2), 163–174.

Pack-Brown, S. P., Whittington-Clark, L. E., & Parker, W. M. (1998). *Images of me: A guide to group work with African-American women*. Boston: Allyn & Bacon.

Russell, J. M. (1978). Sartre, therapy, and expanding the concept of responsibility. *The American Journal of Psychoanalysis, 38*, 259–269.

Russell, J. M. (1979). Sartre's theory of sexuality. *Journal of Humanistic Psychology, 19*(2), 35–45.

Sartre, J. P. (1971). *Being and nothingness*. New York: Bantam.

Sharf, R. S. (2000). *Theories of psychotherapy and counseling: Concepts and cases* (2nd ed.). Pacific Grove, CA: Brooks/Cole.

*Sharp, J. G., & Bugental, J. F. T. (2001). Existential-humanistic psychotherapy. In R. J. Corsini (Ed.), *Handbook of innovative therapies* (2nd ed., pp. 206–217). New York: Wiley.

Tillich, P. (1952). *The courage to be*. New Haven, CT: Yale University Press.

*Vontress, C. E. (1996). A personal retrospective on cross-cultural counseling. *Journal of Multicultural Counseling and Development, 24*(3), 156–166.

*Walsh, R. A., & McElwain, B. (2002). Existential psychotherapies. In D. J. Cain, & J. Seeman, (Eds.), *Humanistic psychotherapies: Handbook of research and practice* (pp. 253–278). Washington, DC: American Psychological Association.

*Yalom, I. D. (1980). *Existential psychotherapy*. New York: Basic Books

CHAPTER 10

The Person-Centered
Approach to Groups

Introduction

The person-centered approach to group counseling (originally known as nondirective counseling and later called client-centered therapy) was developed by the late Carl Rogers. It is grounded on the assumption that human beings tend to move toward wholeness and self-actualization and that individual members, as well as the group as a whole, can find their own direction with a minimal degree of help from the group leader, or "facilitator." The person-centered approach emphasizes the personal qualities of the group leader rather than techniques of leading. The primary function of the facilitator is to create a fertile and healing climate in the group. This therapy is best considered a "way of being" rather than a "way of doing."

The group facilitator establishes a therapeutic climate in the group by creating a relationship based on these attitudes: accurate empathic understanding, acceptance, nonpossessive warmth, caring, and genuineness. As the facilitator projects these attitudes, an accepting and caring climate emerges. Given the establishment of a favorable climate, the group members can be trusted to drop their defenses, to tap their inner resources, and to work toward personally meaningful goals that will lead to significant personal change. To function effectively in a group, the facilitator must trust the abilities of the group members to grow in a favorable direction. If this is not the case, the group leader is likely to apply more control over the group process than is helpful (Page, Weiss, & Lietaer, 2002).

The contemporary person-centered approach to group counseling is the result of an evolutionary process begun more than 60 years ago that continues to remain open to change and refinement (see Cain & Seeman, 2002). In the early 1940s, Rogers developed what was known as *nondirective counseling*, which provided a powerful and revolutionary alternative to the directive approaches to therapy then being practiced. He caused a furor by challenging the basic assumption that the counselor was the expert and the client should be in a passive role. Rogers questioned the validity of such widely used therapeutic procedures as suggestion, giving of advice, teaching, diagnosis, and interpretation. What was new about nondirective counseling was the emphasis given to the therapist's realness and empathy. The therapeutic relationship, rather than the therapist's techniques, was viewed as the central factor leading to change.

A common theme in Rogers's early writings that permeated all of his later works is a basic trust in the client's ability to move forward if conditions fostering growth are present. According to Rogers, there is a *formative tendency* in nature that both maintains and enhances the organism. This central source of energy seeks fulfillment and actualization. A faith in subjective experience and a belief in the basic trustworthiness of human nature go hand in hand. This actualization tendency suggests an internal source of growth and healing. Clients have capacities for self-understanding and constructive change. There is a tendency toward autonomy, which means that the individual moves inherently toward self-regulation and self-determination and away from being controlled. However, the actualizing tendency does not imply a movement away from relationships, interdependence, and connection (Brodley, 1999a). The whole conceptual framework of Rogers's ideas grows out of his experience that human beings become increasingly worthy of trust once they feel at a deep level that they are understood and respected (Thorne, 1992). Although person-centered therapy has changed over the years, this faith in the fundamental actualization tendency of the person has remained at its foundation.

The Relationship Between Existential Therapy and Humanistic Psychology

Some key concepts of existential therapy overlap with the humanistic themes put forth by Rogers and others. Indeed, Rogers constructed his notions of therapeutic practice on existential principles about what it means to be human, the balance between freedom and responsibility, and the client/therapist relationship as a key to change. Both person-centered therapy and Gestalt therapy (the subject of Chapter 11) are experiential, humanistic, phenomenological, and existentially oriented approaches.

The Focus of Humanistic Psychology   A number of humanistic theorists have contributed to a movement often referred to as the "third force" in psychology (in reaction to the psychoanalytic and behavioral forces). They have written on the nature of human existence, on methods for studying human modes of functioning, and on the implications of humanistic assumptions. Synthesizing their theories from many divergent fields and approaches, early humanistic psychologists contended that people could not be studied and understood in segmented fashion. Rather, humans must be studied in complete relation to how they interact with others and with the world. Some key figures in the development of humanistic psychology were Carl Rogers, Rollo May, Abraham Maslow, Sidney Jourard, Fritz Perls, and James Bugental. Many of these psychologists have an existential orientation, but they also applied themes to the practice of psychotherapy that focus on the capacities unique to humans: love, freedom, choice, creativity, purpose, relatedness, meaning, values, growth, self-actualization, autonomy, responsibility, ego transcendence, humor, and spontaneity. According to humanistic psychologists, any therapy that aims at growth must take these human capacities into account.

Several authors (Greenberg & Rice, 1997; Page, Weiss, & Lietaer, 2002) address basic concepts shared by the humanistic approaches to psychotherapy—person-centered group therapy, Gestalt group therapy, and existential group therapy. These authors include these three theories under the humanistic umbrella because they all share common assumptions about human nature and what constitutes key therapeutic processes necessary for effective therapeutic outcomes. Themes of primary importance in all of the humanistic approaches to psychotherapy include these ideas:

1. *Importance of self-awareness.* These theories stress the importance of self-awareness in therapy based on the premise that people who are self-aware can make more life-affirming choices.
2. *Commitment to a phenomenological approach.* This central characteristic involves belief in the uniquely human capacity for reflective consciousness.
3. *Actualization, or growth, tendency.* Both Maslow and Rogers maintain that rather than merely seeking stability human beings strive to grow. People have an innate drive toward growth that enables them to benefit from therapy.
4. *Belief that humans are free, self-determining beings.* Individuals may be influenced by their past and by their environment, but they have a role in who and what they become through the choices they make.
5. *Concern and respect for the subjective experience of each person.* Humanistic therapists attempt to understand and grasp the experiential world of their clients. The humanistic approaches all emphasize the notion that people are capable of acting in responsible and caring ways in interpersonal relationships.

Some Differences Between the Humanistic and Existential Perspectives

Many contemporary existential therapists refer to themselves as *existential-humanistic* practitioners. They often indicate that their strongest roots are in existential philosophy and that they have incorporated many aspects of North American humanistic psychotherapies (Cain, 2002). Although existential and humanistic approaches share common ground, they are not identical. The central difference between existential psychotherapy and humanistic psychotherapy is philosophical. The person-centered approach of the humanist, Rogers, assumes that if positive and nurturing conditions are provided we will automatically grow in positive ways. In contrast, existential thinkers like Kierkegaard and Sartre would not agree that we even have any sort of essential nature or basic needs, nor would they agree that much of anything will happen in life automatically. Where humanists see needs, existentialists see choices; where humanists see the prospect of positive and automatic growth, existentialists see the anxiety of being free and the equal possibilities for growth and decay. Once these philosophical differences are noted, bundling existentialism and humanism together becomes highly problematic.

Historical Background

Rogers's *nondirective approach*, beginning in the early 1940s, focused on reflecting and clarifying the feelings of individual clients. Rogers believed that through an accepting relationship clients were able to gain increasing insight into the nature of their problems and then take constructive action based on their new self-understanding. During the 1950s, Rogers developed and refined his basic hypotheses for psychotherapy, and these principles were later applied to therapy groups. Examples of these applications in the 1950s included groups for physically handicapped children and their parents, parents of retarded children, mothers on public assistance, clients who were involved in individual counseling, psychiatric inpatients, residents of homes for the elderly, and mental health professionals (Raskin, 1986a, p. 277).

Rogers also developed a systematic theory of personality and applied this self-theory to the practice of counseling individuals, which led him to rename his approach *client-centered therapy* (Rogers, 1951). The client-centered approach was broadened to include applications to the teaching/learning situation, affective/cognitive learning in workshops, and organizational development and leadership.

In the 1960s and 1970s Rogers did a great deal to spearhead the development of basic encounter groups and personal growth groups. As the fields of application grew in number and variety, the name "client-centered therapy" was replaced by the term *person-centered approach*. Rogers also broadened his emphasis beyond the therapist's ability to reflect accurately what clients were expressing to include the therapist's congruence and willingness to become increasingly involved in the therapy. The basic encounter groups made it difficult to distinguish between "therapy" and "growth." The group work that Rogers pioneered was mostly in the form of weekend workshops, although some of his workshops lasted two to three weeks. These small groups did much to revolutionize the practice of group work. (For a detailed review of the development of Rogers's approach over the past 55 years, see Bozarth, Zimring, & Tausch, 2002, and Zimring & Raskin, 1992).

Key Concepts

Trust in the Group Process

Rogers (1986b) makes it clear that the person-centered approach rests on a basic trust in human beings' tendency to realize their full potential. Similarly, person-centered therapy is based on a deep sense of trust in the group's ability to develop its own potential by moving in a constructive direction. For a group to move forward, it must develop an accepting and trusting atmosphere in which the members can show aspects of themselves that they usually conceal and move into new behaviors. For example:

• Members move from playing roles to expressing themselves more directly.
• Members move from being relatively closed to experience to becoming more open to outside reality.

- Members move from being out of contact with internal and subjective experience to becoming aware of it.
- Members move from looking for answers outside of themselves to a willingness to direct their own lives from within.
- Members move from lacking trust and being somewhat closed and fearful in interpersonal relationships to being more open and expressive with others.

The Therapeutic Conditions for Growth

The basic tenet underlying the person-centered approach to group work is stated briefly by Rogers (1980): "Individuals have within themselves vast resources for self-understanding and for altering their self-concepts, basic attitudes, and self-directed behavior; these resources can be tapped if a definable climate of facilitative psychological attitudes can be provided" (p. 115). According to Rogers (1986b), the necessary climate that releases our formative, or actualizing, tendency is characterized by three primary attitudes of the therapist: genuineness, unconditional positive regard (also called nonpossessive warmth, or acceptance), and empathy. These three factors are also known as "core conditions," and they will be taken up in detail later in this section.

To the extent that therapists experience genuineness, acceptance, and accurate empathy for their clients and to the extent that the clients perceive these conditions, therapeutic personality change and growth will occur (Braaten, 1986; Thorne, 1992). Hamilton's (2000) research on therapeutic process and outcome of 135 clients seen by 35 different counselors supports Miller, Duncan, and Hubble's (1997) findings, which confirm the significance not only of the therapist's communication of the core conditions but the client's perception of the existence of these conditions. Rogers (1987d) maintains that the core conditions have been put to the test in a wide variety of situations with very divergent groups, different cultures, and different nations. Rogers stresses that the core conditions are not only necessary for effective therapy but also sufficient.

Rogers (1986b) adds another characteristic of a growth-promoting relationship, *presence*, which he concedes cannot as yet be studied empirically. When he is at his best as a group facilitator, he asserts that he is in touch with the unknown in him and that his inner spirit reaches out and touches the inner spirit of the client. The relationship transcends itself and becomes a part of something larger, which releases the most profound growth and healing. Brodley's (2000) qualitative assessment of eight clients' experiences of therapist presence distinguishes between therapeutic and nontherapeutic presence. Although continued research on the curative force of presence is needed to more thoroughly understand its foundations, it seems to embody the client's experience of the combined effects of the core conditions (Hamilton, 2000).

Natiello (1987, 2001) contends that *personal power* is another therapist condition integral to the practice of the person-centered approach. This is a state in which individuals are aware of and can act on their own feelings, needs, and values rather than looking outside of themselves for direction. The greater the degree of autonomy of therapists, the less likely they are to attempt to control others, and the more they can help their clients tap into their own source of power for self-direction. Facilitators share power by actively trusting individuals to direct their own lives and to solve their problems. In training other facilitators in the person-centered approach, Natiello finds that they often experience difficulties translating the concept of personal power into practice. They struggle with how much of themselves to share, and they fear taking over others' power. This fear sometimes leads them to disown their own power or to deny it. To be sure, it is a challenge to learn the balance between accepting one's own power as a therapist and sharing power with clients.

Implications for Training Group Leaders   Bozarth, Zimring, and Tausch (2002) assert that the most important aspect of training is to develop the attitudes of the therapist who will support the client's perception of the world, who will demonstrate faith in the client's inner resources, and who will attend to the therapeutic relationship.

> It is the client who discovers personal power from relationship with the therapist and from his or her own inner resources. The most viable training goal in CCT is that of enabling therapists to develop their own unconditional positive self-regard to experience unconditional positive regard and empathic understanding toward their clients. (p. 179)

Coghlan and McIlduff (1990) maintain that an important aspect of training group facilitators is teaching them the use of personal power. Because the person-centered approach emphasizes an equalization of power, it is critical that the facilitator's behavior in no way diminish the power of members. According to Coghlan and McIlduff, training needs to involve teaching facilitators how to offer alternatives in sensitive ways to group members so that real choice and increased freedom become the property of the group rather than the instrument of the leader.

It is a myth that person-centered therapists are self-abnegating, passive, and uninvolved, merely responding to others by mirroring their responses (Natiello, 1987). Rather, they demonstrate behaviorally the three core therapeutic attitudes: genuineness, acceptance, and empathic understanding. A research review confirms the person-centered assumption that the facilitator's expression of these three conditions is the foundation for positive therapeutic outcomes (Raskin, 1986b). Emphasis is best placed on the art of listening and understanding rather than focusing mainly on teaching techniques and strategies. Thorne (1992) puts the challenge to clinicians well: "The 'core conditions' of congruence, acceptance, and empathy are simple to state, much more difficult to describe and infinitely challenging to practice" (p. 36). Natiello (1987) maintains that "the theory of the person-centered approach is grasped quite readily, but the translation into practice tends to be problematic, diverse, and oversimplified" (p. 203).

The literature generally eschews "how-to" instructions for communicating the therapeutic skills suggested by person-centered theory. However, a growing number of theory-to-practice translations address ways to connect with the theory in a more practical way (see Brodley, 1996, 1997, 1998; Hamilton, Carlson, & Sabol, 2001).

In the following sections I expand on Rogers's three therapeutic conditions as they apply to group leaders' behavior.

Genuineness

The first element is the *genuineness*, realness, or congruence of the therapist (or facilitator of the group). The greater the extent to which facilitators become involved in the group as persons, putting up no professional front, the greater the likelihood that the members will change and grow. What the therapist expresses externally must be *congruent* with his or her inner experience, at least during the time of therapy. In other words, genuine therapists do not pretend to be interested when they are not, don't fake attention or understanding, don't say what they don't mean, and don't adopt behaviors designed to win approval. They can perform their professional functions without hiding behind their professional roles.

According to Natiello (1987), to maintain genuineness, therapists need a high level of self-awareness, self-acceptance, and self-trust. Genuineness is the state of authenticity that results from a deep exploration of self and a willingness to accept the truths of this exploration. In her work with helping professionals in a person-centered training program, Natiello finds that congruence is both complex and difficult to achieve and that it is the condition that is most often ignored. She contends that without congruence the other therapeutic conditions are then offered inauthentically and become mere techniques, which are meaningless, manipulative, and controlling.

Implications for Group Leaders   Genuine therapists, although they are essentially honest in their encounters in the group, are not indiscriminately open, and they know the boundaries of appropriate self-revelation. They realize the importance of taking responsibility for any feelings they express in the group and the importance of exploring with clients any persistent feelings, especially those that may be blocking their ability to be fully present. Through their own authenticity, congruent group leaders offer a model that helps their clients work toward greater realness.

Some group leaders have difficulty with "being themselves." Often that difficulty stems from the misapprehension that genuineness entails expressing every immediate thought or feeling or being spontaneous without any restraint or consideration of the appropriateness and timeliness of one's reactions. Another difficulty arises when leaders, in the name of being "authentic," make themselves the focal point of the group by discussing their personal problems in great detail. As Braaten (1986) has noted, not every kind of genuineness is facilitative for clients. Therapist self-disclosure can be overdone in magnitude and kind. Clearly, even the expression of genuineness must be handled with discretion. Leaders need to examine their motivations for discussing their personal issues and ask themselves whether the disclosure serves the clients' needs or their own. If the leader has had an experience similar to that of a client, sharing feelings about the experience may be therapeutic for the client. When a group leader does engage in self-disclosure, it should be helpful for the group. Leaders who frequently make themselves the focal point of group discussion may be using the group as a platform to talk about their personal problems.

Unconditional Positive Regard and Acceptance

The second core element is the attitude called *unconditional positive regard*, which is an acceptance of and caring for group members. When group facilitators display a positive, nonjudgmental, accepting attitude toward their clients, therapeutic change is more likely (Rogers, 1986b). Positive regard involves communicating a caring that is unconditional and that is not contaminated by evaluation or judgment of the client's feelings and thoughts. In other words, group leaders value and accept members without placing stipulations and expectations on this acceptance; they tell the client, "I accept you as you are," not "I'll accept you when _____." Acceptance, however, is not to be confused with approval; therapists can accept and value their clients as separate persons, with a right to their separateness, without necessarily approving of some of their behavior.

Associated with this attitude of positive regard is an attitude of nonpossessive caring and warmth. This attitude is not dependent on the therapist's own need for approval and appreciation, and it can be expressed in subtle ways such as gestures, eye contact, tone of voice, and facial expression. A genuine expression of caring can be sensed by clients and will promote their development. Artificial warmth can be as readily perceived and is likely to inhibit the client's change and growth. Obviously, once clients sense that the therapist's expression of warmth is more a technique than a genuine feeling, it becomes difficult for them to trust the genuineness of other reactions of the therapist.

Braaten (1986) has written about his struggle with the concept of unconditional positive regard, or even the term *positive regard*. He substitutes the phrase *warm regard*, which includes an expression of both positive and negative feelings. He believes this regard must include a willingness to share one's total self with significant others, including one's anger and possible rejection. Rogers (1987b) does contend that there is room in the person-centered approach for therapists to communicate a range of feelings. This means that boredom and anger, as well as compassion, can be expressed.

Thus, a potential conflict arises between being genuine and maintaining a stance of unconditionality (Lietaer, 1984). It is a rare therapist who can genuinely provide unconditional acceptance for every client on a consistent basis. Unconditionality is not impossible, but it is improbable. Unconditional positive regard can best be thought of as an attitude of receptiveness toward the subjective and experiential world of the client. From Lietaer's perspective, unconditionality means that the therapist values the deeper core of the person. Through the therapist's unconditionality, clients sense that the therapist is on their side and that they will not be let down in spite of their current difficulties. In its optimal form, unconditionality expresses a deep belief in another person. For a scholarly treatment of the controversial concept of unconditional positive regard, see Lietaer (1984).

Related to the concept of accepting the individual group member with unconditional positive regard, caring, and warmth is the idea of developing an attitude of acceptance of the group as a whole. Just as Rogers (1970) believes in the capacity of the individual to find his or her own direction, so does he believe in accepting a group where it is, without attempting to impose a direction on it: "From my experience I know that if I attempt to push a group to a deeper level, it is not, in the long run, going to work" (p. 48).

Implications for Group Leaders   It has been my experience that group leaders in training often struggle with what they see as the monumental task of being able to feel accepting or being able to demonstrate positive regard. Some burden themselves with the unrealistic expectation that they *must always be accepting* and that they must consistently respond with warmth in all situations. Group leaders need to develop an accepting attitude toward themselves as well as toward their clients. At times they won't feel warmth or unconditional positive regard. It is not necessary to feel a high level of warmth and positive regard all the time to be an effective group leader. These attitudes are not an either-or condition; rather, they occur on a graded continuum. Being an effective group leader starts by accepting oneself and continues by bearing in mind that the greater the degree of valuing, caring, and accepting of a client, the greater the opportunity to facilitate change in the client.

Empathy

The third facilitative aspect is an *empathic understanding* of the members' internal and subjective frame of reference. Facilitators show this empathy when they are able to sense accurately the feelings and personal meanings members are experiencing. It is also important for facilitators to be able to communicate this understanding to the members. Rogers (1961) defines empathy as the capacity to see the world of another by assuming the internal frame of reference of that person: "To sense the client's private world as if it were your own but without ever losing the 'as if' quality—this is empathy, and it seems essential to therapy" (p. 284). But sensing, even understanding the client's private world is not enough. The counselor must also be able to communicate this understanding effectively to the client.

Rogers (1975) considers empathy as "an unappreciated way of being" for many group practitioners. He makes a case for regarding empathy as one of the most potent factors in bringing about learning and self-directed change, thus locating power in the person and not in the expert. He summarizes some general research findings concerning empathy as follows:

• Therapists of many different orientations agree that attempting sensitively and accurately to understand others from their viewpoint is a critical factor in being an effective therapist.

• One of the main functions of empathy is to foster client self-exploration. Clients come to a deeper self-understanding through a relationship in which they feel that they are being understood by others. Research has demonstrated that clients who feel understood by their therapists are encouraged to share more of themselves.

• Empathy dissolves alienation, for the person who receives empathy feels connected with others. Furthermore, those who receive empathy learn that they are valued, cared for, and accepted as they are: "Empathy gives that needed confirmation that one does exist as a separate, valued person with an identity" (p. 7).

• The ability to exhibit empathy depends on the personal development of the therapist. Rogers has come to the conclusion that "the more psychologically mature and integrated the therapist is as a person, the more helpful is the relationship he provides" (p. 5).

• Being a skilled diagnostician and making interpretations is not related to empathy, which, at its best, is accepting and nonjudgmental. In fact, for Rogers "true empathy is always free of any evaluative or diagnostic quality" (p. 7).

Our ability to experience anger, joy, fear, and love is what makes it possible to enter the world of another person, even though this person's circumstances may be different from our own. Rogers (1987d) makes it clear that empathy is an active process, yet it is often superficially regarded as passively sitting back and listening:

> To really let oneself go into the inner world of this other person is one of the most active, difficult, demanding things that I know. And yet, it is worth it because it is one of the most releasing, healing things that I have had any occasion to do. (p. 45)

Accurate empathy is central to the practice of the person-centered approach. It is a way for therapists to hear the meanings expressed by their clients that often lie at the edge of their awareness. Empathy that has depth involves more than an intellectual comprehension of what clients are saying. According to Watson (2002), full empathy entails understanding the meaning and feeling of a client's experiencing. Watson states that almost 60 years of research has consistently demonstrated that empathy is the most powerful determinant of client progress in therapy. She puts the challenge to counselors as follows: "Therapists need to be able to be responsively attuned to their clients and to understand them emotionally as well as cognitively. When empathy is operating on all three levels—interpersonal, cognitive, and affective—it is one of the most powerful tools therapists have at their disposal" (pp. 463–464).

A crucial part of achieving empathy is listening with one's total being. Sensitive listening involves suspending judgment of others. It is not done to gain personal advantage or with an ulterior motive. Rather, this kind of listening comes from a genuine interest in making significant contact with others by knowing their reality (Barrett-Lennard, 1988). Braaten (1986) finds that his active listening involves grasping the cognitive and affective messages from his clients on a moment-to-moment basis and trying to verify his understanding with his clients. He asserts that person-centered therapists are unique in their careful monitoring to determine whether they have grasped the full message of their clients.

Active and sensitive listening is what Rogers (1970) *does* when he facilitates a group. "I listen as carefully, accurately, and sensitively as I am able, to each individual who expresses himself. Whether the utterance is superficial or significant, I listen" (p. 47). It is apparent that Rogers "listens" to more than the words; he also hears the meaning behind both the verbal and the nonverbal content. In this regard he is concerned with facilitating the truest expression of the person's subjective experience. Rogers has broadened the meaning of listening and demonstrated the profound healing effect that it has on others.

In a group context, the interpersonal aspects of empathy frequently result in bonding among the members and cohesion in the group as a whole. Although this may be comforting, it should not be thought of as the primary catalyst for change. According to David Cain (personal communication, July 15, 1997), the potent aspect of empathy that leads to change works this way: Empathy, particularly emotionally focused empathy, helps clients (1) pay attention to and value their experiencing; (2) process their experience both cognitively and bodily; (3) view old experiences in new ways that promote shifts in perceptions of the self and one's view of the world; and (4) increase their confidence in their perceptions and their ability to make decisions and take action. In the context of the safety of a group, members' capacity for effective learning about themselves and how they relate to others is gradually restored. For a scholarly discussion of the role of empathy in the person-centered approach, see Bozarth (1984), and for a comprehensive treatment of empathy in therapy, see Bohart and Greenberg (1997).

Implications for Group Leaders   Empathic understanding is essential to foster the climate of acceptance and trust necessary for the success of the group. Empathy is a skill that can be developed—and it is a skill that an effective group leader needs to develop.

In working with group counselors, I have found that many mistakenly assume that unless they themselves have directly experienced the same problems voiced by group members they can't be empathic. Such an assumption can severely limit the leader's potential sphere of influence. Clearly, one need not experience incest to empathize with a group member's anguish over reliving painful sexual experiences. One need not have been abandoned by a parent to feel and experience the sadness of abandonment. It is not necessary to have been divorced to share a client's anger, hurt, and sadness about separation. Such experiences come in many forms and, at one level or another, are common to us all. Situations in every life trigger feelings of isolation, rage, resentment, guilt, sadness, loss, or rejection—to name a few of the feelings that will be expressed in groups. If group leaders remain open to their own emotions, allow themselves to be touched by the emotions of others, and are willing to reexperience certain difficult events, they will increase their capacity to be psychologically present for others.

Barriers to Effective Therapy

In the training workshops that my colleagues and I conduct, the participants typically lead groups and then receive feedback from the members and from us. Many of our students and trainees express feelings of inadequacy as group leaders and a sense of frustration and hopelessness. They see little change occurring in the members of their groups, and they perceive that their clients are resistant and don't enjoy coming to groups. In many instances the problems besetting these students can be traced back to the fact that the conditions of active listening, empathy, and positive regard are in some measure lacking in their groups. Here is a list of specific problems that militate against group progress:

- *Lack of attending and empathy.* Often these prospective group leaders show that they don't really listen; they are preoccupied with a message that they want to impart to their groups and use the group as a vehicle for indoctrination. Or they ask many closed questions and are preoccupied with problem solving rather than problem understanding. In short, many of our students talk too much and listen too little.

- *Absence of counselor self-disclosure.* Some agencies and institutions foster, even require, an aloof and undisclosing leader role. Group counselors are given these messages: "Avoid being personal," "Don't get involved," and "Avoid sharing anything about yourself, even if it affects the relationship." Leaders are expected to change the behavior of members yet keep themselves out of their interactions with group members—clearly an unreasonable and self-defeating expectation.

- *Lack of positive regard, warmth, and acceptance.* Some group counselors are intolerant of the people they are supposedly helping and cling to assumptions that keep their clientele in stereotyped categories. Such prejudice makes client change difficult, if not impossible. Admittedly, it may be hard to maintain positive regard, warmth, and acceptance toward people who are in a treatment program for acts such as spousal abuse, child abuse, or murder. It is not necessary to condone such actions, and it may not even be possible to avoid feeling negatively toward those who have committed such acts. But it is important to try to set aside one's reactions at least during the course of the group.

- *Lack of belief in the therapeutic process.* Underlying the concepts of positive regard and acceptance is the belief that people can change and improve their personal condition. In our in-service group process workshops, we frequently meet practitioners who lead groups only because they are required to do so and who do not believe in the effectiveness of group therapy. In a climate in which enthusiasm, motivation, and faith in groups is absent, is it surprising that leaders find that their groups are somewhat less than successful? How can group members be expected to have faith in a process that the group leader does not believe in?

Implications for Group Leaders   It is essential that leaders examine how their attitudes and behaviors could be barriers to the progress of a group. Here are some questions that can serve as useful catalysts for self-reflection:

- Am I genuinely interested in people?
- What personal needs am I meeting by being a group leader?
- Am I authentically myself in a group, or do I hide behind the role of "leader"?
- Am I able to accept people, or do I need to direct their lives? Do I insist that they look at the world through my eyes?

- Am I willing to take time to understand others, or do I force them to follow my agenda?
- Do I see my main task as helping them get what they want, or getting them to want what I want for them?
- Do I offer a proper model for what I expect the members in my group to become?

Role and Functions of the Group Leader

Rogers (1986b) writes that the therapist's role is to become a companion to clients in their journey toward self-discovery. When the person-centered way of life is lived in therapy, it leads to a process of self-exploration and self-development and less focus on mastery of skills, techniques, and leadership strategies (Bozarth & Brodley, 1986).

The group leader is called a *facilitator*, which reflects the importance of interactions between group members. Person-centered group facilitators use themselves as instruments of change in a group. Their central function is to establish a therapeutic climate in which group members will interact in honest and meaningful ways. Boy and Pine (1999) believe the therapist's role is closely tied to *who* and *what* the therapist is as a person: his or her values, lifestyle, life experiences, and basic philosophy of life. Clearly, the therapist's attitudes and behavior are powerful determinants of the accepting group atmosphere that is conducive to real communication—not any techniques, strategies, or exercises that he or she may employ. Boy and Pine put this emphasis well:

> A person-centered approach to group counseling puts far greater emphasis on the facilitative quality of the counselor *as a person* rather than emphasizing the counselor's knowledge and use of specific and predesigned procedures. It views the counselor's presence as the basic catalyst that prompts group participants to make progress. (p. 150)

Rogers did his best to become a person to the members of his groups, rather than assuming a directive role. In his work as a group facilitator, he functioned somewhat like a guide on a journey. Rogers (1970) emphasizes some of the following characteristics of group facilitators:

- They have a great deal of trust in the group process and believe the group can move forward without their directive intervention.
- They listen carefully and sensitively to each member.
- They do all that is possible to contribute to the creation of a climate that is psychologically safe for the members.
- They attempt to be empathically understanding and accept individuals and the group; they do not push the group to a deeper level.
- They operate in terms of their own experience and their own feelings, which means that they express here-and-now reactions.

- They offer members feedback and, if appropriate, confront members on specifics of their behavior; they avoid judging and, instead, speak about how they are affected by others' behavior.

The person-centered group approach emphasizes certain attitudes and skills as a necessary part of the facilitator's style: listening in an active and sensitive way, accepting, understanding, respecting, reflecting, clarifying, summarizing, sharing personal experiences, responding, encountering and engaging others in the group, going with the flow of the group rather than trying to direct the way the group is going, and affirming a member's capacity for self-determination. The facilitator encourages the members to explore the incongruities between their beliefs and behaviors and the inclinations of their inner feelings and subjective experiencing. As the members become more aware of these incongruities within themselves, their view of themselves expands.

Rogers (1970) maintains that these functions and procedures are counterproductive: (1) manipulating the group toward a particular, but unstated, goal; (2) using planned exercises designed to elicit certain emotions; (3) encouraging and setting up dramatic performances by members; (4) allowing members to attack one another or consistently insisting on expressing hostility; (5) pressuring members to participate in group exercises; (6) consistently interpreting the motives and behaviors of others; (7) making many interpretive comments on the group process; (8) giving of advice; (9) making diagnosis and evaluation as central to the group process; and (10) hiding behind the role of "expert leader" by remaining emotionally distant and anonymous. Although Rogers supports the notion of facilitators being participants in a group by expressing their reactions and concerns, he cautions about the dangers of those with severe problems who use the group to work out their own problems.

Rogers (1970) takes a dim view of the use of techniques or exercises to get a group moving. If and when techniques are used, he believes, the group needs to be made a party to them. He also suggests that facilitators avoid making interpretive comments, because he believes such comments are apt to make the group self-conscious and slow the process down. Group process observations should come from members, a view that is consistent with his philosophy of placing the responsibility for the direction of the group on the members.

It is evident that Rogers (1970) has faith in the capacity of a group to move on its own initiative, although he does admit that anxiety and irritation may result from the lack of a clear and shared structure. He gave his groups permission to determine for themselves how they would spend their time, and he might open a session with the statement "We can make the group experience whatever we want it to be."

Rogers believes members have the resourcefulness for positive movement without the facilitator assuming an active and directive role. The facilitator's presence is far more powerful than the techniques he or she uses to structure the group or to promote interaction within the group. The facilitator's nondirectiveness allows members to demonstrate their typical interpersonal style within the context of the group. The premise is that members will generally reveal their typical behavior if the group is unstructured. Group members, who are accustomed to following authorities, are challenged to rely on themselves to formulate a purpose and a direction. Members are helped to begin listening to themselves and other members by a facilitator who will not act as an expert and give them direction. They are challenged to struggle and to express themselves, and out of this struggle they have a basis for learning how to trust themselves. If the facilitator assumes a role of being too directive or relies on group exercises to get things going in the group, then the members' natural manner of interacting will not evolve as readily.

According to Boy and Pine (1999), the facilitator is challenged to deal with a complexity that is not evident in the more structured and leader-centered process models. The emphasis of a person-centered group is on the natural emergence of the self of each of the participants. This complexity that characterizes the evolution of a person-centered group means that "the counselor is required to be more sensitive, more involved, and generally more attentive to the natural emergence of attitudes and behaviors among group members (pp. 147–148). Tallman and Bohart (1999) maintain that the client is the primary agent of change and that the relationship members have with the facilitator provides a supportive structure within which clients' self-healing capacities are activated. "Clients then are the 'magicians' with the special healing powers. Therapists set the stage and serve as assistants who provide the conditions under which this magic can operate" (p. 95).

Cain (1990b) believes nondirectiveness does not necessarily translate to "freedom" for many participants; rather, it may become a barrier. Given the freedom to choose their own direction, members do not always move toward productive work. For example, a group may be characterized by low energy, and members may choose to stay largely on a superficial and impersonal level. Ultimately, group members have the power to move or not move to a deeper level, yet the leader can encourage them to look at their behavior and decide what they might do differently. Not all persons do well when left primarily to draw on their intrinsic resources. It is essential that therapists modify their therapeutic approach to accommodate the specific needs of each client and the group as a whole. A guiding question Cain (2002) asks of himself and of his clients is "Does it fit?" Cain believes that, ideally, therapists will continually monitor whether what they are doing "fits," especially whether their therapeutic style is compatible with their clients' way of viewing and understanding their problems.

Stages of a Person-Centered Group

Characteristics of the Group

The person-centered group may meet weekly for about two hours for an unspecified number of meetings. Another format consists of a personal growth workshop that meets for a weekend, a week, or longer. The residential aspect of such small personal growth groups affords members opportunities to become a community as a group.

In organizing and conducting a person-centered group, there are generally no rules or procedures for the selection of members. If both the facilitator and the client agree that a group experience would be beneficial, the person is generally included. When the group initially meets, the facilitator does not present ground rules by which members must abide or provide a great deal of information or orientation. It is up to the group members to formulate the rules for their sessions and to establish norms that they agree will assist them in reaching their goals.

Unfolding of the Group Process

On the basis of his experience with numerous groups, Rogers (1970) has delineated 15 process patterns that occur in groups that employ the person-centered approach. It needs to be emphasized, however, that these process patterns, or trends, do not occur in a clear-cut sequence and that they may vary considerably from group to group.

1. *Milling around.* The lack of leader direction inevitably results in some initial confusion, frustration, and "milling around"—either actually or verbally. Questions such as "Who is responsible here?" or "What are we supposed to be doing?" are characteristic and reflect the concern felt at this stage.

2. *Resistance to personal expression or exploration.* Members initially present a public self—one they think will be acceptable to the group. They are fearful of and resistant to revealing their private selves.

3. *Description of past feelings.* Despite doubts about the trustworthiness of the group and the risk of exposing oneself, disclosure of personal feelings does begin—however hesitantly and ambivalently. Generally, this disclosure deals with events outside of the group; members tend to describe feelings in a "there-and-then" fashion.

4. *Expression of negative feelings.* As the group progresses, there is a movement toward the expression of here-and-now feelings. Often these expressions take the form of an attack on the group leader, usually for not providing the needed direction.

5. *Expression and exploration of personally meaningful material.* If the expression of negative reactions is seen by the members as acceptable to the group, a climate of trust is likely to emerge. Members are then able to take the risks involved in disclosing personal material. At this point the participants begin to realize that the group is what they make it, and they begin to experience freedom.

6. *Expression of immediate interpersonal feelings in the group.* Members tend to express a full range of feelings toward one another.

7. *Development of a healing capacity in the group.* Next, members begin to spontaneously reach out to one another, expressing care, support, understanding, and concern. At this stage helping relationships are often formed within

the group that offer members aid in leading more constructive lives outside of the group.

8. *Self-acceptance and the beginning of change.* At this stage participants begin to accept aspects of themselves that they formerly denied or distorted; they get closer to their feelings and consequently become less rigid and more open to change. As members accept their strengths and weaknesses, they drop their defenses and welcome change.

9. *Cracking of facades.* Here individual members begin to respond to the group demand that masks and pretenses be dropped. This revealing of deeper selves by some members validates the theory that meaningful encounters can occur when people risk getting beneath surface interaction. At this stage the group strives toward deeper communication.

10. *Feedback.* In the process of receiving feedback, members acquire a lot of data concerning how others experience them and what impact they have on others. This information often leads to new insights that help them decide on aspects of themselves that they want to change.

11. *Confrontation.* Here members confront one another in what is usually an intensely emotional process involving feedback. Confrontation can be seen as a stepping up of the interactions described in earlier stages.

12. *The helping relationship outside the group sessions.* By this stage members have begun making contacts outside the group. Here we see an extension of the process described in number 7.

13. *The basic encounter.* Because the members come into closer and more direct contact with one another than is generally the case in everyday life, genuine person-to-person relationships occur. At this point members begin to experience how meaningful relationships occur when there is a commitment to work toward a common goal and a sense of community.

14. *Expression of feelings of closeness.* As the sessions progress, an increasing warmth and closeness develops within the group because of the realness of the participants' expression of feelings about themselves and toward others.

15. *Behavior changes in the group.* As members experience increased ease in expressing their feelings, their behaviors, mannerisms, and even their appearance begin to change. They tend to act in an open manner; they express deeper feelings toward others; they achieve an increased understanding of themselves; and they work out more effective ways of being with others. If the changes are effective, the members will carry their new behaviors into their everyday lives.

Some Outcomes of the Group Experience

Based on his vast experience in conducting groups and workshops, as well as his process and outcomes studies, Rogers (1987d) has identified and summarized a number of changes that tend to occur within individuals in a successful group experience. Members become more open and honest. As they feel increasingly understood and accepted, they have less need to defend themselves, and therefore they drop their facades and are willing to be themselves.

Because they become more aware of their own feelings and of what is going on around them, they are more realistic and objective. They tend to be more like the self that they wanted to be before entering a group experience. They are not as easily threatened, because the safety of the group changes their attitude toward themselves and others. Within the group there is more understanding and acceptance of who others are. Members become more appreciative of themselves as they are, and they move toward self-direction. They empower themselves in new ways, and they increasingly trust themselves. The members become more creative because they are willing to accept their own uniqueness. They come to realize that making life change entails both pain and joy.

Application: Therapeutic Techniques and Procedures

Diversity of Methods and Therapeutic Styles

Rogers's original emphasis was on methods of reflecting feelings. As his view of psychotherapy developed, its focus shifted away from therapeutic techniques toward the therapist's personal qualities, beliefs, and attitudes and toward the relationship with the client. Attitudes and qualities that are critical in creating a favorable relationship include therapist's genuineness, transparency, nonjudgmental caring, prizing, respect, and unconditional positive regard (Cain, 2002). It is essential to keep in mind that techniques do not function separately from the person of the group facilitator. Any intervention must be an honest expression of the group facilitator.

As this approach has developed, group facilitators have been allowed greater freedom in participating more actively in the relationship. One of the main ways in which person-centered therapy has evolved is the diversity, innovation, and individualization in practice (Cain, 2002). There is more latitude for therapists to share their reactions, to confront clients in a caring way, and to be active in the therapeutic process (Bozarth, Zimring, & Tausch, 2002; Lietaer, 1984). Current formulations of the approach assign more importance to therapists' bringing in their own here-and-now experiences, which can stimulate members to explore themselves at a deeper level. Although the therapist's receptive attitude is still viewed as being of central importance, this does not exclude the therapist from taking the initiative at times to stimulate a client's experiential process. Lietaer (1984) mentions that even "homework" and other auxiliary techniques may be used in a person-centered manner if the experience of the client remains the touchstone.

These changes from Rogers's original view of the counselor have encouraged the use of a wider variety of methods and a considerable diversity of therapeutic styles. Rogers's personality and style is not the only acceptable way of being. Reflective response is only one way of proceeding; other styles can be equally effective. Rather than restricting themselves by emulating the style of Carl Rogers, those who facilitate groups need to find their own way by developing a unique personal style.

What is basic to this approach is the focus on the members as being the center of the group. The commitment of the therapist to empathically experience the client's frame of reference creates a loyalty to the client's direction and pace. It is the therapist's attitudes and belief in the inner resources of the client that create the therapeutic climate for growth (Bozarth, Zimring, & Tausch, 2002). Members of the person-centered group are often as helpful to the other members as is the leader, and they direct and orchestrate the process and progress.

Whatever techniques one employs or avoids, whatever style one adopts or refrains from, the approach should be adapted to the needs of the group and its members. The diverse range of client populations and the individual differences that characterize members of a group require that any approach be flexibly applied. It almost goes without saying that some clients function better with a high degree of structure, whereas others need very little structure. In addition to the needs of the members, the leadership approach should fit the personality and style of the leader.

Areas of Application

People without advanced psychological education are able to benefit by translating the therapeutic conditions of genuineness, empathic understanding, and unconditional positive regard into both their personal and professional lives. The approach's basic concepts are straightforward and easy to comprehend, and they encourage locating power in the person rather than fostering an authoritarian structure in which control and power are denied to the person. These core skills can be used by many people in the helping professions. These skills are also essential as a foundation for virtually all of the other theoretical orientations covered in this book. If group workers are lacking in these relationship and communication skills, they will not be effective in carrying out their role and functions in a group.

The person-centered approach to groups has been applied to diverse populations including therapy clients, counselors, staff members of entire school systems, administrators, medical students, groups in conflict, drug users and their helpers, people representing different cultures and languages, and job-training groups. As the group movement developed, the person-centered approach became increasingly concerned with reducing human suffering, with cross-cultural awareness, and with conflict resolution on an international basis (Raskin, 1986a).

Applying the Person-Centered Approach to Group Work in the Schools

The person-centered approach can be applied to group counseling with both children and adolescents, since both age groups have a need to be understood, accepted, respected, and given the freedom to grow. In her nondirective client-centered therapy with children, Moon (2001) maintains that the three attitudinal conditions posited in Rogers's theory statements are sufficient for growth to occur in therapy with children. If the therapist is open, available, warm, acceptant, and seeks to follow and understand, then therapeutic gains can occur. It is not necessary to have historical, familial, or presenting problem information about children or from children to be able to conduct effective therapy. Moon does not see it as her function to get children to abide by the demands of reality, to teach manners, to teach appropriate behavior, to dig for feelings, to instruct, or to seek to increase a child's self-understanding.

Moon describes a boy's group in an elementary school with four 11- to 12-year-old boys, all of whom were low academic achievers. Working within a nondirective child therapy framework, Moon found that all but one boy showed improvement in school performance shortly after beginning the group. Her conviction is that the theory works as evidenced by a number of long-term, positive changes in the children. Although she does not strive directly for specific behavioral outcomes, children's grades improve, they become increasingly self-accepting, they become more self-controlled, and they become more self-reliant and freer to grow into a more mature self. Moon claims that she frequently receives "reports from parents or teachers that unwanted behaviors have abated or ceased" (p. 49).

In a person-centered group with children, play therapy is often the medium of expression. Axline's (1964) classic book, *Dibs: In Search of Self*, is an excellent example of a person-centered approach adapted to play therapy. In reading about Dibs, the power of listening, empathy, warmth, and engagement becomes evident. Axline (1964, 1969) demonstrates the healing power of play with children. There are many ways to adapt Axline's basic ideas and methods of person-centered play therapy in small group work. Play can be the medium through which children express their feelings, bring their conflicts to life, explore relationships, and reveal their hopes and fears. In addition to play, other expressive techniques, which are an outgrowth of the person-centered approach, can be used in group work with children such as art, music, and movement. Because children's verbal communication skills may be limited, these nonverbal and expressive approaches can provide clues to what children are feeling and trying to communicate (Thompson & Rudolph, 2000). The essence of person-centered play therapy is captured by Boy and Pine (1999):

> The focus of child-centered play therapy is on the child rather than the problem, the present rather than the past, feelings rather than thoughts or acts, understanding rather than explaining, accepting rather than correcting, the child's direction rather than the therapist's instruction, and the child's insight rather than the therapist's knowledge. (p. 172)

It is possible to create a group using these key principles and, at the same time, bring some degree of structure into the group. Depending on the ages of the children and the main purpose of a specific counseling group, a facilitator may want to assume a more active role rather than being highly nondirective. Generally, if children sense the counselor understands and accepts them, they are likely to open up and become quite responsive. This approach allows for therapist flexibility in working with children in groups.

Applying the Person-Centered Approach with Multicultural Populations

Rogers's interests evolved from working with individuals, to groups, to communities, and to world peace. During the last 15 years of his life, Rogers developed a passion in addressing broader social issues, especially peace. Rogers focused much attention on alternatives to nuclear planetary suicide. He sought alternatives that would reduce psychological barriers that impinge on communication between factions (see Rogers, 1987c; Rogers & Malcolm, 1987).

In 1974 Rogers and some of his colleagues initiated a new form of person-centered group known as the *large community group*. These groups, which began at the Center for Studies of the Person in La Jolla, California, eventually were offered in many communities and places around the world. These large groups, whose size often reached 75 to 800 people, worked and lived together for two to three weeks (Cain, 2002). According to Raskin (1986a), these workshops were designed to build community, to facilitate the members' self-exploration, and to resolve tensions between members representing diverse cultures. These large community groups provided data for understanding how cross-cultural and international differences can be resolved through the application of conditions advocated by the person-centered approach.

The person-centered approach, more than other models, has been applied to bringing people of diverse cultures together for the purpose of developing mutual understanding. One of Rogers's hopes was that people from different cultures would be able to listen to one another and find the common ground that unites them. In 1948 Rogers began developing a theory of reducing tension among antagonistic groups, and he continued this work until his death in 1987.

Shortly before his death, Rogers conducted four-day workshops with Soviet psychologists, educators, and researchers. He maintained that these sessions had demonstrated that the concerns expressed differed little from those felt by a similar professional group in the United States. He found that a psychological climate produced certain predictable results in the United States, Latin America, European countries, and South Africa as well as Russia (Rogers, 1987a).

As we've seen, a major focus of person-centered therapy lies in active listening, which is a key contribution to effective group work. This approach is grounded on the importance of hearing the deeper messages that clients bring to a group. Empathy, being present, and respecting the values of clients are particularly important attitudes and skills in groups with culturally diverse clients.

Therapist empathy has moved far beyond simple "reflection," and therapists now draw from a variety of empathic response modes (Bohart & Greenberg, 1997). Empathy is a pathway to making significant connections with persons of color, and it can be expressed and communicated either directly or indirectly.

There are many ways for therapists to demonstrate an empathic grasp of the client's subjective world and inner experiencing. Clients coming from certain cultures may not be comfortable with direct expression of empathy whereby a therapist engages in intimate self-disclosure. For some clients the most appropriate way to express empathy is for the therapist to demonstrate it indirectly through task-focused interventions (Bohart & Greenberg, 1997).

Empathic understanding, respect, unconditional positive regard, and acceptance are not limited to any one cultural group, but transcend culture. In working with certain Japanese American clients, for example, the leader might learn of their hesitation in revealing their feelings. Person-centered leaders would respect the cultural norm pertaining to showing one's feelings and not be inclined to push clients too quickly to display their feelings. They would help clients work within the framework of their values.

Glauser and Bozarth (2001) remind us about paying attention to the cultural identity that resides within the client. They caution against making assumptions about clients based on their cultural background or the specific group to which they belong and recommend waiting for the cultural context to emerge from the client. Glauser and Bozarth take the position that the use of specific techniques often results in a "specificity myth" that concentrates on specific treatments for particular groups of people. The emphasis then can become a matter of "doing" counseling. There has been too much emphasis on how to *do* counseling rather than how to *be* a counselor. They contend that if counselors use a prescribed approach or predetermined techniques, the therapeutic encounter might well suffer by the distance that is created when the counselor "does" multicultural counseling. Glauser and Bozarth's main message is that counseling in a multicultural context must embody the core conditions associated with all effective counseling. They state: "Person-centered counseling cuts to the core of what is important for therapeutic success in all counseling approaches. The counselor-client relationship and the use of the client's resources are central for multicultural counseling" (p. 146).

Although the person-centered approach has made significant contributions to working with groups representing diverse social, political, and cultural backgrounds, there are also some limitations to practicing exclusively within this framework in community agency settings and outpatient clinics. Many of the clients who come to a community mental health clinic or who are involved in some other type of outpatient treatment may desire or need a more structured group experience. This is especially true of short-term groups, open groups with a rapidly changing membership, task-oriented groups, and groups composed of culturally diverse populations. Clients from a lower socioeconomic status often seek professional help to deal with some current crisis, to alleviate psychosomatic symptoms, to learn certain coping skills (such as stress management), or to find solutions for pressing problems. Some characteristics of ethnic minority clients may include being more concerned with basic security and survival needs, having expectations of getting immediate help from the leader, and waiting for active probing by the group leader or for an expressed invitation to speak. These clients may expect a directive leader who functions in an expert role as an authority, and they can be put off by a leader who does not provide some structure (Chu & Sue, 1984; Leong, 1986, 1992).

According to Leong (1992), those leaders who place a high premium on egalitarian relationships and who provide a low degree of structure are likely to meet with difficulty in working with Asian Americans, for these clients prefer a structured, problem-focused, task-oriented approach to dealing with problems. Such clients may well perceive the person-centered therapist's attempts to create a climate of open and free self-expression as being alien to their cultural values. They are likely to be uncomfortable with this informal and personal style. Leong (1986) cites several studies indicating that Asian Americans perceive counseling as a directive, paternalistic, and authoritarian process. Not only do they expect the professional to take an active and directive role in the counseling process, they also expect the counselor to provide advice and recommend a specific course of action. Moreover, the person-centered approach extols the value of an internal locus of control, and prizes self-determination and autonomy, whereas some cultures place a value on an external locus of evaluation and do not place a high priority on autonomy and self-direction. Such clients may look to family tradition for their answers.

There is a high dropout rate for ethnic minority clients: as many as 52% of them terminate counseling after the first session (Mokuau, 1987). One explanation for this obvious dissatisfaction with professional counseling is that these clients quickly sense that they will not get the help they are looking for from a professional counseling relationship. This is why it is so crucial that the issue of clients' expectations and goals be explored during the first meeting. If leaders simply wait for clients to bring up these issues for themselves, it may be too late, because they may not return for another session. Therefore, more structure may be called for than is usually the case in a person-centered framework, especially in a group. In my opinion, groups can benefit from some orientation by the leader on what groups are about and how best to participate. Members profit from a focused discussion of the general goals and procedures of group process and of how the group might help them deal with their concerns. Leaders who discuss expectations with members are likely to increase the retention rate of their group.

African American, Hispanic, and Native American clients may encounter difficulty in relating to the processes involved in a person-centered group. The communication style emphasizing summarization, reflective listening, and restatement tends to be of limited use in working with many Native American clients (LaFromboise, Trimble, & Mohatt, 1990). In addition to being generally "quiet," Native Americans value restraint of emotion and the acceptance of suffering. Such clients may perceive expressing feelings as a weakness. It would be more consistent with their cultural worldview to treat them within the context of a larger family and community social system.

Although there are distinct limitations to working exclusively within a person-centered perspective with some clients, it should not be concluded that this approach is unsuitable for ethnically and culturally diverse populations. Whereas some clients prefer a directive and active style, others respond well to a less directive leader. The appropriateness and effectiveness of counseling styles depends largely on the cultural values and worldview embraced by an individual (Mokuau, 1987). As mentioned earlier, it is a mistake to assume that one style of group leadership will be effective for all clients. The potential for therapeutic change is maximized when a counselor works with clients in a way that is compatible with their preferred learning style, which is typically influenced by their cultural background (Cain, 1990b).

Evaluation of the Person-Centered Approach to Groups

Contributions and Strengths of the Approach

Because the person-centered approach is very much a phenomenological one, based on the subjective worldview of the client, I consider it an excellent foundation for the initial stages of any type of group. The approach encourages members from the outset to assume responsibility for determining their level of investment in the group and deciding what personal concerns they will raise. A main strength of this approach is the emphasis on truly listening to and deeply understanding the clients' world from their internal frame of reference. Empathy is the cornerstone of this approach and it is a necessary foundation upon which any theory rests (Bohart & Greenberg, 1997). Critical evaluation, analysis, and judgment are suspended, and attention is given to grasping the feelings and thoughts being expressed by the others. I see this form of listening and understanding as a prerequisite to any group approach, particularly during the early stages, when it is essential that members feel free to explore their concerns openly. Unless the participants feel that they are being understood, any technique or intervention plan is bound to fail.

Many of the problems of group leaders in training (as discussed earlier in this chapter) stem from their failure to reach an understanding of the members' subjective world, an understanding that can be achieved only by very careful listening and attending and by restraining the tendency to dive in too quickly to solve members' problems. A major strength of this approach is the central importance placed on the group counselor as a person, and the assumption that the client is the major change agent in a therapy group—both of these assumptions have a great deal to do with determining the outcomes of a group. The therapist's personal development is more important than mastering a set of techniques. Furthermore, the client's capacity for self-healing is in stark contrast with most theories that view the therapist's techniques and procedures as the most powerful agents that lead to change (Tallman & Bohart, 1999).

The leader must develop the ability to be present for members and to encourage them to interact openly. If the leader can create an open and accepting climate within the group, the members' self-healing forces will become operant and they will engage in the kind of work that will enable them to find their own resolutions. Ultimately, group members make their own choices and bring about change for themselves. Yet, with the presence of the facilitator and the support of other members, the realization comes about that one does not have to experience the change process alone.

Rogers and his colleagues engaged in research with personal growth groups when the group movement had reached its zenith in the 1960s, but Page, Weiss, and Lietaer (2002) indicate that there was a decline in the volume of person-centered research in the United States in the 1970s. The overall picture is not bleak, however, as numerous studies of person-centered group therapy have emerged in Europe during the past two decades. The findings of these studies generally support a strong relationship between empathy, warmth, and genuineness, and positive therapeutic outcomes in a group setting.

In summarizing the studies on person-centered group therapy, Page and his colleagues make a number of important points about the efficacy of this approach. Research supports the notion that people with serious problems, such as substance abuse, can assume responsibility for making personal gains in these groups. Hospitalized patients and counseling center clients have also made significant improvement by participating in groups. It is clear that humanistic therapy groups can be used to help clients with a wide range of problems to function better interpersonally and to deal more effectively with their problems. However, humanistic group therapy is an underutilized approach in the managed care era in which practitioners are required to demonstrate concrete and measurable outcomes. Many practitioners are unaware of the research that demonstrates the effectiveness of these kinds of groups with clinical populations. In their conclusions, Page and his colleagues (2002) indicate what kind of research needs to be done:

> The present and future directions of person-centered group psychotherapy seem to point toward ongoing expansions of studies conducted in European countries, as well as an incorporation of more process-oriented, qualitative, and case study research applications. (p. 348)

Consistent with the conclusions of Page and his colleagues, Cain (2002) also concludes that "the large body of research evidence clearly shows that humanistic therapies are as effective or more effective that other major therapeutic approaches in treating a wide range of client problems. Both quantitative and qualitative forms of research have contributed to our ongoing understanding of what works and how it works" (pp. 48–49).

Bozarth, Zimring, and Tausch (2002) provide a comprehensive review of research in person-centered therapy over the various periods in the evolution of its development. Here are some of their conclusions pertaining to the research studies over many years:

- In the earliest years of the approach, the client rather than the therapist was the person in charge. Research showed that nondirective therapy was associated with increased understanding, greater self-exploration, and improved self-concepts.
- Later the approach was characterized by a shift from clarification of feelings to a focus on the client's frame of reference. Research confirmed many

of Rogers's hypotheses, offering strong evidence for the value of the therapeutic relationship and the client's resources as the crux of successful therapy.

- As person-centered therapy developed, research centered on the core conditions of therapy, which were assumed to be both necessary and sufficient conditions for successful therapy. The research strongly supports certain attitudes of the therapist as being basic to successful therapy outcome. A congruent therapist who is able to empathically understand the client's world and communicate a nonjudgmental stance to the client is related to positive outcome.

In assessing the contributions of the person-centered approach, Cain (1990a) points out that when Rogers founded it in the early 1940s very few other therapeutic models were in use. The longevity of this approach is certainly a factor in considering its impact. From Cain's perspective, the most important contribution of the person-centered approach to group work is that it challenges group therapists to trust the resources of group members and to trust the relational characteristics of leaders (and other members) to cultivate these resources. In an age when practitioners are increasingly looking for immediate cures and the techniques that produce quick fixes, the person-centered approach reminds us that it is people who heal people, not techniques (David Cain, personal communication, July 11, 2001). Therapists need to evolve as persons rather than being intent on expanding their repertoire of techniques.

Limitations of the Approach

My central criticism of the person-centered approach, an approach I see as the foundation for practice, involves not what it includes but, rather, what it omits. In my opinion, a weakness is that person-centered therapy does not give sufficient attention to the skills and knowledge required to function as a group leader. I do not subscribe to the notion that technical skills and knowledge are unimportant. However, Boy and Pine (1999) do state that the person-centered counselor must possess knowledge in both the art and the science of counseling: "This means that there is a specific body of knowledge that the counselor must have; knowledge that must continually be expanded, refined, and modified" (p. 124).

Although person-centered theory and practice focuses more on a way of being than a way of doing, significant contributions to the skills domain of person-centered work have been published within the past decade. For instance, Farber, Brink, and Raskin's (1996) edited volume provides a scheme of Rogers's clinical responses, along with detailed critiques of person-centered therapy cases by experts both within and outside the person-centered tradition. In addition, Brodley (1996, 1997, 1998, 1999a,b, 2000) has contributed numerous theory-to-practice translations of the core conditions.

It is clear that person-centered group leaders typically do not employ directive strategies, mainly because of their belief that the members can find their own direction in working through the problems they bring to a group session. Person-centered therapists do not support the notion that it is the facilitator's job to devise and introduce techniques and exercises as a way of structuring a group or getting the group to do its work (Boy, 1990). In disagreement with this view, I prefer the value of action; of therapeutic direction, if it is needed by clients; and of more directive skills than are found in this approach. I see both active support and directive interventions as being extremely helpful for the goal of promoting client change.

In reflecting on what he learned after 40 years of trying to be an effective multimodal therapist, Lazarus (1996) mentions the value of a therapist assuming an active role in blending a flexible repertoire of *relationship styles* with a wide range of techniques as a way to enhance therapeutic outcomes. He maintains that a skilled therapist is able to determine when, and when not, to be confrontational; when to be directive, and when to allow the client to struggle; when to be formal or informal; when to self-disclose or remain anonymous; and when to be gentle or tough. In keeping with a person-centered spirit, Lazarus asserts that *relationships* of choice are no less important than *techniques* of choice.

I am in basic agreement with Lazarus on the importance of being able to draw upon various relationship styles as a way to facilitate movement within a group and to promote member change. I am most effective, and the group seems to be most productive, with a structure that offers some direction yet grants freedom to the members. In my groups I typically provide the most structure at the beginning and ending stages of a group. I generally use techniques to enhance and to highlight the existing material in the group rather than to get things moving. For example, when members talk about a lonely time of their lives and sadness comes up naturally, I am inclined to ask them to do any number of things, a few of which might be looking at another person in the room and talking directly to this person about the sadness, talking to a person as though he or she were a significant other, or reenacting a past event as though it were happening now. I continue to find that when members bring a struggle or some unfinished business with significant people in their lives into the present, whatever they are experiencing is usually intensified. Providing some therapeutic structure affords members the encouragement and support they need to fully experience their personal pain and make a crucial breakthrough.

As you will see in Chapter 11, I favor the active style afforded by the Gestalt approach, which involves creating experiments aimed at heightening the awareness level of group members. I believe I can pay close attention to the core conditions that are an integral part of person-centered approach and, at the same time, use a variety of techniques to bring about cognitive, affective, and behavioral change. There is some support in the literature for this blending of approaches. O'Leary (1997) writes about the advantages of integrating the person-centered and Gestalt approaches, claiming that both therapies offer a broader range of focus for clients to develop both internal and external resources. He maintains that Gestalt-oriented experiments that evolve from the client's current experiencing can be incorporated with person-centered concepts. O'Leary suggests: "Integrating certain concepts in both fields permits a much richer clinical understanding that either would allow on its own" (p. 20).

I believe members can benefit from leader assistance in translating their insights into action programs, and I collaborate with group members in designing homework assignments that will challenge them to do difficult things. Although I generally ask members to come up with their own homework, I am not averse to making suggestions and presenting them in an invitational manner. Most person-centered group facilitators would not feel comfortable with these action-oriented methods, which I find to be very useful.

Where to Go from Here

You might consider joining the Association for the Development of the Person-Centered Approach (ADPCA), an interdisciplinary and international organization. Membership includes a subscription to the *Person-Centered Journal*, the association's newsletter, a membership directory, and information about the annual meeting. It also provides information about continuing education and supervision and training in the person-centered approach. For more information, contact:

The Association for the Development of the Person-Centered Approach,
Inc. (ADPCA)
P. O. Box 3876
Chicago, IL 60690-3876
E-MAIL: adpcaweb@portents.ne.mediaone.net
WEB SITE: http://adpca.org

For information about the *Person-Centered Journal*, contact Jon Rose, editor, at jonmrose@aol.com.

The Center for Studies of the Person (CSP) in La Jolla offers workshops, training seminars, experiential small groups, and sharing of learning in community meetings. The Distance Learning Project and the Carl Rogers Institute for Psychotherapy Training and Supervision provide experiential and didactic training and supervision for professionals interested in developing their own person-centered orientation. To find out more about these workshops, contact:

Joachim Schwarz, Ph.D., Director
Center for Studies of the Person
1150 Silverado, Suite #112
La Jolla, CA 92037
TELEPHONE: (858) 459-3861
E-MAIL: Schwarz@bwn.net
WEB SITE: www.centerfortheperson.org

Recommended Supplementary Readings

Carl Rogers on Encounter Groups (Rogers, 1970) is an excellent introduction to these groups. It is a readable account of their process and outcomes, changes as a result of them, and glimpses of the subjective struggles and experiences of those who participate in them.

On Becoming a Person (Rogers, 1961) is an important work addressing the characteristics of the helping relationship, the philosophy of the person-centered approach, and practical issues related to therapy. I especially recommend Chapters 2–9, 16, and 17.

A Way of Being (Rogers, 1980) contains a series of updated writings on Rogers's personal experiences and perspectives, as well as chapters on the foundations and applications of a person-centered approach. Especially useful are the chapters on person-centered communities, large groups, and perspectives on the world and person of tomorrow.

Humanistic Psychotherapies: Handbook of Research and Practice (Cain & Seeman, 2002) is a very comprehensive discussion of person-centered therapy, Gestalt therapy, and existential therapy. This book provides research evidence for the person-centered theory.

References and Suggested Readings*

Axline, V. (1964). *Dibs: In search of self*. New York: Ballantine.

Axline, V. (1969). *Play therapy* (rev. ed.). New York: Ballantine.

Barrett-Lennard, G. T. (1988). Listening. *Person-Centered Review, 3*(4), 410–425.

*Bohart, A. C., & Greenberg, L. S. (Eds.). (1997). *Empathy reconsidered: New directions in psychotherapy*. Washington, DC: American Psychological Association.

Boy, A. V. (1990). The therapist in person-centered groups. *Person-Centered Review, 5*(3), 308–315.

*Boy, A. V., & Pine, G. J. (1999). *A person-centered foundation for counseling and psychotherapy* (2nd ed.). Springfield, IL: Charles C Thomas.

Bozarth, J. D. (1984). Beyond reflections: Emergent modes of empathy. In R. F. Levant, & J. M. Shlien (Eds.), *Client-centered therapy and the person-centered approach: New directions in theory, research, and practice* (pp. 59–75). New York: Praeger.

Bozarth, J. D., & Brodley, B. T. (1986). Client-centered psychotherapy: A statement. *Person-Centered Review, 1*(3), 262–271.

*Bozarth, J. D., Zimring, F. M., & Tausch, R. (2002). Client-centered therapy: The evolution of a revolution. In D. J. Cain, & J. Seeman, (Eds.), *Humanistic psychotherapies: Handbook of research and practice* (pp. 147–188). Washington, DC: American Psychological Association.

Braaten, L. J. (1986). Thirty years with Rogers's necessary and sufficient conditions of therapeutic personality change: A personal evaluation. *Person-Centered Review, 1*(1), 37–50.

Brodley, B. T. (1996). Empathic understanding and feelings in client-centered therapy. *The Person-Centered Journal, 3*(1), 22–30.

Brodley, B. T. (1997). The nondirective attitude in client-centered therapy. *The Person-Centered Journal, 4*(1), 18–30.

Brodley, B. T. (1998). Congruence and its relation to communication in client-centered therapy. *The Person-Centered Journal, 5*(2), 83–106.

Brodley, B. T. (1999a). The actualizing tendency concept in client-centered theory. *The Person-Centered Journal, 6*(2), 108–120.

Brodley, B. T. (1999b). Reasons for responses expressing the therapist's frame of reference in client-centered therapy. *The Person-Centered Journal, 6*(1), 4–27.

*Books and articles marked with an asterisk are suggested for further study.

Brodley, B. T. (2000). Personal presence in client-centered therapy. *The Person-Centered Journal, 7*(2), 139–149.

Bugental, J. F. T. (1987). *The art of the psychotherapist*. New York: Norton.

Cain, D. J. (1990a). Fifty years of client-centered therapy and the person-centered approach. *Person-Centered Review, 5*(1), 3–7.

Cain, D. J. (1990b). Further thoughts about nondirectiveness and client-centered therapy. *Person-Centered Review, 5*(1), 89–99.

*Cain, D. J. (2002). Defining characteristics, history, and evolution of humanistic psychotherapies. In D. J. Cain, & J. Seeman, (Eds.), *Humanistic psychotherapies: Handbook of research and practice* (pp. 3–54). Washington, DC: American Psychological Association.

*Cain, D. J., & Seeman, J. (Eds.). (2002). *Humanistic psychotherapies: Handbook of research and practice*. Washington, DC: American Psychological Association.

Chu, J., & Sue, S. (1984). Asian/Pacific-Americans and group practice. In L. E. Davis (Ed.), *Ethnicity in social group work practice*. New York: Haworth Press.

Coghlan, D., & McIlduff, E. (1990). Structuring and nondirectiveness in group facilitation. *Person-Centered Review, 5*(1), 13–29.

*Farber, B. A., Brink, D. C., & Raskin, P. M. (Eds.). (1996). *The psychotherapy of Carl Rogers: Cases and commentary*. New York: Guilford.

*Glauser, A. S., & Bozarth, J. D. (2001). Person-centered counseling: The culture within. *Journal of Counseling and Development, 79*(2), 142–147.

*Greenberg, L. S., Korman, L. M., & Paivio, S. C. (2002). Emotion in humanistic psychotherapy. In D. J. Cain, & J. Seeman, (Eds.), *Humanistic psychotherapies: Handbook of research and practice* (pp. 499–530). Washington, DC: American Psychological Association.

*Greenberg, L. S., & Rice, L. N. (1997). Humanistic approaches to psychotherapy. In P. L. Wachtel & S. B. Messer (Eds.), *Theories of psychotherapy: Origins and evolution* (pp. 97–129). Washington, DC: American Psychological Association.

Hamilton, J. C. (2000). Construct validity of the core conditions and factor structure of the client evaluation of counselor scale. *The Person-Centered Journal, 7*(1), 40–51.

Hamilton, J. C., Carlson, M. A., & Sabol, N. L. (2001). A structured learning exercise in person-centered empathy within a counselor training program. *The Person-Centered Journal, 8*(1–2), 71–97.

LaFromboise, T. D., Trimble, J. E., & Mohatt, G. V. (1990). Counseling intervention and American Indian tradition: An integrative approach. *The Counseling Psychologist, 18*(4), 628–654.

Lazarus, A. A. (1996). Some reflections after 40 years of trying to be an effective psychotherapist. *Psychotherapy, 33*(1), 142–145.

Leong, F. T. L. (1986). Counseling and psychotherapy with Asian-Americans: Review of the literature. *Journal of Counseling Psychology, 33*(2), 196–206.

Leong, F. T. L. (1992). Guidelines for minimizing premature termination among Asian American clients. *Journal for Specialists in Group Work, 17*(4), 218–228.

Lietaer, G. (1984). Unconditional positive regard: A controversial basic attitude in client-centered therapy. In R. F. Levant, & J. M. Shlien (Eds.), *Client-centered therapy and the person-centered approach: New directions in theory, research, and practice* (pp. 41–58). New York: Praeger.

Miller, S. D., Duncan, M. A., & Hubble, M. A. (1997). *Escape from Babel: Toward a unifying language for psychological practice*. New York: Norton.

Mokuau, N. (1987). Social workers' perceptions of counseling effectiveness for Asian American clients. *Journal of the National Association of Social Workers, 32*(4), 331–335.

Moon, K. A. (2001). Nondirective client-centered therapy with children. *The Person-Centered Journal, 8*(1), 43–52.

Natiello, P. (1987). The person-centered approach: From theory to practice. *Person-Centered Review, 2*(2), 203–216.

Natiello, P. (2001). *The person-centered approach: A passionate presence.* Herefordshire, UK: PCCS Books.

O'Leary, E. (1997). Towards integrating person-centered and Gestalt therapies. *The Person-Centered Journal, 4*(2), 14–22.

*Page, R. C., Weiss, J. F., & Lietaer, G. (2002). Humanistic group psychotherapy. In D. J. Cain, & J. Seeman, (Eds.), *Humanistic psychotherapies: Handbook of research and practice* (pp. 339–368). Washington, DC: American Psychological Association.

Raskin, N. J. (1986a). Client-centered group psychotherapy, Part 1: Development of client-centered groups. *Person-Centered Review, 1*(3), 272–290.

Raskin, N. J. (1986b). Client-centered group psychotherapy, Part 2: Research on client-centered groups. *Person-Centered Review, 1*(4), 389–408.

Rogers, C. (1951). *Client-centered therapy.* Boston: Houghton Mifflin.

Rogers, C. (1957). The necessary and sufficient conditions of therapeutic personality change. *Journal of Consulting Psychology, 21,* 95–103.

*Rogers, C. (1961). *On becoming a person.* Boston: Houghton Mifflin.

*Rogers, C. (1970). *Carl Rogers on encounter groups.* New York: Harper & Row.

Rogers, C. (1975). Empathic: An unappreciated way of being. *The Counseling Psychologist, 5*(2), 2–9.

*Rogers, C. (1980). *A way of being.* Boston: Houghton Mifflin.

Rogers, C. (1986a). Carl Rogers on the development of the person-centered approach. *Person-Centered Review, 1*(3), 257–259.

Rogers, C. (1986b). Client-centered therapy. In I. L. Kutash, & A. Wolf (Eds.), *Psychotherapist's casebook* (pp. 197–208). San Francisco: Jossey-Bass.

Rogers, C. R. (1987a). Inside the world of the Soviet professional. *Counseling and Values, 32*(1), 46–66.

Rogers, C. R. (1987b). Rogers, Kohut, and Erikson: A personal perspective on some similarities and differences. In J. K. Zeig (Ed.), *The evolution of psychotherapy* (pp. 179–187). New York: Brunner/Mazel.

Rogers, C. R. (1987c). Steps toward world peace, 1948–1986: Tension reduction in theory and practice. *Counseling and Values, 32*(1), 12–16.

Rogers, C. R. (1987d). The underlying theory: Drawn from experience with individuals and groups. *Counseling and Values, 32*(1), 38–45.

Rogers, C. R., & Malcolm, D. (1987). The potential contribution of the behavioral scientist to world peace. *Counseling and Values, 32*(1), 10–11.

*Tallman, K., & Bohart, A. C. (1999). The client as a common factor: Clients as self-healers. In M. A. Hubble, B. L. Duncan, & S. D. Miller, (Eds.), *The heart and soul of change: What works in therapy* (pp. 91–131). Washington, DC: American Psychological Association.

Thompson, C. L., & Rudolph, L. B. (2000). *Counseling children* (5th ed.). Pacific Grove, CA: Brooks/Cole.

*Thorne, B. (1992). *Carl Rogers.* Newbury Park, CA: Sage.

*Watson, J. C. (2002). Re-visioning empathy. In D. J. Cain, & J. Seeman (Eds.), *Humanistic psychotherapies: Handbook of research and practice* (pp. 445–471). Washington, DC: American Psychological Association.

Zimring, F. M., & Raskin, N. J. (1992). Carl Rogers and client/person-centered therapy. In D. K. Freedheim (Ed.), *History of psychotherapy: A century of change* (pp. 629–656). Washington, DC: American Psychological Association.

CHAPTER 11

Gestalt Therapy in Groups

Introduction

Gestalt therapy was developed by Fritz Perls and his wife, Laura, in the 1940s. It is based on the assumption that we are best understood in the context of our environment. The basic goal of a Gestalt group is to provide a context that will enable members to increase their awareness of what they are experiencing and doing. Moment-to-moment awareness of one's experiencing, together with the almost immediate awareness of one's blocks to such experiencing, is seen as therapeutic in and of itself.

Gestalt therapy is existential in that it is grounded in the here-and-now, emphasizes personal choice and responsibility, and gives primacy to existential dialogue. Gestalt therapy gives special attention to existence as people experience it and affirms the human capacity for growth and healing through interpersonal contact and insight (Yontef, 1995a). This approach is *phenomenological* in that it emphasizes how each of us sees the world, how we contribute to creating our experience, and how we organize our world and ourselves. Gestalt is also an *experiential* approach, and group members are able to come to grips with what and how they are thinking, feeling, and doing as they interact with others in the group. Members are encouraged and guided in experimenting with new behaviors as a way to increase self-understanding (Yontef, 1995a).

As clients acquire present-centered awareness and a clearer perception of their blocks and conflicts, significant unfinished business emerges. It is assumed that the way to become an autonomous person is to identify and deal with anything from the past that interferes with current functioning. By reexperiencing past conflicts as if they were occurring in the present, clients expand their level of awareness and are able to integrate denied and fragmented parts of themselves, thus becoming unified and whole.

The Gestalt view is that experiencing is more powerful than the therapist's interpretations (Strumpfel & Goldman, 2002). Therefore, the approach of the Gestalt group is basically noninterpretive. Gestalt therapists do not make intellectual explanations or tell clients why they do things. Instead, group members make their own interpretations and statements and discover the meaning of their experiences. Leaders avoid interfering with client interpretations and deal with whatever the person seems to be experiencing at the moment.

Group members are encouraged to try on a new style of behavior, to give expression to certain dimensions of their personality that are dormant, and to test out alternative modes of behavior to widen their ability to respond in the world. According to Zinker (1978), Gestalt experiments are anchored in the experiential life of the members as they present themselves in the situation and grow out of a living context for the group.

Many of the key concepts of Gestalt therapy were developed by Perls, but it should be noted that Perls never claimed to be doing group therapy. In the 1950s and early 1960s Perls devoted much of his time to conducting workshops as a way to train mental health practitioners in Gestalt theory and techniques as applied to individual therapy. He emphasized one-to-one work—using the "hot seat" style—and discouraged any group interaction. Perls made frequent use of the "empty chair" technique, which was originated by J. L. Moreno (see Chapter 8). Miriam Polster (1997) points out that Perls's work was clearly focused on interaction between himself and a client who volunteered to work *in front of* a group, but not *within* the group. She adds that Perls was not particularly interested in or adept at working with groups, and he rarely recognized the group as a presence in his work. The audience was viewed almost entirely as background for the encounter between the leader and the individual participant (Feder & Ronall, 1994).

Perls demonstrated a style that was highly confrontive, challenging clients to see how they were avoiding responsibility or avoiding feeling. Perls's therapeutic style was characterized by theatrics, abrasive confrontation, and intense catharsis. Yontef (1993) suggests that this dramatic style may have met more of Perls's own narcissistic needs than the needs of his clients. Yontef is critical of this anti-intellectual, individualistic, dramatic, and confrontive flavor that characterized Gestalt therapy in the "anything goes environment" of the 1960s. Yontef (1999) claims that contemporary forms of Gestalt practice have moved away from the harsh and dramatic style of the 1960s and 1970s to an approach that "combines sustained empathic inquiry with crisp, clear, and relevant awareness focusing" (p. 10).

This newer version, labeled "relational Gestalt therapy," includes more support and increased kindness and compassion in therapy (Yontef, 1999). Erving and Miriam Polster (1973, 1999), who are pioneers in relational Gestalt therapy, have made many significant theoretical and practical contributions to the development of contemporary Gestalt therapy. As therapists, supervisors, and trainers, the Polsters employ a style that is supportive, accepting, challenging, and less confrontational than the traditional Gestalt therapy practiced by Perls.

Today, few Gestalt practitioners use the empty chair technique as their *primary* method of conducting groups (Cain, 2002; Frew, 1988; Harman, 1984; Kepner, 1994; Melnick, 1980). The essence of current Gestalt therapy involves honoring and respecting resistance and supporting the client to become more aware of his or her experience without pushing or blaming. Cain (2002) summarizes some major shifts in the development of Gestalt therapy:

> Since Perls's death in 1970, the practice of Gestalt therapy has softened and shifted its emphases toward the quality of the therapist-client relationship, dialogue, empathic attunement, tapping the client's wisdom and resources, an expansion of therapeutic styles, and development of theory, especially field theory and phenomenology. (p. 31)

In keeping with this evolution of Gestalt therapy, in this chapter I emphasize the contemporary developments that characterize this approach in the post-Perls era.

Key Concepts

Therapeutic Goals

The basic aim of Gestalt therapy is to attain awareness, which by and of itself is seen as curative or growth producing. Awareness requires self-knowledge, responsibility for choices, contact with the environment, self-acceptance, and the ability to make contact (Yontef & Jacobs, 2000). Without awareness, clients do not possess the tools for personality change. With awareness, they have the capacity to find within themselves the resources necessary to solve their problems and to discover the conditions that will make change possible.

Gestalt therapy aims not at analysis but at integration of sometimes conflicting dimensions within the individual. This step-by-step process involves "reowning" parts of oneself that have been disowned and then unifying these disparate parts into an integrated whole. As clients become more fully aware, they can carry on with their own personal growth, make informed choices, and live a meaningful existence.

A basic assumption of Gestalt therapy is that individuals can deal with their life problems themselves, especially if they are fully aware of what is happening in and around them. Because of certain problems in development, people find various ways to avoid problems and, therefore, reach impasses in their personal growth. Therapy provides the necessary intervention and challenge to help them proceed toward integration and a more authentic and vital existence.

The Gestalt theory of change posits that the more we attempt to be who or what we are not, the more we remain the same. According to Beisser's (1970) paradoxical theory of change, personal change tends to occur when we become aware of *what we are* as opposed to trying to become *what we are not*. Stated slightly differently, it is important that we accept *who* and *what* we are rather than striving to become what we "should be." What we are is always the starting point for the path we might take. Erv Polster (1995) states that the therapist is called on to see clients as they are, hear them as they are, talk to them as they are, and sense them as they are—to identify with them and create a union.

When we face and become what we are, we open rich possibilities for change. Thus, the challenge for group leaders is not to directly change group participants but rather to engage participants and to assist them in developing their own awareness of how they are in the present moment.

The question of therapeutic goals can be considered from the point of view of personal goals for each member and of group process goals for the group as a whole. Zinker (1994) describes the following *individual* goals:

- Integrating polarities within oneself
- Enriching and expanding awareness
- Achieving contact with self and others
- Learning to provide self-support instead of looking to others for this support
- Defining one's boundaries with clarity
- Translating insights into action
- Being willing to learn about oneself by engaging in creative experiments
- Learning to flow smoothly through the awareness-excitement-contact cycle without serious blockage

Goals for the members to achieve on the *group level* include these:

- Learning how to ask clearly and directly for what they want or need
- Learning how to deal effectively with interpersonal conflicts
- Learning how to give support and energy to one another
- Being able to challenge one another to push beyond the boundaries of safety and what is known
- Creating a community that is based on trust, which allows for a level of deep and meaningful work
- Learning how to give each other feedback
- Learning how to make use of the resources within the group rather than relying on the group leader as the director

The goals of a Gestalt group involve equal attention to both process and content. Miriam Polster (1997) points to the importance of allowing members to talk about aspects of their lives that concern or baffle them and also their way of relating to one another within the group. She states that although it is essential for a member to be able to tell his or her story, the story itself is not enough. What is important is *how* the member tells the story and the way in which others in the group listen and are affected by the story. Polster gives an example of a man in one of her groups who let his sentences simply trail off in such a way that even he was not interested in what he was saying. She asked him to end his sentences with the phrase, "and I *really* mean that!" This led him to put more animation into his speech, which kept the rest of the group interested in what he was saying.

Some Principles of Gestalt Therapy Theory

A number of basic principles underlie the theory of Gestalt therapy. These principles include holism, field theory, the figure-formation process, and organismic self-regulation.

Holism   Holism is one of the foundational principles of Gestalt therapy (Latner, 1986) and is expressed by the dictum: the whole is greater than the sum of its parts. We can only be understood to the extent that we take into consideration all dimensions of human functioning. Because Gestalt therapists are interested in the whole person, they place no superior value on a particular aspect of the individual. Gestalt practice attends to a client's thoughts, feelings, behaviors, body, and dreams. The emphasis is on integration, how the parts fit together and how the individual makes contact with the environment.

Field Theory   Gestalt therapy is based on field theory, which is grounded on the principle that the organism must be seen in its environment, or in its context, as part of the constantly changing field. Everything is relational, in flux, interrelated, and in process, and Gestalt therapists pay particular attention to and explore what is occurring at the boundary between the person and the environment.

The Figure-Formation Process   This process, originally developed in the field of visual perception by a group of Gestalt psychologists, describes how the individual organizes the environment from moment to moment. In Gestalt therapy the undifferentiated field is called the background, or ground. The emerging focus of attention is called the figure. The process of forming this attention is called figure-formation (Latner, 1986). The figure-formation process tracks how some aspect of the environmental field emerges from the background and becomes the focal point of the individual's attention and interest. The needs of an individual at a given moment influence this process (Frew, 1997).

Organismic Self-Regulation   The figure-formation process is intertwined with the principle of "organismic self-regulation," which describes the nature of the relationship between the individual and the environment. When equilibrium is "disturbed" by the emergence of a need, a sensation, or an interest, the organism will distinguish the means required to gratify this need. Organisms will do their best to regulate themselves, given their own capabilities and the resources of their environment (Latner, 1986), and individuals will take actions and make contacts that will both restore equilibrium and contribute to growth and change.

Frew (1997) describes the implications of the principles of figure-formation and organismic self-regulation for the therapy group. Members attempt to self-regulate in the group context by attending to what becomes figural moment to moment. What emerges for each group member is associated with what is of interest or what he or she needs to be able to regain a sense of equilibrium. A main method Gestalt therapists use in working with group members involves directing participants' awareness to the "figures" that emerge from the background during a group session. The therapist uses the figure-formation process as the guide for the focus of exploration and work in the group.

Awareness

The task of members of a Gestalt group is to pay attention to the structure of their experience and to become aware of the *what* and *how* of such experiencing. The psychoanalytic approach is interested in *why* we do what we do; the Gestalt leader asks "what" and "how" questions but rarely "why" questions. By attending to the continuum of awareness—that is, by staying with the moment-to-moment flow of experiencing—clients discover how they are functioning in the world.

Gestalt leaders employ the figure-formation process when they assist members in paying attention to what becomes figural for them. To help members gain a sharper awareness of what they are thinking, feeling, and doing, the Gestalt leader asks questions such as these that lead to present-centeredness:

- What are you experiencing now?
- What's going on inside you as you're speaking?
- How are you experiencing your anxiety in your body?
- How are you attempting to withdraw at this moment, and how are you avoiding contact with unpleasant feelings?
- What's your feeling at this moment—as you sit there and try to talk?
- What's happening to your voice as you talk to your father now?

To attain present-centered awareness of our existence, Gestalt therapy focuses on the obvious—on the surface of behavior—by concentrating on the client's movements, postures, language patterns, voice, gestures, and interactions with others. Polster and Polster (1973) point to the value of attending to the surface of behavior and emphasize the need to provide a climate in which clients can come into contact with their changing awareness from moment to moment.

The Here-and-Now

One of the most important contributions of Gestalt therapy is the emphasis on learning to appreciate and fully experience the present: the present is the most significant tense, for the past is gone, and the future has not yet arrived. The present is lively and exciting. It offers opportunities for real growth and change, which come about from contact with something new. This focus on the present doesn't indicate a lack of interest in the past. The past is important, but only insofar as it is related to our present functioning.

Because of this present-centered emphasis, Gestalt therapists have developed a methodology that helps individuals discover and experiment with new possibilities. This here-and-now focus imbues the group with potency, involvement, and liveliness (Melnick, 1980). In Gestalt groups participants bring past problem situations into the present by reenacting the situation as if it were occurring now. For example, if a group member (Leslie) begins to talk about the difficulty she had when she was younger and attempted to live with her father, the therapist could intervene with a request that Leslie "be here now" with her father and speak directly to him. The therapist might say: "Bring your father into this room now, and let yourself go back to the time when you were a child. Tell him now, as though he were here and you were that child, what you most want to say." The leader might make use of the empty chair technique by suggesting that Leslie imagine that her father is sitting in an empty chair and asking her to talk directly to him. This is merely one of many ways for the leader to encourage this client to attend to the present moment.

Most Gestalt experiments are designed to put clients into closer contact with their ongoing experiencing from moment to moment. There are disadvantages to this exclusive focus if the past and the future are discarded. E. Polster (1987a) observes that too tight a focus, with a highly concentrated emphasis on the here-and-now, will foreclose on much that matters, such as continuity of commitment, the implications of one's acts, dependability, and responsiveness to others.

Unfinished Business and Avoidance

Unfinished business includes unexpressed feelings—such as resentment, hate, rage, pain, hurt, anxiety, guilt, shame, and grief—and events and memories that linger in the background and clamor for completion. Unless these unfinished situations and unexpressed emotions are made figural and dealt with, they keep interfering with present-centered awareness and with our effective functioning.

Because we have a tendency to avoid confronting and fully experiencing our anxiety, grief, guilt, shame, and other uncomfortable emotions, the emotions become a nagging undercurrent that prevents us from being fully alive. The Gestalt therapist might encourage expressing in the therapeutic session intense feelings never directly expressed before. If a client says to the group that she is afraid of getting in touch with her feelings of hatred and spite, she may be encouraged by the therapist to stay with what is truly figural—"I am afraid." The therapist can then design an experiment in which she can deepen her awareness of her fear. For example, she could talk to group members out of her fear, or she might tell each member one of her fears.

During a group session, a member says that he feels empty and powerless. The therapist is likely to encourage him to stay with these uncomfortable feelings, even to exaggerate them—to "be empty," to "be powerless." If this person can endure and truly experience the depth of his feelings, he will probably discover that whatever catastrophic expectations he has with regard to those feelings are more of a fantasy than a reality and that his helplessness and void will not destroy him. Experiencing dreaded emotions leads to integration and growth. By going beyond our avoidances, we make it possible to dispose of unfinished business that interferes with our present life, and we move toward health and integration.

Contact and Resistances to Contact

In Gestalt therapy contact is made by seeing, hearing, smelling, touching, and moving. When we make contact with the environment, change is inevitable. Effective contact means interacting with nature and with other people without losing one's sense of individuality. It is the continually renewed creative adjustment of individuals to their environment (M. Polster, 1987). Prerequisites for good contact are clear awareness, full energy, and the ability to express oneself (Zinker, 1978). Miriam Polster (1987) claims that contact is the lifeblood of growth. It entails zest, imagination, and creativity. There are only moments of this type of contact, so it is most accurate to think of levels of contact rather than a final state to achieve. After a contact experience, there is typically a withdrawal to integrate what has been learned.

The Gestalt therapist also focuses on resistances to contact. From a Gestalt perspective, resistance refers to defenses and interruptions we develop that prevent us from experiencing and staying with the present in a full and real way. Ego-defense mechanisms can prevent people from being authentic. Polster and Polster (1973) describe five major channels of resistance that are challenged in Gestalt therapy: introjection, projection, retroflection, confluence, and deflection.

Introjection involves the tendency to accept others' beliefs and standards uncritically without assimilating them and making them congruent with who we are. These introjects become alien to us because we have not analyzed and restructured them. When we introject, we passively incorporate what the environment provides, spending little time on getting clear what we want or need. During the early stages of a group, introjection is common, for the members tend to look to the leader to provide structure and direction. At this phase of a group's development, members typically do not question the leader's interventions or rules. As the group reaches a working stage, members are less inclined to swallow whole the suggestions of the group leader.

Projection is the reverse of introjection. In projection we disown certain aspects of ourselves by ascribing them to the environment. When we are projecting, we have trouble distinguishing between the inside world and the outside world. Those attributes of our personality that are inconsistent with our self-image are disowned and put onto other people. By seeing in others the very qualities that we refuse to acknowledge in ourselves, we avoid taking responsibility for our own feelings and the person who we are. Of course, projection is the basis of transference. When transference feelings surface early in a group, these dynamics can be fruitfully explored. As members attempt to get a sense of both the leader and other members, they often attribute characteristics to these individuals that really belong to significant others in their lives. During the transition stage, when issues such as the struggle for control and power become central, projection continues to be a primary contacting style. Now participants may disown their own needs to control the group. The conflicts that occur at this phase are difficult to resolve unless those members who are projecting their need to control recognize and own their projections (Frew, 1986).

Retroflection consists of turning back to ourselves what we would like to do to someone else. For example, if we lash out and injure ourselves, we are often directing aggression inward that we are fearful of directing toward others. Typically, these maladaptive styles of functioning are done outside of our awareness; part of the process of Gestalt therapy is to help us discover a self-regulatory system so that we can deal realistically with the world. During the initial phase of a group, retroflection is easily observed in the tendency of some members to "hold back" by saying very little and expressing little emotion.

Confluence involves the blurring of awareness of differentiation between the self and the environment. For people who are confluent, there is no clear demarcation between internal experience and outer reality. Confluence in relationships involves an absence of conflicts, or a belief that all parties experience the same feelings and thoughts. It is a style of contact that is characteristic of group members who have a high need to be accepted and liked. Conflicts can be very anxiety producing for individuals who rely on confluence as a style of contact (Frew, 1986). Confluence makes it difficult for people to have their own thoughts and to speak for themselves. This condition makes genuine contact next to impossible.

Deflection is the interruption of awareness so that it is difficult to maintain a sustained sense of contact. People who deflect attempt to diffuse contact through the overuse of humor, abstract generalizations, and questions rather than statements (Frew, 1986). Deflection involves a diminished emotional experience. People who deflect speak through and for others.

Introjection, projection, retroflection, confluence, and deflection represent styles of contact. These styles can be either healthy or unhealthy, depending on the situation and the group member's level of awareness. Terms such as *resistance to contact* or *boundary disturbance* are used to characterize people who attempt to control their environment. The premise in Gestalt therapy is that contact and withdrawal are both normal and healthy. Therefore, a discussion of these styles of contact focuses on the degree to which these processes are in the individual's awareness. Clients in Gestalt therapy are encouraged to become increasingly aware of their dominant style of blocking contact.

Resistance is a basic concept in Gestalt therapy, and as such resistances are to be welcomed and understood. Latner (1986) makes some excellent points pertaining to how resistance provides valuable material for therapeutic work. The way we resist tells us a great deal about ourselves. Through understanding our resistance, we have opportunities for expanding our awareness and rediscovering aspects of our functioning that we have lost. The purpose of contacting our resistances is not to eliminate them but to gain awareness of ways we developed to meet our needs.

Energy and Blocks to Energy

Because members need energy to work in group sessions, Gestalt leaders pay special attention to where energy is located, how it is used, and how it can be blocked. Blocked energy can be thought of as resistance, and there are a number of ways in which it can show up in the body. One member will experience tension in his neck and shoulders, and another member will experience shortness of breath. Another person will typically speak with a restricted voice, by holding back power. A few other ways that these blocks to energy will manifest themselves are keeping one's mouth shut tightly (as though one were afraid what might slip out); slouching; looking at the ground or in the air as a way of avoiding contact with others' eyes; keeping one's body tight and closed; talking in a fast and staccato fashion; being emotionally flat; or experiencing body sensations such as a lump in the throat, a quivering of the mouth, a hot and flushed feeling, shaking movements of the hands and legs, or dizziness.

Clients may not be aware of their energy or where it is located and may experience it in a negative way. Zinker (1978) suggests that therapy at its best is "a lively process of stoking the client's inner fires of awareness and contact" (p. 24). This process involves a therapeutic relationship that awakens and nourishes the client in such a way that the therapist does not become sapped of his or her own energy. Zinker maintains that it is the therapist's job to help clients locate the ways in which they are blocking energy and to help them transform this blocked energy into more adaptive behaviors. This process is best accomplished when resistance is not viewed as a client's refusal to cooperate and as something simply to be gotten around. Instead, therapists can learn to welcome resistance and use it as a way of deepening therapeutic work. Members can be encouraged to recognize how their resistance is being expressed in their body. Rather than trying to rid themselves of certain bodily symptoms, they can actually delve fully into tension states. By allowing themselves to exaggerate their tight mouth and shaking legs, they are able to discover for themselves how they are diverting energy and keeping themselves powerless.

Experiments can be designed that allow members to try out various body positions. For example, if a member sits with a closed posture, the leader can invite him or her to uncross and experience the feeling, and then cross again. By inviting clients to move out of a particular posture and experiment with a new posture, leaders can facilitate awareness. Members who slouch and who also complain about low self-esteem can be invited to stand and walk erect. In a like way, members can be asked to exaggerate a particular gesture or posture as a way of learning more about themselves. In short, paying attention to the body and energy blockages within the body can be a productive way to explore the meaning of a member's experience.

Role and Functions of the Group Leader

Although Gestalt leaders encourage members to assume responsibility for raising their own level of consciousness, leaders can nevertheless take an active role in creating experiments to help members tap their resources. Gestalt leaders are actively engaged with the members, and leaders frequently engage in self-disclosure as a way to enhance relationships and create a sense of mutuality within the group. Zinker (1978) writes that the therapist, functioning much like an artist, invents experiments with clients to augment their range of behaviors. The leader's function is to create an atmosphere and structure in which the group's own creativity and inventiveness can emerge. For example, a theme of loneliness may come up in a group. Here a central task of the leader is to orchestrate this theme by connecting members with one another and finding ways to involve the group as a whole in exploring loneliness.

Gestalt therapists assume an active role by employing a wide range of interventions and experiments to help clients gain awareness and experience their conflicts fully. Gestalt therapists frequently invite clients to engage in experiments that lead to fresh emotional experiencing and new insights (Strumpfel & Goldman, 2002). It should be made clear, however, that an equally important function of the Gestalt group leader is to promote and create a nurturing environment within the group. Unless the group atmosphere is perceived as being safe, members will keep themselves hidden and therapeutic work will be limited (Feder, 1994). Yontef (1993) contends that although the therapist functions as a guide and a catalyst, suggests experiments, and shares observations, the basic work of exploration is done by the client. Yontef maintains that the therapist's role is to create a climate in which clients will feel free enough to try out new ways of being and behaving.

The Role of the Relationship A number of writers have given central importance to a dialogic relationship marked by an I/Thou attitude. They warn of the dangers of becoming technique-bound and losing sight of their own being as they engage the client. Techniques are not the issue; rather, the therapist's attitudes and behavior and the relationship that is established are what really count (Hycner & Jacobs, 1995; Jacobs, 1989; E. Polster, 1987a, 1987b; M. Polster, 1987; Polster & Polster, 1999; Yontef, 1993, 1995a, 1999). These writers point out that current Gestalt therapy has moved beyond earlier therapeutic practices. Many contemporary Gestalt therapists place increasing emphasis on factors such as presence, authentic dialogue, gentleness, more direct self-expression by the therapist, decreased use of stereotypic exercises, a greater trust in the client's experiencing, and more interest in making full use of the Gestalt group process. In writing about the relationship and therapeutic change, Yontef (1995a) states: "Change is facilitated when the therapist is dialogic in attitude, shows a clear understanding of the patient's subjective experience, is self-disclosing, and is warm and accepting" (p. 284).

Therapists have latitude to invent their own experiments, which are basically an extension of their personalities. Thus, therapists must be grounded and in tune with themselves as well as being present for their clients. If clients are to become authentic, they need contact with an authentic therapist on a genuine "I/Thou" basis. Because Gestalt therapy is part of the existential approach, the mutuality of the I/Thou encounter is seen as essential for therapy to succeed. Healing results from these nonexploitive encounters. The best experiments grow out of the trusting relationship that the leader creates. This approach encourages genuine experimentation and allows for a great deal of creativity on the part of leaders and members (see Zinker, 1978).

In a seminal article, "Dialogue in Gestalt Theory and Therapy," Jacobs (1989) explores the role of the therapeutic relationship as a factor in healing and the extent to which the client/therapist relationship is the focus of therapy. She shows how Martin Buber's philosophy of dialogue, which involves a genuine and loving meeting, is congruent with Gestalt concepts of contact, awareness, and the paradoxical theory of change. Jacobs asserts that a current trend in Gestalt practice is toward greater emphasis on the client/therapist relationship rather than on techniques divorced from the context of this encounter. She believes a therapist who operates from this orientation establishes a present-centered, nonjudgmental dialogue that allows the client to deepen awareness and to find contact with another person. Therapy that takes place within a dialogic relationship affords clients the chance to meet others and to come to know themselves. The experiments therapists employ evolve out of this process. Experiments must always be a phenomenological part of the therapeutic process. The experiments that we consider later in this chapter are aimed at awareness, not at simple solutions to a client's problem. If therapists use experiments when they are frustrated with a client and want to change the person, they are misusing the experiments and will probably thwart rather than foster the client's growth and change (see Hycner & Jacobs, 1995).

Polster and Polster (1973) see the therapist as nothing less than an artist involved in creating new life. Yet in Gestalt, as in most other approaches, the danger exists that the therapist will lose sight of the true meaning of the therapeutic process and become a mere technician. Therapists should use their own experience as an essential ingredient in the therapy process and never forget that they are far more than mere responders, givers of feedback, or catalysts who don't change themselves (Polster & Polster, 1973).

Creative therapists possess a rich personal background, having opened themselves to a range of life experiences and become able to celebrate life fully (Zinker, 1978). In short, they are able to use themselves as a person as they function as a therapist. In addition to being mature and integrated people, creative therapists also possess certain capacities, abilities, and technical skills. Out of their experimental attitude, they use themselves, other group members, and objects and events in the group environment in the service of inventing novel visions of the members. Here are some specific skills Zinker relates to the functioning of creative therapists:

- The capacity to identify energy within the members and to sensitively introduce experiments in a timely and appropriate fashion
- The ability to be flexible by letting go of some things and moving to other areas that are more lively
- The willingness to push and confront members so that they will get their work done, along with the ability to know when to back off
- The ability to help members express their feelings and summarize what they are learning after they complete an experiment
- The wisdom to know when to let members stay confused so that they can learn to find clarity in their own way

From this discussion of the role and functions of the Gestalt group leader, it should be apparent that who the leader is as a person and how he or she functions in the group, creatively drawing on technical expertise, are the critical factors that determine the potency of leadership.

Stages of a Gestalt Group

One way of conceptualizing the role of the Gestalt group leader is to consider the stage of development of the group. Kepner (1994) presents a model that calls for different roles of the leader in working with different dimensions of group process. Gestalt group process aims to create conditions for learning about what it means to be a member of a group. Kepner notes that Gestalt group therapy can accentuate one of three contact boundaries: (1) the *intrapsychic* or *intrapersonal* (what goes on within the individual, such as thoughts, sensations, and feelings); (2) the *interpersonal* (the interactions between and among one another); or (3) the *group level* (the processes that involve the whole group). She maintains that the choice of boundary emphasis is often defined by the leader's choice of role: *therapist* for the intrapersonal dimension; *facilitator* of interpersonal processes; and *consultant* to the group as a whole. In writing about the Gestalt group process, Kepner emphasizes that the leader is committed to working with both the individual and the group for the enhancement of both. She describes the various roles of the leader in the Gestalt process group using a three-stage model.

First Stage In the first stage (initial stage) of a group, the key characteristics are identity and dependence. Each member of the group is dependent on the way he or she is perceived and responded to by other members and the leader. The leader, functioning as a therapist, helps individuals explore questions members have about their identity in the group. During this initial stage, the leader's primary task is to create the conditions that will enable the group members to tap into each other as resources. The leader's activities in the initial stage are directed toward providing a climate of trust that will support risk-taking and making connections between individuals. Once members discover what they have in common with each other, the group is ready to work on differentiation.

Second Stage In the second stage (which is similar to the transition stage) the key characteristics are influence and counterdependence. During this time of transition, the group grapples with issues of influence, authority, and control. The leader's task is to work for increasing differentiation, divergence, and role flexibility among members. The leader assumes the role of facilitator to help members work through reactions they are having toward what is taking place in the group. Some of these facilitative activities include heightening the awareness of the norms operating in the group, encouraging members to challenge norms and openly express differences and dissatisfaction, and differentiating roles from persons.

Third Stage In the third stage (which is similar to the working stage) intimacy and interdependence are the key themes. At this stage of the group's development, real contact occurs within and among members of the group.

Now that the members have worked through the issues of influence, power, and authority, they are ready for a deeper level of work, both individually and with the group as a whole. The group leader is no longer the ultimate authority but now assumes the role of an experienced resource or consultant. The leader helps the group to arrive at closure and also assists members in recognizing unfinished business not worked through in the group.

It is clear that Kepner's model accounts for the reality that the roles and functions of the group leader are rooted in three types of processes that occur simultaneously in groups: intrapersonal, interpersonal, and group as a system. Gestalt leaders have the advantage of being able to intervene at all of these levels (Frew, 1997).

Application: Therapeutic Techniques and Procedures

Gestalt therapy employs a rich variety of interventions designed to intensify what group members are experiencing in the present moment for the purpose of leading to increased awareness. Gestalt therapy encourages "becoming a conflict" or "being what we are feeling" as opposed to merely talking about conflicts, problems, and feelings. Experiments need to be tailored to each individual and used in a timely manner; they also need to be carried out in a context that offers a balance between support and risk. Experiments should be the outgrowth of the therapeutic encounter—an encounter grounded in the mutual experiencing of client and therapist. There are no prescribed techniques that Gestalt group leaders must follow.

The Role of Experiments

It is important to distinguish between *techniques* and *experiments* because the two terms are not synonymous. *Techniques* are exercises or procedures that are often used to bring about action or interaction. Generally, they are not invented in the moment as an integral part of the client's process or the group environment. In contrast, *experiments* are phenomenologically based; that is, they evolve out of what is occurring within a member or members in the present moment, and they usually grow out of the struggles members are experiencing. In Gestalt group experiments, members are invited to try out some new behavior and to pay attention to what they experience. Experiments grow out of the therapeutic relationship and provide a safe context for members to increase their awareness and try out new ways of behaving. A Gestalt-oriented group leader is encouraged to be creative in designing and implementing a wide range of interventions, always using as a guide the client's present experiencing.

It is also useful to differentiate between a group exercise and a group experiment. With group exercises, leaders prepare some kind of structured technique before the group meets. Members might be asked to pair up and talk, or a catalyst might be introduced into the group to provide a specific focus for work during a session. In contrast, a group experiment is a creative happening that grows out of the group experience; as such it cannot be predetermined, and its outcome cannot be predicted (Zinker, 1978). M. Polster (1987) states that experiments are "aimed at restoring momentum to the stuck points of a person's life. It is one way to recover the connection between deliberation and spontaneity by bringing the possibilities for action right into the therapy room" (p. 318). Yontef (1995a) indicates that experiments are aimed at discovering something rather than being aimed at directly controlling behavior change. "Experiments are suggestions for focusing awareness that patients can use to heighten the intensity, power, flexibility, and creativity of their therapy experience" (p. 279).

Some forms that Gestalt experiments might take include dramatizing a painful memory, imagining a dreaded encounter, playing one's parent, creating a dialogue between two parts within oneself, attending to an overlooked gesture, or exaggerating a certain posture (M. Polster, 1987). One of the therapist's functions is to observe whether the experiment appears too safe or too risky. The Polsters (1990) call for sensitivity and careful attention on the therapist's part so that clients are "neither blasted into experiences that are too threatening nor allowed to stay in safe but infertile territory" (p. 104).

Polster (1995) writes that a diversity of Gestalt experiments is available, and therapists can create their own on-the-spot experiments that evolve from therapeutic engagements with clients as well. A loud-voiced client can be asked to experiment with speaking softly. A client grieving over the home she left may be asked to imagine herself walking into her home and report what she sees and feels. M. Polster (1997) describes the experiment as the "safe emergency" that provides group members with the opportunity to explore beyond ways of behaving that have become restrictive and habitual:

> Interactions and experiments within the group setting are not to be taken as scripts or dress rehearsals to be put to use indiscriminately. Within the Gestalt group there are options that a person might not have available in everyday circumstances or might not think of—or dare—to do. (p. 235)

On a similar note, Feder (1994) pays close attention to the balance of safety and danger in the Gestalt group. An experiment is always done within the context of support. Members will not be able to engage in the kind of risk-taking that an experiment entails unless they feel safe in going beyond their comfort zone and venturing into new territory. Feder is particularly concerned about creating a nurturing atmosphere within the group as a whole, and any signs that this safety is lacking warrants the leader's attention.

If members experience the group as being a safe place, they will be inclined to move into the unknown and challenge themselves. It is useful for leaders to provide members with a general understanding of the role of experiments in the group process. To increase the chances that members will benefit from Gestalt methods, group leaders need to communicate the general purpose of these interventions and to create an experimental climate. "Let's try something on for size and see how it fits" or "try it and see what you might learn" conveys this experimental attitude on the part of the leader. The message also says that the leader is not trying to prove a point and that the members are free to try something new and determine for themselves whether it's going to work.

Many problems that members bring to the group relate to unfinished situations with significant people in their lives. Consider the woman who learned to be cautious around men, based largely on her earlier relationship with her father. She may harbor feelings of resentment and mistrust toward men, based on her convictions that men will simply not be there for her in time of need. She may connect this present feeling to old feelings associated with her alcoholic father, who continually let her down and brought much pain into her life. Based on her early decision not to trust men, she may be projecting her negative feelings toward all men now. Concluding that if her own father could not be counted on for love and protection then surely other men will not be more trustworthy, she now looks for evidence to support her hypothesis. The Gestalt group leader might invite her to deal with her father symbolically in the here-and-now. She might have a dialogue with him, becoming both her father and herself. She could now say all the things that she wanted to say to her father as a child but, because of her fear, kept deep inside herself. She might tell her father what she most wanted from him then and what she still wants with him now.

Of course, there are many creative possibilities within the group. She could look at the men in the group, expressing to each some of her resentments. In making contact with each man in the group, she could share her fantasies of all the ways in which they would let her down or of what she would like from them now yet is afraid to ask for. The theoretical rationale for this experiment is rooted in the assumption that the emotions that were overwhelming to her as a child were dealt with by some form of distortion or denial. The Gestalt leader encourages her to reexperience these past events by reliving them in the here-and-now so that emotions that were repressed can come to the surface. With the support of the leader and the group members, she can allow herself to experience feelings that she has sealed off from awareness, and she can now work through some of these feelings and beliefs that are keeping her stuck. By challenging her assumptions of how men are, she is able to establish a new basis for relating to men.

Experiments can be applied to future events as well as dealing with present conflicts and unfinished situations from the past. If the above group member is afraid of a future confrontation with her father, she can be asked to live her expectations in the here-and-now by speaking directly to her father in the group and by expressing her fears and hopes. Thus, she may say to her father: "I want to tell you how much I'd like to be close to you, but I'm afraid that if I do so, you won't care. I'm afraid of saying the wrong things and pushing you even further away from me."

In this example the possibilities are almost endless if there is good contact between the group leader and members, and if there is a climate of safety that encourages trying on a host of ways to deal with unexpressed thoughts and feelings. It is clear that the emphasis is on inviting (not ordering) members to examine their behaviors, attitudes, and thoughts. Leaders can encourage members to look at certain incongruities, especially gaps between their verbal and nonverbal expression. The Gestalt group is characterized by assisting members to pay attention to what they are doing and experiencing in the here-and-now. Asking members to make this kind of examination of what is in the forefront for them could be perceived as challenging to some clients at times. Any time a member is encouraged to take a risk, this must be done in a caring manner. Also, confrontation does not necessarily have to be aimed at weaknesses or negative traits; members can be asked to pay attention to the ways in which they are blocking their strengths and ways in which they are not living as fully as they might. In this sense confrontation can be a genuine expression of caring that results in positive changes in a member, not a brutal assault on a defenseless member.

Members must be prepared for taking part in experiments. They need to know that they can choose to go along and that they can also decide to stop when they want to. Rather than pushing them into experimenting, the spirit is always one of inviting them to discover something new about themselves. It is essential that leaders begin where the client is. By drawing on the support within the client and the group environment, experiments can be graded so that members can move in the direction of becoming more spontaneous.

Keep these introductory comments in mind as you read the following pages, which describe several Gestalt interventions, their rationales, and their applications to group situations. My discussion is based on a variety of sources, among them, Levitsky and Perls (1970), Passons (1975), Perls (1969a), E. Polster (1997), Polster and Polster (1973; 1999), M. Polster (1997), and Zinker (1978). I have modified some techniques to fit the needs of the group situation.

Language Exercises

Gestalt emphasizes the relationship between language patterns and personality. It suggests that our speech patterns are often expressions of our feelings, thoughts, and attitudes and that by focusing on our overt speaking habits we can increase our self-awareness (Passons, 1975). Words can bring us to ourselves, or they can take us away from ourselves. Becoming more aware of some of our speech patterns can enhance self-awareness. It should be noted, however, that these language exercises require a great deal of skill on the part of the leader. Unless the members, through the leader's help, are able to see the value of paying attention to the impact of their language style, they will come to feel that everything they say and do is subject to unnecessary scrutiny. Any one of these interventions based on language may or may not be appropriate with a particular client. These experiments grow out of the phenomenological work with the member; they are not techniques to use in routine and stereotyped ways.

It   "It" talk is a way of depersonalizing language. By using "it" instead of "I," we maintain distance from our experience. When group members say "It's frightening to come to this group," they can be asked to change the sentence to "I'm frightened to come to this group." Substituting personal pronouns for impersonal ones is a way of assuming responsibility for what we say.

You   Group participants often say things like "You feel hurt when someone rejects you." By using "you" talk, people detach themselves from whatever they may be feeling. Ask members to pay attention to the differences between this "you" statement and saying "I feel hurt when someone rebuffs me." By changing a "you" statement to an "I" statement, we reveal ourselves, and we take responsibility for what we are saying. Beginning a sentence with the word "you" tends to put others on the defensive and makes us disown our own experience.

Questions   In a Gestalt group members are discouraged from asking questions. Questions direct attention to other people and can easily put others on the defensive. Also, questions often demand that those being questioned reveal themselves whereas those who ask them are keeping themselves safe behind their interrogation. Group members who tend to ask too many questions can be asked to experiment with any of the following:

- Instead of asking a question, make a direct statement to the person and share your own motivation for your question.
- Avoid "why" questions because they lead to a chain of "why/because" exchanges. Try instead "how" and "what" questions.
- Practice making "I" statements. By doing so, you take responsibility for your position, your opinions, and your preferences.

Qualifiers and Disclaimers   By paying attention to the qualifiers they attach to their statements, group members can increase their awareness of how they diminish the power of their messages. A common example is the use of "but": "I like you, *but* your mannerisms drive me up the wall"; "I often feel depressed, *but* I don't know what to do to change the situation"; "I think this group is helping me, *but* people outside are so different from those in here." In each of these cases the word "but" essentially discounts the statement that precedes it. Without making group members excessively self-conscious, the leader can encourage members to pay attention to the impact of the use of qualifiers and disclaimers.

"Can't" Statements   Group members often say "I can't" when they really mean "I won't." Sally says, "I simply can't talk to my father and tell him what I feel; he'd never understand me." It would be more precise and more honest for Sally to say that she won't make the attempt to talk with her father. Essentially, Sally is unwilling to (won't) take the risk or sees it as not being worth the effort. If a group leader consistently and gently insists that members substitute "won't" for "can't," he or she is helping them own and accept their power by taking responsibility for their decisions.

■ **"Shoulds" and "Oughts"** Some group members seem to be ruled by "shoulds" and "oughts": "I should be interested in what others say in this group"; "I ought to care for everyone, and if I don't, I feel terrible"; "I should express only positive feelings"; and so on. The list of "shouldisms," both in daily life and in a group situation, is endless. Members can at least become aware of the frequency of their "should" and "ought" remarks and of the feelings of powerlessness that accompany their use.

One way of increasing one's awareness of the limitations imposed by a "should" standard is to experiment with changing phrases such as "I have to" or "I should" to "I choose to." For example, if Oscar says, "I hate to stay in school, but I *have* to because my parents expect this of me," he could say instead "I don't like school, but I *choose* to stay in school because I don't want to have a hassle with my parents."

In working with language, it is important to consider the stage of a group's development. If a leader or a member challenges someone's language during the early stages of a group, this can interfere with a sense of safety. Challenging the language of some members may result in their feeling criticized, judged, and not understood. Therefore, sensitivity and appropriate timing must be attended to as language is scrutinized.

Nonverbal Language

Skilled group counselors listen not just to the verbal level of communication but also, and even more keenly, to the message behind the words, which is often conveyed in the voice tone, pitch, and volume, in the speed of delivery, and so forth.

The group setting offers many opportunities to explore the meaning of nonverbal messages. Such explorations are especially useful when participants exhibit nonverbal cues that are incongruent with what they are saying verbally. For example, Dwight tells the group leader that he is angry with him for passing him over, but as he utters his angry words, he is smiling. The leader is likely to call to Dwight's attention the discrepancy between his angry words and his smile. Dwight may then be asked to carry on a dialogue between his words and his smile, or he may be asked to "become his smile" and give this smile a voice: "What is your smile saying?" This procedure gives Dwight the opportunity to discover for himself the meaning of the discrepancy. In fact he may be saying, "I want to let you know that I'm upset that you passed me by, yet I don't want to risk your disapproval by letting you know how angry I am."

Here are some other examples of how the exploration of nonverbal expressions can increase members' awareness of what they are really experiencing in the moment.

• Conrad typically carries himself in a slouched posture. The leader says: "Become aware of your posture; go around the group and tell what your posture says about yourself to each member of the group. Complete the sentence 'I am my posture, and what I am telling you about me is _____!' "

• Maiko tends to speak in a soft voice and with a very tight mouth. The leader invites her to give a speech to the group and consciously exaggerate these mannerisms. She could "become her tight mouth" and say something like: "I'm holding my words and myself back from you. I'm not going to be open, and if you want something from me, you'll have to pry me open."

• Manuel comes across as though he were always delivering a lecture to an audience. Group members have told him that his voice and his style of speaking create a barrier between him and others. He could be asked to stand before the group and give a lecture, perhaps on the value of lecturing people.

Examples of how people deal with nonverbal cues are endless. Creative group leaders can invent a wide variety of experiments designed to help participants become increasingly aware of what they are communicating through their eye contact, mannerisms, subtle gestures, tone of voice, and hand movements, as well as through their whole bodies. Group leaders would do well to avoid making bold interpretations—for example, that keeping one's arms crossed means that one is closed—and instead encourage members to merely pay attention to the nonverbal cues they emit.

Experiments with Internal Dialogues

Because a goal of Gestalt therapy is to achieve integrated function and the acceptance of aspects of one's personality that have been disowned and denied, therapists pay close attention to splits and polarities in personality function. Fantasy dialogues are meant to promote awareness of internal splits and eventual personality integration. These dialogues can take many forms, for example, dialogues between opposing sides or polarities within oneself (like tender/tough, masculine/feminine, loving/hateful, active/passive) and dialogues with a parent or other significant person, fantasized others, or inanimate objects.

Understanding how polarities are related to inner conflicts is central to Gestalt therapy. A variety of experiments with dialogues can help members increase their awareness of the dichotomies within themselves and help them come to terms with dimensions of their personality that seem to oppose each other. Our self-concept often excludes painful awareness of the polarities within us. We would rather think of ourselves as bright than as dull, as kind than as cruel, as loving than as unloving, and as sensitive than as indifferent. Typically, we may resist "seeing" in ourselves those parts that we don't want to accept as being part of who we are. Although we can recognize the altruistic side of ourselves, we might have trouble coming to terms with our self-centered nature. Ideally, as we move closer to becoming psychologically mature and healthy, we are aware of most of the polarities within ourselves, including those thoughts and feelings that society does not sanction. As we become more tolerant of the complexities and seeming contradictions within us, there is less of a tendency to expend energy on fighting to disown those parts of our nature that we don't want to accept.

Dialogue experiments are a powerful method of contacting parts of our nature that we work hard at keeping secret from both ourselves and others.

Learning how to carry on a conversation between our feminine and masculine sides, for instance, is one way of bringing to the surface inner conflicts we might have with these polarities. Alternately becoming each side as fully as we can is a way to *experience* both of these facets of our personality.

Dialogue experiments are typically used to heighten awareness of introjections and projections. In introjection, we uncritically take in aspects of other people, especially parents, and incorporate them into our personality. The danger of uncritical and wholesale acceptance of another's values as our own is that it can prevent personality integration. Gestalt techniques are aimed at getting these introjections out in the open, so that we can take a good look at what we have been swallowing whole without digesting it.

For example, by experimenting with fantasy dialogues, Joaquin becomes aware of some of the messages he has bought into without question: one must be practical; one ought to cling to security and never set out on a new path unless one has carefully assessed all the odds; only irresponsible people seek fun for the sake of fun—in other words, a long list of "dos," "don'ts," "shoulds," and "shouldn'ts" that keep him from enjoying life. At last, Joaquin begins to realize that he has listened to these directives from others and given others the power to direct his life. Through dialogues with the different facets of himself, Joaquin becomes aware that he wants to reclaim this power for himself.

Making the Rounds

A fruitful experiment can be designed that encourages a member to go around to each of the group members and say something that he or she usually does not communicate verbally. For example, assume that Larry sees himself as a self-made man who needs nothing from others. Although he may not say this about himself, the theme of "I can do it by myself" runs through much of his life. For the purpose of seeing how this theme actually determines what he does, he could be asked to stand before each member in the group and tell that person something about himself and then add, "and [or but] I can do everything by myself." Thus, Larry goes to Yesenia and says, "I never ask for emotional support from others, and at times I feel lonely . . . but I can do everything by myself." He then goes to Marie and says, "I make all the decisions in my business . . . and I can do everything by myself." The aim of this experiment is to have him feel fully what it's like for him to be so self-reliant, to the extent that he will not ask help from anyone. Ultimately, he may decide to continue to do things for himself, but with the awareness of the price he pays for doing so. Or he may come to see that he doesn't have to be totally self-reliant and that he can be independent while letting others do things for him from time to time.

Here are a few more examples of the use of making the rounds:

- Paul says that he is afraid of women. He could make the rounds and say to each woman, "I'm afraid of you because _____." or "If I were to get close to you _____."

- Adriana worries about boring people in the group. She might be asked to make the rounds and, for each person, complete the sentence "One way I could bore you is by _____." or "You would be bored if I _____."
- Nisha says that she feels distant from the rest of the group, even though she would like to have a sense of identification. She could make the rounds and experiment with completing the sentence "One way I feel distant from you is _____." or "The way I am different from you is _____."

Fantasy Approaches

Experimenting with a diversity of fantasy situations in a group can lead to significant growth. Fantasy can promote personal awareness in a number of ways, as the following brief list suggests.

- Fantasy can be used when members are too threatened to deal with a problem in concrete terms. For example, members who are afraid to be assertive can imagine themselves in situations in which they are assertive. Thus, they can compare what they feel when they are passive with what they feel when they are able to ask for what they want.
- Fantasy approaches are useful in dealing with catastrophic expectations, which often result in a sense of paralysis. Members who are afraid to express what they think and feel to someone they love can be guided through a fantasy situation in which they say everything they want to say but are afraid to express. Essentially the person speaks in the here-and-now to the loved one (as if he or she were present) in front of the group. The leader may say: "Pick someone in this group to be your mother [or some other significant person]. Borrow this member's eyes and tell your mother what you most want her to hear." There is a possible psychological value in working through these feelings in the safety of the fantasy approach, because the person may be able to release submerged feelings that have become split off. Note that it is not necessary for the person to express these feelings in real life; as a matter of fact, to do so could be unwise.
- Fantasy is a useful and safe way to explore the members' fears about involving themselves in the group. For example, members can be asked to imagine the thing they most fear occurring in the group. If, for example, some members are afraid of being rejected by the group, they can be directed to imagine that everyone is systematically rejecting them and then work with the feelings associated with this fantasy.

There are constructive uses of fantasy that, after having been tried in the group, can be carried outside of it. At times members can be invited to picture themselves as they wish they were in interpersonal situations. They might share their fantasies aloud in the group as they experience themselves in powerful, alive, creative, and dynamic ways. Then they can be asked to try acting in the group as if they were the person they imagined themselves to be. If the experiment is successful, members may feel encouraged enough to try the new behavior in real-life situations.

Rehearsal

In everyday life situations we often rehearse for roles we think we are expected to play, and we worry that we may not say the "right" thing and perform "properly." Internal rehearsing consumes much energy and frequently inhibits spontaneity. By participating in a rehearsal experiment, members say *out loud* what they are thinking silently. This can be especially useful when it is obvious that members are doing a lot of blocking and censoring and when what they say seems carefully measured out for a certain effect. Again, suggesting this kind of experiment must be timed properly, and it must emerge from the situation in which a member is struggling in some way. Rehearsals are not designed to stir up emotions but to bring into sharper awareness a process that is typically done without awareness. For example, during the initial stages of one of my groups, Sherry was quite silent and appeared to be developing an observer's stance. When I asked her if she was indeed saying everything she wanted to say, she shook her head in denial. So I asked her to express aloud some of the random thoughts she had as she was sitting there in silence.

Rehearsal can also be fruitful when a member is anticipating some future confrontation. Assume that Klaus wants to tell his boss that he doesn't feel appreciated and that he wants to be recognized for his accomplishments. Klaus can, in fantasy, picture himself standing before his boss, ready to tell him what he wants to say. Klaus's out-loud rehearsal could go something like: "I'm standing here like a fool. What if I mess up? He won't listen to me, and I don't really have anything to say. How can I let him know what I'm thinking? Right now I feel like running away and apologizing."

In a Gestalt group the participants share their rehearsals with one another to become more aware of the many preparations they go through in performing their social roles. By doing so, they become more aware of how they strive to please others, of the degree to which they want to be accepted and approved, and of the extent of their efforts to avoid alienating others. And then they can decide whether this role playing is worth the effort.

The Reversal Experiment

Certain symptoms and behaviors often represent reversals of underlying or latent impulses. The reversal experiment asks participants to become a side of themselves that they rarely or never express, because they don't want to see it and accept it. The theory underlying the use of this intervention is that integration is possible when people allow themselves to plunge into the very thing that produces anxiety and make contact with those parts of themselves that have been submerged and denied. Groups provide plenty of timely opportunities for using reversal methods.

I remember the case of a young man who was excessively nice, overly polite, and constantly trying to "do things" for other people. I suggested that he experiment with asking other people in the group to do something for him.

He had great difficulty carrying out my suggestion, but eventually he suc-
ceeded. The experiment made him aware of how uncomfortable he was with
accepting something from others. Also, it gave him an increased awareness of
the denied side of himself and a chance to integrate it.

Other examples of the reversal method are asking someone who says almost nothing to take on the role of monopolizer and deliberately interrupt the
group, or inviting someone with inferiority feelings to play the role of being
superior. Often I've found that this and similar techniques truly help people
become aware of and reconcile polarities within themselves.

The Exaggeration Experiment

This experiment involves becoming more aware of the subtle signals and cues
we send through body language. Clients are asked to repeat and intensify a
particular behavior for the purpose of bringing out-of-awareness emotional
processes to awareness (Strumpfel & Goldman, 2002). Movements, postures,
and gestures are exaggerated so that the meanings they communicate become
clearer. By exaggerating the movement or gesture repeatedly, the person experiences more intensely the feelings associated with the behavior and becomes
more aware of its inner meaning.

For example, if the leader notices that Sandy consistently nods her head in
an approving way when people speak, the leader could ask Sandy to go before
each group member and really give in to her head nodding while, at the same
time, putting words with this action. Other examples of behavior that lends
itself to the exaggeration technique are habitually smiling while expressing
painful or negative emotions, trembling, clenching one's fists, tapping one's
foot, crossing one's arms tightly, and pointing a finger at someone.

Berrin, a group member, said, "I feel burdened by listening to everyone's
problems in here!" At an earlier session, Stephen had confronted Berrin for intervening so quickly and trying to make him feel better when he was working
on conflicts he was having with his family. She then revealed that during her
childhood years she typically assumed the role of family arbitrator, always
doing her best to smooth over the battles in her family. Berrin eventually said
that she was sick and tired of carrying everyone's burdens; it weighed her
down and gave her a heavy feeling.

A technique for working with the material that Berrin was providing involved asking her to pick up some heavy objects and hold them as she looked
at each person in the group. She could be invited to allow herself to get into the
experience of the heaviness and being burdened. For example, while holding
the heavy objects, she might make the rounds and complete the sentence
"Looking at you I am burdened by _____." Or she might say something to
each member like "Here, let me take on all your burdens; I really enjoy carrying everyone's problems and I just wouldn't know what to do if I didn't have
all these burdens weighing me down!" Even though she said that she was sick
and tired of carrying around everyone's burdens, we encouraged her to allow
herself to give in to the part of herself that felt burdened and experiment with

telling others all the benefits of being this way. The rationale here was that if she could fully experience being burdened there was a good chance she could allow herself to experience shedding these burdens and being light, at least for a few moments. Again, this experiment is related to the reversal experiment in that the member is asked to play with polarities. Often the best way to discover the aspect of ourselves that we say we'd like to experience more of is to allow ourselves to stay with that part of us that we want to avoid.

Dream Work

Consistent with its noninterpretive spirit, the Gestalt approach does not interpret and analyze dreams. Instead, the intent is to bring the dream back to life, to re-create it, and to relive it as if it were happening now. If you are interested in a detailed presentation of the Gestalt approach to dream work, good sources are Downing and Marmorstein (1973), Perls (1969a), Polster and Polster (1973), Rainwater (1979), and Zinker (1978). Here is a brief description of this approach.

Group members don't report their dreams or talk about them in the past tense. Instead, they are asked to tell the dream as if it were happening in the present. Dreamers become immersed in their dreams with more vitality when they narrate dreams as though they are happening now. Members can be asked to identify with a segment of the dream and to narrate their dream from a subjective perspective. Group members may be asked to transform key elements of the dream into a dialogue and become each part of the dream. The group context allows them to play out parts of the dream as present events.

Dreams contain existential messages; they represent our conflicts, our wishes, and key themes in our lives. By making a list of all the details in a dream—remembering each person, event, and mood—and then acting out ("becoming") each of these parts as fully as possible, one becomes increasingly aware of one's opposing sides and of the range of one's feelings. Eventually the person appreciates and accepts his or her inner differences and integrates the conflicting forces; each piece of work on a dream leads to further assimilation and integration. By avoiding analyzing and interpreting the dream and focusing instead on becoming and experiencing it in all its aspects, the client gets closer to the existential message of the dream. Freud calls the dream "the royal road to the unconscious"; Perls (1969a) calls it "the royal road to integration" (p. 66).

The Polsters (1973) see dreams as a projection of the dreamer. All aspects of the dream are representations of the dreamer. They also view dreams as a road to contact. As dreamers acknowledge their kinship with the many aspects of their dream, they are also extending their own sense of diversity, broadening the experience of self, and centering themselves in the world. Dreams can be used in groups quite creatively "as a starting point for discoveries about present relationships with other group members or the therapist or with a recognition of an existential position which bears exploration using the dream only as a point of departure" (p. 273).

The Polsters give the example of a man (Fred) in a group who dreams a large frog is always watching him and is ready to jump. The group leader can suggest a number of creative experiments to increase contact between Fred and others in the group. The leader might ask Fred to describe his experience of the group as he relates his dream in the present tense. Fred might be asked, "What would you like to say to the members in this group?" If Fred were to indicate that they might see something in him that he doesn't want them to see, he could be asked to imagine what each person sees in him as they watch him. The dream work is an interactive process that enables Fred to experience more intensely his sense of being watched and his fears of being jumped on. It could be that Fred has some unfinished business with the group about a time when he thought they jumped on him.

Here are some suggestions to group leaders for helping members explore their dreams in a group:

- The member can be asked to relive the dream as though it were happening right now.
- After dreamers have had an opportunity to recount a dream in the present tense, they can be asked any one of these questions: "What are you experiencing now?" "What was it like for you to recount your dream?" "What interests you most about the dream?"
- Have members choose an element of the dream that seems most like them and ask, "What element of the dream has the most energy?"
- It is useful to inquire if there is a troublesome part of the dream. If there is, it is important to address it early so that there is time to work on it.
- Members can be encouraged to "become" different parts of a dream. For example, members become all the people in the dream. Are any of them significant people? They can "become" objects in the dream, especially objects that link and join, such as telephone lines and highways. They can identify any powerful force, such as a storm.
- A way for members to become a part of a dream is for them to assume the identity of a person or an object by giving voice and personality to this dream element. For example, Fred might become the frog who is ready to jump and speak for the frog. Fred could create a dialogue between being the frog and being a particular member in the group. It is essential to allow sufficient time for a dialogue between elements in the dream. It is helpful to stay with the dialogue by encouraging the dreamer to have several interchanges between different aspects of the dream.

Rainwater (1979) offers a number of suggestions to dreamers for exploring their dreams:

- Become any two contrasting objects, such as a younger person and an older person.
- Be anything that is missing in the dream. If you don't remember your dreams, then speak to your missing dreams.
- Be alert for any numbers that appear in the dream; become these numbers, and explore associations with them.

Rainwater suggests that in working with a dream, notice how you feel when you wake up. Is your feeling state one of fear, joy, sadness, frustration, surprise, anger? Identifying the feeling tone may be the key to finding the meaning of the dream. In working with dreams in Gestalt style, dreamers can focus on questions such as "What are you doing in the dream?" "What are you feeling?" "What do you want in the dream?" "What are your relationships with other objects and people in the dream?" "What kind of action can you take now?" and "What is your dream telling you?"

Group experiments can emerge out of the dream work of individuals in a group. Zinker (1978) has developed an approach he calls *dream work as theater*, which goes beyond working with an individual's dream. After a dream is reported and worked through by a participant, a group experiment is created that allows other members to benefit therapeutically from the original imagery of the dreamer. Based on his assumption that all the members share certain archetypal themes, Zinker suggests that various images within a dream can be used to enhance self-understanding. Each plays out a part of the dream. This offers the group participants many opportunities for enacting certain dimensions of the dream that relate both to the dreamer and to their own life.

For example, assume that one of the members, Kara, has had a dream that contains a broken-down car, a man shooting at people in the car, and a woman trying to save the passengers. One member may choose to take on the identity of the person doing the shooting, another can take on the role of one of the people in the car being shot at, and still another can be the car that doesn't function. Each of the members can play out his or her part, and the dreamer can help them understand the characters or objects in the dream. The group leader can facilitate the production of the dream as a dramatic and therapeutic experience for the entire group. There are many advantages to this approach in increasing group cohesion and linking one member's work with others.

The dreams of group participants may have implications for how they feel in their group. For example, Kara may discover that she feels frightened in the group and would like to escape. She may feel attacked (shot at) by one or more members, with a woman coming to her rescue. In this case she can act out her dream in the group by selecting the person by whom she feels most seriously attacked and talking to that person directly. She can then become the broken-down car—her powerless vehicle of escape—and see what insights this association brings. She can also pick out the woman in the group by whom she feels most supported and have a dialogue with her. She might reverse roles, becoming the person doing the shooting. Working with the dream in this way has rich potential for dealing with unfinished business with others in the group.

Applying Gestalt Therapy to Group Work in the Schools

Gestalt therapy is grounded on existential principles. The genuineness of the group leader and the quality of the therapeutic relationships between the leader and members (and among the members themselves) are given primary emphasis. This emphasis on creating quality therapeutic relationships fits well with what is required for conducting successful groups with both children and adolescents. More than the techniques group leaders employ, it is the personal dimensions that leaders are able to bring to a group that increase the involvement of young people in a group.

As you have read, Gestalt group work places a premium on the quality of the contact between the individual and the group (M. Polster, 1997). In this respect the Gestalt approach has some common denominators with both the existential and person-centered approaches. I think this is a main strength of Gestalt therapy, and children and adolescents are likely to respond to this collaborative spirit. Specific applications of Gestalt interventions with children can be seen in the works of Lederman (1969), Oaklander (1978), and Owmby (1983). In her book, *Anger in the Rocking Chair*, Lederman (1969) describes her Gestalt awareness work with children by asking them to put people into the rocking chair and express their feelings. Not only are the children able to experience a catharsis if they have feelings of resentment, but they are also able to begin to see other options besides blaming others for their problems.

Although Lederman applies Gestalt techniques with children in a special education setting, the Gestalt awareness interventions she describes can be productively adapted to working with children and adolescents in other school settings as well. In her book, *Windows to Our Children*, Oaklander (1978) describes various Gestalt techniques for children, which can be adapted to group work. Oaklander sees value in projection through art and storytelling as ways of increasing a child's self-awareness. Like Lederman, Oaklander often uses the empty chair technique as a way to assist children in understanding and dealing with frustration, anger, resentment, and other unfinished business. Owmby (1983) has adapted the topdog-underdog technique in working with anger in children. By using the empty chair method, children can put their anger in another chair and gain some awareness of their anger. Children who are afraid of monsters can "become the monster" and explain their motivation for scaring children. Through actually experiencing both projection and retroflection in a group, children frequently come to a greater understanding of their feelings of anger and fear.

Techniques from Gestalt therapy may be limited in working with some adolescent groups, especially in the case of involuntary members. Middle school and high school students are often highly self-conscious and may not take kindly to what they perceive as "weird" techniques. Adolescents who may be reluctant to participate in certain Gestalt activities can be invited by a skillful group leader to take the risk of engaging in here-and-now experiments. The manner in which group leaders introduce role-playing interventions has a great deal to do with enlisting a cooperative spirit among these group members. Instead of adolescents merely talking about problems they have in their relationships, they might be surprised by how real the interactions become when they bring interpersonal difficulties to life by using present-centered methods advocated in Gestalt therapy.

I find that adolescents are generally fascinated with talking about dreams. Group leaders can use Gestalt dream work as an opening to exploring personal meanings within the group context. At first, adolescents are likely to report dreams. With some gentle coaxing, they can be encouraged to talk about their dreams as though they are happening now. Eventually, the members might enjoy and learn from becoming the different aspects of their dreams. Certainly there is value in asking members to attribute the meanings their dreams have for them in light of their present concerns. Through Gestalt dream work, adolescents can gain significant insights into what their dreams are telling them.

Applying Gestalt Therapy with Multicultural Populations

There are many opportunities for Gestalt leaders to exercise their creativity with diverse client populations. People in many cultures give attention to expressing themselves nonverbally rather than emphasizing the content of oral communication. Some clients may express themselves nonverbally to a greater extent than they do with words. For example, group leaders may ask members to focus on their gestures, facial expressions, and the experience within their own body. If a group member, Eduardo, says that he is feeling threatened, the leader may invite him to pay attention to his bodily reactions. Some very creative work can emerge from work with people's gestures and body sensations. If Eduardo is having a struggle between two conflicting parts within himself, one hand could represent one side of the conflict, and the other hand, the other side of the conflict. He might be willing to engage in some Gestalt experiments as a way of heightening his own present experience and of clarifying the nature of his struggle. One of the advantages of drawing on Gestalt experiments is that they can be tailored to fit the unique way in which an individual member perceives and interprets his or her culture. Of course, before Gestalt procedures are introduced, especially with culturally different group members, it is essential that the clients have been adequately prepared.

The use of imagery and fantasy has much potential if members are well prepared and if there is a high degree of trust within the group. Assume that Anita is dealing with unfinished business pertaining to guilt surrounding the death of a loved one. She can make significant inroads into completing this unfinished business by bringing this dead person symbolically into the room and dealing with her in the present. If English is her second language, Anita can be asked to speak in her original language. However, such an exercise may be resisted by the client on two counts: it may be difficult for her to talk about the dead person, let alone "speak directly" to her; she may also argue that it would be more comfortable for her if she spoke in English.

There are certain advantages in using a Gestalt approach with culturally diverse client populations. Gestalt therapy pays attention to how clients view their world, and therapists attend to what is figural for members out of their diverse backgrounds. Because Gestalt therapy is practiced with a phenomenological attitude, therapists are less likely to impose their own values and cultural standards on their clients.

However, there are definite cautions in too quickly utilizing some Gestalt experiments with ethnic minority clients. As is evident from this chapter, these interventions often lead to an expression of emotions. This focus on affect has some limitations with those clients who have been culturally conditioned to be emotionally reserved, or at least not to publicly express their emotions, since doing so is viewed as a sign of weakness and a display of one's vulnerability. Certainly, an effective Gestalt leader would invite such clients to explore their feelings, thoughts, and attitudes surrounding being vulnerable. Ineffective leaders who push for catharsis are likely to find certain clients becoming increasingly resistant, and these members may eventually terminate. For instance, clients who are reluctant to experience and express their emotions will probably not take kindly to the therapist's suggestion that they "talk to the empty chair."

Thompson and Rudolph (2000) point out further limitations of applying Gestalt therapy to diverse cultural groups. People who have experienced oppression may perceive the emphasis on individual responsibility as a minimization of the role of societal factors in contributing to their problems. For example, group members from Latino and Asian cultures may not appreciate the Gestalt emphasis on experiencing and expressing feelings. American Indian clients may object to what they perceive as discounting the past. Although these limitations can be escalated by ill-timed interventions on the leader's part, timely Gestalt interventions can be one approach in helping clients work through some of their deeper resistances and struggles. More than the methods themselves, the manner in which these interventions are presented to members determines the outcomes. The criticisms of Gestalt therapy's value with multicultural populations are often based on misconceptions of this approach as being confrontational and of being a technique-oriented therapy.

Evaluation of the Gestalt Approach to Groups

Contributions and Strengths of the Approach

In his discussion of the distinctive characteristics of Gestalt therapy, Cain (2002) identifies these ideas as being the most significant contributions of this approach:

- The critical importance of contact with oneself, others, and the environment
- The central role of authentic relationship and dialogue in therapy
- The emphasis on field theory, phenomenology, and awareness
- The therapeutic focus on the present; the here-and-now experiencing of the client
- The creative and spontaneous use of active experiments as a pathway to experiential learning

One of the strengths of this approach is the attempt to integrate theory, practice, and research. Strumpfel and Goldman (2002) note that both process and outcome studies have advanced the theory and practice of Gestalt therapy. Process research is appropriate for the process orientation of Gestalt therapy.

Strumpfel and Goldman summarize a number of significant findings based on outcome research:

- Outcome studies have demonstrated Gestalt therapy to be of equal or greater benefit than other therapies for various disorders.
- More recent studies have shown that Gestalt therapy has beneficial effects with personality disturbances, psychosomatic problems, and substance addictions.
- The effects of therapy tend to be stable in follow-up studies one to three years after termination of treatment.
- Gestalt therapy has demonstrated effectiveness in treating a variety of psychological disorders.

Strumpfel and Goldman (2002) conclude: "Within the field of humanistic psychotherapy, research and development in Gestalt therapy have shown how powerful and effective therapy can be in helping people lead healthier and more fulfilling lives (pp. 212–213).

Indeed, I find that Gestalt experiments are powerful and often lead to the expression of immediate emotions and the reexperiencing of old feelings. As is the case with psychodramatic techniques, the Gestalt present-centered methods of reenacting early life experiences bring a certain vitality both to an individual's work and to the participants of the group.

Another distinctive feature of Gestalt therapy is its focus on the body. In an excellent book dealing with the role of the body in psychotherapy, Kepner (1993) demonstrates how a client's posture, movements, and bodily experiences can be incorporated into the practice of Gestalt therapy. Without making interpretations for members, leaders can encourage them to pay attention to what they are experiencing bodily. This focus can provide rich clues to areas members want to avoid, and it also offers a way for members to come in contact with their anxiety. If the leader avoids telling members the meaning of their gestures, postures, and body symptoms, members are more able to stay with what they are experiencing and eventually find their own meaning.

Limitations of the Approach

Gestalt interventions tend to bring out participants' emotions, which makes it tempting for a leader to focus on feelings and sometimes give less attention to cognitive factors. Helping participants discover the meaning of their emotional experiences is a significant factor in producing personality changes that will extend beyond the group. Although the earlier phase of Gestalt therapy's development did not focus on cognitive processes, more recent versions of Gestalt therapy address cognitive factors and integrate the affective and cognitive dimensions of human experiencing (see Harman, 1984; E. Polster, 1987a; M. Polster, 1987; Yontef, 1993; Yontef & Jacobs, 2000). Also, contemporary Gestalt therapy focuses more on relationships and less on techniques.

A major concern I have about Gestalt therapy is the potential misuse of power. Typically, Gestalt therapists are active and directive, and if they do not have the characteristics mentioned by Zinker (1978)—sensitivity, timing, inventiveness, empathy, and respect for the client—the experiments can easily boomerang. Also, the members can grow accustomed to the leader's assuming the initiative in creating experiments for them instead of coming up with some of their own experiments. With an approach that can have powerful effects on members, either constructive or destructive, ethical practice requires adequate training and supervision. The most immediate limitation of Gestalt therapy or any other therapy is the skill, knowledge, training, experience, and judgment of the therapist. Yontef (1995a) indicates that therapists who are poorly trained in Gestalt therapy are likely to use techniques without knowing the goals of therapy, what is central to the client's experience, and what alternative methods might be appropriate.

Inept therapists may use powerful interventions to stir up feelings and open up problems that members have kept from full awareness, only to abandon the members once they have managed to have a dramatic catharsis. Such leaders fail to help members work through what they have experienced and bring some closure to it. Some leaders assume an imposing style, which increases the potential for abuse of power. Those leaders who impose on members are more interested in what they want than in what the members want from them. In the imposing stance, group leaders are less concerned with understanding and respecting the members' experience than they are with making something happen (Frew, 1992).

It is easy to see that many of the Gestalt methods have the potential for offering a tempting place for group leaders to hide their personal responses and forget about the I/Thou relationship, especially those leaders who adopt an imposing style. Through the use of confrontive techniques, leaders can direct the pressure primarily toward the members. It is essential for Gestalt practitioners to learn how to confront in a manner that respects the client's reluctance or resistance. A blend of support and challenge goes a long way in creating the kind of relationship that enables clients to explore their defensiveness.

Some Gestalt practitioners make the mistake of becoming too rigid, pushing such injunctions as "Always be in the present" or "Take responsibility for yourself." There are some situations in which stopping what members are doing and asking them to bring something into the here-and-now is quite counterproductive. Gestalt leaders who have truly integrated their approach are sensitive enough to practice in a flexible way. They strive to help clients experience themselves as fully as possible in the present, yet they are not rigidly bound by dictates, nor do they routinely intervene with a directive whenever members stray from the present. Sensitively staying in contact with a member's flow of experiencing entails the ability to focus on the person and not on the mechanical use of techniques for a certain effect.

Where to Go from Here

If you have become interested in learning more about Gestalt theory and practice, I encourage you to attend a workshop led by a competent professional. You might consider pursuing Gestalt training, which would include attending workshops, seeking out personal therapy from a Gestalt therapist, and enrolling in a Gestalt training program that would involve reading, practice, and supervision.

Here are a few resources for training in Gestalt therapy:

Gestalt Institute of Cleveland, Inc.
1588 Hazel Drive
Cleveland, OH 44106-1791
TELEPHONE: (216) 421-0468
FAX: (216) 421-1729
E-MAIL: gestaltclv@aol.com
WEB SITE: www.gestaltcleveland.org

Gestalt Therapy Institute of the Pacific
1626 Westwood Blvd., Suite 104
Los Angeles, CA 90024
TELEPHONE: (310) 446-9720
FAX: (310) 475-4704
E-MAIL: Lynnejacobs@bigfoot.com
WEB SITE: www.gestalttherapy.org

The Center for Gestalt Development, Inc.
P.O. Box 990
Highland, NY 12528-0990
TELEPHONE: (845) 691-7192
FAX: (209) 671-3843
E-MAIL: tgjournal@gestalt.org
WEB SITE: www.gestalt.org

The Center for Gestalt Development, Inc. publishes *The Gestalt Directory*, which includes information about Gestalt practitioners and training programs throughout the world. The training center's program is described in detail, including admission requirements, costs, length of the program, certifications, and other pertinent data. Single copies of *The Gestalt Directory* are free of charge. Requests for a copy must be in writing or from the Web site. Also available are books, audiotapes, and videotapes dealing with Gestalt practice.

The Gestalt Journal, which is devoted to the theory and practice of Gestalt therapy, is available from the Center for Gestalt Development, Inc. Published twice yearly, it offers articles, reviews, and commentaries of interest to the practitioner, theoretician, academician, and student; the current subscription fee is $35.

Recommended Supplementary Readings

Interactive Group Therapy: Integrating Interpersonal, Action-Oriented and Psychodynamic Approaches (Earley, 2000) develops an action-oriented leadership style for group-centered work. Some Gestalt therapy concepts that are explored in this book are awareness and insight, defenses and resistances, presence and contact, and developmental stages of group process.

Beyond the Hot Seat: Gestalt Approaches to Group (Feder & Ronall, 1994) is the only book published that is exclusively devoted to Gestalt approaches to group work. It discusses the application of Gestalt theory to group practice. Separate chapters are devoted to Gestalt group process, family therapy, training groups, intensive workshops, and other clinical applications.

Creative Process in Gestalt Therapy (Zinker, 1978) is a beautifully written book that is a delight to read. Zinker's concepts are fleshed out with rich clinical examples. The book shows how Gestalt can be practiced in a creative and integrative style.

Gestalt Therapy Integrated: Contours of Theory and Practice (E. Polster & Polster, 1973) is a scholarly and penetrating treatment of some of the concepts underlying Gestalt practice. Theory and practice are successfully integrated in the personal style of the authors.

A Population of Selves: A Therapeutic Exploration of Personal Diversity (E. Polster, 1995) is based on the premise that every person is host to a population of selves. Polster illustrates eight major pathways for therapists to elicit new selves and to help their clients renew neglected or misunderstood selves.

From the Radical Center: The Heart of Gestalt Therapy (E. Polster & Polster, 1999) is an edited collection of central themes in the work of Erving and Miriam Polster. The 20 chapters in this book are taken from the various writings of the Polsters.

References and Suggested Readings*

Beisser, A. R. (1970). The paradoxical theory of change. In J. Fagan & I. L. Shepherd (Eds.), *Gestalt therapy now* (pp. 77–80). New York: Harper & Row (Colophon).

*Cain, D. J. (2002). Defining characteristics, history, and evolution of humanistic psychotherapies. In D. J. Cain, & J. Seeman, (Eds.), *Humanistic psychotherapies: Handbook of research and practice* (pp. 3–54). Washington, DC: American Psychological Association.

Downing, J., & Marmorstein, R. (Eds.). (1973). *Dreams and nightmares: A book of Gestalt therapy sessions*. New York: Harper & Row.

*Earley, J. (2000). *Interactive group therapy: Integrating interpersonal, action-oriented, and psychodynamic approaches*. Philadelphia, PA: Brunner/Mazel (Taylor & Francis Group).

*Feder, B. (1994). Safety and danger in the Gestalt group. In B. Feder & R. Ronall, (Eds.), *Beyond the hot seat: Gestalt approaches to group* (pp. 41–52). Highland, NY: The Gestalt Journal Press.

*Feder, B., & Ronall, R. (Eds.). (1994). *Beyond the hot seat: Gestalt approaches to group*. Highland, NY: The Gestalt Journal Press.

Frew, J. E. (1986). The functions and patterns of occurrence of individual contact styles during the development phase of the Gestalt group. *The Gestalt Journal, 9*(1), 55–70.

*Books and articles marked with an asterisk are suggested for further study.

*Frew, J. E. (1988). The practice of Gestalt therapy in groups. *The Gestalt Journal, 11*(1), 77–96.

Frew, J. E. (1992). From the perspective of the environment. *The Gestalt Journal, 15*(1), 39–60.

*Frew, J. E. (1997). A Gestalt therapy theory application to the practice of group leadership. *Gestalt Review, 1*(2), 131–149.

Greenberg, L. S., & Rice, L. N. (1997). Humanistic approaches to psychotherapy. In P. L. Wachel & S. B. Messer (Eds.), *Theories of psychotherapy: Origins and evolution* (pp. 97–129). Washington, DC: American Psychological Association.

Harman, R. L. (1984). Recent developments in Gestalt group therapy. *International Journal of Group Psychotherapy, 34*(3), 473–483.

*Hycner, R., & Jacobs, L. (1995). *The healing relationship in Gestalt therapy*. Highland, NY: The Center for Gestalt Development.

*Jacobs, L. (1989). Dialogue in Gestalt theory and therapy. *The Gestalt Journal, 12*(1), 25–67.

*Kepner, E. (1994). Gestalt group process. In B. Feder & R. Ronall, (Eds.), *Beyond the hot seat: Gestalt approaches to group* (pp. 5–24). Highland, NY: The Gestalt Journal Press.

Kepner, J. I. (1993). *Body process: Working with the body in psychotherapy*. San Francisco: Jossey-Bass.

Latner, J. (1986). *The Gestalt therapy book*. Highland, NY: Center for Gestalt Development.

Lederman, J. (1969). *Anger in the rocking chair*. New York: McGraw-Hill.

Levitsky, A., & Perls, F. (1970). The rules and games of Gestalt therapy. In J. Fagan & I. Shepherd (Eds.), *Gestalt therapy now*. New York: Harper & Row (Colophon).

Melnick, J. (1980). Gestalt group process therapy. *The Gestalt Journal, 3*(2), 86–96.

Oaklander, V. (1978). *Windows to our children*. Moab, UT: Real People Press.

Owmby, R. L. (1983). Gestalt therapy with children. *Journal of Gestalt Therapy, 6*, 51–58.

Passons, W. R. (1975). *Gestalt approaches in counseling*. New York: Holt, Rinehart & Winston.

*Perls, F. (1969a). *Gestalt therapy verbatim*. New York: Bantam. (Note: In 1992, published by The Gestalt Journal Press, Highland, NY)

Perls, F. (1969b). *In and out of the garbage pail*. New York: Bantam.

Polster, E. (1987a). Escape from the present: Transition and storyline. In J. K. Zeig (Ed.), *The evolution of psychotherapy* (pp. 326–340). New York: Brunner/Mazel.

*Polster, E. (1987b). *Every person's life is worth a novel*. New York: Norton.

*Polster, E. (1995). *A population of selves: A therapeutic exploration of personal diversity*. San Francisco: Jossey-Bass.

*Polster, E. (1997). The therapeutic power of attention: Theory and technique. In J. K. Zeig (Ed.), *The evolution of psychotherapy: The third conference* (pp. 221–229). New York: Brunner/Mazel.

*Polster, E., & Polster, M. (1973). *Gestalt therapy integrated: Contours of theory and practice*. New York: Brunner/Mazel.

*Polster, E., & Polster, M. (1999). *From the radical center: The heart of Gestalt therapy*. Cambridge, MA: The Gestalt Institute of Cleveland Press.

Polster, M. (1987). Gestalt therapy: Evolution and application. In J. K. Zeig (Ed.), *The evolution of psychotherapy* (pp. 312–322). New York: Brunner/Mazel.

*Polster, M. (1997). Beyond one-to-one. In J. K. Zeig (Ed.), *The evolution of psychotherapy: The third conference* (pp. 233–241). New York: Brunner/Mazel.

Polster, M., & Polster, E. (1990). Gestalt therapy. In J. K. Zeig & W. M. Munion (Eds.), *What is psychotherapy? Contemporary perspectives* (pp. 103–107). San Francisco: Jossey-Bass.

Rainwater, J. (1979). *You're in charge! A guide to becoming your own therapist.* Los Angeles: Guild of Tutors Press.

*Strumpfel, U., & Goldman, R. (2002). Contacting Gestalt therapy. In D. J. Cain, & J. Seeman, (Eds.), *Humanistic psychotherapies: Handbook of research and practice* (pp. 189–219). Washington, DC: American Psychological Association.

Thompson, C. L., & Rudolph, L. B. (2000). *Counseling children* (5th ed.). Pacific Grove, CA: Brooks/Cole.

*Yontef, G. (1993). *Awareness, dialogue and process: Essays on Gestalt therapy.* Highland, NY: The Gestalt Journal Press.

*Yontef, G. (1995a). Gestalt therapy. In A. S. Gurman & S. B. Messer (Eds.), *Essential psychotherapies: Theory and practice* (pp. 261–303). New York: Guilford.

Yontef, G. (1995b). Shame and guilt in Gestalt therapy: Theory and practice. In R. Lee & G. Wheeler (Eds.), *The voice of shame: Silence and connection in psychotherapy* (pp. 351–380). San Francisco: Jossey-Bass.

Yontef, G. (1999). Awareness, dialogue and process: Preface to the 1998 German edition. *The Gestalt Journal, 22*(1), 9–20.

*Yontef, G., & Jacobs, L. (2000). Gestalt therapy. In R. Corsini & D. Wedding (Eds.), *Current psychotherapies* (6th ed., pp. 303–339). Itasca, IL: F. E. Peacock.

*Zinker, J. (1978). *Creative process in Gestalt therapy.* New York: Random House (Vintage).

Zinker, J. (1994). The developmental process of a Gestalt therapy group. In B. Feder & R. Ronall (Eds.), *Beyond the hot seat: Gestalt approaches to group* (pp. 55–77). Highland, NY: The Gestalt Journal Press.

CHAPTER 12

Transactional Analysis

Introduction

Transactional analysis (TA) is both a theory of personality and an organized system of interactional therapy. It is grounded on the assumption that we make current decisions based on past premises—premises that were at one time appropriate to our survival needs but that may no longer be valid. TA emphasizes the cognitive, rational, and behavioral aspects of the therapeutic process. Within TA there are three recognized schools—classical, Schiffian (or reparenting), and redecisional—and two unofficial schools identified as self-reparenting and corrective parenting. The redecisional school has gained in prominence and is the focus of this chapter.

The goal of transactional analysis is autonomy, which is defined as awareness, spontaneity, and the capacity for intimacy. In achieving autonomy people have the capacity to make new decisions (redecide), thereby empowering themselves and altering the course of their lives. In therapy groups, TA participants learn how to recognize the three ego states—Parent, Adult, and Child—in which they function. Group members also learn how their current behavior is being affected by the rules and regulations they received and incorporated as children and how they can identify the "lifescript" that is determining their actions. Ultimately, they come to realize that they can now redecide and initiate a new direction in life, changing what is not working while retaining what serves them well.

TA provides an interactional and contractual approach to groups. It is interactional in that it emphasizes the dynamics of transactions between people, and it is contractual in that group members develop clear statements of what they will change and how they will be different as a result of being in group. Members establish their goals and direction and describe how they will be different when they complete their contract. Contracting allows for a more equal footing between client and therapist and demonstrates that the responsibility for change is shared between group member and therapist.

Historical Background

Transactional analysis was originally developed by the late Eric Berne (1961), who was trained as a Freudian psychoanalyst and psychiatrist. TA evolved out of Berne's dissatisfaction with the slowness of psychoanalysis in curing people of their problems. Berne's major objections to psychoanalysis were that it was time consuming, complex, and poorly communicated to clients. Historically, TA developed as an extension of psychoanalysis with concepts and techniques especially designed for group treatment. Berne discovered that by using TA his clients were making significant changes in their lives. As his theory of personality evolved, Berne parted ways with psychoanalysis to devote himself full time to the theory and practice of TA (Dusay, 1986).

Berne formulated most of the concepts of TA by paying attention to what his clients were saying. He began to see an ego state emerge that correlated to the childhood experiences of his patients. He concluded that there was a Child ego state that was different from the "grown-up" ego state. Later, he postulated that there were two "grown-up" states: one, which seemed to be a copy of the person's parents, he called the Parent ego state; the other, which was the rational part of the person, he named the Adult ego state.

One of Berne's contributions is his perspective on how young children develop a personal plan for their life as a strategy for physical and psychological survival. His view is that people are shaped from their first few years by a script that they follow during the rest of their lives.

Contemporary TA practitioners have moved in various directions and modified many of the basic concepts Berne formulated, and it is difficult to discuss practices that apply to all of them. This chapter will highlight the expansion of Berne's approach by Mary and the late Robert Goulding (1979), leaders of the redecisional school of TA. The Gouldings differ from the classical Bernian approach in a number of ways. They have combined TA with the principles and techniques of Gestalt therapy, family therapy, psychodrama, and behavior therapy. The redecisional approach helps group members experience their impasse, or the point at which they feel stuck. They relive the context in which they made earlier decisions, some of which were not functional, and they make new decisions that are functional. Redecisional therapy is aimed at helping people challenge themselves to discover ways in which they perceive themselves in victimlike roles and to take charge of their lives by deciding for themselves how they will change.

Basic Assumptions and Rationale for a Group Approach

Underlying the practice of TA group work is the premise that awareness is an important first step in the process of changing our ways of thinking, feeling, and behaving. In the early stages of a group, techniques are aimed at increasing participants' awareness of their problems and their options for making substantive changes in their lives.

Another basic assumption of TA is that all of us are in charge of what we do, of the ways in which we think, and of how we feel. Others do not make us feel in a certain way; rather, we respond to situations largely by our choices (R. Goulding, 1987).

The practice of TA is ideally suited for groups. Berne believed that group therapy yielded information about one's personal plan for life much more quickly than individual therapy. Redecision therapy, as introduced by the Gouldings, is conducted in a group context in which members can experience their script coming to life by reliving early memories and by interacting with others in the group. From a redecisional perspective, group therapy is the treatment of choice. People change more rapidly than they do in individual therapy, and groups seem to add a human quality to therapy (R. Goulding, 1987).

There are many avenues of self-understanding through analyzing transactions within the group. In the same way that Gestalt groups function in the here-and-now, TA groups bring past issues into the present. Group members facilitate action by representing both family members from the past and contemporaries. Because of the interaction within the TA group, members have easier access to their script content by virtue of others' more personal work. By identifying early decisions and appreciating how valuable they were at the time they were made, members are challenged to see what they would prefer given the reality of today. The redecision is a decision that is truly empowering. For Robert Goulding, one rationale for a group is that it provides a living experience that members can take out to their family, friends, and community.

Key Concepts

The Ego States

An ego state is a set of related thoughts, feelings, and behaviors in which part of an individual's personality is manifested at a given time (Stewart & Joines, 1987). All transactional analysts work with ego states, which encompass important facets of the personality and are considered to be essential and distinguishing characteristics of TA therapy (Dusay, 1986). Each person has a basic trio of Parent, Adult, and Child (P-A-C). According to TA, people are constantly shifting from one of these states to another, and their behavior at any one time is related to the ego state of the moment. One definition of autonomy is the capacity to move with agility and intention through ego states and to operate in the one most appropriate to the reality of the given situation.

The Parent ego state contains the values, morals, core beliefs, and behaviors incorporated from significant authority figures, primarily one's parents. Outwardly, this ego state is expressed toward others in critical or nurturing behavior. Inwardly, it is experienced as old parental messages that continue to influence the inner Child. When we are in the Parent ego state, we react to situations as we imagine our parents might have reacted, or we may act toward others the way our parents acted toward us. The Parent contains all the "shoulds" and "oughts" and other rules for living. When we are in that ego state, we may act in ways that are strikingly similar to those of our parents or other significant people in our early life. We may use some of their very phrases, and our posture, gestures, voice, and mannerisms may replicate those that we experienced in our parents.

The Parent ego state is divided into Nurturing Parent (NP) and Controlling Parent (CP), both of which have positive and negative aspects. The positive aspect of Nurturing Parent is to affirm individuals for both being and doing. The negative aspect is called Marshmellow Parent, which can sound syrupy and discounts others with phrases such as "Oh, you poor thing." The positive aspect of Controlling Parent is to provide structure intended for the benefit or success of the individual, such as "Complete your homework before you watch television." The negative aspect of Controlling Parent is to be critical and often to discount the Child ego state in others.

The Adult ego state is the objective and computerlike part of our personality that functions as a data processor; it computes possibilities, makes decisions, and represents what we have learned and thought out for ourselves. The state is not related to chronological age. The Adult is a thinking state oriented toward current reality; the Adult is objective in gathering information, is nonemotional, and works with the facts of the external reality as perceived by that individual. The Adult often negotiates between the Child's wants and the Parent's shoulds.

The Child ego state is the original part of us and is most naturally who we are. It is the part of ourselves we use to form long-lasting relationships. The Child ego state consists of feelings, impulses, and spontaneous actions and includes "recordings" of early experiences. The Child ego state is divided into Natural Child (NC) and Adapted Child (AC), both of which have positive and negative aspects. The positive aspects of the Natural Child are the spontaneous, ever so lovable, loving and charming parts of all of us. The negative aspect of the Natural Child is to be impulsive to the degree our safety is compromised. The positive aspect of the Adapted Child is that we respond appropriately in social situations. The negative aspect of the Adapted Child involves overadapting wherein we give up our power and discount our value, worth, and dignity. Some TA theorists include the Rebellious Child in the domain of Adapted Child because one who continuously attempts to solve problems by rebelling is overadapting.

In a TA group, members are first taught how to recognize in which of the five ego states they are functioning at any given time: Nurturing Parent, Controlling Parent, Adult, Nurturing Child, or Adapted Child. The aim is to enable them to decide consciously whether that state or another state is most appropriate or useful. For example, a member who typically responds to others in a Controlling Parent style and who has contracted to become more tolerant toward others must recognize his or her habitual ego state before any steps can be taken to change.

The Need for Strokes

Humans need to be stimulated physically, socially, and intellectually. As we grow and develop, we need to be recognized for who we are and what we do. This need for stimulation and recognition is referred to as "strokes"; a stroke is any act of recognition or source of stimulation.

A basic premise of the TA approach is that humans need to receive both physical and psychological "strokes" to develop a sense of trust in the world and a basis for loving themselves. There is ample evidence that lack of physical contact can impair infant growth and development and, in extreme cases, can lead to death. Psychological strokes—verbal and nonverbal signs of acceptance and recognition—are also necessary to people as confirmations of their worth.

Strokes can be classified as verbal or nonverbal, unconditional (being) or conditional (doing), and positive or negative. Positive strokes that express warmth, affection, or appreciation verbally or with a look, smile, touch, or gesture are necessary for the development of psychologically healthy people. Negative strokes can be useful in that they set limits: "I don't like it when you use my computer without asking." Negative strokes are a way to give feedback to people about their behavior. They are sometimes essential in protecting children: "Stop right there! Don't go out into the street until I get to the curb and take your hand." Interestingly, negative strokes are considered preferable to no strokes at all—that is, to being ignored. We are all familiar with instances when children's actions elicit negative strokes from their parents. Even these responses are preferable to being ignored or dismissed.

Steiner (1974) describes strokes as exchanges. They can be offered, accepted or taken in, refused or rejected, and directly requested, such as "Will you tell me that you appreciate that I cooked dinner for you?" Another way strokes are exchanged is to self-stroke, such as "I did the best I could in putting my kids through college." TA group members are introduced to how they live the "stroke economy"; members can then examine their own use of these five restrictive rules about stroking:

- Don't give strokes when you have them to give.
- Don't ask for strokes when you need them.
- Don't accept strokes when you want them (and they are offered).
- Don't reject (negative) strokes when you don't want them.
- Don't give yourself strokes.

When group members understand how these exchanges affect their behavior, they can choose the kinds of exchanges they want to make. For example, Sabrina continually puts herself down with self-deprecating remarks. She either doesn't hear or soon forgets the positive feedback she gets from others in her group. When paid a sincere compliment, Sabrina finds some way to play it down or make a joke of it. If she is the focus of positive attention or receives any display of tenderness, affection, or caring, she becomes extremely uncomfortable, yet she remembers and stores up any critical remarks and feels depressed. As Steiner (1974) would put it, Sabrina collects the "cold pricklies" rather than the "warm fuzzies."

In her TA group Sabrina is confronted with the fact that she discounts her worth and doesn't allow others to give her positive strokes. She is also challenged to decide whether she wants to change her behavior. If she accepts the challenge to change, the group can help her learn how to ask for and accept positive strokes.

Injunctions and Counterinjunctions

The Gouldings' redecision work is grounded in the TA concepts of injunctions and early decisions (M. Goulding, 1987). When parents are excited by a child's behavior, the messages given are often *permissions*. However, when parents feel threatened by a child's behavior, the messages expressed are often *injunctions*, which are issued from the parents' Child ego state. Such messages—expressions of disappointment, frustration, anxiety, and unhappiness—establish the "don'ts" by which children learn to live. Out of their own pain, parents can issue this short, but profound list of general injunctions: "Don't." "Don't be." "Don't be close." "Don't be separate from me." "Don't be the sex you are." "Don't want." "Don't need." "Don't think." "Don't feel." "Don't grow up." "Don't be a child." "Don't succeed." "Don't be you." "Don't be sane." "Don't be well." "Don't belong" (M. Goulding, 1987; M. Goulding & Goulding, 1979). These messages are predominantly given nonverbally and at the psychological level between birth and 7 years of age.

According to Mary Goulding (1987), children decide either to accept these parental messages or to fight against them. If they do accept them, they decide precisely *how* they will accept them. The decisions children make about these injunctions become a basic part of their permanent character structure.

When parents observe their sons or daughters not succeeding, or not being comfortable with who they are, they attempt to "counter" the effect of the earlier messages with *counterinjunctions*. These messages come from the parents' Parent ego state and are given at the social level. They convey the "shoulds," "oughts," and "dos" of parental expectations. Examples of counterinjunctions are "Be perfect." "Try hard." "Hurry up." "Be strong." "Please me." The problem with these counterinjunctions is that no matter how much we try to please we feel as though we still are not doing enough or being enough. This demonstrates the rule that the messages given at the psychological level are far more powerful and enduring than those given at the social level.

In TA groups members explore the "shoulds" and "shouldn'ts," the "dos" and "don'ts" by which they have been trained to live. The first step in freeing oneself from behaviors dictated by the often irrational and generally uncritically received parental messages is awareness of the specific injunctions and counterinjunctions that one has accepted as a child. Once group participants have identified and become aware of these internalized "shoulds," "oughts," "dos," "don'ts," and "musts," they are in a better position to critically examine them to determine whether they are willing to continue living by them.

Decisions and Redecisions

As indicated earlier, transactional analysis emphasizes our cognitive, rational, and behavioral aspects, especially our ability to become aware of decisions that govern our behavior and of the capacity to make new decisions that will beneficially alter the course of our life. This section addresses the decisions made in response to parental injunctions and counterinjunctions and explains how TA group members learn to relive these early decisions and make new ones.

Let's look at an example of decision making that has been dictated by parental injunctions. A TA group member, Alejandro, apparently received the parental injunction, "Don't trust anybody." The decisions about behavior resulting from this injunction were implicit in many of Alejandro's characteristic pronouncements: "If you don't let yourself care, you won't be hurt." "If I keep to myself, I won't need anything from anyone." "Whenever I've wanted something from another, I've been hurt. It's just not worth getting involved with, or even close to, others." Indeed, it became clear in group sessions that by accepting his parents' injunctions against trusting people Alejandro consistently made decisions that caused him to avoid others. To support these decisions, Alejandro was able to find plenty of data—both in the group and in his everyday life—to maintain his view that trust would inevitably lead to hurt. Consequently he continued, often unwittingly, to abide by his parents' injunction.

In the TA group Alejandro not only had the opportunity to become aware of his decisions and of the injunctions behind them but was also helped to investigate whether these decisions were still appropriate. At one time the decisions to avoid people might have been necessary for Alejandro's physical and psychological safety—a matter of sheer survival. In the group Alejandro was able to question whether such decisions were serving any purpose now, or whether they were, instead, thwarting his development. He made a new decision to trust people and to approach them as friends, not enemies.

Even though injunctions and counterinjunctions carry the weight of parental authority, the Gouldings (1978, 1979) point out that the child must accept these messages if they are to have an impact on his or her personality. The Gouldings add that many injunctions under which children live are not issued by the parents but derive instead from the children's own fantasies and misinterpretations. It is important to note that a single parental injunction may foster a variety of decisions on the part of the child, ranging from reasonable to pathological. For example, the injunction "Don't be sane or well" may be responded to by one child deciding she'll become a psychiatrist; another may decide she actually is crazy and later collapse as a grown person and need residential care. Similarly, the injunction "Don't be you" may evoke decisions ranging from "I'll hide who I really am" to "I'll be someone else" to "I'll be a nobody" to "I'll kill myself, and then they'll accept me and love me." The injunction "Don't be you" is sometimes offered and taken as "Don't be the sex you are," resulting in gender-role confusion.

Whatever injunctions people have received, and whatever the resulting life decisions were, transactional analysis maintains that people can change by changing their decisions—by redeciding in the moment. A basic assumption of TA is that anything that has been learned can be relearned. In their groups the Gouldings develop an atmosphere in which members are challenged from the outset to make new decisions for themselves. Early in the course of a group, Robert Goulding (1975) would ask, "What did you decide to do to screw up your life, and what are you going to decide now to unscrew it?" (p. 246).

The group work related to making new decisions frequently requires members to return to the childhood scenes in which they arrived at self-limiting decisions. The group leader may facilitate this process with any of the following interventions: "As you are speaking, how old do you feel?" "Is what you are saying reminding you of any times when you were a child?" "What pictures are coming to your mind right now?" "Could you exaggerate that frown on your face? What are you feeling? What scene comes to mind as you experience your frowning?" Mary Goulding (1987) says that there are many ways of assisting a member to return to some critical point in childhood. "Once there," she adds, "the client reexperiences the scene; and then she relives it in fantasy in some new way that allows her to reject old decisions" (p. 288). After members experience a redecision from being in an old scene, they design experiments so that they can practice new behavior to reinforce their redecision both in and out of group.

Consider Helga, for example, who relives scenes with her parents when she was positively stroked for failing or was negatively stroked for succeeding. It was apparently at those times that she accepted the injunction "Don't succeed." The group challenges her to examine whether the decision, which may have been functional or even necessary in the past, is currently appropriate. She may redecide that "I will make it, and I am successful, even though it is not what you want from me."

Another group member, Kieran, is able to see that he responded to his father's injunction "Don't grow" by deciding to remain helpless and immature. He recalls learning that when he was independent his dad shouted at him and, when he was helpless, he was given his father's attention. Because he wanted his father's approval, Kieran decided, "I'll remain a child forever." During a group session, Kieran goes back to a childhood scene in which he was stroked for his helplessness, and he talks to his father now in a way that he never did as a child: "Dad, even though I still want your approval, I don't need it to exist. Your acceptance is not worth the price I'd have to pay. I'm capable of deciding for myself and of standing on my own two feet. I'll be the man that I want to be, not the boy that you want me to be."

In this redecision work Helga and Kieran enter the past and create fantasy scenes in which they can safely give up old and currently inappropriate early decisions, because both are armed with an understanding in the present that enables them to relive the scene in a new way. According to the Gouldings, it is possible to give a *new ending* to the scenes in which original decisions were made—a new ending that often results in a *new beginning* that allows clients to think, feel, and act in revitalized ways.

Games

A transaction, which is considered the basic unit of communication, consists of an exchange of strokes between two or more people. A game is an ongoing series of transactions that ends with a negative payoff called for by the script that concludes the game and advances some way of feeling badly. By their very nature, games are designed to prevent intimacy. Games consist of three basic elements: a series of complementary transactions that on the surface seem plausible; an ulterior transaction that is the hidden agenda; and a negative payoff that concludes the game and is the real purpose of the game.

Berne (1964) described an anthology of games originating from three positions: persecutor, rescuer, and victim. For example, people who have decided they are helpless may play some version of "Poor Me" or "Kick Me." A student "loses" or "forgets" her homework for the second time this week and makes the announcement publicly in class. The teacher gets angry, and the student takes the payoff and gets paid attention to in the process. People who feel superior may either persecute or rescue. The persecutor plays some form of "Gotcha" or "Blemish" (looking for the flaw), whereas the rescuer plays some form of "I am only trying to help you." Berne described a variety of common games, including "Yes, but," "Kick me," "Harassed," "If it weren't for you," "Martyr," "Ain't it awful," "I'm only trying to help you," "Uproar," and "Look what you made me do!" Games always have some payoff (or else they wouldn't be perpetuated), and one common payoff is support for the decisions described in the preceding section. For example, people who have decided that they are helpless may play the "Yes, but" game. They ask others for help and then greet any suggestions with a list of reasons why the suggestions won't work; thus, they feel free to cling to their helplessness. Addicts of the "Kick me" game are often people who have decided to be rejected; they set themselves up to be mistreated by others so that they can play the role of the victim whom nobody likes.

By engaging in game playing, people receive strokes and also maintain and defend their early decisions. They find evidence to support their view of the world, and they collect bad feelings. These unpleasant feelings that people experience after a game are known as *rackets*. A racket feeling is a familiar emotion that was learned and encouraged in childhood and experienced in many different stress situations, but it is maladaptive as an adult means of problem solving (Stewart & Joines, 1987). Rackets have much the same quality as feelings the people had as children. These rackets are maintained by actually choosing situations that will support them. Therefore, those who typically feel depressed, angry, or bored may be actively collecting these feelings and feeding them into long-standing feeling patterns that often lead to stereotypical ways of behaving. They also choose the games they will play to maintain their rackets. When people "feel bad," they often get sympathy from others or control others by their bad moods.

A group situation provides an ideal environment for the participants to become aware of the specific ways in which they choose game-playing strategies as a way of avoiding genuine contact and choose patterns of thinking, feeling, and behaving that are ultimately self-defeating. Group members can learn about their own games and rackets by observing the behavior of others in the group, as well as by analyzing how their responses in the group are connected to their responses to life situations in early childhood. By using the games they are currently playing in the group, members begin to understand that these games often give the appearance of intimacy but their actual effect is to create distance between people. Later, as members become aware of the more subtle aspects of game playing, they begin to realize that games prevent close human interaction. Consequently, if the members decide that they want to relate more closely to others, they also have to decide not to play games anymore.

Eventually, members are taught to make connections between the games they played as children and those they play now—for example, how they attempted to get attention in the past and how those past attempts relate to the games they play now to get stroked. The aim of this TA group process is to offer members the chance to drop certain games in favor of responding honestly—an opportunity that may lead them to discover ways of changing negative strokes and to learn how to give and receive positive strokes.

Basic Psychological Life Positions and Lifescripts

Decisions about oneself, one's world, and one's relationships to others are crystallized during the first five years of life. Such decisions are basic for the formulation of a life position, which develops into the roles of the lifescript. Generally, once a person has decided on a life position, there is a tendency for it to remain fixed unless there is some intervention, such as therapy, to change the underlying decisions. Games are often used to support and maintain life positions and to play out lifescripts. People seek security by maintaining that which is familiar, even though the familiar may be highly unpleasant. As we have seen earlier, games such as "Kick me" may be unpleasant, but they have the virtue of allowing the player to maintain a familiar position in life, even though this position is negative.

Transactional analysis identifies four basic life positions, all of which are based on decisions made as a result of childhood experiences, and all of which determine how people feel about themselves and how they relate to others:

1. I'm OK—You're OK.
2. I'm OK—You're not OK.
3. I'm not OK—You're OK.
4. I'm not OK—You're not OK.

The *I'm OK—You're OK* position is generally game-free. It is the belief that people have basic value, worth, and dignity as human beings. That people are OK is a statement of their essence, not necessarily their behavior. This position is characterized by an attitude of trust and openness, a willingness to give and take, and an acceptance of others as they are. People are close to themselves and to others. There are no losers, only winners.

I'm OK—You're not OK is the position of people who project their problems onto others and blame them, put them down, and criticize them. The games that reinforce this position involve a self-styled superior (the "I'm OK") who projects anger, disgust, and scorn onto a designated inferior, or scapegoat (the

"You're not OK"). This position is that of the person who needs an underdog to maintain his or her sense of "OKness."

I'm not OK—You're OK is known as the depressive position and is characterized by feeling powerless in comparison with others. Typically such people serve others' needs instead of their own and generally feel victimized. Games supporting this position include "Kick me" and "Martyr"—games that support the power of others and deny one's own.

The *I'm not OK—You're not OK* quadrant is known as the position of futility and frustration. Operating from this place, people have lost interest in life and may see life as totally without promise. This self-destructive stance is characteristic of people who are unable to cope in the real world, and it may lead to extreme withdrawal, a return to infantile behavior, or violent behavior resulting in injury or death of themselves or others.

In reality each of us has a favorite position we operate from under stress. The challenge is to become aware of how we are attempting to make life real through our basic life existential position and create an alternative. Related to the concept of basic psychological positions is the *lifescript*, or plan for life. A personal lifescript is an unconscious life plan made in childhood, reinforced by the parents, "justified" by subsequent events, and culminating in a chosen alternative (Stewart & Joines, 1987). This script, as we have seen, is developed early in life as a result of parental teaching (such as injunctions and counterinjunctions) and the early decisions we make. Among these decisions is selecting the basic psychological position, or dramatic role, that we play in our lifescript. Indeed, lifescripts are comparable to a dramatic stage production, with a cast of characters, a plot, scenes, dialogues, and endless rehearsals. In essence, the lifescript is a blueprint that tells people where they are going in life and what they will do when they arrive.

According to Berne (1972), through our early interactions with parents and others we receive a pattern of strokes that may be either supporting or disparaging. Based on this stroking pattern, we make a basic existential decision about ourselves; that is, we assume one of the four life positions just described. This existential decision is then reinforced by messages (both verbal and nonverbal) that we continue to receive during our lifetime. It is also reinforced by the results of our games, rackets, and interpretations of events. During our childhood years we also make the decision whether people are trustworthy. Our basic belief system is thus shaped through this process of deciding about ourselves and others. If we hope to change the life course that we are traveling, it helps to understand the components of this script, which to a large extent determine our patterns of thinking, feeling, and behaving.

Through a process known as *script analysis*, the TA group helps members become aware of how they acquired their lifescript and to see more clearly their life role (basic psychological life position). Script analysis helps members see the ways in which they feel compelled to play out their lifescript and offers them alternative life choices. Put in another way, the group process relieves participants of the compulsion to play games that justify behavior called for in their lifescript.

Script analysis demonstrates the process by which group members acquired a script and the strategies they employ to justify their actions based on it. The aim is to help members open up possibilities for making changes in their early programming. The participants are asked to recall their favorite stories as children, to determine how they fit into these stories or fables, and to see how these stories fit their current life experiences.

Steiner (1967) developed a lifescript questionnaire that can be used as a catalyst for script analysis in group situations to help members explore significant components of their lifescript—among them, life positions and games. In completing this script checklist, members provide basic information such as the general direction of their life, the models in their life, the nature of their injunctions, the payoffs they seek, and the tragic ending they expect from life.

The analysis of the lifescript of a group member is based on the drama of his or her original family. Through the process of acting out portions of their lifescript in the group sessions, members learn about the injunctions they uncritically accepted as children, the decisions they made in response to these messages, and the games and rackets they now employ to keep these early decisions alive. The group leader can gather information about the family drama by taking a history of the childhood experiences of the members. Members can be asked the kind of drama that would probably result if their family were put on the stage. Other group members can be given a part to play in this family play.

These and other cognitive and emotive techniques often help group participants recall early events and the feelings associated with them. The group setting provides a supportive place to explore the ways in which these past situations are influencing the participants. By being part of the process of self-discovery of other members, each member increases the opportunities for coming to a deeper understanding of his or her own unfinished psychological business.

The group situation allows members to analyze the positions they often take and the games they play, both in the group and in everyday life. As a result, group participants gain the capacity to take some initial steps to break out of self-defeating patterns. As the group members analyze their own life from a TA perspective, they can check the accuracy of their self-interpretations by asking for feedback from the leader and the other members.

Role and Functions of the Group Leader

Although TA is designed to develop both emotional and intellectual awareness, the focus is clearly on the cognitive aspects. As a teacher, the TA therapist explains concepts such as structural analysis, script analysis, and game analysis. The TA therapist functions as a consultant. As noted earlier, TA stresses the importance of equality in the client/therapist relationship, an equality that is manifested through contractual agreements between the group leader and the individual members, which make them mutual allies in the therapeutic process. Consequently, the role of the therapist is to apply his or her knowledge to fulfilling the contract the client initiates.

From the perspective of redecision therapy, the group leader's function is to create a climate in which people can discover for themselves how the games they play are supporting chronic bad feelings and how they hold on to these feelings to support their lifescript and early decisions. Another function of the TA therapist is challenging group members to discover and experiment with more effective ways of being. In short, the role of the therapist is to help members acquire the tools necessary to effect change.

The therapist's style in a TA group tends to promote individual work within a group setting rather than facilitating interaction between group members and thus encouraging therapy by the members. TA group leaders assume an active role and occupy a central position in the group. The focus tends to be on interactions between the group leader and individual members rather than on promoting free interaction among members. Although the transactional analyst is active in structuring the group sessions, is an active catalyst for the redecision, and confronts impasses, the group member does most of the actual work. It is assumed that group members have the power to change negative childhood decisions by developing their positive ego state forces.

Stages of a Transactional Analysis Group

The following summary of the redecisional approach to TA groups is based on an adaptation of some of the chief works of the Gouldings (1976, 1978, 1979; M. Goulding, 1987; R. Goulding, 1982). The core of the work in this approach consists of helping clients make redecisions while they are in their Child ego state. This is done by having them reexperience an early scene as if the situation were occurring in the present. Merely talking about past events or understanding early feelings and decisions from the Adult ego state is not sufficient to push members beyond the places where they are stuck. How the leader helps members get into their Child ego state and make a new decision can best be seen by examining the stages of redecisional group therapy.

The Initial Stage

The first step in the group process consists of establishing good contact. To a large extent, the outcome for group members depends on the quality of the relationship the group leader is able to establish with the members and on the leader's competence. Even when the group leader makes good contact with the members and is competent, the members' most important symptom is typically not brought forward initially (R. Goulding, 1982). Group participants sometimes tell what they think is significant but avoid addressing more pertinent issues. Therefore, the leader attempts to get at the chief complaint of the client. Obviously, the trust factor in the group has a lot to do with the willingness of clients to get to their chief complaint.

The next step in the process consists of making an inquiry into the group member's actual contract for change. A typical question is, "What are you going to change about yourself today?" Notice that members are not asked to state what they hope to change or what the therapist will do to bring about change; nor are they asked what changes they want in the future. The emphasis is on the client taking action now to do something that will bring about change.

The Working Stage

After contracts have been formulated, the Gouldings' approach to group explores rackets the members use to justify their lifescripts and, ultimately, their decisions (M. Goulding & Goulding, 1979). The aim is to expose the rackets of group members and have them take responsibility for them. For example, a person with an "anger racket"—one who is chronically angry—may be asked, "What do you do to maintain your anger?" Beginning with recent events, the person is led back through his or her life in an attempt to remember early situations involving anger. As in Gestalt therapy, members are asked to be in these situations—to recall them not as observers but as participants in the here-and-now. Members are asked to act out both their own responses and the responses of other significant people in the scene.

During this stage of group work, games are analyzed, mainly to see how they support and maintain rackets and how they fit with one's lifescript. In this connection much work is devoted to looking for evidence of the participants' early decisions, discovering the original injunction that lies at the base of these early decisions, and determining the kinds of strokes the person received to support the original injunction.

A major function of the TA group leader is to alert the members to take responsibility for their thinking, feeling, and behaving. Members are challenged when they use "cop-out language," such as "can't," "perhaps," "if it weren't for," "try," and other words that keep members from claiming their own power. The leader also creates a group climate in which the members rapidly become aware of how they maintain their chronic bad feelings by their behavior and fantasy. It is the therapist's task to challenge them to discover alternate choices.

The Gouldings take the position that clients can change *rapidly*, without years of analysis. It is clear that TA groups can be short term, solution focused, and structured in such a way that members acquire skills in addressing current and future problems. The Gouldings stress the decisional aspects of TA therapy on the assumption that when clients perceive that they are responsible for their early decisions they also have it in their power to change those decisions—and they can make these decisional shifts without drawing out the therapeutic process. This approach emphasizes helping participants reexperience early, highly emotional situations to generate the energy to break through the places where they are stuck (M. Goulding & Goulding, 1979). Such breakthroughs, according to the Gouldings, usually require that participants remember and relive situations involving real parenting figures. Through the use of fantasy, in which group members reexperience how their parents sounded, acted, and looked, the therapist creates a psychological climate that enables members to feel the same emotional intensity they felt when, as children, they made their original decisions. If participants are to be successful in going beyond an impasse, the Gouldings stress that they must be in the Child ego state and allow themselves to psychologically relive earlier scenes. Remaining in their Adult ego state and merely thinking about new insights is not enough for change to occur.

The Final Stage

Once a redecision is made from the Child ego state, the changes in one's voice, body, and facial expressions are obvious to everyone in the group. However, Robert Goulding (1982) emphasizes the importance of reinforcement of this redecision by the client and by the others in the group. The group process provides support for members who begin to feel and behave in new ways. Group members are encouraged to tell a new story in the group to replace their old story, and they typically receive verbal and nonverbal stroking to support their new decision. Attention is also given to ways that members might devise other support systems outside the group. It is also important for members to plan specific ways in which they will change their thinking, feeling, behavior, and body.

The focus during the final phase of group work is on challenging members to transfer their changes from the therapy situation to their daily life and then supporting them in these changes. Before members set out on their own, it is important that they fantasize about how some of their changes are likely to lead to other changes. It is well for them to prepare themselves for the new situations they will face when they leave the group and to develop support systems that will help them creatively deal with new problem situations as they arise. Lastly, it is important for group members to structure their departure with brags and appreciations and claim time to say meaningful good-byes.

Application: Therapeutic Techniques and Procedures

Contracts: The Structure of the Therapeutic Relationship

Transactional analysis is based largely on the capacity and willingness of group participants to understand and design a therapeutic contract that requires them to state their intentions and set personal goals. Contracts are the key to all TA treatment. The initiation of a contract begins with group participants creating a vision (from the Child) of how they will be different as a result of their time in group. From the creation of the vision, the contract becomes specific and measurable and contains a concrete statement of the objectives group participants intend to attain and how and when these goals are to be met. Contracts place the responsibility on members for clearly defining what, how, and when *they* want to change. Thus, from the very beginning, members learn that therapy is a shared responsibility and that they cannot passively wait for the leader to direct the group. In short, the members' contracts establish the departure point for group activity.

Group members agree to work on specific issues within the group. For example, a woman who reacts to others in a highly critical way can design a contract that will lead to changing such behavior. Her contract describes *what* she will do in the group to change her actions and experiences, *when* she will do it, and *how many times*. The contract can then be expanded to include situations outside the group.

Dusay (1983) asserts that a well-stated treatment contract will make it clear whether clients are obtaining what they want from therapy. The key question is, "How will you know and how will I know when you get what you are coming to the group for?" This question implies a therapeutic partnership aimed at accomplishing a mutual goal. Since everyone in the group knows the other participants' contracts, a productive focus can be developed in the group sessions. The process of TA treatment focuses primarily on change as defined by the contract, and there is an Adult-to-Adult agreement between the therapist and the client about what the process and the desired goal will be (Dusay & Dusay, 1989).

Contracts are intended to be practical tools for helping people change themselves; they cannot be rigid and should be open to revision. Because long-term contracts can be limiting, contracts are developed in steps and are subject to modification as members penetrate more deeply into the areas in which they are seeking to change. These short-term contracts fit well with the requirements of limited therapy and brief therapy characteristic of many community agencies. Contracts can guide the course of brief therapy and can provide a basis for evaluation of outcomes.

Well-trained TA clinicians know that sustainable change and meaningful redecisions do not occur without the client closing what are termed "escape hatches," ways to universally escape if things really get bad. These escape hatches include (1) Harm or kill myself, (2) Harm or kill you, (3) Provoke you to harm or kill me, (4) Go crazy, and (5) Run away. If things get bad enough, the script will call for one of these as an "escape." Any client with an escape hatch remaining open will not change, or the changes observed will more than likely be cosmetic. Contracts can be instrumental in closing these escape hatches.

Applying Transactional Analysis to Group Work in the Schools

Many of the basic ideas found in TA groups can easily be understood even by very young children. For example, children in the first grade are generally able to understand the ego states when they are explained as the "critical me" (Parent), the "thinking me" (Adult), and the "feeling me" (Child) (Freed & Freed, 1998). Children are also able to understand the concept of the need for human strokes. Even children in the early grades are able to understand that acting-out children are striving to get attention (strokes). Children soon learn that negative strokes are better than receiving no strokes. Both children and adolescents can easily distinguish between a "warm fuzzy" (a pleasant or positive stroke that makes them feel good), and a "cold prickly" (an unpleasant or negative stroke that hurts or feels bad). In children's groups the story *A Warm Fuzzy Tale* (Steiner, 1969) typically leads to lively discussion and interaction.

TA concepts and techniques can be usefully applied in guidance classes in schools or in group counseling sessions with children ages 5 to 12 (Thompson & Rudolph, 2000). For example, exploring parental injunctions can be a useful exercise with both children and adolescent groups. Young people can learn a great deal about the messages they have incorporated from their family of origin. TA provides a structured approach that allows children and adolescents to see connections between what they learned in their family and their attitudes toward others. Many young people are likely to find this type of structure useful, for it helps them understand how their family and culture have influenced them. Consider these injunctions, which you may hear from children and adolescents in your groups:

- Don't cry, or at least don't shed tears in public.
- Live up to the expectations of your parents and your family.
- Be perfect in all that you do.
- Don't be too concerned about yourself.
- Don't stand out or be noticed.
- Don't brag.
- Think of what is best for family [community] rather than focusing on your self-interests.
- Don't talk about your family or about family problems with strangers.

These injunctions provide a good starting place for exploration in groups in the school setting. It is essential for leaders to be aware of the cultural context that may limit confronting certain cultural injunctions. A competent group leader can create a climate in which the members can begin to question the degree to which they have accepted these messages and how certain injunctions influence their present behavior. A main goal of a TA group with students is to facilitate insight so that they are able to assume increased control of their thoughts, feelings, and actions. As children and adolescents develop this self-understanding, they also acquire the ability to make changes both within themselves and in their transactions with others. If you are interested in group work with young people from preschool through high school, you will find useful resources to be Freed and Freed (1998) and Freed (1992, 1998).

Applying Transactional Analysis with Multicultural Populations

The contractual approach used in a TA group has much to offer in a multicultural context. Group members' contracts act as a safeguard against therapists' imposing their cultural values. A contract increases the chances that members will become empowered in a group, for they eventually identify specific problem areas they want to bring into the group.

Thompson and Rudolph (2000) indicate a number of multicultural applications of TA, one of which is the user-friendly nature of TA in transcending cultural barriers. Thompson and Rudolph add that TA has been successfully applied in several different cultures. People from a variety of cultures who prefer a direct and educational approach to personal development are likely to find TA an appropriate modality. For example, African American and Latino clients tend to prefer a psychoeducational context that emphasizes learning practical skills. Asian Americans generally find the cognitive emphasis an attractive feature of TA. When TA is used across cultures, the method is generally the same. Members learn the basic terminology and formulate contracts that guide their work in a group.

A number of factors in TA groups make them particularly useful in working with women. Some of these elements are the use of contracts, the egalitarian relationships between the members and the leader, the emphasis on providing members with knowledge of the TA group process, and the value placed on empowering the group members. Feminist therapists are often concerned about the inappropriate imposition of the therapist's values on clients (Enns, 1993). It appears that a TA group has some distinct advantages in exploring gender-role socialization (Enns, 1993), including its emphasis on empowering members. Additionally, in a TA group the power differential between the leader and members is less pronounced than in most forms of individual therapy. From a feminist perspective, when women are in groups, they have more opportunities to challenge the therapist's ideas, and they are able to compare their reality with those of other women (Enns, 1993).

A strength of TA is that its concepts are congruent with a gender-sensitive approach to group work. When women and men enter a group, they often are unaware of the role that gender plays in their lives. Furthermore, not all practitioners are aware of the detrimental effects of gender socialization when working with individuals in a group. If leaders hope to avoid reinforcing the cultural status quo, they must learn how traditional gender socialization can hurt both women and men. It is important that gender-sensitive group therapists clearly understand how gender messages are transmitted by cultures and then absorbed by individuals so that they can explain this process to the group members. A TA therapist is in a good position to assist members in exploring how they are affected today by the messages they have incorporated regarding what it means to be a woman or a man in this society (Philpot, Brooks, Lusterman, & Nutt, 1997).

In a TA group, both women and men can identify societal messages and stereotypes of what it means to be a female or a male. The book *I Never Knew I Had a Choice* (Corey & Corey, 2002) describes some of these messages that both men and women hear and accept in growing up. The stereotypic view of males includes characteristics such as emotional unavailability, independence, aggressiveness, denial of fears, protection of inner self, invulnerability, lack of bodily self-awareness, remoteness with other men, drive to succeed, denial of "feminine" qualities, avoidance of physical contact, rigid perceptions, devotion to work, and loss of the male spirit.

Men often hide their feelings of vulnerability and are ever watchful of others' reactions, looking for indications that they might be exposed to ridicule. This theme of men hiding their true nature is characteristic of many men, regardless of their racial, ethnic, and cultural background. Many men have become prisoners of a stereotypical role that they feel they must live by. A TA group provides a context where men are able to challenge the restrictions of these traditional roles and where they can take on new attitudes and beliefs that can lead to behavioral change.

Just as is the case with men, traditional gender stereotypes of women are still alive and well in our culture. Women, too, have been restricted by their cultural conditioning and by accepting gender-role stereotypes that keep them in an inferior position. Adjectives often associated with women include gentle, tactful, neat, sensitive, talkative, emotional, unassertive, indirect, and caring. Too often women have defined their own preferences as being the same as those of their partners, and they have had to gain their identity by protecting, helping, nurturing, and comforting.

Despite the staying power of these traditional female role expectations, more and more women are rejecting the limited vision of what a woman is "expected" to be. A TA group lends itself to critically examining the degree to which women have bought into self-limiting messages. Both men and women can interact with each other in the group in new ways. Just as they can examine the influence of a host of injunctions and decisions they have made based on certain messages, group members can fruitfully examine how they can free themselves from the bondage of restrictive gender socialization. A group leader would do well to avoid too quickly challenging the messages about gender roles that have influenced members because this may be interpreted as a sign that the leader does not respect the clients' values or is attempting to impose his or her own value system on the members.

In working with a diverse group, leaders need to be aware that the terminology may seem foreign to some members. Even though TA therapists assert that TA is simple and easy to understand, clients may have difficulty with the complexity of concepts such as the structure and dynamics of games and the subcomponents of the various ego states. Before TA group leaders challenge the lifescripts of group members, which are frequently rooted in their cultural heritage, it is well for them to make sure that a trusting relationship has been established and that these clients have demonstrated a readiness to question their family traditions. In some cultures it is considered taboo to doubt family traditions, let alone talk about such matters in a nonfamily group or have these traditions challenged by others. The contract approach can be useful in empowering these clients by giving them the responsibility for deciding what aspects of their family life they are willing to share as well as deciding which family values they are ready to question or explore. If group members assume this responsibility for defining clear contracts, the chances of inappropriate confrontations by the leader are lessened.

Evaluation of Transactional Analysis in Groups

Contributions and Strengths of the Approach

Transactional analysis provides a cognitive basis for group process that is often missing in experientially oriented groups. The insistence of this approach on having members get out of their victimlike positions and realize that they don't have to continue to live by their early decisions is, I believe, crucial to effective therapy. In my opinion TA, especially redecision therapy, provides a useful conceptual framework for understanding how these early decisions are made, and how they are related to present self-defeating life stances.

Many people are restricted by their early decisions: they cling to parental messages, live their lives by unexamined injunctions, and frequently are not even aware that they are living in a psychological straitjacket. Conceptually, redecision therapy offers tools members can use to free themselves from an archaic lifescript and achieve a successful and meaningful life.

One of the strengths of the TA approach to group counseling is the emphasis on contracts as a way to guide each member's work. The contractual arrangement places the responsibility for deciding what to change clearly on the group members rather than on the leader. Contracts equalize the power base between the leader and the members; they also remove much of the mystery that surrounds what a group is all about. To its credit, TA groups work toward empowerment of members. Members are able to see their responsibility in contributing to their problems, and they also learn new ways of thinking and acting.

Because TA is a structured, psychoeducational approach, the group format lends itself well to agencies within a managed care system. Members identify specific areas they are interested in changing, they formulate a specific contract that guides their work in a group, and they make action plans to reach their goals in the briefest amount of time. A great deal of progress on member goals can be accomplished in about 10 group sessions, which gives TA clear advantages for brief treatment and a focus on specific problems and goals (Thompson & Rudolph, 2000).

Group leaders who work within a managed care framework generally have less time to gather client information, make an assessment, provide an orientation to the therapy process, establish rapport, and intervene in a therapeutic manner (Davis & Meier, 2001). It is essential that a TA leader explain the program policies and limits to the members and how the policies are likely to affect the process, type, and length of the therapy.

TA groups allow a range of possibilities for both preventive and remedial work; they also provide for both an educational and a therapeutic structure. It is important that the information given in TA groups be balanced by experiential work aimed at involving the members both cognitively and emotionally. Therapy interventions are more likely to succeed and produce enduring change if they involve the emotional realm rather than being aimed purely at a cognitive level (Greenberg, Korman, & Paivio, 2002).

Personally, I favor integrating TA concepts and practices with Gestalt and psychodrama techniques. Doing so can integrate the cognitive and emotive dimensions quite naturally. Many of the specific techniques in psychodrama—such as role reversal, self-presentation, doubling, soliloquy, and future projection—are ideal methods of exploring the affective dimensions of injunctions and early decisions. TA concepts can be brought to life by the enactment methods that are typical of psychodrama. Of course, this is what the Gouldings have accomplished. Working from a theoretical base provided by TA, they have used a combination of therapeutic methods, including psychodrama, fantasy and imagery, Gestalt techniques, behavior therapy, desensitization, family therapy procedures, and psychosynthesis. The Gouldings contend that pure Gestaltists may fail to give cognitive feedback and that pure TA therapists seldom encourage the intense emotional work that leads to breaking through those impasses that prevent further growth.

How comprehensive is TA as a theory that can provide a foundation for practice? According to Dusay (1986), TA is recognized as a complete theory of personality and an entire system of psychotherapy. From Dusay's perspective, TA has two major advantages as a therapeutic system. First, there is a complete and easily communicated theory of personality, and second, because of this foundation, the therapist is free to develop an innovative style of treatment utilizing his or her own strengths. He adds, if one were to observe trained transactional analysts in action, one may see therapeutic styles ranging from a more "intellectual" cognitive approach to an emotive "feeling" approach.

TA's regulatory body, the International Transactional Analysis Association, certifies therapists who enroll in its rigorous training program. TA is practiced internationally, both by professionals and paraprofessionals. It is applied to business and organizational development. Prison inmates, schizophrenic patients, and people in drug rehabilitation programs and outpatient clients from all socioeconomic levels have participated in TA treatment programs (Dusay & Dusay, 1989).

Limitations of the Approach

Like most of the other approaches that have been discussed so far, TA can be criticized on the ground that its theory and procedures have not been adequately subjected to empirical validation. Indeed, many of Berne's concepts were stated in such a manner that it would be impossible to design a research study to test them. It appears that most of the claims of success rest on clinical observations and testimonials. Conducting well-designed research studies to evaluate the process and outcome of group therapy has surely not been one of the strengths of TA. This is not to say that no one has attempted to study the outcomes of TA group therapy; research studies are described in various issues of the *Transactional Analysis Journal*. Some TA therapists contend that the use of specific contracts provides built-in accountability. Measures can be taken to determine the extent to which members have fulfilled their contract and benefited from group therapy. In my opinion TA could profit by integrating the commitment to research that is characteristic of behavior therapy.

Transactional analysis group leaders have the potential of working primarily in a cognitive way and not allowing enough room for exploration of feelings. A further concern relates to the way in which some practitioners use the structure and vocabulary of this system to avoid genuine contact with their clients or to keep from revealing their reactions. A therapist can use the structure of TA to avoid person-to-person interactions and to focus on labeling ego states, devising contracts, and directing traffic between transactions. I have also observed some group members who seem to be using TA jargon to deceive themselves into believing that they are becoming self-actualized when, in reality, they are only learning new terms to identify old processes. Some TA clients also tend to slip into the use of jargon as an intellectual front behind which they can safely hide. The danger of becoming lost in the structure and vocabulary of TA can be lessened if the therapist is willing to challenge members when they use jargon.

Where to Go from Here

If you want to learn more about TA group work, I encourage you to take an introductory transactional analysis course or participate in a TA group as a member. Experiencing TA as a member could benefit you personally by bringing many of the concepts in this chapter to life in a concrete way. Also, you may want to consider attending an educational workshop where you can apply TA principles in a group setting.

For further information, contact:

International Transactional Analysis Association
436 14th St., Suite 1301
Oakland, CA 94612-2710
TELEPHONE: (510) 625-7720
FAX: (510) 625-7725
E-MAIL: itaa@itaa-net.org
WEB SITE: www.itaa-net.org

This association provides information on training and certification in transactional analysis. There are approximately 1,500 members in some 60 countries. TA practitioners are involved in clinical and mental health professions as well as in business, education, and industry. Certification in transactional analysis requires that the candidate pass both a written and an oral examination. Work samples are reviewed by a board of examiners to determine the therapist's level of clinical competence.

The *Transactional Analysis Journal* is a good source for keeping current with the developments of TA theory, clinical applications, and research. For information concerning dues for various membership classifications and for journal subscriptions, contact the ITAA office.

Recommended Supplementary Readings

TA Today: A New Introduction to Transactional Analysis (Stewart & Joines, 1987) is a comprehensive text on transactional analysis theory.

Changing Lives Through Redecision Therapy (M. Goulding & Goulding, 1979) is the work I would recommend to a practitioner who had time to read only one book on the TA approach to group work. The authors describe their successful integration of Gestalt and behavioral techniques in their TA theoretical framework.

Scripts People Live: Transactional Analysis of Life Scripts (Steiner, 1974) is a comprehensive discussion of lifescripts that can be applied to group work.

Principles of Group Treatment (Berne, 1966) provides a useful discussion of group structure and process from the TA perspective.

References and Suggested Readings*

Berne, E. (1961). *Transactional analysis in psychotherapy*. New York: Grove Press.

Berne, E. (1964). *Games people play*. New York: Grove Press.

Berne, E. (1966). *Principles of group treatment*. New York: Oxford University Press.

Berne, E. (1972). *What do you say after you say hello?* New York: Grove Press.

Corey, G., & Corey, M. S. (2002). *I never knew I had a choice* (7th ed.). Pacific Grove, CA: Brooks/Cole.

Davis, S. R., & Meier, S. T. (2001). *The elements of managed care: A guide for helping professionals*. Pacific Grove, CA: Brooks/Cole.

Dusay, J. M. (1983). Transactional analysis in groups. In H. I. Kaplan & B. J. Sadock (Eds.), *Comprehensive group psychotherapy* (2nd ed.). Baltimore: Williams & Wilkins.

Dusay, J. M. (1986). Transactional analysis. In I. L. Kutash & A. Wolf (Eds.), *Psychotherapist's casebook* (pp. 413–423). San Francisco: Jossey-Bass.

Dusay, J. M., & Dusay, K. M. (1989). Transactional analysis. In R. J. Corsini (Ed.), *Current psychotherapies* (4th ed., pp. 405–453). Itasca, IL: F. E. Peacock.

Enns, C. Z. (1993). Twenty years of feminist counseling and therapy: From naming biases to implementing multifaceted practice. *The Counseling Psychologist, 21*(1), 3–87.

Freed, A. (1992). *TA for teens and other important people*. (rev. ed.). Rolling Hills Estates, CA: Jalmar Press.

Freed, A. (1998). *TA for tots: And other prinzes*. Rolling Hills Estates, CA: Jalmar Press. [Originally published 1973]

Freed, A., & Freed, M. (1998). *TA for kids: And grown ups too*. Rolling Hills Estates, CA: Jalmar Press. [Originally published 1971]

Goulding, M. M. (1987). Transactional analysis and redecision therapy. In J. K. Zeig (Ed.), *The evolution of psychotherapy* (pp. 285–299). New York: Brunner/Mazel.

*Goulding, M., & Goulding, R. (1979). *Changing lives through redecision therapy*. New York: Brunner/Mazel.

Goulding, R. (1975). The formation and beginning process of transactional analysis groups. In G. Gazda (Ed.), *Basic approaches to group psychotherapy and group counseling* (2nd ed., pp. 234–264). Springfield, IL: Charles C Thomas.

*Books and articles marked with an asterisk are suggested for further study.

Goulding, R. (1982). Transactional analysis/Gestalt/redecision therapy. In G. Gazda (Ed.), *Basic approaches to group psychotherapy and group counseling* (3rd ed., pp. 319–351). Springfield, IL: Charles C Thomas.

Goulding, R. L. (1987). Group therapy: Mainline or sideline? In J. K. Zeig (Ed.), *The evolution of psychotherapy* (pp. 300–311). New York: Brunner/Mazel.

Goulding, R., & Goulding, M. (1976). Injunctions, decisions, and redecisions. *Transactional Analysis Journal, 6*(1), 41–48.

*Goulding, R., & Goulding, M. (1978). *The power is in the patient*. San Francisco: TA Press.

*Greenberg, L. S., Korman, L. M., & Paivio, S. C. (2002). Emotion in humanistic psychotherapy. In D. J. Cain, & J. Seeman, (Eds.), *Humanistic psychotherapies: Handbook of research and practice* (pp. 499–530). Washington, DC: American Psychological Association.

James, M., & Jongeward, D. (1971). *Born to win: Transactional analysis with Gestalt experiments*. Reading, MA: Addison-Wesley.

Kapur, R., & Miller, K. (1987). A comparison between therapeutic factors in TA and psychodynamic therapy groups. *Transactional Analysis Journal, 17*(1), 294–300.

Karpman, S. (1968). Fairy tales and script drama analysis. *Transactional Analysis Bulletin, 7*(26), 39–43.

*Philpot, C. L., Brooks, G. R., Lusterman, D. D., & Nutt, R. L. (1997). *Bridging separate gender worlds: Why men and women clash and how therapists can bring them together*. Washington, DC: American Psychological Association.

Steiner, C. (1967). A script checklist. *Transactional Analysis Bulletin, 6*(22), 38–39.

Steiner, C. (1969). *A warm fuzzy tale*. Available online at www.claudesteiner.com/fuzzy.htm (accessed March 24, 2001).

Steiner, C. (1974). *Scripts people live: Transactional analysis of life scripts*. New York: Grove Press.

*Stewart, I., & Joines, V. (1987). *TA today: A new introduction to transactional analysis*. Nottingham, England: Lifespace Publishing.

Thompson, C. L., & Rudolph, L. B. (2000). *Counseling children* (5th ed.). Pacific Grove, CA: Brooks/Cole.

Tudor, K. (1991). Children's groups: Integrating TA and Gestalt perspectives. *Transactional Analysis Journal, 21*(1), 12–20.

CHAPTER 13

The Behavioral Approach to Groups

Introduction

Behavioral approaches are becoming increasingly popular in group work. One of the reasons for this popularity is the emphasis these approaches place on teaching clients self-management skills they can use to control their lives, deal effectively with present and future problems, and function well without continued therapy. Writers with a behavioral orientation, such as Watson and Tharp (2002), have devoted books to the subject of helping people work toward "self-directed behavior." This goal is achieved through a wide variety of cognitive and behavioral action-oriented techniques. Most of these therapeutic techniques are procedures that clients can use on their own to solve interpersonal, emotional, and decision problems.

The term *behavior therapy* refers to the application of a diversity of techniques and procedures that are rooted in a variety of learning theories. Since no single theory undergirds the practice of contemporary behavior therapy, there is no single group model that, strictly speaking, can be called a "behavioral group." Rather, various types of groups operate on behavioral and learning principles. Behavior therapy is best conceptualized as a general orientation to clinical practice that is based on the experimental approach to the study of behavior.

A basic assumption of the behavioral perspective is that most problematic behaviors, cognitions, and emotions have been learned and can be modified by new learning. This process is often called "therapy," yet it is more properly an educational experience. Individuals are involved in a teaching/learning process and are taught how to develop a new perspective on ways of learning. They are encouraged try out more effective behaviors, cognitions, and emotions. Problems may also arise due to a skills deficit—adaptive behaviors or cognitive strategies that have not been learned—and clients can acquire coping skills by participating in this educational experience. Many of the techniques employed by groups of different orientations (such as rational emotive behavior therapy, cognitive therapy, reality therapy, and transactional analysis) share this basic assumption of group therapy as an educational process, and they stress the teaching/learning values inherent in a group.

Another assumption of the behavioral orientation is that the behaviors that clients express are the problem (not merely symptoms of the problem). Successful resolution of these problematic behaviors resolves the problem, and a new set of problems does not necessarily arise. This behavioral perspective is in contrast to the relationship-oriented and insight-oriented approaches, which place considerable emphasis on clients' achieving insight into their problems as a prerequisite for change. Whereas the insight-oriented approaches assume that if clients understand the nature and causes of their symptoms they will be better able to control their lives, the behavioral approach assumes that change can take place without insight. Behavior therapists operate on the premise that changes in behavior can occur prior to understanding of oneself and that behavioral changes may well lead to an increased level of self-understanding.

Behavioral group leaders may develop strategies from diverse theoretical viewpoints, provided that their effectiveness in meeting therapeutic goals can be demonstrated. These leaders follow the progress of group members through the ongoing collection of data before, during, and after all interventions. Such an approach provides both the group leader and members with continuous feedback about therapeutic progress. In this sense, the behavioral leader is both a clinician and a scientist who is concerned with testing the efficacy of his or her techniques.

Group leaders who operate from a behavioral perspective draw on a wide variety of interventions derived from social learning theory, and for the most part, these are *cognitive behavioral* groups rather than traditionally oriented behavior therapy groups. The cognitive behavioral approach to groups now represents the mainstream of contemporary behavior therapy. Since the early 1970s, the behavioral movement has broadened to give cognitive factors a central role in understanding and treating behavioral problems. As Foreyt and Goodrick (2001) have noted, cognitive processes have become scientifically respectable within behavior therapy. There has been a shift away from the environmental deterministic position and toward viewing individuals as active participants in influencing their development. *Cognitive-Behavioral Group Therapy for Specific Problems and Populations* (White & Freeman, 2000) is an excellent resource that illustrates how cognitive behavioral group therapy is becoming one of the most feasible and efficient forms of treatment for a wide range of specific problems for diverse client populations.

In keeping with the developments within this field, this chapter deals more with *cognitive behavior therapy* than it does with traditional behavior therapy. The groups for social skills training, assertiveness training, cognitive therapy, stress management training, and multimodal group therapy discussed here all represent the cognitive behavioral perspective. Chapter 14 is devoted to one specific cognitive behavioral branch, rational emotive behavior therapy (REBT), founded by Albert Ellis.

Key Concepts

Behavior therapy has some unique characteristics that set it apart from most of the other group approaches discussed in this book. It relies on the principles and procedures of the scientific method, and these experimentally derived principles of learning are systematically applied to help people change mal-adaptive behaviors. The distinguishing characteristic of behavioral practition-ers is their systematic adherence to specification and measurement. Concepts and procedures are stated explicitly, tested empirically, and revised continu-ally. Assessment and treatment occur simultaneously. The specific unique char-acteristics of behavior therapy include (1) conducting a behavioral assessment, (2) precisely spelling out treatment goals, (3) formulating a specific treatment procedure appropriate to a particular problem, and (4) objectively evaluating the outcomes of therapy.

Behavioral Assessment

Behavioral assessment consists of a set of procedures used to get information that will guide the development of a tailor-made treatment plan for each client and help measure the effectiveness of treatment. According to Spiegler and Guevremont (2003), behavioral assessment procedures share five characteris-tics that are consistent with behavior therapy. They (1) are aimed at gathering unique and detailed information about a client's problem, (2) focus on the client's current functioning and life conditions, (3) are concerned with taking samples of a client's behaviors to provide information about how the client typically functions in various situations, (4) are narrowly focused rather than dealing with a client's total personality, and (5) are an integral and continuous part of therapy.

Precise Therapeutic Goals

In most behavior therapy groups, the initial stages of group work are devoted to clients' expanding the final step of their assessment by formulating specific statements of the personal goals they want to achieve. The identification of goals determines the direction of therapeutic movement. Although the group leader guides the discussion of goals, the personal goals originate from the group members themselves (White, 2000b). Group members spell out concrete problematic behaviors they want to change and new skills they want to learn. Personal goals that clients might set include reducing anxiety in test-taking situations, eliminating phobias that interfere with effective functioning, coping with depression, losing weight, and getting rid of addictions (to smoking, alco-hol, or other drugs). Here are some examples of new skills clients may want to acquire:

- Learn to ask clearly and directly for what they want.
- Acquire habits that lead to physical and psychological relaxation.
- Develop specific methods of self-control, such as exercising regularly, con-trolling eating patterns, and eliminating stress.
- Learn to be assertive without becoming aggressive.
- Monitor their behavior or cognitions as a means to change.
- Learn to give and receive both positive and negative feedback.

- Be able to recognize and to challenge self-destructive thought patterns and beliefs.
- Learn communication and social skills.
- Develop problem-solving strategies to cope with a variety of situations encountered in daily life.
- Learn more effective behaviors to cope with stress or anger-inducing situations.

The task of the leader is to help group members break down broad, general goals into specific, concrete, measurable goals that can be pursued in a systematic fashion. For example, if Albert says that he'd like to feel more adequate in social situations, the leader asks: "What do you mean by inadequate? What are you doing or not doing that seems to be related to your feeling of inadequacy? What are the conditions under which you feel inadequate? Can you give me some concrete examples of the situations in which you feel inadequate? In what specific ways would you like to change your behavior?" The group can be used to help members such as Albert formulate answers to these difficult questions by giving him an opportunity to explore these questions, practice new behaviors in the group sessions, and get feedback from others in the group.

Treatment Plan

After members have specified their goals, a treatment plan to achieve these goals is formulated. Behavioral techniques are action-oriented; therefore, members are expected to do things, not just reflect passively and engage in merely talking about their problems. Initially, these plans are generally developed for clients by the group leader. After an initial assessment, and as the members learn the necessary skills, the group members together with the group leader brainstorm intervention strategies that might be used or specific actions that might be taken. Ultimately, the client with the problem is the judge of the strategy or actions he or she must take. The most commonly used techniques are those that lend themselves to group interaction, such as modeling, shaping, behavioral rehearsal, coaching, homework, feedback, cognitive restructuring, desensitization, relaxation training, and information giving. (These are defined and discussed later in this chapter.)

Objective Evaluation

Once target behaviors have been clearly identified, treatment goals specified, and therapeutic procedures delineated, the outcomes of therapy can be objectively assessed. Because behavioral groups emphasize the importance of evaluating the effectiveness of the techniques they employ, assessment of clients' progress toward their goals is continual. If a group is going to meet 10 weeks for social skills training, for example, baseline data on these skills are likely to be taken at the initial session. At every subsequent session an assessment of behavioral changes may be made so members can determine how successfully their objectives are being met. Providing members with ongoing feedback is a vital part of behavioral group therapy.

The decision to use certain techniques is based on their demonstrated effectiveness. The range of these techniques is quite wide, and many behaviorally oriented group counselors are very eclectic in their choices of treatment procedures. They are willing to draw techniques from many of the therapeutic approaches in helping members change their patterns of thinking, feeling, and acting.

Role and Functions of the Group Leader

Behavioral groups are structured in ways that are detailed, concrete, and problem oriented. They tend to utilize short-term interventions, and leaders need to be skilled in drawing on a wide variety of brief interventions aimed at efficiently and effectively solving problems and assisting members in developing new skills. Because of their short-term nature, behavioral groups are most effective when goals are limited and realistic. Actually, the time limitation can be a catalyst for members to make the best use of group time to achieve their goals.

Behavioral group leaders assume the role of teacher and encourage members to learn and practice social skills in the group that they can apply to everyday living. Group leaders are expected to assume an active, directive, and supportive role in the group and to apply their knowledge of behavioral principles and skills to the resolution of problems. Through their conduct in a group, therapists model active participation and collaboration. They do this through their involvement with members in creating an agenda, generating adaptive responses, designing homework, and teaching skills (White, 2000a). Group leaders carefully observe and assess behavior to determine the conditions that are related to certain problems and the conditions that will facilitate change. Members in behavioral groups identify specific skills that they lack or would like to enhance. They proceed through a series of training sessions that involve interventions such as modeling the skill, behavioral rehearsal and coaching, feedback, practicing skills both in the group sessions and through homework, and self-monitoring.

In discussing the social learning that occurs in therapy through modeling and imitation, Bandura (1969, 1977, 1986) suggests that most of the learning that takes place through direct experience can also be acquired by observing the behavior of others. In Bandura's view, one of the fundamental processes by which clients learn new behavior is imitation of the social modeling provided by the therapist. Therefore, group leaders need to be aware of the impact of their values, attitudes, and behaviors on group members. If they are unaware of their power in actually influencing and shaping their clients' ways of behaving, they deny the central importance of their influence as human beings in the therapeutic process.

In addition to these broad functions, the behaviorally oriented group leader is also expected to perform a number of specific educational and therapeutic functions and tasks:

- Group leaders conduct intake interviews with prospective members, during which the preliminary assessment and orientation to the group takes place.
- Teaching participants about the group process and how to get the most from the group is another leader function. The leader explains the purpose of the group, reviews the expectations of the members, and gives them suggestions on how the group can be personally useful.
- Group leaders conduct an ongoing assessment of member problems.
- Leaders draw on a wide array of techniques designed to achieve the members' stated goals.
- A major function of leaders is serving as a model of appropriate behaviors. Also, leaders prepare and coach members to model by role playing for one another how an individual might respond in a particular situation.
- Leaders provide reinforcement to members for their newly developing behavior and skills by making sure that even small achievements are recognized.
- Leaders teach group members that they are responsible for becoming actively involved both in the group and outside of therapy. The behavioral approach emphasizes a plan for change. Leaders help members understand that verbalizations and insight are not enough to produce change. To broaden their repertoire of adaptive behaviors, members are urged to experiment in the group and to practice homework assignments.
- The leader helps members prepare for termination well ahead of the group's ending date. Thus, members have adequate time to discuss their reactions, to consolidate what they have learned, and to practice new skills to apply at home and work. Appropriate referrals are made when reasonable goals have not been achieved.

White (2000a) describes the role of a cognitive behavioral group therapist as akin to a film director or an orchestra conductor. "Similar to the director and the conductor in these artistic venues, the therapist guides a creative process produced by other people" (p. 34). Operating in this role, the therapist makes the most valuable contribution to a group when he or she facilitates a process whereby the members create their own therapy. The ability of the group leader to establish solid relationships within the group has a major bearing on the level of productivity within the group.

A basic assumption of behavioral group therapy is that a good working relationship between the leader and members is a necessary, but not a sufficient, condition for change. It is unfair to cast behavior therapists in a cold and impersonal role that reduces them to programmed machines. Many in the behavioral camp stress the value of establishing a collaborative working relationship between members and the leader. For example, Lazarus (1993, 1996a) believes a flexible repertoire of relationship styles, plus a wide range of techniques, enhances treatment outcomes. He suggests that it is appropriate to discuss the client/therapist relationship at those times when there is reason to think that relationship issues are getting in the way of therapeutic progress.

What are the implications of this view of relationship styles for group leaders? More than simply drawing on a variety of cognitive, affective, and behavioral techniques, group leaders need to make choices regarding different styles of relating to group members. They must decide when and how to be directive or supportive, cold or warm, formal or informal, and tough or tender. The ability to blend appropriate and effective techniques with the most suitable relationship style is one of the most difficult challenges therapists face (Lazarus, 1996a). In short, behavioral group leaders must be skilled technicians who also possess the human qualities that lead to the climate of trust and care necessary for the effective use of these therapeutic techniques.

Stages of a Behavior Therapy Group

This discussion of stages of a group is especially geared to the "multimethod group approach," which has been developed by Rose and his associates. (See Rose, 1989, 1998; Rose & Edleson, 1987.) The multimethod group approach uses various coping strategies for dealing with specific problems: training group members in systematic problem solving, cognitive restructuring, assertion training, relaxation training, behavioral rehearsal, and other strategies that are appropriate for specific problems. This approach involves gradually increasing members' participation and involvement in setting specific goals, planning, decision making, and mutual helping of others. The process progresses from a high degree of leader structure to a low degree of structure. Each client is helped to establish individualized goals and coping skills. Behavioral groups often have a common theme, such as stress management, anger control, or pain management. The goal goes beyond demonstrating change within the group setting. The ultimate goal is the transfer of change into the real world. Later group sessions are structured to make this generalization of learning more likely. How this transfer and generalization are facilitated is addressed in the section describing the final stage of a group.

The following material on the stages of a behaviorally oriented group is based largely on the works of Sheldon Rose (1982, 1983, 1986, 1989, 1998) and Rose and Edleson (1987).

Initial Stage

Prospective clients usually know very little about behavioral programs, so it is important that they be given all the pertinent information about the group process before they join. Pregroup individual interviews and the first group session are devoted to exploring the prospective members' expectations and to helping them decide whether they will join the group. Those who decide to join negotiate a treatment contract, spelling out what the group leader expects from the member over the course of the group, as well as what the client can expect from the leader.

During the initial phase of a group, members learn how the group functions and how each of the sessions is structured. Key tasks at this stage deal with helping members get acquainted, orienting members, building cohesiveness, increasing the motivation of group members, and identifying problematic behaviors that need to be corrected (Rose, 1998). Generally, each session opens with group members checking in by stating significant developments during the week, reporting on their homework, and identifying topics or issues they would like to put on the agenda for the session.

Building cohesion is the foundation for effective work during each stage of a group's development, and the leader has a central role in establishing trust. Cohesiveness is high when people want to be in the group and when they openly relate to one another.

According to Rose (1989, 1998), the leader must initially strive to make the group attractive to its members; create group situations that require social competence on the part of the members; create many functional roles that members can play in the group; delegate the leadership responsibility to the members in a gradual and appropriate manner; present situations in which the members function as therapeutic partners for each other; control excessive group conflict; and find ways of involving all members in group interactions. As the group evolves, leaders move from being directive to training the members in performing these functions for themselves.

Working Stage: Treatment Plan and Application of Techniques

Treatment planning involves choosing the most appropriate set of procedures from among specific strategies that have been demonstrated to be effective in achieving behavioral change. It should be emphasized that assessment and evaluation continue throughout the working stage. Group leaders must continually evaluate the degree of effectiveness of the sessions and how well treatment goals are being attained. To make this evaluation during the working stage, they continue to collect data on matters such as participation, member satisfaction, attendance, and completion of agreed-on assignments between sessions. These assessments also include gathering data to determine whether problems exist within the group and the degree to which group goals are being attained. Throughout the course of a group, individuals monitor their behaviors and the situations in which they occur. In this way they can quickly determine those strategies that are effective or ineffective. By means of this continuing evaluation process, both the members and the leader have a basis for looking at alternative and more effective strategies. Some of the strategies typically used during the working stage are discussed next.

Reinforcement   Reinforcement is a specified event that strengthens the tendency for a response to be repeated. Reinforcement is a key intervention procedure in behavioral groups. In addition to the reinforcement provided by the group leader, other members reinforce one another through praise, approval, support, and attention. It is a good idea to begin each session with members reporting their successes rather than their failures. This sets a positive tone in the group, provides reinforcement to those who did well in everyday life, and reminds the group that change is possible. Reports of success, no matter how modest, are especially important when the members are improving but are still falling short of their expectations and when their changing behavior is being met with disapproval in their everyday environments. In these cases the reinforcement and support of the group are critical if members are to maintain their gains.

Shaping

Social reinforcement is a powerful method of shaping desired behaviors. In addition, self-reinforcement is a key method of helping members change. Participants are taught how to reinforce themselves to increase their self-control and become less dependent on others.

Contingency Contracts   Contingency contracts spell out the behaviors to be performed, changed, or discontinued; the rewards associated with the achievement of these goals; and the conditions under which rewards are to be received. Whenever possible, contracts also specify a time period for achieving the desired behaviors. Effective contingency contracts should have the following features: (1) a clear description of the specific behaviors to be performed in the assignments; (2) a specification of the immediate reinforcement to be received as well as the group reinforcement; and (3) a description of the means by which the assignment is to be observed, measured, and recorded (Rose & Edleson, 1987). Contingency contracts are often used with children, but some adults find them patronizing.

Modeling   Modeling is a process in which clients learn through observation and imitation. Role modeling is one of the most powerful teaching tools available to the group leader. As we have seen with other approaches, an advantage of group counseling over individual counseling is that it offers members a variety of social and role models to imitate. The modeling is performed by both the leader and the participants. Modeling is a technique that is incorporated into a number of behavioral groups, especially in skills training groups and assertion training groups.

What are the characteristics of effective models? Reviews of research (Bandura, 1969) indicate that a model similar to the observer in age, sex, race, and attitudes is more likely to be imitated than a model who is unlike the observer. Models who have a degree of prestige and status are more likely to be imitated. If the client is too different from the model in many of these characteristics, the client tends to perceive the model's behavior as unrealistic. Also, models who are competent in their performance and who exhibit warmth tend to increase modeling effects. As much as possible, models should be reinforced in the presence of the observer, and observers should be reinforced for their imitation of the behavior that is modeled.

Modeling of specific behavior is carried out in role playing during the sessions and practiced *in vivo*. For example, Henry has difficulty initiating contacts with women and would like to feel freer in approaching them in his college classes. He can observe another member modeling at least one way of effectively starting conversations with women. He can then practice in the sessions, using skills he has learned from the model. Then, he can make a contract to initiate several conversations in his classes. Modeling is especially useful in assertion training groups and in teaching clients how to make more constructive self-statements and change cognitive structures. The effect of modeling is enhanced by four other procedures: behavior rehearsal, homework, coaching, and group feedback (Rose, 1989).

Behavior Rehearsal   Behavioral rehearsal is a technique consisting of practicing in a group session a new behavior that will be used in everyday situations. The aim of behavior rehearsal is to prepare members to perform the desired behaviors outside the group, when modeling cues will not be available. New behaviors are practiced in a safe context that simulates the real world. Not only are members protected from adverse consequences while they are learning, but they can also benefit from positive reinforcement, which is likely to increase their willingness to experiment with the new behavior in their daily life (Rose, 1989). The actual practicing of desirable behaviors should take place under conditions that are as similar as possible to the situations that occur in the client's environment, so that maximum generalization from the group to the real world will take place.

Behavior rehearsal, which can be thought of as a gradual shaping process, is useful in teaching social skills. As Goldfried and Davison (1994) indicate, effective social interaction includes many behavioral components besides simply knowing what to say in a particular social situation. Specific factors such as vocal quality, rate of speech, gestures, body posture, eye contact, and other mannerisms are significant aspects. Goldfried and Davison suggest that it is wise to select only a few of these specific behaviors at a given time during a behavior rehearsal. They add that feedback is a useful mechanism of change during behavior rehearsals. Once members achieve successful performance in the group situation, they need to be made aware that application in real life is a basic part of behavior rehearsal. This can be accomplished by reminding members of the importance of completing homework assignments, by devoting some time in each session to deciding on appropriate assignments, and by routinely beginning each group session by checking on the assignments of each member.

Coaching   In addition to modeling and behavior rehearsal, group members sometimes require coaching. This process consists of providing the members with general principles for performing the desired behavior effectively. Coaching seems to work best when the coach sits behind the client who is rehearsing. When a member gets stuck and does not know how to proceed, another group member can whisper suggestions. After one or two coached rehearsals, the coaching is reduced in subsequent role playing. Members rehearse independently before trying out a new role in the real world (Rose, 1998).

Homework In cognitive behavioral groups, homework is encouraged, but not required. Therapeutic homework is aimed at putting into action what members explore during a group session. Homework seeks to integrate what goes on within the group with everyday life. In short, therapeutic progress requires both talking and doing (White, 2000a).

Unless group members participate in designing their own homework assignments, it is unlikely that they will retain a cooperative spirit and keep the motivation needed to carry out the homework. If group members feel they are being forced to do homework, White (2000b) believes the homework is probably going to fail. White suggests that it takes artistic skill on the part of the group leader to guide members in finding homework they are willing to do. Following up on the homework is essential, for all group members can benefit from the homework experiences of each other. White points out the importance of focusing on homework:

> The group therapist needs to follow up on homework with each individual because this conveys the therapist's priorities that homework is important. If members cannot or will not do the homework, it is important to explore the real reasons why—without making it a matter of shame or blame. (p. 22)

Feedback After members practice a new behavior in a group session or report on their homework assignments in daily life, others can provide them with verbal reactions to their performances. These impressions can be given by fellow group members or by the group leader. There are typically two aspects to feedback: praise and encouragement for the behavior and specific suggestions for correcting or modifying errors. Feedback is a useful part of learning new behaviors, especially if it is constructive, specific, and positive. Rose and Edleson (1987) provide these guidelines for offering feedback on a group member's rehearsal performance:

- Before group members are encouraged to offer feedback, they are trained in group exercises in how to give and receive it.
- Positive feedback is given first, so that the member can be reinforced immediately.
- In criticizing a performance, the observer says what could have been done differently.
- Useful feedback is specific and focuses on behaviors.
- Either the group leader or a group member reviews the feedback.

Cognitive Restructuring An individual's cognitive processes have implications for behavior change. Indeed, group members often reveal self-defeating thoughts and negative self-talk when they find themselves in stressful situations. Cognitive restructuring is the process of identifying and evaluating one's cognitions, understanding the negative behavioral impact of certain thoughts, and learning to replace these cognitions with more realistic and appropriate thoughts. Both cognitive therapy and rational emotive behavior therapy use cognitive restructuring as a core procedure in changing an individual's interpretations and thinking processes, which have a powerful effect on his or her feelings and actions. Later in this chapter, cognitive therapy groups are briefly discussed.

Initially, members may be taught through group exercises how to differentiate between self-defeating and self-enhancing statements. Typically, members provide one another with feedback and various models of a cognitive analysis. After clients decide on a set of realistic cognitive statements, cognitive modeling is used, in which the members imagine themselves in stressful situations and substitute self-enhancing statements for self-defeating remarks. In cognitive rehearsal, members imitate the model and get feedback from others in the group. After several trials in the group, they are given the assignment to practice a new set of statements at home before they try out a new style in the real world. In the final step of cognitive restructuring, homework is assigned at the end of each session and then monitored at the beginning of the following session. As members make progress, assignments can be developed at successive levels of difficulty.

Problem Solving   Problem-solving therapy is a cognitive behavioral strategy that teaches individuals ways to deal with problems in their daily lives. The main goal is to identify the most effective solution to a problem and to provide systematic training in cognitive and behavioral skills so the client can apply them and also cope effectively with future problems. The five stages in the problem-solving process are described by Spiegler and Guevremont (2003):

1. The first step in the problem-solving process is adopting a problem-solving orientation. Clients need to understand that it is essential to identify problems when they occur so that action can be taken. Clients must also be convinced that skills can be acquired to cope with daily problems. Finally, it is important to carefully assess alternative courses of action when problem solving.

2. The second stage deals with a definition of the problem and the formulation of specific goals. At this time, clients are helped to understand why certain problem situations are likely to occur and are given the expectation that they can learn ways to cope.

3. In the third stage clients are taught to brainstorm alternative solutions to the problem. The objective is to think of many possible solutions to maximize the chances of finding an adequate solution to a problem. Clients are discouraged from evaluating any of the possible solutions until all the suggestions have been presented.

4. In the fourth stage clients make a decision based on the alternatives they generated in the third stage. In making their choice, they examine the potential consequences of each course of action.

5. In the final stage clients implement the chosen solution and evaluate its effects. They are encouraged to act on this decision and then to verify the degree of effectiveness of their course of action. This verification phase consists of having clients observe and evaluate the consequences of their actions in everyday life situations.

Procedures such as modeling, coaching, and reinforcement are used during problem-solving training. Throughout the therapy process, clients are taught self-control techniques, and they are encouraged to reinforce their own successful performance. Further, once clients have had an opportunity to observe the therapist (or other models) demonstrate effective problem-solving procedures, they are expected to assume a more active role. At this time, the therapist functions largely as a consultant, providing guidance, giving feedback, and encouraging and evaluating real-life applications (Rose, 1989, 1998).

The Buddy System   Rose (1998) makes reference to the "buddy system" as a form of therapeutic alliance between members. Typically, a client is assigned or chooses another as a monitor and coach throughout the group treatment process. The members monitor each other's behavior in the group and remind each other between meetings to stick to their commitments and practice their assignments. In this way they play a supportive role both in and out of the group. Buddies are trained in giving reinforcement for achievements and in giving and receiving criticism. The most important part of treatment occurs outside of the group with the practice of homework assignments. Members assist each other in designing these tasks and monitoring their completion. This arrangement offers members opportunities to be helpful to others and to practice their newly learned leadership skills. The buddy system becomes a self-help network that functions after the group terminates (Rose & Edleson, 1987).

Final Stage

During the final stage of the behavioral group, the leader is primarily concerned with having members transfer the changes they have exhibited in the group to their everyday environment. Practice sessions involving simulations of the real world are used to promote this transfer. Members rehearse what they want to say to significant people in their life and practice alternative behaviors. Feedback from others in the group, along with coaching, can be of the utmost value at this final stage. Sessions are systematically designed so that new behaviors are gradually carried into daily life. Although preparation for generalization and maintenance of change is given a special focus in the final stage, it is a characteristic of all phases of the group.

Transferring changes from the therapy group to daily life is accomplished largely by the following actions taken by the group leader (Rose, 1989; Rose & Edleson, 1987):

- Encouraging members to assume an increasing share of responsibility for their own treatment
- Providing many varied practice situations for the members simulating the real world in the training context
- Preparing members for facing a nonaccepting environment and for dealing with possible regressions
- Overtraining members in the desired target behaviors

- Instructing members in practicing generalization
- Helping clients to help each other to design personalized generalization plans

Self-responsibility is emphasized throughout the life of the group, but it is especially critical in planning for termination. The leader changes from a direct therapist to a consultant in the final stage. Members are typically encouraged to join various social groups where they can practice and develop their newly acquired skills under less controlled conditions than those offered in a therapy group. In addition, they are taught self-help cognitive skills such as self-reinforcement and problem solving as a way of preparing them for situations they have not encountered in the group. This move toward member independence from the group is essential if clients are to gain confidence in their ability to cope effectively with new problems. As the time of termination approaches, many of the initial assessment instruments are repeated as a way of evaluating the effectiveness of the group program.

Termination and follow-up are issues of special concern to behaviorally oriented group leaders. Short- and long-term follow-up interviews are scheduled, which can serve as "booster sessions" for maintaining the changed behaviors and continuing to engage in self-directed change. Follow-up group sessions provide rich opportunities for members to review what they have learned, to update the group on how they are doing, and to encourage them to be accountable for their changes or lack of them. Knowing that they will be accountable, members feel some pressure to maintain and use the discipline they learned in the group. They are encouraged to make use of their buddies and to discover alternative resources (which may include other groups or other forms of counseling) for continuing their progress.

An important advantage of scheduling booster sessions is that doing so provides a way to predict and plan for the inevitable setbacks members are likely to encounter after terminating a group. Relapse prevention is an essential part of terminating a therapy group. It is easy for members to revert to ingrained patterns of old learning, especially when they are faced with a new crisis or when stress escalates. Occasional group sessions in the future assist members in keeping up with their commitments and plans. In addition, reconnecting with members is a form of positive reinforcement to stay on track (White, 2000b).

Application: Therapeutic Techniques and Procedures

There is a growing trend toward "giving psychology away"—that is, a tendency to teach people how to apply interpersonal skills to their everyday life. This trend implies that practitioners will share their knowledge with consumers so that people can lead increasingly self-directed lives and not be dependent on the experts for the effective management of the problems they encounter.

Behaviorally oriented groups offer great promise for those who want to learn the skills necessary for self-management. Areas in which one can learn to control behavior and bring about self-directed change are controlling excessive eating, drinking, and smoking, and learning self-discipline at work or in school. Some people cannot accomplish certain goals in their work because their efforts are hindered by lack of organization; they do not know where to begin with a project, how to sustain their efforts, or how to avoid the crippling discouragement they experience when they fail to attain their goals. It is in these and similar areas that behavioral groups for self-directed change can provide the guidelines and planning necessary to bring about change.

This section deals with some common behavioral techniques that are applicable to group work. For the purpose of this discussion, the techniques have been grouped under five general types of behavioral groups: (1) social skills groups, (2) assertiveness groups, (3) cognitive therapy groups, (4) stress management groups, and (5) multimodal group therapy.

Social Skills Training Groups

Social skills training is a broad category that deals with one's ability to interact effectively with others in a variety of social situations. Social skills training in groups involves the application of many of the behavioral techniques discussed earlier in this chapter. The group offers unique advantages over individual counseling for the development of new social skills. What follows is a summary of the process Rose (1986) uses in structuring social skills training.

Before beginning the social skills training process, the group leader discusses with the members the general purposes of the group and the main procedures that are likely to be used. The members are given a variety of examples and are encouraged to ask questions. The group leader attempts to draw on the experiences of those members who have used these procedures themselves. If the members have had no prior experience with role playing, the leader generally provides them with some training. Then situations are given to the group, and experienced members from previous groups are asked to demonstrate how to role play. Once members learn role-playing skills, they are then trained to develop situations that lend themselves to social skills training. After the group is trained in the development of problem situations, the members are asked to keep a diary of situations as they occur during the course of the week. Each week at least one situation of each member is handled by the group.

Either the therapist or some group member models the desired verbal and nonverbal behaviors in a brief demonstration. Clients then practice their roles in the situation by using the agreed-on behaviors. If clients have trouble using a strategy during the rehearsal, they can be coached by the group leader or other members. When coaching is used, it is generally eliminated in later rehearsals. After each rehearsal, clients receive feedback from the group pertaining to their strengths and weaknesses. Clients assign themselves homework to carry out in the real world. As they complete these assignments, they are asked to observe themselves in new situations and to keep a diary of problems. Behavioral procedures such as modeling, rehearsal, and homework are used to restructure cognitions.

Assertiveness Training Groups

A behavioral approach that has gained increasing popularity is teaching people how to be assertive in a variety of social situations. Alberti and Emmons (2001a) provide this working definition of assertive behavior:

> Assertive behavior promotes equality in human relationships, enabling us to act in our own best interests, to stand up for ourselves without undue anxiety, to express honest feelings comfortably, [and] to exercise personal rights without denying the rights of others. (p. 6)

The basic assumption underlying the practice of assertion training is that people have the right—but not the obligation—to express their feelings, thoughts, beliefs, and attitudes. Assertiveness training can be especially useful for people who cannot ask others for what they want; who are unable to resist inappropriate demands; and who have difficulty expressing feelings of love, gratitude, and approval as well as feelings of irritation, anger, and disagreement. Alberti and Emmons identify three particularly difficult barriers to self-expression: (1) people may not believe they have the right to have or express their thoughts and feelings, (2) people may be anxious about being assertive, and (3) people may sometimes lack the skills for effectively expressing to others what they think and feel.

The goal of assertion training is to increase the group members' behavioral repertoire so that they can make the choice of being assertive or not. Another goal of assertion training is teaching people how to express themselves in a way that reflects sensitivity to the feelings and rights of others. Truly assertive individuals do not rigidly stand up for their rights at all costs, riding roughshod over the feelings and opinions of others. Assertion training attempts to equip clients with the skills and attitudes necessary to deal effectively with a wide range of interpersonal situations. These are some specific outcome goals of this type of training:

- Recognize and change self-defeating or irrational beliefs concerning one's right to be assertive.
- Develop an attitude that places value on one's right to express oneself and on respect for the rights of others.
- Learn how to identify and discriminate among assertive, aggressive, and nonassertive behaviors.
- Be able to apply newly learned assertive skills to specific interpersonal situations

Most assertion training programs focus on clients' negative self-statements, self-defeating beliefs, and faulty thinking. Effective assertion training programs do more than give people skills and techniques for dealing with difficult situations. These programs challenge people's beliefs that accompany their lack of assertiveness and teach them to make constructive self-statements and to adopt a new set of beliefs and self-talk that will result in assertive behavior.

Assertion training is often conducted in groups, with modeling and instructions being presented to the entire group. The members then rehearse behavioral skills in role-playing situations. After the rehearsal, the member is given feedback from the leader and other members. This feedback is especially useful to members in learning how to correct aspects of their behavior and in improving their assertive style. Each member engages in further rehearsals of assertive behaviors until the skills are performed adequately in a variety of simulated situations (Miltenberger, 2001).

For those who are interested in learning the specifics of planning, setting up, conducting, and evaluating assertion training groups, Alberti and Emmons's (2001a, 2001b) books are especially useful.

Cognitive Behavioral Therapy Groups

Cognitive behavioral therapy utilizes a group dynamics format, in conjunction with standard cognitive behavioral techniques, to change maladaptive and dysfunctional beliefs, interpretations, behaviors, and attitudes (Petrocelli, 2002). Some of the most common interventions include automatic thought records, disputing beliefs, monitoring moods, developing an arousal hierarchy, monitoring activities, problem solving, Socratic questioning, relaxation methods, risk assessment, and relapse prevention (Petrocelli, 2002; White, 2000b). Two of the best-known models of cognitive behavioral group therapy are based on the theories of Albert Ellis's rational emotive behavior therapy (the subject of the next chapter) and Aaron Beck's cognitive therapy, which is described next.

Aaron Beck (1976, 1997), a practicing psychoanalytic therapist for many years, grew interested in his clients' "automatic thoughts" (personalized notions that are triggered by particular stimuli that lead to emotional responses). Beck asked his clients to observe negative automatic thoughts that persisted even though they were contrary to objective evidence and from this developed the most comprehensive theory on depression in the world.

Beck (1976) contends that people with emotional difficulties tend to commit characteristic "logical errors" that tilt objective reality in the direction of self-deprecation. Cognitive therapy perceives psychological problems as stemming from commonplace processes such as faulty thinking, making incorrect inferences on the basis of inadequate or incorrect information, and failing to distinguish between fantasy and reality.

The cognitive model of group therapy is based on a theory that emphasizes the interaction of thoughts, feelings, and behaviors; these components are interrelated and multidirectional (White, 2000b). For Beck the most direct way to change dysfunctional emotions and behaviors is to modify inaccurate and dysfunctional thinking. The cognitive therapist teaches clients how to identify these distorted and dysfunctional cognitions through a process of evaluation. Through a collaborative effort, clients learn to discriminate between their own thoughts and events that occur in reality. They learn the influence that cognition has on their feelings and behaviors and even on environmental events. In a group counseling context, members are taught to recognize, observe, and monitor their own thoughts and assumptions, especially their negative automatic thoughts.

Group members often engage in catastrophic thinking by choosing to dwell on the most extreme negative scenarios in many situations. Group leaders can assist members in detecting those times when they get stuck imagining the worst possible outcome of a situation by asking these questions: "What is the worst thing that could occur?" and "If this happens, what would make this such a negative outcome?"

Group members can learn to engage in more realistic thinking, especially if they consistently notice times when they tend to get caught up in catastrophic thinking. Assisting group members to look for evidence to support or refute some of their core beliefs and faulty thinking can also be useful. Once individuals identify a number of self-defeating beliefs, they can begin to monitor the frequency with which these beliefs intrude in situations in everyday life. This simple question can be frequently asked, "Where is the evidence for _____?" If this question is raised often enough, members are likely to make it a practice to ask themselves this question, especially as they become more adept at spotting dysfunctional thoughts and paying attention to their cognitive patterns.

After group members have gained insight into how their unrealistically negative thoughts are affecting them, they are trained to test these automatic thoughts against reality by examining and weighing the evidence for and against them. This process involves empirically testing their beliefs by actively participating in a variety of methods, such as engaging in a Socratic dialogue with the therapist, carrying out homework assignments, gathering data on assumptions they make, keeping a record of activities, and forming alternative interpretations (Freeman & Dattilio, 1994). Members in a cognitive therapy group are expected to form hypotheses about their behavior and eventually learn to employ specific problem-solving and coping skills. Through a process of guided discovery, they acquire insight about the connection between their thinking and the ways they feel and act.

In a cognitive therapy group, the emphasis is on the present and the approach is time limited. Group sessions are focused on current problems, regardless of diagnosis. The past may be brought into group work under certain circumstances: when the member expresses a strong desire to talk about a past situation; when work on current problems results in little or no cognitive, behavioral, and emotional change; and when the therapist considers it essential to understand how and when certain dysfunctional beliefs originated and how these ideas have a current impact on the group member. With this present-centered focus, cognitive group therapy tends to be both brief and task oriented. The therapeutic goals that guide group interventions include providing symptom relief, assisting members in resolving their most pressing problems, and teaching them relapse prevention strategies.

Stress Management Training in Groups

Stress is a basic part of contemporary life. Although it is not realistic to assume that we can eliminate stress, it is realistic for us to learn how to control how we view and cope with stressful events. Stress management training has potentially useful applications for a wide variety of problems and client populations, both for remediation of stress disorders and for prevention. Stress management training is especially useful in dealing with problems with anger, anxiety, phobias, and medical problems; the training is appropriate for victim populations and for professional groups.

The goal of stress management programs is not to eliminate stress but to educate clients about its nature and effects and to teach them a variety of intrapersonal and interpersonal skills to deal with stress constructively (Meichenbaum, 1985). A basic assumption of stress management programs is that we are not simply victims of stress; rather, what we do and what we *think* actively contribute to how we experience stress. In other words, how we appraise events in life determines whether stress will affect us positively or negatively.

Meichenbaum's Stress Inoculation Training   Meichenbaum (1985, 1986, 1993) is concerned with more than merely teaching people specific coping skills. His program is designed to prepare clients for intervention and motivate them to change, and it deals with issues such as resistance and relapse. Stress inoculation training (SIT) consists of a combination of elements of information giving, Socratic discussion, cognitive restructuring, problem solving, relaxation training, behavioral and imaginal rehearsals, self-monitoring, self-instruction, self-reinforcement, and modifying environmental situations. This approach is designed to teach coping skills that can be applied to both present problems and future difficulties.

Meichenbaum (1985, 1993) has designed a three-stage model for SIT: (1) conceptualization, (2) coping skills acquisition, and (3) application. During the initial stage of SIT (conceptualization), the primary focus is on creating a working relationship with clients by educating them to gain a better understanding of the nature of stress and to reconceptualize it in social interaction terms. During this phase, clients are educated about the transactional nature of stress and coping. They learn about the role that cognitions and emotions play in creating and maintaining stress. After an assessment process in which they take an active role, they determine specific goals that will guide treatment. Self-monitoring, which begins at this time, continues throughout the training. Clients typically keep an open-ended diary in which they systematically record their specific thoughts, feelings, and behaviors. Training includes teaching clients to become aware of their own role in creating their stress. This provides clients with a basis for learning ways to reduce the negative effects of stress.

During the second phase of SIT (coping skills acquisition), the client learns and rehearses coping strategies. Some of these specific techniques include relaxation training; cognitive restructuring; problem solving; social skills training; time management; self-instructional training; guided self-dialogue; and lifestyle changes such as reevaluating priorities, developing support systems, and taking direct action to alter stressful situations. Clients are introduced to a variety of methods of relaxation and are taught to use these skills to decrease arousal due to stress. Through teaching, demonstration, and guided practice, they learn the skills of progressive relaxation. They are expected to practice these skills regularly. These activities may include meditation, yoga, tensing and relaxing muscle groups, and breath-control techniques. They can also include walking, jogging, gardening, knitting, or other physical activities. Meichenbaum stresses that it is essential that both clients and trainers understand that relaxation is as much a state of mind as a physical state.

In cognitive restructuring, clients become aware of the role that their cognitions and emotions play in creating and maintaining stress. The cognitive restructuring approach used in SIT is based on Beck's (1976) cognitive therapy. The goal of cognitive therapy is to identify clients' unrealistic, maladaptive thought patterns and to replace them with rational and adaptive modes of thinking. Beck places emphasis on the clients' capacity and responsibility for discovering these maladaptive thought patterns. Beck systematically uses strategies such as modeling and behavior rehearsal in teaching constructive cognitive and coping skills.

Another method used to teach coping skills is a graded task assignment—a shaping strategy in which clients are encouraged to perform small sequential steps leading to a goal. In treating stress-related problems, SIT uses three core techniques: (1) eliciting the client's thoughts, feelings, and interpretations of events; (2) gathering evidence with the client to either support or disprove these interpretations; and (3) designing homework assignments to test the validity of the interpretations and to gather more data for discussion.

Through cognitive therapy techniques, clients learn that cognitions leading to maladaptive behavior have become automatic and often operate out of their awareness. They also learn to detect negative and stress-engendering thoughts, and to challenge their "automatic thoughts," which compound their stress. Clients are also given self-instructional training, which teaches them to instruct themselves, often silently, in coping with challenging situations. Through self-instructional training, clients learn guided self-dialogue techniques to replace negative self-statements. Through training, clients develop a new set of coping self-statements that they can apply when they encounter stressors. If the thinking of clients can make them worse, it is assumed that they can adopt a different set of self-statements to reduce, avoid, or constructively use stress.

In the third phase of SIT (application), the focus is on carefully arranging for transfer and maintenance of change from the therapeutic situation to daily life. The assumption is that coping skills that are practiced in the clinic will not automatically generalize to everyday life situations. To consolidate the lessons learned in the training sessions, clients participate in a variety of activities, including imagery and behavior rehearsal, role playing, modeling, and graduated *in vivo* practice. Clients are asked to write down the homework assignments, or personal experiments, that they are willing to complete. The outcomes of these assignments are carefully checked at subsequent meetings; if clients do not follow through with them, the trainer and the members collaboratively consider the reasons for these failures. Clients are provided with training in relapse prevention, which consists of procedures for dealing with the inevitable setbacks they are likely to experience as they apply their learnings to daily life. A more detailed discussion of the techniques typically used during this phase of treatment was presented in the section describing the final stage of a behavioral group.

Multimodal Group Therapy

The previously described behavioral approaches to groups tend to be short term (6 to 12 sessions) and deal with a homogeneous population. In assertion training groups, for example, the members are alike in wanting to learn ways of being assertive. Stress management training consists of 8 sessions. Pain management training may last for 10 sessions. Likewise, many of the self-directed groups are homogeneous, and the treatment program is relatively brief. Members are taught skills they can apply once they complete these specific training groups.

Lazarus (1997a) has addressed the important subject of brief multimodal therapy. The essence of the broad-spectrum multimodal approach is the premise that human beings are complex in that they move, feel, sense, imagine, think, and relate. Although most of the writing about multimodal therapy has been from the perspective of individual psychotherapy, Lazarus's formulation can be applied to group counseling and therapy. Each client is unique, and Lazarus stresses that care must be taken to avoid fitting clients to a preconceived treatment mode. Instead, a careful attempt is made to determine precisely what relationship with the therapist and what treatment strategies would work best with each particular client and under which particular circumstances. The basic question is who or what is best for this particular client? Therapeutic flexibility and versatility, along with breadth in treatment, are valued highly in the multimodal orientation (Lazarus, 1987, 1989, 1992a, 1992b, 1997a, 2000).

According to Lazarus (1989, 2000), there are seven major areas of personality functioning. Although these modalities are interactive, they can be considered discrete functions and defended as useful divisions. A complete assessment and treatment program must account for each of the seven modalities of the BASIC I.D., which stands for Behavior, Affect, Sensations, Imagery, Cognition, Interpersonal Relationships, and Drugs/Biology. Thus, the BASIC I.D. is the cognitive map that ensures that each aspect of personality receives explicit and systematic attention.

Comprehensive therapy entails the correction of irrational beliefs, deviant behaviors, unpleasant feelings, bothersome images, stressful relationships, negative sensations, and possible biochemical imbalances. It is assumed that clients are troubled by a number of specific problems; therefore, it is best to employ a number of specific treatments. If therapists fail to tune in to a client's presenting modality, the client often feels misunderstood. It is axiomatic that therapy should start where the client is and then move into more productive areas of discourse (Lazarus, 1989). Enduring change is seen as a function of combined techniques, strategies, and modalities. The goal of multimodal therapy is to reduce suffering and promote personal growth as rapidly as possible (Lazarus, 1992b).

Some other basic assumptions underlie multimodal therapy. First, therapists must be effective as people. Second, they need a repertoire of skills and techniques to deal with the range of problems posed by their clients. Third, they must be technically eclectic; that is, they should be able to employ techniques, but not theories, from any disciplines that have been demonstrated to be effective in dealing with specific problems. Fourth, they need to have a consistent theoretical framework that guides their practice. Fifth, it is assumed that groups will be enhanced if therapists take on an active role during group sessions. Thus, therapists function as trainers, educators, consultants, facilitators, and role models.

In calling for technical eclecticism, Lazarus (1997a) endorses using a variety of techniques within a theoretical structure that is open to verification and disproof. He adds that useful techniques can be derived from many sources. Technical eclectics draw strategies from a variety of approaches without having to embrace any of the diverse theoretical positions.

Lazarus (1987) maintains that scientific technical eclecticism requires three other qualities: breadth, depth, and specificity. Practitioners can spell out precisely what interventions they might employ with various clients, as well as the means by which they are selecting these procedures.

Multimodal group therapy begins with a comprehensive assessment of all the modalities of human functioning. The BASIC I.D. assessment allows therapists to utilize types of interventions that are most likely to be helpful to clients in particular circumstances. Ideally, multimodal therapists are broadly trained so that they can work with individuals, couples, families, and groups; they are also skilled in specific behavioral, affective, sensory, imagery, cognitive, interpersonal, and somatic techniques. (See Lazarus, 1989, for a list of the most frequently used techniques.) Here is an adaptation of Lazarus's description of this first phase of group therapy. Members are asked questions pertaining to the BASIC I.D.:

Behavior. This area refers primarily to overt behaviors, including acts, habits, gestures, and motor reactions that are observable and measurable. Some questions asked are "What would you like to change? What behaviors would you like to decrease or eliminate? What behaviors would you like to increase or acquire? What are your chief strengths? What specific behaviors are keeping you from getting what you want?"

Affect. This modality refers to emotions, moods, and strong feelings. Questions sometimes asked include "What emotions do you experience most often? What makes you laugh? What makes you sad? What are some emotions that are problematic for you?"

Sensations. This aspect refers to the five basic senses of touch, taste, smell, sight, and hearing. Examples of questions asked are "Do you suffer from unpleasant sensations, such as pains, aches, dizziness, and so forth? What do you particularly like or dislike in the way of seeing, smelling, hearing, touching, and tasting?"

Imagery. This modality pertains to ways we picture ourselves, and it includes dreams, fantasies, and vivid memories. Some questions asked are "What are some bothersome recurring dreams and vivid memories? How do you view your body? How do you see yourself now? How would you like to be able to see yourself in the future? What are some past, present, or future mental pictures that are troubling you?"

Cognition. This aspect refers to insights, philosophies, ideas, and judgments that constitute one's fundamental values, attitudes, and beliefs. Questions include "What are the values that are most significant in your life? What are some ways in which you meet your intellectual needs? What is the nature of your self-talk? What are some of your central irrational beliefs? What are the main 'shoulds,' 'oughts,' and 'musts' in your life? Do they get in the way of effective living for you? How does your thinking influence what you are doing and how you are feeling?"

Interpersonal Relationships. This term refers to interactions with other people (relatives, lovers, friends, and co-workers). Examples of questions are "What do you expect from the significant others in your life? What do they expect of you? What do you give to these people, and what do you get from them? Are there any relationships with others that you want to change? If so, what changes would you like to see?"

Drugs/Biology. This modality includes more than drugs; it takes into consideration one's nutritional habits and exercise patterns. Some questions asked are "What is the state of your health? Do you have any medical concerns? Do you take any prescribed drugs? What are your diet and exercise habits?"

A preliminary investigation into a client's BASIC I.D. brings out some central and significant themes that can be productively explored in a group. The preliminary questioning is followed by a detailed life history questionnaire. Once the main profile of a person's BASIC I.D. has been established, the next step consists of an examination of the interactions among the different modalities. This second phase of work intensifies specific facets of the person's problem areas and permits the group therapist to understand the person more fully as well as to devise effective coping and treatment strategies.

Group therapy is seen as particularly appropriate (and the treatment of choice) when there is some reason to believe that other people will enhance the processes of learning, unlearning, and relearning. If the BASIC I.D. assessment reveals that the client has a negative self-image and feelings of inadequacy, then multimodal group therapy can be useful. Likewise, for clients whose assessment reveals interpersonal difficulties, group therapy would offer some distinct advantages over individual treatment.

A major premise of multimodal therapy is that *breadth* is often more important than *depth*. The more coping responses a person learns in therapy, the less are the chances for a relapse (Lazarus, 1996a). Thus, for short-term groups it would be well to identify one specific aspect from each element of the BASIC I.D. framework as a target for exploration. An important part of the group process involves teaching members a range of techniques they can use to combat faulty thinking, to learn to relax in stressful situations, and to acquire effective interpersonal skills.

Lazarus endorses an eclectic position and uses a variety of techniques in group work. The multimodal approach to group work requires that the leader be flexible in using various methods and in conducting the group. Thus, discussion, role playing, relaxation exercises, behavior rehearsal, cognitive restructuring, modeling, assertion training exercises, and identifying feelings are but a few of the techniques employed. Lazarus emphasizes, however, that most substantial changes occur outside of the group; therefore, he relies heavily on homework assignments and other performance-based methods rather than exclusively using verbal and cognitive procedures. (For a more detailed discussion of these procedures, see Lazarus, 1989, 1997a, 1997b.)

In summary, one of the values of the multimodal approach to group work is that it does provide a comprehensive view of assessment and treatment. It allows for the incorporation of diverse techniques that are amenable to brief treatment. If a technique has demonstrated efficacy for a given problem, it can become part of the multimodal therapist's approach. Thus, this model appears to foster openness on the part of practitioners.

Applying the Behavioral Approach to Group Work in the Schools

The framework of a present-centered, short-term, action focused, reeducative, behaviorally oriented approach lends itself to the requirements of a diverse range of groups on the elementary school to high school level. A variety of behavioral methods are useful tools for cognitive behavioral group counseling with K through 12 school-age students. These groups typically include an emphasis on operationally defined treatment objectives. In working toward these treatment objectives, the group leader uses a wide range of methods, some of which include reinforcement, contingency management, individual and group contracts, modeling, behavior rehearsal, coaching, homework, feedback, cognitive restructuring, problem solving, and the buddy system. However, as Thompson and Rudolph (2000) have noted, an exclusive reliance on behavioral counseling methods is inadequate to address the full range of problems young people face. Instead, a multimodal approach is generally preferable because of the counselor's commitment to draw from a wide range of techniques espoused by a variety of theoretical models.

A book that group leaders who work with adolescents will find useful is Sheldon Rose's (1998) *Group Therapy with Troubled Youth: A Cognitive-Behavioral Interactive Approach*. Rose describes how a group for adolescents and preadolescents can be structured from a cognitive and behavioral perspective to address several general targets of intervention: interpersonal skills, problem-solving skills, cognitive coping skills, and self-management skills. Rose provides many case examples of a diverse range of young people who are treated in groups. Some of these youth were court ordered and were being seen in the community. Others were being treated in groups in residential facilities or in day treatment centers.

The group work with troubled youth that Rose addresses goes beyond a behavioral orientation. Certainly Rose uses behavioral assessment and treatment interventions, but he makes the assumption that the behavior of youth is not merely due to their beliefs but also a product of their immediate environment, family, community, gender, race, and ethnicity. He assumes that the interaction among the group members is as important as that between the group leader and the members. According to Rose, a broad-based treatment provides the greatest benefit to young people. Members are not, however, bombarded in an unsystematic way with an arsenal of cognitive and behavioral techniques. His model includes these phases of group work: planning for group treatment, orienting the members to the group process and building cohesion, assessing the presenting problems of each member, selecting and applying interventions to bring about change, dealing with group process concerns as they arise, and generalization of changes to the real world and preparing for termination. The group methods and phases of a group's development that Rose describes in these various settings can be applied to group work with students in middle schools and high schools.

Shechtman (2002) reviewed existing studies in educational, counseling, and psychotherapy groups with children in the school setting and found that the cognitive behavioral approach is the most popular theoretical base for interventions in children's groups. This is due to a number of factors: the structured nature of cognitive behavioral interventions, the emphasis given to a time-limited framework, and the demonstrated accountability of this approach. Shechtman states that the results of process research indicate that children and adolescents are generally willing to engage in self-disclosure, even during the early stages of a group. In addition, children tend to react negatively to confrontation, but they react positively to feedback given in a caring and supportive manner. Adolescents are interested in interpersonal learning that they can apply to their social interactions; they also express a need for practical guidance and training. For these reasons, the school setting is very suitable for a variety of behavioral groups with both children and adolescents.

Applying the Behavioral Approach with Multicultural Populations

Behavioral group therapy, especially cognitive behavioral group therapy, has some clear advantages in work with multicultural populations. Behavioral groups deal more with patterns of thinking and behaving, and do not focus on experiencing and expressing intense feelings. Clients who might find catharsis distasteful due to cultural inhibitions against displays of strong emotion are not immediately put off by being expected to emote. In addition, behavioral groups are often short term and highly structured, and thus clients have a good chance of knowing what they are getting into when they agree to participate. Behavioral practitioners typically spend time preparing members to participate in the group experience. The group process is demystified and norms are made clear. This approach may appeal to clients who are somewhat suspicious of the value of a group experience.

Other factors that contribute to the usefulness of the behavioral approach to group work with diverse client populations include its specificity, task orientation, focus on objectivity, focus on cognition and behavior, action orientation, dealing with the present more than the past, emphasis on brief interventions, and problem-solving orientation. Clients learn coping strategies and acquire survival techniques. According to Organista (2000), Latinos who are a part of a cognitive behavioral therapy group (CBT) are likely to find some of the interventions consistent with their expectations. The emphasis on symptom relief, guidance and advice, directiveness, focus on dealing with problems, brevity, and tailoring treatment to the client's particular circumstances are all facets they may appreciate and find useful.

The attention given to transfer of learning and the principles and strategies for maintaining new behavior in daily life are crucial. Because behavior therapy fits into a short-term group format, it is applicable to a variety of practical problems that certain client populations face, and the time frame makes it possible to deal with day-to-day concerns that these clients bring to therapy.

It is important for group leaders to help their clients assess the possible consequences of some of their newly acquired social skills within a particular cultural context. Fukuyama and Coleman (1992) describe Asian cultural norms that may influence levels of assertiveness, such as deference to authority, interpersonal harmony, modesty, and avoidance of public shame. Chinese culture places a premium on compliance with tradition, and being assertive can lead to problems. Individuals who grow up in a traditional Chinese family have little opportunity to develop assertiveness or decision-making skills. Instead, the parents and the elderly are invested with the power to make decisions; children are expected to be obedient and respectful. It is clear that assertion training groups had better take into consideration cultural values and norms. Group leaders need to be mindful of how cultural values can influence the behaviors of clients, and they will also do well to help these members assess the advantages and disadvantages of developing a more assertive style. Members can learn to use what they already have to their advantage. It is also important that members have opportunities to talk about the problems they encounter as they acquire new attitudes and behaviors in their home and at work.

Assertion training groups for women have been viewed with optimism by some, for they provide a vehicle for women to learn how to express themselves more fully, but there has been some criticism of this type of group from a feminist perspective. Enns (1993) comments that women experience frustration when they adopt new roles and then meet with resistance or are given negative labels. From such experiences, it has been learned that social change does not always follow individual change. Enns cites research suggesting that a traditional masculine model of mental health permeates the culture to such a degree that there are few advantages for women if they incorporate behaviorally expressive traits. Although assertiveness training can be an important feminist intervention to empower women, the training needs to consider sociocultural and political dimensions if it is to be effective. Skill development alone is not enough for many individuals with minority status. Even if they succeed in making significant internal changes, they are likely to meet with frustration if social and cultural conditions remain static.

Organista (2000) indicates that cognitive behavioral models of assertiveness training have some limitations when groups include members who come from a traditional Latino culture. The basic concepts of assertive behavior might well be foreign to the nonegalitarian family and friendship systems of Latino clients. Assertive communication can be oppositional to the Latino cultural emphasis on communication that is polite, nonconfrontational, deferential, and even purposefully indirect. Organista proposes an alternative way to motivate Latino members of a group to consider potential values of being assertive in certain situations. These members can be asked to describe what happens to them when they hold negative feelings inside. Latino clients who hold in anger often describe the experience of a range of physical symptoms such as high blood pressure, heart disease, and other somatic symptoms. Once group members become clearer about the price they are paying for denying expression of some of their thoughts and feelings, they might be more likely to consider ways of expressing themselves in a way that is congruent with their cultural framework.

From a multicultural perspective, a potential problem of a behavior group pertains to a leader's imposition of values and goals. If the goals of a group are not consistent with the cultural values of the members, it is not likely that these members will benefit from the group process. Behavioral approaches are often instrumental in helping ethnic minorities make specific changes they desire. However, there is also the possibility that they may feel manipulated to change in the group therapist's direction unless he or she is clear and honest in establishing the premise that clients make their own decisions.

Evaluation of Behavioral Group Therapy

Contributions and Strengths of the Approach

One of the contributions of behavioral group therapy is the emphasis given to education and prevention. A strength of behavior therapy is its precision in specifying goals and procedures, which are defined in unambiguous and measurable terms. This specificity allows for links among assessment, treatment, and evaluation strategies.

The behavioral tradition seeks to tailor specific strategies to each client. Consider how specificity applies to a stress management group. Because behavioral group leaders favor specificity, they take a general term such as stress and break it down into its component parts. Thus, they would not say, "I'm treating Alfonso for stress" but "I'm addressing Alfonso's unassertiveness at work, his tendency to catastrophize, his habit of placing demands on himself, and his fears of rejection, all of which contribute to his feeling stressed out." Leaders attempt to fit the treatment to the client's primary processing style.

More than any of the other therapies discussed in this book, behavior therapy is to be credited for conducting research to determine the efficacy of its techniques. There is a commitment to the systematic evaluation of the procedures used in a group. Those interventions that do not work are eliminated, and techniques are continually being improved. Behavioral interventions can be incorporated effectively into both heterogeneous and homogeneous groups and can be used with groups that have a wide variety of specific purposes. Both behavioral group therapy and cognitive behavioral groups have been extensively used with inpatient populations with demonstrated success in teaching social skills (Klein, Brabender, & Fallon, 1994). Cognitive behavioral group therapy has been demonstrated to have beneficial applications for some of the following specific problems: depression, panic and phobia, obesity, eating disorders, dual diagnoses, dissociative disorders, and adult attention deficit disorders (see White & Freeman, 2000). Based on his survey of outcome studies of cognitive behavioral group therapy, Petrocelli (2002) concluded that this approach to groups is effective for treating a wide range of emotional and behavioral problems.

A behavioral group is a concrete example of a humanistic approach in action. The members are involved in the selection of both goals and treatment strategies. In many groups, the leader helps members move toward independence by delegating leadership functions to them. Members in a behavioral group typically carry out part of the therapy independently of the group in homework assignments and in transferring what they are learning in the sessions to everyday living. Therapy then becomes a place where members learn how to learn and are encouraged to develop the skills necessary to solve future problems.

The behavioral approach allows for evaluation of intervention methods. With the focus on research, these techniques are made more precise so that they can be used with specific clients with a variety of specific problems. Regardless of which models influence our style of group leadership, the spirit of behavior therapy can encourage us to strive for accountability rather than simply relying on faith and intuition that our practices are working.

Advantages of a Group Approach   According to Brabender and Fallon (1993), even though the focus of a behavioral group is on individual goals, the group setting permits and augments individual behavior changes in ways that are not possible in individual therapy. They add that the group facilitates progress toward individual goals by providing enhanced reinforcement options.

Given the protected group environment, the members are encouraged to practice their newly acquired or modified behaviors spontaneously without fear of negative consequences. Because of the level of control of the leader, it is easier to orchestrate the group process so that members respond to one another in accepting rather than rejecting ways.

The population that is suited to behavioral group therapy includes clients with one or more of the following problems: social skills deficits, depression, phobias, anxiety, stress, sexual disorders, pain, anger, eating disorders, substance abuse, psychological trauma, and difficulty managing children (Rose, 1986). Clearly, many complex problems are the focus of treatment in behavioral groups. There is growing empirical support for the utility of various components of behavioral and cognitive behavioral group therapy (Petrocelli, 2002; White & Freeman, 2000). Group therapy appears to be at least as effective and more efficient in terms of therapist cost than individual therapy (Rose, 1989).

Using Behavioral Methods with Other Approaches There is a trend toward broadening the scope of behavior therapy while retaining its essential features. Spiegler and Guevremont (2003) state that behavior therapists are increasingly recognizing that in many cases optimal treatment may require more than one behavioral approach. Moreover, the growing trend toward psychotherapeutic integration involves incorporating treatment strategies from two or more different orientations. In keeping with this trend, behavior therapists are now incorporating nonbehavioral methods in the treatment plans they devise.

It is also possible to combine techniques of the behavioral therapies with the conceptual framework of contemporary psychoanalytic therapies (see Chapter 6). One illustration of how this might be done is provided by Morgan and MacMillan (1999), who developed an integrated counseling model based on theoretical constructs of object relations and attachment theory that incorporates behavioral techniques. Morgan and MacMillan state that there is increasing support in the literature that integrating contemporary psychodynamic theory with behavioral and cognitive behavioral techniques can lead to observable, constructive client changes. If treatment goals are well defined, it is possible to work through the various phases of therapy in a reasonable amount of time. Adapting the conceptual foundation of psychoanalytic thinking to relatively brief therapy makes this approach useful in time-limited therapy.

Dialectical behavior therapy (DBT) is a particularly promising blend of cognitive behavior and psychoanalytic techniques. Linehan (1993a, 1993b) formulated DBT for clients whose symptoms include behaviors resulting in nonfatal self-harm. These symptoms are most typical of clients diagnosed as borderline personality but may also be encountered with other clients. Like analytic therapy, DBT emphasizes the importance of the psychotherapeutic relationship, validation of the client, and the etiologic importance of the client having experienced an "invalidating environment" as a child. The learning emphasis in DBT is an "empirically validated" treatment approach. DBT integrates cognitive behavioral concepts not only with analytic notions but also with the mindfulness training of "Eastern psychological and spiritual practices (primarily Zen practice)" (Linehan, 1993b, p. 6). DBT skills training is not a "quick fix" approach, for it generally involves a minimum of one year of treatment. The group work must be accompanied by individual therapy. Linehan allows for the "integration of DBT skills training with individual psychodynamic therapy" in some settings (p. 14).

As mentioned earlier, another trend in the practice of behavioral group work is to incorporate cognitive factors. Behavior therapists are reformulating their techniques in cognitive and social learning terms instead of the traditional conditioning terms. Many groups are designed primarily to increase the client's degree of control and freedom in specific aspects of daily life. For example, cognitive factors are stressed in the self-control and independence of individuals in groups designed for stress management training, assertion training, social skills training, and self-directed behavior change.

A therapist need not subscribe totally to behavior therapy to derive practical benefits from the use of specific behavioral techniques. As a matter of fact, certain experiential and humanistic models can be enhanced by systematically incorporating some of the behavioral techniques into their relationship-oriented frameworks. I am convinced that an understanding of the learning principles that operate within a group is critical for effective group leadership, regardless of one's orientation.

For example, behavioral principles operate behind such therapeutic procedures as modeling and reinforcement, which are used in almost any kind of group. Members are supported (reinforced) in their attempts to be honest, to take risks, to experiment with new behavior, to be active, to take the initiative, and to participate fully in the group. Behavioral principles are instrumental in fostering group cohesion, which enables members to feel that they are not alone with their problems. The mutual learning and exploration of personal concerns bind the members of a group in a meaningful way. Also, the specificity of the approach helps group members translate fuzzy goals into concrete plans of action, and it helps the group leader keep these plans clearly in focus.

Another strength of the behavioral model is the wide range of techniques that participants can use to specify their goals and to develop the skills needed to achieve these goals. Techniques such as role playing, behavioral rehearsal, coaching, guided practice, modeling, feedback, learning by successive approximations, and homework assignments can be included in any group leader's repertoire, regardless of his or her theoretical orientation. These behavioral principles and techniques lend themselves to short-term groups, which is certainly a strength of the approach.

Limitations of the Behavioral Approach

Behavioral groups do have their disadvantages. For example, when groups are too highly structured, as behavioral groups can often become, individual clients can be prevented from meeting their personal needs. Even minimal effectiveness with groups requires that leaders have training and supervision and that they develop an extensive repertoire of skills (Rose, 1986, 1989; Rose & Edleson, 1987).

Some critics of the behavioral approach to group work argue that this model ignores the historical causes of present behavior and does not work with the past in the therapeutic process. There is some truth to this criticism. It seems clear that the behavior therapist opposes the traditional psychoanalytic approach, which assumes that early traumatic events are at the root of present dysfunction. Behavior therapists may acknowledge that the deviant responses have historical origins, but they maintain that the responses are still in effect because they are being maintained by reinforcing stimuli. They assume that past events seldom maintain current problems. Therefore, they place most of their emphasis on providing the client with new learning experiences. It is clear that the focus is on learning new responses and changing environmental conditions as necessary prerequisites for behavior change.

Although I think it is unfair to accuse behavior therapists of ignoring the past or considering it unimportant, I do believe they fail to work with the past sufficiently. In my own work I have found that most of the contemporary struggles of participants appear to be firmly rooted in their childhood experiences. I see it as particularly important that group members have opportunities to express and explore the feelings that are attached to past traumatic events. I have found that it seems necessary for members to relive certain past experiences and resolve some basic conflicts that have lingered since childhood before new learning can proceed. For this depth of emotional work, techniques from psychodrama and Gestalt therapy are especially useful. I believe behavioral practitioners tend to give insufficient attention to the role unexpressed emotional material plays in behavior.

Another of the limitations of the behavioral model is that, if it is too rigidly applied, it can lead the therapist to lose sight of the people in the group by focusing exclusively on techniques and on the details of the members' specific problems. In my opinion, this focus on problems and symptoms can result in a failure to understand the meaning behind an individual's behavior. This is not to say that group therapy should focus on the "underlying causes" of behavior. However, I prefer to deal with factors both in one's external situation that may be eliciting behavioral problems and with one's internal reactions to these environmental variables. For example, in working with a man who has great anxiety over relating to women, I would be interested in knowing what particular situations in his environment lead to this anxiety, and I would be concerned about his reactions to these situations. How does he feel when he is in the presence of women? What are some things he tells himself when he meets women? How does he perceive women in various situations? What are some historical roots of his fear? I would not simply employ techniques to eliminate his anxiety; rather, I would want to explore with him the meaning of this anxiety. I might also encourage him to relive some earlier painful experiences in dealing with women and facilitate deeper expression of his feelings and self-exploration.

In fairness, most behavior therapists now look at the situation and the response. They are interested in exploring cognitions and, to some extent, the affective elements in the context of the client's problem. In other words, behavior therapists are interested in more than merely eliminating symptoms of problem behaviors. Certainly, practitioners from any orientation could profit by drawing on behavioral interventions and including them in their group work.

Where to Go from Here

If you have an interest in further training in behavior therapy, the Association for Advancement of Behavior Therapy (AABT) is an excellent resource. AABT is a membership organization of more than 5,000 mental health professionals and students who are interested in behavior therapy, cognitive behavior therapy, behavioral assessment, and applied behavioral analysis. If you are interested in becoming a member of this organization, contact:

Association for Advancement of Behavior Therapy
305 Seventh Avenue, 16th Floor
New York, NY 10001-6008
TELEPHONE: (212) 647-1890 or (800) 685-AABT
FAX: (212) 647-1865
E-MAIL: membership@aabt.org
WEB SITE: www.aabt.org

Full and associate memberships are $155 and include one journal subscription (to either *Behavior Therapy* or *Cognitive and Behavioral Practice*), AABT's Membership Directory, and a subscription to the *Behavior Therapist* (a newsletter with feature articles, training updates, and association news). Membership also includes reduced registration and continuing education course fees for AABT's Annual Convention, which features workshops, master clinician programs, symposia, and other educational presentations. Student memberships are $30.

Members receive discounts on all AABT publications, some of which are listed below.

Directory of Graduate Training in Behavior Therapy and Experimental-Clinical Psychology is an excellent source for students and job seekers who want information on programs with an emphasis on behavioral training.
Directory of Psychology Internships: Programs Offering Behavioral Training lists training programs having a behavioral component.
Behavior Therapy is an international journal issued quarterly that focuses on original experimental and clinical research, theory, and practice.
Cognitive and Behavioral Practice is a journal that features clinically oriented articles. Issued quarterly.

Recommended Supplementary Readings

Cognitive-Behavioral Group Therapy for Specific Problems and Populations (White & Freeman, 2000) is a comprehensive text describing a cognitive behavioral approach (CBT) dealing with a range of specific problems such as depression, obesity, eating disorders, panic, and phobias. Also addressed is the application of CBT for specific populations.

Group Therapy with Troubled Youth: A Cognitive-Behavioral Interactive Approach (Rose, 1998) offers practical strategies for working with adolescents in a variety of group settings.

Social skills training and assertion training are particularly well suited for group work. The two sources that I consider to be excellent in this area are *Your Perfect Right: A Guide to Assertive Living* (Alberti & Emmons, 2001a) and the companion professional edition, *Your Perfect Right: A Manual for Assertiveness Trainers* (Alberti & Emmons, 2001b). The latter book contains many helpful guidelines for trainers of these groups.

Contemporary Behavior Therapy (Spiegler & Guevremont, 2003) is a comprehensive and up-to-date treatment of basic principles and applications of the behavior therapies. It also contains a fine discussion of ethical issues. Specific chapters deal with procedures that can be usefully applied to group counseling, a few of which are behavioral assessment, modeling therapy, systematic desensitization, cognitive restructuring, and cognitive coping skills.

Brief But Comprehensive Psychotherapy: The Multimodal Way (Lazarus, 1997a) is an excellent source of techniques and procedures for brief interventions, most of which can be adapted to group counseling. It represents an attempt to deal with the whole person by developing assessments and treatment interventions for all the modalities of human experience.

Interviewing and Change Strategies for Helpers: Fundamental Skills and Cognitive Behavioral Interventions (Cormier & Nurius, 2003) is a comprehensive and clearly written textbook dealing with training experiences and skill development. Its excellent documentation offers group practitioners a wealth of material on a variety of topics, such as assessment procedures, selection of goals, development of appropriate treatment programs, and methods of evaluating outcomes.

References and Suggested Readings*

*Alberti, R. E., & Emmons, M. L. (2001a). *Your perfect right: A guide to assertive living* (8th ed.). Atascadero, CA: Impact.

*Alberti, R. E., & Emmons, M. L. (2001b). *Your perfect right: A manual for assertiveness trainers*. Atascadero, CA: Impact.

---

*Books and articles marked with an asterisk are suggested for further study.

Bandura, A. (1969). *Principles of behavior modification*. New York: Holt, Rinehart & Winston.

Bandura, A. (1977). *Social learning theory*. Englewood Cliffs, NJ: Prentice Hall.

Bandura, A. (1986). *Social foundations of thought and action: A social cognitive theory*. Englewood Cliffs, NJ: Prentice Hall.

*Beck, A. T. (1976). *Cognitive therapy and the emotional disorders*. New York: New American Library.

Beck, A. T. (1997). Cognitive therapy: Reflections. In J. K. Zeig (Ed.), *The evolution of psychotherapy: The third conference* (pp. 55–67). New York: Brunner/Mazel.

Brabender, V., & Fallon, A. (1993). *Models of inpatient group therapy*. Washington, DC: American Psychological Association.

*Cormier, S., & Nurius, P. S. (2003). *Interviewing and change strategies for helpers: Fundamental skills and cognitive behavioral interventions* (5th ed.). Pacific Grove, CA: Brooks/Cole.

Enns, C. Z. (1993). Twenty years of feminist counseling and therapy: From naming biases to implementing multifaceted practice. *The Counseling Psychologist, 21*(1), 3–87.

*Foreyt, J. P., & Goodrick, G. K. (2001). Cognitive behavior therapy. In R. J. Corsini (Ed.), *Handbook of innovative therapies* (2nd ed., pp. 95–108). New York: Wiley.

*Freeman, A., & Dattilio, F. M. (1994). Cognitive therapy. In J. L. Ronch, W. Van Ornum, & N. C. Stilwell, (Eds.), *The counseling sourcebook: A practical reference on contemporary issues*. (pp. 60–71). New York: Continuum Press.

Fukuyama, M. A., & Coleman, N. C. (1992). A model for bicultural assertion training with Asian-Pacific American college students: A pilot study. *Journal for Specialists in Group Work, 17*(4), 210–217.

Goldfried, M. R., & Davison, G. C. (1994). *Clinical behavior therapy* (expanded ed.). New York: Wiley Interscience.

*Klein, R., Brabender, V., & Fallon, A. (1994). Inpatient group therapy. In A. Fuhriman & G. Burlingame (Eds.), *Handbook of group psychotherapy: An empirical and clinical synthesis* (pp. 370–415). New York: Wiley.

Lazarus, A. A. (1987). The need for technical eclecticism: Science, breadth, depth, and specificity. In J. K. Zeig (Ed.), *The evolution of psychotherapy* (pp. 164–178). New York: Brunner/Mazel.

*Lazarus, A. A. (1989). *The practice of multimodal therapy*. Baltimore: Johns Hopkins University.

Lazarus, A. A. (1992a). The multimodal approach to the treatment of minor depression. *American Journal of Psychotherapy, 46*(1), 50–57.

Lazarus, A. A. (1992b). Multimodal therapy: Technical eclecticism with minimal integration. In J. C. Norcross & M. R. Goldfried (Eds.), *Handbook of psychotherapy integration* (pp. 231–263). New York: Basic Books.

*Lazarus, A. A. (1993). Tailoring the therapeutic relationship, or being an authentic chameleon. *Psychotherapy, 30*, 404–407.

Lazarus, A. A. (1996a). Some reflections after 40 years of trying to be an effective psychotherapist. *Psychotherapy, 33*(1), 142–145.

Lazarus, A. A. (1996b). The utility and futility of combining treatments in psychotherapy. *Clinical Psychology: Science and Practice, 3*(1), 59–68.

*Lazarus, A. A. (1997a). *Brief but comprehensive psychotherapy: The multimodal way*. New York: Springer.

*Lazarus, A. A. (1997b). Can psychotherapy be brief, focused, solution-oriented, and yet comprehensive? A personal evolutionary perspective. In J. K. Zeig (Ed.), *The evolution of psychotherapy: The third conference* (pp. 83–94). New York: Brunner/Mazel.

*Lazarus, A. A. (2000). Multimodal therapy. In R. J. Corsini & D. Wedding (Eds.), *Current psychotherapies* (6th ed., pp. 340–374). Itasca, IL: F. E. Peacock.

Linehan, M. M. (1993a). *Cognitive-behavioral treatment of borderline personality disorder.* New York: Guilford.

Linehan, M. M. (1993b). *Skills training manual for treating borderline personality disorder.* New York: Guilford.

Meichenbaum, D. (1985). *Stress inoculation training.* New York: Pergamon Press.

Meichenbaum, D. (1986). Cognitive behavior modification. In F. H. Kanfer & A. P. Goldstein (Eds.), *Helping people change: A textbook of methods* (3rd ed.). New York: Pergamon Press.

Meichenbaum, D. (1993). Stress inoculation training: A 20-year update. In P. M. Lehrer & R. L. Woolfolk (Eds.), *Principles and practice of stress management* (2nd ed., pp. 337–406). New York: Guilford.

*Meichenbaum, D. (1997). The evolution of a cognitive-behavior therapist. In J. K. Zeig (Ed.), *The evolution of psychotherapy: The third conference* (pp. 95–106). New York: Brunner/Mazel.

Miltenberger, R. G. (2001). *Behavior modification: Principles and procedures* (2nd ed.). Pacific Grove, CA: Brooks/Cole.

Morgan, B., & MacMillan, P. (1999). Helping clients move toward constructive change: A three-phase integrative counseling model. *Journal of Counseling and Development, 77*(2), 153–159.

*Organista, K. (2000). Latinos. In J. R. White & A. Freeman (Eds.), *Cognitive-behavioral group therapy for specific problems and populations* (pp. 281–303). Washington, DC: American Psychological Association.

Petrocelli, J. V. (2002). Effectiveness of group cognitive-behavioral therapy for general symptomatology: A meta-analysis. *Journal for Specialists in Group Work, 27*(1), 92–115.

Rose, S. D. (1982). Group counseling with children: A behavioral and cognitive approach. In G. M. Gazda (Ed.), *Basic approaches to group psychotherapy and group counseling* (3rd ed., pp. 466–506). Springfield, IL: Charles C Thomas.

Rose, S. D. (1983). Behavior therapy in groups. In H. I. Kaplan & B. J. Sadock (Eds.), *Comprehensive group psychotherapy* (2nd ed.). Baltimore: Williams & Wilkins.

Rose, S. D. (1986). Group methods. In F. H. Kanfer & A. P. Goldstein (Eds.), *Helping people change: A textbook of methods* (3rd ed., pp. 437–469). New York: Pergamon Press.

Rose, S. D. (1989). *Working with adults in groups.* San Francisco: Jossey-Bass.

*Rose, S. D. (1998). *Group therapy with troubled youth: A cognitive-behavioral interactive approach.* Thousand Oaks, CA: Sage.

Rose, S. D., & Edleson, J. (1987). *Working with children and adolescents: A multimodal approach.* San Francisco: Jossey-Bass.

Shechtman, Z. (2002). Child group psychotherapy in the school at the threshold of a new millennium. *Journal of Counseling and Development, 80*(3), 293–299.

*Spiegler, M. D., & Guevremont, D. C. (2003). *Contemporary behavior therapy* (4th ed.). Pacific Grove, CA: Brooks/Cole.

Thompson, C. L., & Rudolph, L. B. (2000). *Counseling children* (5th ed.). Pacific Grove, CA: Brooks/Cole.

*Watson, D. L., & Tharp, R. G. (2002). *Self-directed behavior: Self-modification for personal adjustment* (8th ed.). Pacific Grove, CA: Brooks/Cole.

*White, J. R. (2000a). Depression. In J. R. White & A. Freeman (Eds.), *Cognitive-behavioral group therapy for specific problems and populations* (pp. 29–61). Washington, DC: American Psychological Association.

*White, J. R. (2000b). Introduction. In J. R. White & A. Freeman (Eds.), *Cognitive-behavioral group therapy for specific problems and populations* (pp. 3–25). Washington, DC: American Psychological Association.

*White, J. R., & Freeman, A. (Eds.) (2000). *Cognitive-behavioral group therapy for specific problems and populations*. Washington, DC: American Psychological Association.

CHAPTER 14

Rational Emotive Behavior Therapy in Groups

Introduction

Albert Ellis, who founded rational emotive therapy (RET) in the mid-1950s, was one of the first therapists to emphasize the influential role of cognition in behavior. Ellis later changed the name of his model to rational emotive behavior therapy (REBT) because of his contention that the model had always stressed the reciprocal interactions among cognition, emotion, and behavior.

Based, in part, on his own experiences conquering emotional problems and consequent inhibited behavior during his youth, Ellis pioneered a large number of thinking, feeling, and activity-oriented methods (Ellis, 1996, 2001a). One of his problems, for example, was a fear of speaking in public. As a way of overcoming his anxieties, Ellis developed a cognitive philosophical approach combined with *in vivo* desensitization and homework assignments, which involved speaking in public regardless of how uncomfortable he might initially be. With these cognitive behavioral methods, Ellis says, he has virtually conquered some of his worst blocks. At age 19 he also feared meeting women, so he forced himself to use behavioral methods to overcome his shyness. Ellis (1996) reports: "I made verbal overtures to 100 different women sitting on park benches in the Bronx Botanical Gardens, got rejected for dating by all of them (one woman kissed me in the park, and made a date for later that evening, but never showed up!)" (p. 109). He gave himself "one lousy minute" to talk to each of these women. Ellis believes that taking these actions helped him to overcome his fear of talking to women.

When Ellis began his practice of psychoanalysis, he routinely put his patients on the sofa and proceeded with them in a decidedly orthodox psychoanalytic way. Despite getting generally good results, he reports, he was dissatisfied with this approach (Ellis, 1994). Eventually, Ellis began to persuade and impel his clients to do the very things they were most afraid of doing, such as risking the rejection of significant others. Gradually, he became much more eclectic and more active and directive as a therapist. He combined humanistic and behavior therapy, and his pioneering efforts have earned him the right to be known as the father of REBT and the grandfather of cognitive behavioral therapy. Ellis also acknowledges the heavy existentialist influences on the formulation of his theory, as well as the neo-analytic works of Karen Horney, Alfred Adler, Erich Fromm, and Harry Stack Sullivan (Ellis, 2001b; Yankura & Dryden, 1994).

REBT is based on the assumption that we are not disturbed solely by our early or later environments but that we have strong inclinations to disturb ourselves consciously and unconsciously. We do this largely by taking our goals and values, which we mainly learn from our families and culture, and changing them into "shoulds," "oughts," and "musts" (Ellis, 1992). To overcome this self-indoctrination, which has resulted in irrational thinking, REBT therapists employ active/directive techniques such as teaching, suggestion, persuasion, and homework assignments, and they challenge clients to substitute a rational belief system for an irrational one (Ellis, 2001a).

The rational emotive behavior approach considers the relationship between therapist and client to be important to the therapeutic process, but what is also given great emphasis is the therapist's ability and willingness to challenge, confront, probe, and convince the client to practice activities (both in and outside of therapy) that will lead to constructive changes in thinking and behaving. The approach stresses action—doing something about the insights one gains in the therapy group. Change, it is assumed, will come about mainly by a commitment to practice new behaviors consistently. REBT lends itself to short-term group-oriented procedures, and practitioners frequently use group processes as a method of choice. The group is seen as offering the participants excellent opportunities for challenging self-destructive thinking and for practicing different behaviors. Ellis (2001a, 2001b) contends that REBT can enable clients to make significant changes with brief therapy (10 to 20 sessions).

Key Concepts

Some Hypotheses and Assumptions of REBT

A number of the basic assumptions of REBT can be categorized under these main postulates (Ellis, 1992, 1994, 1996, 1999, 2000a, 2000b, 2001a, 2001b):

- Thinking, feeling, and behaving continually interact with and influence one another.
- Emotional disturbances are caused or contributed to by a complex of biological and environmental factors. To understand and work with human problems it is *not* necessary to spend much time exploring the past or reliving emotional trauma of early childhood.
- Humans are affected by the people and the things around them, and they also intentionally affect the people around them. People decide, or choose, to disturb themselves—or not disturb themselves—in response to the influences of the system in which they live.
- People disturb themselves cognitively, emotionally, and behaviorally. They often think in a manner that defeats their own best interests as well as those of the others in their social group.

- When unfortunate events occur, people tend to create irrational beliefs about these events that are characterized by absolutist and dogmatic thinking. Typically, these irrational beliefs are centered on competence and success, love and approval, being treated fairly, and safety and comfort.
- It is not unfortunate events by themselves that cause emotional disturbance; rather, irrational beliefs often lead to personality problems.
- Most humans have a prodigious tendency to make and keep themselves emotionally disturbed. Thus, they find it virtually impossible to maintain perfectly good mental health. Unless they clearly and tough-mindedly acknowledge this reality, they are likely to sabotage their best efforts at changing.
- When people behave in self-defeating ways, they do have the ability to become aware of ways in which their beliefs are negatively affecting them. With this awareness they also have the capacity to dispute their irrational thoughts and change them into rational beliefs. By changing these beliefs about certain events, people also change their unhealthy feelings and self-defeating behaviors.
- Once irrational beliefs are discovered, they can be counteracted by using a combination of cognitive, emotive, and behavioral methods. REBT has various techniques of showing people how to minimize their self-sabotaging thoughts, feelings, and behaviors.
- Clients had better be willing to (1) acknowledge that they are mainly responsible for their own disturbed thoughts, emotions, and actions; (2) look at how they are thinking, feeling, and behaving when they needlessly disturb themselves; and (3) push themselves to the hard work that it will take to change.

Origins of Emotional Disturbance

A central concept of REBT is the role that absolutist "shoulds," "oughts," and "musts" play in people's becoming and remaining emotionally disturbed. We forcefully, rigidly, and emotionally subscribe to many grandiose "musts" that result in our needlessly disturbing ourselves. According to Ellis (2001a, 2001b), feelings of anxiety, depression, rejection, rage, guilt, and alienation are largely initiated and perpetuated by a belief system based on irrational ideas that were uncritically embraced, often during early childhood. These self-defeating beliefs are supported and maintained by negative, absolutist, and illogical statements that people make to themselves over and over.

In addition to taking on dysfunctional beliefs from others, Ellis stresses that people also invent "musts" on their own. Ellis (1994, 1997; Ellis & Dryden, 1997; Ellis & Harper, 1997) contends that most of our dysfunctional beliefs can be reduced to three main forms of "*must*urbation":

1. "I *absolutely must* do well and be approved by significant others. I must win their approval, or else I am an inadequate, worthless person."
2. "You *must* under all conditions and at all times treat me considerately, kindly, lovingly, and fairly. If you don't, you are no damned good and are a rotten person."

3. "Conditions under which I live *absolutely must* be comfortable, so that I can get what I want without too much effort. If not, it is *awful*; I *can't* stand it and *can't* have any real happiness at all!"

Rational emotive behavior therapy is grounded on existential principles in many respects. Although parents and society play a significant role in contributing to our emotional disturbance, we do not need to be victims of this indoctrination that takes place in our early years. We may not have had the resources during childhood to challenge parental and societal messages. As psychological adults now, however, we can become aware of how adhering to negative and destructive beliefs hampers our efforts to live fully, and we are also in a position to modify these beliefs.

The A-B-C Theory

The A-B-C theory of personality and emotional disturbance is central to REBT theory and practice. The A-B-C theory maintains that when people have an emotional reaction at point C (the emotional Consequence), after some Activating event that occurred at point A, it is not the event itself (A) that causes the emotional state (C), although it may contribute to it. It is the Belief system (B), or the beliefs that people have about the event, that mainly creates C. For example, if you feel rejected and hurt (C) over not getting a promotion at work (A), it is not the fact that you weren't promoted that causes your hurt; it is your belief (B) about the event. By believing that not having received a promotion means that you are a failure and that your efforts have not been appreciated and that they *should* be, you "construct" the emotional consequence of feeling rejected and hurt. Thus, human beings are largely responsible for creating their own emotional disturbances through the beliefs they associate with the events of their lives.

Ellis (1996, 2001b) maintains that people have the capacity to significantly change their cognitions, emotions, and behaviors. According to him, people can best accomplish this goal by avoiding preoccupying themselves with A and by acknowledging and yet resisting the temptation to dwell endlessly on emotional consequences at C. They can choose to examine, challenge, modify, and uproot B—the irrational beliefs they hold about the activating events at A.

The revised A-B-Cs of REBT now define B as "believing, emoting, and behaving." Because what clients believe (B) also involves strong emotional and behavioral elements, Ellis (2001a) added these latter two components to this framework.

Confronting Irrational Beliefs

The REBT therapeutic process begins by teaching clients the A-B-C theory. When they have come to see how their irrational beliefs and values are causally linked to their emotional and behavioral disturbances, they are ready to Dispute (D) these beliefs and values. D represents the application of scientific principles to challenge self-defeating philosophies and to dispose of unrealistic and unverifiable hypotheses. This is a form of cognitive therapy. One of the most effective methods of helping people reduce their emotional disturbances is to show them how to actively and forcefully dispute these irrational beliefs until they surrender them. This process of disputation involves three other Ds: (1) detecting irrational beliefs and seeing that they are illogical and unrealistic, (2) debating these irrational beliefs and showing oneself how they are unsupported by evidence, and (3) discriminating between irrational thinking and rational thinking (Ellis, 1994, 1996).

After D comes E, or the Effect of disputing—the relinquishing of self-destructive ideologies, the acquisition of effective new beliefs, and a greater acceptance of oneself, of others, and of the inevitable frustrations of everyday life. This new philosophy of life has, of course, a practical side—a concrete E, if you wish. In the previous example, E would translate into a rational and empirically based conclusion: "Well, it's too bad that I didn't get that promotion, but it's not the end of the world. There may be other opportunities. Besides, not getting the promotion doesn't mean that I'm a failure. So I don't need to keep telling myself all that nonsense." Or a person might make a rational statement such as this: "I'd like to have gotten the job, but I didn't. I regret that, but it's not awful, terrible, and horrible. It's bad enough that I lost it; I don't have to make myself miserable as well. I'm disappointed, but it's not awful unless I make it awful." According to REBT theory, the ultimate desired result is the reduction of feelings of depression and rejection.

Group members learn to separate their rational (or functional) beliefs from their irrational (or dysfunctional) beliefs and to understand the origins of their emotional disturbances as well as those of other members. Participants are taught the many ways in which they can (1) free themselves of their irrational life philosophy so that they can function more effectively as an individual and as a relational being and (2) learn more appropriate ways of responding so that they won't needlessly feel upset about the realities of living. The group members help and support one another in these learning endeavors.

Self-Rating and Learning Self-Acceptance

According to Ellis (2001b; Ellis & Harper, 1997), we have a strong tendency not only to rate our acts and behaviors as "good" or "bad," "worthy" or "unworthy" but also to rate ourselves as a total person on the basis of our performances. He contends that people oftentimes rate their performances as ineffectual. They then illogically overgeneralize by rating themselves as incompetent and worthless beings. This is an example of self-rating: "If I fail at something, I'm a failure in life." This self-rating process constitutes one of the main sources of our emotional disturbances. REBT group leaders teach members how to separate the evaluation of their behaviors from the evaluation of themselves—their essence and their totality—and how to accept themselves in spite of their imperfections.

Ellis contends that this kind of self-rating inevitably leads to a number of problems—among them, self-centeredness and self-consciousness; low self-esteem; a tendency to prove oneself rather than enjoying oneself; a tendency to damn oneself and others; the feeling that no matter what one accomplishes, it is never enough; attempts to manipulate others; and the sabotaging of one's goals. If people are able to assess their performances honestly and accurately without rating themselves as persons, he hypothesizes, they will experience minimal disturbance and gain the maximum enjoyment from life (Ellis, 1994, 1996; Ellis & Dryden, 1997).

The opposite of self-rating is *unconditional self-acceptance*, which REBT favors. It is not necessary for individuals to prove their worth by being loved and approved of by others because of their actions. Therapists teach clients the importance of unconditional self-acceptance. Ellis (1999, 2000b; Ellis & Blau, 1998; Ellis & Crawford, 2000) identify some of the pathways of realistic acceptance:

• Accepting the fact that change is the product of hard work and practice
• Unwhining acceptance of what we cannot change
• Accepting the reality that we are imperfect
• Avoiding damnation of ourselves and others

Goals of a REBT Group

According to Ellis (2001b), two of the main goals of REBT are to assist clients in the process of achieving unconditional self-acceptance (USA) and unconditional other acceptance (UOA), and to see how these are interrelated. To the degree that clients are able to accept themselves, they are able to accept others. Further goals are to teach clients how to change their dysfunctional emotions and behaviors into healthy ones and to cope with almost any unfortunate event that may arise in their lives (Ellis, 2001b). Ideally, REBT develops the following characteristics of a mentally and emotionally healthy individual: self-interest, social interest, self-direction, tolerance, acceptance of ambiguity and uncertainty, flexibility, scientific thinking, commitment, risk taking, self-acceptance, long-range hedonism, the willingness to be imperfect, and responsibility for one's own emotional disturbance (Ellis, 1994, 1996, 2001a, 2001b).

REBT aims at providing group members with tools for reducing or eliminating unhealthy emotions (such as depression and anxiety) so that they can live richer and more satisfying lives. To accomplish this basic objective, it offers clients practical ways to identify their underlying faulty beliefs, to critically evaluate such beliefs, and to exchange them for constructive beliefs.

Basically, group members are taught that they are responsible for their own emotional reactions; that they can reduce their emotional disturbances by paying attention to their self-verbalizations and by changing their beliefs and values; and that if they acquire a new and more realistic philosophy, they can cope effectively with most of the unfortunate events in their lives. Although the therapeutic goals of REBT are essentially the same for both individual and group therapy, the two differ in some of the specific methods and techniques employed, as you will see in the pages that follow.

Role and Functions of the Group Leader

The therapeutic activities of an REBT group are carried out with one central purpose: helping the participants internalize a rational philosophy of life, just as they internalized a set of dogmatic and false beliefs derived from their sociocultural environment and from their own invention. In working toward this ultimate aim, the group leader has several specific functions and tasks. The first task is to show group members how they have created their own misery. This is done by clarifying the connection between their emotional and behavioral disturbances and their values, beliefs, and attitudes. The leader confronts them with the beliefs they originally unquestioningly accepted, demonstrates how they are continuing to indoctrinate themselves with unexamined assumptions, and shows them how to think constructively.

To help members move beyond the mere recognition that they originally incorporated irrational thoughts, the therapist helps them modify their thinking. REBT assumes that people's illogical beliefs are so deeply ingrained that they will not change easily. Thus, it is the role of the leader to teach members how to challenge their assumptions and how to stop the vicious circle of the self-rating and other-blaming process.

But getting rid of symptoms of disturbances is not enough. If only specific problems or symptoms are dealt with, other fears are likely to appear. Thus, the final step in the therapeutic process is to teach members how to avoid becoming victims of future irrational beliefs. The therapist challenges the core of clients' faulty thinking and teaches them how to apply realistic and constructive thinking when coping with future problems.

REBT employs many cognitive and emotive techniques, which are best carried out in an active manner (Ellis, 1996, 2001b; Ellis & Dryden, 1997). REBT group workers favor interventions such as questioning, challenging, assigning homework, and helping members experiment with new ways of thinking, feeling, and doing. The therapist assumes the role of a teacher and not that of an intensely relating partner. REBT group leaders tend to avoid relating too closely to their members and thus avoid having them increase their dependency tendencies. However, REBT practitioners demonstrate respect for their clients and also tend to be highly collaborative, encouraging, supportive, and mentoring. A group member learns that the leader is not thinking disapprovingly and can be trusted. Leaders often engage in self-disclosure in cases where doing so would help the members work through their problems (Brabender & Fallon, 1993).

REBT group leaders are active in teaching the theoretical model, proposing methods of coping, and teaching members strategies for testing hypotheses and solutions. Leaders also orchestrate each session to ensure that no one member dominates, that no one becomes disruptive, and that antitherapeutic statements are not allowed to stand. This active role is clearly evident in every session unless the leader elects to be silent or to function as a coach (Brabender & Fallon, 1993).

REBT practitioners employ a directive role in getting members to commit themselves to practicing in everyday situations what they are learning in the group sessions. They view what goes on during the group as important, but they realize that the hard work in between sessions and after therapy is terminated is even more crucial (Ellis, 1996). The group context provides members with the tools that they can use in learning to become self-reliant and to accept themselves unconditionally as they encounter new problems in daily living.

Application: Therapeutic Techniques and Procedures

From the origin of the approach, REBT has always utilized a wide range of cognitive, emotive, and behavioral methods with most clients. Like other cognitive behavioral therapies, REBT blends techniques to change clients' patterns of thinking, feeling, and acting. It is an integrative therapy, selectively adapting various methods that are also used in existential, humanistic, and other therapeutic approaches, but the emphasis is on the cognitive and behavioral dimensions (Ellis, 2001b). REBT focuses on specific techniques for changing a client's self-defeating thoughts in concrete situations. In addition to modifying beliefs, REBT helps group members see how their beliefs influence what they feel and what they do; thus, there is also a concern for changing feelings and behaviors that flow from dysfunctional thinking patterns. REBT aims to minimize symptoms by bringing about a profound change in philosophy.

Problems Treated in REBT

A wide range of disorders can be addressed in REBT groups: anxiety, depression, anger, marital problems, poor interpersonal skills, perfectionism, morbid jealousy, parenting skills, character disorders, obsessive/compulsive disorders, eating disorders, psychosomatic disorders, addictive behaviors, posttraumatic stress disorders, and psychotic disorders (Ellis, 2001b; Ellis & Blau, 1998; Ellis & Crawford, 2000). In the case of clients who are involuntarily referred, it is necessary to find ways of motivating them by showing them that they can benefit in some way by taking REBT seriously (Ellis & Velten, 1992).

Interventions Used in REBT

An international survey of REBT therapists found that the techniques they most frequently used were humor, didactic presentations of REBT theory, cognitive rehearsal of desired behaviors, and unconditional acceptance (Warren & McLellarn, 1987). This same study found the following in-session techniques also being used: strong and forceful language, disputing methods, assertiveness training, social skills training, role playing, behavioral rehearsal, teaching rational coping self-statements, rational emotive imagery, modeling, relaxation training, rational role reversal, problem-solving training, imaginal desensitization, contingency contracting, operant methods, cognitive restructuring, cognitive therapy, *in vivo* desensitization, and information giving.

Applications of REBT to Brief Group Therapy

Ellis (1996, 2001b) demonstrates that REBT mainly employs interventions in groups that are both brief and intensive. He has always maintained that the best therapy is one that is efficient in that clients are taught in a brief time how to tackle practical problems of living. He stresses the following characteristics of REBT methods that constitute brief interventions in a group:

- Group members can quickly learn how they disturb themselves. The A-B-Cs of their problems can be clearly and simply shown, easily grasped, and quickly put to use in therapy.
- Because of the active/directive nature of REBT, members can alleviate their disturbances in the shortest feasible time.
- By using the cognitive, emotive, and behavioral methods of REBT for even a brief time, members can internalize a constructive philosophy that shows them new ways of approaching situations.

Ellis originally developed REBT to try to make psychotherapy shorter and more efficient than most other systems of therapy; hence, it is intrinsically a brief therapy. Since 1959 he has seen thousands of clients in brief therapy beyond the dyadic relationship, ranging from 1 to 10 sessions, including demonstration sessions he has given with hundreds of volunteers at his regular Friday Night Problems of Daily Living in New York and in his public demonstrations throughout the world. He has also used REBT successfully in groups in one- and two-day marathons and in nine-hour REBT intensives (Ellis, 1996; Ellis & Dryden, 1997). The theory and methods of REBT brief therapy are detailed in *Better, Deeper, and More Intensive Brief Therapy* (Ellis, 1996) and in *Brief Rational Emotive Behaviour Therapy* (Dryden, 1995).

Cognitive Methods of REBT

From a cognitive perspective REBT demonstrates to clients that their beliefs and self-talk are keeping them disturbed. It has various techniques for dispelling these self-defeating cognitions and teaching people how to acquire a rational approach to living. As mentioned earlier, in an REBT group there is a heavy emphasis on thinking, disputing, debating, challenging, persuading, interpreting, explaining, and teaching. Some of the cognitive techniques that are often used in an REBT group are described next.

Teaching the A-B-Cs of REBT The A-B-C theory, mentioned earlier, is taught to clients undergoing individual or group therapy. Members are taught that no matter how and where they originally acquired their irrational "shoulds," "oughts," and "musts," they have the power now to begin to surrender these dysfunctional beliefs. They are shown ways to apply the A-B-C theory to practical problems they encounter in everyday life.

Active Disputation of Faulty Beliefs Clients are taught how to check and modify their values and attitudes about themselves and others. Therapists show clients how to detect their "awfulizing," and their "self-downing." In their active and didactic role, REBT leaders focus on disputing the irrational, logically inconsistent, absolutist, catastrophic, and faulty ideas of clients. They demonstrate how such ideas bring about unnecessary disturbances, and they persuade clients to change or surrender these dysfunctional behaviors. For best results, active disputation needs to go beyond the cognitive level and include emotional disputing. Members *forcefully* question and challenge their faulty thinking, and they also engage in a number of emotive methods (described later) as a way of extending the impact of disputing beliefs.

Teaching Coping Self-Statements   Group members are taught how self-destructive beliefs can be countered by sensible coping statements. They are expected to monitor their manner of speaking by writing down and analyzing the quality of their language. For example, a member might tell herself: "I *must* perform well, which means being perfect. If I make any mistakes, it would be *horrible*. I simply *can't stand it* when I don't attain perfection immediately. People will give me approval and love only when I'm perfect, and I *absolutely* need this acceptance from others to feel worthwhile." By becoming aware of the absolutist and demanding quality of her internal and external speech, she can learn how what she tells herself is setting her up for failure. It is possible for her to learn that her demands of being perfect will inevitably result in disillusionment and heartache. She can replace these self-destructive statements with coping statements: "I can still accept myself in spite of my imperfections. Although I *prefer* doing my best, I don't *have* to drive myself to unrealistically high performances. Besides, even if I were to fail in a task, I could still accept myself. I don't have to do everything perfectly well to feel worthwhile as a person."

Psychoeducational Methods   Members of REBT groups are encouraged to practice and work hard outside of the therapy sessions as a pathway to personal change. Ellis, Abrams, and Dengelegi (1992) have found that clients who read cognitive behavioral literature, use REBT audio- and videocassettes, and attend lectures and workshops usually learn to apply REBT better than those who do not. REBT offers many resources for dealing with general emotional problems and specific concerns, such as overcoming addictions, dealing with depression, managing anger, understanding and coping with weight problems, becoming assertive, and overcoming procrastination. Two examples of these self-help books are *How to Stubbornly Refuse to Make Yourself Miserable About Anything—Yes, Anything!* (Ellis, 1988) and *Feeling Better, Getting Better, and Staying Better* (Ellis, 2001a). Ellis has made many tapes, a few of which cover ways of refusing to be ashamed of anything, ways to stop worrying, conquering the dire need for love, and overcoming low tolerance for frustration. Sources of REBT materials that are available from the Albert Ellis Institute are listed at the end of this chapter.

Cognitive Homework   Clients participating in REBT groups are given cognitive homework assignments, which consist of ways of applying the A-B-C theory to many of the problems in daily life. Members may be given the "REBT

Self-Help Form" (reproduced in the Student Manual that accompanies this text), on which they list their irrational beliefs. In an adjoining column they write down a disputing statement for each irrational belief. In another column they record an effective rational belief to replace the irrational belief. Finally, they record the feelings and behaviors that they experienced after arriving at an effective rational belief. For example, the statement "I *must* be approved of and accepted by all the significant people in my life" can be disputed with statements such as "Where is it written that I *must* have this approval?" or "Why must I have their total approval to feel like a worthwhile individual?" An effective rational belief might include the statement "There is no evidence that I *absolutely must* have approval from others, though I would like to be approved of by those whom I respect." During the week, group members make the time to record and think about how their beliefs contribute to their personal problems, and they work hard at uprooting these self-defeating cognitions. When they return to the group, they can bring up specific situations in which they did well or in which they experienced difficulty. Group members often teach each other ways of disputing beliefs based on material that grows out of the REBT Self-Help Form.

Emotive Methods in REBT Groups

As we have seen, REBT is almost always a multimodal approach to change; it rarely treats individuals without using several cognitive, behavioral, and emotive methods (Ellis, 1996, 2001a; Kwee & Ellis, 1997). Emotive techniques include unconditional acceptance, rational emotive imagery, the use of humor, shame-attacking exercises, and rational emotive role playing. These techniques are explored in more detail in the following sections.

Unconditional Acceptance   Clients are given full and unconditional acceptance, no matter how badly they behave inside and outside of therapy, and leaders teach members how to achieve unconditional self-acceptance (USA). Group members often burden themselves with fears of being "discovered" for what they really are and then being rejected. Group leaders can model an accepting attitude that goes beyond what members have done or felt. The therapist can strongly show group members that, even though their behavior might be inappropriate or immoral, they are never *rotten people* or *total fools*. This kind of REBT-flavored unconditional acceptance creates a group atmosphere that allows members to feel personally accepted, even though some of their beliefs and behaviors will likely be challenged vigorously. Ellis shows group members that they are never stupid, inept, or worthless individuals. They are more than what they think and do (Ellis, 1994, 1996, 2001b, 2002, Ellis & Blau, 1998).

Rational Emotive Imagery   Using the technique of rational emotive imagery (REI), clients are asked to vividly imagine one of the worst things that might happen to them. They imagine themselves in specific situations where they experience disturbing feelings. Then they are shown how to train themselves to develop healthy emotions in place of disruptive ones. Clients work actively on changing these feelings to healthy ones and, consequently, changing their behavior in the situation. For example, therapists can induce even resistant clients to imagine vividly that they keep failing and keep getting criticized and can thereby produce in them extreme feelings of inadequacy. Then these clients are induced to change their feelings to mere regret and disappointment instead of worthlessness. Members practice this process for at least 30 days in a row until they have trained themselves to feel regretful and disappointed automatically when they experience failure instead of feeling devastated. Members might imagine some of their worst fears coming true. Within the group, they can share these fears, gain some emotional insight on how such fears control much of what they do and say, and eventually learn to respond in different ways. Imagery work is a safe prelude to actually confronting one's fears in daily life. (For a more detailed discussion of REI, see Ellis, 2001a).

Use of Humor   Humor has both cognitive and emotional benefits in bringing about change. When people disturb themselves, Ellis (2001a) believes they usually lose their sense of humor and take themselves far too seriously. As one of its main techniques to combat the kind of exaggerated thinking that leads people into trouble, REBT employs a good deal of humor. It teaches group members to laugh—not at themselves but at their self-defeating beliefs and their "ridiculous" behavior. REBT reduces certain ideas that clients hold onto tenaciously by showing how contradictory and ridiculous these views really are. Although introducing humor inappropriately or too soon in a group can present problems, once trust has been established, the members are generally far more ready to see the folly of some of their ways and can actually enjoy laughing at some of their behaviors. One example of employing humor is having group members sing comical songs published by Ellis in his songbook, *A Garland of Rational Songs* (1977). The whole group, as an exercise, might sing some of these humorous songs. As a homework exercise, some clients find benefit in singing these songs to themselves when they experience anxiety or depression in daily life situations. (For a more detailed discussion of humor and comical songs, see Ellis, 2001a).

Shame-Attacking Exercises   The rationale underlying shame-attacking exercises is that anxiety often results from shame, guilt, embarrassment, and self-damnation. Thus, the more that people directly face and deal with the irrational beliefs behind these feelings, the less likely they are to remain emotionally disturbed. In REBT group therapy, many kinds of self-disclosing, risk-taking, and shame-attacking exercises are introduced (Ellis, 1996). Members in REBT groups are often encouraged to participate in risk-taking activities as a way to challenge their fears of looking foolish. Practitioners employ shame-attacking exercises as a way of teaching clients to accept themselves in spite of reactions from others. These exercises are aimed at increasing self-acceptance and mature responsibility, as well as helping members to see that much of what they think of as being shameful has to do with the way they define reality for themselves.

The main thing clients learn from shame-attacking exercises is that they are no different when they are experiencing disapproval than when they are not. In other words, disapproval does not have to affect their worth or change them, nor does the fear of disapproval have to prevent them from doing things they consider right. In the course of doing "shameful" things in a group, members move toward unconditional self-acceptance, which is heavily stressed in group therapy.

Group members frequently admit that they are inhibiting themselves from doing many things they would like to do because of their fear of what others might think. In a group situation other members might exert therapeutic pressure and also provide support for individuals to experiment with risky behaviors, first in the group and then in daily situations. Ellis (2002) describes a few exercises that clients might be induced to perform in public. These include wearing outlandish clothes, borrowing money from a stranger, or shouting out the stops in the train or bus. Ellis contends that if clients will do these acts over and over and also work on their feelings so that they don't feel ashamed or humiliated, they will then be able to conquer the powerful feelings that paralyze them and keep them from doing things they would like to do. He suggests that it is better to combine cognitive homework with these *in vivo* shame-attacking exercises. Here are a few other examples of possible shame-attacking exercises:

- Walk through a park singing at the top of your voice.
- In a crowded elevator, tell people that you are glad they could attend this important meeting that you have called.
- Talk to animals, and pretend that they are talking back to you.
- Ride in a crowded elevator standing backward (facing the rear).
- Tie a ribbon around a banana and "walk it" down a street.
- In public, shout out the exact time by saying, "The time is 11:11 and 20 seconds."
- Go to a drugstore, and in a loud voice say to the pharmacist, "I want a gross of condoms, and since I use so many of them, you should give me a special discount!" (This is one of Ellis's favorites.)
- After finishing a meal in a restaurant say, "Ah, I feel a fart coming on!" (This is one of my favorites.)

Role Playing   There are emotional, cognitive, and behavioral components in role playing. One way of assisting clients to experience and cope with feelings of fear is to ask them to reverse roles. For example, if a member is experiencing anxiety over an upcoming job interview, he can assume the role of the interviewer. He can also play himself in both a fearful stance and in a confident manner. Rather than having members simply talk about their problems or think about their beliefs, they can become emotionally involved if they allow themselves to role-play. Of course, some members will be faced with challenging their fears of looking foolish during the role playing or of not engaging in the activity as they think they should. Not only can role playing free members up emotionally, but it can also provide them with opportunities to act in a host of new ways. Indeed, role playing can result in modifying a member's way of thinking, feeling, and behaving.

In an REBT group, role playing also involves a cognitive evaluation of the feelings and beliefs that are experienced. Thus, if a member is trying to deal more effectively with a rejecting father who demands perfection, he can adopt a role quite different from his usual one, a role in which he no longer feels victimized by his father's lack of approval. Afterward, this person undertakes a cognitive analysis of the feelings experienced during the role enactment. To that effect, he may try to answer questions such as these:

• Do I need my father's approval to survive?
• Will I ever be able to attain the level of perfection that my father demands?
• Can I accept myself although I'll never be perfect? Can I avoid destructive self-rating and self-blaming because of my imperfection?
• Do I really have to be perfect before I can accept myself?

Ellis believes role playing is more effective if it entails a cognitive restructuring of the attitudes revealed by the experience.

Behavioral Methods in REBT Groups

According to Ellis (1996, 2001a), the behavioral methods of REBT work best when they are used in combination with emotive and cognitive methods. Also, self-management methods work best when clients control their own behavior rather than allowing themselves to be controlled by the leader.

Homework Assignments   Earlier, I described cognitive homework assignments, which involve reading, listening to audiotapes, and doing a written A-B-C-D-E analysis. In an REBT group there is a frequent use of activity-oriented homework assignments to help people behave more rationally. Group leaders assist members in doing these assignments in their head, through the imagination process, and then encourage members to carry them into real life. REBT favors *in vivo desensitization* and urges members to do repetitively the very things they are afraid of doing as a way to overcome their crippling fears (Ellis, 2001b).

Group participants engage in the PYA (push your ass) technique, deliberately forcing themselves to confront "dangerous" pursuits until they can learn how to cope when they encounter fearful situations. Partly by doing the fearful thing many times, they eventually conquer their fears by carrying out their homework assignments (Ellis, Gordon, Neenan, & Palmer, 1998). These assignments, which are given by the leader as well as other group members, may be carried out in the group itself or outside of it; in the latter case, the person is supposed to report the results to the group. Here are some examples of in-group assignments:

• Members who tend to view the group leader as a superbeing who is to be believed without question are invited to challenge the leader and to deal with their attitude toward authority figures. This assignment allows members to see how, by maintaining a helpless attitude in the presence of such figures, they keep themselves from being empowered.

   • A man who is shy around women is encouraged to approach the female group members and systematically challenge his fears and expectations by talking about them.

   • A woman who is very quiet during the group sessions because she is self-conscious about her accent can be asked to disclose and explore her fears and embarrassment about speaking out. She can also be challenged to work on changing her beliefs about her inability to contribute something of value because of her accent.

   • A group member who is convinced that others in the group will reject him if they know about his shameful side can be encouraged to disclose some of the fears that are keeping him hidden.

   In addition to these in-group assignments, leaders challenge members to carry out homework assignments. Individuals who are afraid of riding in the subway, flying on airplanes, or riding in elevators are encouraged to engage repeatedly in these anxiety-producing activities. For example, people with elevator fears might be encouraged to enter 20 elevators daily for one month while forcefully telling themselves that they can stand it even if the damn elevator gets stuck.

   Ellis (2001b) typically begins a group session by asking members to read their homework assignments to discover whether they have done the assignment and, if not, why not. After homework is reviewed and discussed, members generally bring up some problem they want to explore, discuss their goals and plans, or report on their progress. Both Ellis and the other group members listen carefully for dogmatic "shoulds." As these dysfunctional core beliefs are identified, members are challenged to dispute them vigorously, and they learn rational coping statements. Then another homework assignment is suggested as a way to continue uprooting dysfunctional thinking and replacing it with effective thoughts and behaviors.

Reinforcement and Penalties   Both reinforcers and penalties are used to help clients change. Reinforcements can involve reading a novel, watching a movie, going to a concert, or eating a favorite food. Clients can be taught to reinforce themselves with something they like, but only after they have carried out a specific homework assignment that they have promised themselves to do but that they tend to avoid doing. One of REBT's goals is to teach clients better methods of self-management. Members' ultimate success depends on how effectively they can take charge of their lives beyond the group sessions. Using principles of reinforcement often helps members develop consistency in applying rational principles to the new problems they encounter. In this sense, they become their own therapists and continually teach themselves how to manage their lives.

   REBT also recommends the use of self-imposed penalties when members do not carry out agreed-upon homework. Ellis (2001b) may suggest that "difficult customers" (DCs) penalize themselves after their destructive indulgences. For example, they might be urged to donate a $100 to an organization they violently disagree with when they fail to keep their promises to themselves to change their behavior, or they can spend an hour with a boring person when they gamble, or they can light every cigarette with a $50 bill.

Skills Training   Training clients in specific skills in which they are deficient has long been espoused, as long as this training is done in the context of challenging them to uproot their dysfunctional thinking (Ellis, 1996, 2001b). The assumption is that by acquiring skills they formerly lacked clients will feel more confident about themselves and will experience significant changes in the way they think, feel, and behave (Bernard & Wolfe, 2000; Ellis, 2000a). Group members have opportunities to learn and practice important interpersonal skills in the group sessions. They are encouraged to acquire personal and interpersonal skills by taking courses and practicing outside of the group (Ellis, 2001b).

Advantages of REBT Applied to Group Work

More than 40 years of experience in conducting and leading REBT groups has confirmed Ellis's belief that a group is particularly effective in helping participants make constructive personality and behavior changes. Ellis (2001b) discusses many of the advantages of applying REBT techniques to groups, some of which are briefly summarized here:

- The activity-oriented homework assignments that are a vital component of REBT are more effectively carried out in the group context than in one-to-one therapy.
- The group offers an effective milieu for several active/directive procedures, such as role playing, assertion training, behavior rehearsal, modeling, and risk-taking exercises.
- The group serves as a laboratory in which behavior can be directly observed in action. Because the group exists in a social context, many problems of members can be more easily assessed and explored than they might be in individual therapy.
- Clients are often asked to complete homework report forms, which require going over the A-B-Cs of upsetting situations and then learning how to correct faulty thinking and behaving. By hearing other members' reports and learning how they have dealt with the situations in question, participants can better deal with their own issues. The members can then practice together the behaviors they would like to increase or decrease in the real world.
- By watching other members, participants are able to see that treatment can be effective, that people can change, that they can take steps to help themselves, and that successful therapy is the product of hard and persistent work.
- Disclosing intimate problems, some of which the person considers shameful, is therapeutic in itself. Self-disclosure enables participants to realize

that taking risks pays off: their "revelations" generally don't have the dire consequences they feared so much, and even if someone does criticize them, it is certainly not catastrophic.

• Since REBT is highly educational and didactic, it typically includes information giving and discussion of problem-solving strategies. Economically and practically, this is better done in a group than in an individual setting. The group also encourages participants to become actively involved in their treatment.

• Group procedures are especially useful for people who are rigidly bound by old patterns of dysfunctional behavior; the group setting provides the challenge necessary to reevaluate these patterns and adopt healthier ones.

Even though Ellis uses this list of reasons to support his view that REBT is especially suitable for group work, these same reasons can be adduced to support the group application of most of the other therapeutic models covered in this book. Therefore, the points discussed by Ellis can be usefully considered by any group practitioner who is in the process of developing a rationale for a group counseling program, even if he or she has an orientation other than REBT.

Applying Rational Emotive Behavior Therapy to Group Work in the Schools

The principles and the techniques of REBT have direct application for group counseling with students of varying ages. Because REBT is a form of education that uses methods to reeducate clients, there are a number of direct applications to group counseling with students. As an example, consider a group for children of alcoholics; these kinds of groups are often conducted in elementary, middle, and high schools. A main benefit of a group based on a cognitive behavioral model is that it helps members deal with situations beyond their control. Quite often children and adolescents in such groups feel personally responsible for the disruptions in their family, when in reality the adults' substance abuse is the primary cause of the family turmoil. School counselors leading these groups can assist members in identifying and changing beliefs that put the main blame on themselves and can help members create new self-talk.

The educational aspects of REBT hold promise as a preventive intervention for children, adolescents, and adults who are inclined to exaggerate negative events (Thompson & Rudolph, 2000). Consider the faulty beliefs that many adolescents harbor that would provide grist for the mill in an REBT high school group. Adolescents often tell themselves that they cannot stand rejection. They may believe that if they fail at something important they are basically worthless. They may have little acceptance of themselves if they are less than perfect. Cognitive interventions, such as learning to dispute certain faulty beliefs that are held tenaciously, can be most useful in helping adolescents to think differently. If they learn how to challenge self-limiting beliefs, they will begin to feel better and to get better. A group is an ideal place to work on unconditional self-acceptance and also to increase one's acceptance of others, which are pressing concerns of students.

The goal of a cognitive behavioral group is for students to identify the thoughts and behaviors that bring about undesirable consequences and to help them develop and use strategies that are likely to result in more desirable consequences. The group offers a context for behavior change through modeling, coaching, and reinforcement. Kahn (1999) states that in a cognitive behavioral group the students operationally define their outcome goals. Students are expected to describe evidence of the attainment of their goals by answering questions such as "What will I be doing, and where and when will I be doing it?" For decreasing behaviors, they will answer the question, "What will I be doing instead?" In such a group each student builds an action plan aimed at bringing about behavioral change by drawing on cognitive, emotive, and behavioral techniques. Kahn's work draws on techniques described in the previous chapter and this chapter as well. He asserts that a wide variety of behavioral and cognitive techniques can be applied to group work with school-age students, both from developmental and remedial contexts.

As you know from this chapter, psychoeducational methods are frequently used in REBT groups. Most of the groups in a school setting are educational in nature. The general purpose of the group is to teach the participants coping skills for daily living, as well as to assist students in modifying certain cognitions, emotions, and behaviors. In these groups the participants soon learn that change is the result of practice and hard work outside of the group meetings. Groups oriented around key concepts in REBT can be useful in dealing not only with problems at school but in a student's interpersonal relationships and home environment. A useful resource for teaching REBT concepts to students in both developmental and remedial groups is Ann Vernon's (1989) book *Thinking, Feeling, and Behaving: An Emotional Education for Children*.

Applying Rational Emotive Behavior Therapy with Multicultural Populations

REBT has certain advantages in working with multicultural populations. If members are not challenged too quickly, they can be invited to examine the premises on which they behave. Consider a group composed of members from a culture that stresses doing one's best, cooperation, interdependence, respect for the family, and working hard. Some members of this group may be struggling with feelings of shame and guilt if they perceive that they are not living up to the expectations set for them by their parents and families. Leaders who confront the cultural values of such clients too quickly are likely to see counterproductive results. In fact, these clients may drop out of therapy, based largely on feeling misunderstood. A sensitive REBT group practitioner can, however, encourage such clients to begin to question how they may have uncritically accepted as truth all of the messages from their culture. Without encouraging them to abandon respect for their cultural heritage, the therapist can still challenge them to examine their beliefs and understand their consequences.

Similar to the behavioral group therapist, the REBT group leader functions in the role of a teacher. This image would seem ideal for certain cultural groups, because it detracts from the stigma of being mentally ill and focuses on problems of living. Life can be more fulfilling if clients learn better ways to think about the issues that confront them. With the help of the therapist and other group members, clients learn new ways of thinking and behaving, which result in new feelings.

Challenging faulty beliefs and the cognitive restructuring process involve confronting group members with their self-defeating thinking and certain of their core beliefs. In using these cognitive interventions with Latino group members, Organista (2000) indicates the value of empathy in softening the A-B-C-D approach so frequently used in REBT groups. Organista teaches Latino group members the difference between "helpful" thoughts that ameliorate symptoms and lead to constructive thinking and adaptive behavior and "unhelpful" thoughts that do the opposite. Rather than provoking defensiveness by labeling client beliefs "irrational" or "distorted," in this context it is well for therapists to demonstrate that client thought patterns may be understandable in light of their circumstances.

The literature provides other examples of applying REBT from a multicultural perspective. Sapp (1994, 1996) addresses ways of applying cognitive behavior therapy, mainly REBT, to the academic failure of African American middle school students. Sapp, McNelly, and Torres (1998) applied REBT to the process of death and dying with elderly African Americans and Latinos.

Pack-Brown, Whittington-Clark, and Parker (1998) suggest that a cognitive behavioral approach can be effectively used in African American women's groups because of the emphasis given to cognition and changing behavior:

> Cognitive-behavioral group approaches overlaid with Afrocentric philosophy would be an excellent place for African-American women to think through many of their conflicting and troubling issues in an understanding and supportive environment. Thinking through issues can often reduce the size of certain gigantic issues to more manageable levels. (p. 84)

Pack-Brown and her colleagues add that group leaders can make the mistake of emphasizing the cognitive dimensions to the extent that they might neglect facilitating emotional exploration on the part of clients.

REBT is a forceful approach, and the therapist must exert caution in challenging clients about their beliefs and behaviors. Active-directive therapists might adopt an authoritarian style, which is likely to result in neglecting important individual and multicultural influences (Ellis, 2001b). What may seem like an irrational belief to a therapist may be a long-cherished value that influences the individual. The client may say: "All my life I've been taught to respect my father. Although I do have respect and love for him, I'm thinking that I want to make some choices about my life that aren't in line with his choice for me. I've always told myself that I simply can't disappoint my father, so I've suppressed my wishes and followed his will." A group leader who insensitively hammered away at the irrational quality of this woman's respect would not be upholding her values. Even though it might be therapeutic for her to question some of her beliefs, the therapist must not err by imposing his or her standards on this person.

Ellis (2001b) takes the position that an essential part of people's lives consists of group living and that their happiness depends largely on the quality of their functioning within their community. Thus, individuals can make the mistake of being too self-centered and self-indulgent. REBT stresses the relationship of individuals to the family, community, and other systems. This orientation is consistent with valuing diversity and the interdependence of being an individual and a productive member of the community.

Evaluation of Rational Emotive Behavior Therapy in Groups

Contributions and Strengths of the Approach

I consider several aspects of REBT valuable enough to use in my own approach to group practice. Although I do believe that events and significant persons in our past play a critical role in shaping our present beliefs about ourselves, I agree with Ellis that we are responsible for maintaining self-destructive and irrational convictions. True, we may have learned that unless we were everything others expected us to be we could never hope to be loved and accepted. But the fact that at one time we uncritically accepted certain premises doesn't exempt us now from the responsibility of scrutinizing these and other irrational assumptions and replacing them with more rational ones, which will lead to different and more effective behavior. In this sense, REBT is based on the existential assumption that we are ultimately free and responsible rather than being controlled by our past conditioning. Groups are a particularly useful format both for exploring the ways in which we have bought into self-defeating beliefs and for providing a climate where we can construct new beliefs.

I often ask group members to express the beliefs or assumptions that underlie the problems they are experiencing. One of the most common answers is that making mistakes is a terrible, unforgivable thing and that we should arrange our lives in such a way that we won't make mistakes. After probing to find out how the person came to accept such a belief, I generally pursue the issue with these questions: "Does this belief really make sense to you now? What would your life be like if you continued to live by these assumptions? Do you think you'd be different if you could change some of these basic beliefs? If so, in what ways? What actions can you take now, in this group and in your everyday life, that will help you change some of the beliefs you hold?"

Another contribution of REBT relates to training group leaders. REBT can be used effectively in helping trainees learn how to identify and challenge their internal dialogue, which sometimes gets in the way by creating self-doubt and blocking optimal functioning. Corey, Ellis, and Cooker (1998) provide some examples of the self-talk that blocks the effectiveness of students who are learning how to facilitate groups:

- I *must* have love and approval from all the members in my group. My worth as a counselor and as a person is dependent on the affirmation of my clients.
- As a group facilitator, I *must* always perform competently and perfectly. There is absolutely no room for serious mistakes, for this implies failing, and notable failure always means that I am a failure.
- If I do not get what I want from each member, it is terrible and I *cannot stand it*. The group *must* act exactly the way I want when I want it.
- I should always know what to say, and it is *essential* that I have the right answers.
- I *must* be the perfect role model.
- I fear that I may look foolish, and this *should* never happen!
- I *must* have the right technique for each situation, or else everything might fall flat, and the consequences would be a disaster.

It is likely that student group leaders will discover a core of dysfunctional beliefs that affect both their personal lives and the manner in which they lead their groups. By using some of the concepts and methods of REBT, beginning group leaders can learn how to transform dysfunctional thinking into more productive beliefs. The more capable you are of exploring your own self-limiting thoughts, the more able you will be to challenge the thought patterns of the members of your groups (Corey et al., 1998).

I value REBT's emphasis on thinking because of the crucial role that conceptualizing plays in bringing about behavioral and emotional changes. Experiencing a catharsis and expressing pent-up feelings can have a significant impact only when it is followed by an attempt to understand the meaning of the experience. REBT provides a framework for this vital cognitive dimension.

Like any other action-oriented approach, REBT insists that newly acquired insights be put into action. REBT's use of the homework method is an excellent avenue for translating insights into concrete action programs. In my own groups I often suggest assignments that can be carried out outside the group and that allow clients to practice new behaviors and experiment with a different style of being. Note that these assignments do not have to be "given" by the leader; members can be encouraged to set tasks for themselves. Some of the best homework will consist of activities that members suggest. From my perspective, it is essential that homework assignments be tailored to members' specific problems and that these activities be collaboratively developed by both the member and the leader.

Once members have identified unsupported conclusions and faulty beliefs, they can be encouraged to record and think about how their beliefs contribute to their personal problems. In this way members can work diligently at critically examining their self-defeating cognitions. When members come to the next group session, they can bring up specific situations in which they did well or in which they experienced difficulty. As members consistently question the actual evidence for situations they encounter, they become more effective in challenging their beliefs and behavior.

In my view, much of the group counseling endeavor deals with educating members, teaching them coping skills, and enabling them to see the connection to what they are learning in the group to everyday living. I particularly value the emphasis REBT puts on psychoeducational assignments such as listening to tapes, reading self-help books, and keeping a record of what members are doing and thinking. By working outside of the group, members can further the process of change without becoming excessively dependent on the group itself. In this way they are using the group as a means to an end instead of making the group an end in itself.

Ellis (1996) admits that REBT has its limitations, but his discussion of this topic points more to limitations within the client (such as resistance) rather than any limitations in theory and practice. He mentions some benefits and strengths of REBT:

- It is an intrinsically brief therapy, for in a few sessions clients who are willing to work typically experience significant gains.
- It aims not only for effectiveness but also for efficiency, using many cognitive, emotive, and behavioral techniques that may be uniquely effective for difficult clients.
- It has been incorporated into education, business, and communications and is evolving from individual and group therapy into the general field of educational and mass media therapy. Its principles are ideally suited for applications in homes, schools, social institutions, community centers, and hospitals (Ellis, 1994, 1996).

Limitations of the Approach

A major reservation I have with regard to REBT concerns the dangers inherent in the therapist's confrontive and persuasive stance and the possibility of imposing the leader's values on the members. Persuasion of members is more possible in REBT than in less directive approaches. Members may be subjected to group pressure to change their thinking, even if they are not convinced that they hold irrational beliefs. Although feedback is potentially of great value, ultimately it is really up to the person receiving the feedback to decide what to do about it. If members push and persuade and attempt to do the thinking for another member, the results are at least questionable, since the very integrity of the individual member is at stake.

Ellis (2001b) acknowledges that among the possible disadvantages of an active-directive therapy is that clients may be pressured to adopt goals and values that the therapist sells as opposed to operating within the framework of their own value system. Furthermore, active-directive therapy can result in excessive amounts of power and responsibility on the therapist's part and also disrupt a collaborative and cooperative client/therapist relationship. Ellis emphasizes that clients' beliefs are "irrational" or "dysfunctional" because such beliefs (1) include absolutist "musts" and (2) don't work and are self-defeating. If REBT is *practiced correctly*, the group leader judges these elements, not the person or the person's beliefs in their own right. However, it is possible that some group leaders will assume that it is their function to decide if someone's beliefs are irrational, and they might then work hard at converting that member to "sound thinking."

Aside from the very relevant issue of what constitutes rational thinking and who is the judge of it, I question the value of getting rid of one system of irrational beliefs only to adopt a new set of questionable beliefs, particularly if these values are pushed by the group leader or, in some instances, by other group members. Therefore, it is essential that REBT practitioners be highly aware of themselves and their own motivations. The therapist's level of knowledge, training, perceptiveness, and accuracy of judgment are particularly important. Perhaps one ethical safeguard is for group leaders using REBT procedures to discuss the issue of values openly and to caution members to beware of pressure to change in a definite direction, one that might be alien to their value system.

A key limitation of REBT group therapy for some clients is that they could become dependent on the leader to make decisions about what constitutes rationality. It would be easy for a group leader who is not well qualified to assume a highly active stance that would keep the client passive. This is especially true if the therapist does most of the talking, while the members do most of the listening. Therefore, it seems important that leaders teach their clients to question and to assume an active role in the therapeutic process.

It is well to underscore that REBT can be done by many people in a manner different from Ellis's style. It is worth distinguishing between the principles and techniques of REBT and Ellis's somewhat confrontational way of using them. A therapist can be soft-spoken and gentle and still use REBT concepts and methods.

Where to Go from Here

The *Journal of Rational-Emotive and Cognitive-Behavior Therapy* is published by Kluwer/Academic Human Sciences Press, Inc. This quarterly journal is an excellent way to keep informed about the work of a wide variety of cognitive behavioral specialists. Subscriptions can be obtained from the Albert Ellis Institute for $60 per year.

The Albert Ellis Institute in New York City offers a variety of professional training programs involving a primary (3-day) certificate, an intermediate (5-day) certificate, an associate fellowship, and a fellowship program. The institute also offers a "home study" primary certificate program. Students get direct hands-on training supervision in REBT disputing and assessment techniques. Each of these programs has requirements in the areas of clinical experience, supervision, and personal experience in therapy. Therapists who wish to practice REBT are encouraged to participate in some form of directly supervised training.

You can get a catalog describing REBT professional training programs, workshops, books, cassettetapes, films, self-help forms, software items, and an order form for publications from the institute:

Albert Ellis Institute
45 East 65th Street
New York, NY 10021-6593
TELEPHONE: (212) 535-0822 or toll free at (800) 323-4738
FAX: (212) 249-3582
E-MAIL: info @ rebt.org
WEB SITE: www.rebt.org

The institute and many affiliated centers throughout the United States provide official training programs for professionals. Training centers are located in Chicago; Denver; Tampa; Jamesville, Iowa; Lake Oswego, Oregon; Wilkes-Barre, Pennsylvania; and Salt Lake City as well as elsewhere throughout the country. For a list of these centers and information regarding international affiliated training centers, contact the Albert Ellis Institute. Training outside the United States is available through centers in Argentina, Australia, Canada, England, France, Germany, India, Israel, Italy, Mexico, the Netherlands, Peru, Romania, and Yugoslavia.

The *Journal of Cognitive Psychotherapy: An International Quarterly*, edited by John Riskind, also provides information on theory, practice, and research in cognitive behavior therapy. Information about the journal is available from the International Association of Cognitive Psychotherapy (http://iacp.asu.edu) or by contacting John Riskind directly:

Dr. John Riskind
George Mason University
Department of Psychology, MSN 3F5
Fairfax, VA 22030-4444
TELEPHONE: (703) 993-4094
PRIVATE PRACTICE TELEPHONE: (703) 280-8060
FAX: (703) 993-1359
E-MAIL: jriskind@gmu.edu

Recommended Supplementary Readings

Reason and Emotion in Psychotherapy (Ellis, 1994) is a comprehensive and updated work that deals with the theoretical and conceptual foundations of REBT, the dynamics of emotional disturbance, specific techniques to promote change, and applications of the approach.

Better, Deeper, and More Enduring Brief Therapy: The Rational Emotive Behavior Therapy Approach (Ellis, 1996) applies REBT to brief therapy and shows how it helps clients and readers not only to make themselves less disturbed but, if they keep working at it, how to get better rather than merely feel better.

Feeling Better, Getting Better, and Staying Better (Ellis, 2001a) is a self-help book that describes a wide range of cognitive, emotive, and behavioral approaches to not only feeling better but getting better.

Overcoming Destructive Beliefs, Feelings, and Behaviors (Ellis, 2001b) brings REBT up to date and shows how this approach helps neurotic clients and those suffering from severe personality disorders.

A Guide to Rational Living (Ellis & Harper, 1997) is a self-help book that presents a straightforward approach to REBT based on homework assignments and self-questioning. It is easy reading, and many of the principles discussed can be applied to group work.

The RET Sourcebook for Practitioners (Bernard & Wolfe, 2000) includes many REBT methods that can be used in group therapy as well as in individual and brief therapy.

References and Suggested Readings*

*Bernard, M. E., & Wolfe, J. L. (Eds.). (2000). *The RET sourcebook for practitioners*. New York: Albert Ellis Institute.

Brabender, V., & Fallon, A. (1993). *Models of inpatient group therapy*. Washington, DC: American Psychological Association.

Corey, G., Ellis, A., & Cooker, P. G. (1998). Challenging the internal dialogue of group counselors. *Journal of the Mississippi Counseling Association, 16*(1), 36–44.

Dryden, W. (1995). *Brief rational emotive behaviour therapy*. London: Wiley.

*Dryden, W. (1999). *Rational emotive behavior therapy: A training manual*. New York: Springer.

Ellis, A. (1977). *A garland of rational songs*. New York: Albert Ellis Institute.

Ellis, A. (1988). *How to stubbornly refuse to make yourself miserable about anything—Yes, anything!* Secaucus, NJ: Lyle Stuart.

Ellis, A. (1992). Group rational-emotive and cognitive-behavioral therapy. *International Journal of Group Psychotherapy, 42*(1), 63–80.

*Ellis, A. (1994). *Reason and emotion in psychotherapy* (rev. ed.). New York: Kensington.

*Ellis, A. (1996). *Better, deeper, and more enduring brief therapy: The rational emotive behavior therapy approach*. New York: Brunner/Mazel.

Ellis, A. (1997). The evolution of Albert Ellis and rational emotive behavior therapy. In J. K. Zeig (Ed.), *The evolution of psychotherapy: The third conference* (pp. 69–82). New York: Brunner/Mazel.

*Ellis, A. (1999). *How to make yourself happy and remarkably less disturbable*. Atascadero, CA: Impact.

*Ellis, A. (2000a). *How to control your anxiety before it controls you*. New York: Citadel Press.

Ellis, A. (2000b). Rational emotive behavior therapy. In R. Corsini & D. Wedding (Eds.), *Current psychotherapies* (6th ed., pp. 168–204). Itasca, IL: F. E. Peacock.

*Ellis, A. (2001a). *Feeling better, getting better, and staying better*. Atascadero, CA: Impact.

*Ellis, A. (2001b). *Overcoming destructive beliefs, feelings, and behaviors*. Amherst, NY: Prometheus Books.

*Books and articles marked with an asterisk are suggested for further study.

*Ellis, A. (2002). *Overcoming resistance:* A rational emotive behavior therapy integrated approach (2nd ed.). New York: Springer.

Ellis, A., Abrams, M., & Dengelegi, L. (1992). *The art and science of rational eating.* New York: Barricade Books.

Ellis, A., & Blau, S. (Eds.). (1998). *The Albert Ellis reader.* New York: Kensington.

*Ellis, A., & Crawford, T. (2000). *Making intimate connections: Seven guidelines for great relationships and better communication.* Atascadero, CA: Impact.

*Ellis, A., & Dryden, W. (1997). *The practice of rational-emotive therapy* (2nd. ed.). New York: Springer.

*Ellis, A., Gordon, J., Neenan, M., & Palmer, S. (1998). *Stress counseling: A rational emotive behavior approach.* New York: Springer.

*Ellis, A., & Harper, R. A. (1997). *A guide to rational living* (3rd ed.). North Hollywood, CA: Melvin Powers/Wilshire Books.

Ellis, A., & Velten, E. (1992). *When AA doesn't work: Rational steps for quitting alcohol.* New York: Barricade Books.

*Kahn, W. J. (1999). *The A-B-C's of human experience: An integrative model.* Pacific Grove, CA: Brooks/Cole.

Kwee, M. G. T., & Ellis, A. (1997). Can multimodal and rational emotive behavioral therapy be reconciled? *Journal of Rational-Emotive and Cognitive Behavior Therapy, 15,* 95–132.

*Organista, K. (2000). Latinos. In J. R. White & A. Freeman (Eds.), *Cognitive-behavioral group therapy for specific problems and populations* (pp. 281–303). Washington, DC: American Psychological Association.

Pack-Brown, S. P., Whittington-Clark, L. E., & Parker, W. M. (1998). *Images of me: A guide to group work with African-American women.* Boston: Allyn & Bacon.

Sapp, M. (1994). Cognitive-behavioral counseling: Applications for African American middle school students who are academically at-risk. *Journal of Instructional Psychology, 21*(2), 161–171.

Sapp, M. (1996). Irrational beliefs that can lead to academic failure for African American middle school students who are academically at-risk. *Journal of Rational-Emotive and Cognitive-Behavioral Therapy, 14*(2), 123–134.

Sapp, M., McNeely, R. L., & Torres, J. B. (1998). Rational emotive behavior therapy in the process of dying: Focus on aged African Americans and Latinos. *Journal of Human Behavior in the Social Environment, 1*(213), 229–315.

Thompson, C. L., & Rudolph, L. B. (2000). *Counseling children* (5th ed.). Pacific Grove, CA: Brooks/Cole.

Vernon, A. (1989). *Thinking, feeling, and behaving: An emotional education for children* (Two editions: Grades 1 to 6 and Grades 7 to 12). Champaign, IL: Research Press.

Warren, R., & McLellarn, R. W. (1987). What do RET therapists think they are doing? An international survey. *Journal of Rational-Emotive Therapy, 5*(2), 71–91.

Yankura, J., & Dryden, W. (1994). *Albert Ellis.* Thousand Oaks, CA: Sage.

Reality Therapy in Groups

Introduction

Like many of the founders of other therapeutic approaches described in this book, William Glasser was immersed in Freudian psychology during his training. He quickly became disenchanted with this approach, however, and began to experiment with innovative methods, which later came to be called reality therapy. The essence of reality therapy, now taught all over the world, is that we are responsible for what we choose to do. Because all problems are in the present, reality therapy spends very little time in the past. Glasser believes we can only control what we are presently doing. We may be the product of our past, but we are not the victims of our past unless we so choose.

Reality therapy is based on the assumption that people strive to gain control of their lives to fulfill their needs. Like transactional analysis, behavior therapy, and rational emotive behavior therapy, reality therapy is active, directive, didactic, and focuses on doing and action plans. It does not emphasize attitudes, feelings, insight, transference, one's past, or unconscious motivations. Reality therapy focuses on solving problems and on coping with the demands of reality in society by making more effective choices. People can improve the quality of their lives through honestly examining their wants, needs, and perceptions. Group members are challenged by the leader and other members to evaluate the quality of their behavior, formulate a plan for change, commit themselves to their plan, and follow through with their commitment.

From the 1960s to the late 1970s, reality therapy was aimed at putting a few basic concepts of the approach to work in a variety of settings, such as correctional institutions, schools, private practice, marital and family therapy, group work, and counseling in community clinics. In the early 1980s Glasser developed control theory as an explanation for human behavior, which served as the foundation for the practice of reality therapy. In March 1996 he changed the name from control theory to choice theory.

Glasser's (2000) basic premise is that the source of almost all clients' problems is the lack of satisfying present relationships. In short, Glasser believes the core problem most of us experience is an inability to get along with others as well as we want to. Furthermore, because the core of choice theory is that

421

everything we do is chosen, we can learn to make better choices. Reality therapy is the methodology for implementing the key concepts of choice theory. The focus of this chapter is on applying key concepts of choice theory to the practice of reality therapy in groups.

Key Concepts

Human Needs and Purposeful Behavior

Choice theory is built on the notion that human behavior is purposeful and originates from within the individual rather than from external forces. We are motivated by innate forces, and all of our behavior is aimed at fulfilling basic needs. Glasser (1998, 2000, 2001) identifies five essential human needs: survival, love and belonging, power, freedom, and fun. *Survival* is concerned with maintaining life and good health. *Love and belonging* is the need for involvement with people and the need for loving others and being loved. *Power* is the need for achievement and accomplishment, or the need for a sense of being in charge of one's own life. *Freedom* is the need to make choices. *Fun* involves the need to enjoy life, to laugh, and to experience humor. We spend all our life attempting to satisfy these basic needs.

When we are born, we do not know how to satisfy these needs. What we do know is how we feel and, if we feel pain or discomfort, we want to feel better. Choice theory is based on the premise that all our behavior is basically our best attempt to control the world around us for the purpose of satisfying these five basic needs, which are built into our genetic structure.

Although we all possess these basic needs, we have them to differing degrees, and we fulfill them in various ways. For example, we all have a need for love, but some people need more love than others. We develop an inner "picture album" (or "quality world") of specific wants as well as precise ways to satisfy these wants. We are attempting to choose to behave in a way that gives us the most effective control over our lives, which means being able to behave in a way that reasonably satisfies the pictures in our quality world (Glasser, 1998).

People behave for a purpose: to mold their environment, as a sculptor molds clay, to match their own inner pictures of what they want. An essential part of reality therapy consists of teaching people about their needs and how to more effectively meet these needs. These goals are achievable only through hard work (Wubbolding, 1988, 2000). We have a significant degree of control over our lives, and the more effectively we put this control into action, the more fulfilled we will be. The essence of reality therapy in groups consists of teaching members to help each other to accept responsibility through effective choices.

Choice theory explains that we do not satisfy our needs directly. What we do, beginning shortly after birth and continuing all our lives, is to keep close track of anything we do that feels very good and to store this knowledge in a special place in our brain called our quality world. Our quality world is not large, but it contains the people we are closest to and most enjoy being with.

It may also contain people we don't know but whom we imagine it would be very pleasurable to know, as well as things we own or would like to own and even things like a beautiful sunset that we couldn't own but that may be important to us. Also included are systems of belief that give us pleasure, such as our religious, political, or personal beliefs. This world is our personal Shangri-La—the world we would like to live in if we could. It is completely based on the needs; but, unlike the needs, which are general, it is very specific. We need love, but we put the actual people we want to love in our quality world. People are, by far, the most important components of this world, and these are the people we most want to connect with.

Choice theory provides both an explanation of our nature and a method for achieving the relationships we need all through our lives. Choice theory, with its emphasis on connection and interpersonal relationships is well suited for therapy in a group situation. Group counseling provides individuals with many opportunities for exploring ways to meet their needs through the relationships formed within the group.

Existential/Phenomenological Orientation

In many ways choice theory is grounded on phenomenological and existential premises. We perceive the world in the context of our own needs, not as it really is. It is important for group counselors to teach members the difference between the world as they perceive it and the world as other people perceive it. On this point, Glasser (1998) writes: "Choice theory is an internal control psychology; it explains why and how we make the choices that determine the course of our lives" (p. 7).

In addition to this focus on the subjective world, contemporary choice theory continues to have a strong existential orientation. We are viewed as choosing our own goals and as being responsible for the kind of world we create for ourselves. We are not helpless victims, and we can create a better life. Glasser (1997, 1998, 2000) does not accept the notion that misery simply happens to us; rather, it is something that we often choose, not because we want to suffer but because suffering may give us more control over our lives, or it often appears to be the only choice available. Glasser believes clients are typically quick to complain that they are upset because people are not behaving as they would like them to. It is a powerful lesson for people to recognize that they choose their behaviors, including feeling miserable and thinking that they are victims. But why does it make sense to choose misery? Glasser's (1997) answer to this question includes these three reasons: (1) to keep anger under control, (2) to get others to help us, and (3) to excuse our unwillingness to do something more effective.

Glasser (1998, 2000) speaks of people *depressing* or *angering* themselves rather than being depressed or being angry. With this perspective, depression can be explained as an active choice that we make rather than the result of being a passive victim. This process of "depressing" keeps anger in check, and it also allows us to ask for help. As long as we cling to the notion that we are victims of depression and that misery is something that happens to us, Glasser contends that we will not change for the better. We can change only when we recognize and act on the reality that what we are doing is the result of our choices. By adding the "ing" word ending, Glasser replaces a static state with an active one and emphasizes that feelings are behaviors that are generated. According to Glasser, if we want to stop choosing a painful behavior such as depressing, we can change what we want, change what we are doing, or change both.

Robert Wubbolding (personal communication, January 6, 2002) believes people have a difficult time accepting that there is an element of choice when it comes to depressing. When he asks them if they could make their lives worse, they typically say that they could. Then he leads them to the conclusion that if they can make their situation worse, they could make it better, which is a very empowering promise.

Total Behavior

According to Glasser's latest formulation of choice theory (1998, 2000), we always have control over what we do. This basic premise is clarified in the context of understanding our total behavior, which always includes four insepara- ble, but distinct, components: *acting* (things that we do such as talking or jogging); *thinking* (voluntary thoughts and self-statements); *feeling* (such as anger, joy, depression, anxiety); and *physiology* (such as sweating, "headaching," or developing other psychosomatic symptoms). Although these behaviors are interrelated, one of them is often more prominent than the others.

If we think of our behavioral choices as a car, the motor is the basic needs, the steering wheel allows us to steer the car in the direction of our quality world; acting, thinking, feeling, and physiology are the wheels. Acting and thinking, both obviously chosen, are the front wheels; they steer the car. Feel- ing and physiology are the back wheels, which have to follow the front wheels. They can't be independently or directly steered any more than we can directly choose how we feel or our physiology.

Choice theory is grounded on the assumption that it is impossible to choose a total behavior and not choose all of its components. Although all total behavior is chosen, we have direct control over only the *acting* and *thinking* components. If we hope to change a total behavior (such as experiencing the emotional and physiological consequences of depressing ourselves), it is nec- essary to change what we are doing and what we are thinking. Reality thera- pists accept that people feel badly or that their physiology may not be healthy, as in a psychosomatic disease. However, they do not focus on these compo- nents because they cannot be directly changed. For example, we might feel upset and then depress ourselves if we fail to get a job that we applied for. We do not have the ability to directly change how we are feeling, independently of what we are doing or thinking. But we can change how we are acting, and we have some ability to change what we are thinking, in spite of how we might be feeling. Therefore, the key to changing a total behavior lies in choosing to change how we are acting and thinking, for these are the behaviors we can control. If we markedly change the acting and thinking components, then the feeling and physiological components will change as well (Glasser, 1998, 2000).

The Essence of Choice Theory

Choice theory teaches that the only person whose behavior we can control is our own. The only way we can control events in our environment is through what we choose to do. How we feel is not controlled by others or by events. We are not psychological slaves to others, nor are we trapped by our past or present—unless we choose to be. An axiom of choice theory is that although the past may have contributed to a current problem the past is never the problem. Regardless of what occurred in the past, to function effectively we need to live and plan in the present. Our task is to do what we can to correct our present relationships (Glasser, 1998, 2000). For example, if we have had an unsatisfying relationship in the past—perhaps due to being abused as a child—what actually happened cannot be changed. Glasser contends that all we have control over is our own behavior, and all we can do is try to change our present behavior so that we can get along with people we now need. We can neither change what we did to others nor what others did to us. Reality therapists often say to clients: "The past is over, and it can't be changed. Let's not talk endlessly about the past. Instead, let's face your current problems and search for solutions."

What are the implications of choice theory for the practice of reality therapy group counseling? Group leaders can help members recognize that what they are doing is not working for them, help them accept themselves as they are, and guide them in making realistic plans to do better and to help others in the group to do the same. Practitioners provide help through skillful questioning that is aimed at getting members to assess what they want. If group leaders are not skillful enough to get clients to see that their total behavior is not getting them what they want, therapy will not be effective.

Leaders need to challenge members continually with this basic reality therapy question: "Is what you are now choosing to do (your actions and thoughts) getting you what you want?" Here are some other questions often posed to members:

- Do you want to change?
- How would you most like to change your life?
- What do you want in your life that you are not getting?
- Is your current behavior getting you closer or further from people in your environment?
- If you changed, how would you feel better?
- What would you have in your life if you were to change?
- What do you have to do now to make the changes happen?

Members can more easily choose better behavior if they come to realize that what they are doing, thinking, and feeling is not simply happening to them but that they are, indeed, making choices.

Role and Functions of the Group Leader

Group leaders strive to create a good relationship with the members. From this relationship, the leader is able to help members improve the quality of their relationships. Reality therapy teaches that people are most able to gain effective control of their lives when they recognize and accept accountability for their own chosen behaviors and make better choices. The group leader helps participants understand that they have some indirect control over their feelings by choosing to act and think differently. The group leader encourages members to consider different choices in the following ways:

- Actively promotes discussion of members' current behavior and actively discourages excuses for irresponsible or ineffective behavior
- Helps members make inner self-evaluations
- Introduces and fosters the process of evaluating which wants are realistically attainable
- Teaches members to formulate and carry out plans to change their behaviors
- Helps participants evaluate their level of commitment to their action plans
- Encourages members to identify how to continue making the changes they want once the group ends

Reality therapy group leaders assume a verbally active and directive role in the group. In carrying out their functions, they focus on the strengths and potentials of the members rather than on their misery. They assume that dwelling on limitations, problems, and failures tends to reinforce clients' low self-esteem and ineffective control. Therefore, they challenge members to look at their unused potential and to discover how to work toward more effective choices and, thus, more effective control.

It is important for group leaders to develop their own individual therapeutic style. Sincerity and being comfortable with their style are crucial traits in carrying out the therapeutic functions associated with their role. Developing a personal style does take time and experience in working with a variety of groups. In establishing this style, effective practitioners are aware of their own value system and of the cultural differences and worldviews of the members. The unique needs of culturally diverse members can be met by adapting and adjusting the procedures used in practice. Group practitioners can continue their growth by being open to challenge and by exploring their own values with the groups they facilitate.

Application: Therapeutic Techniques and Procedures

The practice of reality therapy consists of two major components: (1) the counseling environment and (2) specific procedures that lead to changes in behavior. The art of counseling is to weave these components together in ways that lead clients to evaluate their lives and decide to move in more effective directions. Wubbolding (1988, 2000, 2002) describes these two elements as the "cycle of counseling." The cycle illustrates that there is an overall sequence to translating reality therapy's theory into practice. The counseling environment, which consists of specific guidelines for implementing interventions, is the foundation from which the procedures are built.

Several points are important to keep in mind. First, although the concepts discussed here may seem clear and simple as they are presented in written form, they are difficult to translate into actual therapeutic practice. It takes skill and creativity to apply these concepts successfully in group work. Although the principles will be the same when used by any certified reality therapist, the manner in which they are applied does vary depending on the therapist's style and personal characteristics.

Reality therapy is a process, and it is a mistake to apply these methods in a rigid, step-by-step, or "cookbook" fashion. According to Glasser's (2000) current formulations of the "new reality therapy," there are no absolute patterns, questions, techniques, or timing that the therapist must follow. Procedures are means to an end, not the end in themselves (personal communication, Robert Wubbolding, January 10, 2002). Guided by the principles of choice theory, group counselors tailor their interventions to what the group members present. Although the leader does not operate with preordained techniques, the move in the direction of satisfying relationships is kept in the foreground.

The discussion that follows is an integrated summary and adaptation of material from various sources (Glasser, 1992, 1998, 2000; Wubbolding, 1988, 1991, 2000, 2001). In addition, the Student Manual that accompanies this textbook contains a chart by Wubbolding (2002) that highlights issues and tasks to be accomplished at each of the stages of a reality therapy group. This discussion provides a look at reality therapy in group work, but it should not be thought of as a replacement for the extensive training that is needed to counsel effectively using this approach.

Stages of a Reality Therapy Group

The stages of group development, which were discussed in detail in Chapters 4 and 5, are quite applicable to reality therapy groups. Effective reality therapists are aware that need fulfillment should be facilitated at each of the stages of a group and that various needs are more prominent at different stages of the group (Wubbolding & Brickell, 1999). During the initial stage of a reality therapy group, key leader functions include developing a comfortable psychological atmosphere, discussing informed consent, and exploring rules and boundaries. When a group is in transition, the leader will have to be prepared to deal effectively with anxiety, conflict, control issues, and resistance. At the working stage, the role of the leader includes encouraging feedback among members, helping members to evaluate their level of commitment, assisting members in reframing failure, encouraging the development of action plans, and teaching members how to confront without criticism. As is the case during the final stage of any group, important functions of the reality therapy group leader center around consolidation and termination issues, such as dealing with feelings about the ending of the group, completing unfinished business, and carrying learning further. Other aspects of the leader's role during the final stage involve helping members to evaluate their program, to develop a future map that will help members deal with new problems, and to assist members in summarizing their perceptions of the future. For a more detailed discussion of the role of group leaders at the various stages of a reality therapy group, see Wubbolding and Brickell (1999).

The Counseling Environment

Personal Involvement with the Client   The practice of reality therapy begins with the group counselor's efforts to create a supportive environment within which clients can begin to make life changes. To create this therapeutic climate, counselors need to establish good working relationships with the members of a group, which implies getting involved in their lives and creating the rapport that will be the foundation of the therapeutic relationship. It is essential for the counselor to see the world as the clients see it. In a sense, this is the most important and demanding aspect of a group, for in the absence of personal involvement there can be no effective therapy. When reality group therapy is ineffective, it is usually because genuine involvement has not been established. Caring on the part of the group leader can go a long way toward building the bonds of trust that will be needed for clients to commit themselves to the challenges of making positive changes. When a working relationship is established, members are generally able to evaluate both what they want and the total behavior they are presently choosing.

For real involvement to take place, the leader must have certain personal qualities, including warmth, understanding, acceptance, concern, respect for the client, openness, and the willingness to be challenged by others. One of the best ways to develop this goodwill and therapeutic friendship is simply by listening to clients. Yet, as Wubbolding (2000) mentions, this high level of empathy is shown more by skillful questioning than by reflective listening. Involvement is also promoted by talking about a wide range of topics that have relevance for group members, topics that relate to the members' current everyday behaviors and experiences and that play down misery and past failures.

In his description of the cycle of counseling, Wubbolding (2000, 2002) identifies specific ways for counselors to create a climate that leads to involvement with clients, emphasizing that the cycle of counseling cannot be applied in the same way with every client. Some of the approaches to establishing a therapeutic environment include using attending behavior, suspending judgment of clients, doing the unexpected, using humor appropriately, being oneself as a counselor, engaging in facilitative self-disclosure, listening for metaphors in the client's mode of self-expression, listening for themes, summarizing and focusing, and being an ethical practitioner. The basis for therapeutic interventions to work rests on a fair, firm, friendly, and trusting environment.

For most clients this choice theory atmosphere will be a new experience. Many will distrust it and try to replace it with the more coercive atmosphere they are used to. If the counselor resists all these self-destructive attempts, in a short period of time the client will begin to enjoy this caring, accepting, noncoercive environment. It is from this confronting yet always noncriticizing, nonblaming, noncomplaining, caring environment that the client learns to create the satisfying environment that leads to successful relationships.

Because of the opportunity to form relationships with several other people besides the therapist, there is a definite advantage in practicing reality therapy in groups. The essence of reality group therapy consists of a process of self-evaluation, and the group atmosphere can foster involvement and can help members make an honest evaluation of what they are doing. Fellow group members provide both support and an honest challenge to look at one's life. Group interaction is especially important in helping individual members break the vicious circle of failure experiences. According to reality therapy theory, people cannot make more effective choices and gain more effective control by isolating themselves. What they do must fulfill the need for belonging.

One effective way to create a therapeutic climate for participants in involuntary groups is for the leader to explain to members some specific ways in which the group process can be of personal value to them. For example, if participants see the group as a place where they can learn to escape their particular pattern of repeated failures, they may take the first step toward involvement. Such involvement is fostered by the reality therapist, who actively participates in defining the nature and the purpose of the group as well as the limits of its activities. However, the leader encourages the members to participate in establishing the goals that guide their group, even in correctional settings.

Counselor Attitudes and Behaviors That Promote Change   In addition to the positive attributes of counselors to establish a climate conducive to positive change, counselors who hope to enhance involvement and create a therapeutic alliance avoid behaviors such as arguing, belittling, criticizing, demeaning, finding fault, imposing external control, accepting excuses, instilling fear, and giving up easily. Instead, the emphasis is on accepting clients as they are and encouraging them to focus on what they can control.

Counselors hope to teach their clients to value the attitude of accepting responsibility for their total behaviors. Thus, they accept no excuses for harmful choices such as not doing what they said they would do. If clients do not follow through with their plans for change, counselors do not ask fruitless questions about why the plan failed. Instead, they teach members that excuses are a form of self-deception that may offer temporary relief but will ultimately lead to failure and to the cementing of a failure identity.

Reality therapy holds that reasonable consequences are necessary and useful, but punishment is not a useful means of effecting behavioral change. Instead of using punishment, the therapist challenges clients to see the consequences that flow from their actions and to behave in ways that reduce the necessity for negative consequences. Doing this is educational and leads to responsibility and rehabilitation (Wubbolding, 2000).

It is important that counselors not give up easily in their belief in the client's ability to find a more responsible life, even if the client makes little effort to follow through on plans or is faced with external obstacles. Reality therapists simply do not include giving up as one of their options, for if they did, it would tend to confirm the client's belief that no one cared enough to help. Those with a history of failure expect others to give up on them. It is a real challenge to refuse to give up easily on clients who are resistant, passive/ aggressive, uncooperative, hostile, or apathetic. It is unhelpful for a therapist to assume that another person will never change or that a person is hopeless. Regardless of what clients say or do, it is therapeutically helpful for the therapist not to lose faith in their capacity to change.

Procedures in a Reality Therapy Group: The WDEP System

Wubbolding (2000, 2001, 2002) uses an acronym—WDEP—to illustrate key procedures that can be applied in the practice of reality therapy groups. Each of the letters refers to a cluster of strategies: W = wants; D = direction and doing; E = self-evaluation; and P = planning. These strategies are designed to promote change.

Wants (W)   Reality therapists ask, "What do you want?" Through the therapist's skillful questioning, clients are encouraged to recognize, define, and refine how they wish to meet their needs. The use of questioning is a cornerstone in the practice of reality therapy. Well-timed and strategic questions can get members to think about what they want and to evaluate whether their behavior is leading them in the direction they want to go. Because reality therapy makes use of questioning to a greater degree than many other counseling approaches, it is important for group leaders to develop extensive questioning skills. The art of group counseling requires that leaders know *what* questions to ask, *how* to ask them, and *when* to ask them.

Questioning is often misused by group leaders. Some leaders' questions appear to have no point other than to keep the members talking. Those leaders use the question-and-answer technique mainly because they don't know what else to do. Wubbolding (1996b) writes that the excessive use of questions can result in irritated clients, resistance, and defensiveness. If questioning becomes the main technique a leader uses, it tends to create distance and keep the leader anonymous. Wubbolding asserts that relationships are enhanced when questioning is combined with reflective thinking, checking perceptions, and other techniques.

Part of counseling consists of the exploration of clients' "picture albums" and the ways in which their behavior is aimed at moving the external world closer to their inner world of wants. It is essential that this exploration continue throughout the entire counseling process because the client's pictures change.

Clients are given the opportunity to explore every facet of life, including what they want from their family, friends, and work. Furthermore, it is useful for clients to define what they expect and want from the counselor and from themselves (Wubbolding, 1996a; Wubbolding & Brickell, 1999).

In a group, members explore what they want, what they have, and what they are not getting. Throughout the process, the focus is on getting members to make a self-evaluation to determine the direction in which their behavior is taking them. This assessment provides a basis for making specific changes that will enable the members to reduce their frustrations. Useful questions can help them pinpoint what they want: "What kind of person do you wish you were?" "What would your family be like if your wants and their wants matched?" "What would you be doing if you were living the way you wished?" "Is this choice to your best short-term and long-term advantage, and is it consistent with your values?" This line of questioning sets the stage for the application of other procedures in reality therapy.

Doing and Direction (D)   After clients explore their quality world (wants) and needs, they are asked to look at their current behavior to determine if what they are doing is getting them what they want. Wubbolding (1991) writes that the therapist holds a mirror before group members and asks: "Will this choice get you where you want to go? Is your destination truly helpful to you?" (p. 93).

The group leader consistently attempts to focus clients on what they are doing now. The leader does not allow clients to talk about events in the past unless these events can be easily related to present situations. The focus would be on what clients learned from past experiences. Once involvement has been established, the leader encourages the group members to confront themselves with the reality and consequences of their current behavior. Although problems may originate in the past, they all occur in the present. Therefore, problems must be solved either in the present or through a plan for the future. The past may be discussed if doing so will help clients plan for a better tomorrow. When problems are solved, it is the result of clients learning how to modify their thinking and choosing better ways of acting than when they began therapy.

Reality therapists also avoid discussing clients' feelings or their physiological reactions as though these were separate from their total behavior. That doesn't imply that attitudes are dismissed as unimportant; rather, the approach is that behavioral change is easier than attitudinal change and of greater value in the therapeutic process. The counselor relates clients' feelings or physical symptoms to their concurrent actions and thoughts, over which they have more direct control. For that reason, a client who expressed feelings of helplessness would not be questioned about the reasons for these feelings or encouraged to explore them. Although the counselor might encourage members to discuss feelings, the focus would clearly be on urging them to identify actions that accompany or support the feelings. When members change their actions, the feelings will change.

The aim of this emphasis on current behavior is to help clients understand their responsibilities for their own feelings. As a way of encouraging clients to look at what they are actually doing to contribute to their feelings, these questions might be asked:

- What are you doing now?
- What did you actually do this past week?
- What did you want to do differently this past week?
- What stopped you from doing what you say you wanted to do?
- What will you do tomorrow?

Getting members to focus on what they are doing has the aim of teaching them that they can gain conscious control over their behavior, can make choices, and can change their lives. Although they may want to talk in detail about how others are not living up to their expectations and how, if only the world would change, they could be happy, such talk will only solidify their victimlike position.

Self-Evaluation (E)   It is the therapist's task to confront clients with the consequences of their behavior and to get them to judge the quality of their actions. Indeed, unless clients eventually evaluate their own behavior, they will not change. Self-evaluation is the core of reality therapy. After clients make an evaluation about the quality of their behavior, they can determine what may be contributing to their failures and what changes they can undertake to promote success.

It is important that therapists remain nonjudgmental about clients' behavior and do not assume the responsibility for the client in making these value judgments. Instead, they best serve clients when they challenge them to stop, look, and listen. If therapists can stimulate client self-questioning, the client will be more likely to begin to make changes. Asking clients to evaluate each component of their total behavior is a major task in reality therapy. The skillful reality therapy group leader helps members evaluate their own behavior by involving the group in this self-evaluation process.

From the reality therapist's perspective, it is acceptable to be directive with certain clients in the beginning of treatment. Reality therapists sometimes express what they think will be helpful. In treating children of alcoholics and even alcoholics themselves, for example, it is necessary to say straightforwardly what will work and what will not work. Certain clients do not have the thinking behaviors in their choice system to be able to make consistent evaluations. These clients are likely to have blurred pictures and may not always be aware of what they want or whether their wants are realistic. As clients grow and continually interact with the counselor, they learn to make evaluations with less help.

Planning (P)   Much of the work in reality therapy consists of helping members identify specific ways to change their failure choices into success choices. Once a client has made an evaluation about his or her behavior and decided to change it, the therapist is in a position to assist the client in developing a plan for behavioral changes. The best plan is one that is initiated by the client. The second best plan is one that is initiated by the therapist and the client. And the third best plan is one that is initiated by the therapist (Wubbolding, 2000). Regardless of who initiates the plan, the art of planning is to establish practical short-term goals that have a high probability of being successfully attained, because such successes will positively reinforce the client's efforts to achieve long-range goals.

Planning for responsible behavior is an essential part of the helping process. This is clearly a teaching phase of therapy. Therefore, therapy is best directed toward providing clients with new information and helping them discover more effective ways of getting what they want. A large portion of the therapy time consists of making plans and then checking to determine how these plans are working. In a group context, members learn how to plan realistically and responsibly through contact with both the other members and the leader. The members are encouraged to experiment with new behaviors, to try out different ways of attaining their goals, and to carry out an action program. It is important that these plans not be too ambitious, for people need to experience success. The purpose of the plan is to arrange for successful experiences. Once a plan works, feelings of self-esteem will increase. It is clear that helpful plans are modest in the beginning and specify what is to be done, when it will be done, and how often. In short, plans are meant to encourage clients to translate their talk and intentions into actions.

A plan that fulfills wants and needs is central to effective group counseling. The process of creating and carrying out plans enables people to gain effective control over their lives. Wubbolding (2002) summarizes the characteristics of a good plan: simple, attainable, measurable and precise, immediate, involved, controlled by the doer of the plan, consistent and repetitive, committed to, short range or long range, able to be revised, personal, positive, evaluated, process centered, want and need fulfilling, and timely. The characteristics of effective planning are identified and described by Wubbolding (1988, 1991, 2000):

• Good plans are simple and easy to understand. Although plans need to be specific, concrete, and measurable, they should be flexible and open to modification as clients gain a deeper understanding of the specific behaviors that they want to change. In short, it is vital that clients run their plans, not vice versa.

• Plans should be realistic and attainable. Leaders can help members recognize that even small plans can help them take significant steps toward their desired changes.

• An effective plan involves doing something rather than not doing something. That is, the plan should involve a positive plan of action, and it should be stated in terms of what will be done.

• The group leader encourages members to develop plans that they can carry out independently of what others do. Therefore, the leader's task is to focus on the members rather than on the world external to them, which is often beyond their control.

- Group leaders can help members develop specific and concrete plans through their skillful questioning. Key questions often used include "What?" "Where?" "With whom?" "When?" and "How often?"

- Effective plans are repetitive; that is, they are performed regularly, if not daily. People do not change by practicing new behaviors only when the spirit moves them but, rather, by continuously repeating the positive elements of their program.

- Plans should have a sense of immediacy; that is, they should be put into action as soon as possible. Leaders may ask their members questions such as "What are you willing to do today to begin to change your life?" or "You say that you would like to have more fun. So, what are you going to do now to enjoy yourself?" The message behind these questions is that members do have the capacity to control their lives by making immediate changes.

- Effective planning involves process-centered activities. For example, members may say that they can do any of the following: pay their child three compliments, jog 30 minutes a day, devote two hours a week to volunteer work, or take a vacation that they have been wanting.

- Before members carry out a plan, it is a good idea to evaluate the plan in the group and get feedback from other members and the leader. After the plan has been carried out in real life, it is useful to evaluate it again. Members can return to the group and talk about the degree to which their plan has been successful. With input from the group, they can figure out what the plan might be lacking, how it needs to be more specific, or how it might need to be modified in some other way.

- For clients to commit themselves to their plan, it is useful for them to firm it up—for example, by writing it down. Furthermore, both the group leader and other members can help by providing reinforcement for an effective plan.

Most members do not formulate an ideal plan like the one just described. The better the plan, however, the better the chances are that members will attain their wants. Toward this end, it is essential that they commit themselves to following through with their plans.

Although the burden of responsibility for formulating and carrying out plans for change rests with the group members, it is the task of the leader to create an accepting and nourishing atmosphere for planning. It needs to be emphasized that throughout this planning phase, the group leader continually encourages members to assume responsibility for their own choices and actions. This calls for considerable skill and inventiveness.

Commitment   Clearly, formulating even the most reasonable and practical plan is a waste of time if the client lacks the willingness to implement it. As is true for transactional analysis groups, plans can be put in the form of a contract that will assist group members in holding themselves and others accountable for carrying them out.

Once individual members make plans and announce them, the group is in a position to help members evaluate and review these plans and to offer support and encouragement when needed. If individual members fall short of their commitments or in any way fail to implement their plans, that fact cannot be hidden from others or, more important, from themselves. If some members are able to follow through with their plans, they serve as models for the rest of the group. If their peers can do what they have set out to do, others may realize that they can succeed too.

Asking clients to determine what they want for themselves, to make a self-evaluation, and to follow through with action plans includes assisting them in determining how intensely they are willing to work to attain the changes they desire. Wubbolding (2000, p. 142) describes five levels of commitment:

Level 1: "I don't want to be here. You can't help me."
Level 2: "I want the outcome. But I don't want to exert any effort."
Level 3: "I'll try. I might. I could."
Level 4: "I will do my best."
Level 5: "I will do whatever it takes."

Commitment is not an all-or-nothing matter; it exists in degrees. Leaders can encourage members who have a low level of commitment to move in the direction of increasing their level of commitment to do what it takes to bring about change. It is essential that members who are reluctant to make a commitment be helped to express and explore their fears of failing. Members can be encouraged to begin each group session by reporting on the activities of the week, including the difficulties they encountered in sticking with their plans as well as the successes they had in trying out new behaviors in the real world. Just as in behavioral groups, where the buddy system is used, reality therapy can encourage members to make contacts with each other during the week if they have trouble sticking by their commitments.

Some group members may be unwilling to make any commitments. Therapists cannot force change, but they can help such group members look at what is stopping them from making a commitment to change. Sometimes people are convinced that they cannot change, that they cannot stick to any decision, and that they are destined to remain a failure. In such cases it is important that the group member be helped to see clearly the consequences of not changing and then be guided to formulate very short-range, limited plans with goals that are easy to reach.

Commitment places the responsibility for changing directly on the clients. If members say over and over that they want to change and hope to change, they can be asked the question, "Will you do it, and when will you do it?" The danger, of course, is that the member's plan may not be carried out, which leads to an increase of frustrations and adds to the person's failures. Reality therapy tries to avoid this problem by not asking for any commitment that is unreasonable or impossible.

Solution-Focused Therapy

Although not a part of reality therapy, solution-focused therapy shares many of the principles and techniques of reality therapy. Solution-focused therapy differs from traditional therapies by eschewing the past—and even the present—in favor of the future. It is so focused on what is possible that it has little or no interest in understanding the problem. Both reality therapy and solution-focused therapy can be applied to groups with a time-limited focus.

De Shazer (1991), perhaps the most radical proponent of the solution-focused group, has suggested that therapists do not need to know a problem to solve it and that there is no necessary relationship between problems and their solutions. If knowing and understanding problems is unimportant, so is searching for "right" solutions. O'Hanlon and Weiner-Davis (1989) assert that any person might consider multiple solutions and that what is right for one person may not be right for others. As is the case in reality therapy groups, in this model clients choose the goals they wish to accomplish.

In many groups the participants will come with a "problem-oriented" frame of mind. Even the few solutions they have considered are wrapped in the power of the problem orientation. Group leaders who draw on ideas from a solution-focused perspective tend to intervene by asking people to create optimistic conversations that highlight the belief that it is possible to quickly achieve usable goals. These goals are developed by using what de Shazer (1985, 1988) calls the *miracle question:* Essentially, if a miracle happened and the problem you have was solved overnight, how would you know it was solved, *and what would be different*? Clients are then encouraged to enact "what would be different" in spite of perceived problems. This process reflects O'Hanlon and Weiner-Davis's (1989) belief that changing the *doing* and *viewing* of the perceived problem changes the problem. The miracle question can be used in a reality therapy group when members are asked to think about what they are moving toward and how they would like to be living differently.

Solution-focused therapists ask *exception questions* that direct clients to times in their lives when the problem did not exist. This exploration helps clients see that problems are not all-powerful and have not existed forever; it also provides a field of opportunity for evoking resources, engaging strengths, and positing possible solutions. Both solution-focused therapists and reality therapists focus on small, achievable changes that may lead to additional positive outcomes. Their language joins with the client's, using similar words, pacing, and tone, but also involves questions that presuppose change, suggest multiple answers, and remain goal directed and future oriented.

Solution-focused therapists also employ the technique of *scaling questions*. For example, a woman reporting feelings of panic or anxiety might be asked this question: "On a scale of zero to 10, with zero being how you felt when you first came to therapy and 10 being how you feel the day after your miracle occurs and your problem is gone, how would you rate your anxiety right now?" Even if the client has only moved away from zero to 1, she has improved.

How did she do that? What does she need to do to move another number up the scale? This technique of scaling questions can be applied at all phases of the WDEP model of reality therapy.

Some clients want to justify their belief that life can't be changed or, worse, that life is moving them further and further away from where they would like to be in their life. De Shazer (1991) prefers to engage clients in conversations whereby people create situations in which they can make steady gains toward their goals. In doing this, a therapist might say: "Tell me about times when you feel good, when things are going your way, and when you enjoy your family and friends." It is in these stories of life worth living that the power of problems is deconstructed and new solutions are manifest and made possible. Solution-focused therapists believe that life is *change* and that change is inevitable. Their function is to guide the changer and the changed in a self-chosen direction.

Applying Reality Therapy to Group Work in the Schools

Reality therapy is very relevant for group work with children and adolescents in school settings. Glasser has been generally openly received by educators who wanted him to apply his basic ideas of reality therapy to the classroom (Wubbolding & Brickell, 1999). Glasser's (1969) first book on applying reality therapy to groups in the classroom was *Schools Without Failure*. In his *Control Theory in the Classroom*, Glasser (1986) showed how teachers could be managers whose main task was to motivate students by empowering them with the responsibility for their learning. Later developments of ways that reality therapy could be applied to schools are found in *The Quality School: Managing Students Without Coercion* (Glasser, 1990) and *The Quality School Teacher* (Glasser, 1993).

Currently about 200 schools in North America are members of the Quality School Consortium and structure their school program using choice theory and reality therapy (Wubbolding & Brickell, 1999). The quality school models a democratic structure as opposed to an autocratic structure. In "boss management" teachers use coercion and punishment in an attempt to get children to learn; in "lead management" teachers function in democratic and straightforward ways. Lead management involves all individuals in decisions that affect them. All viewpoints are considered before decisions are made. Teachers and counselors who use lead management are mainly interested in empowering students. Glasser (1998) believes a quality school will reduce the problems that characterize so many schools today. He states: "In a quality school, where students are led instead of bossed, they acquire a lot of knowledge by using what they learn, and they retain it" (p. 239). Wubbolding (1997) writes about ways to improve the school environment by empowering students by (1) creating a curriculum that aims to fulfill the basic needs of survival, belonging, power, freedom, and fun; (2) emphasizing the rights of students to make choices for themselves and to accept the consequences that result from their choices; (3) teaching students the art of self-evaluation; (4) conducting class meetings that encourage students to provide input in the formulation of class rules; and (5) creating and consistently enforcing schoolwide rules and policies that are clear, simple, reasonable, and known by all students.

Although much of what has been written about applying choice theory and reality therapy to schools pertains to working with the classroom and the overall structure of a school system, the basic philosophy of choice theory is highly applicable to group counseling with both children and adolescents. Any counseling group can be designed to assist students in exploring the degree to which they are meeting their needs for love and belonging, power, freedom, and fun. The WDEP system described earlier in this chapter is relevant to working with both children and adolescents. In a group situation, young people can be invited to explore their wants, needs, and perceptions. They can be asked to take an honest look at what they are doing and to clarify whether their behavior is getting them what they say they want. The emphasis on present behavior is a plus when it comes to school counseling, because groups are generally time limited in the school context. Depending on their developmental level, children and adolescents can be taught how to make evaluations of what they are doing and how to use self-evaluation to determine if they want to behave in any different ways. Once young people get a clearer picture of what they want, they can begin to make plans that will help them attain their goals. Much of the time in a counseling group can be devoted to assisting students in designing useful action plans in changing their behavior. Again, the earlier detailed discussion of planning can be applied to group counseling with students. In short, most of the key concepts of choice theory and most of the interventions used in reality therapy can be part and parcel of working with students of varying ages in many different kinds of groups.

How effective is reality therapy in the schools? Thompson and Rudolph (2000) consider the best validation of reality therapy to be Glasser's success early in his career in conducting both individual and group counseling at the Ventura School for Girls. Before he became associated with this institution, the school's recidivism rate approached 90%. Shortly after his work with the girls, this rate fell to 20%. It is crucial for group counselors who work in school settings to create a trusting climate within their groups. The personal characteristics of the group leader really matter in creating an open climate. The principles of the counseling environment based on personal involvement discussed in this chapter are the essence of establishing and maintaining a safe atmosphere that will allow productive work to occur in school groups.

Applying Reality Therapy with Multicultural Populations

Wubbolding (1990, 2000) has expanded the practice of reality therapy to both group counseling and multicultural situations. He believes reality therapy needs to be modified to fit the cultural context of people from areas other than North America. Besides teaching reality therapy workshops in North America, Wubbolding's experiences conducting reality therapy workshops in Slovenia,

Croatia, Italy, Japan, Taiwan, Hong Kong, Singapore, Korea, India, Kuwait, Australia, and Europe have taught him the difficulty of making generalizations about other cultures.

Based on these experiences, Wubbolding (1990, 2000) adapted the cycle of counseling to working with Japanese clients. He points to some basic language differences between Japanese and Western cultures. North Americans are inclined to say what they mean, to be assertive, and to be clear and direct in asking for what they want. In Japanese culture, assertive language is not appropriate between a child and a parent or between an employee and a supervisor. Ways of communicating are more indirect. Because of this indirect style, some specific adaptations are needed to make the practice of reality therapy relevant to Japanese clients.

First, it is not necessary to have clients verbally define their specific wants or express their goals. Also, the reality therapist's tendency to ask direct questions may need to be softened, and questions could be posed more elaborately and indirectly. Confrontation will be used to a much lesser degree. For example, in counseling American students the counselor might ask, "Is what you are doing helping or hurting you?" However, in counseling an Asian youth in Singapore, more emphasis would be placed on questions such as "What does your family think about your actions?" or "Do your actions bring shame or honor on your parents?" The teaching and the practice of reality therapy must be adjusted to people's values, wants, and manner of expression (personal communication, Robert Wubbolding, January 10, 2002).

Second, there is no exact translation for the word *plan*, nor is there an exact word for the term *accountability*, yet both of these are key dimensions in the practice of reality therapy. Finally, as counselors present dimensions such as wants of the client, the evaluation process, making plans, and committing to them, it is useful to employ a more indirect style of communication than is typically practiced in the Western version of reality therapy. For example, in working with Western clients, counselors would not settle for a response of "I'll try." In Japan, however, the counselor is likely to accept "I'll try" as a firm commitment.

These are but a few illustrations of ways in which reality therapy might be adapted to non-Western clients. Although reality therapy assumes that the basic needs (survival, belonging, power, freedom, and fun) are universal, the ways in which these needs are expressed depend largely on the cultural context. When working with culturally diverse clients, it is essential that group leaders allow latitude for a diverse range of acceptable behaviors to satisfy these needs.

Now, let's focus on some of the broader applications of the core concepts of reality therapy from a multicultural perspective. Once clients have evaluated for themselves whether their wants are realistic and whether their behavior is helping them, they can make realistic plans that are consistent with their cultural values. This focus clearly empowers clients. It is a sign of respect that the group leader refrains from deciding what behavior should be changed. Through skillful and sensitive questioning, the leader can help clients determine the degree to which they have acculturated into the dominant society. Members can then make a personal assessment of the degree to which their wants and needs are being satisfied by having made this decision. It is possible for them to find their own balance of retaining their ethnic and cultural identity and at the same time integrating some of the values and practices of the dominant group. Again, the group leader does not determine this for these clients but challenges them to arrive at their own answers based on their own value system.

Practitioners who lead groups composed of culturally diverse members may find such clients reluctant to share their feelings during the early phase of the group. Because of their cultural values, some clients are likely to react more positively and to cooperate to a greater degree if the focus is on what they are doing and wanting rather than on what they are feeling. For example, some clients may be experiencing depression and anxiety, and they may hope to gain relief from these symptoms by being in a group. Thinking of these symptoms from a reality therapy perspective, the leader could guide the members to look at what they are doing (or not doing) that is contributing to their emotional state. There is no pressure to experience a catharsis and to do emotional work within the group. Yet members eventually realize that they are "depressing" and "anxietying" rather than having these things simply happen to them. Once they realize that certain behaviors are not functional for their purposes, they are in a better position to make changes that will lead to different outcomes.

As is true for the cognitive behavioral approaches, reality therapy often utilizes contracts. In this way the group members eventually specify particular problems that are causing them difficulty and that they would like to explore in the group. Thus, group counseling is typically cast in the framework of a teaching/learning process, which appeals to many ethnically diverse client groups. A specific focus—namely, a certain behavioral pattern—becomes the target for intervention. The reality therapy leader is interested in helping members discover better ways to meet their needs. To its credit, choice theory/reality therapy provides group members with tools for making the desired changes, especially during the planning phase. With the support and help of other members and the group leader, clients can develop specific and workable plans for action. Within this context, members can be assisted in taking specific steps to move the external world closer to the inner world of their wants. If their plans do not always meet with success in everyday reality, these members can then bring concrete situations back to the group sessions. This type of specificity, and the direction provided by an effective plan, is certainly an asset in working with minority clients in groups.

One of the limitations of using choice theory/reality therapy with ethnic minorities, gays and lesbians, and women is that these clients may not feel that real environmental forces that are operating against them in everyday life are being taken into consideration. For example, discrimination, racism, sexism, homophobia, ageism, and negative attitudes toward disabilities are unfortunate realities, and these forces do limit many minority clients in getting what they want from life. If the group leader does not accept these environmental restrictions or is not interested in social change as well as individual change, members are likely to feel misunderstood. There is a danger that some reality therapists may overstress the ability of these clients to take charge of their lives and not pay enough attention to systemic issues. Such clients may interpret the group leader's line of questioning as "If you try hard enough, you can pull yourself up by your bootstraps and become anything you choose." Group members who get such messages may prematurely leave the group in the belief that the leader and other members are not fully appreciating their everyday struggles. Rather than being a fault of choice theory/reality therapy, this is more a limitation of some who practice it.

In writing about the multicultural applications of reality therapy, Wubbolding (1998) notes that it is critical that the user of reality therapy demonstrate a willingness and skill in adapting the methodology to each individual client:

> Choice theory and reality therapy can be applied to any culture. It is a theory and a method based on universal motivation. Nevertheless, it needs to be adapted when used and taught in a multicultural setting. To do this effectively, teachers, counselors, therapists, or trainers need to be aware of their own values, skills and knowledge. They are also well-advised to learn about the customs, history, sociopolitical forces, and methods of communication which are part of other cultures. (p. 6)

Wubbolding and his colleagues (1998) put forth the following ethical principles for adapting reality therapy to culturally diverse client populations:

- Reality therapy is most ethically and effectively practiced in a multicultural setting when its principles and procedures are adapted to the individual client.
- Because of the need for adaptation, reality therapy should not be viewed as a rigid and closed system that is applied in the same manner to everyone or to every cultural group but as an open system that allows for flexibility in application.
- The skill in this adaptation process requires more than knowing the concepts and procedures of reality therapy. It requires an understanding of how to apply these principles and procedures to the client's culture and worldview.
- Practitioners are advised to examine their own attitudes, knowledge, and skills with a view to learning more about how other cultures impact the behaviors of individuals.

In summary, the specific skills that are a part of the WDEP system should be viewed as flexible procedures to be adapted to the personality of the leader and to the specific wants of members of various cultures. The challenge is to find ways of adapting reality therapy to the diversity we encounter in our groups rather than expecting (or forcing) these clients to adapt to and neatly correspond with the theory. As with other theories and the techniques that flow from them, flexibility is a foremost requirement.

Evaluation of Reality Therapy in Groups

Contributions and Strengths of the Approach

A characteristic of reality therapy that I especially favor is its stress on accountability. When a group participant indicates a desire to change certain behaviors, for example, the leader confronts the member with a question about what is keeping the person from doing so. I appreciate the fact that it is the members, not the leader, who evaluate their own behavior and decide whether they want to change. It seems to me that many group leaders meet with resistance because they have suggestions and plans for how the members should best live their lives. To their credit, reality therapists keep challenging the members to evaluate for themselves whether what they are doing is getting them what they want. If the members concede that what they are doing is not working for them, their resistance is much more likely to melt, and they tend to be more open to trying different behaviors.

Once the members make some change, reality therapy provides the structure for them to formulate specific plans for action and to evaluate their level of success. In most of my groups I have found it useful to employ these action-oriented procedures to help members carry what they are learning in the group into their everyday lives. I also ask members to state the terms of their contract clearly in the group and to report to the group the outcome of their efforts to fulfill it.

Other aspects of reality therapy that I endorse include the idea of not accepting excuses for failure to follow through with contracts and the avoidance of any form of punishment and blaming. As I see it, if people don't carry out a plan, it is important to discuss with them what got in their way. Perhaps they set their goals unrealistically high, or perhaps there is a discrepancy between what they say they want to change and what they actually want to change.

I also like reality therapy's insistence that change will not come by insight alone; rather, members will have to begin doing something different once they determine that their behavior is not working for them. I have become increasingly skeptical about the value of catharsis as a therapeutic vehicle unless the release of pent-up emotions is eventually put into some kind of cognitive framework and is also followed up with an action plan. My colleagues and I have worked in groups with people who seem to have immobilized themselves by dwelling excessively on their negative feelings and by being unwilling to take action to change. Therefore, we continue to challenge such members to look at the futility of waiting for others to change. Increasingly, we have asked them to assume that the significant people in their life may never change, which means that they will have to take a more active stance in shaping their own destiny. I appreciate the emphasis of reality therapy on teaching clients that the only person's life they can control is their own. Thus, the focus is not on what others are doing or on getting others to be different; instead, it is on helping clients change their own patterns of acting and thinking.

Group members are encouraged to look inward and search for alternatives. Since other members and the group leader will not accept rationalizations for their failing behavior, the members are forced to choose for themselves whether to change. I consider the challenging and skillful questioning by reality therapists to be a major strength of this approach. Of course, it is important for leaders to ask open-ended questions that get members to search inwardly and to avoid the "district attorney" style of questioning in which they feel grilled and bombarded.

Reality therapy encourages clients to look at the range of freedom they do possess, along with the responsibilities of this freedom. In this sense reality therapy is a form of existential therapy. As it is currently practiced, the emphasis is on the inner needs, wants, self-evaluation, and choices made by clients (Wubbolding, 2000). Because of this focus on the perceptual and behavioral systems, reality therapy can also be considered as a cognitive behavioral approach. A strength of the approach is its emphasis on understanding the subjective inner world of clients. This phenomenological view helps the therapist understand more fully how clients perceive their world, and such a perspective is an excellent means of establishing the rapport needed for creating an effective client/therapist relationship. Understanding the personal world of the client does not mean that therapists have to adopt a "soft" approach; on the contrary, they can demonstrate their caring by refusing to give up on the client. A therapist who consistently maintains a sense of hope that clients can change is often the catalyst who instills and activates a sense of optimism.

One of the strengths of reality therapy is that it is a straightforward and clear approach. Although its key principles are simple, basic, and practical, you should not conclude that the method is necessarily simple to apply in group counseling situations. Skills need to be mastered and practiced. Using the methods effectively in groups requires training and supervision—the kind that is provided by the William Glasser Institute or the Center for Reality Therapy in the basic intensive week program (both of which are listed at the end of this chapter).

Reality therapy has much to offer groups of parents, groups composed of children and adolescents who are having behavioral problems and who continually get in trouble at school, groups of teachers who work with a variety of students, groups of people who recognize that their lifestyle is not working for them, and groups of people in institutions for criminal behavior. The approach is well suited to brief interventions in crisis counseling situations. Because reality therapy deals with what clients are presently doing—and asks clients to make an evaluation of what they want to change—the approach fits into the managed care programs that restrict the number of sessions. Clients are expected to identify specific problem areas they want to explore, which also lends this approach to short-term methods. Groups designed on reality therapy principles can fit into a 10- to 12-week format.

Groups based on choice theory can be useful in working with clients who see themselves as the victims of the abusive actions of others. It is also widely used in addiction counseling and in groups with substance abusers. In many situations with these populations, it would be inappropriate to embark on long-term therapy that delves into unconscious dynamics and an intensive exploration of one's past. Reality therapy focuses on making changes in the present and is an effective, short-term approach that fits into the structure of many kinds of psychoeducational groups.

Choice theory and reality therapy work effectively for a variety of practitioners in a diversity of groups, and this approach has been successfully used in educational settings, in correctional institutions, in various mental health agencies, and in private practice. Choice theory can be used by parents, social welfare workers, counselors, marriage and family therapists, school administrators, the clergy, and youth workers. Glasser (1992, 2000) has successfully applied reality therapy principles and procedures with schools, youth custodial institutions, drug addiction clinics, and rehabilitation centers.

In summary, I see some unique values and contributions of reality therapy for group leaders. Most of its principles can be fruitfully integrated into several of the other systems that have been discussed in this book. Reality therapy can also be practiced by incorporating techniques from other approaches such as cognitive behavior therapy, transactional analysis, and solution-focused therapy. As is true of all models, the practitioner must examine the concepts of choice theory and the procedures of reality therapy to determine what elements can be effectively incorporated into his or her individual therapeutic style of facilitating groups.

Limitations of the Approach

Some critics object to choice theory/reality therapy as being simplistic and superficial. I have to admit that I, too, have been critical of this orientation to group work on those grounds; however, I no longer feel that way. The therapeutic procedures of reality therapy are simple and clear-cut to talk about, but actually putting them into practice is not a simple matter. Because of the simple language used in reality therapy, some might mistakenly conclude that this approach is simple to practice. A concern I still have about this approach is the danger that group practitioners will abuse the theory by applying the principles simplistically in their work. There is the danger of the group leader's assuming the role of a "preacher," or moral expert, who judges for the members how they should change. This can be considered an abuse of reality therapy. Clearly, if group members accept the leader's standards of behavior instead of questioning and struggling, they don't have to look within themselves to discover their own values. From my perspective this is a very undesirable outcome. I assume that what people need is more than advice or solutions to problems; they need to learn how to draw upon their own resources to find creative ways of living fully.

Though I agree that an action program is essential for changes in behavior, my personal preference is to give more attention to the realm of expressing and exploring feelings than choice theory/reality therapy calls for. Once involvement is attained in a group, my inclination is to give members many opportunities to express emotions that they may have kept buried for years. As I've mentioned several times before, my assumption is that therapeutic work is deepened by paying attention to the realm of feelings. Therefore, I draw heavily on techniques from the experiential approaches as a way of helping the members fully experience their feelings. However, I go along with transactional analysis, rational emotive behavior therapy, and the other cognitive behavioral therapies in placing emphasis on the role of thinking as a key determinant of behavior. Reality therapy emphasizes self-evaluation, which is a cognitive function. Many problems that show up behaviorally have a connection to the self-defeating statements that we often repeat to ourselves. In addition to encouraging members to come into full contact with the range of their feelings, I also try to get them to look at the thoughts and beliefs that are contributing to their emotional and behavioral problems.

Another limitation I see is the tendency to carry valid points to an invalid extreme. For example, although it is true that dwelling on the past can constitute avoidance of present responsibility, discounting the role of the past can easily lead to a superficial treatment of certain problems. Glasser (1998) asserts: "What happened in the past that was painful has a great deal to do with what we are today, but revisiting this painful past can contribute little or nothing to what we need to do now: improve an important present relationship" (p. 334). Glasser grants that we are products of our past, but argues that we are not able to change our past. Many therapeutic approaches are based on the assumption that adequate functioning in the present demands an understanding of our past. Another premise is that unless we revisit our past we can't understand it. Glasser (1998) maintains that we should discard the notion that it is important to know our past before we can deal with the present. He adds, "It is good to revisit the parts of our past that were satisfying, but leave what was unhappy alone" (p. 334).

From my perspective, Glasser's view of the past is flawed. As I have maintained throughout the critiques of each approach, unrecognized and unexplored issues from our past will bring a shadow to our present experiencing and behavior. Thus, I see it as critical to explore the ways in which our experiences are manifested in our present and in our future.

Some reality therapists do make it a practice to talk about the past if it is tied to the present. For example, they are likely to help an adult who was abused as a child to talk about it, for this is not really purely a past event, even though it happened many years ago. The event results in a present source of pain, and therefore it is present behavior rather than past behavior. If a group member has never discussed this abuse with anyone, then this is still currently influencing behavior. Similarly, there are some advantages to focusing on the conscious aspects of behavior, yet carried to an extreme this emphasis denies the powerful place of the unconscious in human experience. I don't see choice theory as adequately explaining unconscious dynamics, dealing with ways in which the unconscious affects conscious behavior, or addressing how unconscious factors are played out within a group setting.

Where to Go from Here

The programs offered by the William Glasser Institute are designed to teach the concepts of choice theory and the practice of reality therapy. The institute offers a certification process, which starts with a four- to five-day introductory course known as "The Basic Intensive Week" in which participants become involved in discussions, demonstrations, and role playing. For those wishing to pursue more extensive training, the institute offers a five-part sequential course of study leading to certification in reality therapy: the basic intensive week, the basic practicum, the advanced intensive week, the advanced practicum, and the certification week. For further information about these training programs, contact either of these two organizations:

The William Glasser Institute
Dr. William Glasser, President and Founder
22024 Lassen Street, Suite #118
Chatsworth, CA 91311-3600
TELEPHONE: (818) 700-8000
TOLL FREE: (800) 899-0688
FAX: (818) 700-0555
E-MAIL: wginst@earthlink.net
WEB SITE: www.wglasser.com

Center for Reality Therapy
Dr. Robert E. Wubbolding, Director
7672 Montgomery Road #383
Cincinnati, OH 45236-4258
TELEPHONE: (513) 561-1911
FAX: (513) 561-3568
E-MAIL: wubsrt@fuse.net
WEB SITE: www.realitytherapywub.com

A useful videotape, *Using Reality Therapy in Group Counseling*, has been prepared by Robert Wubbolding and is available through the Center for Reality Therapy. The first part of this two-hour video consists of an explanation of the basic concepts of choice theory and of the stages involved in a reality therapy group. The second part is a demonstration of a group, with a commentary from the perspective of a practicing reality therapist.

Recommended Supplementary Readings

Glasser has written little on group counseling; however, the principles and concepts discussed in his books easily translate to group work. I would highly recommend *Choice Theory: A New Psychology of Personal Freedom* (Glasser, 1998). In this popular and easy-to-read book, the author deals with a theory of personal freedom and with a range of topics, including love and marriage, family, workplace, schooling and education, and community.

Counseling with Choice Theory: The New Reality Therapy (Glasser, 2000) uses many cases to give readers a sense of how choice theory principles can actually be applied in helping people establish better relationships. He develops the existential theme that because we are responsible for our behavior we are capable of acquiring more effective coping styles.

Reality Therapy for the 21st Century (Wubbolding, 2000) is a comprehensive and practical book that represents major extensions and developments of reality therapy. The practical formulation of the WDEP system of reality therapy is highlighted, much of which can be adapted to group counseling. Included are multicultural adaptations and summaries of research studies validating the theory and practice of reality therapy.

Understanding Reality Therapy (Wubbolding, 1991) is a practical book containing stories, metaphors, and anecdotes for increasing knowledge of choice theory and reality therapy.

The *International Journal of Reality Therapy* began semiannual publication in September 1981. The journal publishes manuscripts concerning research, theory development, and specific descriptions of the successful application of reality therapy principles in field settings. If you are interested in subscribing, contact:

Dr. Lawrence Litwack, Editor (Journal of Reality Therapy)
203 Lake Hall
Boston-Bouve College
Northeastern University
360 Huntington Avenue
Boston, MA 02115

References and Suggested Readings*

de Shazer, S. (1985). *Keys to solutions in brief therapy.* New York: Norton.
de Shazer, S. (1988). *Clues: Investigating solutions in brief therapy.* New York: Norton.
de Shazer, S. (1991). *Putting difference to work.* New York: Norton.
Glasser, N. (Ed.). (1980). *What are you doing? How people are helped through reality therapy.* New York: Harper & Row.
Glasser, N. (Ed.). (1989). *Control theory in the practice of reality therapy: Case studies.* New York: Harper & Row (Perennial).
Glasser, W. (1965). *Reality therapy: A new approach to psychiatry.* New York: Harper & Row.
Glasser, W. (1969). *Schools without failure.* New York: Harper & Row.
Glasser, W. (1976). *Positive addiction.* New York: Harper & Row.
Glasser, W. (1985). *Control theory: A new explanation of how we control our lives.* New York: Harper & Row (Perennial).
Glasser, W. (1986). *Control theory in the classroom.* New York: Harper & Row.
Glasser, W. (1989). Control theory. In N. Glasser (Ed.), *Control theory in the practice of reality therapy: Case studies* (pp. 1–15). New York: Harper & Row (Perennial).
Glasser, W. (1990). *The quality school: Managing students without coercion.* New York: Harper & Row.
Glasser, W. (1992). Reality therapy. *New York State Journal for Counseling and Development, 7*(1), 5–13.

---

*Books and articles marked with an asterisk are suggested for further study.

Glasser, W. (1993). *The quality school teacher*. New York: Harper & Row.

Glasser, W. (1995). *Staying together*. New York: HarperCollins.

Glasser, W. (1997). Teaching and learning reality therapy. In J. K. Zeig (Ed.), *The evolution of psychotherapy: The third conference* (pp. 123–133). New York: Brunner/Mazel.

*Glasser, W. (1998). *Choice theory: A new psychology of personal freedom*. New York: HarperCollins.

*Glasser, W. (2000). *Counseling with choice theory: The new reality therapy*. New York: HarperCollins.

Glasser, W. (2001). *Fibromyalgia: Hope from a completely new perspective*. Chatsworth, CA: William Glasser Institute.

Glasser, W., & Wubbolding, R. E. (1995). Reality therapy. In R. Corsini & D. Wedding (Eds.), *Current psychotherapies* (5th ed., pp. 293–321). Itasca, IL: F. E. Peacock.

Thompson, C. L., & Rudolph, L. B. (2000). *Counseling children* (5th ed.). Pacific Grove, CA: Brooks/Cole.

*O'Hanlon, W. H., & Weiner-Davis, M. (1989). *In search of solutions: A new direction in psychotherapy*. New York: Norton.

*Wubbolding, R. E. (1988). *Using reality therapy*. New York: Harper & Row (Perennial).

Wubbolding, R. E. (1990). *Expanding reality therapy: Group counseling and multicultural dimensions*. Cincinnati: Center for Reality Therapy.

*Wubbolding, R. E. (1991). *Understanding reality therapy*. New York: Harper & Row (Perennial).

*Wubbolding, R. E. (1996a). Reality therapy: Theoretical underpinnings and implementation in practice. *Directions in Mental Health Counseling, 6*(9), 4–16.

Wubbolding, R. E. (1996b). Professional issues: The use of questions in reality therapy. *Journal of Reality Therapy, 16*(1), 122–127.

Wubbolding, R. E. (1997). The school as a system: Quality linkages. *Journal of Reality Therapy, 16*(2), 76–79.

*Wubbolding, R. E. (2000). *Reality therapy for the 21st century*. Philadelphia, PA: Brunner-Routledge (Taylor & Francis).

Wubbolding, R. E. (2001). *Reality therapy training* (12th revision). Cincinnati, OH: Center for Reality Therapy.

Wubbolding, R. E. (2002). *Cycle of managing, supervising, counseling and coaching* (chart, 13th revision). Cincinnati, OH: Center for Reality Therapy.

Wubbolding, R. E., Al-Rashidi, B., Brickell, J., Kakitani, M., Kim, R. I., Lennon, B., Lojk, L., Ong, K. H., Honey, I., Stijacic, D., & Tham, E. (1998). Multicultural awareness: Implications for reality therapy and choice theory. *International Journal of Reality Therapy, 17*(2), 4–6.

Wubbolding, R. E., & Brickell, J. (1998). Qualities of the reality therapist. *International Journal of Reality Therapy, 17*(2), 47–49.

*Wubbolding, R. E., & Brickell, J. (1999). *Counselling with reality therapy*. London: Winslow.

Wubbolding, R. E., & Brickell, J. (2000a). Misconceptions about reality therapy. *International Journal of Reality Therapy, 19*(2), 64–65.

*Wubbolding, R. E., & Brickell, J. (2000b). *A set of directions for putting and keeping yourself together*. Minneapolis, MN: Educational Media Corporation.

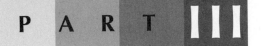

PART **III**

INTEGRATION AND APPLICATION

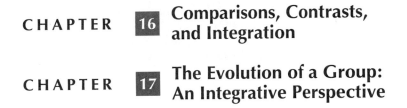

CHAPTER 16

Comparisons, Contrasts, and Integration

The purpose of this chapter is fourfold: (1) to compare and contrast the various models as they apply to issues special to group work; (2) to raise some basic questions that you'll need to answer now and throughout the course of your practice; (3) to challenge you to attempt an integration of the various perspectives that is consistent with your personality; and (4) to stimulate your thinking about ways of developing and refining group techniques that reflect your leadership style. This chapter will help you answer these questions:

- Is it possible to achieve some integration of the diverse group models by focusing on their commonalities?
- How would an integrated view of the various perspectives actually help you define your own goals of group counseling?
- How do you go about blending concepts and techniques from several approaches to achieve your own definition of the leader's role and your own unique leadership style?
- How can you achieve an optimum balance between responsible leadership and responsible membership?
- What kind of structuring do you want to provide for a group? How do you determine how much structure is appropriate?
- How do you develop techniques that are consonant with your personality and style and are also appropriate for the kinds of groups you lead?
- How can the techniques of the theoretical approaches be modified to fit the cultural backgrounds of various clients?
- What are the advantages and the disadvantages of an integrative approach to group practice?

The Goals of Group Counseling: Various Perspectives

To impart meaningful direction to their groups, leaders need to address themselves to the issue of goals. What should be the specific goals of a given group, and who should determine them? How can the leader help group members develop meaningful goals for themselves? How does the leader's theoretical orientation influence the process of goal setting? Is it possible to set group goals based on a variety of theoretical orientations? To help you find common denominators among the goals stressed by the various theoretical models and to guide you in your attempt to integrate these models, Table 16-1 (p. 467) lists the essential therapeutic goals of each of the group approaches discussed in Part II. As you read the table, keep in mind that the diversity of goals can be simplified by seeing the goals as existing on a continuum from general, global, and long-term objectives to specific, concrete, and short-term objectives. Existential and relationship-oriented group approaches tend to deal with broad goals that are formulated by the members, and behavioral and cognitively oriented systems focus on short-term, observable, and precise goals that are formulated collaboratively with the members and the leader. The goals at opposite ends of the continuum are not necessarily contradictory; it is just a matter of how specifically the goals are defined. Thus, a convergence is possible if practitioners view concrete short-term goals as components of broad, long-range goals.

Most theoretical perspectives agree on the importance of group members' formulating their own specific goals. When leaders decide that they know what is best for the participants and force their own goals on them, they typically encounter resistance. To be sure, leaders need to have some overall goals for the group, but such goals should in no way infringe on the members' freedom to select personal goals that will give direction to their work in the group. Individual goal setting is an ongoing process that needs to be constantly reevaluated. The leader can be of invaluable assistance in this regard by encouraging members to formulate clear and specific goals for themselves and by helping them determine how they can work toward achieving these goals. In this way, goal setting is an ongoing process that is done in a collaborative manner.

Role and Functions of the Group Leader: Various Perspectives

Should the leader be a facilitator? a therapist? a teacher? a catalyst? a coach? a guide? a fellow explorer? a technician? a director? an evaluator? some or all of these?

How you answer these questions will depend in part on your theoretical perspective, but ultimately your answers will be based on your own definition of the leader's role and on your own assessment of what the most significant functions of the leader are. Certain criteria also cut across all the theoretical approaches-for example, the type of group and its goals, the setting, the nature of the participants, and the demands of your job.

Before discussing the various perspectives on the group leader's role and functions, let's briefly review some of the tasks I consider essential to successful group leadership:

1. Group leaders initiate and promote interaction by the way they structure the group and model behaviors. Thus, they demonstrate how to share, take risks, relate honestly, and involve others in interactions.

2. Group leaders have the task of orienting members to the group process, teaching them how to get the most from their group, and helping them become aware of the group dynamics.

3. Group leaders must be capable of sensitive, active listening. Only by paying full attention to the members' verbal and nonverbal communication can they help participants move toward a deeper level of self-exploration and self-understanding.

4. Group leaders are responsible for creating a safe and supportive climate conducive to exploring personally significant issues.

5. Group leaders are responsible for setting limits, establishing group rules, informing members of their rights and responsibilities, and protecting members.

As we have seen, each therapeutic approach stresses different functions for the group leader. For example, the person-centered approach emphasizes the role of facilitator. Since in this model the group is seen as having the resources to direct itself, the leader is supposed to facilitate rather than direct group process. Other approaches see the leader as a teacher. Rational emotive behavior therapy, reality therapy, Adlerian therapy, behavior therapy, and transactional analysis are all based on the assumption that group counseling is essentially an educational and learning process, and consequently the leader's key function is teaching skills and providing a cognitive framework that will lead to reeducation and behavioral changes.

Other models, such as the psychoanalytic approach, focus on the role of the group leader as a technical expert who interprets intrapsychic and interpersonal processes as they manifest themselves in a group. Still other models, such as the existential, person-centered, and Gestalt approaches, stress the leader's role in helping members gain an experiential awareness of their conflicts through meaningful relationships with the leader and others in the group. As we have seen, your roles and functions as a group leader are many; which of them you choose to emphasize is partly determined by your theoretical orientation. As you review the different perspectives summarized in Table 16-2 (p. 468), consider what elements you want to incorporate from each of them in defining your own role as group leader.

Degree of Structuring and Division of Responsibility: Various Perspectives

Group leaders often struggle with the question of what constitutes the optimum degree of structure in a group. It should be clear that all groups have a structure. Even the least directive group leaders, who avoid imposing a format on the group, do make the choice of having an open structure and letting the participants determine the course of the group.

Group structuring exists on a continuum, from extremely nondirective to highly directive. On the nondirective end of the continuum are psychoanalytic groups, person-centered groups, and some existential groups. In these groups the leader tends to assume a less directive stance and encourages group members to assume much of the responsibility for the direction they take.

At the opposite end of the continuum are those leaders who provide a high degree of structure for the group. They often use structured exercises to open the group sessions; also, they employ techniques to focus members on specific themes or problem areas and to intensify certain emotions and conflicts. Many behavior therapy groups are characterized by a very active and directive group leadership. This is also true of reality therapy groups and REBT groups. Typically, there is a progression from session to session, the meetings are organized in accordance with a predetermined agenda, and certain procedures are used to direct the group toward exploration and resolution of specific problem areas.

Like structuring, division of responsibility can be conceptualized in terms of a continuum. At one end are those group leaders who see themselves as experts and who believe they should actively intervene to keep the group moving in productive ways. The group's outcomes are largely seen as being dependent on the leader's skills. Since therapy is considered an educative process, the group leader is seen mainly as a teacher in charge of the reeducation of group members. For effective results, group therapists are expected to employ a didactic and challenging methodology aimed at cognitive restructuring and behavioral change. Group leaders who embrace this perspective include those with orientations such as behavior therapy, rational emotive behavior therapy, and reality therapy. However, despite the active and directive role assigned to the leader, these approaches also place a considerable share of responsibility for directing the group on the members, who are expected to be active, work hard, and practice between group sessions.

At the other end of the continuum are group leaders who expressly announce at the beginning of a group that the members are responsible to define the direction the group takes. This type of leadership is characteristic of the person-centered leader, who sees the participants as the ones who truly know what is best for them. Rather than assume the role of directing the course a group takes, the therapist functions as a facilitator by attempting to create a trusting climate wherein members can safely explore significant personal issues and search for the necessary resources within themselves.

Somewhat in the middle of the continuum are Gestalt group leaders. They are typically active, in that they intervene with techniques that provide the group with structure, but they also expect members to participate in the creation of experiments that will heighten their awareness. Group leaders are responsible for being aware of their own experience throughout the group process and for suggesting appropriate experiments to intensify group work. Members are responsible for bringing up issues that they want to investigate in the group and for making their own interpretations. Table 16-3 (p. 469) gives you an idea of the variety of theoretical positions on structuring and division of responsibility.

My view is that group leaders need to achieve a balance between assuming too much responsibility for the direction of the group and assuming too little. If clients are perceived by the leader as not having the capacity to take care of themselves, they soon begin to live up to this expectation. Besides undermining members' independence, leaders who assume an inordinate amount of responsibility burden themselves greatly. They tend to blame themselves for whatever failures or setbacks the group suffers. If members do little productive work, these leaders view this as a reflection of their lack of skill. This style of leadership is draining, and the leaders who use it may soon lose the energy required to lead groups.

In contrast, leaders who place all the responsibility for the direction and outcomes of a group on the participants may simply be trying to avoid their own role in the outcomes their groups. Thus, if a group seems to flounder and not engage in productive work, these leaders are not likely to reflect on their role in the group process.

The Use of Techniques: Various Perspectives

Techniques are quite useful both as catalysts for group action and as devices to keep the group moving. But techniques are just tools, and like all tools they can be used properly or misused. When leaders fall into a pattern of employing methods mechanically, they become technicians and are not responding to the needs of the particular group they are leading. Also, indiscriminate use of techniques tends to increase the resistance level of the group instead of facilitating deeper communication and exploration. Some leaders, overly eager to use new methods, rely too much on techniques to bring energy to the group and provide it with a direction. Others, out of anxiety over not knowing how to deal with certain problems that arise in a group, try technique after technique in helter-skelter fashion. In general, group leaders should have sound reasons for using particular methods of intervention, and an overreliance on technique is, in my view, questionable. Techniques need to be an extension of who the leader is as a person, and group leaders should not force themselves to use methods that don't suit their personality and their unique leadership style.

My basic assumption is that techniques should facilitate group process, not artificially create action in a group. I also assume that they are most effective when the group leader learns how to pay attention to the obvious. They can deepen feelings that are already present, and they should grow out of what is going on in the group at the time. There is always something going on in a group, and this material can suggest appropriate methods. I like the notion of leaders and members collaboratively creating experiments that grow out of what is happening presently within a group, which is a perspective shared by Gestalt therapists. Although my colleagues and I sometimes use techniques to introduce material at the initial stage of a group and often use them to integrate what members have learned at the final stage, we generally do not have a preset agenda. We take our cues from what is occurring within the group and flow with that rather than attempting to direct the group to pursue a specific theme. For example, if I notice that there is little energy in the room and that nobody appears willing to be engaged in significant work, I do not introduce an exercise designed to stir up feelings or promote interaction. Instead, I tend to let the group know that I am feeling strained from taking too much responsibility for keeping the group alive, and I try to get some assessment of what each person is experiencing.

In choosing techniques to facilitate group process, you must consider several factors. Your theory, of course, will influence what methods you employ. If it focuses on cognitive aspects, your techniques are likely to encourage clients to look for the connection between their thought patterns and their actions. If you have an experiential orientation, your techniques will tend to promote an awareness of present feelings and an intensification of these feelings. If you are behaviorally oriented, many of your techniques will be geared to getting members to monitor their actions and experiment with specific behaviors. Your style of leadership also has much to do with what methods you will use. Finally, the population with whom you are working, the purpose of your group, and the stage of development of the group are all factors to consider in the selection of techniques. Regardless of your theory, you need to understand the relationship between techniques and theoretical concepts and be fully aware of why you are using certain methods. You also need to continually assess the effects of these techniques.

As illustrated by Table 16-4 (p. 470), the various group models offer a variety of strategies for initiating and maintaining group interaction. There is no reason for group practitioners to restrict themselves to the techniques of a single approach simply because that's the approach they favor. For example, group leaders with an existential orientation can draw on techniques from the cognitive behavioral approaches. In summary, leaders need to use their imagination to discover ways of adapting techniques from various theoretical models to the specific type of group they lead and of modifying them to suit their leadership style.

Group Work in a Multicultural Context: Various Perspectives

Each of the theories presented in this book has been briefly examined for its relevance to culturally diverse populations. As can be seen in Table 16-5 (p. 471), each perspective has certain concepts or techniques that can contribute to effective multicultural group counseling. Yet they all have some limitations, and caution is needed in using certain techniques that flow from a given theory (see Table 16-6, p. 472). Technical eclecticism seems especially necessary in working with a diverse range of cultural backgrounds. Harm can come to group participants who are expected to fit all the specifications of a given theory, whether or not the values espoused by the theory are consistent with their own cultural values. Rather than stretching the client to fit the dimensions of a single theory, leaders must make their theory and practice fit the unique needs of the client. This requirement calls for group leaders who possess knowledge of various cultures, awareness of their own cultural heritage, and skills to assist diverse clients in meeting their needs within the realities of their culture.

It is essential for leaders to be able to assess the special needs of clients. Depending on the group member's ethnicity and culture and also on the individual concerns that bring a member to a group, the leader will need to show flexibility in utilizing diverse therapeutic strategies. At times, some clients will need more direction, and even advice. Others will be very hesitant in talking about themselves in personal ways, especially during the early phase of a group. Leaders need to be patient and to avoid quickly pushing members to "open up and be real." Furthermore, leaders need to recognize that what may appear to be resistance is very likely to be the client's response to years of cultural conditioning and respect for certain values and traditions. Group leaders need to be familiar with a variety of theoretical approaches and be able to employ and adapt their techniques to fit the person-in-the-environment. It is not enough to merely assist members in gaining insight, expressing suppressed emotions, or making certain behavioral changes. The challenge for leaders is to find practical strategies for adapting the techniques they have developed to enable clients to question the impact their culture continues to have on their life and to make decisions about what facets of their life they want to change. Being an effective group leader involves reflecting on how your own culture influences you and your interventions in your groups. This awareness will be a critical factor in your becoming more sensitive to the cultural backgrounds of the members in your groups.

Applications of the Integrative Eclectic Model

The term *integrative eclectic model* refers to a perspective based on concepts and techniques from the various theoretical approaches. It is the model I use in my own practice of group work. This section describes how I apply my synthesis at each stage of a group's development. This model is designed to address the three factors of thinking, feeling, and doing. As you've seen, some of the 10 theories discussed in Part II focus on cognition, others on experiencing feelings, and others on behavior. My goal is to blend the unique contributions of these approaches so that all three dimensions of human experiencing are given attention at each phase of a group. At the same time, it is important to avoid the trap of emerging with a hodgepodge of unamalgamated theories hastily thrown together. Your goal should be to develop a consistent conceptual framework that you can use as a basis for selecting from the multiple techniques that you have studied.

Theories Applied to the Pregroup Stage

The preparatory period in the formation of a group may be the most critical of all. If the group's foundation is weak, the group may never get off the ground. Effective groups do not simply "happen." The hard work and careful organization that go into planning a group are bound to have payoffs once the group gets under way. At this point it would be a good idea for you to review the major considerations in forming groups, found in Chapter 4.

The behavioral theories are particularly relevant at the pregroup stage, for they emphasize assessing both the need for a particular kind of group and the participant's readiness and appropriateness for a group. As a group leader, you must have clear expectations, a rationale for why and how a group is an effective approach, and a sense of how to design a specific group tailored to the unique needs and interests of the members. If you are clear about how a group can benefit prospective members, you'll be better able to help them decide whether to join. If members know what they are getting into, the chances are increased that they will become active and committed participants.

In this regard, the therapeutic approaches that structure a group on a contractual basis have much to offer. A contract can help demystify the group process, can increase the members' sense of responsibility to become active agents in their own change, and can structure the course a group takes. Contracts set forth the division of responsibility between the members and the leader, and they are a useful springboard for productive work. As you will remember, the cognitively and behaviorally oriented therapies stress contracts as a way of beginning the process. TA groups, behavioral group therapy, and, sometimes, rational emotive behavior therapy and reality therapy groups work on a contractual basis. Whatever your theoretical orientation, open-ended and flexible contracts can be drawn up before the group actually meets as a whole.

Theories Applied to the Initial Stage

Basic Characteristics   The early phase of a group is a time for orientation and exploration. Some of the distinguishing characteristics at this time are these: Members are attempting to find a place in the group. They are trying to get acquainted and learn what a group is all about. They are gradually learning the norms and expectations. Interactions tend to be of a socially acceptable nature and somewhat on the surface, and there is a certain tentativeness within the group. Perhaps the most basic issue pertains to creating and maintaining trust. The attitudes and behaviors of the group leader are directly related to the creation of a level of trust that will promote significant interaction.

Drawing on Theories   The relationship-oriented approaches (especially person-centered therapy, existential therapy, and Gestalt therapy) provide an excellent foundation for building a community characterized by trust and the willingness to take the risks that are necessary for change. The leader's modeling is especially important, for it is my belief that members learn more from what the leader does than from what he or she says. Here is where enthusiasm about groups can be communicated to the members by a dedicated, competent, and caring group leader. A basic sense of respect for what the members are experiencing as they approach a new group can best be demonstrated by a leader's willingness to allow members to express what they are thinking and feeling in the here-and-now. Typically, members do have some initial anxieties. They may fear an unfamiliar situation, rejection, or closeness. Some may fear opening up more than they will be able to manage, disrupting their life outside the group, or incurring the disapproval of others in the group. A genuine interest in listening to these feelings sets the tone for caring, attentiveness, and compassion and goes a long way toward creating a climate in which members can be free to share what they feel and think.

Besides encouraging members to express their feelings, I draw on the cognitive therapies. Thus, members come to a group with certain expectations of themselves and of what they think a group can do for them. Some may expect others to provide them with answers to their problems. Others may expect to get from the group what is missing in everyday living. Then there are some who may be convinced that a group will not really help them. Such expectations need to be stated and addressed at the early sessions.

Defining Personal Goals   It is during the initial stage that the *behavioral* approaches and the *cognitive* therapies have special relevance. I like the behavioral emphasis on helping members identify concrete aspects of their behavior that they most want to change. From there the leader may do some teaching to show members how involvement in the group can be instrumental in attaining their goals. I see it as counterproductive for leaders to impose on members specific goals that they should work toward, for unless the members really want to change, there is little hope that change can be forced on them. For this reason I value the Adlerian concept of goal alignment. Adlerians make special efforts to negotiate a congruence of goals between the client and the therapist. TA groups are also characterized by mutually agreed-on therapeutic goals. In reality therapy groups there is emphasis on asking members to evaluate their wants and to determine whether these desires are realistic. Reality therapy also challenges members to look at their behavior and decide whether it is working for them. If members make the evaluation that their current behavior is not working, the process of making specific behavioral changes can begin.

If members are not aided in making an evaluation of their wants, needs, and current behavior, they find it very difficult to know where to begin. Careful consideration of this personal evaluation is a way to engage the group members and to motivate them to do something different. Of course, the skill in group leading involves showing members how a group can help them get what they say they want. I cannot overstress the importance of inducing the members to decide if they really want to change some of their thoughts, feelings, and behaviors.

Although I am very sympathetic toward the existential goal of learning how to live more creatively by accepting freedom and responsibility, I think such broad goals need to be narrowed down so that members have a clear idea of what thoughts, feelings, and actions they are willing to change and can learn how to make such changes. A way to help members specify their goals is to ask them to write them down.

Theories Applied to the Transition Stage

◼ **Learning to Deal with Conflict and Resistance**   One of the most challenging and often frustrating periods in the life of a group is the transition phase. Before a group can progress to the working stage, it typically must learn to recognize and deal with anxiety, defensiveness, resistance, conflict, the struggle for control, challenges to the leader, and various other problematic behaviors. Some groups reach the transitional period only to remain stuck there. This impasse can be traced either to an earlier failure to establish norms or to inept handling of resistance and conflict within the group. It is essential that conflict be both recognized and then dealt with therapeutically if the group is to move forward. One way to recognize resistance is to regularly assess the group members' level of satisfaction with their participation in the group. This can be done in a brief written evaluation, which can then be tabulated and brought back to the group. It is useful to get members used to regular assessments, for in this way problems within the group can be detected and then worked on in the sessions. Specific questions can be asked about each member's level of investment, satisfaction with the sessions, trust level, and willingness to take risks. Refer to the Student Manual of this text for ideas about inventories that can be used to assess group process. Of course, this type of assessment is consistent with behavioral approaches that stress specificity of behavior, outcomes, and regular feedback about the process as a way to determine whether the group interventions are effective.

Again, the role of leader modeling is critical when it comes to accepting and dealing with resistance. At times, leaders create resistance or make it worse by what they say or do. If leaders take too personally any problems that occur within the group, they burden themselves and tend to become defensive. It is essential to give members some room to maneuver, to avoid responding sharply or defensively, and, most certainly, to avoid sarcasm. The manner in which the group leader deals with the inevitable resistance that manifests itself in various avoidances and defensive maneuvers will determine how well the group meets the developmental tasks at the transition phase. I hope you will learn how to respect resistance by seeing it as a normal and healthy sign of a group's movement toward autonomy. Rather than viewing resistance as a nuisance to be gotten around, you can help members deal with the sources of their resistance in a therapeutic way.

◼ **Ways of Conceptualizing Resistance**   Several theoretical perspectives shed some light on the dynamics of resistance and suggest methods of dealing with it constructively. From a psychoanalytic perspective, resistance is seen as anything that prevents members from dealing with unconscious material. It is the unconscious attempt to defend oneself from the anxiety that would arise if the unconscious were uncovered. It helps me to remember that members have to struggle with intrapsychic conflicts as well as interpersonal conflicts. A leader who is sensitive to the ambivalence that members experience—both wanting to be a part of the process of self-discovery and fearing self-knowledge—can help participants begin to look at their fears and defenses.

I see ways of combining the psychoanalytic and Adlerian views of resistance. Group members typically reexperience some of the old feelings they had in their original family. Sibling rivalry, position in the group, acceptance/rejection feelings, strivings for attention and success, authority issues, managing negative feelings, and childhood traumas all surface in the group experience. People are often stuck in a developmental sense because of these unfinished situations that now intrude on their ability to function effectively. In many ways the group resembles one's family of origin. By working with their projections, transferences, attractions, and other feelings toward others in the group, the members can experiment with new ways of thinking about themselves and others.

A Thinking, Feeling, Behaving Perspective   When a group is in transition, I appreciate the freedom given by the person-centered approach to express any feelings and have this expression accepted. My hope is that members will allow themselves to *feel* the ways in which they are resisting and to intensify those feelings. Here is where I draw on some of the action-oriented techniques of Gestalt therapy and psychodrama so that clients will have a way to experience as fully as possible whatever they feel. It is important to assess what clients need, however, and to work within the framework of their cultural background. Some members, because of their cultural injunctions, would have a difficult time getting involved in the emotional aspects of Gestalt experiments or emotionally intense psychodramas. It is certainly not therapeutically productive to push clients to experience emotions, but it could be helpful to explore with them their reluctance to share their emotions.

At some point I would also want to work with the belief systems and self-talk of the members. Here is where I find transactional analysis, rational emotive behavior therapy, and the cognitive therapies of value. For example, a member might participate very little in a group because she is following certain parental injunctions, such as these: "Don't show other people what you feel." "Don't talk in public about your family and personal problems." "Don't trust others." "Be strong, and don't give in to feelings of self-pity." I think TA provides a useful framework within which members can gain awareness of these parental messages and their early decisions. Although a group experience can help these clients eventually challenge the validity of certain messages, it is important to avoid confronting some of these values too quickly. Patience and respect are extremely important at this time.

REBT is also of value in helping members challenge some of the self-defeating beliefs that lead to an entrenchment of their defensiveness in the group. Some members may say very little because of their fear of disapproval or because they are convinced that they must say things "perfectly" if they hope to be understood. Once members allow themselves to experience their resistance on a feeling level, they are better able to genuinely challenge their cognitions. Here is where writing helps again. If members can be encouraged to keep a journal of their thoughts (and how these thoughts lead to some unwanted behaviors and feelings), they can then do some in-depth exploration of certain self-talk that is not productive. They can learn new and more functional cognitions, and they can practice them both in and out of group. Related to this is their willingness to begin to behave in different ways. I like the emphasis of reality therapy on paying attention to what one is *doing* and REBT's emphasis on *practicing* new behaviors as the basis for making lasting changes. Reality therapy provides some particularly useful questions that can lead members to make plans for change. This planning can be one way for members to actually begin to act differently.

Theories Applied to the Working Stage

During the working stage there is a commitment by members to explore the significant problems that they bring to the sessions and to express their reactions to what is taking place within the group. I find that this stage requires the least degree of structuring. In part this is because members bring up issues they want to work on, freely interact with one another, have the feeling of being a group rather than a bunch of strangers, and assume responsibility to keep the sessions moving.

Concepts and Techniques   My preference is to let the members raise the issues they are willing to pursue seriously rather than taking the responsibility for calling on them, drawing them out, or telling them what they should talk about. I still find it helpful to ask members to create their own agenda for each meeting, and I like to begin a group session by asking each person to declare in a clear sentence what he or she wants for the session. This does not imply a passive stance, however, for during the working stage I am very willing to suggest experiments and to invite members to take part in a technique that is designed to heighten whatever it is that they are experiencing. Again, my concern is with the thinking, feeling, and doing dimensions, and the techniques I suggest reflect this type of integration. Once members declare that they do want to work and we decide what it is they want to accomplish, I typically ask them if they are willing to participate in an experiment.

Generally, I prefer to begin with helping members get into contact with what they are feeling in the here-and-now. Gestalt experiments are most useful in focusing on present-centered awareness and bringing any unfinished business from the past to the surface. I favor the approach that asks members to bring any past issue into the present, as is true of both psychodrama and Gestalt. There is a lively quality to the work, and members rather quickly begin to experience what they feel rather than talking abstractly about feelings and thoughts. For example, if a woman becomes aware that she is afraid that she is growing up to be just like the mother she resents, a good place to begin is to ask her to "bring your mother into the group" symbolically. Again, Gestalt therapy and psychodrama offer a rich range of techniques to help her get into focus and intensify her experience. She might experiment with assuming her mother's identity and actually speaking to others in the group "as her mother." Although I value the contact with feelings, I think it is of limited value to stop with catharsis or the mere expression of her feelings. I am likely to suggest that she identify some of the beliefs that she has picked up from her mother. Perhaps she has uncritically accepted some irrational ideas that she is clinging to and is keeping herself upset by living by untested assumptions.

Coupled with her emotional work, some exploration of her cognitions is likely to reveal how her daily behavior is limiting her. Therefore, I see debates as productive in a group. Especially valuable are debates that members can learn to have with themselves. They can challenge untested assumptions, argue the pros and cons of a given issue, and think about how they sometimes set themselves up for defeat. Finally, working at a behavioral level is an excellent way to correct faulty thinking and emotional disturbances.

My particular emphasis during the working phase is to focus on what members are doing outside of the sessions. Therefore, I like to allow time toward the end of each session to ask every member to respond to questions such as these: "What did you learn about yourself in today's session?" "What kind of behaviors can you practice during the week?" "What is one specific homework assignment that you are willing to give yourself and carry out?" This approach reinforces in-group learning, and it helps members continually think about how to apply new ways of thinking and behaving in everyday situations.

Theories Applied to the Final Stage

Review of Tasks   The final stage of the group's evolution is critical, for members have an opportunity to clarify the meaning of their experiences in the group, to consolidate the gains they have made, and to revise their decisions about what newly acquired behaviors they want to transfer to their daily life. The major task facing members during this consolidation stage is to learn ways of maintaining these changed behaviors in the outside world. My focus is on getting the members to review the nature of any changes on a thinking, feeling, and behaving level. Have they learned the value of expressing negative feelings rather than swallowing them? Have they learned that repressing their feelings results in some indirect expression of them? What cognitions have they modified? Have they let go of some dysfunctional cognitions that lead to emotional upsets? Have they challenged their beliefs and values and made them their own? What concrete behavioral changes have they made that they value? How did they make these changes? How can they continue to behave in ways that are productive? What plan for action can they devise now that the group is coming to an end so that they can continue to make progress?

Theoretical Perspectives   I tend to use the most structure during the beginning and ending phases of a group. I don't believe members will automatically transfer specific cognitive, emotional, and behavioral changes from the group to the outside world. Therefore, I provide a structure that I hope will promote this transfer of learning. I have mentioned that in ongoing groups I do whatever I can to promote action on the part of the members by getting them to create their own homework assignments and then to report on their progress at the next group meeting. This is a way of continually using the group as a place to learn how to be different and then of carrying this new behavior into life. The group is a means to an end and should never become an end in itself.

Whereas I tend to use experiential therapies and exploration of feelings during the working phase, during the final stage I lean toward the cognitive behavioral therapies and toward putting one's learning into some type of conceptual framework. From the behavioral therapies I draw techniques such as practice and rehearsal for leaving a group, self-monitoring procedures, building a support system beyond the group, and learning methods of self-reinforcement. I see therapy as a teaching/learning process, and I try to help members devise a conceptual framework that will ensure that they make sense of what they have experienced. Therefore, at the final stage I tend to ask over and over, "What did you learn in this group that you valued, and how did you learn it?" I don't want members attributing their changes to the magic of the group but, rather, to specific actions that they took to change. Both REBT and reality therapy are relevant models at this point in a group's history, because they stress the importance of developing specific plans for change, making a commitment to do what is needed to bring about change, and evaluating the outcomes of the therapeutic process.

Although members are urged to try out a plan of action during the working phase, it is during the final stage that such a plan is essential. It is also important to help members find ways to continue to build on their newly acquired skills. Members can promote their change by deciding toward the end of the group on other paths for growth. They can make decisions about specific activities that will keep challenging them. They can make contracts to behave in certain ways once the group ends.

I emphasize cognitive work and behavioral plans for action during the final stage, but I do not assume that feelings are unimportant at this time. It is critical that members deal with their feelings about separation and termination, that they express any fears or reservations they may have about making it in the world without the support of the group, and that they learn how to say good-bye. Also, the opportunity to complete any unfinished business is paramount at this time.

Toward the end of a group's history there is a place for the role of the leader as a teacher. Leaders can caution members and provide them with practical strategies for dealing with setbacks once they leave a group. Members need to learn that the path toward growth is bumpy and uneven. At this time they can be taught how to evaluate the impact of the group on themselves as well as assess the progress they have made as a group.

Theories Applied to Postgroup Issues

After the group comes to an end, the members' main task is applying their in-group learning to an action program in their daily life so that they can function in self-directed ways. I value setting aside time for individual interviews with each member, if possible, along with arranging for a follow-up group session.

Such procedures build in accountability, for both the members and the leader can more accurately assess the impact of the group. Again, the behavioral approaches stress this accountability and evaluation, which enable the leader to make modifications in future groups based on what seemed to work. Follow-up procedures also provide a safety valve. If members left the group with unresolved or negative feelings, they can at least discuss them with the group leader.

The Pros and Cons of an Integrative Model

As I've said many times, I'm convinced that as a group practitioner you need to find a style that fits you as a person; the model I've described is the result of my own search for an approach to groups that fits me both professionally and personally. It reflects my view of groups as entities that express in an integrated fashion the thinking, feeling, and doing dimensions of individual members. It also combines the didactic with the experiential, because I believe what we experience in a group needs to be supported by a conceptual framework. Without such a framework, it would be difficult for us to make sense of the experience and to understand its implications for our daily existence. My model brings together the action-oriented, the insight-oriented, and the experientially oriented approaches—that is, the cognitive, affective, and behavioral dimensions—to pursue more effectively the basic goal of any therapeutic group: change.

Although I believe an integration of therapeutic perspectives provides the best way to develop your interventions in a group, creating an eclectic stance is truly a challenge, for it does not simply mean picking bits and pieces from theories in a random and fragmented manner. In forming an integrative perspective, it is important to ask yourself these questions: Which theories provide a basis for understanding the cognitive dimensions? the feeling aspects? the behavioral dimension? Most of the 10 therapeutic orientations I have presented focus on a single dimension of human experience. Although the other dimensions are not necessarily ignored, they are often given short shrift.

Developing an integrative theoretical perspective requires much reading, thinking, and actual counseling experience. Unless you have an accurate and in-depth knowledge of these theories, you cannot formulate a true synthesis. A central message of this book has been to encourage you to remain open to each theory, to do further reading, and to reflect on how the key concepts of each theory fit your personality. Building your personalized theory of counseling, based on what you consider to be the best features of several theories, is a long-term venture. Effective leaders are continually defining and refining a personalized group theory that guides them in their practice and allows them to make sense of what occurs in groups. Of course, the specific type of group that you are leading and the makeup of the clients in your group are critical variables in deciding what strategies are most appropriate. Be open to modifying your techniques so that they fit the needs of the members of the group, including their social and cultural background.

Having said all that, I wish to add that there are dangers in encouraging the development of an integrative model, as opposed to sticking primarily with one theory. At its worst, eclecticism can be an excuse for sloppy practice—a practice that lacks a systematic rationale for what you actually do in your work. If you merely pick and choose according to whims, it is likely that your selections will just reflect your biases and preconceived ideas. At its best, however, eclecticism can be a creative synthesis of the unique contributions of diverse approaches, dynamically integrating concepts and techniques that fit the uniqueness of your personality and style.

Summary and Review Tables

At this point it would be useful for you to reflect on the major insights you have gained through taking this course and reading this book. Most of all, think about what theories seemed to have the most practical application in helping you understand your present life situation. You might consider what changes you are interested in making and which approaches could provide you with strategies to modify specific thoughts, feelings, and behaviors. This is a good time to review what you may have learned about your ability to establish effective relationships with other people. Especially important is a review of any personal characteristics that could either help or hinder you in developing solid working relationships with the members in your groups.

After you make this review of significant personal learning, I suggest that you also ponder what you have learned about group process. It has been my experience that between the first and the last day of an introductory course in group counseling, students find that what seems at first to be an overwhelming mass of knowledge and a bewildering array of theories eventually becomes a manageable store of understanding about the basis of counseling. Moreover, I hope you will be patient enough to recognize that much of the theoretical foundation you have received in this book will take on new meanings when you gain more practical experience in leading various groups. The same is true for the many professional and ethical issues that were discussed in the book. I think it is essential that you reflect on these basic issues, that you begin to formulate your own position on them, and that you discuss them with fellow students and instructors. Even though experience will teach you many new lessons, you will be far better equipped to deal with these and related issues when you meet them if you have reflected on them now.

As you review the tables (Tables 16-1 through 16-6) summarizing the 10 theories, consider which particular approaches you would be most inclined to draw from with respect to these dimensions: (1) goals of group counseling, (2) group leader's role and function, (3) degree of structuring and division of responsibility, (4) group techniques, and (5) adapting theories to the practice of multicultural group counseling.

Table 16-1 ■ Comparative Overview of Group Goals

Model	Goals
Psychoanalytic	To provide a climate that helps clients reexperience early family relationships. To uncover buried feelings associated with past events that carry over into current behavior. To facilitate insight into the origins of faulty psychological development and stimulate a corrective emotional experience.
Adlerian	To create a therapeutic relationship that encourages participants to explore their basic life assumptions and to achieve a broader understanding of lifestyles. To help clients recognize their strengths and their power to change. To encourage them to accept full responsibility for their chosen lifestyle and for any changes they want to make.
Psychodrama	To facilitate the release of pent-up feelings, to provide insight, and to help clients develop new and more effective behaviors. To open up unexplored possibilities for solving conflicts.
Existential	To provide conditions that maximize self-awareness and reduce blocks to growth. To help clients discover and use freedom of choice and assume responsibility for their own choices.
Person-centered	To provide a safe climate wherein members can explore the full range of their feelings. To help members become increasingly open to new experiences and develop confidence in themselves and their own judgments. To encourage clients to live in the present. To develop openness, honesty, and spontaneity. To make it possible for clients to encounter others in the here-and-now and to use the group as a place to overcome feelings of alienation.
Gestalt	To enable members to pay close attention to their moment-to-moment experiencing, so they can recognize and integrate disowned aspects of themselves.
Transactional analysis	To assist clients in becoming free of scripts and games in their interactions. To challenge members to reexamine early decisions and make new ones based on awareness.
Behavior therapy	To help group members eliminate maladaptive behaviors and learn new and more effective behavioral patterns. (Broad goals are broken down into precise subgoals.)
Rational emotive behavior therapy	To teach group members that they are responsible for their own disturbances and to help them identify and abandon the process of self-indoctrination by which they keep their disturbances alive. To eliminate the clients' irrational and self-defeating outlook on life and replace it with a more tolerant and rational one.
Reality therapy	To guide members toward learning realistic and responsible behavior. To assist group members in evaluating their behavior and in deciding on a plan of action for change.

Table 16-2 ■ Comparative Overview of Leader's Role and Functions

Model	Leader's Roles
Psychoanalytic	Facilitates group interaction by helping create an accepting and tolerant climate. Remains relatively anonymous and objective, so that members will develop projections toward him or her. Signals indications of resistance and transference and interprets their meanings. Helps members work through unfinished business. Sets limits for the group.
Adlerian	Uses procedures such as confrontation, self-disclosure, interpretation, and analysis of prevailing patterns to challenge beliefs and goals. Observes social context of behavior. Models attentive caring. Helps members accept and utilize their assets. Encourages members to develop the courage needed to translate what is learned in the group to behavior outside of the group.
Psychodrama	Has the job of warming up the group, helping set up a psychodrama, directing the enactment, and then processing the outcomes with the participants. Specific tasks include facilitating, observing, directing, and producing.
Existential	Has the central role of being fully present and available to individuals in the group and of grasping their subjective being-in-the-world. Functions by creating a person-to-person relationship, by disclosing him- or herself, and by confronting members in a caring way.
Person-centered	Facilitates the group (as opposed to directing it)—deals with barriers to communication, establishes a climate of trust, and assists the group in functioning effectively. Central task is to be genuine in the sessions and demonstrate caring, respect, and understanding. Has the primary role of creating a climate of tolerance and experimentation. Often becomes directly involved by sharing personal feelings and impressions about what is happening in the group.
Gestalt	Suggests techniques designed to help participants intensify their experience and be alert to their body messages. Assists clients in identifying and working through unfinished business from the past that interferes with current functioning. Focuses on members' behaviors and feelings.
Transactional analysis	Has a didactic role. Teaches clients how to recognize the games they play to avoid intimacy, the ego state in which they are functioning in a given transaction, and the self-defeating aspects of early decisions and adopted life plans.
Behavior therapy	Functions as an expert in behavior modification; thus, must be directive and often functions as teacher or trainer. Imparts information and teaches coping skills and methods of modifying behavior so that members can practice outside group sessions.
Rational emotive behavior therapy	Functions didactically: explains, teaches, and reeducates. Helps members see and rigorously confront their illogical thinking and identify its connection with self-defeating behavior. Teaches them to change their patterns of thinking and behaving.
Reality therapy	Encourages members to evaluate their behavior and make choices that will allow them to fulfill their needs in socially acceptable ways. Helps members by establishing a personal relationship with them, by firmly expecting that they will formulate and implement a plan for change.

Table 16-3 ■ **Comparative Overview of Degree of Structuring and Division of Responsibilities**

Model	Structuring and Responsibilities
Psychoanalytic	*Leader* shies away from directive leadership and allows the group to determine its own course; interprets the meaning of certain behavioral patterns.
	Members raise issues and produce material from the unconscious; assume increasing responsibility for interacting spontaneously, making interpretations, and sharing insights about others; become auxiliary therapists for one another.
Adlerian	*Leader*, at the outset, works toward goal alignment; takes active steps to establish and maintain a therapeutic relationship, to explore and analyze the individual's dynamics, and to communicate a basic attitude of concern and hope.
	Members develop insight about themselves; assume the responsibility for taking positive measures to make changes; consider alternative beliefs, goals, and behaviors.
Psychodrama	*Director/leader* suggests specific techniques designed to intensify feelings, re-create past situations, and provide increased awareness of conflicts; makes sure that the protagonist is not ignored and that other members of the group have a chance to share what they experienced during the psychodrama.
	Members produce the material for psychodramas and, when in the role of protagonist, direct their own psychodramas.
Existential	*Leader* may structure the group along the lines of certain existential themes such as freedom, responsibility, anxiety, and guilt; shares here-and-now feelings with the group.
	Members are responsible for deciding the issues they want to explore, thus determining the direction of the group.
Person-centered	*Leader* provides very little structuring or direction.
	Members are seen as having the capacity to find a meaningful direction, of being able to help one another, and of moving toward constructive outcomes.
Gestalt	*Leader* is responsible for being aware of his/her present-centered experience and for using it in the context of the group; brings structure to the group by introducing appropriate techniques to intensify emotions.
	Members must be active and make their own interpretations.
Transactional analysis	Because of the stress on an equal relationship between leader and members, responsibility is shared, as specified in a contract.
	Members and *leader* spell out in the contract what changes members want to make and what issues they want to explore in the group.
Behavior therapy	*Leader* is responsible for active teaching and for having the group proceed according to a predetermined set of activities.
	Members are expected to be active, to apply what they learn to everyday life situations, and to practice new behaviors outside the group.
Rational emotive behavior therapy	*Leader* is responsible for challenging any signs of member behavior based on faulty thinking; structures the group experience so that members stay with the task of making constructive changes.
	Members are responsible for attacking their own self-defeating thinking and that of fellow group members; are expected to carry out self-confrontation outside the group and work hard at changing illogical thoughts.
Reality therapy	*Leader* teaches members to assume responsibility for how they live their life; structures the group by focusing on present behavior and ways of making specific behavioral changes; influences members by modeling success-oriented behavior; confronts clients who are not living realistically.
	Members decide on specific changes they want to make and are held responsible for implementing desired changes.

Table 16-4 ■ **Comparative Overview of Group Techniques**

Model	Techniques
Psychoanalytic	Interpretation, dream analysis, free association, analysis of resistance, and analysis of transference—all designed to make the unconscious conscious and bring about insight.
Adlerian	Analysis and assessment, exploration of family constellation, reporting of earliest recollections, confrontation, interpretation, cognitive restructuring, challenging of one's belief system, and exploration of social dynamics and of one's unique style of life.
Psychodrama	Self-presentation, presentation of the other, interview in the role of the other and interview in the role of the self, soliloquy, role reversal, double technique and auxiliary egos, mirroring, and, future projection.
Existential	Since this approach stresses understanding first and techniques second, no specific set of methods is prescribed. However, leaders can borrow techniques from other therapies to better understand the world of clients and to deepen the level of therapeutic work.
Person-centered	The stress is on the facilitator's attitudes and behavior, and few structured or planned techniques are used. Basic techniques include active listening, reflection of feelings, clarification, support, and "being there" for the client.
Gestalt	Many action-oriented techniques are available to the leader, all of which intensify immediate experiencing and awareness of current feelings. Techniques include confrontation, empty chair, game of dialogue, making the rounds, fantasy approaches, reversal procedures, rehearsal techniques, exaggerating a behavior, staying with feelings, dialogues with self or significant others in the present, and dream work. Experiments are designed to enable participants to become increasingly aware of bodily tensions and of the fear of getting physically and emotionally close, to give members a chance to experiment with new behavior, and to release feelings. Guided fantasy, imagery, and other techniques designed to stimulate the imagination may be used.
Transactional analysis	Techniques include the use of a script-analysis checklist or questionnaire to detect early injunctions and decisions, games, and life positions; family modeling; role playing; and structural analysis.
Behavior therapy	The main techniques, which are based on behavioral and learning principles and are aimed at behavioral changes and cognitive restructuring, include systematic desensitization, implosive therapy, assertion training, aversive techniques, operant-conditioning methods, self-help techniques, reinforcement and supportive measures, behavior rehearsal, coaching, modeling, feedback, and procedures for challenging and changing cognitions.
Rational emotive behavior therapy	The essential technique is active teaching. Leaders probe, confront, challenge, and forcefully direct. They model and teach rational thinking, and they explain, persuade, and lecture clients. They use a rapid-fire style that requires members to constantly use their cognitive skills. REBT uses a wide range of behavioral techniques such as deconditioning, role playing, behavior rehearsal, homework assignments, and assertion training.
Reality therapy	A wide range of techniques is used, such as role playing, confrontation, modeling, use of humor, contracts, and specific plans for action.

Table 16-5 ■ Comparative Overview of Contributions to Multicultural Counseling

Model	Contributions
Psychoanalytic	Focus on family dynamics is appropriate for working with many minority groups. Therapist formality appeals to those clients who expect professional distance. Notion of defense is helpful in understanding inner dynamics and dealing with environmental stresses.
Adlerian	Culture is viewed as a perspective and background from which meaning in life can be derived. Each individual will make a different meaning out of his or her personal cultural experience.
Psychodrama	For reserved clients, this approach invites self-expression in the present. Director can create scenes that are culturally sensitive and assist members in understanding the impact of their culture on them. Through enactment, nonverbal clients have other means of communication. Opportunities arise for developing spontaneity and creativity within the framework of one's culture.
Existential	A core value is the emphasis on understanding the member's phenomenological world, including cultural background. This approach leads to empowerment in an oppressive society. It can help members examine their options for change within the context of their cultural realities.
Person-centered	Rogers made significant contributions to breaking cultural barriers and facilitating open dialogue among diverse cultural populations. Main strengths are respect for client's values, active listening, welcoming of differences, nonjudgmental attitude, understanding, willingness to allow clients to determine what will be explored in sessions, and prizing cultural pluralism.
Gestalt	Focus on expressing oneself nonverbally is congruent with those cultures that look beyond words for messages. Approach provides many techniques in working with clients who have cultural injunctions against freely expressing feelings. Focus on bodily expressions is a subtle way to help clients recognize their conflicts.
Transactional analysis	Contractual method acts as a safeguard against therapist imposition of values that may not be congruent with a client's culture. This approach offers a basis for understanding the impact of cultural and familial injunctions. It provides a structure that many clients will value.
Behavior therapy	Focus on behavior, rather than on feelings, is compatible with many cultures. Strengths include preparation of members by teaching them purposes of group; assisting members in learning practical skills; educational focus of groups; and stress on self-management strategies.
Rational emotive behavior therapy	This approach provides ways of questioning one's beliefs and identifying values that may no longer be functional. Its focus on thinking and rationality (as opposed to expressing feelings) is likely to be acceptable to many clients. Focus on teaching/learning process tends to avoid the stigma of mental illness. Many clients may value the leader directiveness and stress on homework.
Reality therapy	Focus is on members' making own evaluation of behavior (including how they respond to their culture). Through personal assessment they can determine the degree to which their needs and wants are being satisfied; they can find a balance between retaining their own ethnic identity and integrating some of the values and practices of the dominant society.

Table 16-6 ■ Comparative Overview of Limitations in Multicultural Counseling

Model	Limitations
Psychoanalytic	Focus on insight, intrapsychic dynamics, and long-term treatment is often not valued by clients who prefer to learn coping skills in dealing with pressing environmental concerns. Internal focus is often in conflict with cultural values that stress an interpersonal and environmental focus.
Adlerian	This approach's detailed interview about one's family background can conflict with cultures that have injunctions against disclosing family matters. Leader needs to make certain that the goals of members are respected and that these goals are congruent with the goals of a given group.
Psychodrama	Emphasis on experiencing and expressing feelings, on catharsis, and on enacting past problems in the present can be highly threatening for some clients. Caution needed in encouraging clients to display their intense emotions in presence of others.
Existential	Its values of individuality, freedom, autonomy, and self-realization often conflict with cultural values of collectivism, respect for tradition, deference to authority, and interdependence. Some may be deterred by absence of specific techniques. Others will expect more focus on surviving in their world.
Person-centered	Some of the core values of this approach may not be congruent with the client's culture. Lack of leader direction and structure are unacceptable for many clients who are seeking help and immediate answers from knowledgeable leader.
Gestalt	Clients who have been culturally conditioned to be emotionally reserved may not embrace Gestalt techniques. It is important not to push quickly for expressing feelings until relationship is established. Some may not see how "being aware of present experiencing" will lead to solving their problems.
Transactional analysis	Terminology of TA may distract clients from some cultures with a different perspective. Leader must establish clear contract of what client wants before challenging client's lifescripts, cultural and familial injunctions, and decisions. Caution required in probing into family patterns.
Behavior therapy	Leaders need to help members assess the possible consequences of making behavioral changes. Family members may not value clients' newly acquired assertive style, so clients must be taught how to cope with resistance by others.
Rational emotive behavior therapy	If leader has a forceful and directive leadership style, members may retreat. It is necessary to understand client's world before forcefully attacking beliefs perceived as irrational by leader.
Reality therapy	Approach stresses taking charge of one's own life, yet some members hope to change their external environment. Leader needs to appreciate the role of discrimination and racism and help clients deal with social and political realities.

CHAPTER 17

The Evolution of a Group: An Integrative Perspective

Co-authored by Marianne Schneider Corey and Gerald Corey

Introduction

To give you a better picture of how the various approaches discussed in Part II actually work, this chapter provides glimpses of an actual group. This three-day residential group, co-facilitated by Marianne and Jerry Corey, was convened for the purpose of making an educational video, *Evolution of a Group*. This video and its accompanying workbook are designed to bring to life the unfolding of a group from the initial to the final stage.

In this chapter we model the integrative perspective, demonstrating how theory can be applied to practice. We pay special attention to working with individual members, and we attempt to link members with common personal issues. Many of the themes that emerged in this weekend workshop are described to show a variety of ways of exploring personal issues at the various stages of a group. However, not all of the themes discussed grew out of the actual group proceedings. Some material is expanded and modified for teaching purposes. We present each theme and then illustrate ways we draw from various theoretical perspectives. This chapter reflects our own personal integration. Our hope is that this illustration will encourage you to reflect on how you might draw from several orientations to develop your own personal style of group practice.

About the Group

The participants in this group are not actors. They were not following a script, nor were they merely role-playing fictitious cases. They were willing to be themselves and explore some of their real concerns.

The group we describe in this chapter is a closed and time-limited intensive group that met for about 20 working hours. It consists of eight members (five women and three men) and two co-leaders. Although this particular group was a residential workshop, the process we describe (both in the video and in this chapter) does not necessarily differ a great deal from the process of a group that meets weekly. Certainly, the techniques we demonstrate can be used in groups that meet weekly. Many of the concerns raised by these group members are no different from personal issues that are typically explored in therapy groups.

The Emerging Themes

We have selected the following themes to discuss in this chapter from among the many that typically emerge during the life of a group:

- Clarifying personal goals
- Creating and maintaining trust
- Bringing interactions into the here-and-now
- Dealing with fears and resistances
- Making internal dialogue explicit
- Exploring feelings of isolation
- Dealing with parents
- Dealing with feelings of separation and loss

These themes are developed by describing how they apply in concrete ways to various members of our group. We demonstrate the use of interventions drawn from the various theoretical approaches as they apply to the individual members and the group as a whole.

We are not suggesting that we would make all of the interventions we have included here. However, for teaching purposes, in this chapter we describe many different ways of pursuing group themes with one individual. Sometimes we will draw on relationship-oriented approaches or the experiential therapies. At other times we may rely on psychoanalytic or Adlerian perspectives when employing interventions. And sometimes we will utilize cognitive behavioral techniques with an individual's work. The chapter concludes with a description of how we would use concepts and techniques from these various approaches to deal with some issues characteristic of the ending stages of a group.

Formation of the Group

The Pregroup Meeting

All the participants in this group had some prior group experience. Before making the decision to be a part of this group, the members participated in a pregroup meeting in which they met each other and both co-leaders. At this time they had the opportunity to get acquainted with one another and to determine whether they wanted to participate in this type of special group experience.

Of course, all the participants knew in advance that the purpose of this workshop was to produce an educational video. We also discussed at length the special circumstances associated with participating in a group that is being videotaped, such as informed consent, confidentiality, and revealing of sensitive personal information. We wanted members to be themselves by sharing their real concerns, yet we emphasized it was for them to decide what specific personal subjects they would be willing to introduce. Furthermore, we reassured them that they had control over what would or would not be included in the final video. Throughout the weekend workshop, group members had opportunities to tell us if they wanted to omit any portion of their actual work. The members' veto power was pointed out to them at the pregroup meeting, during the weekend workshop, and after they returned home. Furthermore, all of the group members had a chance to review this chapter and to suggest changes.

Importance of Preliminary Preparation

It is ideal to arrange for a pregroup meeting after members have been screened and selected. This meeting is an orientation session where leaders can provide further information regarding the group to help the members decide if this group is suitable for them. If a pregroup meeting is impractical, then the first group meeting can be used to orient and prepare members for a successful group experience.

Many groups that get stuck at some point do so because the foundations were poorly laid at the outset. What is labeled as "resistance" on the part of group members is often the result of the leader's failure to provide adequate orientation. This preparation can begin at the individual screening and can be continued during the initial session. Although building pregroup preparation into the design of a group takes considerable effort, the time involved pays dividends as the group evolves. Many potential barriers to a group's progress can be avoided by careful planning and preparation.

Initial Stage

As you'll recall from Chapter 4, the initial stage of a group is a period for members to get to know one another. It is difficult to build a climate of safety if members do not have a sense of one another. It is not our intention to immediately get members to focus on exploring their deeper personal issues at the first meeting, but to heighten their awareness of the atmosphere in the room. This is a time for getting acquainted, learning how the group functions, developing the norms that will govern the group, exploring fears and expectations pertaining to the group, identifying personal goals, and determining if this group is a safe place. The manner in which the leader deals with the reactions of members determines the degree of trust that can be established in the group.

In these early sessions we are shaping up specific group norms—working in the here-and-now, talking directly to one another, expressing persistent reactions, dealing with expectations and fears, establishing personal goals, and so on. As co-leaders, our main attention is on establishing a foundation of trust. We do this by getting members to talk about afterthoughts, by teaching them how to pay attention to what they are experiencing in the here-and-now, by noticing their reactions to others in the group, and by verbalizing these reactions. We do considerable teaching about how the participants can most productively involve themselves in the ongoing group process.

Theme: Clarifying Personal Goals

In most groups the initial sessions are devoted to exploring group goals and clarifying the members' personal goals. We also ask members to identify what might get in their way of accomplishing those goals.

We usually begin a group by having the members state their goals as clearly and concretely as possible. Our aim is to help the members formulate specific contracts for their own work, which will provide a direction for the group. We are also interested in assisting members to make an evaluation of their current behavior to determine the degree to which their behavior is getting them what they want (drawing from reality therapy). Here are some of the questions we are likely to pose to the members to stimulate this self-evaluation:

- What do you have in your life now that you most value?
- What is at least one thing that is missing in your life?
- If you had what you wanted now, how would your life be different?
- What can you begin to do today to get what you say you want?
- How can you best use this group to get what you want?

The aim of this line of questioning is to get members to realize that if what they are thinking, feeling, and doing is not satisfactory to them, they have the power to change and choose better behaviors.

Our attempt during the early stage of this group is to work cooperatively and collaboratively on the goals that will govern the direction the group takes (which is characteristic of the Adlerian perspective). For example, one of us might say: "Since this is your group, I'd like to hear from each of you what you expect from this group. After each of you has a chance to state your expectations, perhaps we can spend some time formulating group norms that will help us accomplish these goals." Cooperation on a common therapeutic task is essential if change is to occur. Resistance is to be expected if group leaders impose an agenda on the group rather than helping the members create their own agenda.

Each individual may experience overlapping goals or a combination of goals. Here is a summary of what each member of this group hoped to get from participating:

Jacqueline (late 40s) sometimes does not feel a part of various groups in which she is involved. She refers to herself as an African American woman who, at times, finds it difficult to relate to others and states that she often feels "marginalized." One of her goals is to explore ways she seeks approval from others.

SusAnne (age 27), of Hispanic background, would like to explore relationships in her life. At times she feels that she has put a wall around herself to prevent herself from getting hurt. She wants to explore the price she is paying for staying safe and not taking the risks of pursuing the relationships she wants.

Jyl (age 39), a Euro-American, is willing to deal with struggles pertaining to perfectionism. She also wants to explore the impact of significant losses in her life. Jyl experiences difficulty in asking others for what she wants or in letting others care for her.

James (age 35) describes himself as an educated Latino who has to "prove himself." Because of his cultural background, he often feels oppressed. He also is considering working on significant relationships (mother, brother).

Andrew (age 35), a Euro-American, is struggling with issues of trust and with deciding how close he wants to get to people, especially women in an intimate relationship. Having been betrayed in marriage, he is very protective of his feelings, which keeps him safe, but somewhat lonely.

Darren (age 27), of Hispanic background, sometimes worries about how he expresses himself and is concerned about the impression he makes. He realizes he rehearses before he talks so that he will sound intelligent. He is willing to work on "talking out loud" more often in the group. Many times he feels like an outsider, and he wants to belong.

Casey (age 23) refers to herself as a Vietnamese American. She struggles with messages she received as a child that now get in her way. She worries about others' judging her, and she sometimes keeps herself separate in social situations. She would like to challenge her fears of feeling judged, which she feels keep her back at times.

Jackie (age 43), a Euro-American, puts a lot of pressure on herself to be perfect, to get everyone to like her, and to keep everyone happy. She sometimes feels that she is not enough, no matter what she accomplishes.

Theme: Creating and Maintaining Trust

As a group gets under way, members will often question their ability to trust the group leaders, the other members, and even themselves. To create a climate of trust, we typically ask members to share what they are thinking and feeling at this first meeting, especially as it pertains to what they are aware of in this group. They are also asked to share their expectations pertaining to the group experience.

We also mention to members that it does not make sense to open up too quickly without a foundation of trust. A good way to create trust is to get members to verbalize their fears, concerns, and here-and-now reactions during the early sessions. We emphasize that it is up to each member to decide what to talk about and how far to pursue a topic. During the early phase of a group, we are not likely to make interventions that lead to in-depth exploration of what members are saying. Rather than focusing immediately on the first member who speaks, we make sure that everybody has a chance to briefly introduce him- or herself.

The following excerpts are typical of what members are sometimes thinking during the first or second group meeting. Our goal is to assist members in talking more openly about what might get in the way of their ability to trust themselves and others in this particular group.

Jackie: My expectation is to go through this group without making anyone mad at me or without crying. I want feedback that I am okay, and I want to be liked and valued.

Jacqueline: I'm afraid I won't say things well. I tend to beat up on myself after a group, telling myself that I didn't say what I wanted to say clearly enough.

SusAnne: I am not sure that I trust that people in here will care about me if I let my pain and hurt show, so I censor what I say.

James: In a group I sometimes feel on the outside. You won't know this, because most of the time I won't let you know.

Andrew: I also sometimes feel like an outsider. I'm concerned I will censor my emotions and isolate myself from the group if I feel I'm being judged while talking about the pains of my past.

Darren: I feel young and invisible. I don't know how to get in with you guys.

Jyl: It's scary when I think of opening up. I'm afraid I'll lose control and start crying and not stop.

Casey: When I'm in a group, I observe a lot. I rehearse in my head before I speak. I'm afraid I can't articulate myself and that you won't understand me. I want to sound intelligent.

Typically, during their early stages, groups focus on issues of trust such as those illustrated by these examples. If members are to drop their defenses and reveal themselves—as indeed they must if the group is to be effective—they need assurance that the group is a safe place to do this. Members can learn that by being open and taking risks, they have the potential to live fully.

We know that confidentiality is essential if members are to feel a sense of safety in a group. Even if no one raises this issue, we raise the topic. We caution members about how confidentiality can be broken and provide guidelines for maintaining the confidential nature of the exchanges. Specifically, we emphasize how easy it might be to break confidentiality without intending to do so. We ask members to refrain from talking about what others are doing in the group. We ask members about any concerns they may have about confidentiality. Furthermore, we provide them with information on how to best maintain confidentiality and discuss the limitations of confidentiality. We emphasize to members that it is their responsibility to make the room safe by continuing to address their concerns regarding how their disclosures will be treated. If they do not feel trusting because they are afraid that others will talk, this doubt will certainly hamper their ability to fully participate.

For this particular group confidentiality took on special significance. Because they were being videotaped and being written about in a textbook and a workbook, group members had an opportunity to eliminate any portions of their work they did not want to make public.

Helping to build trust in the group is a vital task at the early stages of a group, and as co-leaders, we realize that the way in which we approach the group is of crucial importance. Our main aim is to give members opportunities to express their reactions about the level of trust in the group and to talk about ways that they can feel safe so that they can move into personally meaningful work. To illustrate some of the messages we want to get across early on in this group, here are some sample comments from various theoretical orientations that we might use to open a group:

Psychoanalytic: "In this group I'll be paying a lot of attention to what is going on in the here-and-now, with particular attention on your reactions to one another. I'll look for patterns in the way you relate, and my job is to help you see how your earlier experiences often influence the way you perceive others and react to them."

Existential and psychodrama: "This group will assist you in examining choices you've made about how you are living. In this group I'll be encouraging you to enact—not just talk about—your conflicts and the problems you'd like to explore. By releasing your feelings about a particular reenactment of an event in your life, you are likely to come to a different understanding of that event. You will be encouraged to experiment with different ways of behaving."

Gestalt therapy: "We will pay particular attention to the here-and-now and deal with whatever prevents you from maintaining a present-centered awareness. The focus will be on the *what* and *how* rather than the *why* of behavior. One of my functions is to assist you in identifying your unfinished business from the past, bringing it into the present, and achieving greater awareness of how your past may be impeding your present experiencing."

TA and behavior therapy: "Each of you is my colleague in your own therapy. I don't presume the right to special knowledge about you; rather, I assume that you will decide on the course of your work in here, largely by developing clear contracts that will specify what you want to change and how you want to do it. The group will offer a context for this learning and give you the support you need to reinforce any changes you make so that they become an integral part of you."

Reality therapy and behavior therapy: "My main goal in this group is to assist you in determining whether your current behavior meets your needs adequately. If you discover that it doesn't and if you decide to change, we will work collaboratively to formulate a plan of action designed to promote change. The group will offer you a place to practice this plan for change."

Theme: Bringing Interactions into the Here-and-Now

During the initial stage of a group, we pay attention to here-and-now reactions and teach members the importance of sharing these reactions with one another. In this particular group some important racial and cultural issues emerged that needed to be addressed as a prerequisite for building a safe and accepting environment. We ask members what they were thinking since we first met as a group at the preliminary orientation session, or pregroup meeting, and what they were aware of as they were driving to this residential workshop.

James: I often feel that I have to prove myself, especially since I am an educated Chicano. I've experienced discrimination in a number of places, so I wonder about how I'll fit into a group.

We suggest that James pay attention to ways that he might feel that he has to prove himself in this group.

Marianne: James, how do you feel in this group? Will you let people know how you are experiencing them in this group? Are you willing to let us know when you do not feel a part of this group?

As James talks about his awareness of being different from some others in this group, Jacqueline brings herself into the discussion.

Jacqueline: As an African American woman, there are times when I feel marginalized. And because of this I feel that I am not taken seriously. As I look at some of you, I feel different from you.

Jyl brings herself into the interactions, for she has reactions to what both James and Jacqueline are saying. She feels that she is not being given a chance to be herself with them.

Jyl: Being with you [Jacqueline] is not safe. I am going to have to protect myself, for I am aware of feeling judged by you. [and to James] You know, I don't know what it is like to be an educated Chicano. But I do know what it's like to be an educated white woman who is sometimes treated like a piece of fluff.

Jyl goes on to talk about some of the ways that she can identify with the feelings of both James and Jacqueline.

Dealing with diversity issues can bring the group together. However, if members do not talk about the ways they may feel different from others in this group, a hidden agenda is likely to develop. When members are willing to express their here-and-now thoughts and feelings as they pertain to the group, the energy level increases. Once members are willing to deal with the present, there is plenty to explore. Even if participants have problems in their past, it is still useful to try to get them to relate these concerns to how these past issues might influence how they are in this present group.

Here are some comments group members made relatively early in the life of this group:

- I have a tendency to think that what others have to say is more important than what is on my mind.
- When I look around the room, I wonder if I will fit in this group.
- I'm afraid of what people in here will think if I show my emotions.
- It's hard for me to ask for time in group.
- When others are talking, it's difficult for me to bring myself into the group.

We consistently ask members to pay attention to their present reactions and perceptions about one another. For a group to achieve a genuine level of trust, it is essential that they express persistent reactions that pertain to what is going on in the context of the group. We underscore the importance of members saying what is on their mind, even if they fear that what they have to say might be interruptive. When members keep their reservations to themselves, the group cannot deal with their concerns. When participants share certain reactions that could get in their way of participating fully in the group, we have a basis to do some productive work. For instance, Jackie lets us know that she tends to be cautious as a way to avoid hurting anyone's feelings or of creating a conflict. With this information now being public, she is in a good position to use reactions that will emerge for her as a reference point for some intensive work.

We are interested in both a here-and-now focus and a there-and-then focus. However, we find that members usually are not ready to take the risk of dealing with significant personal issues outside the group until they first deal with their reactions to one another in the room. When members bring up either a present or past problem situation outside of the group, we explore how this might be played out in the context of the present group. For example, James says that he often feels that he has to prove himself at work. Both Jacqueline and Jackie inform us that they often seek approval. Andrew talks about feeling isolated. All these members are asked to take note of when they experience these feelings or thoughts in the group.

Although we emphasize here-and-now reactions, we also ask members to explore how their present reactions in the group may reflect how they feel away from the group. Jackie expresses her concern that she will not live up to our expectations, nor will she get our approval. Eventually, as the group becomes more established, we hope she will also increase her awareness of how her struggles operate in her everyday life.

Developing a here-and-now orientation in a group is consistent with person-centered therapy, existential therapy, Gestalt therapy, and psychodrama. Dealing with here-and-now concerns does not exclude exploring the past. As you recall, both Gestalt therapy and psychodrama are present-centered approaches in that they require members to bring either past or future concerns into the present tense. Thus, we frequently remind participants that if they become aware of something or someone in the group it is best to talk about it. When it comes to expressing reactions pertaining to what is going on in the group, we prefer members say too much rather than too little.

Transition Stage

The Challenges of the Transition Phase

Before groups progress to a working stage, they typically go through a transition phase, which is characterized by anxiety, defensiveness, resistance, the struggle for control, and intermember conflicts. During the transition phase, it is the members' task to monitor their thoughts, feelings, and actions and to learn to express them verbally. Leaders can help members come to recognize and accept their reluctance and at the same time encourage members to challenge their tendencies toward avoidance. For members to progress to a deeper level of exploration, they must talk about any anxiety and defensiveness they may be experiencing. Some fears members may have during the early or transition stages of a group include the fear of rejection, losing control, being inappropriate, being involved in a conflict, or looking foolish. These fears may be manifested as resistance, and it is important that group leaders understand there is a purpose for this resistance. Above all, members' struggles need to be respected, understood, and explored.

Leaders should not directly attack resistance, but it is a mistake to bypass or ignore problematic behaviors exhibited by members. Some groups remain stuck at the transition stage because resistance is unnoticed, ignored, or poorly dealt with by the group leader. Teaching members how to challenge themselves is a basic task at this time, yet it is also essential that members learn how to respectfully confront others in a caring and constructive fashion. We teach members the importance of talking more about themselves and how they are affected by the behaviors of a member they are confronting rather than telling a member how he or she is, or judging that person.

We model how to remain open and nondefensive in receiving feedback from others. If conflicts arise, it is essential that members recognize these conflicts and develop the skills to resolve them. Again, what leaders model when addressing conflict in a firm and respectful manner is every bit as important as what they tell members about conflict resolution. If conflict is not addressed, it then becomes a hidden agenda, which blocks open group interaction. How group leaders intervene is crucial to building trust.

During the initial stage, members generally address their fears or reservations about participating in the group. However, during the transition stage, there is a more extensive and more specific discussion of how these fears are manifested within the group. Doing this enables members to feel the support and safety that is required for the intense work they are getting ready to do.

Theme: Dealing with Fears and Resistances

As a group moves into a transition stage, members typically express fears about getting involved and are reluctant to delve into personal concerns. Some members keep their fears about becoming involved in the group to themselves, whereas others seem eager to express their fears and put them to rest so that they can begin to work. Whether or not the fears are expressed, they tend to give rise to some ambivalence—the desire to reveal oneself is balanced by a reluctance to expose oneself. Here are some typical expressions of ambivalence:

- I tend to isolate at times. Part of me wants to let others know me in here, yet another part of me wants to pull back and check things out quietly.

- I'm afraid to get involved because I may make a fool of myself, and then people will judge me negatively.
- I'm afraid that if I say what I really think and feel people in here will not accept or like me.
- If I see myself as I really am, I may not like what I find.
- I'm afraid that by becoming too involved in this group, I may make my problems bigger than they really are.
- If I get too involved in the group, I'm afraid I'll become too dependent on it for solving problems that I have to handle alone.
- Right now my life is rather comfortable; if I become too involved in the group, I may open up a can of worms that I can't handle. I'm afraid that I might be left feeling vulnerable.
- I'm somewhat afraid of disclosing myself to others, not only because of what they may think but also because of what I might find out about myself.
- I want to protect myself by not letting myself care. If I get too close to people in the group, I'll feel a real loss when it ends.

We encourage members to express their concerns and fears by talking directly to each other. When members talk to us (as leaders) about an individual in the group, we instruct them to look at and talk directly to that person.

Co-Leader: I'd like each of you to share some of your fears about being in this group. As you do so, look at different members in the group. Share any fears you may be experiencing with the group members.

This strategy is borrowed from the experiential approaches and is aimed at building group cohesion.

Depending on what emerges in individuals within the group, we may work on a feeling level or we may focus on members' thoughts, or both. Using a Gestalt orientation, we deal with resistance by inviting members to rehearse their fears out loud.

SusAnne: I'm not sure I trust that people in here will care if I share some hurtful experiences. What I generally do is keep most of my hurt to myself.

Co-Leader: What do you usually do when you feel uncertain about others?

SusAnne: My first instinct is to disappear. But I really would like to be able to trust people more fully.

Operating within the spirit of reality therapy, we offer a challenge to SusAnne:

Co-Leader: What would happen if during this weekend you try something different? Instead of withdrawing, you could experiment with opening up. If what you typically do doesn't work too well, are you willing to make some changes and see what that would be like?

SusAnne: I'm willing to push myself a bit and give voice to some of the fears that I typically keep to myself. I feel lighter and I'm not quite as afraid. It helps to verbalize my thoughts.

Note that it is SusAnne who makes the evaluation of what she is currently doing and what she may want to change. It is not our function, as group leaders, to make these decisions for SusAnne.

Casey brings herself into the group by saying that she is having reactions to SusAnne. We invite Casey to tell SusAnne directly how she is being affected by SusAnne.

Casey: I feel afraid that if you know certain things about me you will judge me, that you won't want anything to do with me, and that you'll not like me.

Through this kind of dialogue, we want to provide Casey with the opportunity to identify and challenge ways that she often stops herself from being herself because she fears judgment from others, especially SusAnne. Both SusAnne and Casey are actually making the room safer for themselves by expressing the fears and reservations that they typically keep to themselves. This process allows them to check out the reality of some of their assumptions about each other, as well as others in the group.

Darren holds back because of his fear of being rejected by the group. We ask him to talk to each group member and complete this sentence: "You could reject me by _____ ." By completing the sentence in a different way with each member, Darren can express the full spectrum of the fears of rejection he normally keeps inside of himself. Doing this exercise gives Darren an insight that many of his fears of rejection lie within him rather than coming from others in the group (Gestalt therapy).

Another way to begin with Darren would be to pursue cognitive work. Drawing from a rational emotive behavioral orientation, we might challenge Darren with questions such as "What would be so terrible if everyone in here did reject you?" or "What is the worst thing that you can imagine if you were to be rejected?" The attempt here is to show Darren that he has uncritically bought the self-defeating idea that he would find rejection devastating. With this new insight, Darren may be able to challenge the notion that everyone will reject him. After working with Darren on his fears of rejection, we invite other members to express similar fears and then proceed to teach the group members how they contribute to their problems by subscribing to beliefs that they have accepted without questioning the validity of such beliefs.

Our orientation emphasizes giving members an opportunity to express their feelings and thoughts, and to explore them. We do not think it is useful to provide quick solutions. When a member raises self-doubts, fears, or struggles, we block other members from offering reassurance too quickly. This allows the individual an opportunity to explore his or her concern. For instance, when Jyl is crying as she is talking to James, we do not facilitate members giving her reassurance or telling her that she has no reason to feel embarrassed. Instead, when Jyl says she feels exposed, our intervention leads her to say more about what it is like for her to feel exposed and with whom. Although quick reassuring feedback from members may make Jyl feel good for a brief moment, it is doubtful that this feeling will be long lasting. This is based on the assumption that Jyl's critic lies within her and not primarily with others.

Theme: Making Internal Dialogue Explicit

In many groups it is what members won't say that will bog the group down—not what they do say. We encourage members to identify what they might be silently saying to themselves, both before they come to a session and during the group meeting. If members decide to make their internal dialogue explicit, others often are able to relate to what is being voiced. We want to teach members the value of verbalizing their thoughts and feelings, especially if they have a tendency to observe a great deal and think about how they will present themselves.

A good example of a member who engaged in a great deal of internal dialogue is Casey. At different times in the group, Casey indicates that she carefully thinks about what she wants to say before she speaks. Because of wanting to appear articulate, she censors many of her thoughts. Noticing that Casey is looking down as she speaks, we ask her what she is feeling. She indicates that she is scared of being judged by others. Our work with Casey consists of asking her to select those members whom she fears are judging her and then tell them about the judgment she fears they are making about her. Once she deals with her concerns about who might judge her, she realizes her fears of judgments are imagined more than rooted in reality. This illustrates what the Gestalt therapists refer to as owning one's projections. This exercise creates the safety that is crucial for Casey's deeply personal work later on.

If members experience the group as being a safe place, they will be inclined to move into the unknown and challenge themselves. In our role as co-leaders, we assume that it is useful to provide members with a general understanding of the techniques and methods we may employ in our work with them. To increase the chances that members will benefit from Gestalt methods, we think that group leaders need to communicate the general purpose of these interventions and to create an experimental climate. "Let's try something on for size and see how it fits" conveys this experimental attitude on the part of the leader. It is not our intention to prove a point; rather, our aim is to encourage the members to experiment with novel ways of thinking and acting, and then to determine for themselves how they might expand their behavioral repertoire.

In this section we have given examples of some ways to assist members in exploring their concerns about group participation. For a more complete discussion of group process issues at the transition stage, review Chapter 4.

Working Stage

Moving Toward a Deeper Level of Interaction

There are no arbitrary dividing lines between the phases of a group. In actual practice these phases merge with each other. This is especially true of the movement from the transition stage to the working stage. The line is somewhat thin between expressing anxieties and ways of avoiding, which is so characteristic of the transition stage, and working resistances through to move the group into a more advanced stage of development. If a group does move into the working stage, it can be expected that earlier themes of trust, conflict, and reluctance to participate will surface from time to time. As a group takes on new challenges, deeper levels of trust have to be achieved. Also, considerable conflicts may be settled at the initial stage, yet new conflicts may emerge as the group evolves. A group can be compared to an intimate relationship. Neither is static; both are characterized by a fluid process. Perfection is never achieved in a group, and smooth waters often become stormy for a time. Commitment is necessary to do the difficult work of moving forward.

Even if a group eventually reaches a working stage, this does not imply that all members are able to function at the same level of intensity. Some members may be on the periphery, others may still be holding back, and still others may be more resistant or less willing to take risks. Indeed, there are individual differences among members at all stages of a group. Some members may be very willing to engage in intense emotional exploration, and this can have the effect of drawing more hesitant members into active participation. (For a more detailed discussion of the working stage, review Chapter 5.)

Theme: Exploring Feelings of Isolation

Andrew has mentioned several times that he has a tendency to isolate himself. He refers to being locked up emotionally, yet he realizes that he has the key to open himself to others. Andrew also talks about a wall that surrounds him, which has the effect of keeping him safe, yet isolated. Andrew has asked himself why his marriage did not work out. Because of his divorce, he asks himself: "Am I to blame for what happened? Will I be able to trust anyone again? Will I be able to get over the hurt of the divorce?"

There are a number of ways to work with Andrew. One way (from a person-centered perspective) would be to invite Andrew to tell his story. While he does so, we pay full attention not only to what he is saying but also to his nonverbal expressions of pain over his loss. This attention and the support of the group will allow him to fully experience and share the intensity of his feelings. By letting us in on some of his painful experiences, he is decreasing his feelings of isolation. As Andrew stays connected to others in the group, he becomes aware of their compassion for him, which encourages him to share more of himself.

An alternative approach to dealing with this theme involves drawing on psychodrama techniques. In doing this, Marianne might ask Andrew where he feels most stuck in regard to his divorce. Andrew replies, "There are a lot of things that have gone unsaid—things that I feel stuck with, things that I'm afraid I won't ever say." Marianne asks Andrew to reveal one of the things he might not ever say. Andrew is then asked to select a member to play his ex-wife's role. He picks Jyl and begins by expressing his hurt. Jyl (as his symbolic wife) at first just listens and may later respond. She could respond as if she were his wife or as she imagines his ex-wife might respond. Andrew could provide a few lines of what his wife is likely to say as a way to coach Jyl in playing this role.

In doing the role play, Andrew expresses feelings of being hurt and betrayed, and of being slow to trust again. As he is talking to his symbolic wife, Andrew repeats that he is not good enough to keep a relationship together. At this point Darren, who identifies with Andrew's feelings, is selected as Andrew's double and steps next to Andrew, saying a few of the things that Andrew is not verbalizing. By having someone speak in his behalf, Andrew may eventually find his own words and release some of his deeper feelings.

After engaging in this role play, Marianne asks Andrew to imagine the kind of intimate relationship he would like five years from now. He says that he would like to see himself as feeling trusting enough to form meaningful relationships. In working with Andrew we have attempted to understand his subjective world (existential) and have drawn on the support of the members to further Andrew's work. The use of psychodrama results in intensification of emotions. By expressing his emotions, Andrew will experience some relief from keeping certain feelings bottled up inside. Not only will this emotional release result in his feeling better, but Andrew can decide that he does not have to be isolated and that he can share his pain with caring people in his life. He may learn that he can trust selectively and that everyone will not let him down.

In psychodrama the participants enact conflicts as if they are occurring in the present moment rather than narrating past events. Leaders with a psychodrama orientation frequently say to members, "Don't tell us, show us." A basic tenet of psychodrama is that reliving and reexperiencing a scene from the past gives the participants both the opportunity to examine how that event affected them at the time it occurred and a chance to deal differently with the event *now*. By replaying a past event in the present, Andrew is able to assign new meaning to it. Through this process he can work through unfinished business and put a new and different ending to that earlier situation.

Still another level for working with Andrew is to engage him cognitively. From a rational emotive behavior therapy perspective, Jerry assists Andrew in becoming aware of and challenging his pattern of self-blaming. Having been taught the A-B-C model of therapy, Andrew is in the position to critically evaluate some of his beliefs that get him into trouble. In Andrew's case, the Activating event (A)—that is, his divorce—is not the cause of his unhappiness now. Rather, the cause is his response to the Activating event—namely, his irrational Beliefs (B). Specifically, his response is to keep telling himself that because of his divorce he has failed; that if his wife does not love him nobody will or can; that getting intimate again will only end in more pain; and if only he had been different, his wife would still be with him. Thus, the emotional Consequence (C) of his emotional pain is due not to his divorce but to his faulty, illogical thinking.

In doing this cognitive work, Andrew discovers that he has been avoiding making contacts with other women because he has convinced himself that women may not want to become involved with him, and if they did, they would certainly hurt him. Jerry challenges Andrew's perceptions about the catastrophic consequences of becoming intimate. Even though he has been deeply wounded, it does not stand to reason that he will necessarily be hurt in every close relationship. The future does not have to be a repeat of the past. The aim is to have Andrew put himself in situations where he has to critically appraise his beliefs regarding emotional closeness.

With encouragement and direction, Andrew begins to challenge his self-defeating notions. Jerry suggests that he role-play initiating a conversation with a woman in the group. The purpose of this exercise is to enable him to more freely engage in dialogue with a woman. Andrew discusses his fears of getting involved again, which we then explore further during this session.

There are other ways that we could work with Andrew's ambivalence over wanting to get close to others and also wanting to keep others at a distance. Drawing on concepts from transactional analysis, a productive strategy might be to focus on exposing and working with an early decision that Andrew made, for example: "If you open yourself to being loved by others, or if you let yourself care about others, you are bound to be hurt. Thus, it's best to seal off your feelings and become emotionally numb, because then you won't feel the pain." We engage his thinking processes by asking Andrew to consider when and why he decided to keep his emotions in check as a way to protect himself. He is also asked to think about how that decision most likely gets in the way of current relationships, and if he might like to redecide. Finally, some of his injunctions—"Don't get close." "Don't let people get too close to your feelings." "Be careful who you trust." "Protect yourself."—may be the focal point of some further exploration.

Certain ideas from TA and Gestalt therapy experiments often work well together. We could follow up his work on his early decisions with some Gestalt exploration. Andrew states that he wants to work on his mixed feelings about intimacy with women. First, Marianne asks him to face each woman in the group and state his worst fear about getting close to her. As he does this, he becomes keenly aware of his here-and-now fears toward the women in the group, especially Jyl and SusAnne. Marianne suggests that Andrew look at Jyl and SusAnne, allowing each of them to be the focus of a conflicting side of himself. As he looks at Jyl, he expresses the side of himself that wants to care and get involved.

Andrew: It feels so lonely and cold behind the walls that I build around myself. I work so hard to keep people out. I want to get out of these walls, but I'm afraid of what is out there. Acting this way is really bottling me up because it isn't representative of my true nature. This isn't who I am.

Marianne: Andrew, look at SusAnne and let yourself be the side of you that wants to remain behind those walls.

Andrew: Stay behind those walls that you've worked so hard to build. You're isolated, but at least you're safe. You know what happens whenever you let yourself really care: you get burned, and that pain isn't worth the effort of getting involved.

This dialogue helps Andrew become more aware of the polarities within himself, without forcing him to choose between his two sides. By exaggerating and staying longer with each side, he may be better able to make a decision about which way he wants to live.

We could go in a very different direction with Andrew. Instead of working on his conflicting emotions from a Gestalt framework, we could employ behavioral strategies. Jerry decides to use relaxation and desensitization techniques to approach Andrew's fear of intimacy. Relaxation techniques, which are taught to the entire group, consist of systematically tensing and relaxing all the muscles in the body. They are practiced daily at home.

A practical application of relaxation techniques to Andrew's difficulties may proceed as follows: He is instructed to construct an imaginary hierarchy of interpersonal situations ranging from those that would produce the least amount of anxiety to those that would produce the most. He is then asked to use the techniques he has learned to become extremely relaxed. Next, he is guided through an image about an interpersonal situation that, according to his hierarchy, generates the least degree of anxiety—say, talking with a woman he is attracted to. This is followed by images of situations involving greater and greater anxiety. As soon as Andrew experiences anxiety, he is instructed to "switch off" that scene and relax. In this manner he may manage to work himself up to sustaining images about a high-anxiety-producing situation—for example, starting a relationship with a woman.

In working with Andrew's struggle of wanting to be involved in relationships versus his wanting to keep himself safe, we have illustrated a variety of therapeutic strategies: person-centered, existential, psychodrama, Gestalt, rational emotive behavior therapy, transactional analysis, and behavior therapy. Of course, we are not suggesting that we would make all of these interventions with Andrew. Instead, these illustrations are intended to show how, drawing from different theories, one could work in a variety of ways. It is important to pay attention to the client and what he is willing to do in this particular situation. Certainly we could involve Andrew as a collaborator in designing experiments he could carry out in this group.

Theme: Dealing with Parents

Jyl lets it be known that she is ready to work on feelings about her father. Jyl says that it is so sad that it took her dad so long to tell her what she wanted to hear. As Jyl continues to talk, she expresses her pain over not hearing her father tell her that she could have made it as a musician. Jyl so much wanted her father to believe in her, yet it wasn't until he was dying that he told her that she could have been successful in a music career.

We ask Jyl to pick a person in the group whom she could look at and talk to as her father. The fact that he died recently does not diminish the intensity or meaningfulness of Jyl's talking to a father. The purpose of this psychodrama technique is to provide Jyl with an avenue to give verbal and nonverbal expressions to many of the things she may be keeping inside. If there is unfinished business with Dad, engaging in this dialogue is an effective way to address it.

Once she has done this role play, the work could take any number of directions. We might simply ask: "Jyl, having said what you did, what has this been like for you? What would you like to do next?" Taking our clue from Jyl would be the best way to proceed. As a follow-up experiment, we are likely to ask Jyl to write a letter to her father, even though he is no longer alive. In this letter, Jyl could say what she most wanted from her dad, what she misses about him, and what she wishes she might have said. The rationale for writing a letter is to give Jyl an opportunity to release feelings over not getting what she wanted from her father. Perhaps then she will be able to give herself increased affirmation, and she may be more open to receiving support from others. It seems that Jyl is extremely hard on herself for what she has done or failed to do. Writing the letter may be a way for her to come to appreciate her talents and what she has accomplished.

Jackie is drawn into Jyl's work with parents. One of Jackie's struggles is allowing herself to feel "good enough" as a person, regardless of her performances or accomplishments. It is as though Jackie is operating on the premise that if she were perfect, then she would receive universal approval, and then she would feel adequate as a person.

Jackie: My mom left when I was 7 years old. I always felt responsible. I felt that if I was funnier, more desirable, prettier, then she might have wanted to stay. In my head, I know I wasn't responsible for her leaving, but there are times that I feel that if I were more, then she would have stayed. I wanted to be the center of her world. So, it's not that people don't give to me, but it's that I can't give enough back.

Marianne works with Jackie on her intense feelings about her mother, reflecting Jackie's possible belief that if she were more perfect her mother would not have left.

Even if we do not work with Jackie by using psychoanalytic techniques, the psychoanalytic perspective can provide a context for understanding Jackie's problem. Looking at Jackie's dynamics, we might speculate that in some ways she is looking at others to feed her and nourish her as a person. She has not given up the fantasy of being the type of young girl that her parents wanted; this frustration of her need to be seen as the "ideal daughter" by her parents may bring about feelings of insecurity, disillusionment, and anxiety. We might interpret her behavior as seeking the parents she has always wanted. Jackie may now be treating others in the group as she treated her parents. In fact, at one point she indicates that she is very aware of people in authority and goes on to say that she is particularly aware of Marianne and Jerry and wants to be liked by them. She may look to us as co-leaders for validation of her worth. Certainly, we would pay close attention to this transference.

At the working stage Jackie may regress and reexperience some old and familiar patterns, which will be seen as material to be worked through in the group. How she behaves in the group sessions provides some clues to the historical determinants of her present behavior. It may be useful to make timely interpretations so that some of Jackie's past can be brought to the surface. Another focus will be guiding her in working through her transferences with the co-leaders. In the group situation it is probable that she has re-created her original family; this transference interferes with her accurate appraisal of reality, because she is now projecting onto others in the group feelings she had for her parents. Furthermore, Jackie may be searching for the approval she sought from her mother in many of us in this group.

An Adlerian interpretation would be quite different from this psychoanalytic interpretation. We would not devote time to exploring the possible causes of her struggle to win her parents' approval. Instead, the focus would be on the here-and-now behavior Jackie displays and on ways in which she can begin to challenge her thinking and thus make changes in her behavior. Working within an Adlerian model, she is invited to consider our perceptions, or our interpretation, of her striving for parental approval. She explores her style of life to see how searching for approval may be a theme. The interpretation is focused on her goals, purposes, and intentions, as well as on her private logic and how it works. As she gains insight, through referring to her basic premises and to the ways these beliefs are mistaken, she can begin the process of modifying these cognitions and thus find ways of leading a more satisfying life.

If we were to utilize an action-oriented approach to Jackie's theme, we would employ psychodrama techniques to make the material come alive. We want to know whether Jackie remembers any time as a child when she wanted parental approval and love and didn't receive it. Let's say that Jackie recalls the time (at age 7) when she found out that her mother was leaving. Marianne assists her in reenacting this childhood scene with the help of two group members who play her parents. Here are a few possibilities for a psychodrama format:

- Playing herself as a child, Jackie says all the things now that she thought and felt but never said when her mother left.
- She asks her parents (still as the child) to love her and to stay together.
- The symbolic parents play their roles either as rejecting parents or as accepting parents.
- Other group members stand in for Jackie and say things that she finds difficult to express.
- Jackie projects a scene with her parents in the present that incorporates an interaction with them as she would wish it to be. In this case she coaches others to be the parents she would have wanted at age 7.

Following the psychodrama there is an effort to connect Jackie's present struggles with the feelings she had as a child. The ways in which she seeks approval of others, especially her wanting to be liked and valued by authority figures, could be much like her dynamics as a child. By participating in this psychodrama, she is likely to discover how striving toward perfect performances and winning the approval of everyone has become increasingly problematic. Jackie recognizes that nobody can ever give her the kind of approval she desperately wanted from her mother as a child.

As Jackie's work is coming to closure, Marianne notices that Jacqueline is tearing up and seems involved in Jackie's work. Marianne invites Jacqueline to tell Jackie how she is being affected by the feelings Jackie is expressing.

Jacqueline: No matter how much my mother affirms me and says all the right things, it is just so hard for me to take it in. It's just really hard for me to be close to her. That's all I wanted, to just get rid of these feelings of rejection I've had. I don't even know how to fix it. And she tries, and I try, but we miss the mark every time. I'm just tired of it. I just want to accept her for who she is.

Jacqueline is asked to look at some of her beliefs that are underneath much of what she does in everyday life. From an Adlerian perspective, Jacqueline is operating on the fictional notion that if she were perfect she would get her mother's approval. Eventually, Jacqueline comes to the realization that she has been wanting her mother's approval and she assumes that nobody else is going to give her the approval she seeks.

Marianne says that she suspects that what Jacqueline wants with us in the group is what her mom did not give to her. Jacqueline's need for validation from others is rooted in her need to be told from a significant person (mother) that she is an acceptable person. At this juncture we employ an Adlerian technique of asking Jacqueline to imagine that she is a worthwhile person and that she does have the approval of her mother. Jerry makes the following *as if* intervention.

Jerry: Jacqueline, for two weeks I'd like you to act as if you had all the approval you needed and that you could accept it. Furthermore, I'd like you to stand in front of your mirror each day for the next two weeks and complete this sentence: "Jacqueline, I approve of you because _____."

Jacqueline: Wow! You're asking a lot of me. You want me to stand in front of a mirror and tell myself what I like and approve about me. What if I can't find enough good stuff to say to myself?

Jerry: Let's start right now. List one thing about you that helps you feel approving of yourself.

Jacqueline: Well, I'm a good mother myself.

Jerry: Now list one other trait about you that you like.

Jacqueline: I'm a good student. Even though school has been tough, I have plugged away and now I'm in a doctoral program.

Jerry stays with Jacqueline for a time and asks her to list as many traits as she can that she values. My intention here is to enable Jacqueline to identify for herself what she values about who she is instead of looking externally to find her self-worth. My assumption is that if others give her the approval she is seeking, she won't believe it, or she will soon forget it once she hears it. This experiment is designed to help Jacqueline recognize that the approval she wants is not to be found in others but in herself.

As is the case with a group that has reached the working stage, a number of members can work on common themes. James has been affected by the talk of mothers. He says that he was thinking of his mom as Jackie and Jacqueline were talking about their mothers. Marianne intervenes at this point, suggesting that he talk to Jackie as his mother (since he seems to have been triggered by her exploration). James lets Marianne know that he would like to use both Jackie and Marianne as his mother, since there are things he wants to say to both women. (This shows the importance of asking the client who can be most helpful to him or her in setting up a role-play situation. There is no need to restrict the dialogue to one person, and two or more symbolic mothers can add to the breadth of the work.)

James: If my mom were here, I'd say (hesitatingly and with emotion) that I love you. I haven't told you that recently, and I know that you are really a strong woman. You do a lot of good things for a lot of people. I wish you'd do these things for yourself and believe in yourself. You don't know how special you are.

After James says a few of the things he loves about Mom to Jackie, Marianne asks Jackie how it was for her to hear what James said.

Jackie: When you first started sharing, it felt real good, and those were the things I'd like to hear from my son. But all of a sudden I wanted more from you, and it felt like there was more that you wanted to tell me.

With that James continues talking to Jackie, telling her all the ways she is special.

Whether or not James tells his mother some of what he communicated in the role-playing situation is up to him. He needs to decide how not telling her what is in his heart might be getting in his way in having the relationship he would like with her. If he decides he would like a better relationship, this might be a good time to incorporate some aspects of reality therapy and behavior therapy into his dealings with his mother.

In reality therapy, James is asked: "If nothing changes between you and your mother, how would that be?" or "If you had with your mother what you wanted with her, how would your relationship be different?" If he decides to actually talk to his mother, we could set up a behavioral rehearsal in which he tells her what is most important for him to express. He doesn't need to overwhelm himself or his mother by communicating everything in one encounter with her. Using reality therapy, we would draw on specific methods of making an action plan. His plan would need to be clear, specific, attainable, and realistic. At this juncture, we collaboratively design a plan that will enable him to meet with his mother and tell her some of what he would most like her to hear. His plan might include carrying out a homework assignment, such as scheduling a dinner date with his mother and engaging in the kind of dialogue with her that he would like.

Darren identifies in some ways with James. Darren lets us know that he feels it is hard for him to feel like an adult around his mother. Furthermore, Darren realizes that his relationship with his parents is getting in his way with people in this group. He tells James that he envies what he has with his mother. He finds it difficult to assert himself with us in an adult way, and he adds, "It's like a hole in my soul." Marianne observes his powerful imagery and reflects his phrase "a hole in my soul." She says to Darren: "How about looking at a few people and saying again, I have a hole in my soul."

As Darren repeats "I have a hole in my soul" to a few people, he begins to cry, expressing his feelings of loneliness as a child. "Growing up I didn't feel I could talk to my parents. I just wanted to be understood. I felt so lonely." Darren continues to express intense feelings about his relationships with his parents and how he wasn't sure of where he fit. Later he acknowledges that he is not blaming his parents, since he knows they did the best they could with what they had. However, after staying with his feelings he begins to see how today he often struggles with fitting in and feeling a sense of belongingness. He makes the connection between his way of being with his family and how this is played out with others in a way that is not fulfilling to him.

As Darren continues exploring how his relationship with his parents influences the person he is today, he might well decide that he wants to initiate a discussion with his parents in real life. Drawing on a behavioral rehearsal technique, he could be asked to pick a mom or dad and practice what he most wants to communicate to his parents. We would certainly caution him not to rush out after an intense emotional experience in the group to confront his parents with what they didn't do for him when he was a child. After rehearsal opportunities, Darren may be ready to establish a contract that would involve some form of homework assignment, which he gives to himself. The use of contracts and homework is a part of several modalities, such as transactional analysis, behavior therapy, and reality therapy. These action methods can assist James and Darren in translating their insights into concrete behavioral changes.

All of these themes have emerged from the group interactions or from an individual's explorations. The group provides the encouragement for members to begin listening to themselves and paying attention to their subjective experience. By openly sharing and exploring universal personal concerns, members develop a sense of mutuality. The close ties that they feel with one another give them many opportunities for using the group culture differently from other aspects of their culture. The group becomes a place where people can be together in deeply meaningful ways. Through the process of self-disclosure, the participants grasp the universality of basic human concerns that unite them, in spite of their differences. When they entered the group, some of the members likely felt that they would have a difficult time feeling connected with others. But as members make themselves known to each other, they build alliances. Members come to understand the existential reality that we all experience and share pain, even though the particulars of our stories are different.

Final Stage

To assist you in thinking about ways to integrate these different group models into your personal style, in this section we describe how we would use concepts and techniques from the various approaches in dealing with some typical issues that we observe during the last few sessions of most groups. As a group evolves toward termination, a number of tasks remain: dealing with feelings of separation, saying good-bye, dealing with unfinished business, reviewing the group experience, consolidating learnings, practicing for behavioral change, giving and receiving feedback, talking about ways to carry learnings outside of group, making contracts of what to do after a group ends, and talking about a follow-up meeting. We remind members again about the importance of maintaining confidentiality. We also ask members to talk about what they might do to discount what they actually did during the group, how they might recover from setbacks and how to create support systems.

Theme: Dealing with Feelings of Separation and Loss

The final stage of a group is a difficult time. The members are aware that their community is about to dissolve, and they are beginning to mourn their impending separation. Some of them are pulling back; they are becoming less intense and are no longer contributing much new material to work on. Others wonder whether they'll be able to maintain the openness they have learned in the group once they can't count any longer on the group's encouragement and support. They fear that in their everyday life they won't find people to give them the kind of support they need to keep experimenting with change and, as a consequence, that they may regress to old ways.

In facilitating any group, members need to be given an opportunity to fully express their feelings about the termination of the group, in this case, an intensive weekend workshop. The person-centered approach, which stresses listening actively and giving permission to explore whatever feelings are present, offers a useful model for this phase of group work. The members do not need a great deal of direction; rather, they need to be encouraged to face the reality that after sharing in an intense experience they will soon be going their separate ways. In this particular group, it is necessary to allow members to talk about any unfinished business they may have concerning any work they initiated or any interactions that occurred during the entire weekend. If participants can fully express their feelings about separation, the transition period between leaving the group and carrying what they've learned in the group into their day-to-day life will be made easier.

We have often observed the concern on the part of many group participants that they won't be able to create in their everyday lives that which they have experienced within the group. It seems crucial that we help members come to understand what *they* did to make this group meaningful. If they see their part in creating a group that allowed them to be expressive, there is hope that they can bring this into everyday living. Our goal is to help participants see that their group has been a place where they could learn how to form meaningful interpersonal relationships, a process that is not restricted to the group but that can be applied in any setting.

In this regard there is some value in helping participants understand any connections that might exist between their past and their family, on the one side, and the relationships they have developed within the group, on the other. For that purpose the psychoanalytic approach is useful. In some ways the group represents a new family for its members, and by relating their behaviors in the group "family" to their behaviors in their actual families, members can learn much about themselves. To assist participants in their process of making connections among behaviors, we ask them to reflect on these questions:

- To whom was I drawn in this group, and what did I learn from that?
- With whom did I have the most conflict, and what meaning did that have for me?
- In what ways did my feelings and actions in this group resemble the ways in which I felt and acted as a child in my family?
- Were my reactions to the group leaders in any way similar to my reactions to my parents or others who were significant in my life?
- Did I experience feelings of competitiveness or jealousy within the group, and what insights did that provide?

Looking Ahead

Another tool we use as the group is drawing to a close is the development of a plan of action. We find that too often group members don't allow themselves to imagine creatively how they would like to experience their life. To assist them in their endeavor, we ask members to picture themselves and their lives in some ideal future circumstance, a technique that is used by both the Gestalt and the psychodrama approaches. Applying the fantasy technique to this group, we might suggest these scenarios to members:

- Imagine that you are attending a reunion of the group five years from now and that we are meeting to discuss how our lives have changed. What do you most want to be able to say to us at this reunion?

- Let yourself imagine all the ways in which you want to be different in your everyday life once you leave this group. Close your eyes and carry on a silent dialogue between yourself and the people who are most special in your life. What are you telling them? What are they replying? Imagine that a year has passed since we ended the group. Let yourself consider that nothing has changed in your life—that you have continued the way you have always been. Try to picture how you would feel.

We have found that some members and the group in general might benefit by sharing their hopes of how they want to be different in special relationships. To accomplish this, role-playing exercises are helpful. For example, we sometimes ask participants to select a member of the group to role-play a significant other. The role play begins by having the participant briefly tell the person selected what it is that he or she would like to change in their relationship and how he or she intends to make those changes.

During the final stages of the group, we also ask the members to review what they have learned about their early decisions as a result of participating in this group (an approach characteristic of existential therapy, transactional analysis, and rational emotive behavior therapy). To stimulate this review, we typically ask these questions:

- Do you want to revise any of these early decisions?
- Are these decisions still appropriate for you now?
- What new decisions do you want to make?

In addition, we ask members to identify, even write down, the self-defeating statements they sometimes tell themselves, to share them, and to offer one another feedback concerning the validity of these self-statements, as well as suggestions on how to combat negative thinking.

During the final stages of the group, we rely heavily on the cognitive and action-oriented approaches characteristic of the behavior therapies, reality therapy, rational emotive behavior therapy, and transactional analysis. We see the group as a learning laboratory in which the members have identified the specific changes they are willing to make and have experimented with new behaviors. Assuming that this has indeed occurred, it becomes extremely important that the members carry out their own action-oriented programs outside the group.

Toward the end of the group we have members formulate a specific contract—a brief statement of the plans they have concerning behavioral changes once the group ends. The aim is to have members clearly define what they now want to do and how they specifically intend to do it.

Our experience has taught us that members tend to forget some of what they learned and to discount the actual value of what they did in the group. To help prevent this from occurring and to help members retain whatever they have learned—about others, about human struggling, about life, and about themselves—we ask them at the final session to review specific insights they had throughout the course of the group. It is our contention that unless one articulates and shares with others the specifics of what one has learned in the group, the group experience may soon become an indistinct blur.

Here, again, we find the principles of the behavioral approaches useful during the final session—specifically, application of feedback principles to help members strengthen the perceptions they gained during the course of the group. For example, we often ask members to complete feedback sentences for every member in the group, such as:

- "One of the things I like best about you is _____."
- "One way I see you blocking your strengths is _____."
- "My hope for you is _____."
- "My greatest concern or fear for you is _____."
- "The way I'll remember you in this group is _____."
- "A few things that I hope you'll remember are _____."

Focused feedback, whether verbal or written, can give the participants a good sense of the impact they had on others in the group and how they are viewed by others.

As the final session draws to a close, we give members a message to take with them—a message grounded in the existential approach:

Co-leaders: We hope you have become aware of your role in bringing about change in your life. You can assume power by focusing on changing yourself rather than trying to get others to be different. Many of you have become aware of the choices that are open to you; thus, you can now reflect on the decisions you will make. Even if you decide to remain largely as you are, you now are aware that you can choose, that you don't need to have others design your life for you. Although choosing for yourself can provoke anxiety, it does give you a sense that your life is yours and that you have the power to shape your own future.

Behavioral approaches stress developing clear goals, working on these goals during the sessions, and then evaluating the degree to which these goals are met. What members do after the group ends is as important as the group sessions. Therefore, we tend to devote ample time to suggesting ways in which members might consolidate their learning and carry it into daily living. Specifically, we encourage members to develop the habit of keeping a journal—writing down the problems they are encountering, describing how they feel about themselves in specific situations, and listing their successes and difficulties in following through with their contracts. New ideas can be a powerful catalyst in helping people make the changes they want to make, and we encourage members to select and read books on topics of interest to them as a way of continuing to work on themselves and to grow.

Finally, we schedule a follow-up session—several months after the termination of the group—for the purpose of allowing members to discuss what the group meant to each of them as well as to report on the extent to which they have fulfilled their contracts. We strongly encourage members to attend the follow-up meeting, even if they did not complete some or all of their contracts. The follow-up session provides rich opportunities for evaluation of the process and outcomes of a group. This allows members to evaluate what they learned about themselves, as well as to reflect on the degree to which they are applying what they learned in the group to everyday living. As co-leaders, we continue to find that a follow-up session is one of the best ways to evaluate the effectiveness of a group. Over the years that we have been leading groups, our practice has been influenced by this feedback from members.

Develop Your Own Style of Leadership

In this chapter we have given examples of how we might draw from the various approaches with respect to the themes that have emerged in the illustrative group. Although it is valuable to practice working within the framework of each theory as you learn about it, there is no need to limit yourself to practicing any one model exclusively. Instead, you can integrate various components from all these models and begin to develop your own leadership style—a style that suits your personality and the kind of groups you may lead. The single most important element in effective group leadership is your way of being in a group.

We have described a variety of techniques in dealing with the themes that members introduced, but we use these techniques as means to further the agenda presented to us—not as ends in themselves. Techniques are no better than the person using them, and they are not useful if they are not sensitively adapted to the particular client and context. The outcome of a technique is affected by the climate of the group and by the relationship between the leader and the members. Techniques are merely tools to amplify emerging material that is present and to encourage exploration of issues that have personal relevance to the members.

More important than the techniques we use are the attitudes we have toward members, which are manifested by who we are and what we do in the group. When we are fully present and ourselves, we can be catalysts for members to engage in introspection, relevant self-disclosure, and risk-taking. We believe that our primary function as co-leaders is to support members in their journey of making decisions regarding how they want to live. We work with people who are often struggling, who may be lost, or who are in a lot of psychological pain. The group experience affords members avenues for finding themselves and enables them to live more peacefully with themselves and others. We can be part of their journey as they discover their best.

A Final Word—and a Request!

I hope this book and the Student Manual that accompanies it have stimulated you to think productively about group process, to read more and learn more about the topics we have explored together, and to seek group experience both as a member and as a leader. You may have also used the video, *Evolution of a Group* (and the accompanying workbook), as a supplement to this book, especially to this chapter. The Student Video and Workbook are available from Brooks/Cole.

I am sincerely interested in getting feedback from you regarding this textbook and the accompanying manual as well as your experience in your own training program. I welcome and value any suggestions for making this book more useful in future revisions. You can use the tear-out evaluation at the end of this book, or write to me in care of Brooks/Cole.

NAME INDEX

SUBJECT INDEX